Metaphysics: *The Classic Readings*

PHILOSOPHY: *The Classic Readings*

This series offers a concise collection of the classic readings of philosophy, from ancient times to the first part of the twentieth century, and contains seminal writings from both Western and non-Western traditions. Combined with valuable editorial guidance, including a substantial introduction to each volume and preambles to individual chapters, they serve as core texts for historically orientated philosophy courses.

Already published:

Aesthetics: *The Classic Readings*
Ethics: *The Classic Readings*
Epistemology: *The Classic Readings*
Metaphysics: *The Classic Readings*

Forthcoming:

Philosophy of Religion: *The Classic Readings*
Political Philosophy: *The Classic Readings*

Metaphysics:

The Classic Readings

Edited by David E. Cooper

University of Durham

Advisory Editor
T. L. S. Sprigge

Copyright © Blackwell Publishers Ltd 2000
Introduction and editorial apparatus copyright © David E. Cooper 2000

First published 2000

2 4 6 8 10 9 7 5 3 1

Blackwell Publishers Ltd
108 Cowley Road
Oxford OX4 1JF
UK

Blackwell Publishers Inc.
350 Main Street
Malden, Massachusetts 02148
USA

British Library Cataloguing in Publication Data
A CIP catalogue record for this book is available from the British Library.

Library of Congress Cataloging-in-Publication Data
Metaphysics: the classic readings / edited by David E. Cooper ;
   advisory editor, T. L. S. Sprigge.
         p.   cm. — (Philosophy: the classic readings)
   Includes bibliographical references and index.
   ISBN 0–631–21324–4 (hb : alk. paper). — ISBN 0–631–21325–2 (pbk.
: alk. paper)
   1. Metaphysics.   I. Cooper, David Edward.   II. Sprigge, Timothy L. S.
III. Series.
BD111.M576   1999
110—dc21   99–16130
                                                                      CIP

Typeset in 10 on 12½ pt Galliard
by Ace Filmsetting Ltd, Frome, Somerset
Printed in Great Britain by MPG Books, Bodmin, Cornwall

This book is printed on acid-free paper.

Contents

Series Preface

Philosophers in the English-language world are becoming increasingly aware of the importance of the history of their subject. *Philosophy: The Classic Readings* is a series which provides students and teachers with the central historical texts in the main branches of philosophy. The texts selected range from ancient times to the first part of the twentieth century. In response to a growing and laudable interest in the contributions of non-Western philosophers, the volumes in the series will contain seminal writings from the Indian, Chinese and other traditions as well as the classics of Western philosophical literature.

Each volume in the series begins with a substantial introduction to the relevant area of philosophy and its history, and to the bearing of this history on contemporary discussion. Each selected text is prefaced by a discussion of its importance within the development of that area.

Taken individually, each volume will serve as a core text for courses which adopt a historical orientation towards the relevant branch of philosophy. Taken together, the volumes in the series will constitute the largest treasury of classic philosophical writings available.

The books in the series are edited and introduced by David E. Cooper, Professor of Philosophy at the University of Durham, England, and author of many books, including *World Philosophies: An Historical Introduction*, also published by Blackwell.

Acknowledgements

The source of each reading is given underneath the relevant chapter title. The editor and publishers gratefully acknowledge all copyright holders for permission to reproduce copyright material. The publishers apologize for any errors or omissions in the copyright information, and would be grateful to be notified of any corrections that should be incorporated in the next edition or reprint of this book.

Introduction

Metaphysics today enjoys a contested status. For many writers in the twentieth century, it is a branch of philosophy which should be consigned to the scrap-heap of intellectual history. For others, it deserves to be restored to its 'central position in philosophy as the most fundamental form of rational inquiry'.[1] So, do the 'classic readings' which follow have a proper subject-matter at all, or are they relics of an aberration of human thought.

Clearly there is a prior question to ask. What is that subject-matter, proper or not, supposed to be? What, more simply, is metaphysics? Like most philosophical disciplines, it gets its name from Greek. As we have seen in earlier volumes of this series, the Greek origin does not always afford much help in understanding what a philosophical discipline is about. *Ethos*, for example, means 'character' and did not connote matters of distinctively moral or ethical moment. In the case of metaphysics, the Greek expression affords no direct help at all. It was coined, in the first century BCE, by someone cataloguing the works of Aristotle. To the loosely related writings which, in the catalogue, came after (*meta*) the writings on nature (*Ta Physika*), he gave the name 'Metaphysics' – the works coming after those on nature. People, often its detractors, are therefore mistaken who assume that metaphysics is, by definition or origin, inquiry into what goes 'beyond' or transcends the natural world.

However, because of an ambiguity in the term 'meta-', 'metaphysics' is not an entirely unhappy term for its subject. As in expressions like 'metamathematics' and 'metalogic', it can suggest a 'higher order' inquiry into a 'lower order' one. Metaphysics certainly includes reflective inquiry into the claims and status of physics. Better, perhaps, it comprises inquiry

[1] E. J. Lowe, *The Possibility of Metaphysics: substance, identity, and time*, Oxford: Clarendon Press, 1998, p. 1.

into the foundations of physics and every other form of knowledge, into what the world would have to be like for these forms of knowledge to be possible. Metaphysics, to cite a couple of recent characterizations, is 'the systematic study of the most fundamental structure of reality', or 'the philosophical investigation of the nature, constitution, and structure of reality'.[2]

That the task of metaphysics could be understood in such terms was not, as we saw, due to the original meaning of the expression. But it is largely due to the subject-matter of the writings of Aristotle for which that expression was coined. Aristotle's *Metaphysics* (see chapter 3 below) discusses a wide variety of topics, but at the centre of this exercise in 'primary philosophy', as he called it, is the study of 'being *qua* being', above all of that kind of being, 'substance' (*ousia*), which must exist if anything at all can be said to exist. The particular concepts Aristotle tackles in this connection – substance, property, form, matter, cause, soul, God, and so on – have become staple topics for metaphysical discussion. More than that, however, metaphysics inherits the overall enterprise in which Aristotle saw himself, like Plato before him, engaged: that of articulating the most general and fundamental aspects of reality, and hence of identifying what is only apparent, illusory or, at best, secondary and parasitic.

I

As those who offer them recognize, characterizations of metaphysics as inquiry into the fundamental nature of reality and the like are hardly precise. What exactly, for instance, counts as 'fundamental'? Certainly such characterizations will not determine a precise set of distinctively metaphysical topics. In fact, no two books on metaphysics are likely to address just the same set of issues. One will, a second will not, include a chapter on persons and God, for example. Such differences, however, are less likely to reflect substantial disagreement than relatively arbitrary decisions whether to include a topic under the heading of metaphysics or of some branch of philosophy which has since broken off and achieved a considerable degree of autonomy. Already in the eighteenth century, the German philosopher Christian Wolff was distinguishing between 'general metaphysics' (or 'ontology', the study of being) and several branches of 'special metaphysics' which partially coincide with what, today, we call the philosophies of mind, science and religion respectively.

[2] *Ibid.*, p. 2 and Panayot Butchvarov, 'Metaphysics', in R. Audi (ed.), *The Cambridge Dictionary of Philosophy*, Cambridge: Cambridge University Press, 1995.

The trend, in effect, is to reserve the title 'metaphysics' for the study of the most general and global aspects of reality: for, say, inquiry into what it is to be an object *tout court*, rather than a particular object such as a person; or into what it is to be a property *tout court*, rather than a particular sort of property, such as a colour. It is not that these more particular questions are not metaphysical ones, simply that they get addressed, alongside ones of, say, an epistemological kind, within the more 'special' disciplines of philosophy.

Rather than agonize over just what belongs properly in the province of metaphysics, I shall describe the matters which preoccupy the authors represented in this volume. For if their preoccupations are not metaphysical, none are. The texts I have selected do not, for the most part, have as their main aim that of resolving particular metaphysical issues or elucidating particular metaphysical concepts. They address, rather, that largest of all questions, 'What is the ultimate character of reality?'. They are exercises in 'grand theory' and are 'global', not merely in dealing with a highly general issue, but in advancing total 'world views'. (Some of the texts are not, perhaps, quite that ambitious, but even these purport to identify crucial aspects or structures of reality which any total world view should incorporate.) To mention two contrasting examples, there is the Indian philosopher Śaṁkara's depiction of reality as a seamless, ineffable, spiritual Absolute, of which the world of ordinary experience is an 'illusory' appearance (chapter 5), and there is Bertrand Russell's account of reality as constituted by an infinity of simple 'logical atoms', out of which ordinary objects and persons are somehow 'constructed' (chapter 16).

These texts ask...

Although the texts are primarily concerned with the grand, global question just referred to, this is not to say that more particular metaphysical concepts and topics are left unaddressed. On the contrary, there are a number of these which crop up with regularity, ones which are especially central in attempts to articulate 'grand theories'. One of these is causality. Any world view, it seems, must provide an account of how things or events are related to one another. Is that relation a causal one? If so, what is a causal relation? If not, how does the 'illusion' of causal relations arise? These are issues addressed by, among others, Aristotle, Śaṁkara, Buddhist thinkers (chapter 4), Spinoza (chapter 7), Leibniz (chapter 9), and Whitehead (chapter 17). Another is the issue of 'universals' or properties. In everyday talk, we speak not only of particular things existing, but of there being the properties which these things have. How literally is such talk to be taken? There are, we ordinarily take it, green leaves and just men: but do the colour green and the quality of justice in addition exist, and if they do, is this in the same sense as the men and the leaves exist? Clearly such questions need

Causality (vital topic)

Issue of universals or properties

to be answered in any attempt at a comprehensive account of what reality contains. The *locus classicus* of the view that universals really exist, indeed *more* really exist than particulars, is Plato's doctrine of the Forms, given poetic expression in his *Phaedrus* (chapter 2). This is a doctrine criticized by Aristotle in his *Metaphysics* and one touched upon by several later writers in this volume, including Russell.

But the concept which looms largest is that of substance. This is the term which, somewhat unhappily, was used to translate Aristotle's expression *ousia* (being, entity). By 'first' substance, Aristotle meant those beings which do not depend on anything else, in the way that, say, a smile depends on the existence of the person who is smiling. And this, roughly, is how subsequent metaphysicians, such as Descartes (chapter 6), have understood the notion of substance. Given this understanding, it is unsurprising that the notion should be such a central one. An enquiry into what *ultimately* or *fundamentally* exists could be construed as trying to identify what exists without dependence on anything else – what substance or substances there are, in other words. This is certainly how Spinoza and Leibniz, for example, construe their enquiries. It is unsurprising, as well, that the notion of substance should have been the critical target of other philosophers – such as Bradley (chapter 14), Whitehead, and Heidegger (chapter 18) – for whom the whole idea of reality being composed of independent things or stuffs is misconceived.

II

If certain concepts occur with great frequency in the texts in this volume, so do a number of *polarities*. Indeed, it is various ancient tensions between opposing conceptions of the world which inspired the development of metaphysics in the first place, and which continue to breathe life into it. The names for such opposing conceptions – such as 'idealism' and 'realism', 'monism' and 'pluralism' – have become staples of the metaphysical lexicon. Three such polarities are especially prominent in the following texts.

(a) *The one and the many*. It seems to be an abiding urge of human beings, attested to by most religions, to identify some unity among the immensely diverse furniture of the world. Indeed, it is attested to by the very sense that there is *a* world to which all this furniture belongs. Certainly the search for such unity was characteristic of much early philosophizing in China and India as well as Greece. The famous *Tao Te Ching* (chapter 1), for example, vividly conveys the sense of a 'way' or 'principle' (*tao*) which holds together and informs the apparent diversity of things.

Among some early thinkers – Parmenides in Greece, the Advaitins in India – this sense of unity modulates into a radical monism, according to which plurality and change are merely apparent. Reality is a single, indivisible whole. Such claims were soon to invite criticism, from Aristotle, for example, and the Buddhist composers of the *Abhidharma* texts. But the broad issue of monism *versus* pluralism has continued to divide metaphysicians. We will, for instance, encounter the opposition between Spinoza and Leibniz: the former holding that reality is a single substance, the latter regarding it as an infinity of causally unconnected 'monads'; or between the atomistic phenomenalism of John Stuart Mill (chapter 13) and the 'holism' of F. H. Bradley (chapter 14). William James (chapter 15) and Russell are explicitly concerned with this issue, both siding with the pluralist, while the sections from Heidegger's *Being and Time* advance a 'holistic' view of the world as we 'primordially' encounter it.

(b) *The mental and the material*. The term 'monism' is sometimes used not for the view that there exists only one substance, but for the doctrine that there is just one *type* of substance. It then contrasts not with 'pluralism', but with 'dualism', the doctrine – pre-eminently associated with Descartes – that reality is composed of two fundamental and distinct kinds of substance, mental and material. Monists, in this sense, divide into three schools: holding, respectively, that only the mental fundamentally exists, that only the material does so, and that what fundamentally exists is neutral between the mental and the material. Perhaps the most fiercely debated issues of metaphysics are those which divide these schools from one another, and all them from their dualist rival.

Descartes' many critics in the twentieth century sometimes give the impression that dualism has been the orthodox philosophical position until relatively recently. This is completely inaccurate. Every one of the post-Cartesian philosophers represented in this volume is critical, in one way or another, of Descartes' dualism. What is relatively recent is widespread sympathy for a materialist alternative. It is idealism – the broad thought that fundamental reality is in some sense mental – which, in its various forms, has been by far the more popular direction taken. Qualifiers like 'in some sense' and 'in its various forms' are essential, for idealism is a broad church. In English-language circles, the best-known version is that of Bishop Berkeley (chapter 10), referred to by Kant as 'empirical idealism', according to which all that exists are minds (including God's) and their contents, 'ideas'. So-called physical objects are simply collections of such ideas. (On the important 'phenomenalist' variant of this view, championed by Mill, such objects are enduring 'possibilities of sensation'.)

At least three other varieties of idealism are represented by our authors.

2. Transcendental
   Idealism
(Kant,
Schopenhauer)

First, there is the 'transcendental idealism' advanced by Kant (chapter 11) and subscribed to, with important divergences, by Schopenhauer (chapter 12). The central and difficult tenet of Kant – at its clearest, perhaps, in his remarks on space – is that the world we experience is not reality as it is 'in itself', but one conditioned and structured by mind. Space, for example, is not an aspect of 'things in themselves', but a 'form of sensibility', a condition determining our experience of objects.

3. Absolute
   Idealism

Second, there is 'absolute idealism'. Whereas Kant had insisted on complete agnosticism concerning the nature of reality in itself, idealists of this orientation hold that 'absolute reality' is, if not a mind, then at any rate mind-like or analogous to mind, somehow impregnated with intelligence. I have not included texts by the German absolute idealists, such as Fichte and Schelling, on account of their extreme difficulty when taken out their larger contexts. Absolute idealism is, however, represented both by Śaṁkara and Bradley. For the former, the absolute is *brahman*, about which little can be said: but it can be described as 'consciousness' and 'bliss', in senses of those terms at least analogous to the ones they bear when applied to human mental life. For Bradley, absolute reality is experience as a whole: not a sum total of individual experiences, but a seamless whole from which these are artificial abstractions. Finally, there is the *sui generis* idealism articulated by Leibniz, though partly echoed by Whitehead. Reality consists of an infinity of 'monads': some of these are minds, but even those which are not – like those composing a physical object – are, despite lacking consciousness, mind-like entities displaying 'appetition'.

Given today's enthusiasm for materialist accounts of reality, it may seem strange to have included no out-and-out materialist 'classic'. The fact is that no metaphysician of the first rank has, until very recently, unequivocally espoused materialism. There was a materialist school of Indian thinkers, but it is indicative of their relative unimportance that there are no extant writings of theirs. In the West, the only materialist of the period covered by this volume with a strong claim to have been included in it is Thomas Hobbes. Not only, however, is his defence of the materialist position crude, but relevant passages will be included in the forthcoming *Political Philosophy: the classic readings*.

Scientific
realism
(Locke)

Although our authors include no out-and-out materialist, we find in John Locke (chapter 8), in part following Descartes' lead, enunciating views which have played an important role in generating contemporary 'scientific realism', the view that fundamental reality is simply the world as depicted by physics. In particular, Locke defends the claims that (1) the nature of substances is accessible, in principle, to scientific identification, and (2) the properties of things are either the 'primary' ones, like space, which figure in modern scientific accounts of the world, or 'powers' which these primary qualities have to affect one another and ourselves.

Given the seemingly interminable arguments between idealists and their opponents, many metaphysicians have, unsurprisingly, tried to cut through the debate, pronouncing a plague on both houses. Spinoza, Whitehead, and Heidegger do this in their different ways, and Russell suggests a certain sympathy towards William James's theory of 'neutral monism'. This last position, according to which fundamental reality is neither mental nor physical, is one which is currently enjoying a revival in consequence of the intractable problem, as some see it, of fitting consciousness and mentality into a physicalist picture of the world.

(c) *The real and the apparent.* Any metaphysical position which could be taken seriously must make room for, and respect, the commonsense distinction between how something really is (square and red, say) and how it might merely appear to be (oblong and yellow, say). But, as we have already seen, some metaphysicians, while claiming to be able to do this, nevertheless argue for a general distinction between reality and how it appears to be, even in those perceptions and experiences which, by commonsense standards, are veridical. For Kant, famously, we can never experience things as they are in themselves. These are *noumena*: entities which, if knowable at all, are so only through a special 'intuition', unavailable to us humans.

Philosophers, including several represented in this book, divide over two large issues in connection with such a claim. The first is whether it is true that reality, knowable or not, is, quite generally, different from how things appear to be in ordinary experience. ('Ordinary' is important here, since for some thinkers, like Śaṁkara, absolute reality, though inaccessible to perception, may be divined in extraordinary mystical experience.) For Kant and his follower, in this respect at least, Schopenhauer, it is and must be different. While Schopenhauer is willing to call the thing in itself 'the will', he is quick to add that this 'will' must be very different from the will as we experience it, for example, at work in our own actions. For Berkeley and Mill, by stark contrast, 'external' reality cannot be (generally) different from our perceptions of it, since 'external' objects just are suitable collections of actual or possible perceptions.

The second issue is one which divides those who agree on a general reality *vs.* appearance contrast. Given the contrast, can reality be known at all, at least in the sense of being articulatable, of being accessible to what Kant called 'discursive' intelligence? For Plato, on a familiar if contentious interpretation, the Forms, which constitute the reality of which things as experienced are mere pale 'copies', may be known to the philosopher who has been through a sufficiently rigorous training in rational 'dialectic'. But, for many other thinkers, such as Bradley, the ultimately real is not 'discursible'. To take only the most famous example, furnished by the first line of the first text in this volume, 'The Tao that can be told of is not the eternal Tao'.[3]

The positions taken on these two issues need not be as 'black and white' as those I have so far mentioned. For example, there is Locke's account of primary and secondary qualities, with its seeming implication that far more of the content of perceptual experience than is naively imagined, but not all of it, fails to parallel the real features of things. Nothing in the object itself, for instance, resembles the red which you and I see. Finally, one should mention those philosophers who, as with the mental *vs.* the material debate, aim to dissolve the issues rather than come down on one side or the other. The clearest example in this book is furnished by the Buddhist writer, Nāgārjuna (chapter 4), for whom reality (*nirvana*) is not reducible to the phenomenal order, but is not different from it either. Rather, it is matter of two different ways of conceiving of things, 'conventionally' and *sub specie aeternitatis*.

III

I have described some of the topics and debates which inform and inspire metaphysical enquiry. But are they genuine ones which sensible people should occupy themselves with? The question recalls my opening remark on the tendency, in the century just ended, to regard metaphysics as an impossible and misguided enterprise. To assess that tendency, we must identify the reasons advanced for concluding, as Gilbert Ryle bluntly put it, that 'metaphysics is out!'.

Some of those reasons have a long ancestry. To begin with, there have always been writers *sceptical* of establishing truths about the world which go beyond what might be established, or even rendered probable, by empirical investigation. The classic expression of this scepticism was David

---

[3] Someone might hold that the issue discussed in this paragraph is an epistemological, not a metaphysical, one. Well, the distinction between metaphysics and epistemology is hardly a sharply defined one. Anyway, it is surely possible to modulate from the epistemological-sounding claims to metaphysical-sounding ones: for instance, from the denial of 'discursive' knowledge of reality to denial that reality has that structure, or those features, which make it possible for us 'discursively' to know what it is positively like.

Hume's. Given that 'the mind has never anything present to it but [its] own perceptions', then we must remain ignorant of, *inter alia*, 'the essence of . . . external bodies' and 'the ultimate principle which binds [things] together'. Since metaphysics purports to discover such matters, it is 'sophistry' which should be 'committed to the flames'.[4] Kant, woken from his 'dogmatic slumbers' by Hume, shared a similar attitude towards what he called 'dogmatic' metaphysics, agreeing that it is impossible to penetrate into the nature of things in themselves, since any possible object of knowledge was conditioned by the forms and structures of human experience and understanding. Kant, however, allowed a role for metaphysics: that of articulating the synthetic *a priori* principles which, in effect, formulate those forms and structures. 'Every event has a cause', for example, is a metaphysical truth which expresses a condition which any event must meet in order to be an object of experience.

It was on different grounds that the notorious attack on metaphysics by the logical positivists was launched in the 1920s and '30s. As one of their number, A. J. Ayer, put it, Kant was wrong to make 'the impossibility of a transcendent metaphysic' a matter of *fact* about the limits of our knowledge: rather, it is 'a matter of logic', due to considerations about meaning. 'The utterances of the metaphysician are nonsensical' because they are neither empirically verifiable (or falsifiable) nor analytic (true by definition).[5] Since a proposition only has sense, according to the positivists' principle of meaning, if it is empirically testable or analytic, then metaphysical utterances are not meaningful propositions. Disputes, like those discussed above, between monists and pluralists or idealists and materialists, are therefore pseudo-disputes – so much hot air unless, as is sometimes the case, they can be seen as misleadingly worded and conducted arguments about some empirical or analytic matter.

In retrospect, even the temporary success of this attack on metaphysics seems puzzling. It is hard to take seriously a principle of meaning which, rather obviously, violates the conditions it lays down: *it* is neither empirically testable nor true by definition. One might stipulate that a proposition is meaningful only if verifiable or analytic, but that would betray an unargued and dogmatic privileging of scientific and mathematical discourses, of which the positivists seem only too guilty.

One does not have to be a logical positivist to assign a special authority to science, and in recent years perhaps the most common attack on meta-

[4] *An Enquiry Concerning Human Understanding*, Indianapolis: Hackett, 1977, pp. 105 and 114, and *A Treatise of Human Nature*, Oxford: Clarendon Press, 1960, pp. 267 and 636.
[5] *Language, Truth and Logic*, London: Gollancz, 1967, pp. 34 and 41.

physics comes from those who hold that metaphysics is 'out' because its traditional ambitions have been taken over by the sciences. 'Whatever can be known', writes W. V. Quine, 'can be known by means of science' alone.[6] It is bizarre, however, to suppose that this claim, even if it were coherent and true, puts paid to metaphysics, since, of course, it is itself a patently metaphysical claim. We should surely distinguish between science itself – a body of procedures, propositions and theories – and a 'scientistic' metaphysics, according to which the world is such that science alone can correctly describe it. As it stands, claims like Quine's, intended to dismiss metaphysical speculation, simply confirm Bradley's insight that those who rubbish metaphysical theories turn out to be peddling one of their own.

There have been plenty of other attacks on metaphysics, but I suspect that all of them involve either an unusual stipulative understanding of the term or a metaphysical position of their own – or, as in the case of Heidegger's later writings, both. He uses 'metaphysics' to label a long tradition of thought guilty, in his view, of both an 'anthropomorphic' conception of being and of understanding being as if it were an entity or set of entities of a special sort – God, say, or substances, or Forms.[7] Maybe his characterization and criticism of this tradition are apposite: however, it is surely arbitrary to label it 'metaphysics', and certainly not all of the authors represented in this book belong to it. Moreover, it is apparent that Heidegger's own difficult account of being, and its difference from beings, is itself an exercise in metaphysics on any less stipulative understanding of the term.

IV

A more covert criticism of traditional metaphysics than the frontal attacks just described is implied by various 'deflationist' conceptions of the subject. The possibility of metaphysics is not denied in name, but the discipline is assigned more modest goals. The effect, in one recent author's view, is to 'enfeeble' and 'downgrade' metaphysics.[8]

Deflationism is already at work in Kant's conception of metaphysics. It is not reality in itself, but only the *a priori* conditions of our objective experience of phenomena, into which a viable metaphysics can enquire. Still more deflationist and distant from the traditional ambitions of metaphysics was

---

[6] 'Philosophical progress in language theory', *Metaphilosophy*, 1, 1970, p. 1.
[7] See, for example, 'Metaphysics and anthropomorphism' in his *Nietzsche*, vol. IV, ed. D. F. Krell, San Francisco: Harper & Row, 1982.
[8] E. J. Lowe, *The Possibility of Metaphysics*, pp. 3 and 6.

the conception advanced by the neo-Kantian followers of the great German. For them, Kant's idea of viable metaphysics was still too ambitious,
for it assumed that the *a priori* conditions of experience were universal and
eternal, rather than historically contingent and relative to practices of enquiry. The best-known statement of this conception of metaphysics is R.
G. Collingwood's: 'Metaphysics is the attempt to find out what absolute
presuppositions have been made by this or that person or group of persons, on this or that occasion . . . , in the course of this or that piece of
thinking'. Questions about the truth of such varying presuppositions
belong to 'pseudo-metaphysics'.[9] Metaphysics, on this view, lies closer to
anthropology and sociology than to traditional ontology.

Two remarks should be made about these deflationist attitudes. The first
is that it may, in fact, make rather little difference in practice, or to the
kinds of arguments deployed, whether a metaphysician adopts a traditional
or deflationist view of his enquiries. The arguments which two philosophers use to establish that every event must have a cause can be similar
even though the one takes himself or herself simply to be identifying a
presupposition of modern scientific enquiry, the other to be delineating
the abiding structure of reality. Again, similar considerations might be
employed to show either that our concepts of physical objects are analysable
into sensory concepts or that physical objects are 'composed' of sense-
data. Russell, for example, moves smoothly between those two ways of
talking, conceptual and ontological.

Second, it is hard to see that deflationists, despite their protests, avoid
making metaphysical claims of a traditional kind, albeit ones of a pretty
negative type. Thus Kant's insistence that reality in itself cannot have any
empirically accessible features is surely a metaphysical one in the old style,
as is that of some neo-Kantians, to the effect that no sense can be made of
the notion of a way things anyway are independent of historically conditioned conceptual schemes.

Whether sceptical, deflationist, or unequivocally hostile attitudes towards
the possibility of metaphysics have any warrant, readers of the texts in this
volume must judge for themselves. If current philosophical practice is to
be a guide, then metaphysics has ridden out the storms of criticism which
blew strong for several decades.

---

[9] *An Essay on Metaphysics*, Chicago: Regnary, 1972, p. 47. A related deflationist view is defended by P. F. Strawson, *Individuals: an essay in descriptive metaphysics*, London: Methuen,
1959. The kind of viable metaphysics intended by the subtitle – and contrasted with 'revision-
ary' metaphysics – is confined to illuminating *description*, without *adjudication*, of the conceptual scheme we employ.

One reason I have dwelt, in this Introduction, on those storms, besides the obvious one of suggesting that this volume has a genuine subject matter, is that I have not included any texts by out-and-out critics of metaphysics. My advisory editor, Timothy Sprigge, wisely persuaded me that the book should consist *of* metaphysics (in action, as it were) and exclude musings *about* metaphysics (meta-metaphysics, I suppose).

Various further considerations, some already mentioned, have influenced my selection of texts. Rather than invidiously choose just one or two texts addressed to this or that narrow metaphysical issue, I have preferred to fill the volume with texts which offer general conceptions of reality, or at any rate of crucial, global aspects of reality. Next, I judged several texts which were certainly serious candidates to be insufficiently intelligible taken out of the context of the larger works to which they belong. This was true of the writings of the German absolute idealists, and also of the writings of medieval philosophers. Finally, some other candidate texts are better located, in my judgement, in other volumes in the *Philosophy: the classic readings* series. For example, Edmund Husserl's metaphysical position can be found articulated in his lectures included in the earlier volume on epistemology, while aspects of St Thomas Aquinas' metaphysics will be apparent in his discussion of God's existence in the forthcoming volume on philosophy of religion.

As ever with anthologies, the present selection of texts has reflected predilections and enthusiasms of their editor. But I hope that the selection may serve to convince readers that, in the words of one contemporary writer, metaphysics has deserved to be 'neither destroyed nor . . . silenced' by its detractors.[10]

---

[10] Ernest Sosa, 'Metaphysics, problems of', in T. Honderich (ed.), *The Oxford Companion to Philosophy*, Oxford: Oxford University Press, 1995, p. 563.

Tao Te Ching (selected chapters)

From A Source Book in Chinese Philosophy, trans. and compiled by Wing-Tsit Chan. Princeton: Princeton University Press, 1969, pp. 139–50, 152–54, 156–64, 166, 172 (some notes and passages omitted; asterisked notes are the translator's).

Hardly any books in world literature have inspired more translations and commentaries than the short work (only 5,000 Chinese characters) known as the *Tao Te Ching* (*Dao De Jing*, in Pinyin transliteration). The usual English rendition of the title is 'The Book of the Way (*tao*) and Its Virtue (*te*)', though some translators prefer 'power' to 'virtue' – for the virtue of which the book speaks is, for the most part, not moral excellence, but something more akin to the 'efficacy' of a plant or mineral to which scientists referred of old as its virtue. Opinions on the book's date and authorship vary wildly: some commentators cling to the traditional view that it was written by Lao Tzu (Laozi, or 'Old Master'), a contemporary of Confucius in the sixth century BCE, while others hold that Lao Tzu was a mythical figure and the book a fourth- or third-Century compilation. A compromise opinion is that Lao Tzu may have been real enough, but most of the chapters are later accretions.[1]

What is not similarly in dispute is the massive influence of the book – immediately on Taoist thinkers such as Chuang Tzu and later on almost every development in Chinese philosophy, including Chan or Zen Buddhism. Its influence has not been confined, moreover, to the East. In our own century, that influence is palpable in the later writings of Martin Heidegger, who even embarked on an abortive project to translate the work.[2]

Like other famous works from the 'classic age' of Chinese philosophy, such as Confucius' *Analects*, the *Tao Te Ching* has a primarily practical purpose: to advise the author's contemporaries in those troubled and bellicose times,

---

[1] The three opinions mentioned are those of, respectively, Wing-Tsit Chin in his preamble to the translation I have selected, Arthur Waley, *The Way and Its Power*, London: Unwin, 1977, and Fung Yu-Lan, *A Short History of Chinese Philosophy*, New York: Free Press, 1966.

[2] See Reinhold May, *Heidegger's Hidden Sources: East Asian influences on his work*, London: Routledge, 1996.

especially the rulers of states, on how to live – and enable others to live – prudently, safely and contentedly. The advice given by Lao Tzu (assuming he was the author) is, on the surface, no different from that offered by other authors of the time. The wise person or ruler must live 'in accord with' the Tao, the Way, for 'whatever is contrary to Tao will soon perish' (ch. 55). Lao Tzu, however, invested the notion of Tao with much greater metaphysical significance than had other writers, for whom the Way was often no more than the natural order of the world. As the resounding opening lines of the *Tao Te Ching* tell us, the Tao is the eternal, nameless and ultimate origin of everything. (In the original text, whose chapters were later reordered, such metaphysical passages came after the advisory ones, which indicates that the book's purpose was primarily practical, but hardly, as some have held, that the metaphysics was only an 'afterthought'.)[3]

The *Tao Te Ching* makes at least four claims of metaphysical interest – claims of a general kind, moreover, which has had recurrent appeal to thinkers during the whole history of philosophy. First and foremost there is the idea that, in order for any thing, any being, to exist, there must be a 'profound' origin or source that cannot itself be conceived as a thing or a being. This is the point of the references to the Tao as 'non-being' or 'no-thing'. The Tao is not some remarkable entity or person, a God, who created the universe *ex nihilo*. While it is the source of all things, their precondition, it is nothing over and above or outside them – no more than the melody which, so to speak, holds the notes together, is something *in addition to* those notes.[4] Second, there is the insistence that the 'eternal Tao' is ineffable, 'nameless' in the sense of resisting informative description. It was to be left to Chuang Tzu, with his reflections on the limits of language, to clarify why the Tao must be ineffable, but hints are afforded in the *Tao Te Ching* – in Chapters 14 and 25, for example, where it is implied that the Tao is too 'undifferentiated' and 'vague' for informative descriptions to be given of it.

Third, there is the claim that, while the 'eternal Tao' is unknowable and ineffable, it nevertheless presents aspects to us – the 'named Tao' – which can be discerned in the operations of the natural world. We can discern, for instance, that the Tao operates according to a principle of 'reversal', an oscillation back and forth between 'opposites', like heat and cold, which prevents things going beyond limits in a way fatal for the stability of the natural order. We can discern, too, that the Tao's 'actions', like that of water (Ch. 8), display that spontaneity and effortlessness which Taoists call *wu wei* ('actionless

---

[3] See Charles Wei-hsun Fu, 'Daoism in Chinese philosophy', in Brian Carr and Indira Mahalingam (eds.), *Companion Encyclopedia of Asian Philosophy*, London: Routledge, 1997, p. 554.
[4] The analogy is Raymond M. Smullyan's, *The Tao is Silent*, San Francisco: Harper, 1977, p. 20.

action'). Finally, there is the claim, required if the metaphysical claims are to be of practical import, that insight into the Way enables a proper human life. The good and sage person is one who, in certain respects, emulates the Way, above all by renouncing those conventions or artifices (so admired by Confucians) and a febrile striving antithetical to *wu wei*, which indicate that the Tao has been 'lost'.

The *Tao Te Ching*, then, is one of philosophy's earliest invitations to share a metaphysical vision of a source of all things which, while ineffable, affords us intimations of its nature – a nature which to ignore or oppose is to 'perish'.

Tao-Te Ching

1. The Tao (way) that can be told of is not the eternal Tao;
   The name that can be named is not the eternal name.
   The Nameless is the origin of Heaven and Earth;
   The Named is the mother of all things.
   Therefore let there always be non-being so we may see their
       subtlety [or mystery].
   And let there always be being so we may see their outcome.
   The two are the same,
   But after they are produced, they have different names.
   They both may be called deep and profound (*hsüan*).
   Deeper and more profound,
   The door of all subtleties!

2. When the people of the world all know beauty as beauty,
       There arises the recognition of ugliness.
   When they all know the good as good,
       There arises the recognition of evil.
   Therefore:
       Being and non-being produce each other;
       Difficult and easy complete each other;
       Long and short contrast each other;
       High and low distinguish each other;
       Sound and voice harmonize with each other;
       Front and back follow each other.
   Therefore the sage manages affairs without action (*wu-wei*)
   And spreads doctrines without words.
   All things arise, and he does not turn away from them.
   He produces them, but does not take possession of them.

He acts, but does not rely on his own ability.
He accomplishes his task, but does not claim credit for it.
It is precisely because he does not claim credit that his
accomplishment remains with him. . . .

4. Tao is empty (like a bowl),
It may be used but its capacity is never exhausted.
It is bottomless, perhaps the ancestor of all things.
It blunts its sharpness,
It unties its tangles.
It softens its light.
It becomes one with the dusty world.
Deep and still, it appears to exist forever.
I do not know whose son it is.
It seems to have existed before the Lord. . . .

6. The spirit of the valley never dies.
    It is called the subtle and profound female.
The gate of the subtle and profound female
    Is the root of Heaven and Earth.
It is continuous, and seems to be always existing.
Use it and you will never wear it out. . . .

8. The best (man) is like water.
Water is good; it benefits all things and does not
    compete with them.
It dwells in (lowly) places that all disdain.
This is why it is so near to Tao.
[The best man] in his dwelling loves the earth.
    In his heart, he loves what is profound.
    In his associations, he loves humanity.
    In his words, he loves faithfulness.
    In government, he loves order.
    In handling affairs, he loves competence.
    In his activities, he loves timeliness.
    It is because he does not compete that he is
        without reproach. . . .

10. Can you keep the spirit and embrace the One without departing
        from them?
Can you concentrate your vital force (*ch'i*) and achieve the

highest degree of weakness like an infant?

Can you clean and purify your profound insight so it will be
    spotless?

Can you love the people and govern the state without knowledge
    (cunning)?

Can you play the role of the female in the opening and closing
    of the gates of Heaven?

Can you understand all and penetrate all without taking any
    action?

    To produce things and to rear them,
      To produce, but not to take possession of them,
    To act, but not to rely on one's own ability,
    To lead them, but not to master them –
    This is called profound and secret virtue (*hsüan-te*).

11. Thirty spokes are united around the hub to make a wheel,
    But it is on its non-being that the utility of the carriage
      depends.
  Clay is molded to form a utensil,
    But it is on its non-being that the utility of the utensil
      depends.
  Doors and windows are cut out to make a room,
    But it is on its non-being that the utility of the room
      depends.
  Therefore turn being into advantage, and turn non-being
  into utility. . . .

14. We look at it and do not see it;
    Its name is The Invisible.
  We listen to it and do not hear it;
    Its name is The Inaudible.
  We touch it and do not find it;
    Its name is The Subtle (formless).
  These three cannot be further inquired into,
  And hence merge into one.
  Going up high, it is not bright, and coming down low, it is
    not dark.
  Infinite and boundless, it cannot be given any name;
  It reverts to nothingness.
  This is called shape without shape,
  Form (*hsiang*) without object.

Tao as riddle, mystery — the possibility of being(s)

It is The Vague and Elusive.
Meet it and you will not see its head.
Follow it and you will not see its back.
Hold on to the Tao of old in order to master the things of
    the present.
From this one may know the primeval beginning [of the
    universe].[1]
This is called the bond [*chi*] of Tao.*

15. Of old those who were the best rulers were
        subtly mysterious and profoundly penetrating;
        Too deep to comprehend.
    And because they cannot be comprehended,
        I can only describe them arbitrarily:
        Cautious, like crossing a frozen stream in the winter,
        Being at a loss, like one fearing danger on all sides,
        Reserved, like one visiting,
        Supple and pliant, like ice about to melt,
        Genuine, like a piece of uncarved wood,†
        Open and broad, like a valley,
        Merged and undifferentiated, like muddy water.

    Who can make muddy water gradually clear through
        tranquillity?
    Who can make the still gradually come to life through
        activity?
    He who embraces this Tao does not want to fill himself
        to overflowing.
    It is precisely because there is no overflowing that he is
        beyond wearing out and renewal.

16. Attain complete vacuity,
    Maintain steadfast quietude.
    All things come into being,
    And I see thereby their return.
    All things flourish,

---

* *Chi*, literally a thread, denotes tradition, discipline, principle, order, essence, etc. Generally it means the system, principle, or continuity that binds things together.
† *P'u*, literally an uncarved wood, has come to mean in Taoism simplicity, plainness, genuineness, etc.

But each one returns to its root.
This return to its root means tranquillity.
It is called returning to its destiny.
To return to destiny is called the eternal (Tao).
To know the eternal is called enlightenment.
Not to know the eternal is to act blindly to result in disaster.
He who knows the eternal is all-embracing.
Being all-embracing, he is impartial.
Being impartial, he is kingly (universal).
Being kingly, he is one with Nature.
Being one with Nature, he is in accord with Tao.
Being in accord with Tao, he is everlasting,
And is free from danger throughout his lifetime. . . .

Tao as root – the depths of Being, the way to contentment/flourishing

Tao provides perspective, knowledge towards Nature and Existence

18. When the great Tao declined,
The doctrines of humanity (*jen*) and righteousness (*i*) arose.
When knowledge and wisdom appeared,
There emerged great hypocrisy.
When the six family relationships* are not in harmony,
There will be the advocacy of filial piety and deep love to children.
When a country is in disorder,
There will be praise of loyal ministers. . . .[2]

20. Abandon learning and there will no sorrow.
How much difference is there between "Yes, sir," and "Of course not"?
How much difference is there between "good" and "evil"?
What people dread, do not fail to dread.
But, alas, how confused, and the end is not yet.
The multitude are merry, as though feasting on a day of sacrifice,
Or like ascending a tower at springtime.
I alone am inert, showing no sign (of desires),
Like an infant that has not yet smiled.
Wearied, indeed, I seem to be without a home.
The multitude all possess more than enough,
I alone seem to have lost all.
Mine is indeed the mind of an ignorant man,
Indiscriminate and dull!

* Father, son, elder brother, younger brother, husband, and wife.

Common folks are indeed brilliant;
I alone seem to be in the dark.

Common folks see differences and are clear-cut;
I alone make no distinctions.
I seem drifting as the sea;
Like the wind blowing about, seemingly without destination.
The multitude all have a purpose;
I alone seem to be stubborn and rustic.
I alone differ from others,
And value drawing sustenance from Mother (Tao).

[handwritten margin note: Awareness of Tao makes us strange to others]

21. The all-embracing quality of the great virtue (*te*) follows
    alone from the Tao.
    The thing that is called Tao is eluding and vague.
    Vague and eluding, there is in it the form.
    Eluding and vague, in it are things.
    Deep and obscure, in it is the essence.*
    The essence is very real; in it are evidences.
    From the time of old until now, its name (manifestations)
    ever remains,
    By which we may see the beginning of all things.
    How do I know that the beginnings of all things are so?
    Through this (Tao). . . .

[handwritten margin note: All-embracing as great virtue which follows from Tao]

25. There was something undifferentiated and yet complete,
    Which existed before heaven and earth.
    Soundless and formless, it depends on nothing
        and does not change.
    It operates everywhere and is free from danger.
    It may be considered the mother of the universe.
    I do not know its name; I call it Tao.
    If forced to give it a name, I shall call it Great.
    Now being great means functioning everywhere.
    Functioning everywhere means far-reaching.
    Being far-reaching means returning to the original point.
    Therefore Tao is great.
    Heaven is great.
    Earth is great.

[handwritten margin note: Tao as before heaven/earth]

---

* The word *ching* (essence) also means intelligence, spirit, life-force.

And the king is also great.
There are four great things in the universe, and the king is
   one of them.
Man models himself after Earth.
Earth models itself after Heaven.
Heaven models itself after Tao.
And Tao models itself after Nature. . . .

Nature
↓
Tao
↓
Heaven
↓
Earth
↓
Man

28. He who knows the male (active force) and keeps to the
      female (the passive force or receptive element)
   Becomes the ravine of the world.
   Being the ravine of the world,
   He will never depart from eternal virtue,
   But returns to the state of infancy.
   He who knows the white (glory) and yet keeps to the
      black (humility),
   Becomes the model for the world.
   Being the model for the world,
   He will never deviate from eternal virtue,
   But returns to the state of the Ultimate of Non-being.
   He who knows glory but keeps to humility,
   Becomes the valley of the world.
   Being the valley of the world,
   He will be proficient in eternal virtue,
   And returns to the state of simplicity (uncarved wood).
   When the uncarved wood is broken up, it is turned into
      concrete things (as Tao is transformed into the myriad
      things).
   But when the sage uses it, he becomes the leading official.
   Therefore the great ruler does not cut up. . . .

32. Tao is eternal and has no name.
   Though its simplicity seems insignificant, none in the world
      can master it.
   If kings and barons would hold on to it, all things would
      submit to them spontaneously.
   Heaven and earth unite to drip sweet dew.
   Without the command of men, it drips evenly over all.
   As soon as there were regulations and institutions, there
      were names (differentiation of things).
   As soon as there are names, know that it is time to stop.

It is by knowing when to stop that one can be free from danger.
Analogically, Tao in the world (where everything is embraced
   by it), may be compared to rivers and streams running
   into the sea. . . .

34. The Great Tao flows everywhere.
   It may go left or right.
   All things depend on it for life, and it does not turn away
      from them.
   It accomplishes its task, but does not claim credit for it.
   It clothes and feeds all things but does not claim to be
      master over them.
   Always without desires, it may be called The Small.
   All things come to it and it does not master them;
      it may be called The Great.
   Therefore (the sage) never strives himself for the great, and
      thereby the great is achieved.

35. Hold fast to the great form (Tao),
   And all the world will come.
   They come and will encounter no harm;
   But enjoy comfort, peace, and health.
   When there are music and dainties,
   Passing strangers will stay.
   But the words uttered by Tao,
   How insipid and tasteless!
   We look at Tao; it is imperceptible.
   We listen to it; it is inaudible.
   We use it; it is inexhaustible. . . .

38. . . . , only when Tao is lost does the doctrine of virtue arise.
   When virtue is lost, only then does the doctrine of humanity
      arise.
   When humanity is lost, only then does the doctrine of
      righteousness arise.
   When righteousness is lost, only then does the doctrine of
      propriety [*li*]* arise.
   Now, propriety is a superficial expression of loyalty and

* In a narrow sense, *li* means rites, ritual, ceremonies, etc., but in a broad sense it means rules
of behavior or principles of conduct.

faithfulness, and the beginning of disorder.
Those who are the first to know have the flowers (appearance)
of Tao but are the beginning of ignorance.
For this reason the great man dwells in the thick (substantial),
and does not rest with the thin (superficial).
He dwells in the fruit (reality), and does not rest with the
flower (appearance).
Therefore he rejects the one, and accepts the other.

39. Of old those that obtained the One:
Heaven obtained the One and became clear.
Earth obtained the One and became tranquil.
The spiritual beings obtained the One and became divine.
The valley obtained the One and became full.
The myriad things obtained the One and lived and grew.
Kings and barons obtained the One and became rulers
of the empire.
What made them so is the One.
If heaven had not thus become clear,
It would soon crack.
If the earth had not thus become tranquil,
It would soon be shaken.
If the spiritual beings had not thus become divine,
They would soon wither away.
If the valley had not thus become full,
It would soon become exhausted.
If the myriad things had not thus lived and grown,
They would soon become extinct.
If kings and barons had not thus become honorable and high
in position,
They would soon fall.
Therefore humble station is the basis of honor.
The low is the foundation of the high.
For this reason kings and barons call themselves the orphaned,
the lonely ones, the unworthy.
Is this not regarding humble station as the basis of honor?
Is it not?
Therefore enumerate all the parts of a chariot as you may,
and you still have no chariot.
Rather than jingle like the jade,
Rumble like the rocks.

Obtaining Tao leads to fulfillment

40. Reversion is the action of Tao.
    Weakness is the function of Tao.
    All things in the world come from being.
    And being comes from non-being.

41. . . . Tao is hidden and nameless.
    Yet it is Tao alone that skillfully provides for all and brings
        them to perfection.

42. Tao produced the One.
    The One produced the two.
    The two produced the three.
    And the three produced the ten thousand things.[3]
    The ten thousand things carry the yin and embrace the
        yang,* and through the blending of the material force
        (*ch'i*)† they achieve harmony. . . .

43. The softest things in the world overcome the hardest
        things in the world.
    Non-being penetrates that in which there is no space.
    Through this I know the advantage of taking no action.
    Few in the world can understand teaching without words
        and the advantage of taking no action. . . .

47. One may know the world without going out of doors.
    One may see the Way of Heaven without looking through
        the windows,
    The further one goes, the less one knows.
    Therefore the sage knows without going about,
    Understands without seeing,
    And accomplishes without any action. . . .

51. Tao produces them (the ten thousand things).
    Virtue fosters them.
    Matter gives them physical form.[4]
    The circumstances and tendencies complete them.
    Therefore the ten thousand things esteem Tao and honor
        virtue.

---

* Yin is the passive, female cosmic principle or force while yang is the active or male principle.
† Variously translated as matter, matter-energy, vital force, breath, etc.

Tao is esteemed and virtue is honored without anyone's order.
They always come spontaneously.
Therefore Tao produces them and virtue fosters them.
They rear them and develop them.
They give them security and give them peace.
They nurture them and protect them.
(Tao) produces them but does not take possession of them.
It acts, but does not rely on its own ability.
It leads them but does not master them.
This is called profound and secret virtue.

52. There was a beginning of the universe
    Which may be called the Mother of the Universe.   Tao as mother
    He who has found the mother (Tao)
    And thereby understands her sons (things)
    And having understood the sons,
    Still keeps to its mother,
    Will be free from danger throughout his lifetime. . . .

55. . . . To know harmony means to be in accord with the eternal.
    To be in accord with the eternal means to be enlightened.
    To force the growth of life means ill omen.
    For the mind to employ the vital force without restraint
       means violence.
    After things reach their prime, they begin to grow old,
    Which means being contrary to Tao.
    Whatever is contrary to Tao will soon perish.

56. He who knows does not speak.
    He who speaks does not know.
    Close the mouth.
    Shut the doors (of cunning and desires).
    Blunt the sharpness.
    Untie the tangles.
    Soften the light.
    Become one with the dusty world.
    This is called profound identification. . . .

70. My doctrines are very easy to understand and very easy to
       practice,
    But none in the world can understand or practice them.

My doctrines have a source (Nature); my deeds have a
   master (Tao).
It is because people do not understand this that they do not
   understand me.
Few people know me, and therefore I am highly valued.
Therefore the sage wears a coarse cloth on top and carries
   jade within his bosom.

71. To know that you do not know is the best.
   To pretend to know when you do not know is a disease.
   Only when one recognizes this disease as a disease can one be
      free from the disease.
   The sage is free from the disease.
   Because he recognizes this disease to be disease, he is free
      from it. . . .

Notes

1 References to Tao as the 'beginning' or 'origin' of the universe should not
   be taken in a temporal sense, but an ontological one. Tao is the precondition of 'the dusty world', but does not pre-exist it.
2 The target in this chapter, and several others (e.g. ch. 38), is Confucian
   ethics, in which 'righteousness', 'propriety' and 'filial piety' figure prominently. The point made is that such conventional and 'artificial' virtues would
   not be required had people not forgotten or departed from the Way.
3 The intended referents of 'one', 'two' and 'three' have been much disputed.
   But perhaps, like Chuang Tzu, we should be impatient with attempts to
   determine an exact literal meaning and instead treat the passage as simply
   indicating the development of the Tao from simplicity to complexity and
   differentiation. 'The ten thousand things', incidentally, is a conventional
   Chinese expression for the totality of things.
4 This makes clear that 'virtue' is not necessarily a human and moral feature.
   Here it seems to refer to a thing's essential form as distinct from the matter
   of which it is composed.

Plato, *Phaedrus*, 245–50

From The Dialogues of Plato, Vol. I (trans. B. Jowett). New York: Macmillan & Co., 1892. pp. 451–7 (one note omitted; asterisked note is the translator's).

Although the Way indicated in the *Tao Te Ching* is intangible and invisible, it is not dualistically opposed, as an 'other world', to the everyday 'dusty world'. In the *Phaedrus* dialogue of the great Athenian philosopher, Plato (c. 427–347 BCE), however, we are introduced to just such an opposition – between a realm of 'existence absolute' and the ordinary empirical world whose contents are but 'copies' of the 'universals' or 'essences' comprised in the former (247). Only if the soul were not 'enshrined in that living tomb', the body, could it attain knowledge of the absolute realm – or, rather, fully recapture the knowledge it enjoyed prior to that enshrinement. As it is, nearly all of us are condemned to mere 'opinion' about the world of 'copies'. The Plato of *Phaedrus*, then, is perhaps the earliest and certainly the greatest western thinker to have promulgated the triple dualisms of 'the two worlds', soul *versus* body, and transcendent knowledge *versus* mere 'opinion'.

In *Phaedrus*, as in related writings – notably, Diotima's speech in the *Symposium* and the central Books of *Republic* – Plato represents his metaphysical vision in the form of allegory or 'figure'. Only someone who experiences 'existence absolute' could, if language allowed, provide a literal account of it, and Plato make no personal claim to any such experience. Plato's figurative presentation creates a problem, of course, for as one commentator puts it, it is not 'permissible to extract metaphysics from mythical details . . . [included] for the coherency of the pictorial representation'.[1] The charioteer allegory of *Phaedrus* is 'one of the highest points in Plato's achievement as artist and poet',[2] and presumably we are to take as merely poetic references such as those to a supra-heavenly vault and the ten millennia it takes a soul to grow wings. On the other hand, there is no reason to doubt Plato's commitment to the literal, or near-literal, truth of those doctrines, briefly indicated in the dialogue, which are elaborated and defended elsewhere, notably in *Republic*.[3]

[1] A. E. Taylor, *Plato: the man and his work*, London: Methuen, 1937, p. 307.
[2] Walter Hamilton, Introduction to Plato's *Phaedrus and Letters VII and VIII*, Harmondsworth: Penguin, 1973, p. 10.

These doctrines include: (a) the distinction between the realm of 'universals', or as Plato elsewhere calls them, 'Forms' or 'Ideas', and the world of ordinary things which are their 'copies'; (b) the doctrine of *anamnesis*, according to which our present understanding is due to dim recollection of the 'universals' experienced by the soul prior to its embodiment; (c) the idea that while reason may lead us towards an understanding of 'existence absolute', this is finally a matter of enjoying a 'beatific' or 'mystic' vision; (d) the immortality of the soul; (e) the distinctness of soul from body, in which it unfortunately gets stuck 'like an oyster in its shell' (250); (f) the 'transmigration' of souls from body to body; and (g) the 'tripartite' nature of the soul, rational, 'spirited' and 'appetitive'.

The bulk of *Phaedrus* is concerned not with metaphysics, but with the nature of sexual love and the status of rhetoric. We join the dialogue at the point where Plato's mouthpiece, Socrates,[4] is challenging the view that the 'temperate' person is superior to the lover since the latter is 'mad', 'possessed' or 'beside himself'. He intends to show that there is a divine madness which is manifested in sexual desires of whose real significance the lover is typically unaware, and which can only be understood as a displaced yearning for absolute beauty. Since this is the Form of beauty, Socrates needs, therefore, first to give an account of how the soul, which must be immaterial and immortal, originally encountered it. The charioteer allegory provides that account.

It would be a mistake to think that Plato's admiration for the person of divine madness or passion entails any rejection of reason. 'What emerges with particular clarity from the *Phaedrus* is that it is *reason itself* which longs for Beauty' and the other Forms.[5] It is a prior *knowledge* of Beauty, not the aesthetic thrills it may have afforded, which the lover unconsciously seeks to recollect. And the 'madness' or passion of the philosopher – the lover (from Gk. *philia*) of wisdom (from Gk. *sophia*) – is a rational passion to know and understand 'existence absolute'.

▶ ▶ ▶   **Plato, *Phaedrus***

245   . . . I might tell of many other noble deeds which have sprung from inspired madness. And therefore, let no one frighten or flutter us by saying that the temperate friend is to be chosen rather than the inspired, but let

---

[3] The relevant parts of *Republic*, including the allegory of the cave, are included in my *Epistemology: the classic readings*, Oxford: Blackwell, 1999.

[4] *Phaedrus* belongs to Plato's so-called 'middle period' when, it is generally agreed, many of the views expressed by the character Socrates, especially those of a metaphysically momentous nature, are not those of the historical Socrates.

[5] Christopher Rowe, 'Plato: aesthetics and psychology', in C. C. W. Taylor (ed.), *From the Beginning to Plato*, London: Routledge, 1997, p. 435.

him further show that love is not sent by the gods for any good to lover or beloved; if he can do so we will allow him to carry off the palm. And we, on our part, will prove in answer to him that the madness of love is the greatest of heaven's blessings, and the proof shall be one which the wise will receive, and the witling disbelieve. But first of all, let us view the affections and actions of the soul divine and human, and try to ascertain the truth about them. The beginning of our proof is as follows:–

The soul through all her being is immortal, for that which is ever in motion is immortal; but that which moves another and is moved by another, in ceasing to move ceases also to live. Only the self-moving, never leaving itself, never ceases to move, and is the fountain and beginning of motion to all that moves besides. Now, the beginning is unbegotten, for that which is begotten has a beginning; but the beginning is begotten of nothing, for if it were begotten of something, then the begotten would not come from a beginning. But if unbegotten, it must also be indestructible; for if beginning were destroyed, there could be no beginning out of anything, nor anything out of a beginning; and all things must have a beginning. And therefore the self-moving is the beginning of motion; and this can neither be destroyed nor begotten, else the whole heavens and all creation would collapse and stand still, and never again have motion or birth. But if the self-moving is proved to be immortal, he who affirms that self-motion is the very idea and essence of the soul will not be put to confusion. For the body which is moved from without is soulless; but that which is moved from within has a soul, such motion being inherent in the soul. But if this is true, must not the soul be the self-moving, and therefore of necessity unbegotten and immortal? Enough of the soul's immortality.

Of the nature of the soul, though her true form be ever a theme of large and more than mortal discourse, let me speak briefly, and in a figure. And let the figure be composite – a pair of winged horses and a charioteer.[1] Now the winged horses and the charioteers of the gods are all of them noble and of noble descent, but those of other races are mixed; the human charioteer drives his in a pair; and one of them is noble and of noble breed, and the other is ignoble and of ignoble breed; and the driving of them of necessity gives a great deal of trouble to him. I will endeavour to explain to you in what way the mortal differs from the immortal creature. The soul in her totality has the care of inanimate being everywhere, and traverses the whole heaven in divers forms appearing;– when perfect and fully winged she soars upward, and orders the whole world; whereas the imperfect soul, losing her wings and drooping in her flight at last settles on the solid ground – there, finding a home, she receives an earthly frame which appears to be self-moved, but is really moved by her power; and this composition of soul

[Margin notes, handwritten:]
Immortal Soul as ever moving, unbegotten

246

Divine (perfect soul) cares for inanimate being everywhere; imperfect soul animates earthly frame and body is called a living and mortal creature. For immortal no such union can be reasonably believed to be; although fancy, not having seen nor surely known the nature of God, may imagine an immortal creature having both a body and also a soul which are united throughout all time. Let that, however, be as God wills, and be spoken of acceptably to him. And now let us ask the reason why the soul loses her wings!

The wing is the corporeal element which is most akin to the divine, and which by nature tends to soar aloft and carry that which gravitates downwards into the upper region, which is the habitation of the gods. The divine is beauty, wisdom, goodness, and the like; and by these the wing of the soul is nourished, and grows apace; but when fed upon evil and foulness and the opposite of good, wastes and falls away. Zeus, the mighty lord, holding the reins of a winged chariot, leads the way in heaven, ordering all and taking care of all; and there follows him the array of gods and demi-gods, marshalled in eleven bands; Hestia alone abides at home in the house of heaven;[2] of the rest they who are reckoned among the princely twelve march in their appointed order. They see many blessed sights in the inner heaven, and there are many ways to and fro, along which the blessed gods are passing, every one doing his own work; he may follow who will and can, for jealousy has no place in the celestial choir. But when they go to banquet and festival, then they move up the steep to the top of the vault of heaven. The chariots of the gods in even poise, obeying the rein, glide rapidly; but the others labour, for the vicious steed goes heavily, weighing down the charioteer to the earth when his steed has not been thoroughly trained:– and this is the hour of agony and extremest conflict for the soul. For the immortals, when they are at the end of their course, go forth and stand upon the outside of heaven, and the revolution of the spheres carries them round, and they behold the things beyond. But of the heaven which is above the heavens, what earthly poet ever did or ever will sing worthily? It is such as I will describe; for I must dare to speak the truth, when truth is my theme. There abides the very being with which true knowledge is concerned; the colourless, formless, intangible essence, visible only to mind, who is the pilot of the soul. The divine intelligence, being nurtured upon mind and pure knowledge, and the intelligence of every soul which is capable of receiving the food proper to it, rejoices at beholding reality, and once more gazing upon truth, is replenished and made glad, until the revolution of the worlds brings her round again to the same place. In the revolution she beholds justice, and temperance, and knowledge absolute, not in the form of generation or of relation, which men call existence, but knowledge absolute in existence absolute; and beholding the other true existences in like manner, and feasting upon them, she passes down into the interior of the heavens and returns home; and there the charioteer putting up his horses at the stall, gives them ambrosia to eat and nectar to drink.

Such is the life of the gods; but of other souls, that which follows God best and is likest to him lifts the head of the charioteer into the outer world, and is carried round in the revolution, troubled indeed by the steeds, and with difficulty beholding true being; while another only rises and falls, and sees, and again fails to see by reason of the unruliness of the steeds. The rest of the souls are also longing after the upper world and they all follow, but not being strong enough they are carried round below the surface, plunging, treading on one another, each striving to be first; and there is confusion and perspiration and the extremity of effort; and many of them are lamed or have their wings broken through the ill-driving of the charioteers; and all of them after a fruitless toil, not having attained to the mysteries of true being, go away, and feed upon opinion. The reason why the souls exhibit this exceeding eagerness to behold the plain of truth is that pasturage is found there, which is suited to the highest part of the soul; and the wing on which the soul soars is nourished with this. And there is a law of Destiny, that the soul which attains any vision of truth in company with a god is preserved from harm until the next period, and if attaining always is always unharmed. But when she is unable to follow, and fails to behold the truth, and through some ill-hap sinks beneath the double load of forgetfulness and vice, and her wings fall from her and she drops to the ground, then the law ordains that this soul shall at her first birth pass, not into any other animal, but only into man; and the soul which has seen most of truth shall come to the birth as a philosopher, or artist, or some musical and loving nature; that which has seen truth in the second degree shall be some righteous king or warrior chief; the soul which is of the third class shall be a politician, or economist, or trader; the fourth shall be a lover of gymnastic toils, or a physician; the fifth shall lead the life of a prophet or hierophant; to the sixth the character of a poet or some other imitative artist will be assigned; to the seventh the life of an artisan or husbandman; to the eighth that of a sophist or demagogue; to the ninth that of a tyrant;— all these are states of probation, in which he who does righteously improves, and he who does unrighteously, deteriorates his lot.

Ten thousand years must elapse before the soul of each one can return to the place whence she came, for she cannot grow her wings in less; only the soul of a philosopher, guileless and true, or the soul of a lover, who is not devoid of philosophy, may acquire wings in the third of the recurring periods of a thousand years;— these, if they choose this higher life three times in succession, have wings given them, and go away at the end of

248

249   three thousand years. But the other souls* receive judgment when they have completed their first life, and after the judgment they go, some of them to the houses of correction which are under the earth, and are punished; others to some place in heaven whither they are lightly borne by justice, and there they live in a manner worthy of the life which they led here when in the form of men. And at the end of the first thousand years the good souls and also the evil souls both come to draw lots and choose their second life, and they may take any which they please. The soul of a man may pass into the life of a beast, or from the beast return again into the man. But the soul which has never seen the truth will not pass into the human form. For a man must have intelligence of universals, and be able to proceed from the many particulars of sense to one conception of reason;– this is the recollection of those things which our soul once saw while following God, when, regardless of that which we now call being, she raised her head up towards the true being.[3] And therefore the mind of the philosopher alone has wings; and this is just, for he is always, according to the measure of his abilities, clinging in recollection to those things in which God abides, and in which abiding He is Divine. And he who employs aright these memories is ever being initiated into perfect mysteries and alone becomes truly perfect. But, as he forgets earthly interests and is rapt in the divine, the vulgar deem him mad, and rebuke him; they do not see that he is inspired.

Thus far I have been speaking of the fourth and last kind of madness, which is imputed to him who, when he sees the beauty of earth, is transported with the recollection of the true beauty; he would like to fly away, but he cannot; he is like a bird fluttering and looking upward and careless of the world below; and he is therefore thought to be mad. And I have shown this of all inspirations to be the noblest and highest and the offspring of the highest to him who has or shares in it, and that he who loves the beautiful is called a lover because he partakes of it. For, as has been already said, every soul of man has in the way of nature beheld true being; 250   this was the condition of her passing into the form of man. But all souls do not easily recall the things of the other world; they may have seen them for a short time only, or they may have been unfortunate in their earthly lot, and, having had their hearts turned to unrighteousness through some corrupting influence, they may have lost the memory of the holy thingsn which once they saw. Few only retain an adequate remembrance of them; and they, when they behold here any image of that other world, are rapt in amazement; but they are ignorant of what this rapture means, because they

---

* The philosopher alone is not subject to judgment, for he has never lost the vision of truth.

do not clearly perceive. For there is no light of justice or temperance or any of the higher ideas which are precious to souls in the earthly copies of them: they are seen through a glass dimly; and there are few who, going to the images, behold in them the realities, and these only with difficulty. There was a time when with the rest of the happy band they saw beauty shining in brightness, – we philosophers following in the train of Zeus, others in company with other gods; and then we beheld the beatific vision and were initiated into a mystery which may be truly called most blessed, celebrated by us in our state of innocence, before we had any experience of evils to come, when we were admitted to the sight of apparitions innocent and simple and calm and happy, which we beheld shining in pure light, pure ourselves and not yet enshrined in that living tomb which we carry about, now that we are imprisoned in the body, like an oyster in his shell.

[handwritten margin notes: "Earthly copies may spark memory of divine realities", "Vision/rapture is re-awareness of Ideas", "Body = prison"]

Notes

1 Jowett's translation ignores the word *sumphutos* in the Greek text, which signifies that the two horses and the charioteer are 'grown together' into an uneasy unity. Plato's figure is to be compared with the tripartite account of the soul in Book IV of the *Republic*. Sections 253–5 of *Phaedrus* make it clearer that the charioteer corresponds to the rational part, while the two horses correspond to 'spiritedness' (or 'mettle', *thumos*) and 'appetite' respectively.
2 Hestia was the goddess of the hearth and a symbol of the earth. Presumably the point of her remaining at home is to emphasize the divide between earth and the realm of the Forms.
3 Plato's most detailed account of 'recollection' is in his *Meno*.

3 Aristotle, *Metaphysics*, Books VII–VIII (selected chapters)

From J. L. Ackrill (ed.), *A New Aristotle Reader*, trans. W. D. Ross (revised by J. Barnes). Oxford: Clarendon Press, 1987, pp. 284–9, 291–6, 306–14 (some passages omitted). Reprinted by permission of Oxford University Press.

Plato's theory of Forms (or Ideas, or Types) was soon to come under attack from his most famous pupil, Aristotle (384–22 BCE), above all in those writings of Aristotle which, in a collected edition, came after (*meta*) his writings on nature (*ta phusika*). *Metaphysics* is a wide-ranging work, but its main concerns are interconnected and each of them comes to centre on the notion of substance (*ousia*), the subject of the work's most famous (and, unfortunately, very difficult) section, Book VII (or Z).

Three main themes are the nature of being or the meaning of 'is', change and the explanation of coming-to-be and ceasing-to-be, and the criteria for identity. Just about anything we speak of can be said to be, including health, smiles and colours: but, for Aristotle, being must belong 'primarily' to what 'underlies' or supports such states, occurrences or properties, for – *pace* the Cheshire Cat's smile – they are incapable of independent existence. 'Substance' is first introduced (Ch. 1) as the name for the underlying entities. It is the name, too, for the relatively stable and persistent things we must assume in order to make sense of the idea of change. For change to occur, there must be something which persists in order to undergo the change. Finally, it is a substance we are trying to specify when answering questions about anything's identity, such as 'What is it?' or 'What makes it the same thing over time and distinguishes it from anything else?'.

Whether or not a single concept of substance can apply to 'underlying', independently existing entities, to the entities which undergo change, and to what anything owes its essential identity to, is a moot question.[1] But it is Aristotle's

---

[1] See Martha C. Nussbaum, 'Aristotle', in Jaegwon Kim and Ernest Sosa (eds), *A Companion to Metaphysics*, Oxford: Blackwell, 1995, pp. 24–31, for a succinct discussion of possible tensions in Aristotle's notion of substance.

view that it can, and in Book VII, especially, he explores this concept with the aim of showing what substance is. With two views of substance – of what, fundamentally, there *is* – he takes issue. First, substance is not, as the 'naturalists' like Democritus had held, *matter*. When we ask what something is, we are asking about something 'separable and individual', not about some general stuff of which it may be composed. (Elsewhere Aristotle had argued that ultimate or 'prime' matter was anyway unknowable, and hence could not be appealed to in identifying a thing's nature. *Physics* 193ff.) Second, and at the other extreme, substance cannot be identified with abstract Platonic Forms or Ideas, held to exist independently of or 'apart from' the particular things which 'participate' in them. For one thing, such Forms would be useless for explaining how things come into being (Ch. 8). For another, insuperable logical problems arise once we press such questions as whether the Form of, say, animals is the same or a different one in the case of each different species, or how particular men relate to the 'man-in-himself' which is alleged to be their Form (Ch. 13ff). Other arguments against Platonic Forms are marshalled in Book XIII.

In *Metaphysics*, moreover, Aristotle is no longer content, it seems, with the 'robustly commonsensical'[2] answer to the question 'What are substances?' offered in his *Categories*, where by 'primary substances' he meant individual concrete things, animals, plants or whatever. (Though see the beginning of Ch. 15.) His considered answer is that a substance is a *form* of something (not to be confused with a (Platonic) Form). By a form, Aristotle means the 'essence' of something – what makes it what it is – rather than the object itself considered as a spatio-temporal particular.[3] It may sound odd to equate substances with essences, but in the first place we should set aside the 'stuff-like' connotations which the word 'substance' acquired in later philosophical and vernacular parlance (the Greek *ousia*, an Aristotelian term of art, was coined from the participle of the verb 'to be'). And, second, we need to recall a main role Aristotle intended the term to play – namely, to refer to what can exist independently (unlike a smile or a colour, which must be *of* somebody or something). His thought seems to be that the concrete individual Socrates is not, in the relevant sense, suitably independent, since his existence depends on his essence. A certain snub-nosed Greek philosopher was only *Socrates* because of a unique essence he embodied. It is hard to exaggerate the importance of Aristotle's 'independence' criterion for substance. Crucially, it helps explain the 'theological' turn in Book XII of *Metaphysics* (comparable, in some respects, to a similar turn at the end of the *Nicomachean Ethics*), where Aristotle intimates that, strictly speaking, only God may be a substance. This is presumably because God, being immaterial, is not dependent, like Socrates, on matter.

---

2 Jonathan Barnes, *Aristotle*, Oxford: Oxford University Press, 1985, p. 46.
3 For a clear discussion of Aristotle on substance as form, see Jonathan Lear, *Aristotle: the desire to understand*, Cambridge: Cambridge University Press, 1988.

[Marginal handwritten notes:]
Opposed to views of substance:
1. Democritus – naturalists
2. Plato – idealists

No longer considers 'substances' to be individual concrete things
Substance defined
↓
essence
↓
that which exists independently

Perhaps only God is truly substance

Despite, or perhaps because of, the difficulties and ambiguities in Aristotle's discussion of substance, it is one which – alongside such related discussions of form *versus* matter, actuality *versus* potentiality, essence *versus* accident – has continued to influence, indeed to shape, all subsequent metaphysical debate in the West.

These discussions continue in metaphysics

▶ ▶ ▶   **Aristotle, *Metaphysics***

Book VII (Z)

Chapter 1

1028ᵃ   There are several senses in which a thing may be said to be, as we pointed out previously in our book on the various senses of the words; for in one sense it means what a thing is or a 'this', and in another sense it means that a thing is of a certain quality or quantity or has some such predicate asserted of it. While 'being' has all these senses, obviously that which is pri-

15   marily is the 'what', which indicates the substance of the thing. For when we say of what quality a thing is, we say that it is good or beautiful, but not that it is three cubits long or that it is a man; but when we say *what* it is, we do not say 'white' or 'hot' or 'three cubits long', but 'man' or 'God'. And all other things are said to be because they are, some of them, quantities of that which *is* in this primary sense, others qualities of it, other affections of

20   it, and others some other determination of it. And so one might raise the question whether 'to walk' and 'to be healthy' and 'to sit' signify in each case something that is, and similarly in any other case of this sort; for none of them is either self-subsistent or capable of being separated from sub-

25   stance, but rather, if anything, it is that which walks or is seated or is healthy that is an existent thing. Now these are seen to be more real because there is something definite which underlies them; and this is the substance or individual, which is implied in such a predicate; for 'good' or 'sitting' are not used without this. Clearly then it is in virtue of this category that each

30   of the others *is*. Therefore that which is primarily and *is* simply (not is something) must be substance.

Now there are several senses in which a thing is said to be primary; but substance is primary in every sense – in formula, in order of knowledge, in time. For of the other categories none can exist independently, but only

35   substance. And in formula also this is primary; for in the formula of each
1028ᵇ   term the formula of its substance must be present. And we think we know each thing most fully, when we know what it is, e.g. what man is or what fire is, rather than when we know its quality, its quantity, or where it is;

Primary sense of 'is' is answered in 'what' – substance

Substance is independent

since we know each of these things also, only when we know *what* the quantity or the quality *is*.

And indeed the question which, both now and of old, has always been raised, and always been the subject of doubt, viz. what being is, is just the question, what is substance? For it is this that some assert to be one, others more than one, and that some assert to be limited in number, other unlimited. And so we also must consider chiefly and primarily and almost exclusively what that is which *is* in this sense.

Chapter 2

Substance is thought to belong most obviously to bodies; and so we say that both animals and plants and their parts are substances, and so are natural bodies such as fire and water and earth and everything of the sort, and all things that are parts of these or composed of these (either of parts or of the whole bodies), e.g. the heaven and its parts, stars and moon and sun. But whether these alone are substances, or there are also others, or only some of these, or some of these and some other things are substances, or none of these but only some other things, must be considered. Some think the limits of body, i.e. surface, line, point, and unit, are substances, and more so than body or the solid. Further, some do not think there is anything substantial besides sensible things, but others think there are eternal substances which are more in number and more real, e.g. Plato posited two kinds of substance – the Forms and the objects of mathematics – as well as a third kind, viz. the substance of sensible bodies. And Speusippus made still more kinds of substance, beginning with the One, and making principles for each kind of substance, one for numbers, another for spatial magnitudes, and then another for the soul; and in this way he multiplies the kinds of substance. And some say Forms and numbers have the same nature, and other things come after them, e.g. lines and planes, until we come to the substance of the heavens and to sensible bodies.

Regarding these matters, then, we must inquire which of the common statements are right and which are not right, and what things are substances, and whether there are or are not any besides sensible substances, and how sensible substances exist, and whether there is a separable substance (and if so why and how) or there is no substance separable from sensible substances; and we must first sketch the nature of substance.

Chapter 3

The word 'substance' is applied, if not in more senses, still at least to four main objects: for both the essence and the universal and the genus are thought to be the substance of each thing, and fourthly the substratum. Now the substratum is that of which other things are predicated, while it is itself not predicated of anything else. And so we must first determine the nature of this; for that which underlies a thing primarily is thought to be in the truest sense its substance. And in one sense matter is said to be of the nature of substratum, in another shape, and in a third sense, the compound of these. By the matter I mean, for instance, the bronze, by the shape the plan of its form, and by the compound of these (the concrete thing) the statue. Therefore if the form is prior to the matter and more real, it will be prior to the compound also for the same reason.

We have now outlined the nature of substance, showing that it is that which is not predicated of a subject, but of which all else is predicated. But we must not merely state the matter thus; for this is not enough. The statement itself is obscure, and further, on this view, *matter* becomes substance. For if this is not substance, it is beyond us to say what else is. When all else is taken away evidently nothing but matter remains. For of the other elements some are affections, products, and capacities of bodies, while length, breadth, and depth are quantities and not substances. For a quantity is not a substance; but the substance is rather that to which these belong primarily. But when length and breadth and depth are taken away we see nothing left except that which is bounded by these, whatever it be; so that to those who consider the question thus matter alone must seem to be substance. By matter I mean that which in itself is neither a particular thing nor of a certain quantity nor assigned to any other of the categories by which being is determined. For there is something of which each of these is predicated, so that its being is different from that of each of the predicates; for the predicates other than substance are predicated of substance, while substance is predicated of matter. Therefore the ultimate substratum is of itself neither a particular thing nor of a particular quantity nor otherwise positively characterized; nor yet negatively, for negations also will belong to it only by accident.

For those who adopt this point of view, then, it follows that matter is substance. But this is impossible; for both separability and individuality are thought to belong chiefly to substance. And so form and the compound of form and matter would be thought to be substance, rather than matter. The substance compounded of both, i.e. of matter and shape, may be dismissed; for it is posterior and its nature is obvious. And matter also is in a sense manifest. But we must inquire into the third kind of substance; for this is the most difficult.

It is agreed that there are some substances among sensible things, so that we must look first among these. For it is an advantage to advance to that which is more intelligible. For learning proceeds for all in this way – through that which is less intelligible by nature to that which is more intelligible . . .   5

Chapter 4

Since at the start we distinguished the various marks by which we deter-   1
mine substance, and one of these was thought to be the essence, we must
investigate this. And first let us say something about it in the abstract. The   13 *Essence*
essence of each thing is what it is said to be in virtue of itself. For being you   *defined*
is not being musical; for you are not musical in virtue of yourself. What,   15
then, you are in virtue of yourself is your essence.

But not the whole of this is the essence of a thing; not that which something is in virtue of itself in the way in which a surface is white, because
being a surface is not being white. But again the combination of both –
being a white surface – is not the essence of surface. Why? Because 'surface'
itself is repeated. The formula, therefore, in which the term itself is not
present but its meaning is expressed, this is the formula of the essence of   20
each thing. Therefore if to be a white surface is to be a smooth surface, to
be white and to be smooth are one and the same. . . .

. . . the essence is what something is; but when one thing is said of another, that is not what a 'this' is, e.g. white man is not what a 'this' is since   5
being a 'this' belongs only to substances. Therefore there is an essence only
of those things whose formula is a definition. But we have a definition not
where we have a word and a formula identical in meaning (for in that case
all formulae would be definitions; for there will be some name for any
formula whatever, so that even the *Iliad* would be a definition), but where
there is a formula of something primary; and primary things are those which   10
do not involve one thing's being said of another. Nothing, then, which is   *Only a*
not a species of a genus will have an *essence* – only species will have it, for in   *species will*
these the subject is not thought to participate in the attribute and to have   15 *have an*
it as an affection, nor to have it by accident; but for everything else as well,   *essence*
if it has a name, there will be a formula of its meaning – viz. that this
attribute belongs to this subject; or instead of a simple formula we shall be
able to give a more accurate one; but there will be no definition nor essence. . . .

. . . essence will belong, just as the 'what' does, primarily and in the
simple sense to substance, and in a secondary way to the other categories   30
also, – not essence simply, but the essence of a quality or of a quantity. For
it must be either homonymously that we say these *are*, or by making qualifications and abstractions (in the way in which that which is not known
may be said to be known), – the truth being that we use the word neither

homonymously nor in the same sense, but just as we apply the word 'medi-
1030ᵇ   cal' when there is a *reference* to one and the same thing, not *meaning* one
and the same thing, nor yet speaking homonymously; for a patient and an
operation and an instrument are called medical neither homonymously nor
in virtue of one thing, but with reference to one thing. But it does not
matter in which of the two ways one likes to describe the facts; this is
5   evident, that definition and essence in the primary and simple sense belong
to substances. Still they belong to other things as well in a similar way, but
not primarily. For if we suppose this it does not follow that there is a definition of every word which means the same as any formula; it must mean
the same as a particular kind of formula; and this condition is satisfied if it
is a formula of something which is one, not by continuity like the *Iliad* or
10   the things that are one by being bound together, but in one of the main
senses of 'one' which answer to the senses of 'is'; now 'that which is' in one
sense denotes an individual, in another a quantity, in another a quality.
And so there can be a formula or definition of white man, but not in the
sense in which there is a definition either of white or of a substance. . . .

Chapter 6

15   We must inquire whether each thing and its essence are the same or different. This is of some use for the inquiry concerning substance; for each
thing is thought to be not different from its substance, and the essence is
said to be the substance of each thing.
20   Now in the case of things with accidental attributes the two would be
generally thought to be different, e.g. white man would be thought to be
different from the essence of white man. For if they are the same, the
essence of man and that of white man are also the same; for a man and a
white man are the same, as people say, so that the essence of white man and
that of man would be also the same. But probably it is not necessary that
25   things with accidental attributes should be the same. For the extreme terms
are not in the same way the same. – Perhaps *this* might be thought to
follow, that the extreme terms, the accidents, should turn out to be the
same, e.g. the essence of white and that of musical; but this is not actually
thought to be the case.
        But in the case of so-called self-subsistent things, is a thing necessarily
30   the same as its essence? E.g. if there are some substances which have no
other substances nor entities prior to them – substances such as some assert
the Ideas to be? If the essence of good is to be different from the Idea of
good, and the essence of animal from the Idea of animal, and the essence
1031ᵇ   of being from the Idea of being, there will, firstly, be other substances and

entities and Ideas besides those which are asserted, and, secondly, these others will be prior substances if the essence is substance. And if the posterior substances are severed from one another, there will be no knowledge of the ones and the others will have no being. (By 'severed' I mean, if the Idea of good has not the essence of good, and the latter has not the property of being good.) For there is knowledge of each thing only when we know its essence. And the case is the same for other things as for the good; so that if the essence of good is not good, neither will the essence of being be, nor the essence of unity be one. And all essences alike exist or none of them does; so that if the essence of being is not, neither will any of the others be. Again, that which has not the property of being good is not good. The good, then, must be one with the essence of good, and the beautiful with the essence of beauty, and so with all things which do not depend on something else but are self-subsistent and primary. For it is enough if they are this, even if there are no Forms; and perhaps all the more if there are Forms. – At the same time it is clear that if there are Ideas such as some people say there are, the substratum of them will not be substance; for these must be substances, and not predicable of a substratum; for if they were they would exist only by being participated in. – Each thing then and its essence are one and the same in no merely accidental way, as is evident both from the preceding arguments and because to *know* each thing, at least, is to know its essence, so that even by the exhibition of instances it becomes clear that both must be one.

(But of an accidental term, e.g. 'the musical' or 'the white', since it has two meanings, it is not true to say that it itself is identical with its essence; for both that to which the accidental quality belongs, and the accidental quality, are white, so that in a sense the accident and its essence are the same, and in a sense they are not; for the essence of white is not the same as the man or the white man, but it is the same as the attribute white.)

The absurdity of the separation would appear also if one were to assign a name to each of the essences; for there would be another essence besides the original one; e.g. to the essence of horse there will belong a second essence. Yet why should not some things be their essences from the start, since essence is substance? But not only are a thing and its essence one, but the formula of them is also the same, as is clear even from what has been said; for it is not by accident that the essence of one, and the one, are one. Further, if they were different, the process would go on to infinity; for we should have the essence of one, and the one, so that in their case also the same infinite regress would be found. Clearly, then, each primary and self-subsistent thing is one and the same as its essence.

Now the sophistical objections to this position, and the question whether

[marginal annotations, handwritten:] 5 ... 10 ... Idea of or essence of good relies upon 15 Particulars ... 20 ... 25 ... 30 ... 1032ᵃ 5

Socrates and to be Socrates are the same thing, are obviously answered in the same way; for there is no difference either in the standpoint from which the question would be asked, or in that from which one could answer it

10   successfully. We have explained, then, in what sense each thing is the same as its essence and in what sense it is not.

Chapter 7

Of things that come to be some come to be by nature, some by art, some spontaneously. Now everything that comes to be comes to be by the agency of something and from something and comes be something. And the something which I say it comes to be may be found in any category; it may come

15   to be either a 'this' or of some quantity or of some quality or somewhere.
Now natural comings to be are the comings to be of those things which come to be by nature; and that out of which they come to be is what we call matter; and that by which they come to be is something which exists naturally; and the something which they come to be is a man or a plant or one

20   of the things of this kind, which we say are substances if anything is. All things that come to be either by nature or by art have matter, for each of them is capable both of being and of not being, and this capacity is the matter in each. And, in general, both that from which they are produced is nature, and the type according to which they are produced is nature (for that which is produced, e.g. a plant or an animal, has a nature), and so is that by which they are produced – the so-called 'formal' nature, which is specifically the same as the nature of the thing produced (though it is in

25   another individual); for man begets man.
Thus, then, are natural products produced; all other productions are called 'makings'. And all makings proceed either from art or from a cap-

30   acity or from thought. Some of them happen also spontaneously or by chance just as natural products sometimes do; for there also the same things sometimes are produced without seed as well as from seed. Concerning

1032ᵇ   these cases, then, we must inquire later, but from art proceed the things of which the form is in the soul. (By form I mean the essence of each thing and its primary substance.) For even contraries have in a sense the same form; for the substance of a privation is the opposite substance, e.g. health is the substance of disease; for it is by its absence that disease exists; and health is the formula and the knowledge in the soul.

30   . . . Therefore, as we say, it is impossible that anything should be produced if there were nothing before. Obviously then some part of the result will pre-exist of necessity; for the matter is a part; for this is present in the

1033ᵃ   process and it is this that becomes something. But do some also of the elements in the *formula* pre-exist? Well, we describe in both ways what bronze circles are; we describe both the matter by saying it is bronze, and the form by saying that it is such and such a figure; and figure is the proximate genus in which it is placed. The bronze circle, then, has its mat- 5 ter *in its formula*.

And as for that out of which as matter they are produced, some things are said, when they have been produced, to be not it but of it, e.g. the statue is not stone but of stone. But though what becomes healthy is a man, a man is not what the healthy product is said to come from. The reason is that though a thing comes both from its privation and from its substratum, which we call its matter (e.g. what becomes healthy is both a 10 man and an invalid), it is said to come rather from its privation (e.g. it is from an invalid rather than from a man that a healthy subject is produced). And so the healthy subject is not said to *be* an invalid, but to be a man, and a healthy man. But as for the things whose privation is obscure and name-less, e.g. in bronze the privation of a particular shape or in bricks and tim- 15 ber the privation of arrangement as a house, the thing is thought to be produced *from* these materials, as in the former case the healthy man is produced *from* an invalid. And so, as there also a thing is not said to be that from which it comes, here the statue is not said to be wood but is said by a verbal change to be not wood but wooden, not bronze but of bronze, not stone but of stone, and the house is said to be not bricks but of bricks (since we should not say without qualification, if we looked at things care- 20 fully, even that a statue is produced from wood or a house from bricks, because its coming to be implies change in that from which it comes, and not permanence). For this reason, then, we use this way of speaking.

Chapter 8

Since anything which is produced is produced by something (and this I call 25 the starting-point of the production), and from something (and let this be taken to be not the privation but the matter; for the meanings we attach to these have already been distinguished), and since something is produced (and this is either a sphere or a circle or whatever else it may chance to be), just as we do not make the substratum – the bronze – so we do not make the sphere, except incidentally, because the bronze sphere is a sphere and 30 we make the former. For to make a 'this' is to make a 'this' out of the general substratum. I mean that to make the bronze round is not to make the round or the sphere, but something else, i.e. to produce this form in something else. For if we make the form, we must make it out of some- **1033ᵇ** thing else; for this was assumed. E.g. we make a bronze sphere; and that in

the sense that out of this, which is bronze, we make this other, which is a
sphere. If, then, we make the sphere itself, clearly we must make it in the
same way, and the processes of making will regress to infinity. Obviously
5   then the form also, or whatever we ought to call the shape of the sensible
thing, is not produced, nor does production relate to it,– i.e. the essence is
not produced; for this is that which is made to be in something else by art
or by nature or by some capacity. But that there is a *bronze sphere*, this we
make. For we make it out of bronze and the sphere; we bring the form into
10   this particular matter, and the result is a bronze sphere. But if the essence
of sphere in general is produced, something must be produced out of something. For the product will always have to be divisible, and one part must
be this and another that, I mean the one must be matter and the other
form. If then a sphere is the figure whose circumference is at all points
15   equidistant from the centre, part of this will be the medium in which the
thing made will be, and part will be in that medium, and the whole will be
the thing produced, which corresponds to the bronze sphere. It is obvious
then from what has been said that the thing, in the sense of form or substance, is not produced, but the concrete thing which gets its name from
this is produced, and that in everything which comes to be matter is present,
and one part of the thing is matter and the other form.
20   Is there then a sphere apart from the individual spheres or a house apart
from the bricks? Rather we may say that no 'this' would ever have been
coming to be, if this had been so. The 'form' however means the 'such',
and is not a 'this' – a definite thing; but the artist makes, or the father
generates, a 'such' out of a 'this'; and when it has been generated, it is a
25   'this such'. And the whole 'this', Callias or Socrates, is analogous to this
bronze sphere, but man and animal to bronze sphere in general. Obviously
then the cause which consists of the Forms (taken in the sense in which
some maintain the existence of the Forms, i.e. if they are something apart
from the individuals) is useless with regard both to comings-to-be and to
substances; and the Forms need not, for this reason at least, be self-subsist-
30   ent substances. In some cases it is even obvious that the producer is of the
same kind as the produced (not, however, the same nor one in number,
but in form), e.g. in the case of natural products (for man produces man),
unless something happens contrary to nature, e.g. the production of a mule
by a horse. And even these cases are similar; for that which would be found
to be common to horse and ass, the genus next above them, has not re-
1034ª   ceived a name, but it would doubtless be both, as the mule is both. Obviously, therefore, it is quite unnecessary to set up a Form as a pattern (for we
should have looked for Forms in these cases if any; for these are substances
5   if anything is so); the begetter is adequate to the making of the product

and to the causing of the form in the matter. And when we have the whole, such and such a form in this flesh and in these bones, this is Callias or Socrates; and they are different in virtue of their matter (for that is different), but the same in form; for their form is indivisible. . . .

Chapter 13

Let us again return to the subject of our inquiry, which is substance. As the substrate and the essence and the compound of these are called substance, so also is the universal. About two of these we have spoken; about the essence and about the substrate, of which we have said that it underlies in two senses, either being a 'this' – which is the way in which an animal underlies its attributes –, or as the matter underlies the complete reality. The universal also is thought by some to be in the fullest sense a cause, and a principle; therefore let us attack the discussion of this point also. For it seems impossible that any universal term should be the name of a substance. For primary substance is that kind of substance which is peculiar to an individual, which does not belong to anything else; but the universal is common, since that is called universal which naturally belongs to more than one thing. Of which individual then will this be the substance? Either of all or of none. But it cannot be the substance of all; and if it is to be the substance of one, this one will be the others also; for things whose substance is one and whose essence is one are themselves also one.

Further, substance means that which is not predicable of a subject, but the universal is predicable of some subjects always.

But perhaps the universal, while it cannot be substance in the way in which the essence is so, can be present in this, e.g. animal can be present in man and horse. Then clearly there is a formula of the universal. And it makes no difference even if there is not a formula of everything that is in the substance; for none the less the universal will be the substance of something. Man is the substance of the individual man in whom it is present; therefore the same will happen again, for a substance, e.g. animal, must be the substance of that in which it is present as something peculiar to it. And further it is impossible and absurd that the 'this', i.e. the substance, if it consists of parts, should not consist of substances nor of what is a 'this', but of quality; for that which is not substance, i.e. the quality, will then be prior to substance and to the 'this'. Which is impossible; for neither in formula nor in time nor in coming to be can the affections be prior to the substance; for then they would be separable from it. Further, in Socrates there will be a substance in a substance, so that he will be the substance of two things. And in general it follows, if man and such things are substances,

1038^b

5

10

15

20

25

30

that none of the elements in their formulae is the substance of anything, nor does it exist apart from the species or in anything else; I mean, for instance, that no animal exists apart from the particular animals, nor does any other of the elements present in formulae exist apart.

1039ᵃ   If, then, we view the matter from these standpoints, it is plain that no universal attribute is a substance, and this is plain also from the fact that no common predicate indicates a 'this', but rather a 'such'. If not, many difficulties follow and especially the 'third man'.

The conclusion is evident also from the following consideration – that a
5   substance cannot consist of substances present in it actually (for things that are thus actually two are never actually one, though if they are *potentially* two, they can be one, e.g. the double line consists of two halves – potentially; for the *actualization* of the halves divides them from one another; therefore if the substance is one, it will not consist of substances present in
10   it); and according to the argument which Democritus states rightly; he says one thing cannot come from two nor two from one; for he identifies his indivisible magnitudes with substances. It is clear therefore that the same will hold good of number, if number is a synthesis of units, as is said by some; for two is either not one, or there is no unit present in it actually.

15   The consequence of this view involves a difficulty. If no substance can consist of universals because a universal indicates a 'such', not a 'this', and if no composite substance can be composed of actual substances, every substance would be incomposite, so that there would not even be a formula of any substance. But it is thought by all and has been previously
20   stated that it is either only, or primarily, substance that can be defined; yet now it seems that not even substance can. There cannot, then, be a definition of anything; or rather in a sense there can be, and in a sense there cannot. And what we say will be plainer from what follows.

Chapter 14

25   It is clear also from these very facts what consequences confront those who say the Ideas are substances and can exist apart, and at the same time make the Form consist of the genus and the differentiae. For if the Forms exist and animal is present in man and horse, it is either one and the same in number, or different. (In formula it is clearly one; for he who states the
30   formula unfolds the same formula in either case.) If there is a man-in-himself who is a 'this' and exists apart, the parts of which he consists, e.g. animal and two-footed, must indicate a 'this' and be things existing apart and substances; therefore animal too must be of this sort.

1039ᵇ   Now if animal, which is in the horse and in man, is one and the same, as you are one and the same with yourself, how will the one in things that exist apart be one, and how will this animal escape being divided even from itself?

Further, if it is to share in two-footed and many-footed, an impossible conclusion follows; for contrary attributes will belong at the same time to it although it is one and a this. If it does not, what is the relation implied when one says the animal is two-footed or has feet? But perhaps these are 5 put together and are in contact, or are mixed. Yet all these are absurd.

But suppose the Form to be different in each species. Then there will be practically an infinite number of things whose *substance* is animal; for it is not by accident that man has animal for one of its elements. Further, animal-in-itself will be many. For the animal in each species will be the substance of the species; for it is not dependent on anything else; if it were, 10 that other would be an element in man, i.e. would be the genus of man. And further all the elements of which man is composed will be Ideas. Now nothing can be the Idea of one thing and the substance of another; this is impossible. Each, then, of the Ideas present in the species of animals will be the ideal animal. Further, from what will these Ideas be derived; how will they be derived from the ideal animal? Or how can an Idea of animal whose 15 essence is simply animal exist apart from the ideal animal? Further, in the case of sensible things both these consequences and others still more absurd follow. If, then, these consequences are impossible, clearly there are not Forms of sensible things in the sense in which some maintain their existence.

Chapter 15

Since substance is of two kinds, the concrete thing and the formula (I 20 mean that one kind of substance is the formula taken with the matter, while another kind is the formula in its generality), substances in the former sense are capable of destruction (for they are capable also of generation), but there is no destruction of the formula in the sense that it is ever in course of being destroyed; for there is no generation of it (the being of 25 house is not generated, but only the being of *this* house), but without generation and destruction formulae are and are not; for it has been shown that no one produces nor makes these. For this reason, also, there is neither definition nor demonstration of sensible individual substances, because they have matter whose nature is such that they are capable both of being and of not being; for which reason all the individual instances of 30 them are destructible. If then demonstration is of necessary truths and definition involves knowledge, and if, just as knowledge cannot be sometimes knowledge and sometimes ignorance, but the state which varies thus is opinion, so too demonstration and definition cannot vary thus, but it is opinion that deals with that which can be otherwise than as it is, clearly there can neither be definition nor demonstration of sensible individuals. For perishing things are obscure to those who have knowledge of them, when they have passed from our perception; and though the formulae remain in the soul unchanged, there will no longer be either definition or demonstration. Therefore when one of those who aim at definition defines any individual, he must recognize that his definition may always be overthrown; for it is not possible to define such things.

Nor is it possible to define any Idea. For the Idea is, as its supporters say, an individual, and can exist apart; and the formula must consist of words; and he who defines must not invent a word (for it would be unknown), but the established words are common to each of a number of things; these then must apply to something besides the thing defined; e.g. if one were defining you, he would say 'an animal which is lean' or 'white', or something else which will apply also to some one other than you. If anyone were to say that perhaps all the attributes taken apart may belong to many subjects, but together they belong only to this one, we must reply firstly that they belong also to both the elements, e.g. two-footed animal belongs to animal and to the two-footed. And where the elements are eternal this is even necessary, since the elements are prior to and parts of the compound; what is more, they can also exist apart, if 'man' can exist apart. For either neither or both can. If, then, neither can, the genus will not exist apart from the species; but if it does, the differentia will also. Secondly, we must reply that they are prior in being; and things which are prior to others are not destroyed when the others are.

Again, if the Ideas consist of Ideas (as they must, since elements are simpler than the compound), it will be further necessary that the elements of which the Idea consists, e.g. animal and two-footed, should be predicated of many subjects. If not, how will they be known? For there will then be an Idea which cannot be predicated of more subjects than one. But this is not thought possible – every Idea is thought to be capable of being shared.

As has been said, then, people do not realize that it is impossible to define in the case of eternal things, especially those which are unique, like the sun or the moon. For they err not only by adding attributes after whose removal the sun would still exist, e.g. 'going round the earth' or 'night-hidden' (for from their view it follows that if it stands still or is visible, it will no longer be the sun; but it is strange if this is so; for the 'sun' means a certain *substance*); but also by the mention of attributes

1040ª

5

10

15

20

25

30

which can belong to another subject; e.g. if another thing with the stated attributes comes into existence, clearly it will be a sun; the formula there- **1040ᵇ** fore is general. But the sun was supposed to be an individual, like Cleon or Socrates. Why does not one of the supporters of the Ideas produce a definition of an Idea? It would become clear, if they tried, that what has now been said is true.

Chapter 16

Evidently even of the things that are thought to be substances, most are only   5 potentialities, – e.g. the parts of animals (for none of them exists separately; and when they *are* separated, then they too exist, all of them, merely as matter) and earth and fire and air; for none of them is one, but they are like a heap before it is fused by heat and some one thing is made out of the bits. One might suppose especially that the parts of living things and the corre-   10 sponding parts of the soul are both, i.e. exist both actually and potentially, because they have sources of movement in something in their joints; for which reason some animals live when divided. Yet all the parts must exist only potentially, when they are one and continuous by nature, – not by force   15 or even by growing together, for such a phenomenon is an abnormality.

Since the term 'unity' is used like the term 'being', and the substance of that which is one is one, and things whose substance is numerically one are numerically one, evidently neither unity nor being can be the substance of things, just as being an element or a principle cannot be the substance, but we seek *what* the principle is, that we may refer the thing to something   20 more intelligible. Now of these things being and unity are more substantial than principle or element or cause, but not even the former are substance, since in general nothing that is common is substance; for substance does not belong to anything but to itself and to that which has it, of which it is the substance. Further, that which is one cannot be in many things at the   25 same time, but that which is common is present in many things at the same time; so that clearly no universal exists apart from the individuals.

But those who say the Forms exist, in one respect are right, in saying the Forms exist apart, if they are substances; but in another respect they are not right, because they say the one *in* many is a Form. The reason for their   30 doing this is that they cannot say what are the substances of this sort, the imperishable substances which exist apart from the individual and sensible substances. They make them, then, the same in kind as the perishable things (for this kind of substance we know) – man himself and the horse itself, adding to the sensible things the word 'itself'. Yet even if we had not seen the stars, none the less, I suppose, would there be eternal substances be-   **1041ᵃ**

sides those which we knew; so that now also if we do not know what eternal substances there are, yet it is doubtless necessary that some should exist. Clearly, then, no universal term is the name of a substance, and no
5   substance is composed of substances.

Chapter 17

We should say what, and what sort of thing, substance is, taking another starting-point; for perhaps from this we shall get a clear view also of that substance which exists apart from sensible substances. Since, then, sub-
10   stance is a principle and a cause, let us attack it from this standpoint. The 'why' is always sought in this form – 'why does one thing attach to another?' For to inquire why the musical man is a musical man, is either to inquire – as we have said – why the man is musical, or it is something else.
15   Now 'why a thing is itself' is doubtless a meaningless inquiry; for the fact or the existence of the thing must already be evident (e.g. that the moon is eclipsed), but the fact that a thing is itself is the single formula and the single cause to all such questions as why the man is man, or the musical musical, unless one were to say that each thing is inseparable from itself; and its being one just meant this. This, however, is common to all things
20   and is a short and easy way with the question. But we *can* inquire why man is an animal of such and such a nature. Here, then, we are evidently not inquiring why he who is a man is a man. We are inquiring, then, why something is predicable of something; that it is predicable must be clear; for if not, the inquiry is an inquiry into nothing. E.g. why does it thunder?
25   – why is sound produced in the clouds? Thus the inquiry is about the predication of one thing of another. And why are certain things, i.e. stones and bricks, a house? Plainly we are seeking the cause. And this is the essence (to speak abstractly), which in some cases is that for the sake of which,
30   e.g. perhaps in the case of a house or a bed, and in some cases is the first mover; for this also is a cause. But while the efficient cause is sought in the case of genesis and destruction, the final cause is sought in the case of being also.

The object of the inquiry is most overlooked where one term is not
1041ᵇ   expressly predicated of another (e.g. when we inquire why man is), because we do not distinguish and do not say definitely 'why do these parts form this whole?' But we must distinguish the elements before we begin to inquire; if not, it is not clear whether the inquiry is significant or unmeaning.
5   Since we must know the existence of the thing and it must be given, clearly the question is *why* the matter is some individual thing, e.g. why are these materials a house? Because that which was the essence of a house is present.

And why is this individual thing, or this body in this state, a man? There-fore what we seek is the cause, i.e. the form, by reason of which the matter is some definite thing; and this is the substance of the thing. Evidently, then, in the case of simple things no inquiry nor teaching is possible; but we must inquire into them in a different way.

As regards that which is compounded out of something so that the whole is one – not like a heap, however, but like a syllable, – the syllable is not its elements, *ba* is not the same as *b* and *a*, nor is flesh fire and earth; for when they are dissolved the wholes, i.e. the flesh and the syllable, no longer exist, but the elements of the syllable exist, and so do fire and earth. The syllable, then, is something – not only its elements (the vowel and the consonant) but also something else; and the flesh is not only fire and earth or the hot and the cold, but also something else. Since, then, that something must be either an element or composed of elements, if it is an element the same argument will again apply; for flesh will consist of this and fire and earth and something still further, so that the process will go on to infinity; while if it is a compound, clearly it will be a compound not of one but of many (or else it will itself be that one), so that again in this case we can use the same argument as in the case of flesh or of the syllable. But it would seem that this is something, and not an element, and that it is the cause which makes *this* thing flesh and *that* a syllable. And similarly in all other cases. And this is the substance of each thing; for this is the primary cause of its being; and since, while some things are not substances, as many as are substances are formed naturally and by nature, their substance would seem to be this nature, which is not an element but a principle. An *element* is that into which a thing is divided and which is present in it as matter, e.g. *a* and *b* are the elements of the syllable.

Book VIII (H)

Chapter 1

We must draw our conclusions from what has been said, and sum up our results, and put the finishing touch to our inquiry. We have said that the causes, principles, and elements of substances are the object of our search. And some substances are recognized by all thinkers, but some have been advocated by particular schools. Those generally recognized are the natural substances, i.e. fire, earth, water, air, etc., the simple bodies; secondly, plants and their parts, and animals and the parts of animals; and finally the heavens and the parts of the heavens. Some particular schools say that Forms and the objects of mathematics are substances. And it follows from our arguments that there are other substances, the essence and the substratum. Again, in another way the genus seems more substantial than the species, and the universal than the particulars. And with the universal and the genus the Ideas are connected; it is in virtue of the same argument that they are thought to be substances. And since the essence is substance, and the definition is formula of the essence, for this reason we have discussed definition and essential predication. Since the definition is a formula, and a formula has parts, we had to consider with respect to the notion of part, what are parts of the substance and what are not, and whether the same things are also parts of the definition. Further, then, neither the universal nor the genus is a substance; we must inquire later into the Ideas and the objects of mathematics; for some say these exist apart from sensible substances.

But now let us resume the discussion of the generally recognized substances. These are the sensible substances, and sensible substances all have matter. The substratum is substance, and this is in one sense the matter (and by matter I mean that which, not being a 'this' actually, is potentially a 'this'), and in another sense the formula or form (which being a 'this' can be separately formulated), and thirdly the complex of matter and form, which alone is generated and destroyed, and is, without qualification, capable of separate existence; for of substances in the sense of formulae some are separable and some are not.

But clearly matter also is substance;[1] for in all the opposite changes that occur there is something which underlies the changes, e.g. in respect of place that which is now here and again elsewhere, and in respect of increase that which is now of one size and again less or greater, and in respect of alteration that which is now healthy and again diseased; and similarly in respect of substance there is something that is now being generated and again being destroyed, and now underlies the process as a 'this' and again underlies it as the privation of positive character. In this last change the others are involved. But in either one or two of the others this is not involved; for it is not necessary if a thing has matter for change of place that it should also have matter for generation and destruction.

Note

1 This is hard to square with the earlier denial that matter is substance, e.g. in Book VII, Ch. 3. Critics will see, in this apparent inconsistency, an indication that no one concept of substance can do all the work to which Aristotle would like to put it.

(A) Gotama (the Buddha), Sayings on 'Conditioned Genesis'
(B) *Lalitavistara*, XIII, 95–117
(C) Nāgārjuna, *Madhyamaka-Kārikā*, Dedication and Chapter 25

(A) and (B) *From* Edward Conze (trans. and ed.), *Buddhist Texts Through the Ages*, Boston: Shambhala, 1990, pp. 65–70, 91–4, 158–61 (some notes omitted). (C) From Theodore Stcherbatsky, *The Conception of Buddhist Nirvana*, Delhi: Motilal Banarsidass, 1977, pp. 77, 81–4.

In chapter 3, we saw the important place occupied in Aristotle's *Metaphysics* by causality, broadly construed. A similarly broad notion played an even more central part in a remarkably rich eastern metaphysical tradition, Buddhism – from the Buddha himself (Siddhatha Gotama, c. sixth to fifth century BCE) to the greatest of Buddhist philosophers, the south Indian monk Nāgārjuna (c. second to third century CE), and beyond.

Among the wider public, the best known doctrines of the Buddha are those of the Four Noble Truths, concerning the origin and elimination of 'suffering', and the Eightfold Path ('right action' etc.; see p. 56 below), which details the means to the ending of 'suffering'.[1] But neither doctrine, widespread in Indian religion at large, was distinctive of the Buddha's thought in the way that two underlying doctrines of a more metaphysical character were. These were the theses of 'conditioned genesis' (*paṭiccasamuppāda* in Pali; alternatively translated, *inter alia*, as 'dependent arising' and 'relative conditioning') and of 'not-self' (*anatta*). What distinguishes Buddhism from other Indian schools is the insistence that it is through grasping these two theses that 'suffering' may be

[1] Useful introductory accounts of the Buddha's thought are Walpola Rahula, *What the Buddha Taught*, New York: Grove, 1962 and Peter Harvey, *An Introduction to Buddhism*, Cambridge: Cambridge University Press, 1990.

ended and 'liberation' from the everyday world (saṃsāra) achieved. 'Who sees Conditioned Genesis', spoke the Buddha, 'sees Dhamma [true doctrine]'.

The two theses are closely related: it is because people and things are not self-subsistent, because everything is reciprocally conditioned in a circular chain,[2] that there are no 'selves', in the sense of enduring, unchanging substances (mental or physical) underlying the changing phenomena we observe. (Compare the positions of Spinoza and Leibniz in chapters 9 and 10 below.) Hence, for example, we must reject the Vedantin view (see chapter 5 below) that people have 'true selves' which are identical with absolute reality, Brahman.

The two theses are also intimately connected with other famous Buddhist concepts, notably those of Nirvana and 'emptiness' (śūnyatā). Nirvana, the goal of the Eightfold Path, is 'the stopping of [conditioned] becoming', of the cycle of birth-and-death, and the world is 'empty' because everything is 'empty of self', a 'no-thing' if 'thing' is understood as 'substance'.

The Buddha regarded abstract metaphysical speculation about reality as 'unprofitable', so that it was left to later thinkers to develop the implications of his remarks on 'conditioned genesis' and related notions into a systematic position. Early Theravada Buddhists, for example, tended towards a 'realist' interpretation of things, but with an insistence that these are analysable into the constituents or 'atoms' on which they depend. By contrast, later Buddhists of the 'mind only' school understood the Buddha's account of the chain of dependence to imply that reality is an interconnected process of mental events. In one text I have chosen, the Lalitavistara, one discerns the 'atomist' approach, but with a pronounced tendency as well to regard a world of merely conditioned things as a 'mock show'.[3]

Perhaps the most interesting and radical interpretation of the Buddha's sayings was that of Nāgārjuna, the main representative of the Mahayana school known as Madhyamaka ('middle way').[4] (Nāgārjuna's equally radical views on

---

[2] As in the extract from the Vinaya-piṭaka on p. 55f below, 'conditioned genesis' is often explained in terms of a 12-link chain of mutually dependent factors (consciousness, mind-and-body, craving, etc.). The general point, though, is the one stated in the previous extract: 'If this is that comes to be; from the arising of this that arises . . .'.

[3] This work, of uncertain date, is, in the main, an account of the Buddha's life and the primary inspiration, incidentally, for Sir Edwin Arnold's long poem, The Light of Asia. Commentators vary on where to 'place' it philosophically, marking as it does a relatively early work with anticipations of later Mahayana themes.

[4] It is the 'middle school' since it attempts to steer between robust assertion of the world's reality and nihilistic denial of this. Inspiration was sought from such remarks of the Buddha as: '" Everything exists", this is one extreme; "Nothing exists", this is the other extreme. Avoiding both extremes the [Buddha] teaches a doctrine of the middle' (Samyutta Nikāya, 2.12.15). On Nāgārjuna, see Paul Williams, Mahayana Buddhism, London: Routledge, 1989, and Kenneth K. Inada, Nāgārjuna, Tokyo: Hokuseido, 1970, which offers a more scholarly, but less accessible, translation of the Madhyamaka-Kārikā than the one from which I have selected.

knowledge were included in an earlier volume in this series, *Epistemology: the classic readings*). He is often described as a 'nihilist' – unsurprisingly, perhaps, when one reads the 'Dedication' on p. 64 below, which seems to deny the existence of anything whatever. But his position is a good deal more subtle. Nāgārjuna's insight was that, with 'selves' or substances rejected, it is hard to see what sense to make of causality and conditioning, in which case we cannot rest content with a view of reality as a causally conditioned whole.

This does not mean, however, that we can regard the familiar world as an illusion, as non-existent. For one thing, that would imply a contrast with some true world, of Nirvana perhaps: but postulating such an 'other world' is to remain in the grip of the substantialist idea of self. Nirvana is not any kind of entity, but rather the familiar world considered in abstraction from all causal concepts (Ch. 25, Verse IX). As such, it is a 'limit' to thought, about which nothing informative can be said. For another thing, dismissing the world as illusory or non-existent would wrongly assume that words like 'illusion' and 'exist', which have a use *within* the everyday world, can be used to talk about that world as a whole. For Nāgārjuna, as for Wittgenstein in his *Tractatus Logico-Philosophicus*, the world as a whole is not a mere nothing, but we must greet it with silence, with 'the cessation of all thought'. Therein, for the Buddhist, lies 'bliss'.

(A) Gotama, Sayings on 'Conditioned Genesis'

Who sees Conditioned Genesis sees Dhamma [true doctrine]; who sees Dhamma sees Conditioned Genesis.

Majjhima-nikāya I, 190–91

This body, monks, is not yours, nor does it belong to others. It should be regarded (as the product of) former karma,[1] effected through what has been willed and felt. In regard to it, the instructed disciple of the Ariyans well and wisely reflects on Conditioned Genesis itself: If this is that comes to be; from the arising of this that arises; if this is not that does not come to be; from the stopping of this that is stopped. That is to say: . . . (*continue as in next extract*).

Samyutta-nikāya II, 64–65

Conditioned by ignorance are the karma-formations;* conditioned by the karma-formations is consciousness; conditioned by consciousness is mind-

* The Saṁkhāra are karma-formations or karmical formations, in the sense of 'forming', as opposed to 'formed'. As such they may be said to represent the volitional activity (cetanā) of body (kāya), speech (vacì) and mind (mano).

and-body; conditioned by mind-and-body are the six sense-fields; conditioned by the six sense-fields is impression; conditioned by impression is feeling; conditioned by feeling is craving; conditioned by craving is grasping; conditioned by grasping is becoming; conditioned by becoming is birth; conditioned by birth there come into being ageing and dying, grief, sorrow, suffering, lamentation and despair. Thus is the origin of this whole mass of suffering.

But from the stopping of ignorance is the stopping of the karma-formations; from the stopping of the karma-formations is the stopping of consciousness; from the stopping of consciousness is the stopping of mind-and-body; from the stopping of mind-and-body is the stopping of the six sense-fields; from the stopping of the six sense-fields is the stopping of impression; from the stopping of impression is the stopping of feeling; from the stopping of feeling is the stopping of craving; from the stopping of craving is the stopping of grasping; from the stopping of grasping is the stopping of becoming; from the stopping of becoming is the stopping of birth; from the stopping of birth, ageing and dying, grief, sorrow, suffering, lamentation and despair are stopped. Thus is the stopping of this whole mass of suffering.

Vinaya-piṭaka I, 1

From the arising of ignorance is the arising of the karma-formations; from the stopping of ignorance is the stopping of the karma-formations. This ariyan[2] eightfold Way is itself the course leading to the stopping of the karma-formations, that is to say: right view, right thought, right speech, right action, right mode of livelihood, right endeavour, right mindfulness, right concentration.

When an ariyan disciple comprehends 'condition' thus, its arising, its stopping and the course leading to its stopping thus, he is called an ariyan disciple who is possessed of right view, of vision, one who has come into this true Dhamma, who sees this true Dhamma, who is endowed with the knowledge and lore of a learner, who has attained the stream of Dhamma, who is an Ariyan of penetrating wisdom, and who stands knocking at the door of the Deathless.

Samyutta-nikāya II, 43

And what is ageing and dying? Whatever for this or that class of beings is ageing, decrepitude, breaking up, hoariness, wrinkling of the skin, dwindling of the life-span, overripeness of the sense-faculties: this is called ageing. Whatever for this or that being in this or that class of beings is the falling and deceasing, the breaking, the disappearance, the mortality and dying, the passing away, the breaking of the khandhas,[3] the laying down of the body: this is called dying. This is called ageing and dying.

And what is birth? Whatever for this or that being in this or that class of beings is the conception, the birth, the descent, the production, the appearance of the khandhas, the acquiring of the sensory fields: this is called birth.

And what is becoming? There are these three becomings: sensuous becoming, fine-material becoming, immaterial becoming.

And what is grasping? There are four graspings: after sense-pleasures, after speculative view, after rite and custom, after the theory of self.

And what is craving? There are six classes of craving: for material shapes, sounds, smells, tastes, touches and mental objects.

And what is feeling? There are six classes of feeling: feeling due to visual, auditory, olfactory, gustatory, physical and mental impact.

And what is impression? There are six classes of impression: visual, auditory, olfactory, gustatory, physical and mental.

And what are the six sensory fields? The field of the eye, ear, nose, tongue, body, mind.

And what is mind-and-body? Feeling, perception, volition, impression, wise attention: this is called mind. The four great elements* and the material shape derived from them: this is called body. Such is mind and such is body. This is called mind-and-body.

And what is consciousness? There are six classes of consciousness: visual, auditory, olfactory, gustatory, physical and mental consciousness.

And what are the karma-formations? There are three: karma formations of body, of speech, of thought.

And what is ignorance? Whatever is the unknowing in regard to suffering, its arising, its stopping and the course leading to its stopping – this is called ignorance.

Majjhima-nikāya I, 49–54

"Is suffering wrought by oneself, good Gotama?"

"No, Kassapa."

"Then by another?"

"No."

"Then by both oneself and another?"

"No, Kassapa."

"Well then, has the suffering that has been wrought neither by myself nor by another come to me by chance?"

* Earth, water, fire and air.

"No, Kassapa."

"Then, is there not suffering?"

"No, Kassapa, it is not that there is not suffering. For there *is* suffering."

"Well then, the good Gotama neither knows nor sees suffering."

"It is not that I do not know suffering, do not see it. I know it, I see it."

"To all my questions, good Gotama, you have answered 'No', and you have said that you know suffering and see it. Lord, let the Lord explain suffering to me, let him teach me suffering."

"Whoso says, 'He who does (a deed) is he who experiences (its result)', is thereby saying that from the being's beginning suffering was wrought by (the being) himself – this amounts to the Eternity-view. Whoso says, 'One does (a deed), another experiences (the result)', is thereby saying that when a being is smitten by feeling the suffering was wrought by another – this amounts to the Annihilation-view.

"Avoiding both these dead-ends, Kassapa, the Tathagata[4] teaches Dhamma by the man: conditioned by ignorance are the karma-formations . . . *and so on*. Thus is the origin of this whole mass of suffering. By the utter stopping of that very ignorance is the stopping of the karma-formations . . . *and so on*. Thus is the stopping of this whole mass of suffering."

Samyutta-nikāya II, 19–21

Once when the Lord was staying among the Kurus, the venerable Ananda approached him and said: "It is wonderful, Lord, that while Conditioned Genesis is so deep and looks so deep, to me it seems perfectly clear."

"Do not speak like that, Ananda. For this Conditioned Genesis is deep and looks deep too. It is from not awakening to this Dhamma, Ananda, from not penetrating it, that this generation, become tangled like a ball of thread, covered as with blight, twisted up like a grass-rope, cannot overpass the sorrowful state, the bad bourn, the abyss, the circling on (samsara).

Dīgha-nikāya II, 55

"To what extent is the world called 'empty', Lord?"

"Because it is empty of self or of what belongs to self, it is therefore said: 'The world is empty.' And what is empty of self and what belongs to self? The eye, material shapes, visual consciousness, impression on the eye – all these are empty of self and of what belongs to self. So too are ear, nose, tongue, body and mind (and their appropriate sense-data, appropriate consciousness and the impression on them of their appropriate sense-data – *as above*): they are all empty of self and of what belongs to self. Also that feeling which arises, conditioned by impression on the eye, ear, nose, tongue, body, mind, whether it be pleasant or painful or neither painful nor pleasant – that too is empty of self and of what belongs to self. Wherefore is the world called empty because it is empty of self and of what belongs to self."

Samyutta-nikāya IV, 54

And what is the freedom of mind that is empty? As to this, a monk forest-gone or gone to the root of a tree or to an empty place reflects thus: This is empty of self or of what belongs to self. This is called the freedom of mind that is empty. . . . To the extent that the freedoms of mind are immeasurable, are of no-thing, are signless, of them all unshakable freedom of mind is pointed to as chief, for it is empty of passion, empty of aversion, empty of confusion.

Majjhima-nikāya I, 297–98

The stopping of becoming is Nirvana.

Samyutta-nikāya II, 117

It is called Nirvana because of the getting rid of craving.

Samyutta-nikāya I, 39

That monk of wisdom here, devoid of desire and passion, attains to deathlessness, peace, the unchanging state of Nirvana.

Suttanipāta, 204

For those who in mid-stream stay, in great peril in the flood – for those adventuring on ageing and dying – do I proclaim the Isle:
    Where is no-thing, where naught is grasped, this is the Isle of No-beyond. Nirvana do I call it – the utter extinction of ageing and dying.

Suttanipāta, 1093–94

"To what extent, Lord, is one a speaker of Dhamma?"
    "Monk, if one teaches Dhamma for the turning away from material shape, from feeling, perception, the impulses, consciousness, for dispassion in regard to them, for their cessation, it is fitting to call him a monk who is a speaker of Dhamma. If he is himself faring along for the turning away from material shape and so on, for dispassion in regard to them, for their cessation, it is fitting to call him a monk who is faring along in accordance with Dhamma. Monk, if he is freed by this turning away, by dispassion in regard to these things, by their cessation, it is fitting to call him a monk who has attained Nirvana here and now."

Samyutta-nikāya III, 163–64

A wanderer who ate rose-apples spoke thus to the venerable Sariputta:

"Reverend Sariputta, it is said: 'Nirvana, Nirvana.' Now, what, your reverence, is Nirvana?"

"Whatever, your reverence, is the extinction of passion, of aversion, of confusion, this is called Nirvana."

"Is there a way, your reverence, is there a course for the realization of this Nirvana?"

"There is, your reverence."

"What is it, your reverence?"

"This ariyan eightfold Way itself is for the realization of Nirvana, that is to say right view, right thought, right speech, right action, right mode of livelihood, right endeavour, right mindfulness, right concentration."

"Goodly, your reverence, is the Way, goodly the course for the realization of this Nirvana. But for certain it needs diligence."

Samyutta-nikāya IV, 251–52

As this, Ananda, he perceives thus: This is the real, this the excellent, namely the calm of all the impulses, the casting out of all 'basis', the extinction of craving, dispassion, stopping, Nirvana.

Anguttara-nikāya V, 322

There is, monks, that plane where there is neither extension nor . . . motion nor the plane of infinite ether . . . nor that of neither-perception-nor-non-perception, neither this world nor another, neither the moon nor the sun. Here, monks, I say that there is no coming or going or remaining or deceasing or uprising, for this is itself without support, without continuance, without mental object – this is itself the end of suffering.

There is, monks, an unborn, not become, not made, uncompounded, and were it not, monks, for this unborn, not become, not made, uncompounded, no escape could be shown here for what is born, has become, is made, is compounded. But because there is, monks, an unborn, not become, not made, uncompounded, therefore an escape can be shown for what is born, has become, is made, is compounded.[5]

Udāna, 80–81

(B) *Lalitavistara*, XIII, 95–117

The following stanzas were spoken by the Gods to remind the Buddha that the time had come to leave his home:

95. Impermanent and unstable are all conditioned things,
    Essentially brittle, like an unbaked pot.
    Like some borrowed article, like a town built on sand,
    They last for a short while only.

96. These complexes are doomed to destruction,
    Like plaster washed away by the rainy season,
    Like sand on a river's bank.
    They are subject to conditions, and their own-being is hard to
        get at.

97. Like the flame of a lamp are the complexes.
    Suddenly it arises, soon it is doomed to stop.
    Without any staying power they are, like air, or a mass of foam,
    Unsubstantial and weak in themselves.

98. Complexes have no inner might, are void in themselves;
    Rather like the stem of the plantain tree, when reflects on them,
    Like a mock show which deludes the mind,
    Like an empty fist with which a child is teased.

99. Everything that is a complex event
    Proceeds by way of causes and conditions,
    And the events mutually cause and condition each other.
    This fact is not understood by foolish people.

100. Out of pieces of Munja-grass a rope is twisted
    By the force of effort;
    Well-buckets are raised by several revolutions of the wheel;
    Yet each revolution, by itself, can do nothing.

101. Just so, the turning of all the components of becoming
    Results from their mutual interaction;
    In each of them singly it cannot be apprehended,
    Either at the beginning or at the end.

102. Where there is a seed, there is the sprout;
    But the seed is by its nature not the sprout,
    Nor is it other than that, nor just that.
    Just so the true nature of Dharma is neither annihilated nor
        eternal.[6]

103. Ignorance is the condition of all conditioned things;
     But in real truth these conditioned things are not.
     For conditioned things and ignorance are just empty,
     By their own inner nature without any ability to act.

104. One can see the impression made by a seal,
     But the transmission of the seal one cannot apprehend.
     It is not therein, nor anywhere else.
     Just so are conditioned things not annihilated or eternal.

105. Dependent on eye and sight-object
     An act of eye-consciousness springs up here.
     But the sight-object is not based on the eye,
     Nor has any sight-object been transferred to the eye.

106. Without self and impure are these dharmas;
     Yet one imagines that they are with self and pure.
     The act of eye-consciousness springs up from that
     Which is pervertedly seen, which is discriminated although it
         does not exist.

107. The wise discern of an act of consciousness
     The origin and the stopping, the production and the passing away.
     The Yogin sees that it has come from nowhere, gone to
         nowhere,
     That it is empty, and like unto a mock show.

108. Conditioned by the concourse of three factors, –
     The tinderstick, the fuel, the exertion of the hand, –
     Does fire arise; it does its work,
     And then it quickly stops again.

109. Then a wise man searches all around
     Whence it has come and whither it goes.
     Through every region, in every direction he searches.
     He cannot find it as it was before it came or went.

110. Skandhas, sense-fields, elements, craving and ignorance,
     These are the conditions which bring about our deeds.
     Where they are complete one thinks of a being.
     In ultimate truth such a being can never be found.

111. When words are uttered the conditions are
  The throat, the lips, the palate and the rolling of the
    tongue.
  But the words have not come from the throat or the
    palate,
  And in each single of these conditions they cannot be
    found.

112. Speech comes about when all these conditions are
    complete,
  With mind and intellect as the driving force.
  Invisible and immaterial are mind and speech;
  Without or within they cannot be found.

113. The wise man discerns the rise and fall,
  Of speech, or song, or noise, or any sound.
  They are but momentary and empty,
  All speech is similar to an echo.

114. From a lute, or other stringed musical instruments,
  Sound comes forth when three conditions are present –
  The strings, the wooden body, and the hand's exertion.
  It is their concourse which brings forth the sound.

115. Then the wise man searches all around
  Whence it has come and whither it goes.
  Through every region, in every direction he searches,
  He cannot find the sound as it was before it came.

116. Thus immersed in causes and conditions
  Proceeds all that belongs to this conditioned world.
  The Yogin again with his vision of the truly real
  Sees the complexes as empty and without inner might.

117. The skandhas, the sense-fields, the elements
  They are empty inward, empty outward.
  The beings are separated from their self and homeless,
  The dharmas marked with the own-being of space.

Lalitavistara XIII, 95–117

(C) Nāgārjuna, *Madhyamaka-Kārikā*

DEDICATION

The Perfect Buddha,
The foremost of all Teachers I salute.
He has proclaimed
The principle of Universal Relativity [conditioned genesis],
'Tis like blissful (Nirvāṇa),
Quiescence of Plurality.
There is nothing disappears,
Nor anything appears,
Nothing has an end.
Nor is there anything eternal,
Nothing is identical with itself,
Nor is there anything differentiated,
Nothing moves,
Neither hither nor thither.

Chapter XXV

Examination of Nirvāṇa

I[7]

If everything is relative,
No (real) origination, no (real) annihilation,
How is Nirvāṇa, then conceived?
Through what deliverance, through what annihilation?

II

Should every thing be real in substance,
No (new) creation, no (new) destruction,
How should Nirvāṇa then be reached?
Through what deliverance, through what annihilation?

III

What neither is released, nor is it ever reached,
What neither is annihilation, nor is it eternality,
What never disappears, nor has it been created,
This is Nirvāṇa. It escapes precision.

IV

Nirvāṇa, first of all, is not a kind of Ens {entity, substance].
It would then have decay and death.
There altogether is no Ens.
Which is not subject to decay and death.

V

If Nirvāṇa is Ens,
It is produced by causes,
Nowhere and none the entity exists
Which would not be produced by causes.

VI

If Nirvāṇa is Ens,
How can it lack substratum,
There whatsoever is no Ens
Without any substratum.

VII

If Nirvāṇa is not an Ens,
Will it be then a non-Ens?
Wherever there is found no Ens,
There is neither a (corresponding) non-Ens.[8]

VIII

Now, if Nirvāṇa is a non-Ens,
How can it then be independent?
For sure, an independent non-Ens
Is nowhere to be found.

IX

Coordinated here or caused are (separate) things,
We call this world Phenomenal;
But just the same is called Nirvāṇa,
When from causality abstracted.

X

The Buddha has declared
That Ens and non-Ens should both be rejected.
Neither as Ens nor as a non-Ens
Nirvāṇa therefore is conceived.

XI

If Nirvāṇa were both Ens and non-Ens,
Final Deliverance would be also both,
Reality and unreality together,
This never could be possible.

XII

If Nirvāṇa were both Ens and non-Ens,
Nirvana could not be uncaused.
Indeed the Ens and the non-Ens
Are both dependent on causation.

XIII

How can Nirvāṇa represent
An Ens and a non-Ens together?
Nirvana is indeed uncaused,
Both Ens and non-Ens are productions.

XIV

How can Nirvāṇa represent
(The place of Ens and non-Ens together –
As light and darkness in one spot)
They cannot be simultaneously present.

XV

If it were clear, indeed,
What an Ens means, and what a non-Ens,
We could then understand the doctrine.
About Nirvāṇa being neither Ens nor non-Ens.

XVI

If Nirvāṇa is neither Ens nor non-Ens,
No one can really understand
This doctrine which proclaims at once
Negation of them both together.

XVII

What is the Buddha after Nirvāṇa?
Does he exist or does he not exist,
Or both, or neither?
We never will conceive it.

XVIII

What is the Buddha then at life time?
Does he exist, or does he not exist,
Or both, or neither?
We never will conceive it.

XIX

There is no difference at all
Between Nirvāṇa and Saṁsāra,
There is no difference at all
Between Saṁsāra and Nirvāṇa.

XX

What makes the limit of Nirvāṇa
Is also then the limit of Saṁsāra.
Between the two we cannot find
The slightest shade of difference.

XXI

(Insoluble are antinomic) views
Regarding what exists beyond Nirvāṇa,
Regarding what the end of this world is,
Regarding its beginning.

XXII

Since everything is relative (we do not know),
What is finite and what is infinite,
What means finite and infinite at once,
What means negation of both issues?

XXIII

What is identity, and what is difference?
What is eternity what non-eternity,
What means eternity and non-eternity together,
What means negation of both issues?

XXIV

The bliss consists in the cessation of all thought,
In the quiescence of Plurality.
No (separate) Reality was preached at all,
Nowhere and none by Buddha.

Notes

1 *Karma* means intentional action. Buddhism shares the standard Indian view that such action must 'bear fruit', good or bad, in the present or a future lifetime of the agent, according to its moral quality.

2 'Ariyan (or Aryan)' was the name of the central asian invaders of India in the second millennium BCE (and of their language). It came to mean, as here, 'noble' or 'holy'.

3 The *khandhas* (*skhandhas* in Sanskrit) are the 'five aggregates' which comprise a person: matter, sensation, perception, mental formations and consciousness.

4 *Tathagata*, literally 'the thus-gone', is a familiar epithet for a Buddha or 'enlightened one'.

5 This passage reflects a more metaphysically adventurous view of Nirvana than do the Buddha's usual remarks, and for that reason its authenticity has been questioned. The suggestion that Nirvana is some uncompounded plane of existence underlying or transcending the world is one that some Buddhists took up and elaborated, but which others, such as Nāgārjuna, clearly reject.

6 The unpluralizable word *Dharma* (*Dhamma* in Pali), here, does not mean 'true (Buddhist) doctrine', as on p. 55, but 'reality' or 'the world', which is comprised of *dharmas*, in the plural – the constituents of the world (see Verse 106). These three senses of '*dharma*' do not exhaust this versatile word: it can also mean 'law' and 'duty'.

7 Verse I expresses an imagined critic's objection to regarding everything as relative or conditioned. Verse II is in Nāgārjuna's own voice and argues that the critic's worry, concerning the status of Nirvana, remains when things are considered as absolute or unconditioned. If things are unconditioned, how can they be annihilated or extinguished so that Nirvana (literally, 'extinction') is reached?

8 Nāgārjuna is making two points here. (a) Although Nirvana is not an entity or substance, for it is 'empty', one cannot just bluntly deny its existence. At the same time, (b) it would be an error to reify 'emptiness', to treat what is a 'no-thing', Nirvana, as a special kind of thing.

Śaṁkara, *Brahmasūtrabhāṣya* (selections)

From A Source Book of Advaita Vedānta, ed. Eliot Deutsch and J. A. B. van Buitenen, trans. George Thibaut. Honolulu: University Press of Hawaii, 1971. pp. 151–56, 158–60, 162–65, 173–85, 189–90, 196–98. Copyright © Professor Eliot Deutsch.

Criticism of what he saw as the 'nihilistic' position of Buddhist thinkers such as Nāgārjuna occurs in several writings of the eighth to ninth century CE Indian philosopher Śaṁkara (or Śaṅkara) – the author, despite his short life, of a large corpus of works and perhaps the most revered figure of philosophical Hinduism. But it is his own position which is articulated in the following selections from his greatest work, 'the single most influential text in India today',[1] a massive Commentary (*bhāṣya*) on the *Brahmasūtras* (or *Vedāntasūtras*). These were a collection of short verses, attributed to one Bādarāyana and of uncertain date, which interpreted the doctrines found in the *Upaniṣads*, themselves philosophical reflections on the Vedic scriptures.

Śaṁkara was the leading exponent of the philosophy of Advaita Vedānta (non-dualist Vedānta, with 'Vedānta' (lit: 'end of the Veda') here referring to the systematic interpretation of such texts as the *Upaniṣads* and the *Bhagavadgītā*). As its name implies, Śaṁkara's position was a monistic one, and very radically so. The nearest parallel in the western tradition, perhaps, is the 'absolute idealism' of F. H. Bradley (see chapter 14 below). For Śaṁkara, there is not simply just one *kind* of being, but only one being or entity – Brahman (the favoured term for 'absolute reality', and not to be confused with the Hindu god, Brahmā). Śaṁkara's main metaphysical tenets can be summarized as follows:

(a) Nothing is real other than a unitary, ineffable being, Brahman.
(b) Everything taken to exist by ordinary people or philosophers is either illusion or it is identical with Brahman.

---

[1] Karl H. Potter (ed.), *Encyclopedia of Indian Philosophies: Advaita Vedānta up to Śaṁkara and his pupils*, Delhi: Motilal Banarsidass, 1981, p. 119. This book contains a useful reduction of the *Brahmasūtrabhāṣya*.

(c) Individual selves are only 'appearances' of a single Self or 'pure conscious-ness', Ātman, which is itself identical with Brahman.

To these metaphysical claims, Śaṁkara adds an epistemological one to the effect that:

(d) Failure to recognize the truth of (a)–(c) is due to our mistakenly 'superim-posing' upon Brahman/Ātman features which do not belong to it;

and a soteriological claim to the effect that:

(e) Full appreciation of these metaphysical truths will lead to happiness and 'liberation' (*mokṣa*) from the cycle of rebirth in the 'apparent' world.

Śaṁkara's argument for the above metaphysical claims is almost entirely an argument from testimony. Properly understood, he insists, such famous and authoritative Upaniṣadic utterances as 'That thou art' assert the identity of Self, and everything which truly exists, with Brahman. Not even the scriptures, however, can provide informative descriptions of Brahman: for, although it may be grasped through 'direct intuition' and a 'self-luminous flash', it lacks all those features of the 'apparent' world which language is capable of articu-lating. Thus, although Brahman might be called 'conscious' and 'blissful', the senses of these terms are at best analogous to the ones they bear when ap-plied to minds and their states. Indeed, for Śaṁkara the very existence, albeit only 'apparent', of the pluralistic world of things, properties and persons is the product, in some sense, of the imposition of linguistic classifications on what is, in itself, seamless (II.1.27).

Such religious mysticism might seem to leave little scope for philosophical elaboration. But Śaṁkara displays his philosophical acumen in at least three ways in the passages I have selected. First, in his Introduction, he analyses the notion of 'superimposition' which he will later deploy in order to explain how our ignorance of Brahman, our confusion of reality with the world of illusion or *maya*, arises. Second, especially in Part I, he offers us various analogies – for example, that of Space and the spaces inside jugs and the like – to help give us a handle on his claim that what is really One (Brahman/Ātman) can appear as many (things/selves). Finally, and at most length, he considers and attempts to refute a battery of objections, whether common-sense ones or those levelled by rival Schools, to his position.

The set of objections he takes most seriously concern causality, above all the following one. If, as scripture tells us, Brahman is the cause and origin of the world, how can we deny the real existence of a world distinct from Brahman? Here, in Part II, Śaṁkara defends the view that effects are really identical with causes against both the more moderate Sāṁkhyan view that effects are 'im-plicit' in their causes and the radically opposed view, associated with David Hume, that causes and effects are entirely distinct.[2]

My selection ends with an important discussion of dreams and sleep. Śaṁkara is keen to insist that his position does not entail that the 'apparent' world is no different in status from that of 'the world of dreams'. However, dreams also provide him with a useful analogy. Just as the world of dreams is 'daily sublated' or contradicted by waking experience, so the illusory character of the latter is revealed in direct intuitive experience of Brahman. Ultimately, indeed, it is the testimony of those who have enjoyed such direct experience, as recorded in scripture, which convinces Śaṁkara of the truth of his doctrine of the 'absolute unity' of reality.

The works referred to by Śaṁkara in abbreviated form in the following selections are: the *Taittirīya, Chāndogya, Bṛhadāraṇyaka, Muṇḍaka,* and *Kaṭha Upaniṣads*; the *Aiterya Āraṇyaka*; and Gauḍapāda's *Kārikās on the Māṇḍūkya Upaniṣad.*

Śaṁkara, *Brahmasūtrabhāṣya* ◄◄◄

Introduction

It is a matter not requiring any proof that the object and the subject whose respective spheres are the notion of the 'Thou' (the Non-Ego) and the 'Ego,' and which are opposed to each other as much as darkness and light are, cannot be identified. All the less can their respective attributes be identified. Hence it follows that it is wrong to superimpose upon the subject – whose Self is intelligence, and which has for its sphere the notion of the Ego – the object whose sphere is the notion of the Non-Ego, and the attributes of the object, and vice versa to superimpose the subject and the attributes of the subject on the object. In spite of this it is on the part of man a natural procedure – which has its cause in wrong knowledge – not to distinguish the two entities (object and subject) and their respective attributes, although they are absolutely distinct, but to superimpose upon each the characteristic nature and the attributes of the other, and thus, coupling the Real and Unreal, to make use of expressions such as 'That am I' 'That is mine.' – But what have we to understand by the term 'superimposition?' – The apparent presentation, in the form of remembrance, to consciousness of something previously observed, in some other thing.

Some indeed define the term 'superimposition' as the superimposition of the attributes of one thing on another thing. Others, again, define su-

---
² For an especially useful discussion of Śaṁkara's views on causality, see Brian Carr, 'Śaṅkarācārya', in Brian Carr and Indira Mahalingam (eds.), *Companion Encyclopedia of Asian Philosophy*, London: Routledge, 1997.

perimposition as the error founded on the non-apprehension of the difference of that which is superimposed from that on which it is superimposed. Others, again, define it as the fictitious assumption of attributes contrary to the nature of that thing on which something else is superimposed. But all these definitions agree in so far as they represent superimposition as the apparent presentation of the attributes of one thing in another thing. And therewith agrees also the popular view which is exemplified by expressions such as the following: 'Mother-of-pearl appears like silver,' 'The moon although one only appears as if she were double.' But how is it possible that on the interior Self which itself is not an object there should be superimposed objects and their attributes? For every one superimposes an object only on such other objects as are placed before him (i.e. in contact with his sense-organs), and you have said before that the interior Self which is entirely disconnected from the idea of the Thou (the Non-Ego) is never an object. It is not, we reply, non-object in the absolute sense. For it is the object of the notion of the Ego, and the interior Self is well known to exist on account of its immediate (intuitive) presentation. Nor is it an exceptionless rule that objects can be superimposed only on such other objects as are before us, i.e. in contact with our sense-organs; for non-discerning men superimpose on the ether, which is not the object of sensuous perception, dark-blue colour.

Hence it follows that the assumption of the Non-Self being superimposed on the interior Self is not unreasonable.

This superimposition thus defined, learned men consider to be Nescience (*avidyā*), and the ascertainment of the true nature of that which is (the Self) by means of the discrimination of that (which is superimposed on the Self), they call knowledge (*vidyā*). There being such knowledge (neither the Self nor the Non-Self) are affected in the least by any blemish or (good) quality produced by their mutual superimposition. The mutual superimposition of the Self and the Non-Self, which is termed Nescience, is the presupposition on which there base all the practical distinctions – those made in ordinary life as well as those laid down by the Veda – between means of knowledge, objects of knowledge (and knowing persons), and all scriptural texts, whether they are concerned with injunctions and prohibitions (of meritorious and non-meritorius actions), or with final release. – But how can the means of right knowledge such as perception, inference, &c., and scriptural texts have for their object that which is dependent on Nescience? – Because we reply, the means of right knowledge cannot operate unless there be a knowing personality, and because the existence of the latter depends on the erroneous notion that the body, the sense, and so on, are identical with, or belong to, the Self of the knowing person. For without the employment of the senses, perception and the other means of right knowledge cannot operate. And without a basis (i.e. the body) the senses cannot act. Nor does anybody act by means of a body on which the nature of the Self is not super-imposed. Nor can, in the absence of all that, the Self which, in its own nature is free from all contact, become a knowing agent. And if there is no knowing agent, the means of right knowledge cannot operate (as said above). Hence perception and the other means of right knowledge, and the Vedic texts have for their object that which is dependent on Nescience. . . .

. . . That by superimposition we have to understand the notion of some-thing in some other thing we have already explained. (The superimposi-tion of the Non-Self will be understood more definitely from the following examples.) Extra-personal attributes are superimposed on the Self, if a man considers himself sound and entire, or the contrary, as long as his wife, children, and so on are sound and entire or not. Attributes of the body are superimposed on the Self, if a man thinks of himself (his Self) as stout, lean, fair, as standing, walking, or jumping. Attributes of the sense-organs, if he thinks 'I am mute, or deaf, or one-eyed, or blind.' Attributes of the inter-nal organ when he considers himself subject to desire, intention, doubt, determination, and so on. Thus the producer of the notion of the Ego (i.e. the internal organ) is superimposed on the interior Self, which, in reality, is the witness of all the modifications of the internal organ, and vice versa the interior Self, which is the witness of everything, is superimposed on the internal organ, the senses, and so on. In this way there goes on this natural beginning – and endless superimposition, which appears in the form of wrong conception, is the cause of individual souls appearing as agents and enjoyers (of the results of their actions), and is observed by every one.

(Sūtra. Then therefore the enquiry into Brahman.)

The word 'then' is here to be taken as denoting immediate consecution; not as indicating the introduction of a new subject to be entered upon; for the enquiry into Brahman (more literally, the desire of knowing Brahman) is not of that nature. . . .

If, then, the word 'then' intimates immediate consecution it must be explained on what antecedent the enquiry into Brahman specially depends; just as the enquiry into active religious duty . . . specially depends on the antecedent reading of the Veda.

. . . Well, then, we maintain that the antecedent conditions are the dis-crimination of what is eternal and what is non-eternal; the renunciation of all desire to enjoy the fruit (of one's actions) both here and hereafter; the acquirement of tranquillity, self-restraint, and the other means, and the desire of final release. If these conditions exist, a man may, either before entering on an enquiry into active religious duty or after that, engage in the enquiry into Brahman and come to know it; but not otherwise. The word 'then' therefore intimates that the enquiry into Brahman is subsequent to the acquisition of the above-mentioned (spiritual) means. . . .

But, it may be asked, is Brahman known or not known (previously to the enquiry into its nature)? If it is known we need not enter on an enquiry concerning it; if it is not known we can not enter on such an enquiry.[1]

We reply that Brahman is known. Brahman, which is all-knowing and endowed with all powers, whose essential nature is eternal purity, intelligence, and freedom, exists. For if we consider the derivation of the word 'Brahman,' from the root *brh*, 'to be great,' we at once understand that eternal purity, and so on, belong to Brahman. Moreover the existence of Brahman is known on the ground of its being the Self of every one. For every one is conscious of the existence of (his) Self, and never thinks 'I am not.' If the existence of the Self were not known, every one would think 'I am not.' And this Self (of whose existence all are conscious) is Brahman. But if Brahman is generally known as the Self, there is no room for an enquiry into it! Not so, we reply; for there is a conflict of opinions as to its special nature. Unlearned people and the Lokāyatikas [materialists] are of opinion that the mere body endowed with the quality of intelligence is the Self; others that the organs endowed with intelligence are the Self; others maintain that the internal organ is the Self; others, again, that the Self is a mere momentary idea; others, again, that it is the Void. Others, again (to proceed to the opinion of such as acknowledge the authority of the Veda), maintain that there is a transmigrating being different from the body, and so on, which is both agent and enjoyer (of the fruits of action); others teach that that being is enjoying only, not acting; others believe that in addition to the individual souls, there is an all-knowing, all-powerful Lord. Others, finally, (i.e. the Vedāntins) maintain that the Lord is the Self of the enjoyer (i.e. of the individual soul whose individual existence is apparent only, the product of Nescience).

Thus there are many various opinions, basing part of them on sound arguments and scriptural texts, part of them on fallacious arguments and scriptural texts misunderstood. If therefore a man would embrace some one of these opinions without previous consideration, he would bar himself from the highest beatitude and incur grievous loss. . . . (I, 1, 1)

. . . The full sense of the [next] Sūtra . . . is: That omniscient omnipotent cause from which proceed the origin, subsistence, and dissolution of this world – which world is differentiated by names and forms, contains many agents and enjoyers, is the abode of the fruits of actions, these fruits having their definite places, time, and causes, and the nature of whose arrangement cannot even be conceived by the mind – that cause, we say, is Brahman. . . .

. . . [T]he knowledge of the real nature of a thing does not depend on the notions of man, but only on the thing itself. For to think with regard to a post, 'this is a post or a man, or something else,' is not knowledge of truth; the two ideas, 'it is a man or something else,' being false, and only the third idea, 'it is a post,' which depends on the thing itself, falling under the head of true knowledge. Thus true knowledge of all existing things depends on the things themselves, and hence the knowledge of Brahman all depends altogether on the thing, i.e. Brahman itself. – But, it might be said, as Brahman is an existing substance, it will be the object of the other means of right knowledge also, and from this it follows that a discussion of the Vedānta-texts is purposeless. – This we deny; for as Brahman is not an object of the senses, it has no connection with those other means of knowledge. For the senses have, according to their nature, only external things for their objects, not Brahman. If Brahman were an object of the senses, we might perceive that the world is connected with Brahman as its effect; but as the effect only (i.e. the world) is perceived, it is impossible to decide (through perception) whether it is connected with Brahman or something else. Therefore the Sūtra under discussion is not meant to propound inference (as the means of knowing Brahman), but rather to set forth a Vedānta-text. – Which, then, is the Vedānta-text which the Sūtra points at as having to be considered with reference to the characteristics of Brahman? – It is the passage Taitt. Up. III, 1, 'Bhṛigu Vāruṇi went to his father Varuṇa, saying, Sir, teach me Brahman,' &c., up to 'That from whence these beings are born, that by which, when born, they live, that into which they enter at their death, try to know that. That is Brahman.' The sentence finally determining the sense of this passage is found III, 6: 'From bliss these beings are born; by bliss, when born, they live; into bliss they enter at their death.' Other passages also are to be adduced which declare the cause to be the almighty Being, whose essential nature is eternal purity, intelligence, and freedom. (I, 1, 2)

. . . But how about the objection raised . . . that the information about Brahman cannot be held to have a purpose in the same way as the statement about a rope has one, because a man even after having heard about Brahman continues to belong to this transmigratory world? – We reply as follows: It is impossible to show that a man who has once understood Brahman to be the Self, belongs to the transmigratory world in the same sense as he did before, because that would be contrary to the fact of his being Brahman. For we indeed observe that a person who imagines the body, and so on, to constitute the Self, is subject to fear and pain, but we have no right to assume that the same person after having, by means of the Veda, comprehended Brahman to be the Self, and thus having got over his former imaginings, will still in the same manner be subject to pain and fear whose cause is wrong knowledge. . . . Thus *śruti* [reliable testimony] also declares, 'When he is free from the body, then neither pleasure nor pain touches him' (Ch. Up. VIII, 12, 1). If it should be objected that the condition of being free from the body follows on death only, we demur, since the cause of man being joined to the body is wrong knowledge. For it is not possible to establish the state of embodiedness upon anything else but wrong knowledge. And that the state of disembodiedness is eternal on account of its not having actions for its cause, we have already explained. The objection again, that embodiedness is caused by the merit and demerit effected by the Self (and therefore real), we refute by remarking that as the (reality of the) conjunction of the Self with the body is itself not established, the circumstance of merit and demerit being due to the action of the Self is likewise not established; for (if we should try to get over this difficulty by representing the Self's embodiedness as caused by merit and demerit) we should commit the logical fault of making embodiedness dependent on merit and demerit, and again merit and demerit on embodiedness. And the assumption of an endless retrogressive chain (of embodied states and merit and demerit) would be no better than a chain of blind men (who are unable to lead one another). . . .

. . . As long as the knowledge of the Self, which Scripture tells us to search after, has not arisen, so long the Self is knowing subject; but that same subject is that which is searched after, viz. (the highest Self) free from all evil and blemish. Just as the idea of the Self being the body is assumed as valid (in ordinary life), so all the ordinary sources of knowledge (perception and the like) are valid only until the one Self is ascertained.' (I, 1, 4)

But to raise a new objection, there exists no transmigrating soul different from the Lord and obstructed by impediments of knowledge; for *śruti* expressly declares that 'there is no other seer but he; there is no other knower but he' (Bṛh. Up. III, 7, 23). How then can it be said that the origination of knowledge in the transmigrating soul depends on a body, while it does not do so in the case of the Lord? – True, we reply. There is in reality no transmigrating soul different from the Lord. Still the connexion (of the Lord) with limiting adjuncts, consisting of bodies and so on, is assumed, just as we assume the ether to enter into connexion with divers limiting adjuncts such as jars, pots, caves, and the like. And just as in consequence of connexion of the latter kind such conceptions and terms as 'the hollow (space) of a jar,'

&c. are generally current, although the space inside a jar is not really different from universal space, and just as in consequence thereof there generally prevails the false notion that there are different spaces such as the space of a jar and so on; so there prevails likewise the false notion that the Lord and the transmigrating soul are different; a notion due to the non-discrimination of the (unreal) connexion of the soul with the limiting conditions, consisting of the body and so on. That the Self, although in reality the only existence, imparts the quality of Selfhood to bodies and the like which are Not-Self is a matter of observation, and is due to mere wrong conception, which depends in its turn on antecedent wrong conception. And the consequence of the soul thus involving itself in the transmigratory state is that its thought depends on a body and the like. (I, 1, 5)

. . . The individual soul (*jīva*) is called awake as long as being connected with the various external objects by mean of the modifications of the mind – which thus constitute limiting adjuncts of the soul – it apprehends those external objects, and identifies itself with the gross body, which is one of those external objects. When, modified by the impressions which the external objects have left, it sees dreams, it is denoted by the term 'mind.' When, on the cessation of the two limiting adjuncts (i.e. the subtle and the gross bodies), and the consequent absence of the modifications due to the adjuncts, it is, in the state of deep sleep, merged in the Self as it were, then it is said to be asleep (resolved into the Self). . . . (I, 1, 9)

In what precedes we have shown, availing ourselves of appropriate arguments, that the Vedānta-texts exhibited under Sūtras I, 1–11, are capable of proving that the all-knowing, all-powerful Lord is the cause of the origin, subsistence, and dissolution of the world. And we have explained, by pointing to the prevailing uniformity of view (I, 10), that all Vedānta-texts whatever maintain an intelligent cause. The question might therefore be asked, 'What reason is there for the subsequent part of the *Vedāntasūtras?*' (as the chief point is settled already.)

To this question we reply as follows: Brahman is apprehended under two forms; in the first place as qualified by limiting conditions owing to the multiformity of the evolutions of name and form (i.e. the multiformity of the created world[)]; in the second place as being the opposite of this, i.e. free from all limiting conditions whatever. . . .[2]

Although one and the same Self is hidden in all beings movable as well as immovable, yet owing to the gradual rise of excellence of the minds which form the limiting conditions (of the Self), Scripture declares that the Self, although eternally unchanging and uniform, reveals itself in a graduated series of beings, and so appears in forms of various dignity and power; compare, for instance (Ait. Ār. II, 3, 2, 1), 'He who knows the higher manifestation of the Self in him,' &c. . . . (I, 1, 11)

. . . [W]e see that in ordinary life, the Self, which in reality is never anything but the Self, is, owing to non-comprehension of the truth, identified with the Non-Self, i.e. the body and so on; whereby it becomes possible to speak of the Self in so far as it is identified with the body, and so on, as something not searched for but to be searched for, not heard but to be heard, not seized but to be seized, not perceived but to be perceived, not known but to be known, and the like. Scripture, on the other hand, denies, in such passages as 'there is no other seer but he' (Bṛh. Up. III, 7, 23), that there is in reality any seer or hearer different from the all-knowing highest Lord. (Nor can it be said that the Lord is unreal because he is identical with the unreal individual soul; for) the Lord differs from the soul (*vijñānātman*) which is embodied, acts and enjoys, and is the product of Nescience, in the same way as the real juggler who stands on the ground differs from the illusive juggler, who, holding in his hand a shield and a sword, climbs up to the sky by means of a rope; or as the free unlimited ether differs from the ether of a jar, which is determined by its limiting adjunct, (viz. the jar.) . . . (I, 1, 17)

. . . [A]s the passages, 'I am Brahman,' 'That art thou,' and others, prove, there is in reality no such thing as an individual soul absolutely different from Brahman, but Brahman, in so far as it differentiates itself through the mind (*buddhi*) and other limiting conditions, is called individual soul, agent, enjoyer.
. . . If there were no objects there would be no subjects; and if there were no subjects there would be no objects. For on either side alone nothing could be achieved. . . . (I, 1, 31)

True, we reply, (there is in reality one universal Self only.) But the highest Self in so far as it is limited by its adjuncts, viz. the body, the senses, and the mind (*mano-buddhi*), is, by the ignorant, spoken of as if it were embodied. Similarly the ether, although in reality unlimited, appears limited owing to certain adjuncts, such as jars and other vessels. With regard to this (unreal limitation of the one Self) the distinction of objects of activity and of agents may be practically assumed, as long as we have not learned – from the passage, 'That art thou' – that the Self is one only. As soon, however, as we grasp the truth that there is only one universal Self, there is an end to the whole practical view of the world with its distinction of bondage, final release, and the like. (I, 2, 6)

. . . The declaration of the difference of the embodied Self and the internal ruler has its reason in the limiting adjunct, consisting of the organs of action, presented by Nescience, and is not absolutely true. For the Self within is one only; two internal Selfs are not possible. But owing to its limiting adjunct the one Self is practically treated as if it were two; just as we make a distinction between the ether of the jar and the universal ether. Hence there is room for those scriptural passages which set forth the distinction of knower and object of knowledge, for perception and the other means of proof, for the intuitive knowledge of the apparent world, and for that part of Scripture which contains injunctions and prohibitions. In accordance with this, the scriptural passage, 'Where there is duality, as it were, there one sees another,' declares that the whole practical world exists only in the sphere of Nescience; while the subsequent passage, 'But when the Self only is all this, how should he see another?' declares that the practical world vanishes in the sphere of true knowledge. (I, 2, 20)

. . . That same highest Brahman constitutes – as we know from passages such as 'that art thou' – the real nature of the individual soul, while its second nature, i.e. that aspect of it which depends on fictitious limiting conditions, is not its real nature. For as long as the individual soul does not free itself from Nescience in the form of duality – which Nescience may be compared to the mistake of him who in the twilight mistakes a post for a man – and does not rise to the knowledge of the Self, whose nature is unchangeable, eternal Cognition – which expresses itself in the form 'I am Brahman' – so long it remains the individual soul. But when, discarding the aggregate of body, sense-organs and mind, it arrives, by means of Scripture, at the knowledge that it is not itself that aggregate, that it does not form part of transmigratory existence, but is the True, the Real, the Self, whose nature is pure intelligence; then knowing itself to be of the nature of unchangeable, eternal Cognition, it lifts itself above the vain conceit of being one with this body, and itself becomes the Self, whose nature is unchanging, eternal Cognition. As is declared in such scriptural passages as 'He who knows the highest Brahman becomes even Brahman' (Mu. Up. III, 2, 9). And this is the real nature of the individual soul by means of which it arises from the body and appears in its own form.

. . . Before the rise of discriminative knowledge the nature of the individual soul, which is (in reality) pure light, is non-discriminated as it were from its limiting adjuncts consisting of body, senses, mind, sense-objects and feelings, and appears as consisting of the energies of seeing and so on. Similarly – to quote an analogous case from ordinary experience – the true nature of a pure crystal, i.e. its transparency and whiteness, is, before the rise of discriminative knowledge (on the part of the observer,) non-discriminated as it were from any limiting adjuncts of red or blue colour; while, as soon as through some means of true cognition discriminative knowledge has arisen, it is said to have now accomplished its true nature, i.e. transparency and whiteness, although in reality it had already done so before. (I, 3, 19)

... Brahman has been defined as that from which there proceed the origination, sustentation, and retractation of this world. Now as this definition comprises alike the relation of substantial causality in which clay and gold, for instance, stand to golden ornaments and earthen pots, and the relation of operative causality in which the potter and the goldsmith stand to the things mentioned; a doubt arises to which of these two kinds the causality of Brahman belongs. ...

... Now the knowledge of everything is possible through the cognition of the material cause, since the effect is non-different from the material cause. On the other hand, effects are not non-different from their operative cause; for we know from ordinary experience that the carpenter, for instance, is different from the house he has built. – The illustrative example referred to is the one mentioned (Ch. Up. VI, 1, 4), 'My dear, as by one clod of clay all that is made of clay is known, the modification (i.e. the effect) being a name merely which has its origin in speech, while the truth is that it is clay merely;' which passage again has reference to the material cause. ... The Self is thus the operative cause, because there is no other ruling principle, and the material cause because there is no other substance from which the world could originate. (I, 4, 23)

There is nothing objectionable in our system. – The objection that the effect when being reabsorbed into its cause would inquinate [pollute] the latter with its qualities does not damage our position 'because there are parallel instances' ... of effects not inquinating with their qualities the causes into which they are reabsorbed. Things, for instance, made of clay, such as pots, &c., which in their state of separate existence are of various descriptions, do not, when they are reabsorbed into their original matter (i.e. clay), impart to the latter their individual qualities; nor do golden ornaments impart their individual qualities to their elementary material, i.e. gold, into which they may finally be reabsorbed. Nor does the fourfold complex of organic beings which springs from earth impart its qualities to the latter at the time of reabsorption. You [the objector], on the other hand, have not any instances to quote in your favour. For reabsorption could not take place at all if the effect when passing back into its causal substance continued to subsist there with all its individual properties. And that in spite of the non-difference of cause and effect the effect has its Self in the cause, but not the cause in the effect, is a point which we shall render clear later on, under II, 1, 14.

. . . We can quote other examples in favour of our doctrine. As the magician is not at any time affected by the magical illusion produced by himself, because it is unreal, so the highest Self is not affected by the world-illusion. And as one dreaming person is not affected by the illusory visions of his dream because they do not accompany the waking state and the state of dreamless sleep; so the one permanent witness of the three states (viz. the highest Self which is the one unchanging witness of the creation, subsistence, and reabsorption of the world) is not touched by the mutually exclusive three states. For that the highest Self appears in those three states, is a mere illusion, not more substantial than the snake for which the rope is mistaken in the twilight. With reference to this point teachers knowing the true tradition of the Vedanta have made the following declaration, 'When the individual soul which is held in the bonds of slumber by the beginningless *māyā* awakes, then it knows the eternal, sleepless, dreamless non-duality' (Gauḍap. Kār. I, 16). (II, 1, 11)

. . . Another objection, based on reasoning, is raised against the doctrine of Brahman being the cause of the world. . . .

. . . The distinction of enjoyers and objects of enjoyment is well known from ordinary experience, the enjoyers being intelligent, embodied souls, while sound and the like are the objects of enjoyment. Devadatta, for instance, is an enjoyer, the dish (which he eats) an object of enjoyment. The distinction of the two would be reduced to non-existence if the enjoyer passed over into the object of enjoyment, and vice versa. Now this passing over of one thing into another would actually result from the doctrine of the world being non-different from Brahman. But the sublation of a well-established distinction is objectionable, not only with regard to the present time when that distinction is observed to exist, but also with regard to the past and the future, for which it is inferred. The doctrine of Brahman's causality must therefore be abandoned, as it would lead to the sublation of the well-established distinction of enjoyers and objects of enjoyment.

To the preceding objection we reply, 'It may exist as in ordinary experience.' Even on our philosophic view the distinction may exist, as ordinary experience furnishes us with analogous instances. We see, for instance, that waves, foam, bubbles, and other modifications of the sea, although they really are not different from the sea-water, exist, sometimes in the state of mutual separation, sometimes in the state of conjunction, &c. From the fact of their being non-different from the seawater, it does not follow that they pass over into each other; and, again, although they do not pass over into each other, still they are not different from the sea. So it is in the case under discussion also. The enjoyers and the objects of enjoyment do not pass over into each other, and yet they are not different from the highest Brahman. And although the enjoyer is not really an effect of Brahman, since the unmodified creator himself, in so far as he enters into the effect, is called the enjoyer (according to the passage, 'Having created he entered into it,' Taitt. Up. II, 6), still after Brahman has entered into its effects it passes into a state of distinction, in consequence of the effect acting as a limiting adjunct; just as the universal ether is divided by its contact with jars and other limiting adjuncts. The conclusion is, that the distinction of enjoyers and objects of enjoyment is possible, although both are non-different from Brahman, their highest cause, as the analogous instance of the sea and its waves demonstrates. (II, 1, 13)

The refutation contained in the preceding Sutra was set forth on the condition of the practical distinction of enjoyers and objects of enjoyment being acknowledged. In reality, however, that distinction does not exist because there is understood to be non-difference (identity) of cause and effect. The effect is this manifold world consisting of ether and so on; the cause is the highest Brahman. Of the effect it is understood that in reality it is non-different from the cause, i.e. has no existence apart from the cause. – How so? – 'On account of the scriptural word "origin" and others.' The word 'origin' is used in connexion with a simile, in a passage undertaking to show how through the knowledge of one thing everything is known; viz. Ch. Up. VI, 1, 4, 'As, my dear, by one clod of clay all that is made of clay is known, the modification (i.e. the effect; the thing made of clay) being a name merely which has its origin in speech, while the truth is that it is clay merely; thus,' &c. – The meaning of this passage is that, if there is known a lump of clay which really and truly is nothing but clay, there are known thereby likewise all things made of clay, such as jars, dishes, pails, and so on, all of which agree in having clay for their true nature. For these modifications or effects are names only, exist through or originate from speech only, while in reality there exists no such thing as a modification. In so far as they are names (individual effects distinguished by names) they are untrue; in so far as they are clay they are true. – This parallel instance is given with reference to Brahman; applying the phrase 'having its origin in speech' to the case illustrated by the instance quoted we understand that the entire body of effects has no existence apart from Brahman. . . . We therefore must adopt the following view. In the same way as those parts of

ethereal space which are limited by jars and waterpots are not really different from the universal ethereal space, and as the water of a mirage is not
really different from the surface of the salty steppe – for the nature of that
water is that it is seen in one moment and has vanished in the next, and
moreover, it is not to be perceived by its own nature (i.e. apart from the
surface of the desert –; so this manifold world with its objects of enjoyment, enjoyers and so on has no existence apart from Brahman. – But – it
might be objected – Brahman has in itself elements of manifoldness. As the
tree has many branches, so Brahman possesses many powers and energies
dependent on those powers. Unity and manifoldness are therefore both
true. Thus, a tree considered in itself is one, but it is manifold if viewed as
having branches; so the sea in itself is one, but manifold as having waves
and foam; so the clay in itself is one, but manifold if viewed with regard to
the jars and dishes made of it. On this assumption the process of final
release resulting from right knowledge may be established in connexion
with the element of unity (in Brahman), while the two processes of common worldly activity and of activity according to the Veda – which depend
on the *karmakāṇḍa* [ritual activity] – may be established in connexion
with the element of manifoldness. And with this view the parallel instances
of clay &c. agree very well.

This theory, we reply, is untenable because in the instance (quoted in
the Upaniṣad) the phrase 'as clay they are true' asserts the cause only to be
true while the phrase 'having its origin in speech' declares the unreality of
all effects. And with reference to the matter illustrated by the instance given
(viz. the highest cause, Brahman) we read, 'In that all this has its Self;' and,
again, 'That is true,' whereby it is asserted that only the one highest cause
is true. The following passage again, 'That is the Self; thou art that, O
Śvetaketu!' teaches that the embodied soul (the individual soul) also is
Brahman. (And we must note that) the passage distinctly teaches that the
fact of the embodied soul having its Self in Brahman is self-established, not
be accomplished by endeavour. This doctrine of the individual soul having
its Self in Brahman, if once accepted as the doctrine of the Veda, does away
with the independent existence of the individual soul, just as the idea of the
rope does away with the idea of the snake (for which the rope had been
mistaken). And if the doctrine of the independent existence of the individual soul has to be set aside, then the opinion of the entire phenomenal
world – which is based on the individual soul – having an independent
existence is likewise to be set aside. But only for the establishment of the
latter an element of manifoldness would have to be assumed in Brahman,
in addition to the element of unity. – Scriptural passages also (such as 'When
the Self only is all this, how should he see another?' Bṛh. Up. II, 4, 13)

declare that for him who sees that everything has its Self in Brahman the whole phenomenal world with its actions, agents, and results of actions is non-existent. Nor can it be said that this non-existence of the phenomenal world is declared (by Scripture) to be limited to certain states; for the passage 'Thou art that' shows that the general fact of Brahman being the Self of all is not limited by any particular state.

Other objections are started. – If we acquiesce in the doctrine of absolute unity, the ordinary means of right knowledge, perception, &c., become invalid because the absence of manifoldness deprives them of their objects; just as the idea of a man becomes invalid after the right idea of the post (which at first had been mistaken for a man) has presented itself. Moreover, all the texts embodying injunctions and prohibitions will lose their purport if the distinction on which their validity depends does not really exist. And further, the entire body of doctrine which refers to final release will collapse, if the distinction of teacher and pupil on which it depends is not real. And if the doctrine of release is untrue, how can we maintain the truth of the absolute unity of the Self, which forms an item of that doctrine?

These objections, we reply, do not damage our position because the entire complex of phenomenal existence is considered as true as long as the knowledge of Brahman being the Self of all has not arisen; just as the phantoms of a dream are considered to be true until the sleeper wakes. For as long as a person has not reached the true knowledge of the unity of the Self, so long it does not enter his mind that the world of effects with its means and objects of right knowledge and its results of actions is untrue; he rather, in consequence of his ignorance, looks on mere effects (such as body, offspring, wealth, &c.) as forming part of and belonging to his Self, forgetful of Brahman being in reality the Self of all. Hence, as long as true knowledge does not present itself, there is no reason why the ordinary course of secular and religious activity should not hold on undisturbed. The case is analogous to that of a dreaming man who in his dream sees manifold things, and, up to the moment of waking, is convinced that his ideas are produced by real perception without suspecting the perception to be a merely apparent one. – But how (to restate an objection raised above) can the Vedanta-texts if untrue convey information about the true being of Brahman? We certainly do not observe that a man bitten by a rope-snake (i.e. a snake falsely imagined in a rope) dies, nor is the water appearing in a mirage used for drinking or bathing. – This objection, we reply, is without force (because as a matter of fact we do see real effects to result from unreal causes), for we observe that death sometimes takes place from imaginary venom, (when a man imagines himself to have been bitten by a venomous snake,) and effects (of what is perceived in a dream) such as the bite of a snake or bathing in a river take place with regard to a dreaming person. – But, it will be said, these effects themselves are unreal! – These effects themselves, we reply, are unreal indeed; but not so the consciousness which the dreaming person has of them. This consciousness is a real result; for it is not sublated by the waking consciousness. The man who has risen from sleep does indeed consider the effects perceived by him in his dream such as being bitten by a snake, bathing in a river, &c. to be unreal, but he does not on that account consider the consciousness he had of them to be unreal likewise.

. . . Thus the Lord depends (as Lord) upon the limiting adjuncts of name and form, the products of Nescience; just as the universal ether depends (as limited ether, such as the ether of a jar, &c.) upon the limiting adjuncts in the shape of jars, pots, &c. He (the Lord) stands in the realm of the phenomenal in the relation of a ruler to the so-called jīvas (individual souls) or cognitional Selfs (*vijñānātman*), which indeed are one with his own Self – just as the portions of ether enclosed in jars and the like are one with the universal ether – but are limited by aggregates of instruments of action (i.e. bodies) produced from name and form, the presentations of Nescience. Hence the Lord's being a Lord, his omniscience, his omnipotence, &c. all depend on the limitation due to the adjuncts whose Self is Nescience; while in reality none of these qualities belong to the Self whose true nature is cleared, by right knowledge, from all adjuncts whatever. . . . (II, 1, 14)

That the effect exists before its origination and is non-different from the cause, follows from reasoning as well as from a further scriptural passage.

We at first set forth the argumentation. – Ordinary experience teaches us that those who wish to produce certain effects, such as curds, or earthen jars, or golden ornaments, employ for their purpose certain determined causal substances such as milk, clay, and gold; those who wish to produce sour milk do not employ clay, nor do those who intend to make jars employ milk and so on. But, according to that doctrine which teaches that the effect is non-existent (before its actual production), all this should be possible. For if before their actual origination all effects are equally non-existent in any causal substance, why then should curds be produced from milk only and not from clay also, and jars from clay only and not from milk as well? – Let us then maintain, the *asatkāryavādin* rejoins,[3] that there is indeed an equal non-existence of any effect in any cause, but that at the same time each causal substance has a certain capacity reaching beyond itself (*atiśaya*) for some particular effect only and not for other effects; that, for instance, milk only, and not clay, has a certain capacity for curds; and clay only, and not milk, an analogous capacity for jars. – What, we ask in return, do you understand by that '*atiśaya*'? If you understand by it the antecedent condition of the effect (before its actual origination), you abandon your doctrine that the effect does not exist in the cause, and prove our doctrine according to which it does so exist. If, on the other hand, you understand by the *atiśaya* a certain power of the cause assumed to the end of accounting for the fact that only one determined effect springs from the cause, you must admit that the power can determine the particular effect only if it neither is other (than cause and effect) nor non-existent; for if it were either, it would not be different from anything else which is either non-existent or other than cause and effect, (and how then should it alone be able to produce the particular effect?). Hence it follows that that power is identical with the Self of the cause, and that the effect is identical with the Self of that power. – Moreover, as the ideas of cause and effect on the one hand and of substance and qualities on the other hand are not separate ones, as, for instance, the ideas of a horse and a buffalo, it follows that the identity of the cause and the effect as well as of the substance and its qualities has to be admitted. (Let it then be assumed, the opponent rejoins, that the cause and the effect, although really different, are not apprehended as such, because they are connected by the so-called *samavāya* connexion.) – If, we reply, you assume the *samavāya* connexion between cause and affect,[4] you have either to admit that the *samavāya* itself is joined by a certain connexion to the two terms which are connected by *samavāya*, and then that connexion will again require a new connexion (joining it to the two terms which it binds together), and you will thus be compelled to postulate an infinite series of connexions; or else you will have to maintain that the *samavāya* is not joined by any connexion to the terms which it binds together, and from that will result the dissolution of the bond which connects the two terms of the *samavāya* relation. – Well then, the opponent rejoins, let us assume that the *samavāya* connexion as itself being a connexion may be connected with the terms which it joins without the help of any further connexion. – Then, we reply, conjunction (*saṁyoga*) also must be connected with the two terms which it joins without the help of the *samavāya* connexion; for conjunction also is a kind of connexion. – Moreover, as substances, qualities, and so on are apprehended as standing in the relation of identity, the assumption of the *samavāya* relation has really no purport.

In what manner again do you – who maintain that the cause and the effect are joined by the *samavāya* relation – assume a substance consisting of parts which is an effect to abide in its causes, i.e. in the material parts of which it consists? Does it abide in all the parts taken together or in each particular part? – If you say that it abides in all parts together, it follows that the whole as such cannot be perceived, as it is impossible that all the parts should be in contact with the organs of perception. (And let it not be objected that the whole may be apprehended through some of the parts only), for manyness which abides in all its substrates together (i.e. in all the many things), is not apprehended so long as only some of those substrates are apprehended. – Let it then be assumed that the whole abides in all the parts by the mediation of intervening aggregates of parts. – In that case, we reply, we should have to assume other parts in addition to the primary originative parts of the whole, in order that by means of those other parts the whole could abide in the primary parts in the manner indicated by you. For we see (that one thing which abides in another abides there by means of parts different from those of that other thing), that the sword, for instance, pervades the sheath by means of parts different from the parts of the sheath. But an assumption of that kind would lead us into a regressus in infinitum, because in order to explain how the whole abides in certain given parts we should always have to assume further parts. – Well, then, let us maintain the second alternative, viz. that the whole abides in each particular part. – That also cannot be admitted; for if the whole is present in one part it cannot be present in other parts also; not any more than Devadatta can be present in Śrughna and in Pāṭaliputra on one and the same day. If the whole were present in more than one part, several wholes would result, comparable to Devadatta and Yajñadatta, who, as being two different persons, may live one of them at Śrughna and the other at Pāṭaliputra. – If the opponent should rejoin that the whole may be fully present in each part, just as the generic character of the cow is fully present in each individual cow; we point out that the generic attributes of the cow are visibly perceived in each individual cow, but that the whole is not thus perceived in each particular part. If the whole were fully present in each part, the consequence would be that the whole would produce its effects indifferently with any of its parts; a cow, for instance, would give milk from her horns or her tail. But such things are not seen to take place. . . . (II, 1, 18)

Your assertion that the intelligent Brahman alone, without a second, is the cause of the world cannot be maintained, on account of the observation of employment (of instruments). For in ordinary life we see that potters, weavers, and other handicraftsmen produce jars, cloth, and the like, after having put themselves in possession of the means thereto by providing themselves with various implements, such as clay, staffs, wheels, string, &c.; Brahman, on the other hand, you conceive to be without any help; how then can it act as a creator without providing itself with instruments to work with? – We therefore maintain that Brahman is not the cause of the world.

This objection is not valid, because causation is possible in consequence of a peculiar constitution of the causal substance, as in the case of milk. Just as milk and water turn into curds and ice respectively, without any extraneous means, so it is in the case of Brahman also. And if you object to this analogy for the reason that milk, in order to turn into curds, does require an extraneous agent, viz. heat, we reply that milk by itself also undergoes a certain amount of definite change, and that its turning is merely accelerated by heat. If milk did not possess that capability of itself, heat could not compel it to turn; for we see that air or ether, for instance, is not compelled by the action of heat to turn into sour milk. By the co-operation of auxiliary means the milk's capability of turning into sour milk is merely completed. The absolutely complete power of Brahman, on the other hand, does not require to be supplemented by any extraneous help. . . . (II, 1, 24)

. . . [W]e maintain that the (alleged) break in Brahman's nature is a mere figment of Nescience. By a break of that nature a thing is not really broken up into parts, not any more than the moon is really multiplied by appearing double to a person of defective vision. By that element of plurality which is the fiction of Nescience, which is characterised by name and form, which is evolved as well as non-evolved, which is not to be defined either as the Existing or the Non-existing, Brahman becomes the basis of this entire apparent world with its changes, and so on, while in its true and real nature it at the same time remains unchanged, lifted above the phenomenal universe. And as the distinction of names and forms, the fiction of Nescience, originates entirely from speech only, it does not militate against the fact of Brahman being without parts. – Nor have the scriptural passages which speak of Brahman as undergoing change the purpose of teaching the fact of change; for such instruction would have no fruit. They rather aim at imparting instruction about Brahman's Self as raised above this apparent world; that being an instruction which we know to have a result of its own. . . . (II, 1, 27)

. . . It is not true that the world of dreams is real; it is mere illusion and there is not a particle of reality in it. – Why? – 'On account of its nature not manifesting itself with the totality,' i.e. because the nature of the dream world does not manifest itself with the totality of the attributes of real things. – What then do you mean by the 'totality'? – The fulfilment of the conditions of place, time, and cause, and the circumstance of non-refutation. All these have their sphere in real things, but cannot be applied to dreams. In the first place there is, in a dream, no space for chariots and the like; for those cannot possibly find room in the limited confines of the body. . . . In the second place we see that dreams are in conflict with the conditions of time. One person lying asleep at night dreams that it is day in the Bhārata

Varṣa; another lives, during a dream which lasts one [brief period] only, through many crowds of years. – In the third place there do not exist in the state of dreaming the requisite efficient causes for either thought or action; for as, in sleep, the organs are drawn inward, the dreaming person has no eyes, &c. for perceiving chariots and other things; and whence should he, in the space of the twinkling of an eye, have the power of – or procure the material for – making chariots and the like? – In the fourth place the chariots, horses, &c., which the dream creates, are refuted, i.e. shown not to exist by the waking state. And apart from this, the dream itself refutes what it creates, as its end often contradicts its beginning; what at first was considered to be a chariot turns, in a moment, into a man, and what was conceived to be a man has all at once become a tree. . . . (III, 2, 3)

. . . We only maintain that the world connected with the intermediate state (i.e. the world of dreams) is not real in the same sense as the world consisting of ether and so on is real. On the other hand we must remember that also the so-called real creation with its ether, air, &c., is not absolutely real; for as we have proved before (II, 1, 14) the entire expanse of things is mere illusion. The world consisting of ether, &c. remains fixed and distinct up to the moment when the soul cognizes that Brahman is the Self of all; the world of dreams on the other hand is daily sublated by the waking state. That the latter is mere illusion has, therefore, to be understood with a distinction. (III, 2, 4)

We now attempt to ascertain, on the ground of *śruti*, the nature of that Brahman with which the individual soul becomes united in the state of deep sleep and so on, in consequence of the cessation of the limiting adjuncts. – The scriptural passages which refer to Brahman are of a double character; some indicate that Brahman is affected by difference, so, e.g. 'He to whom belong all works, all desires, all sweet odours and tastes' (Ch. Up. III, 14, 2); others, that it is without difference, so, e.g. 'It is neither coarse nor fine, neither short nor long,' &c. (Bṛh. Up. III, 8, 8). Have we, on the ground of these passages, to assume that Brahman has a double nature, or either nature, and, if either, that it is affected with difference, or without difference? This is the point to be discussed.

The [objector] maintains that, in conformity with the scriptural passages which indicate a double nature, a double nature is to be ascribed to Brahman.

To this we reply as follows. – At any rate the highest Brahman cannot, by itself, possess double characteristics; for on account of the contradiction implied therein, it is impossible to admit that one and the same thing should

by itself possess certain qualities, such as colour, &c., and should not possess them. – Nor is it possible that Brahman should possess double characteristics 'on account of place,' i.e. on account of its conjunction with its
limiting adjuncts, such as earth, &c. For the connexion with limiting adjuncts is unavailing to impart to a thing of a certain nature an altogether
different nature. The crystal, e.g. which is in itself clear, does not become
dim through its conjunction with a limiting adjunct in the form of red
colour; for that it is pervaded by the quality of dimness is an altogether
erroneous notion. In the case of Brahman the limiting adjuncts are, moreover, presented by Nescience merely. Hence (as the upadhis [limitations]
are the product of Nescience) if we embrace either of the two alternatives,
we must decide in favour of that according to which Brahma is absolutely
devoid of all difference, not in favour of the opposite one. For all passages
whose aim it is to represent the nature of Brahman (such as, 'It is without
sound, without touch, without form, without decay,' Ka. Up. I, 3, 15)
teach that it is free from all difference. (III, 2, 11)

Just as the light of the sun or the moon after having passed through
space enters into contact with a finger or some other limiting adjunct, and,
according as the latter is straight or bent, itself becomes straight or bent as
it were; so Brahman also assumes, as it were, the form of the earth and the
other limiting adjuncts with which it enters into connexion. Hence there is
no reason why certain texts should not teach, with a view to meditative
worship, that Brahman has that and that form. . . . (III, 2, 15)

Notes

1 Readers will be reminded here of Plato's puzzle, in the *Meno*, as to how one can
  seek knowledge without already knowing what one is seeking. Śaṁkara's solution is that while we know Brahman in the sense of being acquainted with it in
  form of our true Self, most of us do not know what it is and indeed entertain
  mistaken theories about it.
2 This is the famous distinction between *saguṇa* (qualified/conditioned) and *nirguṇa*
  (unqualified/unconditioned) Brahman or reality. The former is Brahman as manifested in the apparent world; the latter, Brahman as it truly is in itself.
3 *Asatkāryavāda* is the doctrine that the effect does *not* already exist in the cause.
4 *Samavāya* is usually translated as 'inherence'. The argument which follows is
  strikingly similar to F. H. Bradley's 'infinite regress' argument against the possibility of 'external', including causal, relations between different things. See his
  Appearance and Reality, Oxford: Oxford University Press, 1969, ch. 3.

From Descartes: Selected Philosophical Writings, trans. J. Cottingham, R. Stoothoff and D. Murdoch. Cambridge: Cambridge University Press, 1988. pp. 160–66, 169–70, 172–85, 188 (some passages and notes omitted; asterisked notes are the translators').

In my Introduction, I noted that the line between epistemology and metaphysics, hardly a sharp or undisputed one, was something which earlier thinkers were less prone to harp upon than contemporary philosophers. Descartes (1596–1650), generally regarded as the initiator of 'modern philosophy', is often congratulated – or condemned – for putting epistemological concerns at the forefront of philosophy, above all by his systematic subjection of our usual beliefs to 'methodological doubt'. But, for Descartes, investigation of human knowledge and its limits quickly generates metaphysical results. The most prominent example in his writings is the conclusion, drawn from the premise that the existence of my mind cannot, as can that of my body, be doubted, that mind and matter are entirely distinct substances. To take another example, Descartes thinks that the existence of God can be inferred from the fact that we possess a certain concept, that of perfection. In *Principles of Philosophy*, a late and synoptic work, as in other writings, we find, therefore, a shuttling back and forth between what today's philosophers would think of as epistemological and metaphysical concerns.

Part I of the *Principles* provides a virtual overview of most of Descartes' distinctive and influential claims. My selection retains the somewhat *al presto* rehearsal (Articles 1–7) of his methodological doubt and the famous claim that doubt cannot extend to the existence of the 'thinking thing' which is doing the doubting. *Cogito ergo sum*. 'I am thinking, therefore I exist'. (Descartes' more leisurely discussion of these matters, from his *Meditations*, was included in *Epistemology: the classic readings*.) Those Articles are followed by ones in which Descartes not only tries to establish God's existence, but to show that if and only if God exists can we legitimately regain confidence in what was earlier subjected to doubt – at any rate, in those matters which are open to 'clear and distinct perception'.

It is important to note that while Descartes thinks we can know *that* God exists, he insists that our knowledge *of* Him is very limited. This insistence has two significant implications for Descartes' overall metaphsyics. First, it enables him to sidestep a problem about free will.[1] We may not understand how our free will is compatible with divine preordination, but given the opacity of God's powers, it would be 'absurd' to let that puzzle weaken our confidence in our freedom (art. 41). Second, 'we shall entirely banish ... the search for final causes' (art. 28) – the attempt, that is, to explain events in terms of teleological ends – and focus solely on the antecedent, 'efficient' causes of things. (This eschewal of final causes by Descartes, Bacon and other figures of the time is usually regarded as integral to 'modern' thinking.)

The latter half of Part I of the *Principles* consists, primarily, in Descartes' attempts to specify what is 'clearly and distinctly' given to perception or thought, and in effect to delineate the broad structure of reality. As for Aristotle, pride of place in that structure is given to *substance*. Substance is what 'depend[s] on no other thing for its existence' (art. 51) – which means that, as Aristotle again hinted, the only substance strictly speaking is God. Speaking slightly more loosely, however, we can postulate that there are just two further substances – mind and matter, whose 'essences' or 'natures' are thought and extension respectively. Speaking still more loosely, we can talk of the many substances – the individual minds and physical objects – which 'pertain to' mind or matter. On the question of 'Forms' or 'universals' (properties, roughly), which so vexed the ancients and the medievals, Descartes rejects the 'realist' view that these exist independently of thought and the particular things which have properties. They arise, he says, solely from the 'use' towards which we put our 'ideas' (art. 59).

In arts. 69–70 there is a brief, but seminal, articulation of a view which not only indicates Descartes' debt to the emerging, Galilean science of his day, but was to influence John Locke (see chapter 8 below) and later advocates of science as the provider of an 'absolute' account of the world.[2] In effect, Descartes is making the distinction between 'primary' and 'secondary' qualities, though he does not use those expressions, and insisting that only the former – shape, motion, and the like – belong genuinely 'in the objects' themselves. In the case of colour, smell and so on, there is nothing in the objects resembling that 'of which we have sensory awareness'.

In Part I of the *Principles*, then, we are offered, in staccato form, not only an account of the powers and limits of human knowledge, and of the reasons we tend to overstep those limits, but a delineation of Descartes' world: a world

---

[1] It is hard to exaggerate the importance Descartes attaches to our free will, especially to our freedom to withhold belief. It is here, as much as anywhere perhaps, that his 'modernity' resides. See Hans Blumenberg, *The Legitimacy of the Modern Age*, Boston: MIT Press, 1985 Part 2.

[2] On Descartes and the 'absolute', scientific picture of the world, see Bernard Williams, *Descartes*, Harmondsworth: Penguin, 1978.

created and governed by a perfect God who has laid down causal laws for its operation, and consisting of two interacting substances – mind, whose nature is to be explored by introspection, and body, whose nature is to be revealed by the sciences. We are offered, in effect, the epistemology and metaphysics which have set the agenda for modern philosophy and with which, in rest of this volume, most of the authors represented are visibly grappling.

René Descartes, *Principles of Philosophy*

Part One

The principles of human knowledge

1. *The seeker after truth must, once in the course of his life, doubt everything, as far as is possible.*
Since we began life as infants, and made various judgements concerning the things that can be perceived by the senses before we had the full use of our reason, there are many preconceived opinions that keep us from knowledge of the truth. It seems that the only way of freeing ourselves from these opinions is to make the effort, once in the course of our life, to doubt everything which we find to contain even the smallest suspicion of uncertainty.

2. *What is doubtful should even be considered as false.*
Indeed, it will even prove useful, once we have doubted these things, to consider them as false, so that our discovery of what is most certain and easy to know may be all the clearer.

3. *This doubt should not meanwhile be applied to ordinary life.*
This doubt, while it continues, should be kept in check and employed solely in connection with the contemplation of the truth. As far as ordinary life is concerned, the chance for action would frequently pass us by if we waited until we could free ourselves from our doubts, and so we are often compelled to accept what is merely probable. From time to time we may even have to make a choice between two alternatives, even though it is not apparent that one of the two is more probable than the other.

4. *The reasons for doubt concerning the things that can be perceived by the senses.*
Given, then, that our efforts are directed solely to the search for truth, our initial doubts will be about the existence of the objects of sense-perception and imagination. The first reason for such doubts is that from time to time

6   we have caught out the senses when they were in error, and it is prudent never to place too much trust in those who have deceived us even once. The second reason is that in our sleep we regularly seem to have sensory perception of, or to imagine, countless things which do not exist anywhere; and if our doubts are on the scale just outlined, there seem to be no marks by means of which we can with certainty distinguish being asleep from being awake.

5. *The reasons for doubting even mathematical demonstrations.*
Our doubt will also apply to other matters which we previously regarded as most certain – even the demonstrations of mathematics and even the principles which we hitherto considered to be self-evident. One reason for this is that we have sometimes seen people make mistakes in such matters and accept as most certain and self-evident things which seemed false to us. Secondly, and most importantly, we have been told that there is an omnipotent God who created us. Now we do not know whether he may have wished to make us beings of the sort who are always deceived even in those matters which seem to us supremely evident; for such constant deception seems no less a possibility than the occasional deception which, as we have noticed on previous occasions, does occur. We may of course suppose that our existence derives not from a supremely powerful God but either from ourselves or from some other source; but in that case, the less powerful we make the author of our coming into being, the more likely it will be that we are so imperfect as to be deceived all the time.

6. *We have free will, enabling us to withhold our assent in doubtful matters and hence avoid error.*
But whoever turns out to have created us, and however powerful and however deceitful he may be, in the meantime we nonetheless experience within us the kind of freedom which enables us always to refrain from believing things which are not completely certain and thoroughly examined. Hence we are able to take precautions against going wrong on any occasion.

7. *It is not possible for us to doubt that we exist while we are doubting; and this is the first thing we come to know when we philosophize in an orderly way.*
7   In rejecting – and even imagining to be false – everything which we can in any way doubt, it is easy for us to suppose that there is no God and no heaven, and that there are no bodies, and even that we ourselves have no hands or feet, or indeed any body at all. But we cannot for all that suppose that we, who are having such thoughts, are nothing. For it is a contradiction to suppose that what thinks does not, at the very time when it is think-

ing, exist. Accordingly, this piece of knowledge – *I am thinking, therefore I exist* – is the first and most certain of all to occur to anyone who philosophizes in an orderly way.

8. *In this way we discover the distinction between soul and body, or between a thinking thing and a corporeal thing.*
This is the best way to discover the nature of the mind and the distinction between the mind and the body. For if we, who are supposing that everything which is distinct from us is false, examine what we are, we see very clearly that neither extension nor shape nor local motion, nor anything of this kind which is attributable to a body, belongs to our nature, but that thought alone belongs to it. So our knowledge of our thought is prior to, and more certain than, our knowledge of any corporeal thing; for we have already perceived it, although we are still in doubt about other things.

9. *What is meant by 'thought'.*
By the term 'thought', I understand everything which we are aware of as happening within us, in so far as we have awareness of it. Hence, *thinking* is to be identified here not merely with understanding, willing and imagining, but also with sensory awareness. For if I say 'I am seeing, or I am walking, therefore I exist', and take this as applying to vision or walking as bodily activities, then the conclusion is not absolutely certain. This is because, as often happens during sleep, it is possible for me to think I am seeing or walking, though my eyes are closed and I am not moving about; such thoughts might even be possible if I had no body at all. But if I take 'seeing' or 'walking' to apply to the actual sense or awareness of seeing or walking, then the conclusion is quite certain, since it relates to the mind, 8 which alone has the sensation or thought that it is seeing or walking.

10. *Matters which are very simple and self-evident are only rendered more obscure by logical definitions, and should not be counted as items of knowledge which it takes effort to acquire.*
I shall not here explain many of the other terms which I have already used or will use in what follows, because they seem to me to be sufficiently self-evident. I have often noticed that philosophers make the mistake of employing logical definitions in an attempt to explain what was already very simple and self-evident; the result is that they only make matters more obscure. And when I said that the proposition *I am thinking, therefore I exist* is the first and most certain of all to occur to anyone who philosophizes in an orderly way, I did not in saying that deny that one must first know what thought, existence and certainty are, and that it is impossible that that

which thinks should not exist, and so forth. But because these are very simple notions, and ones which on their own provide us with no knowledge of anything that exists, I did not think they needed to be listed.

11. *How our mind is better known than our body.*
In order to realize that the knowledge of our mind is not simply prior to and more certain than the knowledge of our body, but also more evident, we should notice something very well known by the natural light: nothingness possesses no attributes or qualities. It follows that, wherever we find some attributes or qualities, there is necessarily some thing or substance to be found for them to belong to; and the more attributes we discover in the same thing or substance, the clearer is our knowledge of that substance. Now we find more attributes in our mind than in anything else, as is manifest from the fact that whatever enables us to know anything else cannot but lead us to a much surer knowledge of our own mind. For example, if I judge that the earth exists from the fact that I touch it or see it, this very fact undoubtedly gives even greater support for the judgement that my mind exists. For it may perhaps be the case that I judge that I am touching the earth even though the earth does not exist at all; but it cannot be that, when I make this judgement, my mind which is making the judgement does not exist. And the same applies in other cases <regarding all the things that come into our mind, namely that we who think of them exist, even if they are false or have no existence>.

12. *Why this fact does not come to be known to all alike.*
Disagreement on this point has come from those who have not done their philosophizing in an orderly way; and the reason for it is simply that they have never taken sufficient care to distinguish the mind from the body. Although they may have put the certainty of their own existence before that of anything else, they failed to realize that they should have taken 'themselves' in this context to mean their minds alone. They were inclined instead to take 'themselves' to mean only their bodies – the bodies which they saw with their eyes and touched with their hands, and to which they incorrectly attributed the power of sense-perception; and this is what prevented them from perceiving the nature of the mind.

13. *The sense in which knowledge of all other things depends on the knowledge of God.*
The mind, then, knowing itself, but still in doubt about all other things, looks around in all directions in order to extend its knowledge further. First of all, it finds within itself ideas of many things; and so long as it

merely contemplates these ideas and does not affirm or deny the existence outside itself of anything resembling them, it cannot be mistaken. Next, it finds certain common notions from which it constructs various proofs; and, for as long as it attends to them, it is completely convinced of their truth. For example, the mind has within itself ideas of numbers and shapes, and it also has such common notions as: *If you add equals to equals the results will be equal;* from these it is easy to demonstrate that the three angles of a triangle equal two right angles, and so on. And so the mind will be convinced of the truth of this and similar conclusions, so long as it attends to the premises from which it deduced them. But it cannot attend to them all the time; and subsequently,* recalling that it is still ignorant as to whether it may have been created with the kind of nature that makes it go wrong   10 even in matters which appear most evident, the mind sees that it has just cause to doubt such conclusions, and that the possession of certain knowledge will not be possible until it has come to know the author of its being.

14. *The existence of God is validly inferred from the fact that necessary existence is included in our concept of God.*

The mind next considers the various ideas which it has within itself, and finds that there is one idea – the idea of a supremely intelligent, supremely powerful and supremely perfect being – which stands out from all the others. <And it readily judges from what it perceives in this idea, that God, who is the supremely perfect being, is, or exists. For although it has distinct ideas of many other things it does not observe anything in them to guarantee the existence of their object.> In this one idea the mind recognizes existence – not merely the possible and contingent existence which belongs to the ideas of all the other things which it distinctly perceives, but utterly necessary and eternal existence. Now on the basis of its perception that, for example, it is necessarily contained in the idea of a triangle that its three angles should equal two right angles, the mind is quite convinced that a triangle does have three angles equalling two right angles. In the same way, simply on the basis of its perception that necessary and eternal existence is contained in the idea of a supremely perfect being, the mind must clearly conclude that the supreme being does exist.[1]

15. *Our concepts of other things do not similarly contain necessary existence, but merely contingent existence.*

The mind will be even more inclined to accept this if it considers that it

---

* '... when it happens that it remembers a conclusion without attending to the sequence which enables it to be demonstrated' (added in French version).

cannot find within itself an idea of any other thing such that necessary existence is seen to be contained in the idea in this way. And from this it understands that the idea of a supremely perfect being is not an idea which was invented by the mind, or which represents some chimera, but that it represents a true and immutable nature which cannot but exist, since necessary existence is contained within it.

16. *Preconceived opinions prevent the necessity of the existence of God from being clearly recognized by everyone.*

Our mind will, as I say, easily accept this, provided that it has first of all completely freed itself from preconceived opinions. But we have got into the habit of distinguishing essence from existence in the case of all other things; and we are also in the habit of making up at will various ideas of things which do not exist anywhere and have never done so. Hence, at times when we are not intent on the contemplation of the supremely perfect being, a doubt may easily arise as to whether the idea of God is not one of those which we made up at will, or at least one of those which do not include existence in their essence.

17. *The greater the objective perfection in any of our ideas, the greater its cause must be.*

When we reflect further on the ideas that we have within us, we see that some of them, in so far as they are merely modes of thinking, do not differ much one from another; but in so far as one idea represents one thing and another represents another, they differ widely; and the greater the amount of objective* perfection they contain within themselves, the more perfect their cause must be. For example, if someone has within himself the idea of a highly intricate machine, it would be fair to ask what was the cause of his possession of the idea: did he somewhere see such a machine made by someone else; or did he make such a close study of mechanics, or is his own ingenuity so great, that he was able to think it up on his own, although he never saw it anywhere? All the intricacy which is contained in the idea merely objectively – as in a picture – must be contained in its cause, whatever kind of cause it turns out to be; and it must be contained not merely objectively or representatively, but in actual reality, either formally or eminently,† at least in the case of the first and principal cause.

---

* If an idea represents some object which is F, the idea is said to possess 'objective' F-ness, or to contain F-ness 'objectively'.
† To possess a property *formally* is to possess it strictly as defined; to possess it *eminently* is to possess it in some higher or more perfect form.

18. *This gives us a second reason for concluding that God exists.*

Since, then, we have within us the idea of God, or a supreme being, we may rightly inquire into the cause of our possession of this idea. Now we find in the idea such immeasurable greatness that we are quite certain that it could have been placed in us only by something which truly possesses the sum of all perfections, that, by a God who really exists. For it is very evident by the natural light not only that nothing comes from nothing but also that what is more perfect cannot be produced by – that is, cannot have as   12
its efficient and total cause – what is less perfect. Furthermore, we cannot have within us the idea or image of anything without there being some- where, either within us or outside us, an original which contains in reality all the perfections belonging to the idea. And since the supreme perfec- tions of which we have an idea are in no way to be found in us, we rightly conclude that they reside in something distinct from ourselves, namely God – or certainly that they once did so, from which it most evidently follows that they are still there. . . .

28. *It is not the final but the efficient causes of created things that we must inquire into.*

When dealing with natural things we will, then, never derive any explana- tions from the purposes which God or nature may have had in view when creating them <and we shall entirely banish from our philosophy the search for final causes>. For we should not be so arrogant as to suppose that we can share in God's plans. We should, instead, consider him as the efficient   16
cause of all things; and starting from the divine attributes which by God's will we have some knowledge of, we shall see, with the aid of our God- given natural light, what conclusions should be drawn concerning those effects which are apparent to our senses.* At the same time we should remember, as noted earlier, that the natural light is to be trusted only to the extent that it is compatible with divine revelation.

29. *God is not the cause of our errors.*

The first attribute of God that comes under consideration here is that he is supremely truthful and the giver of all light. So it is a complete contradiction to suppose that he might deceive us or be, in the strict and positive sense, the cause of the errors to which we know by experience that we are prone. For although the ability to deceive may perhaps be regarded among us men as a

---

* '. . . and we shall be assured that what we have once clearly and distinctly perceived to belong to the nature of these things has the perfection of being true' (added in French ver- sion, which also omits the last sentence of this article).

sign of intelligence, the will to deceive must undoubtedly always come from malice, or from fear and weakness, and so cannot belong to God.

30. *It follows that everything that we clearly perceive is true; and this removes the doubts mentioned earlier.*

It follows from this that the light of nature or faculty of knowledge which God gave us can never encompass any object which is not true in so far as it is indeed encompassed by this faculty, that is, in so far as it is clearly and distinctly perceived. For God would deserve to be called a deceiver if the faculty which he gave us was so distorted that it mistook the false for the true <even when we were using it properly>. This disposes of the most serious doubt, which arose from our ignorance about whether our nature might not be such as to make us go wrong even in matters which seemed to us utterly evident. Indeed, this argument easily demolishes all the other reasons for doubt which were mentioned earlier. Mathematical truths should no longer be suspect, since they are utterly clear to us. And as for our senses, if we notice anything here that is clear and distinct, no matter whether we are awake or asleep, then provided we separate it from what is confused and obscure we will easily recognize – whatever the thing in question – which are the aspects that may be regarded as true.

39. *The freedom of the will is self-evident.*

That there is freedom in our will, and that we have power in many cases to give or withhold our assent at will, is so evident that it must be counted among the first and most common notions that are innate in us. This was obvious earlier on when, in our attempt to doubt everything, we went so far as to make the supposition of some supremely powerful author of our being who was attempting to deceive us in every possible way. For in spite of that supposition, the freedom which we experienced within us was nonetheless so great as to enable us to abstain from believing whatever was not quite certain or fully examined. And what we saw to be beyond doubt even during the period of that supposition is as self-evident and as transparently clear as anything can be.

40. *It is also certain that everything was preordained by God.*

But now that we have come to know God, we perceive in him a power so immeasurable that we regard it as impious to suppose that we could ever do anything which was not already preordained by him. And we can easily get ourselves into great difficulties if we attempt to reconcile this divine preordination with the freedom of our will, or attempt to grasp both these things at once.

41. *How to reconcile the freedom of our will with divine preordination.*
But we shall get out of these difficulties if we remember that our mind is
finite, while the power of God is infinite – the power by which he not only
knew from eternity whatever is or can be, but also willed it and preordained it. We may attain sufficient knowledge of this power to perceive
clearly and distinctly that God possesses it; but we cannot get a sufficient
grasp of it to see how it leaves the free actions of men undetermined. Nonetheless, we have such close awareness of the freedom and indifference which
is in us, that there is nothing we can grasp more evidently or more perfectly. And it would be absurd, simply because we do not grasp one thing,
which we know must by its very nature be beyond our comprehension, to
doubt something else of which we have an intimate grasp and which we
experience within ourselves.

42. *Although we do not want to go wrong, nevertheless we go wrong by our
own will.*
Now that we know that all our errors depend on the will, it may seem
surprising that we should ever go wrong, since there is no one who wants   21
to go wrong. But there is a great difference between choosing to go wrong
and choosing to give one's assent in matters where, as it happens, error is
to be found. And although there is in fact no one who expressly wishes to
go wrong, there is scarcely anyone who does not often wish to give his
assent to something which, though he does not know it, contains some
error. Indeed, precisely because of their eagerness to find the truth, people
who do not know the right method of finding it often pass judgement on
things of which they lack perception, and this is why they fall into error.

43. *We never go wrong when we assent only to what we clearly and distinctly
perceive.*
It is certain, however, that we will never mistake the false for the true provided we give our assent only to what we clearly and distinctly perceive. I
say that this is certain, because God is not a deceiver, and so the faculty of
perception which he has given us cannot incline to falsehood; and the same
goes for the faculty of assent, provided its scope is limited to what is clearly
perceived. And even if there were no way of proving this, the minds of all of
us have been so moulded by nature that whenever we perceive something
clearly, we spontaneously give our assent to it and are quite unable to doubt
its truth. . . .

45. *What is meant by a clear perception, and by a distinct perception.*
Indeed there are very many people who in their entire lives never perceive

anything with sufficient accuracy to enable them to make a judgement
about it with certainty. A perception which can serve as the basis for a
certain and indubitable judgement needs to be not merely clear but also
distinct. I call a perception 'clear' when it is present and accessible to the
attentive mind – just as we say that we see something clearly when it is
present to the eye's gaze and stimulates it with a sufficient degree of strength
and accessibility. I call a perception 'distinct' if, as well as being clear, it is
so sharply separated from all other perceptions that it contains within itself
only what is clear.

46. *The example of pain shows that a perception can be clear without being*
    distinct, but cannot be distinct without being clear.

For example, when someone feels an intense pain, the perception he has of
it is indeed very clear, but is not always distinct. For people commonly
confuse this perception with an obscure judgement they make concerning
the nature of something which they think exists in the painful spot and
which they suppose to resemble the sensation of pain; but in fact it is the
sensation alone which they perceive clearly. Hence a perception can be
clear without being distinct, but not distinct without being clear.

47. *In order to correct the preconceived opinions of our early childhood we*
    must consider the simple notions and what elements in each of them are
    clear.

In our childhood the mind was so immersed in the body that although
there was much that it perceived clearly, it never perceived anything distinctly. But in spite of this the mind made judgements about many things,
and this is the origin of the many preconceived opinions which most of us
never subsequently abandon. To enable us to get rid of these preconceived
opinions, I shall here briefly list all the simple notions which are the basic
components of our thoughts; and in each case I shall distinguish the clear
elements from those which are obscure or liable to lead us into error.

48. *All the objects of our perception may be regarded either as things or affec-*
    tions of things, or as eternal truths. The former are listed here.

All the objects of our perception we regard either as things, or affections of
things, or else as eternal truths which have no existence outside our thought.
The most general items which we regard as things are *substance, duration,*
order, number and any other items of this kind which extend to all classes
of things. But I recognize only two ultimate classes of things: first, intellectual or thinking things, i.e. those which pertain to mind or thinking substance; and secondly, material things, i.e. those which pertain to extended

substance or body. Perception, volition and all the modes both of perceiving and of willing are referred to thinking substance; while to extended substance belong size (that is, extension in length, breadth and depth), shape, motion, position, divisibility of component parts and the like. But we also experience within ourselves certain other things which must not be referred either to the mind alone or to the body alone. These arise . . . from the close and intimate union of our mind with the body. This list includes, first, appetites like hunger and thirst; secondly, the emotions or passions of the mind which do not consist of thought alone, such as the emotions of anger, joy, sadness and love; and finally, all the sensations, such as those of pain, pleasure, light, colours, sounds, smells, tastes, heat, hardness and the other tactile qualities.

49. *It is not possible – or indeed necessary – to give a similar list of eternal truths.*
Everything in the preceding list we regard either as a thing or as a quality or mode of a thing. But when we recognize that it is impossible for anything to come from nothing, the proposition *Nothing comes from nothing* is regarded not as a really existing thing, or even as a mode of a thing, but as an eternal truth which resides within our mind. Such truths are termed common notions or axioms. The following are examples of this class: *It is impossible for the same thing to be and not to be at the same time; What is done cannot be undone; He who thinks cannot but exist while he thinks,* and countless others. It would not be easy to draw up a list of all of them; but nonetheless we cannot fail to know them when the occasion for thinking about them arises, provided that we are not blinded by preconceived opinions. . . .

51. *What is meant by 'substance' – a term which does not apply univocally to God and his creatures.*
In the case of those items which we regard as things or modes of things, it is worthwhile examining each of them separately. By *substance* we can understand nothing other than a thing which exists in such a way as to depend on no other thing for its existence. And there is only one substance which can be understood to depend on no other thing whatsoever, namely God. In the case of all other substances, we perceive that they can exist only with the help of God's concurrence. Hence the term 'substance' does not apply *univocally*, as they say in the Schools, to God and to other things; that is, there is no distinctly intelligible meaning of the term which is common to God and his creatures. <In the case of created things, some are of such a nature that they cannot exist without other things, while some

need only the ordinary concurrence of God in order to exist. We make this distinction by calling the latter 'substances' and the former 'qualities' or 'attributes' of those substances.>

52. *The term 'substance' applies univocally to mind and to body. How a substance itself is known.*

25   But as for corporeal substance and mind (or created thinking substance), these can be understood to fall under this common concept: things that need only the concurrence of God in order to exist. However, we cannot initially become aware of a substance merely through its being an existing thing, since this alone does not of itself have any effect on us. We can, however, easily come to know a substance by one of its attributes, in virtue of the common notion that nothingness possesses no attributes, that is to say, no properties or qualities. Thus, if we perceive the presence of some attribute, we can infer that there must also be present an existing thing or substance to which it may be attributed.

53. *To each substance there belongs one principal attribute; in the case of mind, this is thought, and in the case of body it is extension.*

A substance may indeed be known through any attribute at all; but each substance has one principal property which constitutes its nature and essence, and to which all its other properties are referred. Thus extension in length, breadth and depth constitutes the nature of corporeal substance; and thought constitutes the nature of thinking substance. Everything else which can be attributed to body presupposes extension, and is merely a mode of an extended thing; and similarly, whatever we find in the mind is simply one of the various modes of thinking. For example, shape is unintelligible except in an extended thing; and motion is unintelligible except as motion in an extended space; while imagination, sensation and will are intelligible only in a thinking thing. By contrast, it is possible to understand extension without shape or movement, and thought without imagination or sensation, and so on; and this is quite clear to anyone who gives the matter his attention.

54. *How we can have clear and distinct notions of thinking substance and of corporeal substance, and also of God.*

Thus we can easily have two clear and distinct notions or ideas, one of created thinking substance, and the other of corporeal substance, provided
26   we are careful to distinguish all the attributes of thought from the attributes of extension. We can also have a clear and distinct idea of uncreated and independent thinking substance, that is of God. Here we must simply avoid

supposing that the idea adequately represents everything which is to be found in God; and we must not invent any additional features, but concentrate only on what is really contained in the idea and on what we clearly perceive to belong to the nature of a supremely perfect being. And certainly no one can deny that we possess such an idea of God, unless he reckons that there is absolutely no knowledge of God to be found in the minds of men.

55. *How we can also have a distinct understanding of duration, order and number.*

We shall also have a very distinct understanding of *duration, order* and *number*, provided we do not mistakenly tack on to them any concept of substance. Instead, we should regard the duration of a thing simply as a mode under which we conceive the thing in so far as it continues to exist. And similarly we should not regard order or number as anything separate from the things which are ordered and numbered, but should think of them simply as modes under which we consider the things in question.

56. *What modes, qualities and attributes are.*

By *mode*, as used above, we understand exactly the same as what is elsewhere meant by an *attribute* or *quality*. But we employ the term *mode* when we are thinking of a substance as being affected or modified; when the modification enables the substance to be designated as a substance of such and such a kind, we use the term *quality*; and finally, when we are simply thinking in a more general way of what is in a substance, we use the term *attribute*. Hence we do not, strictly speaking, say that there are modes or qualities in God, but simply attributes, since in the case of God, any variation is unintelligible. And even in the case of created things, that which always remains unmodified – for example existence or duration in a thing which exists and endures – should be called not a quality or a mode but an attribute.

57. *Some attributes are in things and others in thought. What duration and time are.*

Now some attributes or modes are in the very things of which they are said to be attributes or modes, while others are only in our thought. For example, when time is distinguished from duration taken in the general sense and called the measure of movement, it is simply a mode of thought. For the duration which we understand to be involved in movement is certainly no different from the duration involved in things which do not move. This is clear from the fact that if there are two bodies moving for an hour, one 27 slowly and the other quickly, we do not reckon the amount of time to be greater in the latter case than the former, even though the amount of movement may be much greater. But in order to measure the duration of all things, we compare their duration with the duration of the greatest and most regular motions which give rise to years and days, and we call this duration 'time'. Yet nothing is thereby added to duration, taken in its general sense, except for a mode of thought.

58.   *Number and all universals are simply modes of thinking.*
In the same way, number, when it is considered simply in the abstract or in general, and not in any created things, is merely a mode of thinking; and the same apples to all the other *universals*, as we call them.

59.   *How universals arise. The five common universals: genus, species, differentia, property, accident.*
These universals arise solely from the fact that we make use of one and the same idea for thinking of all individual items which resemble each other: we apply one and the same term to all the things which are represented by the idea in question, and this is the universal term. When we see two stones, for example, and direct our attention not to their nature but merely to the fact that there are two of them, we form the idea of the number which we call 'two'; and when we later see two birds or two trees, and consider not their nature but merely the fact that there are two of them, we go back to the same idea as before. This, then, is the universal idea; and we always designate the number in question by the same universal term 'two'. In the same way, when we see a figure made up of three lines, we form an idea of it which we call the idea of a triangle; and we later make use of it as a universal idea, so as to represent to our mind all the other figures made up of three lines. Moreover, when we notice that some triangles have one right angle, and others do not, we form the universal idea of a right-angled triangle; since this idea is related to the preceding idea as a special case, it is termed a *species*. And the rectangularity is the universal *differentia* which distinguishes all right-angled triangles from other triangles. And the fact that the square on the hypotenuse is equal to the sum of the squares on the other two sides is a *property* belonging to all and only right-angled triangles. Finally, if we suppose that some right-angled triangles are in motion while others are not, this will be a universal *accident* of such triangles. Hence five universals are commonly listed: *genus, species, differentia, property* and *accident*.

60. *Three sorts of distinction: firstly, what is meant by a 'real distinction'.*

Now number, in things themselves, arises from the distinction between them. But *distinction* can be taken in three ways: as a *real* distinction, a *modal* distinction, or a *conceptual* distinction. Strictly speaking, a *real* distinction exists only between two or more substances; and we can perceive that two substances are really distinct simply from the fact that we can clearly and distinctly understand one apart from the other. For when we come to know God, we are certain that he can bring about anything of which we have a distinct understanding. For example, even though we may not yet know for certain that any extended or corporeal substance exists in reality, the mere fact that we have an idea of such a substance enables us to be certain that it is capable of existing. And we can also be certain that, if it exists, each and every part of it, as delimited by us in our thought, is really distinct from the other parts of the same substance. Similarly, from the mere fact that each of us understands himself to be a thinking thing and is capable, in thought, of excluding from himself every other substance, whether thinking or extended, it is certain that each of us, regarded in this way, is really distinct from every other thinking substance and from every corporeal substance. And even if we suppose that God has joined some corporeal substance to such a thinking substance so closely that they cannot be more closely conjoined, thus compounding them into a unity, they nonetheless remain really distinct. For no matter how closely God may have united them, the power which he previously had of separating them, or keeping one in being without the other, is something he could not lay aside; and things which God has the power to separate, or to keep in being separately, are really distinct.

61. *What is meant by a 'modal distinction'.*

A *modal distinction* can be taken in two ways: firstly, as a distinction between a mode, properly so called, and the substance of which it is a mode; and secondly, as a distinction between two modes of the same substance. The first kind of modal distinction can be recognized from the fact that we can clearly perceive a substance apart from the mode which we say differs from it, whereas we cannot, conversely, understand the mode apart from the substance. Thus there is a modal distinction between shape or motion and the corporeal substance in which they inhere; and similarly, there is a modal distinction between affirmation or recollection and the mind. The second kind of modal distinction is recognized from the fact that we are able to arrive at knowledge of one mode apart from another, and *vice versa*, whereas we cannot know either mode apart from the substance in which they both inhere. For example, if a stone is in motion and is square-shaped,

I can understand the square shape without the motion and, conversely, the motion without the square shape; but I can understand neither the motion nor the shape apart from the substance of the stone. A different case, however, is the distinction by which the mode of one substance is distinct from another substance or from the mode of another substance. An example of this is the way in which the motion of one body is distinct from another body, or from the mind; or the way in which motion differs from doubt. It seems more appropriate to call this kind of distinction a real distinction, rather than a modal distinction, since the modes in question cannot be clearly understood apart from the really distinct substances of which they are modes.

30

62. *What is meant by a 'conceptual distinction'.*

Finally, a *conceptual distinction* is a distinction between a substance and some attribute of that substance without which the substance is unintelligible; alternatively, it is a distinction between two such attributes of a single substance. Such a distinction is recognized by our inability to form a clear and distinct idea of the substance if we exclude from it the attribute in question, or, alternatively, by our inability to perceive clearly the idea of one of the two attributes if we separate it from the other. For example, since a substance cannot cease to endure without also ceasing to be, the distinction between the substance and its duration is merely a conceptual one. And in the case of all the modes of thought which we consider as being in objects, there is merely a conceptual distinction between the modes and the object which they are thought of as applying to; and the same is true of the distinction between the modes themselves when these are in one and the same object. I am aware that elsewhere I did lump this type of distinction with the modal distinction, namely at the end of my Replies to the First Set of Objections to the *Meditations on First Philosophy*; but that was not a suitable place for making a careful distinction between the two types; it was enough for my purposes to distinguish both from the real distinction.

63. *How thought and extension may be distinctly recognized as constituting the nature of mind and of body.*

Thought and extension can be regarded as constituting the natures of intelligent substance and corporeal substance; they must then be considered as nothing else but thinking substance itself and extended substance itself – that is, as mind and body. In this way we will have a very clear and distinct understanding of them. Indeed, it is much easier for us to have an understanding of extended substance or thinking substance than it is for us to

31

understand substance on its own, leaving out the fact that it thinks or is extended. For we have some difficulty in abstracting the notion of substance from the notions of thought and extension, since the distinction between these notions and the notion of substance itself is merely a conceptual distinction. A concept is not any more distinct because we include less in it; its distinctness simply depends on our carefully distinguishing what we do include in it from everything else.

64. *How thought and extension may also be distinctly recognized as modes of a substance.*

Thought and extension may also be taken as modes of a substance, in so far as one and the same mind is capable of having many different thoughts; and one and the same body, with its quantity unchanged, may be extended in many different ways (for example, at one moment it may be greater in length and smaller in breadth or depth, and a little later, by contrast, it may be greater in breadth and smaller in length). The distinction between thought or extension and the substance will then be a modal one; and our understanding of them will be capable of being just as clear and distinct as our understanding of the substance itself, provided they are regarded not as substances (that is, things which are separate from other things) but simply as modes of things. By regarding them as being in the substances of which they are modes, we distinguish them from the substances in question and see them for what they really are. If, on the other hand, we attempted to consider them apart from the substances in which they inhere, we would be regarding them as things which subsisted in their own right, and would thus be confusing the ideas of a mode and a substance.

65. *How the modes of thought and extension are to be known.*   32

There are various modes of thought such as understanding, imagination, memory, volition, and so on; and there are various modes of extension, or modes which belong to extension, such as all shapes, the positions of parts and the motions of the parts. And, just as before, we shall arrive at the best perception of all these items if we regard them simply as modes of the things in which they are located. As far as motion is concerned, it will be best if we think simply of local motion, without inquiring into the force which produces it. . . .

66. *How sensations, emotions and appetites may be clearly known, despite the fact that we are frequently wrong in our judgements concerning them.*

There remains sensations, emotions and appetites [see art. 48]. These may be clearly perceived provided we take great care in our judgements concerning them to include no more than what is strictly contained in our perception – no more than that of which we have inner awareness. But this is a very difficult rule to observe, at least with regard to sensations. For all of us have, from our early childhood, judged that all the objects of our sense-perception are things existing outside our minds and closely resembling our sensations, i.e. the perceptions that we had of them. Thus, on seeing a colour, for example, we supposed we were seeing a thing located outside us which closely resembled the idea of colour that we experienced within us at the time. And this was something that, because of our habit of making such judgements, we thought we saw clearly and distinctly – so much so that we took it for something certain and indubitable.

67. *We frequently make mistakes, even in our judgements concerning pain.*
The same thing happens with regard to everything else of which we have sensory awareness, even to pleasure and pain. For, although we do not suppose that these exist outside us, we generally regard them not as being in the mind alone, or in our perception, but as being in the hand or foot or in some other part of our body. But the fact that we feel a pain as it were in our foot does not make it certain that the pain exists outside our mind, in the foot, any more than the fact that we see light as it were in the sun, makes it certain the light exists outside us, in the sun. Both these beliefs are preconceived opinions of our early childhood, as will become clear below.

68. *How to distinguish what we clearly know in such matters from what can lead us astray.*
In order to distinguish what is clear in this connection from what is obscure, we must be very careful to note that pain and colour and so on are clearly and distinctly perceived when they are regarded merely as sensations or thoughts. But when they are judged to be real things existing outside our mind, there is no way of understanding what sort of things they are. If someone says he sees colour in a body or feels pain in a limb, this amounts to saying that he sees or feels something there of which he is wholly ignorant, or, in other words, that he does not know what he is seeing or feeling. Admittedly, if he fails to pay sufficient attention, he may easily convince himself that he has some knowledge of what he sees or feels, because he may suppose that it is something similar to the sensation of colour or pain which he experiences within himself. But if he examines the nature of what is represented by the sensation of colour or pain – what is represented as existing in the coloured body or the painful part – he will realize that he is wholly ignorant of it.

69. *We know size, shape and so forth in quite a different way from the way in which we know colours, pains and the like.*

This will be especially clear if we consider the wide gap between our knowledge of those features of bodies which we clearly perceive, as stated earlier [in art. 48], and our knowledge of those features which must be referred to the senses, as I have just pointed out. To the former class belong the size of the bodies we see, their shape, motion, position, duration, number and so on (by 'motion' I mean local motion: philosophers have imagined that there are other kinds of motion distinct from local motion, thereby only making the nature of motion less intelligible to themselves).* To the latter class belong the colour in a body, as well as pain, smell, taste and so on. It is true that when we see a body we are just as certain of its existence in virtue of its having a visible colour as we are in virtue of its having a visible shape; but our knowledge of what it is for the body to have a shape is much clearer than our knowledge of what it is for it to be coloured.

70. *There are two ways of making judgements concerning the things that can be perceived by the senses: the first enables us to avoid error, while the second allows us to fall into error.*

It is clear, then, that when we say that we perceive colours in objects, this is really just the same as saying that we perceive something in the objects whose nature we do not know, but which produces in us a certain very clear and vivid sensation which we call the sensation of colour. But the way in which we make our judgement can vary very widely. As long as we merely judge that there is in the objects (that is, in the things, whatever they may turn out to be, which are the source of our sensations) something whose nature we do not know, then we avoid error; indeed, we are actually guarding against error, since the recognition that we are ignorant of something makes us less liable to make any rash judgement about it. But it is quite different when we suppose that we perceive colours in objects. Of course, we do not really know what it is that we are calling a colour; and we cannot find any intelligible resemblance between the colour which we suppose to be in objects and that which we experience in our sensation. But this is something we do not take account of; and, what is more, there are many other features, such as size, shape and number which we clearly perceive to be actually or at least possibly present in objects in a way exactly corre-

* By 'local motion' is meant, roughly, movement from place to place. Scholastic philosophers, following Aristotle, sometimes classifed any alteration (e.g. a quantitative or a qualitative change) as a type of motion; various other distinctions, e.g. that between 'natural' and 'violent' motion, were also commonplace.

sponding to our sensory perception or understanding. And so we easily fall
35   into the error of judging that what is called colour in objects is something
exactly like the colour of which we have sensory awareness; and we make
the mistake of thinking that we clearly perceive what we do not perceive at
all. . . .

75. *Summary of the rules to be observed in order to philosophize correctly.*
In order to philosophize seriously and search out the truth about all the
things that are capable of being known, we must first of all lay aside all our
preconceived opinions, or at least we must take the greatest care not to put
our trust in any of the opinions accepted by us in the past until we have first
scrutinized them afresh and confirmed their truth. Next, we must give our
attention in an orderly way to the notions that we have within us, and we
must judge to be true all and only those whose truth we clearly and distinctly recognize when we attend to them in this way. When we do this we
shall realize, first of all, that we exist in so far as our nature consists in
thinking; and we shall simultaneously realize both that there is a God, and
that we depend on him, and also that a consideration of his attributes enables us to investigate the truth of other things, since he is their cause. Finally, we will see that besides the notions of God and of our mind, we have
within us knowledge of many propositions which are eternally true, such as
'Nothing comes from nothing'. We shall also find that we have knowledge
both of a corporeal or extended nature which is divisible, moveable, and so
on, and also of certain sensations which affect us, such as the sensations of
pain, colours, tastes and so on (though we do not yet know the cause of
our being affected in this way). When we contrast all this knowledge with
the confused thoughts we had before, we will acquire the habit of forming
clear and distinct concepts of all the things that can be known. These few
39   instructions seem to me to contain the most important principles of human
knowledge. . . .

Note

1   This 'ontological argument' for God's existence reminds one, of course, of St
Anselm's reasoning. According to him, God's 'essence' – that of a supremely
great being – requires that God actually exist, since an imaginary or fictional
God would not be as great as an existing one.

From Benedict de Spinoza, *Ethics*, ed. and trans. E. Curley. Harmondsworth: Penguin, 1996. pp. 1–10, 13–23, 25 (some passages omitted).

In the Preface to Part V of his *Ethics*, the Dutch philosopher of Jewish–Spanish descent, Benedict de Spinoza (1632–77), accuses Descartes' 'interactionist' account of mental and material substances of being an 'occult' doctrine unworthy of 'so great a man'. Like other critical admirers of Descartes, such as Thomas Hobbes, Spinoza's metaphysics was largely inspired by an ambition to articulate a system that would be free from the implausibility, as they saw it, of the Frenchman's mind–body dualism. It is in Part II of his posthumously published *Ethics* that Spinoza develops his own, extremely difficult view of mind and body, or thought and extension, as two 'attributes' or 'aspects' of a single substance, as two incommensurable ways in which we humans are compelled to view and describe the same reality. In Part I, entitled 'Of God', Spinoza undertakes the prior tasks of establishing that there is just one substance and of drawing out crucial implications of that claim.

'Of God' has a somewhat musical structure, with the first part constituting a crescendo which climaxes in the Propositions (14 and 15) that there is a single substance, God, and that 'whatever is, is in God', while the remaining sections explore those themes and their modulations (the eternal nature of substance, for example). Spinoza, then, was a 'monist', but of a different type from Śaṁkara (chapter 5 above). For one thing, he has no tendency to relegate physical objects and people, which are 'modes' of, or 'in', the one substance, to the realm of illusion. Nor does he appeal, by way of argument, to any special 'mystical experience' of oneness or unity. Indeed, he eschews appeal to experience of any sort. Spinoza was an arch-rationalist, as the Euclidean lay-out of *Ethics*, with its apparatus of axioms, corollaries, lemmas, scholia etc., might indicate. It was not simply that Spinoza thought that pure reason, unaided by empirical evidence, was the proper tool for arriving at metaphysical truth. He was also a 'causal rationalist',[1]

[1] See Jonathan Bennett, *A Study in Spinoza's* Ethics, Cambridge: Cambridge University Press, 1984.

holding it to be clearer than 'the noon light that there is absolutely nothing . . . contingent (P. 33), so that to the fully rational mind everything which is or happens will be recognizable as strictly necessary.

The ascent to the central Propositions 14–15 is achieved, above all, by reflection on the notion of substance, specifically by taking to its logical conclusion, in Spinoza's view, the traditional idea, stemming from Aristotle (chapter 3 above), that substance is 'independent' – or, as he himself puts it, what is 'in itself' and 'whose concept does not require the concept of another thing' (Definition 3). Descartes himself had said that, on such a characterization, there is, strictly speaking, only one substance, God. For Spinoza, we should never speak less than strictly. Hence, if we stick to the 'independence' criterion, we are forced to concede that there must be exactly one substance. There must be *at least* one, since it belongs to the notion of substance that it is a cause of itself, and so must exist. There cannot be *more* than one since, *inter alia*, a second would 'limit', and hence be incompatible with, the complete 'independence' of, the first.

It is less easy to understand why Spinoza calls this one substance 'God', a difficulty compounded for some readers by his later remark that this 'eternal and infinite being' may be called 'God *or* Nature' (IV Preface). In some commentators' view, Spinoza was in effect a closet atheist who, for reasons of prudence in an intolerant age, needed to retain the rhetorical trappings of religion. But it is more plausible to hold that Spinoza, if not the 'God-intoxicated' figure described by Novalis, regarded his one substance as enjoying sufficiently many of the essential features traditionally associated with God – necessity, eternity, self-causation, freedom (in the sense of being unlimited by anything else), and so on. It is true that Spinoza's God is, under one aspect, extended matter, but as one commentator points out, the effect of his 'conception rather raises our conception of matter than lowers our conception of God', in somewhat the same manner as does Wordsworth's pantheistic picture of the world as 'rolled through' by 'something far more deeply interfused'.[2] In this connection, one should remark that the 'Nature' which seems, for Spinoza, to be synonymous with 'God', is *natura naturans*, the dynamic 'expression' of a 'free' causal process, not *natura naturata*, the finished products, as it were – trees, stones, people – of that process (P. 29). (I have had to omit some of the more obviously 'theological' passages where Spinoza compares and contrasts his view with traditional ones).

Spinoza's *Ethics* is rationalist metaphysics on the grand and ambitious scale. It will be intriguing to compare his position to the very different one reached by an equally ambitious rationalist, Leibniz (chapter 9 below), on the basis, ironically, of strikingly similar premises.

---

[2] T. L. S. Sprigge, *Theories of Existence: a sequence of essays on the fundamental questions of philosophy*, Harmondsworth: Penguin, 1984, p. 157.

In the following text, the abbreviations used are: D = definition, A = axiom, P = proposition, Dem = demonstration, Exp = explanation, Cor = corollary, Schol = scholium, NS = *Nagelate Schriften* (i.e. material from a Dutch translation of the original Latin).

Spinoza, *Ethics*

First Part of the Ethics: Of God

DEFINITIONS

D1: By cause of itself I understand that whose essence involves existence, *or* that whose nature cannot be conceived except as existing.

D2 : That thing is said to be finite in its own kind that can be limited by another of the same nature.

For example, a body is called finite because we always conceive another that is greater. Thus a thought is limited by another thought. But a body is not limited by a thought nor a thought by a body.

D3: By substance I understand what is in itself and is conceived through itself, that is, that whose concept does not require the concept of another thing, from which it must be formed.

D4: By attribute I understand what the intellect perceives of a substance, as constituting its essence.

D5: By mode I understand the affections of a substance, *or* that which is in another through which it is also conceived.

D6: By God I understand a being absolutely infinite, that is, a substance consisting of an infinity of attributes, of which each one expresses an eternal and infinite essence.

Exp.: I say absolute infinite, not infinite in its own kind; for if something is only infinite in its own kind, we can deny infinite attributes of it [NS: (i.e., we can conceive infinite attributes which do not pertain to its nature)]; but if something is absolutely infinite, whatever expresses essence and involves no negation pertains to its essence.

D7: That thing is called free which exists from the necessity of its nature alone, and is determined to act by itself alone. But a thing is called necessary, or rather compelled, which is determined by another to exist and to produce an effect in a certain and determinate manner.

D8: By eternity I understand existence itself, insofar as it is conceived to follow necessarily from the definition alone of the eternal thing.

Exp.: For such existence, like the essence of a thing, is conceived as an eternal truth, and on that account cannot be explained by duration or time, even if the duration is conceived to be without beginning or end.

AXIOMS

A1: Whatever is, is either in itself or in another.

A2: What cannot be conceived through another, must be conceived through itself.

A3: From a given determinate cause the effect follows necessarily; and conversely, if there is no determinate cause, it is impossible for an effect to follow.

A4: The knowledge of an effect depends on, and involves, the knowledge of its cause.

A5: Things that have nothing in common with one another also cannot be understood through one another, *or* the concept of the one does not involve the concept of the other.

II/47   A6: A true idea must agree with its object.

A7: If a thing can be conceived as not existing, its essence does not involve existence.

P1: *A substance is prior in nature to its affections.*
   Dem.: This is evident from D3 and D5.

P2: *Two substances having different attributes have nothing in common with one another.*
   Dem.: This is also evident from D3. For each must be in itself and be conceived through itself, *or* the concept of the one does not involve the concept of the other.

P3: *If things have nothing in common with one another, one of them cannot be the cause of the other.*
   Dem.: If they have nothing in common with one another, then (by A5) they cannot be understood through one another, and so (by A4) one cannot be the cause of the other, q.e.d.

P4: *Two or more distinct things are distinguished from one another, either by a difference in the attributes of the substances or by a difference in their affections.*

Dem.: Whatever is, is either in itself or in another (by A1), that is (by D3 and D5), outside the intellect there is nothing except substances and their affections. Therefore, there is nothing outside the intellect through which a number of things can be distinguished from one another except sub- II/48 stances, *or* what is the same (by D4), their attributes and their affections, q.e.d.

P5: *In Nature there cannot be two or more substances of the same nature* or *attribute.*

Dem.: If there were two or more distinct substances, they would have to be distinguished from one another either by a difference in their attributes, or by a difference in their affections (by P4). If only by a difference in their attributes, then it will be conceded that there is only one of the same attribute. But if by a difference in their affections, then since a substance is prior in nature to its affections (by P1), if the affections are put to one side and [the substance] is considered in itself, that is (by D3 and A6), considered truly, one cannot be conceived to be distinguished from another, that is (by P4), there cannot be many, but only one [of the same nature *or* attribute], q.e.d.

P6: *One substance cannot be produced by another substance.*

Dem.: In Nature there cannot be two substances of the same attribute (by P5), that is (by P2), which have something in common with each other. Therefore (by P3) one cannot be the cause of the other, *or* cannot be produced by the other, q.e.d.

Cor.: From this it follows that a substance cannot be produced by anything else. For in Nature there is nothing except substances and their affections, as is evident from A1, D3, and D5. But it cannot be produced by a substance (by P6). Therefore, substance absolutely cannot be produced by anything else, q.e.d.

Alternatively: This is demonstrated even more easily from the absurdity of its contradictory. For if a substance could be produced by something else, the knowledge of it would have to depend on the knowledge of its cause (by A4). And so (by D3) it would not be a substance.

P7: *It pertains to the nature of a substance to exist.* II/49

Dem.: A substance cannot be produced by anything else (by P6C); therefore it will be the cause of itself, that is (by D1), its essence necessarily involves existence, *or* it pertains to its nature to exist, q.e.d.

P8: *Every substance is necessarily infinite.*

Dem.: A substance of one attribute does not exist unless it is unique (P5), and it pertains to its nature to exist (P7). Of its nature, therefore, it will exist either as finite or as infinite. But not as finite. For then (by D2) it would have to be limited by something else of the same nature, which would also have to exist necessarily (by P7), and so there would be two substances of the same attribute, which is absurd (by P5). Therefore, it exists as infinite, q.e.d.

Schol. 1: Since being finite is really, in part, a negation, and being infinite is an absolute affirmation of the existence of some nature, it follows from P7 alone that every substance must be infinite. [NS: For if we assumed a finite substance, we would, in part, deny existence to its nature, which (by P7) is absurd.]

Schol. 2: I do not doubt that the demonstration of P7 will be difficult to conceive for all who judge things confusedly, and have not been accustomed to know things through their first causes – because they do not distinguish between the modifications of substances and the substances themselves, nor do they know how things are produced. So it happens that they fictitiously ascribe to substances the beginning which they see that natural things have; for those who do not know the true causes of things confuse everything and without any conflict of mind feign that both trees and men speak, imagine that men are formed both from stones and from seed, and that any form whatever is changed into any other. So also, those who confuse the divine nature with the human easily ascribe human affects to God, particularly so long as they are also ignorant of how those affects are produced in the mind.

II/50   But if men would attend to the nature of substance, they would have no doubt at all of the truth of P7. Indeed, this proposition would be an axiom for everyone, and would be numbered among the common notions. For by substance they would understand what is in itself and is conceived through itself, that is, that the knowledge of which does not require the knowledge of any other thing. But by modifications they would understand what is in another, those things whose concept is formed from the concept of the thing in which they are.

This is how we can have true ideas of modifications which do not exist; for though they do not actually exist outside the intellect, nevertheless their essences are comprehended in another in such a way that they can be conceived through it. But the truth of substances is not outside the intellect unless it is in them themselves, because they are conceived through themselves.

Hence, if someone were to say that he had a clear and distinct, that is true, idea of a substance, and nevertheless doubted whether such a substance existed, that would indeed be the same as if he were to say that he had a true idea, and nevertheless doubted whether it was false (as is evident to anyone who is sufficiently attentive). Or if someone maintains that a substance is created, he maintains at the same time that a false idea has become true. Of course nothing more absurd can be conceived. So it must be confessed that the existence of a substance, like its essence, is an eternal truth.

And from this we can infer in another way that there is only one [substance] of the same nature, which I have considered it worth the trouble of showing here. But to do this in order, it must be noted,

I. that the true definition of each thing neither involves nor expresses anything except the nature of the thing defined.

From which it follows,

II. that no definition involves or expresses any certain number of individuals,

since it expresses nothing other than the nature of the thing defined. For example, the definition of the triangle expresses nothing but the simple nature of the triangle, but not any certain number of triangles. It is to be noted,

III. that there must be, for each existing thing, a certain cause on account of which it exists.

Finally, it is to be noted,

IV. that this cause, on account of which a thing exists, either must be contained in the very nature and definition of the existing thing (*viz. that it pertains to its nature to exist*) or must be outside it.

From these propositions it follows that if, in Nature, a certain number of individuals exists, there must be a cause why those individuals, and why neither more nor fewer, exist.

For example, if twenty men exist in Nature (*to make the matter clearer, I assume that they exist at the same time, and that no others previously existed in Nature*), it will not be enough (i.e., *to give a reason why twenty men exist*) to show the cause of human nature in general; but it will be necessary in addition to show the cause why not more and not fewer than twenty exist. For (by III) there must necessarily be a cause why each [NS: particular man] exists. But this cause (by II and III) cannot be contained in human nature itself, since the true definition of man does not involve the number 20. So (by IV) the cause why these twenty men exist, and consequently, why each of them exists, must necessarily be outside each of them.

For that reason it is to be inferred absolutely that whatever is of such a

II/51

nature that there can be many individuals [of that nature] must, to exist, have an external cause to exist. Now since it pertains to the nature of a substance to exist (by what we have already shown in this scholium), its definition must involve necessary existence, and consequently its existence must be inferred from its definition alone. But from its definition (as we have shown from II and III) the existence of a number of substances cannot follow. Therefore it follows necessarily from this, that there exists only one of the same nature, as was proposed.

P9: *The more reality or being each thing has, the more attributes belong to it.*
Dem.: This is evident from D4.

P10: *Each attribute of a substance must be conceived through itself.*
Dem.: For an attribute is what the intellect perceives concerning a substance, as constituting its essence (by D4); so (by D3) it must be conceived through itself, q.e.d.

II/52   Schol.: From these propositions it is evident that although two attributes may be conceived to be really distinct (i.e., one may be conceived without the aid of the other), we still cannot infer from that that they constitute two beings, *or* two different substances. For it is of the nature of a substance that each of its attributes is conceived through itself, since all the attributes it has have always been in it together, and one could not be produced by another, but each expresses the reality, *or* being of substance.

So it is far from absurd to attribute many attributes to one substance. Indeed, nothing in Nature is clearer than that each being must be conceived under some attribute, and the more reality, or being it has, the more it has attributes which express necessity, *or* eternity, and infinity. And consequently there is also nothing clearer than that a being absolutely infinite must be defined (as we taught in D6) as a being that consists of infinite attributes, each of which expresses a certain eternal and infinite essence.

But if someone now asks by what sign we shall be able to distinguish the diversity of substances, let him read the following propositions, which show that in Nature there exists only one substance, and that it is absolutely infinite. So that sign would be sought in vain.

P11: *God,* or *a substance consisting of infinite attributes, each of which expresses eternal and infinite essence, necessarily exists.*
Dem.: If you deny this, conceive, if you can, that God does not exist. Therefore (by A7) his essence does not involve existence. But this (by P7) is absurd. Therefore God necessarily exists, q.e.d.

Alternatively: For each thing there must be assigned a cause, *or* reason, both for its existence and for its nonexistence. For example, if a triangle exists, there must be a reason *or* cause why it exists; but if it does not exist, II/53 there must also be a reason *or* cause which prevents it from existing, *or* which takes its existence away.

But this reason, *or* cause, must either be contained in the nature of the thing, or be outside it. For example, the very nature of a square circle indicates the reason why it does not exist, namely, because it involves a contradiction. On the other hand, the reason why a substance exists also follows from its nature alone, because it involves existence (see P7). But the reason why a circle or triangle exists, or why it does not exist, does not follow from the nature of these things, but from the order of the whole of corporeal Nature. For from this [order] it must follow either that the triangle necessarily exists now or that it is impossible for it to exist now. These things are evident through themselves; from them it follows that a thing necessarily exists if there is no reason or cause which prevents it from existing. Therefore, if there can be no reason or cause which prevents God from existing, or which takes his existence away, it must certainly be inferred that he necessarily exists.

But if there were such a reason, *or* cause, it would have to be either in God's very nature or outside it, that is, in another substance of another nature. For if it were of the same nature, that very supposition would concede that God exists. But a substance which was of another nature [NS: than the divine] would have nothing in common with God (by P2), and therefore could neither give him existence nor take it away. Since, then, there can be, outside the divine nature, no reason, *or* cause, which takes away the divine existence, the reason will necessarily have to be in his nature itself, if indeed he does not exist. That is, his nature would involve a contradiction [NS: as in our second example]. But it is absurd to affirm this of a Being absolutely infinite and supremely perfect. Therefore, there is no cause, *or* reason, either in God or outside God, which takes his existence away. And therefore, God necessarily exists, q.e.d.

Alternatively: To be able not to exist is to lack power, and conversely, to be able to exist is to have power (as is known through itself). So, if what now necessarily exists are only finite beings, then finite beings are more powerful than an absolutely infinite Being. But this, as is known through itself, is absurd. So, either nothing exists or an absolutely infinite Being also exists. But we exist, either in ourselves, or in something else, which necessarily exists (see A1 and P7). Therefore an absolutely infinite Being – that is (by D6), God – necessarily exists, q.e.d.

Schol.: In this last demonstration I wanted to show God's existence a II/54 posteriori, so that the demonstration would be perceived more easily – but not because God's existence does not follow a priori from the same foundation. For since being able to exist is power, it follows that the more reality belongs to the nature of a thing, the more powers it has, of itself, to exist. Therefore, an absolutely infinite Being, *or* God, has, of himself, an absolutely infinite power of existing. For that reason, he exists absolutely.

Still, there may be many who will not easily be able to see how evident this demonstration is, because they have been accustomed to contemplate only those things that flow from external causes. And of these, they see that those which quickly come to be, that is, which easily exist, also easily perish. And conversely, they judge that those things to which they conceive more things to pertain are more difficult to do, that is, that they do not exist so easily. But to free them from these prejudices, I have no need to show here in what manner this proposition – *what quickly comes to be, quickly perishes* – is true, nor whether or not all things are equally easy in respect to the whole of Nature. It is sufficient to note only this, that I am not here speaking of things that come to be from external causes, but only of substances that (by P6) can be produced by no external cause.

For things that come to be from external causes – whether they consist of many parts or of few – owe all the perfection or reality they have to the power of the external cause; and therefore their existence arises only from the perfection of their external cause, and not from their own perfection. On the other hand, whatever perfection substance has is not owed to any external cause. So its existence must follow from its nature alone; hence its existence is nothing but its essence.

Perfection, therefore, does not take away the existence of a thing, but on the contrary asserts it. But imperfection takes it away. So there is nothing of whose existence we can be more certain than we are of the existence of an absolutely infinite, *or* perfect, Being – that, God. For since his essence excludes all imperfection, and involves absolute perfection, by that very fact it takes away every cause of doubting his existence, and gives the greatest certainty concerning it. I believe this will be clear even to those who are only moderately attentive.

P12: *No attribute of a substance can be truly conceived from which it follows that the substance can be divided.*

Dem.: For the parts into which a substance so conceived would be divided either will retain the nature of the substance or will not. If the first [NS: viz. they retain the nature of the substance], then (by P8) each part will have to be infinite, and (by P7) its own cause, and (by P5) each part will have to consist of a different attribute. And so many substances will be able to be formed from one, which is absurd (by P6). Furthermore, the parts (by P2) would have nothing in common with their whole, and the whole (by D4 and P10) could both be and be conceived without its parts, which is absurd, as no one will be able to doubt.

But if the second is asserted, namely, that the parts will not retain the nature of substance, then since the whole substance would be divided into equal parts, it would lose the nature of substance, and would cease to be, which (by P7) is absurd.

P13: *A substance which is absolutely infinite is indivisible.*

Dem.: For if it were divisible, the parts into which it would be divided will either retain the nature of an absolutely infinite substance or they will not. If the first, then there will be a number of substances of the same nature, which (by P5) is absurd. But if the second is asserted, then (as above [NS: P12]), an absolutely infinite substance will be able to cease to be, which (by P11) is also absurd.

Cor.: From these [propositions] it follows that no substance, and consequently no corporeal substance, insofar as it is a substance, is divisible.

Schol.: That substance is indivisible, is understood more simply merely from this, that the nature of substance cannot be conceived unless as infinite, and that by a part of substance nothing can be understood except a   II/56
finite substance, which (by P8) implies a plain contradiction.

P14: *Except God, no substance can be or be conceived.*

Dem.: Since God is an absolutely infinite being, of whom no attribute which expresses an essence of substance can be denied (by D6), and he necessarily exists (by P11), if there were any substance except God, it would have to be explained through some attribute of God, and so two substances of the same attribute would exist, which (by P5) is absurd. And so except God, no substance can be or, consequently, be conceived. For if it could be conceived, it would have to be conceived as existing. But this (by the first part of this demonstration) is absurd. Therefore, except for God no substance can be or be conceived, q.e.d.

Cor. 1: From this it follows most clearly, first, that God is unique, that is (by D6), that in Nature there is only one substance, and that it is absolutely infinite (as we indicated in P10S).

Cor. 2: It follows, second, that an extended thing and a thinking thing are either attributes of God, or (by A1) affections of God's attributes.

P15: *Whatever is, is in God, and nothing can be or be conceived without God.*

Dem.: Except for God, there neither is, nor can be conceived, any substance (by P14), that is (by D3), thing that is in itself and is conceived through itself. But modes (by D5) can neither be nor be conceived without substance. So they can be in the divine nature alone, and can be con-

II/57   ceived through it alone. But except for substances and modes there is nothing (by A1). Therefore, [NS: everything is in God and] nothing can be or be conceived without God, q.e.d.

Schol.: [I] There are those who feign a God, like man, consisting of a body and a mind, and subject to passions. But how far they wander from the true knowledge of God, is sufficiently established by what has already been demonstrated. Them I dismiss. For everyone who has to any extent contemplated the divine nature denies that God is corporeal. They prove this best from the fact that by body we understand any quantity, with length, breadth, and depth, limited by some certain figure. Nothing more absurd than this can be said of God, namely, of a being absolutely infinite. But meanwhile, by the other arguments by which they strive to demonstrate this same conclusion they clearly show that they entirely remove corporeal, *or* extended, substance itself from the divine nature. And they maintain that it has been created by God. But by what divine power could it be created? They are completely ignorant of that. And this shows clearly that they do not understand what they themselves say. At any rate, I have demonstrated clearly enough – in my judgment, at least – that no substance can be produced or created by another thing (see P6C and P8S2). Next, we have shown (P14) that except for God, no substance can either be or be conceived, and hence [in P14C2] we have concluded that extended substance is one of God's infinite attributes. . . .

II/60   . . . All things, I say, are in God, and all things that happen, happen only through the laws of God's infinite nature and follow (as I shall show) from the necessity of his essence. So it cannot be said in any way that God is acted on by another, or that extended substance is unworthy of the divine nature, even if it is supposed to be divisible, so long as it is granted to be eternal and infinite. But enough of this for the present.

P16: *From the necessity of the divine nature there must follow infinitely many things in infinitely many modes, (i.e., everything which can fall under an infinite intellect).*

Dem.: This proposition must be plain to anyone, provided he attends to the fact that the intellect infers from the given definition of any thing a number of properties that really do follow necessarily from it (that is, from the very essence of the thing); and that it infers more properties the more the definition of the thing expresses reality, that is, the more reality the essence of the defined thing involves. But since the divine nature has absolutely infinite attributes (by D6), each of which also expresses an essence infinite in its own kind, from its necessity there must follow infinitely many things in infinite modes (i.e., everything which can fall under an infinite intellect), q.e.d.

Cor. 1: From this it follows that God is the efficient cause of all things which can fall under an infinite intellect.

Cor. 2: It follows, second, that God is a cause through himself and not an accidental cause. II/61

Cor. 3: It follows, third, that God is absolutely the first cause.

P17: *God acts from the laws of his nature alone, and is compelled by no one.*

Dem.: We have just shown (P16) that from the necessity of the divine nature alone, or (what is the same thing) from the laws of his nature alone, absolutely infinite things follow, and in P15 we have demonstrated that nothing can be or be conceived without God, but that all things are in God. So there can be nothing outside him by which he is determined or compelled to act. Therefore, God acts from the laws of his nature alone, and is compelled by no one, q.e.d.

Cor. 1: From this it follows, first, that there is no cause, either extrinsically or intrinsically, which prompts God to action, except the perfection of his nature.

Cor. 2: It follows, second, that God alone is a free cause. For God alone exists only from the necessity of his nature (by P11 and P14C1), and acts from the necessity of his nature (by P17). Therefore (by D7) God alone is a free cause, q.e.d.

Schol.: [I.] Others think that God is a free cause because he can (so they think) bring it about that the things which we have said follow from his nature (i.e., which are in his power) do not happen or are not produced by him. But this is the same as if they were to say that God can bring it about that it would not follow from the nature of a triangle that its three angles are equal to two right angles; *or* that from a given cause the effect would II/62 not follow – which is absurd.

Further, I shall show later, without the aid of this proposition, that neither intellect nor will pertain to God's nature. Of course I know there are many who think they can demonstrate that a supreme intellect and a free will pertain to God's nature. For they say they know nothing they can ascribe to God more perfect than what is the highest perfection in us.

Moreover, though they conceive God to actually understand in the highest degree, they still do not believe that he can bring it about that all the things he actually understands exist. For they think that in that way they would destroy God's power. If he had created all the things in his intellect (they say), then he would have been able to create nothing more, which they believe to be incompatible with God's omnipotence. So they prefer to maintain that God is indifferent to all things, not creating anything except what he has decreed to create by some absolute will.

But I think I have shown clearly enough (see P16) that from God's supreme power, *or* infinite nature, infinitely many things in infinitely many modes, that is, all things, have necessarily flowed, or always follow, by the same necessity and in the same way as from the nature of a triangle it follows, from eternity and to eternity, that its three angles are equal to two right angles. So God's omnipotence has been actual from eternity and will remain in the same actuality to eternity. And in this way, at least in my opinion, God's omnipotence is maintained far more perfectly.

Indeed – to speak openly – my opponents seem to deny God's omnipotence. For they are forced to confess that God understands infinitely many creatable things, which nevertheless he will never be able to create. For otherwise, if he created everything he understood [NS: to be creatable] he would (according to them) exhaust his omnipotence and render himself imperfect. Therefore to maintain that God is perfect, they are driven to maintain at the same time that he cannot bring about everything to which his power extends. I do not see what could be feigned which would be more absurd than this or more contrary to God's omnipotence. . . .

P18: *God is the immanent, not the transitive, cause of all things.*

II/64   Dem.: Everything that is, is in God, and must be conceived through God (by P15), and so (by P16C1) God is the cause of [NS: all] things, which are in him. That is the first [thing to be proven]. And then outside God there can be no substance (by P14), that is (by D3), thing which is in itself outside God. That was the second. God, therefore, is the immanent, not the transitive cause of all things, q.e.d.

P19: *God is eternal, or all God's attributes are eternal.*

Dem.: For God (by D6) is substance, which (by P11) necessarily exists, that is (by P7), to whose nature it pertains to exist, or (what is the same) from whose definition it follows that he exists; and therefore (by D8), he is eternal.

Next, by God's attributes are be understood what (by D4) expresses an essence of the divine substance, that is, what pertains to substance. The attributes themselves, I say, must involve it itself. But eternity pertains to the nature of substance (as I have already demonstrated from P7). Therefore each of the attributes must involve eternity, and so, they are all eternal, q.e.d.

Schol.: This proposition is also as clear as possible from the way I have demonstrated God's existence (P11). For from that demonstration, I say, it is established that God's existence, like his essence, is an eternal truth. And then I have also demonstrated God's eternity in another way (*Descartes' Principles* IP19), and there is no need to repeat it here.

P20: *God's existence and his essence are one and the same.*

Dem.: God (by P19) and all of his attributes are eternal, that is (by D8), each of his attributes expresses existence. Therefore, the same attributes of God which (by D4) explain God's eternal essence at the same time explain his eternal existence, that is, that itself which constitutes God's essence at the same time constitutes his existence. So his existence and his essence are one and the same, q.e.d.

II/65

Cor. 1: From this it follows, first, that God's existence, like his essence, is an eternal truth.

Cor. 2: It follows, second, that God, *or* all of God's attributes, are immutable. For if they changed as to their existence, they would also (by P20) change as to their essence, that is (as is known through itself), from being true become false, which is absurd.

P21: *All the things which follow from the absolute nature of any of God's attributes have always had to exist and be infinite, or are, through the same attribute, eternal and infinite.*

Dem.: If you deny this, then conceive (if you can) that in some attribute of God there follows from its absolute nature something that is finite and has a determinate existence, *or* duration, for example, God's idea in thought. Now since thought is supposed to be an attribute of God, it is necessarily (by P11) infinite by its nature. But insofar as it has God's idea, [thought] is supposed to be finite. But (by D2) [thought] cannot be conceived to be finite unless it is determined through thought itself. But [thought can] not [be determined] through thought itself, insofar as it constitutes God's idea, for to that extent [thought] is supposed to be finite. Therefore, [thought must be determined] through thought insofar as it does not constitute God's idea, which [thought] nevertheless (by P11) must necessarily exist. Therefore, there is thought which does not constitute God's idea, and on that account God's idea does not follow necessarily from the nature [of this thought] insofar as it is absolute thought (for [thought] is conceived both as constituting God's idea and as not constituting it). [That God's idea does not follow from thought, insofar as it is absolute thought] is contrary to the hypothesis. So if God's idea in thought, or anything else in any attribute of God (for it does not matter what example is taken, since the demonstration is universal), follows from the necessity of the absolute nature of the attribute itself, it must necessarily be infinite. This was the first thing to be proven.

Next, what follows in this way from the necessity of the nature of any attribute cannot have a determinate [NS: existence, or] duration. For if you deny this, then suppose there is, in some attribute of God, a thing

II/66

which follows from the necessity of the nature of that attribute – for example, God's idea in thought – and suppose that at some time [this idea] did not exist or will not exist. But since thought is supposed to be an attribute of God, it must exist necessarily and be immutable (by P11 and P20C2). So beyond the limits of the duration of God's idea (for it is supposed that at some time [this idea] did not exist or will not exist) thought will have to exist without God's idea. But this is contrary to the hypothesis, for it is supposed that God's idea follows necessarily from the given thought. Therefore, God's idea in thought, or anything else which follows necessarily from the absolute nature of some attribute of God, cannot have a determinate duration, but through the same attribute is eternal. This was the second thing [NS: to be proven]. Note that the same is to be affirmed of any thing which, in some attribute of God, follows necessarily from God's absolute nature.

P22: *Whatever follows from some attribute of God insofar as it is modified by a modification which, through the same attribute, exists necessarily and is infinite, must also exist necessarily and be infinite.*

Dem.: The demonstration of this proposition proceeds in the same way as the demonstration of the preceding one.

P23: *Every mode which exists necessarily and is infinite has necessarily had to follow either from the absolute nature of some attribute of God, or from some attribute, modified by a modification which exists necessarily and is infinite.*

Dem.: For a mode is in another, through which it must be conceived (by D5), that is (by P15), it is in God alone, and can be conceived through God alone. So if a mode is conceived to exist necessarily and be infinite, [its necessary existence and infinity] must necessarily be inferred, *or* perceived through some attribute of God, insofar as that attribute is conceived to express infinity and necessity of existence, *or* (what is the same, by D8) eternity, that is (by D6 and P19), insofar as it is considered absolutely. Therefore, the mode, which exists necessarily and is infinite, has had to follow from the absolute nature of some attribute of God – either immediately (see P21) or by some mediating modification, which follows from its absolute nature, that is (by P22), which exists necessarily and is infinite, q.e.d.

P24: *The essence of things produced by God does not involve existence.*

Dem.: This is evident from D1. For that whose nature involves existence (considered in itself), is its own cause, and exists only from the necessity of its nature.

Cor.: From this it follows that God is not only the cause of things' beginning to exist, but also of their persevering in existing, *or* (to use a Scholastic term) God is the cause of the being of things. For – whether the things [NS: produced] exist or not – so long as we attend to their essence, we shall find that it involves neither existence nor duration. So their essence can be the cause neither of their existence nor of their duration, but only God, to whose nature alone it pertains to exist [, can be the cause] (by P14C1).

P25: *God is the efficient cause, not only of the existence of things, but also of their essence.*

Dem.: If you deny this, then God is not the cause of the essence of things; and so (by A4) the essence of things can be conceived without God. But (by P15) this is absurd. Therefore God is also the cause of the essence of things, q.e.d.   II/68

Schol.: This proposition follows more clearly from P16. For from that it follows that from the given divine nature both the essence of things and their existence must necessarily be inferred; and in a word, God must be called the cause of all things in the same sense in which he is called the cause of himself. This will be established still more clearly from the following corollary.

Cor.: Particular things are nothing but affections of God's attributes, *or* modes by which God's attributes are expressed in a certain and determinate way. The demonstration is evident from P15 and D5.

P26: *A thing which has been determined to produce an effect has necessarily been determined in this way by God; and one which has not been determined by God cannot determine itself to produce an effect.*

Dem.: That through which things are said to be determined to produce an effect must be something positive (as is known through itself). And so, God, from the necessity of his nature, is the efficient cause both of its essence and of its existence (by P25 and 16); this was the first thing. And from it the second thing asserted also follows very clearly. For if a thing which has not been determined by God could determine itself, the first part of this [NS: proposition] would be false, which is absurd, as we have shown.

P27: *A thing which has been determined by God to produce an effect, cannot render itself undetermined.*

Dem.: This proposition is evident from A3.

P28: *Every singular thing, or any thing which is finite and has a determinate*   II/69
existence, can neither exist nor be determined to produce an effect unless it is determined to exist and produce an effect by another cause, which is also finite

and has a determinate existence; and again, this cause also can neither exist not be determined to produce an effect unless it is determined to exist and produce an effect by another, which is also finite and has a determinate existence, and so on, to infinity.

Dem.: Whatever has been determined to exist and produce an effect has been so determined by God (by P26 and P24C). But what is finite and has a determinate existence could not have been produced by the absolute nature of an attribute of God; for whatever follows from the absolute nature of an attribute of God is eternal and infinite (by P21). It had, therefore, to follow either from God or from an attribute of God insofar as it is considered to be affected by some mode. For there is nothing except substance and its modes (by A1, D3, and D5) and modes (by P25C) are nothing but affections of God's attributes. But it also could not follow from God, or from an attribute of God, insofar as it is affected by a modification which is eternal and infinite (by P22). It had, therefore, to follow from, or be determined to exist and produce an effect by God or an attribute of God insofar as it is modified by a modification which is finite and has a determinate existence. This was the first thing to be proven.

And in turn, this cause, *or* this mode (by the same reasoning by which we have already demonstrated the first part of this proposition) had also to be determined by another, which is also finite and has a determinate existence; and again, this last (by the same reasoning) by another, and so always (by the same reasoning) to infinity, q.e.d.

II/70   Schol.: Since certain things had to be produced by God immediately, namely, those which follow necessarily from his absolute nature, and others (which nevertheless can neither be nor be conceived without God) had to be produced by the mediation of these first things, it follows:

I. That God is absolutely the proximate cause of the things produced immediately by him, and not [a proximate cause] in his own kind, as they say. For God's effects can neither be nor be conceived without their cause (by P15 and P24C).

II. That God cannot properly be called the remote cause of singular things, except perhaps so that we may distinguish them from those things that he has produced immediately, or rather, that follow from his absolute nature. For by a remote cause we understand one which is not conjoined in any way with its effect. But all things that are, are in God, and so depend on God that they can neither be nor be conceived without him.

P29: *In nature there is nothing contingent, but all things have been determined from the necessity of the divine nature to exist and produce an effect in a certain way.*

Dem.: Whatever is, is in God (by P15); but God cannot be called a contingent thing. For (by P11) he exists necessarily, not contingently. Next, the modes of the divine nature have also followed from it necessarily and not contingently (by P16) – either insofar as the divine nature is considered absolutely (by P21) or insofar as it is considered to be determined to act in a certain way (by P28). Further, God is the cause of these modes not only insofar as they simply exist (by P24C), but also (by P26) insofar as they are considered to be determined to produce an effect. For if they have not been determined by God, then (by P26) it is impossible, not contingent, that they should determine themselves. Conversely (by P27) if they have been determined by God, it is not contingent, but impossible, that they should render themselves undetermined. So all things have been determined from the necessity of the divine nature, not only to exist, but to exist in a certain way, and to produce effects in a certain way. There is nothing contingent, q.e.d.

II/71

Schol.: Before I proceed further, I wish to explain here – or rather to advise [the reader] – what we must understand by *Natura naturans* and *Natura naturata*. For from the preceding I think it is already established that by *Natura naturans* we must understand what is in itself and is conceived through itself, *or* such attributes of substance as express an eternal and infinite essence, that is (by P14C1 and P17C2), God, insofar as he is considered as a free cause.

But by *Natura naturata* I understand whatever follows from the necessity of God's nature, *or* from any of God's attributes, that is, all the modes of God's attributes insofar as they are considered as things which are in God, and can neither be nor be conceived without God.

P30: *An actual intellect, whether finite or infinite, must comprehend God's attributes and God's affections, and nothing else.*

Dem.: A true idea must agree with its object (by A6), that is (as is known through itself), what is contained objectively in the intellect must necessarily be in Nature. But in Nature (by P14C1) there is only one substance, namely, God, and there are no affections other than those which are in God (by P15) and which can neither be nor be conceived without God (by P15). Therefore, an actual intellect, whether finite or infinite, must comprehend God's attributes and God's affections, and nothing else, q.e.d.

P31: *The actual intellect, whether finite or infinite, like will, desire, love, and the like, must be referred to* Natura Naturata, *not to* Natura naturans.

Dem.: By intellect (as is known through itself) we understand not absolute thought, but only a certain mode of thinking, which mode differs from the others, such as desire, love, and the like, and so (by D5) must be conceived through absolute thought, that is (by P15 and D6), it must be

II/72

so conceived through an attribute of God, which expresses the eternal and infinite essence of thought, that it can neither be nor be conceived without [that attribute]; and so (by P29S), like the other modes of thinking, it must be referred to *Natura naturata*, not to *Natura naturans*, q.e.d.

Schol.: The reason why I speak here of actual intellect is not because I concede that there is any potential intellect, but because, wishing to avoid all confusion, I wanted to speak only of what we perceive as clearly as possible, that is, of the intellection itself. We perceive nothing more clearly than that. For we can understand nothing that does not lead to more perfect knowledge of the intellection.

P32: *The will cannot be called a free cause, but only a necessary one.*

Dem.: The will, like the intellect, is only a certain mode of thinking. And so (by P28) each volition can neither exist nor be determined to produce an effect unless it is determined by another cause, and this cause again by another, and so on, to infinity. Even if the will be supposed to be infinite, it must be determined to exist and produce an effect by God, not insofar as he is an absolutely infinite substance, but insofar as he has an attribute that expresses the infinite and eternal essence of thought (by P23). So in whatever way it is conceived, whether as finite or as infinite, it requires a cause by which it is determined to exist and produce an effect. And so (by D7) it cannot be called a free cause, but only a necessary or compelled one, q.e.d.

II/73

Cor. 1: From this it follows, first, that God does not produce any effect by freedom of the will.

Cor. 2: It follows, second, that will and intellect are related to God's nature as motion and rest are, and as are absolutely all natural things, which (by P29) must be determined by God to exist and produce an effect in a certain way. For the will, like all other things, requires a cause by which it is determined to exist and produce an effect in a certain way. And although from a given will, *or* intellect infinitely many things may follow, God still cannot be said, on that account, to act from freedom of the will, any more than he can be said to act from freedom of motion and rest on account of those things that follow from motion and rest (for infinitely many things also follow from motion and rest). So will does not pertain to God's nature any more than do the other natural things, but is related to him in the same way as motion and rest, and all the other things which, as we have shown, follow from the necessity of the divine nature and are determined by it to exist and produce an effect in a certain way.

P33: *Things could have been produced by God in no other way, and in no other order than they have been produced.*

Dem.: For all things have necessarily followed from God's given nature (by P16), and have been determined from the necessity of God's nature to exist and produce an effect in a certain way (by P29). Therefore, if things could have been of another nature, or could have been determined to produce an effect in another way, so that the order of Nature was different, then God's nature could also have been other than it is now, and therefore (by P11) that [other nature] would also have had to exist, and consequently, there could have been two or more Gods, which is absurd (by P14C1). So things could have been produced in no other way and no other order, and so on, q.e.d.

Schol. 1: Since by these propositions I have shown more clearly than the noon light that there is absolutely nothing in things on account of which they can be called contingent, I wish now to explain briefly what we must understand by contingent – but first, what [we must understand] by necessary and impossible. II/74

A thing is called necessary either by reason of its essence or by reason of its cause. For a thing's existence follows necessarily either from its essence and definition or from a given efficient cause. And a thing is also called impossible from these same causes – namely, either because its essence, *or* definition, involves a contradiction, or because there is no external cause which has been determined to produce such a thing.

But a thing is called contingent only because of a defect of our knowledge. For if we do not know that the thing's essence involves a contradiction, or if we do know very well that its essence does not involve a contradiction, and nevertheless can affirm nothing certainly about its existence, because the order of causes is hidden from us, it can never seem to us either necessary or impossible. So we call it contingent or possible.

Schol. 2: From the preceding it clearly follows that things have been produced by God with the highest perfection, since they have followed necessarily from a given most perfect nature. Nor does this convict God of any imperfection, for his perfection compels us to affirm this. Indeed, from the opposite, it would clearly follow (as I have just shown), that God is not supremely perfect; because if things had been produced by God in another way, we would have to attribute to God another nature, different from that which we have been compelled to attribute to him from the consideration of the most perfect being. . . .

P34: *God's power is his essence itself.* II/77

Dem.: For from the necessity alone of God's essence it follows that God is the cause of himself (by P11) and (by P16 and P16C) of all things. Therefore, God's power, by which he and all things are and act, is his essence itself, q.e.d.

P35: *Whatever we conceive to be in God's power, necessarily exists.*

Dem.: For whatever is in God's power must (by P34) be so comprehended by his essence that it necessarily follows from it, and therefore necessarily exists, q.e.d.

P36: *Nothing exists from whose nature some effect does not follow.*

Dem.: Whatever exists expresses the nature, *or* essence of God in a certain and determinate way (by P25C), that is (by P34), whatever exists expresses in a certain and determinate way the power of God, which is the cause of all things. So (by P16), from [NS: everything which exists] some effect must follow, q.e.d.

John Locke, *An Essay Concerning Human Understanding*, Book II, Chapters 8 and 23 (§§1–11)

8

From John Locke, *An Essay Concerning Human Understanding* Vol. I, ed. J. W. Yolton. London: J. M. Dent & Sons, 1961, pp. 103–11, 244–50 (opening paragraphs of Ch. 8 omitted).

A seventeenth-century philosopher more congenial than Descartes and Spinoza to the predominant temper of our times is John Locke (1632–1704). Both as the 'father' of British Empiricism and as one of the first to appreciate the philosophical significance of modern science, Locke's *Essay* has great appeal in an age whose received wisdom is that of an empirically and scientifically minded intelligentsia. Indeed, Locke is frequently hailed as the prime inspiration for a metaphysics of 'scientific realism' whose central tenet is that objective reality is what is articulated by the natural sciences, at any rate by an 'ideal' physics.[1] Scientific realists sometimes need reminding that their position *is* a metaphysical one. It is one thing to subscribe to various propositions of physics, quite another to hold that those propositions uniquely describe how the world objectively is.

There are two discussions of Locke's in particular which have been inspirational for scientific realists. The first of these, found in Book II, Ch. 8, argues for a radical distinction between 'primary' qualities, such as shape and motion, and 'secondary' ones, such as colour and smell. We briefly encountered this distinction, though not drawn in those terms, in Descartes' *Principles* (p. 111 above), but Locke's discussion owes more to the scientist Robert Boyle, who had made the distinction on the basis of his 'corpuscular theory' of the material world. For many years, the tendency was to interpret Locke as holding that only primary qualities belong to external objects, with secondary ones belonging 'in the mind', to our perceptual 'ideas' or sensations. Certainly some of Locke's remarks suggest that interpretation, as when he asserts that yellow-

[1] See, for example, Michael Devitt, *Realism and Truth*, Oxford: Blackwell, 1991, for an expression of one scientific realist's debt to Locke.

ness, unlike solidity, say, is 'not actually in gold'. But his more considered view seems to be that colour does belong to objects, but only as a 'power' which they have, due to their primary features, to produce certain sensations in the mind. The crucial difference between primary and secondary qualities is, therefore, that only the former have any 'resemblance' to our 'ideas' or experiences of them – a claim sharply criticized, as we will see (Ch. 10), by Berkeley. From the scientific realist's point of view, it perhaps matters little in which of these ways the distinction is drawn. Either way – whether colour is 'in the mind' or reduced to primary qualities and their powers – we are not required to include, in our basic account of material reality, any concepts which do not figure in the physicist's mathematicized depiction of the universe.[2]

Locke's second discussion, scattered at various places in the *Essay*, but beginning with Book II, Ch. 23, is not unrelated to the first: it concerns substances and our concepts of them. Unlike Descartes and Spinoza, Locke's main emphasis is not upon substances as entities capable of existing 'independently', but as what 'stand under', 'support' or 'hold together' the various properties attributed to, say, gold or some animal. Locke complains that earlier, Aristotelian and medieval, views of 'substantial forms' fail to honour a crucial distinction between our *idea* of a substance like gold and the intrinsic nature of that substance. They have wrongly conflated what, in Book III, he calls 'nominal' and 'real' essence, for they have failed to distinguish between the question of our usual criteria for judging that something is gold and that of gold's underlying nature. A person's concept of a substance is a combination of an idea of its properties and 'a supposition of he knows not what support' these properties have. The substance itself, Locke seems to suggest, might be identified with that 'real constitution', inaccessible to ordinary perception but available in principle to scientific investigation, which serves as that 'support'.

The appeal of this position to the scientific realist is not hard to discern. If the above interpretation of Locke is right then, in order to know what a thing or a creature really and basically is, it is not our everyday understanding of its 'manifest' features which should be consulted, but scientific understanding of a physical constitution underlying such features. Indeed, the possibility is always there that everyday allocation of objects or creatures to species and kinds may be overturned by scientific discoveries concerning the inner physical constitutions. 'Natural kinds', defined in terms of such constitutions, may have no close fit with the prescientific categories employed for dividing up the world's furniture.[3]

For Locke himself, his claim about the (presently) unknown natures of sub-

---

[2] For a clear discussion of Locke's distinction and its relation to science, see John Mackie, *Problems From Locke*, Oxford: Clarendon Press, 1976 and E. J. Lowe, *Locke on Human Understanding*, London: Routledge, 1995.
[3] See Saul A. Kripke, *Naming and Necessity*, Cambridge, MA: Harvard University Press, 1980, for the best known contemporary development of this line of thought.

stances had further and welcome implications for the philosophy of mind. First, we should not deny that there exists mental substance simply because its nature is unknown, for the position is no different in the case of material substance. Second, it was premature of Descartes to insist that mind and body were substances of radically different kinds. Granted, mental properties and spatial ones are strikingly different, but for Locke there can be no a *priori* reason to insist that the substances which 'hold together' or 'stand under' both sets of properties are themselves of different natures.

Locke, *An Essay Concerning Human Understanding*

Chapter VIII

SOME FURTHER CONSIDERATIONS CONCERNING OUR SIMPLE IDEAS

...7.   To discover the nature of our *ideas* the better, and to discourse of them intelligibly, it will be convenient to distinguish them as they are *ideas* or perceptions in our minds, and as they are modifications of matter in the bodies that cause such perceptions in us: that so we *may not* think (as perhaps usually is done) that they are exactly the images and *resemblances* of something inherent in the subject: most of those of sensation being in the mind no more the likeness of something existing without us, than the names that stand for them are the likeness of our *ideas*, which yet upon hearing they are apt to excite in us.

8.   Whatsoever the mind perceives in itself, or is the immediate object of perception, thought, or understanding, that I call *idea*; and the power to produce any *idea* in our mind, I call *quality* of the subject wherein that power is. Thus a snowball having the power to produce in us the *ideas* of *white*, *cold*, and *round*, the power to produce those *ideas* in us as they are in the snowball I call *qualities*; and as they are sensations or perceptions in our understandings, I call them *ideas*; which *ideas*, if I speak of sometimes as in the things themselves, I would be understood to mean those qualities in the objects which produce them in us.

9.   Qualities thus considered in bodies are:

First, such as are utterly inseparable from the body, in what state soever it be; such as in all the alterations and changes it suffers, all the force can be used upon it, it constantly keeps; and such as sense constantly finds in every particle of matter which has bulk enough to be perceived; and the mind finds inseparable from every particle of matter, though less than to make itself singly be perceived by our senses. V.g., take a grain of wheat, divide it into two parts, each part has still *solidarity, extension, figure*, and *mobility*; divide it again, and it retains still the same qualities; and so divide it on, till the parts become insensible: they must retain still each of them all those qualities. For division (which is all that a mill or pestle or any other body does upon another in reducing it to insensible parts) can never take away either solidity, extension, figure, or mobility from any body, but only makes two or more distinct separate masses of matter, of that which was but one before; all which distinct masses, reckoned as so many distinct bodies, after division make a certain number. These I call *original* or *primary qualities* of body; which I think we may observe to produce simple *ideas* in us, viz. solidity, extension, figure, motion or rest, and number.

10.   Secondly, such *qualities* which in truth are nothing in the objects themselves but powers to produce various sensations in us by their *primary qualities*, i.e. by the bulk, figure, texture, and motion of their insensible parts, as colours, sounds, tastes, etc. These I call *secondary qualities*. To these might be added a third sort, which are allowed to be barely powers, though they are as much real qualities in the subject as those which I, to comply with the common way of speaking, call *qualities*, but for distinction, *secondary qualities*. For the power in fire to produce a new colour, or consistency in wax or clay, by its primary qualities, is as much a quality in fire as the power it has to produce in me a new *idea* or sensation of warmth or burning, which I felt not before, by the same primary qualities, viz. the bulk, texture, and motion of its insensible parts.

11.   The next thing to be considered is how *bodies* produce *ideas* in us; and that is manifestly *by impulse*, the only way which we can conceive bodies operate in.

12.   If then external objects be not united to our minds when they produce *ideas* in it and yet we perceive *these original qualities* in such of them as singly fall under our senses, it is evident that some motion must be thence continued by our nerves or animal spirits, by some parts of our bodies, to the brains or the seat of sensation, there to *produce in our minds the particular* ideas *we have of them*. And since the extension, figure, number, and motion of bodies of an observable bigness may be perceived at a distance *by* the sight, it is evident some singly imperceptible bodies must come from them to the eyes, and thereby convey to the brain some *motion*, which produces these *ideas* which we have of them in us.

13.   After the same manner that the *ideas* of these original qualities are produced in us, we may conceive that the *ideas of secondary qualities* are also *produced*, viz. *by the operation of insensible particles on our senses*. For it being manifest that there are bodies and good store of bodies, each whereof

are so small that we cannot by any of our senses discover either their bulk, figure, or motion, as is evident in the particles of the air and water and others extremely smaller than those, perhaps as much smaller than the particles of air or water as the particles of air or water are smaller than peas or hail-stones: let us suppose at present that the different motions and figures, bulk and number, of such particles, affecting the several organs of our senses, produce in us those different sensations which we have from the colours and smells of bodies: v.g. that a violet, by the impulse of such insensible particles of matter, of peculiar figures and bulks, and in different degrees and modifications of their motions, causes the *ideas* of the blue colour and sweet scent of that flower to be produced in our minds. It being no more impossible to conceive that God should annex such *ideas* to such motions, with which they have no similitude, than that he should annex the *idea* of pain to the motion of a piece of steel dividing our flesh, with which that *idea* hath no resemblance.

14.   What I have said concerning *colours* and *smells* may be understood also of *tastes* and *sounds, and other the like sensible qualities,* which, whatever reality we by mistake attribute to them, are in truth nothing in the objects themselves but powers to produce various sensations in us, and depend *on those primary qualities,* viz. bulk, figure, texture, and motion of parts, as I have said.

15.   From whence I think it easy to draw this observation: that the *ideas of primary qualities* of bodies *are resemblances* of them, and their patterns do really exist in the bodies themselves; but the *ideas produced* in us *by* these *secondary qualities have no resemblance* of them at all. There is nothing like our *ideas* existing in the bodies themselves. They are, in the bodies we denominate from them, only a power to produce those sensations in us; and what is sweet, blue, or warm in *idea* is but the certain bulk, figure, and motion of the insensible parts in the bodies themselves, which we call so.

16.   *Flame* is denominated *hot* and *light; snow, white* and *cold;* and *manna, white* and *sweet,* from the *ideas* they produce in us. Which qualities are commonly thought to be the same in those bodies that those *ideas* are in us, the one the perfect resemblance of the other, as they are in a mirror, and it would by most men be judged very extravagant if one should say otherwise. And yet he that will consider that *the same fire* that at one distance *produces* in us the sensation of *warmth* does, at a nearer approach, produce in us the far different sensation of *pain,* ought to bethink himself what reason he has to say that his *idea* of *warmth,* which was produced in him by the fire, is actually *in the fire;* and his *idea* of *pain,* which the same fire produced in him the same way, is *not* in the *fire.* Why are whiteness and coldness in snow, and pain not, when it produces the one and the other

idea in us; and can do neither, but by the bulk, figure, number, and motion of its solid parts?

17.   The particular *bulk, number, figure, and motion of the parts of fire or snow are really in them*, whether anyone's senses perceive them or no; and therefore they may be called *real qualities*, because they really exist in those bodies. But *light, heat, whiteness,* or *coldness are no more really in them than sickness or pain is in* manna. Take away the sensation of them; let not the eyes see light or colours, nor the ears hear sounds; let the palate not taste, nor the nose smell; and all colours, tastes, odours, and sounds, as they are such particular *ideas*, vanish and cease, and are reduced to their causes, i.e. bulk, figure, and motion of parts.[1]

18.   A piece of *manna* of a sensible bulk is able to produce in us the *idea* of a round or square figure; and by being removed from one place to another, the *idea* of motion. This *idea* of motion represents it as it really is in the *manna* moving; a circle or square are the same, whether in *idea* or existence, in the mind or in the *manna*; and this, both *motion and figure, are really in the manna*, whether we take notice of them or no: this everybody is ready to agree to. Besides, *manna*, by the bulk, figure, texture, and motion of its parts, has a power to produce the sensations of sickness, and sometimes of acute pains or gripings in us. That these *ideas* of *sickness and pain are not in the* manna, but effects of its operations on us, and are nowhere when we feel them not: this also everyone readily agrees to. And yet men are hardly to be brought to think that *sweetness and whiteness are not really in manna*, which are but the effects of the operations of *manna*, by the motion, size, and figure of its particles, on the eyes and palate, as the pain and sickness caused by *manna* are confessedly nothing but the effects of its operations on the stomach and guts, by the size, motion, and figure of its insensible parts (for by nothing else can a body operate, as has been proved): as if it could not operate on the eyes and palate and thereby produce in the mind particular distinct *ideas* which in itself it has not, as well as we allow it can operate on the guts and stomach and thereby produce distinct *ideas* which in itself it has not. These *ideas* being all effects of the operations of *manna* on several parts of our bodies by the size, figure, number, and motion of its parts, why those produced by the eyes and palate should rather be thought to be really in the *manna* than those produced by the stomach and guts; or why the pain and sickness, *ideas* that are the effects of *manna*, should be thought to be nowhere, when they are not felt: and yet the sweetness and whiteness, effects of the same *manna* on other parts of the body by ways equally as unknown, should be thought to exist in the *manna*, when they are not seen nor tasted, would need some reason to explain.

19.   Let us consider the red and white colours in *porphyry*. Hinder light but from striking on it, and its colours vanish: it no longer produces any such *ideas* in us; upon the return of light it produces these appearances on us again. Can anyone think any real alterations are made in the *porphyry* by the presence or absence of light; and that those *ideas* of whiteness and redness are really in *porphyry* in the light, when it is plain *it has no colour in the dark*? It has, indeed, such a configuration of particles, both night and day, as are apt, by the rays of light rebounding from some parts of that hard stone, to produce in us the *idea* of redness, and from others the *idea* of whiteness; but whiteness or redness are not in it at any time, but such a texture that hath the power to produce such a sensation in us.

20.   Pound an almond, and the clear white *colour* will be altered into a dirty one, and the sweet *taste* into an oily one. What real alteration can the beating of the pestle make in any body, but an alteration of the *texture* of it?

21.   *Ideas* being thus distinguished and understood, we may be able to give an account how the same water, at the same time, may produce the *idea* of cold by one hand and of heat by the other, whereas it is impossible that the same water, if those *ideas* were really in it, should at the same time be both hot and cold. For if we imagine *warmth* as it is *in our hands* to be *nothing but a certain sort and degree of motion in the minute particles of our nerves, or animal spirits*, we may understand how it is possible that the same water may at the same time produce the sensation of heat in one hand and cold in the other; which yet figure never does, that never producing the *idea* of a square by one hand which has produced the *idea* of a globe by another. But if the sensation of heat and cold be nothing but the increase or diminution of the motion of the minute parts of our bodies, caused by the corpuscles of any other body, it is easy to be understood that, if that motion be greater in one hand than in the other, if a body be applied to the two hands, which has in its minute particles a greater motion than in those of one of the hands, and a less than in those of the other, it will increase the motion of the one hand and lessen it in the other, and so cause the different sensations of heat and cold that depend thereon.

22.   I have in what just goes before been engaged in physical inquiries a little further than perhaps I intended. But, it being necessary to make the nature of sensation a little understood; and to make the *difference between the qualities in bodies, and the* ideas *produced by them in the mind*, to be distinctly conceived, without which it were impossible to discourse intelligibly of them: I hope I shall be pardoned this little excursion into natural philosophy, it being necessary in our present inquiry to distinguish the *primary* and *real qualities* of bodies, which are always in them (viz. solidity,

extension, figure, number, and motion or rest; and are sometimes perceived by us, viz. when the bodies they are in are big enough singly to be
discerned), from those *secondary* and *imputed qualities*, which are but the
powers of several combinations of those primary ones, when they operate
without being distinctly discerned; whereby we also may come to know
what *ideas* are, and what are not, resemblances of something really existing
in the bodies we denominate from them.

23.   The *qualities*, then, that are in *bodies*, rightly considered, are of *three
sorts*:

First, The *bulk*, *figure*, *number*, *situation*, and *motion or rest* of their
solid parts. Those are in them, whether we perceive them or no; and when
they are of that size that we can discover them, we have by these an *idea* of
the thing as it is in itself, as is plain in artificial things. These I call *primary
qualities*.

Secondly, The *power* that is in any body, by reason of *its* insensible *primary qualities*, to operate after a peculiar manner on any of our senses, and
thereby *produce in us* the *different ideas* of several colours, sounds, smells,
tastes, etc. These are usually called sensible qualities.

Thirdly, The *power* that is in any body, *by* reason of the particular constitution of *its primary qualities*, *to* make such a *change* in the *bulk, figure,
texture, and motion of another body*, as to make it operate on our senses
differently from what it did before. Thus the sun has a power to make wax
white, and fire to make lead fluid. These *are* usually called powers.

The first of these, as has been said, I think may be properly called *real,
original*, or *primary qualities*, because they are in the things themselves,
whether they are perceived or no; and upon their different modifications it
is that the secondary qualities depend.

The other two are only powers to act differently upon other things, which
powers result from the different modifications of those primary qualities.

24.   But though *these two latter sorts of qualities are powers barely*, and
nothing but powers relating to several other bodies and resulting from
the different modifications of the original qualities, yet they are generally
otherwise thought of. For *the second sort*, viz. the powers to produce several
ideas in us by our senses, *are looked upon as real qualities in the things* thus
affecting us; but *the third sort are called and esteemed barely powers*, v.g. the
idea of heat or light which we receive by our eyes or touch from the sun are
commonly thought *real qualities* existing in the sun and something more
than mere powers in it. But when we consider the sun in reference to wax,
which it melts or blanches, we look upon the whiteness and softness produced in the wax not as qualities in the sun but effects produced by *powers*
in it: whereas, if rightly considered, these qualities of light and warmth,

which are perceptions in me when I am warmed or enlightened by the sun, are no otherwise in the sun than the changes, made in the wax when it is blanched or melted, are in the sun. They are all of them equally powers in the sun, depending on its primary qualities; whereby it is able in the one case so to alter the bulk, figure, texture, or motion of some of the insensible parts of my eyes or hands as thereby to produce in me the *idea* of light or heat; and in the other, it is able so to alter the bulk, figure, texture, or motion of the insensible parts of the wax, as to make them fit to produce in me the distinct *ideas* of white and fluid.

25. The reason *why the one are ordinarily taken for real qualities and the other only for bare powers* seems to be because the *ideas* we have of distinct colours, sounds, etc., containing nothing at all in them of bulk, figure, or motion, we are apt to think them the effects of these primary qualities which appear not to our senses to operate in their production, and with which they have not any apparent congruity or conceivable connexion. Hence it is that we are so forward to imagine that those *ideas* are the resemblances of something really existing in the objects themselves, since sensation discovers nothing of bulk, figure, or motion of parts in their production, nor can reason show how bodies by their bulk, figure, and motion should produce in the mind the *ideas* of blue or yellow, etc. But in the other case, in the operations of bodies changing the qualities one of another, we plainly discover that the quality produced hath commonly no resemblance with anything in the thing producing it; wherefore we look on it as a bare effect of power. For, though receiving the *idea* of heat or light from the sun, we are apt to think it is a perception and resemblance of such a quality in the sun: yet when we see wax or a fair face receive change of colour from the sun, we cannot imagine that to be the reception or resemblance of anything in the sun, because we find not those different colours in the sun itself. For, our senses being able to observe a likeness or unlikeness of sensible qualities in two different external objects, we forwardly enough conclude the production of any sensible quality in any subject to be an effect of bare power, and not the communication of any quality which was really in the efficient, when we find no such sensible quality in the thing that produced it. But our senses not being able to discover any unlikeness between the *idea* produced in us and the quality of the object producing it, we are apt to imagine that our *ideas* are resemblances of something in the objects, and not the effects of certain powers placed in the modification of their primary qualities, with which primary qualities the *ideas* produced in us have no resemblance.

26. To conclude, beside those before-mentioned *primary qualities* in bodies, viz. bulk, figure, extension, number, and motion of their solid parts:

all the rest, whereby we take notice of bodies and distinguish them one from another, are nothing else but several powers in them, depending on those primary qualities; whereby they are fitted, either by immediately operating on our bodies to produce several different *ideas* in us, or else, by operating on other bodies, so to change their primary qualities as to render them capable of producing *ideas* in us different from what before they did. The former of these, I think, may be called *secondary qualities immediately perceivable*, the latter *secondary qualities, mediately perceivable*.

Chapter XXIII

OF OUR COMPLEX IDEAS OF SUBSTANCES

1.   The mind being, as I have declared, furnished with a great number of the simple *ideas* conveyed in by the *senses*, as they are found in exterior things, or by *reflection* on its own operations, takes notice also that a certain number of these simple *ideas* go constantly together; which, being presumed to belong to one thing, and words being suited to common apprehensions and made use of for quick dispatch, are called, so united in one subject, by one name; which, by inadvertency, we are apt afterward to talk of and consider as one simple *idea*, which indeed is a complication of many *ideas* together: because, as I have said, not imagining how these simple *ideas* can subsist by themselves, we accustom ourselves to suppose some *substratum* wherein they do subsist, and from which they do result; which therefore we call *substance*.

2.   So that if anyone will examine himself concerning his *notion of pure substance in general*, he will find he has no other *idea* of it at all, but only a supposition of he knows not what support of such qualities which are capable of producing simple *ideas* in us; which qualities are commonly called accidents. If anyone should be asked what is the subject wherein colour or weight inheres, he would have nothing to say but, the solid extended parts; and if he were demanded what is it that that solidity and extension adhere in, he would not be in a much better case than the *Indian* before-mentioned who, saying that the world was supported by a great elephant, was asked what the elephant rested on, to which his answer was, a great tortoise; but being again pressed to know what gave support to the broad-backed tortoise, replied, something, he knew not what. And thus here, as in all other cases where we use words without having clear and distinct *ideas*, we talk like children who, being questioned what such a thing is which they know not, readily give this satisfactory answer, that it is *some-*

thing; which in truth signifies no more, when so used, either by children or men, but that they know not what, and that the thing they pretend to know and talk of is what they have no distinct *idea* of at all, and so are perfectly ignorant of it and in the dark. The *idea* then we have, to which we give the general name substance, being nothing but the supposed, but unknown, support of those qualities we find existing, which we imagine cannot subsist *sine re substante,* without something to support them, we call that support *substantia;* which, according to the true import of the word, is, in plain *English, standing under* or *upholding.*

3.   An obscure and relative *idea* of substance in general being thus made, we come to have the *ideas of particular sorts of substances* by collecting such combinations of simple *ideas* as are, by experience and observation of men's senses, taken notice of to exist together, and are therefore supposed to flow from the particular internal constitution or unknown essence of that substance. Thus we come to have the *ideas* of a man, horse, gold, water, etc.; of which substances, whether anyone has any other clear *idea,* further than of certain simple *ideas* co-existent together, I appeal to everyone's own experience. It is the ordinary qualities observable in iron, or a diamond, put together that make the true complex *idea* of those substances, which a smith or a jeweller commonly knows better than a philosopher; who, whatever substantial forms he may talk of, has no other *idea* of those substances than what is framed by a collection of those simple *ideas* which are to be found in them: only we must take notice that our complex *ideas* of substances, besides all these simple *ideas* they are made up of, have always the confused *idea* of *something* to which they belong, and in which they subsist; and therefore when we speak of any sort of substance, we say it is a *thing* having such or such qualities: as body is a *thing* that is extended, figured, and capable of motion; a spirit, a *thing* capable of thinking; and so hardness, friability, and power to draw iron, we say, are qualities to be found in a loadstone. These and the like fashions of speaking intimate that the substance is supposed always *something* besides the extension, figure, solidity, motion, thinking or other observable *ideas,* though we know not what it is.

4.   Hence, when we talk or think of any particular sort of corporeal substances, as *horse, stone,* etc., though the *idea* we have of either of them be but the complication or collection of those several simple *ideas* of sensible qualities, which we use to find united in the thing called *horse* or *stone:* yet, because we cannot conceive how they should subsist alone, nor one in another, we suppose them existing in and supported by some common subject; *which support we denote by the name substance,* though it be certain we have no clear or distinct *idea* of that *thing* we suppose a support.

5.   The same thing happens concerning the operations of the mind, viz. thinking, reasoning, fearing, etc., which we concluding not to subsist of themselves, nor apprehending how they can belong to body or be produced by it, we are apt to think these the actions of some other *substance*, which we call *spirit*; whereby yet it is evident that, having no other *idea* or notion of matter but *something* wherein those many sensible qualities which affect our senses do subsist, by supposing a substance wherein *thinking, knowing, doubting*, and a power of moving, etc., do subsist, *we have as clear a notion of the substance of spirit as we have of body*: the one being supposed to be (without knowing what it is) the *substratum* to those simple *ideas* we have from without; and the other supposed (with a like ignorance of what it is) to be the *substratum* to those operations which we experiment in ourselves within. It is plain then that the *idea* of corporeal *substance* in matter is as remote from our conceptions and apprehensions as that of spiritual *substance*, or *spirit*; and therefore, from our not having any notion of the *substance* of spirit, we can no more conclude its non-existence than we can, for the same reason, deny the existence of body: it being as rational to affirm there is no body, because we have no clear and distinct *idea* of the *substance* of matter, as to say there is no spirit, because we have no clear and distinct *idea* of the *substance* of a spirit.

6.   Whatever therefore be the secret and abstract nature of *substance* in general, all *the* ideas *we have of particular distinct sorts of substances* are nothing but several combinations of simple *ideas*, co-existing in such, though unknown, cause of their union as makes the whole subsist of itself. It is by such combinations of simple *ideas* and nothing else that we represent particular sorts of *substances* to ourselves; such are the *ideas* we have of their several species in our minds; and such only do we, by their specific names, signify to others, v.g. *man, horse, sun, water, iron*; upon hearing which words, everyone who understands the language frames in his mind a combination of those several simple *ideas* which he has usually observed or fancied to exist together under that denomination, all which he supposes to rest in and be, as it were, adherent to that unknown common subject which inheres not in anything else. Though in the meantime it be manifest, and everyone upon inquiry into his own thoughts will find, that he has no other *idea* of any *substance*, v.g., let it be *gold, horse, iron, man, vitriol, bread*, but what he has barely of those sensible qualities which he supposes to inhere, with a supposition of such a *substratum* as gives, as it were, a support to those qualities or simple *ideas* which he has observed to exist united together. Thus, the *idea* of the *sun*, what is it but an aggregate of those several simple *ideas*, bright, hot, roundish, having a constant regular motion, at a certain distance from us, and perhaps some other: as he who

thinks and discourses of the *sun* has been more or less accurate in observing those sensible qualities, *ideas*, or properties, which are in that thing which he calls the *sun*.

7. For he has the perfectest *idea* of any of the particular sorts of *substances*, who has gathered and put together most of those simple *ideas* which do exist in it; among which are to be reckoned its active powers and passive capacities, which, though not simple *ideas*, yet in this respect, for brevity's sake, may conveniently enough be reckoned amongst them. Thus, the power of drawing iron is one of the *ideas* of the complex one of that substance we call a *loadstone*; and a power to be so drawn is a part of the complex one we call *iron*: which powers pass for inherent qualities in those subjects. Because every *substance*, being as apt, by the powers we observe in it, to change some sensible qualities in other subjects as it is to produce in us those simple *ideas* which we receive immediately from it, does, by those new sensible qualities introduced into other subjects, discover to us those powers which do thereby mediately affect our senses, as regularly as its sensible qualities do it immediately: v.g. we immediately by our senses perceive in *fire* its heat and colour, which are, if rightly considered, nothing but powers in it to produce those *ideas* in us; we also by our senses perceive the colour and brittleness of *charcoal*, whereby we come by the knowledge of another power in fire, which it has to change the colour and consistency of wood. By the former, fire immediately, by the latter, it mediately discovers to us these several powers; which therefore we look upon to be a part of the qualities of fire, and so make them a part of the complex *idea* of it. For all those powers that we take cognizance of terminating only in the alteration of some sensible qualities in those subjects on which they operate, and so making them exhibit to us new sensible *ideas*, therefore it is that I have reckoned these powers amongst the simple *ideas* which make the complex ones of the sorts of *substances*, though these powers considered in themselves are truly complex *ideas*. And in this looser sense, I crave leave to be understood when I name any of these *potentialities amongst the simple ideas, which we recollect in our minds when we think of particular substances.* For the powers that are severally in them are necessary to be considered, if we will have true distinct notions of the several sorts of substances.

8. Nor are we to wonder that *powers make a great part of our complex* ideas *of substances*, since their secondary qualities are those which in most of them serve principally to distinguish substances one from another, and commonly make a considerable part of the complex *idea* of the several sorts of them. For, our senses failing us in the discovery of the bulk, texture, and figure of the minute parts of bodies, on which their real constitutions and differences depend, we are fain to make use of their secondary

qualities as the characteristical notes and marks whereby to frame *ideas* of them in our minds and distinguish them one from another: all which secondary qualities, as has been shown, are nothing but bare powers. For the colour and taste of *opium* are, as well as its soporific or anodyne virtues, mere powers, depending on its primary qualities, whereby it is fitted to produce different operations on different parts of our bodies.

9.   The ideas *that make our complex ones of corporeal substances* are of these three sorts. *First,* the *ideas* of the primary qualities of things, which are discovered by our senses, and are in them even when we perceive them not; such are the bulk, figure, number, situation, and motion of the parts of bodies, which are really in them, whether we take notice of them or no. *Secondly,* the sensible secondary qualities, which, depending on these, are nothing but the powers those substances have to produce several *ideas* in us by our senses; which *ideas* are not in the things themselves otherwise than as anything is in its cause. *Thirdly,* the aptness we consider in any substance to give or receive such alterations of primary qualities, as that the substance so altered should produce in us different *ideas* from what it did before: these are called active and passive powers; all which powers, as far as we have any notice or notion of them, terminate only in sensible simple *ideas.* For whatever alteration a *loadstone* has the power to make in the minute particles of iron, we should have no notion of any power it had at all to operate on iron, did not its sensible motion discover it; and I doubt not but there are a thousand changes that bodies we daily handle have a power to cause in one another, which we never suspect, because they never appear in sensible effects.

10.   *Powers* therefore justly *make a great part of our complex* ideas *of substances.* He that will examine his complex *idea* of gold will find several of its *ideas* that make it up to be only powers, as the power of being melted, but of not spending itself in the fire, of being dissolved in *aqua regia,* are *ideas* as necessary to make up our complex *idea* of gold as its colour and weight; which, if duly considered, are also nothing but different powers. For, to speak truly, yellowness is not actually in gold, but is a power in gold to produce that *idea* in us by our eyes, when placed in a due light; and the heat, which we cannot leave out of our *idea* of the sun, is no more really in the sun, than the white colour it introduces into wax. These are both equally powers in the sun, operating, by the motion and figure of its insensible parts, so on a man as to make him have the *idea* of heat; and so on wax, as to make it capable to produce in a man the *idea* of white.

11.   Had we senses acute enough to discern the minute particles of bodies and the real constitution on which their sensible qualities depend, I doubt not but they would produce quite different *ideas* in us; and that which is

now the yellow colour of gold would then disappear, and instead of it we should see an admirable texture of parts, of a certain size and figure. This microscopes plainly discover to us; for what to our naked eyes produces a certain colour is, by thus augmenting the acuteness of our senses, discovered to be quite a different thing; and the thus altering, as it were, the proportion of the bulk of the minute parts of a coloured object to our usual sight produces different *ideas* from what it did before. Thus sand, or pounded glass, which is opaque and white to the naked eye, is pellucid in a microscope; and a hair seen this way loses its former colour and is in a great measure pellucid, with a mixture of some bright sparkling colours, such as appear from the refraction of diamonds and other pellucid bodies. Blood to the naked eye appears all red, but by a good microscope, wherein its lesser parts appear, shows only some few globules of red, swimming in a pellucid liquor; and how these red globules would appear, if glasses could be found that yet could magnify them a thousand or ten thousand times more, is uncertain. . . .

Note

1 In this paragraph there is clearly oscillation between denying that secondary qualities belong to objects and identifying them with the causal powers of the objects' primary qualities.

9 G. W. Leibniz, *Monadology*

From Gottfried Wilhelm Leibniz, *Philosophical Writings*, ed. G. H. R. Parkinson, trans. M. Morris and G. H. R. Parkinson. London: J. M. Dent & Sons, 1973. pp. 179–94 (asterisked note is the translators').

In Bertrand Russell's opinion, it was the 'lamentable waste of time in the endeavour to please' his princely patrons which prevented the German polymath, Gottfried Wilhelm Leibniz (1646–1716), from writing an extensive exposition of his metaphysical system.[1] On a more generous view, the reason was Leibniz's 'unachievable ambition to excel in every sphere of intellectual and political activity'.[2] But while Leibniz left no extended account, he did, in his *Monadology* of 1714, provide a virtually complete statement of his views. The work defies useful summary, since it is itself a useful summary, bold and clear, of one of the most comprehensive and ambitious of metaphysical systems. Most of Leibniz's distinctive theses – the Principles of Sufficient Reason and of the Identity of Indiscernibles, for example – are all there. More valuable, by way of a preamble, than an attempt at summary is to place Leibniz's position in relation to those of his predecessors, above all Spinoza.

Leibniz was a critical admirer of the three seventeenth-century philosophers represented in this volume (chapter 6–8). As with Spinoza and Locke, an aim was to develop a philosophy which would not entail Descartes' dualistic dichotomy between mind and body. Against Locke, however, Leibniz sided with the two rationalists in holding up the self-evident truths of reason, and their logical implications, as the only proper objects of knowledge. (Leibniz's defence of innate ideas against Locke's insistence that all knowledge derives from experience was included in *Epistemology: the classic readings*.) As for Spinoza, Leibniz shared the widespread and almost certainly mistaken view that he was a 'brutal' materialist whose references to God were little more than decorative.

In fact, there are deep similarities between Spinoza's and Leibniz's metaphysics: and this is so despite some apparently radical differences. Whereas for

[1] Quoted in John Cottingham, *The Rationalists*, Oxford: Oxford University Press, 1990, p. 26.
[2] G. MacDonald Ross, *Leibniz*, Oxford: Oxford University Press, 1984, p. 26.

the Dutchman there is just one substance ('God or Nature'), for the German reality is composed of countless simple substances ('monads'). For Spinoza, the idea of God as a creator of independent substances is absurd, while for Leibniz that is precisely what God is. And whereas, for Spinoza, there are no contingencies, for Leibniz we need to distinguish between the necessary truths of reason and contingent truths.

Reflection on what Leibniz intends by that latter distinction, however, soon begins to soften the contrast between the two thinkers. For Leibniz, the truth that, say, Adam ate the apple is, as it were, only contingent *for us*, with our limited understanding. Had we a 'complete concept' of Adam, in the way God does, we would recognize that eating the apple belonged to that concept, so that someone who refused Eve's offer, however like Adam in other respects, could not have *been* Adam. Moreover, though lacking 'complete concepts', we can reflect that everything which happens does so in accordance with a necessity to which God, by his nature, is subject – namely to determine everything 'for the best'.

Furthermore, while Spinoza and Leibniz disagree about the number of substances, their concepts of substance are similar. A substance is 'independent', so that it cannot be causally affected by anything outside it. In Leibniz's famous remark, 'monads have no windows, by which anything could come in or go out' (§7 below). As such, the development of any monadic substance must be due to something internal to it, which Leibniz calls 'appetition'. 'In a manner of speaking', remarks one commentator, 'monads were gonads'.[3]

Spinoza and Leibniz's disagreement over the number of substances – one *versus* an infinity – is due to the following difference. Spinozan substance is independent *tout court*, while for Leibniz – here following Descartes – a (simple) substance is something which 'does not depend on anything except . . . God'.[4] Nor is this a disagreement which prevents Leibniz's conception of reality being almost as *holistic* as Spinoza's. While there really are distinct monads, not just 'modes' of a single substance, each of these 'mirrors' or 'expresses' all other monads in a grand system of 'pre-established harmony'. Were we to possess divine knowledge, we could 'read off' from our knowledge of each monad how everything else in the universe must be.

Leibniz cannot subscribe, in so many words, to Spinoza's alternative to Cartesian dualism, for this requires treating mind and body as merely different 'attributes' of God/Nature. Instead, he argues that matter does not exist at the level of ultimate reality, being a 'chimera' constructed out of 'incorporeal' monads. At a less deep level, however, it is in order to speak of bodies, rather in the

---

[3] Ibid., p. 107.
[4] *Metaphysical Consequences of the Principle of Reason*, also in Leibniz's *Philosophical Writings*, p. 175.

way it is unobjectionable to speak of flocks or armies, even though these have no existence beyond their individual members. But it would remain a mistake to suppose, with Descartes, that souls and bodies 'interact'. Rather, there is a 'pre-established harmony' between mental and bodily events: in particular between events in a given mind and events in a given body where the harmony is sufficiently obvious to permit speaking – at the conventional level – of the body in question as that mind's, or person's, body. *My* body, that is, is an aggregate of events which are 'mirrored' with special vivacity and clarity in the mental events which take place in the monad which *I* am.

Leibniz's philosophy, like Spinoza's, is metaphysics on the grand, speculative scale. Unlike Spinoza, Leibniz became a major influence on eighteenth-century philosophy. It is unsurprising, therefore, that he was also to become, as we shall see in chapter 11, one of the main targets of Immanuel Kant's attack on 'dogmatic' metaphysics.

 ### Leibniz, *Monadology*

1.   The *monad*, of which we shall speak here, is nothing but a simple substance which enters into compounds; *simple*, that is to say, without parts.

2.   And there must be simple substances, because there are compounds; for the compound is nothing but a collection or *aggregatum* of simples.

3.   Now where there are no parts, there neither extension, nor shape, nor divisibility is possible. And these monads are the true atoms of nature and, in a word, the elements of things.

4.   Moreover, there is no fear of dissolution, and there is no conceivable way in which a simple substance could perish in the course of nature.

5.   For the same reason there is no way in which a simple substance could begin in the course of nature, since it cannot be formed by means of compounding.

6.   Thus it may be said that monads can only begin and end all at once, that is to say they can only begin by creation and end by annihilation, whereas what is compound begins or ends by parts.

7.   There is also no means of explaining how a monad can be altered or changed within itself by any other created thing, since it is impossible to displace anything in it or to conceive of the possibility of any internal motion being started, directed, increased, or diminished within it, as can occur in compounds, where change among the parts takes place. Monads have no windows, by which anything could come in or go out. Accidents cannot become detached, or wander about outside substances, as the

'sensible species' of the Scholastics used to do.[1] Thus neither substance nor accident can enter a monad from without.

8.   Monads, however, must have some qualities, otherwise they would not be beings at all. And if simple substances did not differ by their qualities, there would be no way of perceiving any change in things, since what is in the compound can only come from its simple ingredients; and if monads were without qualities, they would be indistinguishable from one another, since they do not differ in quantity either. And consequently, supposing space to be a plenum, each place would always only receive, when motion occurred, the equivalent of what it had before; and one state of things would be indistinguishable from another.

9.   Indeed, every monad must be different from every other. For there are never in nature two beings which are precisely alike, and in which it is not possible to find some difference which is internal, or based on some intrinsic denomination.[2]

10.   I also take it as granted that every created thing, and consequently the created monad also, is subject to change, and indeed that this change is continual in each one.

11.   It follows from what we have just said, that the natural changes of monads come from an *internal principle*, since an external cause would be unable to influence their inner being.

12.   But besides the principle of change, there must be *differentiation within that which changes*, to constitute as it were the specification and variety of simple substances.

13.   This differentiation must involve a plurality within the unity or the simple. For since very natural change takes place by degrees, something changes, and something remains; and consequently the simple must contain a large number of affections and relations, although it has no parts.

14.   The passing state, which involves and represents a plurality within the unity or simple substance, is nothing other than what is called *perception*, which must be carefully distinguished from apperception or consciousness, as will appear presently. And herein lies the great mistake of the Cartesians, that they took no account of perceptions which are not apperceived. It is this also which made them believe that minds alone are monads, and that neither brutes nor other entelechies [see §18] have souls. For the same reason also they fell into the common error of confusing death, properly so called, with a prolonged unconsciousness; and this made them favour the Scholastic conviction that souls are entirely separate from bodies, and even confirmed some ill-balanced minds in the opinion that souls are mortal.

15.   The action of the internal principle which produces the change or passage from one perception to another may be called *appetition*; it is true that the appetite cannot always attain completely the whole of the perception towards which it tends, but it always attains something of it, and arrives at new perceptions.

16.   We ourselves experience plurality within a simple substance, when we find that the least thought which we apperceive involves a variety in its object. So everyone who acknowledges that the soul is a simple substance must acknowledge this plurality within the monad; and M. [Pierre] Bayle should not have found any difficulty in this, as he does in his *Dictionary*, in the article 'Rorarius'.

17.   We are moreover obliged to confess that *perception* and that which depends on it *cannot be explained mechanically*, that is to say by figures and motions. Suppose that there were a machine so constructed as to produce thought, feeling, and perception, we could imagine it increased in size while retaining the same proportions, so that one could enter as one might a mill. On going inside we should only see the parts impinging upon one another; we should not see anything which would explain a perception. The explanation of perception must therefore be sought in a simple substance, and not in a compound or in a machine. Moreover, there is nothing else whatever to be found in the simple substance except just this, viz. perceptions and their changes. It is in this alone that all the *internal actions* of simple substances must consist.

18.   We may give the name *entelechies* to all created simple substances or monads. For they have in themselves a certain perfection (ἔχουσι τὸ ἐντελές), there is a self-sufficiency (αὐτάρκεια) in them which makes the sources of their internal actions – incorporeal automata, if I may so put it.

19.   If we wish to give the name 'soul' to everything which has *perceptions* and *appetites* in the general sense I have just explained, all created simple substances or monads might be called souls; but as feeling is something more than a simple perception, I agree that the general name – monad or entelechy – should be enough for simple substances which have no more than that, and that those only should be called souls, whose perception is more distinct and is accompanied by memory.

20.   For we experience within ourselves a state, in which we remember nothing and have no distinguishable perception; as when we fall into a swoon, or when we are overcome by a deep dreamless sleep. In this state the soul does not sensibly differ from a simple monad; but as this state is not permanent, and as the soul emerges from it, the soul is something more.

21.   And it does not follow that when in that state the simple substance

has no perception at all. Indeed, that is not possible for the above reasons; for it cannot perish, nor can it subsist without some affection in some way, and this affection is nothing but its perception. But when there are a very great number of small perceptions with nothing to distinguish them, we are stupefied, just as it happens that if we go on turning round in the same direction several times running, we become giddy and go into a swoon, so that we can no longer distinguish anything at all. And death can throw animals* into this state for a time.

22. And as every state of a simple substance is a natural consequence of its preceding state, so that the present state of it is big with the future,

23. and since, on awakening from our stupor, we apperceive our perceptions, it must be the case that we received the perceptions the moment before, though we did not apperceive them; for a perception cannot arise in the course of nature except from another perception, as one motion can only arise in the course of nature from another motion.

24. From this we see that if we had nothing in our perceptions to distinguish them, nothing so to speak heightened and of a keener savour, we should always be in this stupor. And this is the state of bare monads.

25. We see also that Nature has given heightened perceptions to animals from the care she has taken to provide them with organs which collect several rays of light, or several undulations of the air, so as to make these more effective by being united. There is something of the kind in smell, taste, and touch, and perhaps in many other senses which are unknown to us. I will explain later how what occurs in the soul represents what takes place in the organs.

26. Memory provides souls with a kind of *consecutiveness*, which copies reason but must be distinguished from it. What I mean is this: we often see that animals, when they have a perception of something which strikes them, and of which they had a similar perception previously, are led, by the representation of their memory, to expect what was united with his perception before, and are moved to feelings similar to those they had before. For example, when dogs are shown a stick, they remember the pain which it has caused them in the past, and howl or run away.

27. The powerful imagination, which strikes and moves them, arises either from the magnitude or from the number of the preceding perceptions. For often a vivid impression has in a moment the effect of long *habit*, or of many moderate perceptions oft repeated.

28. Men act like brutes in so far as the sequences of their perceptions

---

* By 'animals' Leibniz means all living creatures up to and including man. The lower animals as distinguished from man, he refers to as 'brutes'.

arise through the principle of memory only, like those empirical physicians who have mere practice without theory. We are all merely empiricists as regards three-fourths of our actions. For example, when we expect it to be day tomorrow, we are behaving as empiricists, because until now it has always happened thus. The astronomer alone knows this by reason.

29.   But it is the knowledge of necessary and eternal truths which distinguishes us from mere animals, and gives us *reason* and the sciences, raising us to knowledge of ourselves and God. It is this in us which we call the rational soul or *mind*.

30.   Further it is by the knowledge of necessary truths and by their abstractions that we are raised to *acts of reflection*, which make us think of what is called the *self*, and consider that this or that is within *us*. And it is thus that in thinking of ourselves, we think of being, of substance, of the simple and the compound, of the immaterial and of God himself, conceiving that what is limited in us, in him is limitless. And these acts of reflection provide the chief objects of our reasonings.

31.   Our reasonings are based on two great principles: the *principle of contradiction*, by virtue of which we judge to be false that which involves a contradiction, and true that which is opposed or contradictory to the false;

32.   and the *principle of sufficient reason*, by virtue of which we consider that no fact can be real or existing and no proposition can be true unless there is a sufficient reason, why it should be thus and not otherwise, even though in most cases these reasons cannot be known to us.

33.   There are also two kinds of *truths*: truths of *reasoning* and truths of *fact*. Truths of reasoning are necessary and their opposite is impossible; those of fact are contingent and their opposite is possible. When a truth is necessary, the reason for it can be found by analysis, that is, by resolving it into simpler ideas and truths until the primary ones are reached.

34.   It is in this way that in mathematics speculative *theorems* and practical *canons* are reduced by analysis to *definitions*, *axioms*, and *postulates*.

35.   Finally there are simple ideas of which no definition can be given; there are also axioms and postulates, or in a word *primary principles*, which cannot be proved and have no need of proof. These are *identical propositions*, whose opposite contains an express contradiction.[3]

36.   But a *sufficient reason* also must be found in the case of *contingent truths* or *truths of fact*; that is to say, in the case of the series of things spread over the universe of created things; here resolution into particular reasons might go on into endless detail on account of the immense variety of things in nature and the division of bodies *ad infinitum*. There are an infinite number of shapes and motions, both present and past, which enter into the efficient cause of my present writing; and there are an infinite

number of minute inclinations and dispositions of my soul, both present and past, which enter into its final cause.

37. And as all this differentiation involves only other prior or more differentiated contingent things, all of which need a similar analysis to explain them, we are no further advanced: and the sufficient or ultimate reason must be outside the succession or *series* of this differentiation of contingent things, however infinite it may be.

38. This is why the ultimate reason of things must lie in a necessary substance, in which the differentiation of the changes only exists eminently as in their source; and this is what we call *God*.

39. Now since this substance is a sufficient reason of all this differentiation, which it itself likewise all connected, *there is only one God, and this God is enough*.

40. We may also judge that since this Supreme Substance, who is unique, universal, and necessary, has nothing outside himself independent of himself, and is a simple consequence of possible being, he must be incapable of being limited, and must contain just as much reality as is possible.

41. Whence it follows that God is absolutely perfect, since *perfection* is nothing but magnitude of positive reality, in the strict sense, setting aside the limits or bounds in things which are limited. And there, where there are no bounds, that is to say in God, perfection is absolutely infinite.

42. It follows also that created things owe their perfections to the influence of God, but that they owe their imperfections to their own nature, which is incapable of being without limits. For it is in this that they are distinguished from God.

43. It is true likewise, that in God is the source not only of existences but also of essences, in so far as they are real, that is of all the reality there is in possibility. This is because the Understanding of God is the region of eternal truths or of the ideas on which they depend, and because without him there would be nothing real in the possibilities – not only nothing existent, but also nothing possible.

44. For if there is a reality in essences or possibilities, or indeed in eternal truths, this reality must be founded on something existent and actual; and consequently on the existence of the Necessary Being in whom essence involves existence, or in whom it is enough to be possible in order to be actual.

45. Thus God alone (or the Necessary Being) has the privilege that he must exist if he is possible. And as nothing can prevent the possibility of that which has no limits, no negation, and consequently no contradiction, this alone is sufficient for us to know the existence of God *a priori*. We have proved it also by the reality of eternal truths. And we have now just

proved it *a posteriori* also, since there exist contingent beings, which can only have their ultimate or sufficient reason the Necessary Being, who has the reason for his existence in himself.

46.   We must not, however, imagine, as some do, that because the eternal truths are dependent on God, they are therefore arbitrary and depend on his will, as Descartes, and after him M. [Pierre] Poiret, seem to have thought. This is true only of contingent truths, whose principle is *fitness* or the choice of *the best*; whereas necessary truths depend solely on his understanding, of which they are the internal object.

47.   Thus God alone is the primary Unity, or original simple substance, from which all monads, created and derived, are produced, and are born, so to speak, by continual fulgurations of the Divinity from moment to moment, limited by the receptivity of the created being, which is of its essence limited.

48.   There is in God *power*, which is the source of everything, *knowledge*, which contains the differentiation of the ideas, and finally *will*, which causes changes and productions according to the principle of what is best. And these correspond to what provides the ground or basis in created monads, the perceptive faculty and the appetitive faculty. But in God these attributes are absolutely infinite or perfect, while in created monads or in *entelechies* (or *perfectihabiae*, as Hermolaus Barbarus translated this word) there are only limitations of them, in proportion to the perfection there is in the monad.

49.   The created thing is said to *act* outwardly in so far as it has perfection, and to be *passively affected* by another in so far as it is imperfect. Thus *activity* is attributed to the monad in so far as it has distinct perceptions, and *passivity* in so far as it has confused perceptions.

50.   And one created thing is more perfect than another when there is found in it that which explains *a priori* what happens in the other; and it is because of this that we say that it acts upon the other.

51.   But in simple substances the influence of one monad over another is *ideal* only; it can have its effect only through the intervention of God, inasmuch as in the ideas of God a monad rightly demands that God, in regulating the rest from the beginning of things, should have regard to itself. For since it is impossible for a created monad to have a physical influence on the inner nature of another, this is the only way in which one can be dependent on another.

52.   And this is why actions and passions are mutual between created things. For when God compares two simple substances he finds in each reasons which oblige him to adapt the other to it, and consequently what is active in certain aspects is passive from another point of view: *active* in so

far as what is distinctly known in it explains what occurs in another, and *passive* in so far as the reason for what occurs in it is found in what is distinctly known in another.

53. Now as there is an infinite number of possible universes in the ideas of God, and as only one can exist, there must be a sufficient reason for God's choice, determining him to one rather than to another.

54. And this reason can only be found in the *fitness*, or in the degrees of perfection, which these worlds contain, each possible world having the right to claim existence in proportion to the perfection which it involves.

55. And it is this which causes the existence of the best, which God knows through his wisdom, chooses through his goodness, and produces through his power.

56. Now this *connexion* or adaptation of all created things with each, and of each with all the rest, means that each simple substance has relations which express all the others, and that consequently it is a perpetual living mirror of the universe.

57. And just as the same town, when looked at from different sides, appears quite different and is, as it were, multiplied *in perspective*, so also it happens that because of the infinite number of simple substances, it is as if there were as many different universes, which are however but different perspectives of a single universe in accordance with the different point of view of each monad.

58. And this is the means of obtaining as much variety as possible, but with the greatest order possible; that is to say, it is the means of obtaining as much perfection as possible.

59. Further it is this hypothesis alone (which I venture to regard as proved) which properly exalts the greatness of God. This M. Bayle recognised, when in his *Dictionary* (in the article 'Rorarius') he made objections, in which he was even inclined to believe that I attributed too much to God, and more than is possible. But he could not advance any reason why this universal harmony, which causes each substance exactly to express all the others through the relations which it has with them, should be impossible.

60. Moreover, there are evident from what I have just said the *a priori* reasons why things could not be otherwise than they are: namely, because God in regulating the whole had regard to each part, and particularly to each monad. The nature of the monad is representative, and consequently nothing can limit it to representing a part of things only, although it is true that its representation is confused as regards the detail of the whole universe and can only be distinct as regards a small part of things; that is to say as regards those which are either the nearest or the largest in relation to

each of the monads; otherwise each monad would be a divinity. It is not in the object, but in the modification of the knowledge of the object, that monads are limited. In a confused way they all go towards the infinite, towards the whole; but they are limited and distinguished from one another by the degrees of their distinct perceptions.

61.   And in this the compounds agree with the simples. For as the whole is a plenum, which means that the whole of matter is connected, and as in a plenum every movement has some effect on distant bodies in proportion to their distance, so that each body not only is affected by those which touch it, and is in some way sensitive to whatever happens to them, but also by means of them is sensitive to those which touch the first bodies by which it is itself directly touched; it follows that this communication stretches out indefinitely. Consequently every body is sensitive to everything which is happening in the universe, so much so that one who saw everything could read in each body what is happening everywhere, and even what has happened or what will happen, by observing in the present the things that are distant in time as well as in space; σύμπνοια πάντα ['Everything is in League'], as Hippocrates said. But a soul can read in itself only what is distinctly represented there; it is unable to develop all at once all the things that are folded within it, for they stretch to infinity.

62.   Thus although each created monad represents the whole universe, it represents more distinctly the body which is particularly affected by it, and whose entelechy it is: and as this body expresses the whole universe by the connexion of all matter in the plenum, the soul represents the whole universe also in representing the body which belongs to it in a particular way.

63.   The body belonging to a monad, which is that body's entelechy or soul, constitutes together with the entelechy what may be called a *living thing*, and with the soul what is called an *animal*. Now this body of a living thing or animal is always organic; for since every monad is in its way a mirror of the universe, and since the universe is regulated in a perfect order, there must also be an order in that which represents it, that is to say in the perceptions of the soul, and consequently in the body, according to which order the universe is represented therein.

64.   Thus each organic body of a living thing is a kind of divine machine, or natural automaton, which infinitely surpasses all artificial automata. Because a machine which is made by the art of man is not a machine in each of its parts; for example, the tooth of a metal wheel has parts or fragments which as far as we are concerned are not artificial and which have about them nothing of the character of a machine, in relation to the use for which the wheel was intended. But the machines of nature, that is to say living bodies, are still machines in the least of their parts *ad infinitum*. This

it is which makes the difference between nature and art, that is to say between Divine art and ours.

65.   And the Author of nature was enabled to practise this divine and infinitely marvellous artifice, because each portion of matter is not only infinitely divisible, as the ancients recognised, but is also actually subdivided without limit, each part into further parts, of which each one has some motion of its own: otherwise it would be impossible for each portion of matter to express the whole universe.

66.   Whence it is evident that there is a world of created beings – living things, animals, entelechies, and souls – in the least part of matter.

67.   Each portion of matter may be conceived as a garden full of plants, and as a pond full of fish. But every branch of each plant, every member of each animal, and every drop of their liquid parts is itself likewise a similar garden or pond.

68.   And although the earth and the air interspersed between the plants in the garden, or water interspersed between the fish in the pond, are neither plant nor fish, yet they still contain them, though most usually of a subtlety which renders them imperceptible to us.

69.   Thus there is nothing waste, nothing sterile, nothing dead in the universe; no chaos, no confusions, save in appearance. We might compare this to the appearance of a pond in the distance, where we can see the confused movement and swarming of the fish, without distinguishing the fish themselves.

70.   Thus we see that each living body has a dominant entelechy, which in the case of an animal is the soul, but the members of this living body are full of other living things, plants and animals, of which each has in turn its dominant entelechy or soul.

71.   But we must not imagine, as some have done who have misunderstood my view, that each soul has a mass or portion of matter appropriate or attached to itself for ever, and that it consequently possesses other inferior living things, for ever destined to its service. For all bodies are in a perpetual flux like rivers, and parts are passing in and out of them continually.

72.   Thus the soul only changes its body bit by bit and by degrees, so that it is never despoiled of all its organs all together; in animals there is often metamorphosis, but never metempsychosis, nor transmigration of souls: neither are there any entirely *separate souls*, nor *superhuman spirits* without bodies. God alone is entirely detached from body.

73.   It is because of this also that there is never, strictly speaking, absolute generation nor perfect death, consisting in the separation of the soul. And what we call *generation* is a development and a growth, while what we call *death* is an envelopment and a diminution.

74.   Philosophers have been much embarrassed over the origin of forms, entelechies or souls. But today when exact researches on plants, insects, and animals have revealed the fact that the organic bodies of nature are never produced from a chaos or from putrefaction, but always from seeds, wherein there was certainly some *preformation*, we conclude not only that the organic body was already present before conception, but also that there was a soul in this body; that, in a word, the animal itself was present, and that by means of conception it was merely prepared for a great transformation, so as to become an animal of another kind. We even see something of this kind apart from birth, as when worms become flies, and caterpillars become butterflies.

75.   The *animals*, of which some are raised by means of conception to the rank of the larger animals, may be called *spermatic*; but those among them which remain in their own kind (and they are the greater number) are born, multiply, and are destroyed like the large animals; and there is only a small number of elect ones who pass into a greater theatre.

76.   But this is only half the truth. And so I have judged that if the animal never begins naturally, neither does it end naturally; and that not only will there be no birth, but also no complete destruction, no death, strictly speaking. And these reasonings, which are *a posteriori* and derived from experience, agree perfectly with the principles which I have deduced *a priori* above.

77.   Thus one may say that not only is the soul (the mirror of an indestructible universe) itself indestructible, but so also is the animal itself, although its machine may often perish in part, and cast off or put on particular organic integuments.

78.   These principles provide me with a way of explaining naturally the union, or rather the conformity, of the soul and the organic body. The soul follows its own laws, and the body its own likewise, and they accord by virtue of the *harmony pre-established* among all substances, since they are all representations of one and the same universe.

79.   Souls act according to the laws of final causes by appetitions, ends, and means. Bodies act according to the laws of efficient causes by motions. And the two kingdoms, of efficient and of final causes, are in harmony with one another.

80.   Descartes recognised that souls cannot give force to bodies because there is always the same quantity of force in matter. He believed, however, that the soul could change the direction of bodies. But this is because in his day the law of nature was not known which affirms the conservation of the same total direction in matter.[4] Had he noticed this, he would have stumbled upon my system of Pre-established Harmony.

81.   Under this system, bodies act as though, *per impossibile*, there were no souls: and souls act as if there were no bodies, and both act as if each influenced the other.

82.   As for minds or rational souls, although I find that what I have just been saying is at bottom true of all living beings and animals (that is to say that the animal and the soul only begin with the world and do not come to an end any more than the world comes to an end), yet rational animals are peculiar in this, that their little spermatic animals, so long as they are that merely, have only ordinary or sensitive souls; but as soon as those which are, so to speak, elect arrive by an actual conception at human nature, then their sensitive souls are raised to the rank of reason and to the prerogative of minds.

83.   Among other differences which exist between ordinary souls and minds, some of which I have already pointed out, there is also this, that souls in general are the living mirrors or images of the universe of created things, whereas minds are also images of the Divinity himself, or the Author of nature, capable of knowing the system of the universe, and of imitating something of it by architectonic patterns, each mind being as it were a little divinity in its own department.

84.   This it is which renders minds capable of entering into a kind of society with God, and makes his relation to them not only that of an inventor to his machine (which is God's relation to the rest of created things) but also that of a prince to his subjects, and even of a father to his children.

85.   From this it is easy to conclude that the assemblage of all minds must make up the City of God, that is to say the most perfect possible state under the most perfect of monarchs.

86.   This City of God, this truly universal monarchy, is a moral world in the natural world, and is the most exalted and the most divine of God's works, and in it truly consists his glory, since he could not be glorified if his greatness and goodness were not known and wondered at by minds: it is also in relation to this divine City that he may properly be said to have goodness, whereas his wisdom and power are manifested everywhere.

87.   As we have established above a perfect harmony between two natural kingdoms, the one of efficient and the other of final causes, we ought here also to point out another harmony between the physical kingdom of nature and the moral kingdom of grace; that is to say between God as Architect of the machine of the universe, and God as Monarch of the divine City of Minds.

88.   This harmony means that things conduce to grace by the very ways of nature, and that this globe, for example, must be destroyed and repaired by natural ways at the times demanded by the government of minds for the chastisement of some and the reward of others.

89.   It can further be said that God as Architect satisfies God as Law-

giver in everything, and that thus sins carry their punishment with them by the order of nature, and by virtue of the mechanical structure of things itself; and that in the same way noble actions will attract their rewards by ways which are mechanical as far as bodies are concerned, although this cannot and should not always happen immediately.

90. Finally, under this perfect government there will be no good action without reward, no evil action without punishment, and everything must turn out for the good of the righteous, of those, that is, who are not dissatisfied in this great State, who trust in Providence when they have done their duty, and who love and imitate fittingly the Author of all good, delighting in the consideration of his perfections after the manner of true *pure love*, which makes us take pleasure in the happiness of the beloved. This it is which makes the wise and virtuous work for whatever seems to conform with the presumptive or antecedent will of God, and yet leaves them satisfied with what God in fact causes to happen by his secret will, which is consequent and decisive,[5] recognising as they do that if we could sufficiently understand the order of the universe, we should find that it surpasses all the desires of the most wise, and that it is impossible to make it better than it is, not only for the whole in general, but also for ourselves in particular, if we are attached as we should be to the Author of the whole, not merely as to the Architect and efficient Cause of our being, but also as to our Master and the final Cause which must constitute the whole end of our will, and which alone can constitute our happiness.

Notes

1 The reference here is probably to the properties which, according to some medieval philosophers, transferred themselves from objects on to the mind.

2 This is one of Leibniz's many statements of his principle of 'the identity of indiscernibles'. If x and y are different objects, x must possess at least one property which y lacks.

3 The point in these sections is that a 'truth of reasoning' is such that, on analysis of its terms, denial of it would be an explicit contradiction. For example, 'All vixens are foxes' can be analysed as 'All female foxes are foxes', a statement whose denial is plainly a contradiction. Leibniz's view, in later philosophical parlance, is that all necessary truths are 'analytic'.

4 This somewhat obscure point is explained at greater length in 'Explanation of the New System', §20, also in Leibniz's *Philosophical Writings*.

5 The translator explains that ' "Consequent will" ' refers to God's decisions (hence it is called 'decisive' in the *Monadology*), whereas the antecedent will only inclines'.

George Berkeley, *The Principles of Human Knowledge*, Part I (§§1–37)

From George Berkeley, *Philosophical Works*, ed. M. R. Ayers, London: J. M. Dent & Sons, 1995. pp. 77–87 (notes omitted).

Idealism – the broad view that reality is 'mental' – can, as pointed out in my Introduction, come in many shapes and sizes. We have encountered idealist systems in earlier chapters: in Śaṁkara's view that Brahman or the Absolute is consciousness, the familiar physical world being some kind of 'illusion' (chapter 5), and in Leibniz's claim that everything ultimately consists in monads, all of which are, if not minds, then certainly 'incorporeal' and mind*like* (chapter 9). Neither Śaṁkara nor Leibniz were concerned to deny the offence to commonsense caused by their theories. The Irish-born Bishop Berkeley (1685–1752), on the other hand, despite attracting charges of insanity and being a butt of Dr Johnson's jokes, argued that a main merit of his empiricist idealism was its consonance with commonsense. While noting the 'opinion strangely prevailing' that houses and mountains exist independently of being perceived (§4), he insists that this conflicts with the far more deeply and generally rooted convictions that we really do perceive such objects and do know for certain that they exist – convictions, he argues, which his own immaterialism alone can secure. For him, it is 'obvious', on just a little reflection, that all the things which compose the world have no existence 'without a mind, that their being is to be perceived' (§6).

Berkeley's claim, spelt out at the beginning of Part I of the *Principles*, is that we never perceive anything but our own 'ideas', and that objects such as houses are nothing but 'collections of ideas' which minds do or might experience. He goes on to argue that belief in a material world independent of perception is at best unsupported and superfluous, at worst incoherent. Our ideas do have an outside cause, but this is God, not matter. My selection ends with the early stages of Berkeley's attempt to show that his position is perfectly consonant with commonsense assumptions which it might seem to threaten, such as that there is a genuine difference between veridical and illusory experiences.

A main target is John Locke (chapter 8). Already in his Introduction, Berkeley has rejected Locke's doctrine of 'abstract general ideas' (see n. 1, p. 179 below). In Part I, Locke's distinction between primary and secondary qualities and his notion of material substances which 'support' qualities are both dismissed. Features which Locke takes to distinguish secondary qualities, such as their relativity to perceivers, are, Berkeley argues, equally true of size, solidity and other allegedly primary qualities. More crucially, Locke's claim that, in the case of primary qualities, our ideas of them 'resemble' qualities possessed by mind-independent objects, is declared to be absurd, for 'an idea can be like nothing but an idea' (§8). As for the notion of substances or substrata, this is declared to be unintelligible.

Although Berkeley spends some time attacking Locke's views (though not as much as in his *Three Dialogues Between Hylas and Philonous*), he states (§22) that he has been 'needlessly prolix' and that, 'in a line or two', the immaterialist thesis can be secured by another argument. This so-called 'master argument' is to the effect that the attempt even to conceive of unperceived or unthought things is self-defeating, for in imagining them you in effect perceive or think them, so that they turn out simply to be ideas of yours. As it stands, this argument has unwelcome implications for Berkeley's own philosophy. It would seem to show, for example, that in trying to conceive of God you turn Him into an idea in your mind. On a charitable interpretation, however, the argument is driving at an important thought: the impossibility of conceiving of anything except from *perspectives* which cannot be transcended in order to arrive at a conception of how anything in itself is.[1]

In the pages I have selected, one finds Berkeley apparently proposing two very different accounts of what it is for a tree or a house to exist when no one is perceiving it. (Clearly, if Berkeley is to succeed in reconciling his idealism with commonsense, *some* account of this is imperative.) In §3, the suggestion seems to be the 'phenomenalist' one – taken up by David Hume and elaborated by J. S. Mill (chapter 13 below) – that something can exist, though unperceived, only in the sense that I or someone else *would* perceive it if suitably placed to do so so.[2] But Berkeley's more considered and constant view is the one indicated in Ronald Knox's famous limerick about the unperceived tree in the Quad:

---

[1] See Howard Robinson, 'Berkeley', in N. Bunnin and E. P. Tsui-James (eds), *The Blackwell Companion to Philosophy*, Oxford: Blackwell, 1996, pp. 564ff. See, also, the same author's *Objections to Physicalism*, Oxford: Oxford University Press, 1995, and John Foster, *The Case for Idealism*, London: Routledge, 1982, for modern-day defences of Berkelian idealism.

[2] See G. J. Warnock, *Berkeley*, Harmondsworth: Penguin, 1953, for a phenomenalist reading of Berkeley.

I am always about in the Quad.
And that's why the tree
Will continue to be,
Since observed by *Yours Faithfully*, GOD.

More prosaically, an actual object unperceived by any human or animal ob-server is nevertheless always being perceived, as ideas in the mind of God.

For Berkeley, God's existence is not a matter of mere faith. As he argues in Part I (§§29ff), there must be some extremely powerful cause of the ideas I perceive, since I am aware of myself as the passive recipient of most of these. Since that cause cannot be matter, it must be an immaterial mind – a cause which has the further advantage of being intelligible to me, unlike matter, by way of analogy with my own self. Berkeley, arguably, is at his philosophically and theologically most acute, when showing the sheer redundancy of materi-alist hypotheses in accounting for our experiences once the existence of God is admitted. And the vision he offers is surely one that, for religious persons, might be a deeply satisfying one: the vision of human beings, whenever they see, smell, touch, taste or think being in direct receipt of ideas granted to them by God.

Berkeley, *Of the Principles of Human Knowledge*

Part I

1.   It is evident to anyone who takes a survey of the objects of human knowledge, that they are either ideas actually imprinted on the senses, or else such as are perceived by attending to the passions and operations of the mind, or lastly ideas formed by help of memory and imagination, either compounding, dividing, or barely representing those originally perceived in the aforesaid ways. By sight I have the ideas of light and colours with their several degrees and variations. By touch I perceive, for example, hard and soft, heat and cold, motion and resistance, and of all these more and less either as to quantity or degree. Smelling furnishes me with odours; the palate with tastes, and hearing conveys sounds to the mind in all their variety of tone and composition. And as several of these are observed to accompany each other, they come to be marked by one name, and so to be reputed as one thing. Thus, for example, a certain colour, taste, smell, figure and consistence having been observed to go together, are accounted one distinct thing, signified by the name *apple*. Other collections of ideas constitute a stone, a tree, a book, and the like sensible things; which, as

they are pleasing or disagreeable, excite the passions of love, hatred, joy, grief, and so forth.

2.   But besides all that endless variety of ideas or objects of knowledge, there is likewise something which knows or perceives them, and exercises divers operations, as willing, imagining, remembering about them. This perceiving, active being is what I call *mind, spirit, soul* or *myself*. By which words I do not denote any one of my ideas, but a thing entirely distinct from them, wherein they exist, or, which is the same thing, whereby they are perceived; for the existence of an idea consists in being perceived.

3.   That neither our thoughts, nor passions, nor ideas formed by the imagination, exist without the mind, is what everybody will allow. And it seems no less evident that the various sensations or ideas imprinted on the sense, however blended or combined together (that is, whatever objects they compose) cannot exist otherwise than in a mind perceiving them. I think an intuitive knowledge may be obtained of this, by anyone that shall attend to what is meant by the term *exist* when applied to sensible things. The table I write on, I say, exists, that is, I see and feel it; and if I were out of my study I should say it existed, meaning thereby that if I was in my study I might perceive it, or that some other spirit actually does perceive it. There was an odour, that is, it was smelled; there was a sound, that is to say, it was heard; a colour or figure, and it was perceived by sight or touch. This is all that I can understand by these and the like expressions. For as to what is said of the absolute existence of unthinking things without any relation to their being perceived, that seems perfectly unintelligible. Their *esse* is *percipi*, nor is it possible they should have any existence, out of the minds or thinking things which perceive them.

4.   It is indeed an opinion strangely prevailing amongst men, that houses, mountains, rivers, and in a word all sensible objects have an existence natural or real, distinct from their being perceived by the understanding. But with how great an assurance and acquiescence soever this principle may be entertained in the world; yet whoever shall find in his heart to call it in question, may, if I mistake not, perceive it to involve a manifest contradiction. For what are the forementioned objects but the things we perceive by sense, and what do we perceive besides our own ideas or sensations; and is it not plainly repugnant that any one of these or any combination of them should exist unperceived?

5.   If we thoroughly examine this tenet, it will, perhaps, be found at bottom to depend on the doctrine of *abstract ideas*.[1] For can there be a nicer strain of abstraction than to distinguish the existence of sensible objects from their being perceived, so as to conceive them existing unperceived? Light and colours, heat and cold, extension and figures, in a word the

things we see and feel, what are they but so many sensations, notions, ideas or impressions on the sense; and is it possible to separate, even in thought, any of these from perception? For my part I might as easily divide a thing from itself. I may indeed divide in my thoughts or conceive apart from each other those things which, perhaps, I never perceived by sense so divided. Thus I imagine the trunk of a human body without the limbs, or conceive the smell of a rose without thinking on the rose itself. So far I will not deny I can abstract, if that may properly be called *abstraction*, which extends only to the conceiving separately such objects, as it is possible may really exist or be actually perceived asunder. But by conceiving or imagining power does not extend beyond the possibility of real existence or perception. Hence as it is impossible for me to see or feel anything without an actual sensation of that thing, so is it impossible for me to conceive in my thoughts any sensible thing or object distinct from the sensation or perception of it.

6. Some truths there are so near and obvious to the mind, that a man need only open his eyes to see them. Such I take this important one to be, to wit, that all the choir of heaven and furniture of the earth, in a word all those bodies which compose the mighty frame of the world, have not any subsistence without a mind, that their being is to be perceived or known; that consequently so long as they are not actually perceived by me, or do not exist in my mind or that of any other created spirit, they must either have no existence at all, or else subsist in the mind of some eternal spirit: it being perfectly unintelligible and involving all the absurdity of abstraction, to attribute to any single part of them an existence independent of a spirit. To be convinced of which, the reader need only reflect and try to separate in his own thoughts the being of a sensible thing from its being perceived.

7. From what has been said, it follows, there is not any other substance than *spirit*, or that which perceives. But for the fuller proof of this point, let it be considered, the sensible qualities are colour, figure, motion, smell, taste, and such like, that is, the ideas perceived by sense. Now for an idea to exist in an unperceiving thing, is a manifest contradiction; for to have an idea is all one as to perceive: that therefore wherein colour, figure, and the like qualities exist, must perceive them; hence it is clear there can be no unthinking substance or *substratum* of those ideas.

8. But say you, though the ideas themselves do not exist without the mind, yet there may be things like them whereof they are copies or resemblances, which things exist without the mind, in an unthinking substance. I answer, an idea can be like nothing but an idea; a colour or figure can be like nothing but another colour or figure. If we look but ever so little into our thoughts, we shall find it impossible for us to conceive a likeness except only between our ideas. Again, I ask whether those supposed originals or

external things, of which our ideas are the pictures or representations, be themselves perceivable or no? If they are, then they are ideas, and we have gained our point; but if you say they are not, I appeal to anyone whether it be sense, to assert a colour is like something which is invisible; hard or soft, like something which is intangible; and so of the rest.

9.   Some there are who make a distinction betwixt *primary* and *secondary* qualities: by the former, they mean extension, figure, motion, rest, solidity or impenetrability and number: by the latter they denote all other sensible qualities, as colours, sounds, tastes, and so forth. The ideas we have of these they acknowledge not to be the resemblances of anything existing without the mind or unperceived; but they will have our ideas of the primary qualities to be patterns or images of things which exist without the mind, in an unthinking substance which they call *matter*. By matter therefore we are to understand an inert, senseless substance, in which extension, figure, and motion, do actually subsist. But it is evident from what we have already shewn, that extension, figure and motion are only ideas existing in the mind, and that an idea can be like nothing but another idea, and that consequently neither they nor their archetypes can exist in an unperceiving substance. Hence it is plain, that the very notion of what is called *matter* or *corporeal substance*, involves a contradiction in it.

10.   They who assert that figure, motion, and the rest of the primary or original qualities do exist without the mind, in unthinking substances, do at the same time acknowledge that colours, sounds, heat, cold, and such like secondary qualities, do not, which they tell us are sensations existing in the mind alone, that depend on and are occasioned by the different size, texture and motion of the minute particles of matter. This they take for an undoubted truth, which they can demonstrate beyond all exception. Now if it be certain, that those original qualities are inseparably united with the other sensible qualities, and not, even in thought, capable of being abstracted from them, it plainly follows that they exist only in the mind. But I desire anyone to reflect and try, whether he can by any abstraction of thought, conceive the extension and motion of a body, without all other sensible qualities. For my own part, I see evidently that it is not in my power to frame an idea of a body extended and moved, but I must withal give it some colour or other sensible quality which is acknowledged to exist only in the mind. In short, extension, figure and motion, abstracted from all other qualities, are inconceivable. Where therefore the other sensible qualities are, there must these be also, to wit, in the mind and nowhere else.

11.   Again, *great* and *small*, *swift* and *slow*, are allowed to exist nowhere without the mind, being entirely relative, and changing as the frame or

position of the organs of sense varies. The extension therefore which exists without the mind, is neither great nor small, the motion neither swift nor slow, that is, they are nothing at all. But say you, they are extension in general, and motion in general: thus we see how much the tenet of extended, moveable substances existing without the mind, depends on that strange doctrine of *abstract ideas*. And here I cannot but remark, how nearly the vague and indeterminate description of matter or corporeal substance, which the modern philosophers are run into by their own principles, resembles that antiquated and so much ridiculed notion of *materia prima* ['prime matter'], to be met with in Aristotle and his followers. Without extension solidity cannot be conceived; since therefore it has been shewn that extension exists not in an unthinking substance, the same must also be true of solidity.

12.   That number is entirely the creature of the mind, even though the other qualities be allowed to exist without, will be evident to whoever considers, that the same thing bears a different denomination of number, as the mind views it with different respects. Thus, the same extension is one or three or thirty-six, according as the mind considers it with reference to a yard, a foot, or an inch. Number is so visibly relative, and dependent on men's understanding, that it is strange to think how anyone should give it an absolute existence without the mind. We say one book, one page, one line; all these are equally units, though some contain several of the others. And in each instance it is plain, the unit relates to some particular combination of ideas arbitrarily put together by the mind.

13.   Unity I know some will have to a simple or uncompounded idea, accompanying all other ideas into the mind. That I have any such idea answering the word *unity*, I do not find; and if I had, methinks I could not miss finding it; on the contrary it should be the most familiar to my understanding, since it is said to accompany all other ideas, and to be perceived by all the ways of sensation and reflexion. To say no more, it is an *abstract idea*.

14.   I shall farther add, that after the same manner, as modern philosophers prove certain sensible qualities to have no existence in matter, or without the mind, the same thing may be likewise proved of all other sensible qualities whatsoever. Thus, for instance, it is said that heat and cold are affections only of the mind, and not at all patterns of real beings, existing in the corporeal substances which excite them, for that the same body which appears cold to one hand, seems warm to another. Now why may we not as well argue that figure and extension are not patterns or resemblances of qualities existing in matter, because to the same eye at different stations, or eyes of a different texture at the same station, they appear various, and cannot therefore be the images of anything settled and determinate with-

out the mind? Again, it is proved that sweetness is not really in the sapid thing, because the thing remaining unaltered the sweetness is changed into bitter, as in case of a fever or otherwise vitiated palate. Is it not as reasonable to say, that motion is not without the mind, since if the succession of ideas in the mind become swifter, the motion, it is acknowledged, shall appear slower without any alteration in any external object.

15.   In short, let anyone consider those arguments, which are thought manifestly to prove that colours and tastes exist only in the mind, and he shall find they may with equal force, be brought to prove the same thing of extension, figure, and motion. Though it must be confessed this method of arguing doth not much prove that there is no extension or colour in an outward object, as that we do not know by sense which is the true extension or colour of the object. But the arguments foregoing plainly shew it to be impossible that any colour or extension at all, or other sensible quality whatsoever, should exist in an unthinking subject without the mind, or in truth, that there should be any such thing as an outward object.

16.   But let us examine a little the received opinion. It is said extension is a mode or accident of matter, and that matter is the *substratum* that supports it. Now I desire that you would explain what is meant by matter's *supporting* extension: say you, I have no idea of matter, and therefore cannot explain it. I answer, though you have no positive, yet if you have any meaning at all, you must at least have a relative idea of matter; though you know not what it is, yet you must be supposed to know what relation it bears to accidents, and what is meant by its supporting them. It is evident *support* cannot here be taken in its usual or literal sense, as when we say that pillars support a building: in what sense therefore must it be taken?

17.   If we inquire into what the most accurate philosophers declare themselves to mean by *material substance*; we shall find them acknowledge, they have no other meaning annexed to those sounds, but the idea of being in general, together with the relative notion of its supporting accidents. The general idea of being appeareth to me the most abstract and incomprehensible of all other; and as for its supporting accidents, this, as we have just now observed, cannot be understood in the common sense of those words; it must therefore be taken in some other sense, but what that is they do not explain. So that when I consider the two parts or branches which make the signification of the words *material substance*, I am convinced there is no distinct meaning annexed to them. But why should we trouble ourselves any farther, in discussing this material *substratum* or support of figure and motion, and other sensible qualities? Does it not suppose they have an existence without the mind? And is not this a direct repugnancy, and altogether inconceivable?

18.   But though it were possible that solid, figured, moveable substances may exist without the mind, corresponding to the ideas we have of bodies, yet how is it possible for us to know this? Either we must know it by sense, or by reason. As for our senses, by them we have the knowledge only of our sensations, ideas, or those things that are immediately perceived by sense, call them what you will: but they do not inform us that things exist without the mind, or unperceived, like to those which are perceived. This the materialists themselves acknowledge. It remains therefore that if we have any knowledge at all of external things, it must be by reason, inferring their existence from what is immediately perceived by sense. But what reason can induce us to believe the existence of bodies without the mind, from what we perceive, since the very patrons of matter themselves do not pretend, there is any necessary connexion betwixt them and our ideas? I say it is granted on all hands (and what happens in dreams, phrensies, and the like, puts it beyond dispute) that it is possible we might be affected with all the ideas we have now, though no bodies existed without, resembling them. Hence it is evident the supposition of external bodies is not necessary for the producing our ideas: since it is granted they are produced sometimes, and might possibly be produced always in the same order we see them in at present, without their concurrence.

19.   But though we might possibly have all our sensations without them, yet perhaps it may be thought easier to conceive and explain the manner of their production, by supposing external bodies in their likeness rather than otherwise; and so it might be at least probable there are such things as bodies that excite their ideas in our minds. But neither can this be said; for though we give the materialists their external bodies, they by their own confession are never the nearer knowing how our ideas are produced: since they own themselves unable to comprehend in what manner body can act upon spirit, or how it is possible it should imprint any idea in the mind. Hence it is evident the production of ideas or sensations in our minds, can be no reason why we should suppose matter or corporeal substances, since that is acknowledged to remain equally inexplicable with, or without this supposition. If therefore it were possible for bodies to exist without the mind, yet to hold they do so, must needs be a very precarious opinion; since it is to suppose, without any reason at all, that God has created innumerable beings that are entirely useless, and serve to no manner of purpose.

20.   In short, if there were external bodies, it is impossible we should ever come to know it; and if there were not, we might have the very same reasons to think there were that we have now. Suppose, what no one can deny possible, an intelligence, without the help of external bodies, to be

affected with the same train of sensations or ideas that you are, imprinted in the same order and with like vividness in his mind. I ask whether that intelligence hath not all the reason to believe the existence of corporeal substances, represented by his ideas, and exciting them in his mind, that you can possibly have for believing the same thing? Of this there can be no question; which one consideration is enough to make any reasonable person suspect the strength of whatever arguments he may think himself to have, for the existence of bodies without the mind.

21.   Were it necessary to add any farther proof against the existence of matter, after what has been said, I could instance several of those errors and difficulties (not to mention impieties) which have sprung from that tenet. It has occasioned numberless controversies and disputes in philosophy, and not a few of far greater moment in religion. But I shall not enter into the detail of them in this place, as well because I think, arguments *a posteriori* are unnecessary for confirming what has been, if I mistake not, sufficiently demonstrated *a priori*, as because I shall hereafter find occasion to say somewhat of them.

22.   I am afraid I have given cause to think me needlessly prolix in handling this subject. For to what purpose is it to dilate on that which may be demonstrated with the utmost evidence in a line or two, to anyone that is capable of the least reflexion? It is but looking into your own thoughts, and so trying whether you can conceive it possible for a sound, or figure, or motion, or colour, to exist without the mind, or unperceived. This easy trial may make you see, that what you contend for, is a downright contradiction. Insomuch that I am content to put the whole upon this issue; if you can but conceive it possible for one extended moveable substance, or in general, for any one idea or anything like an idea, to exist otherwise than in a mind perceiving it, I shall readily give up the cause: and as for all that *compages* of external bodies which you contend for, I shall grant you its existence, though you cannot either give me any reason why you believe it exists, or assign any use to it when it is supposed to exist. I say, the bare possibility of your opinion's being true, shall pass for an argument that it is so.

23.   But say you, surely there is nothing easier than to imagine trees, for instance, in a park, or books existing in a closet, and nobody by to perceive them. I answer, you may so, there is no difficulty in it: but what is all this, I beseech you, more than framing in your mind certain ideas which you call *books* and *trees*, and at the same time omitting to frame the idea of anyone that may perceive them? But do not you yourself perceive or think of them all the while? This therefore is nothing to the purpose: it only shows you have the power of imagining or forming ideas in your mind; but

it doth not shew that you can conceive it possible, the objects of your thought may exist without the mind: to make out this, it is necessary that you conceive them existing unconceived or unthought of, which is a manifest repugnancy. When we do our utmost to conceive the existence of external bodies, we are all the while only contemplating our own ideas. But the mind taking no notice of itself, is deluded to think it can and doth conceive bodies existing unthought of or without the mind; though at the same time they are apprehended by or exist in itself. A little attention will discover to anyone the truth and evidence of what is here said, and make it unnecessary to insist on any other proofs against the existence of material substance.

24.   It is very obvious, upon the least inquiry into our own thoughts, to know whether it be possible for us to understand what is meant, by the *absolute existence of sensible objects in themselves, or without the mind.* To me it is evident those words mark out either a direct contradiction, or else nothing at all. And to convince others of this, I know no readier or fairer way, than to entreat they would calmly attend to their own thoughts: and if by this attention, the emptiness or repugnancy of those expressions does appear, surely nothing more is requisite for their conviction. It is on this therefore that I insist, to wit, that the absolute existence of unthinking things are words without a meaning, or which include a contradiction. This is what I repeat and inculcate, and earnestly recommend to the attentive thoughts of the reader.

25.   All our ideas, sensations, or the things which we perceive, by whatsoever names they may be distinguished, are visibly inactive, there is nothing of power or agency included in them. So that one idea or object of thought cannot produce, or make any alternation in another. To be satisfied of the truth of this, there is nothing else requisite but a bare observation of our ideas. For since they and every part of them exist only in the mind, it follows that there is nothing in them but what is perceived. But whoever shall attend to his ideas, whether of sense or reflexion, will not perceive in them any power or activity; there is therefore no such thing contained in them. A little attention will discover to us that the very being of an idea implies passiveness and inertness in it, insomuch that it is impossible for an idea to do anything, or, strictly speaking, to be the cause of anything: neither can it be the resemblance or pattern of any active being, as is evident from *Sect.* 8. Whence it plainly follows that extension, figure and motion, cannot be the cause of our sensations. To say therefore, that these are the effects of powers resulting from the configuration, number, motion, and size of corpuscles, must certainly be false.

26.   We perceive a continual succession of ideas, some are anew ex-

cited, others are changed or totally disappear. There is therefore some cause of these ideas whereon they depend, and which produces and changes them. That this cause cannot be any quality or idea or combination of ideas, is clear from the preceding section. It must therefore be a substance; but it has been shewn that there is no corporeal or material substance: it remains therefore that the cause of ideas is an incorporeal active substance or spirit.

27.   A spirit is one simple, undivided, active being: as it perceives ideas, it is called the *understanding*, and as it produces or otherwise operates about them, it is called the *will*. Hence there can be no idea formed of a soul or spirit: for all ideas whatever, being passive and inert, *vide Sect.* 25, they cannot represent unto us, by way of image or likeness, that which acts. A little attention will make it plain to anyone, that to have an idea which shall be like that active principle of motion and change of ideas, is absolutely impossible. Such is the nature of *spirit* or that which acts, that it cannot be of itself perceived, but only by the effects which it produceth. If any man shall doubt of the truth of what is here delivered, let him but reflect and try if he can frame the idea of any power or active being; and whether he hath ideas of two principal powers, marked by the names *will* and *understanding*, distinct from each other as well as from a third idea of substance or being in general, with a relative notion of its supporting or being the subject of the aforesaid powers, which is signified by the name *soul or spirit*. This is what some hold; but so far as I can see, the words *will, soul, spirit*, do not stand for different ideas, or in truth, for any idea at all, but for something which is very different from ideas, and which being an agent cannot be like unto, or represented by, any idea whatsoever. Though it must be owned at the same time, that we have some notion of soul, spirit, and the operations of the mind, such as willing, loving, hating, in as much as we know or understand the meaning of those words.

28.   I find I can excite ideas in my mind at pleasure, and vary and shift the scene as oft as I think fit. It is no more than willing, and straightway this or that idea arises in my fancy: and by the same power it is obliterated, and makes way for another. This making and unmaking of ideas doth very properly denominate the mind active. Thus much is certain, and grounded on experience: but when we talk of unthinking agents, or of exciting ideas exclusive of volition, we only amuse ourselves with words.

29.   But whatever power I may have over my own thoughts, I find the ideas actually perceived by sense have not a like dependence on my will. When in broad day-light I open my eyes, it is not in my power to choose whether I shall see or no, or to determine what particular objects shall present themselves to my view; and so likewise as to the hearing and other

senses, the ideas imprinted on them are not creatures of my will. There is therefore some other will or spirit that produces them.

30. The ideas of sense are more strong, lively, and distinct than those of the imagination; they have likewise a steadiness, order, and coherence, and are not excited at random, as those which are the effects of human wills often are, but in a regular train or series, the admirable connexion whereof sufficiently testifies the wisdom and benevolence of its Author. Now the set rules or established methods, wherein the mind we depend on excites in us the ideas of sense, are called the *Laws of Nature*: and these we learn by experience, which teaches us that such and such ideas are attended with such and such other ideas, in the ordinary course of things.

31. This gives us a sort of foresight, which enables us to regulate our actions for the benefit of life. And without this we should be eternally at a loss: we could not know how to act anything that might procure us the least pleasure, or remove the least pain of sense. That food nourishes, sleep refreshes, and fire warms us; that to sow in the seed-time is the way to reap in the harvest, and, in general, that to obtain such or such ends, such or such means are conducive, all this we know, not by discovering any necessary connexion between our ideas, but only by the observation of the settled laws of Nature, without which we should be all in uncertainty and confusion, and a grown man no more know how to manage himself in the affairs of life, than an infant just born.

32. And yet this consistent uniform working, which so evidently displays the goodness and wisdom of that governing spirit whose will constitutes the Laws of Nature, is so far from leading our thoughts to him, that it rather sends them a wandering after second causes. For when we perceive certain ideas of sense constantly followed by other ideas, and we know this is not of our doing, we forthwith attribute power and agency to the ideas themselves, and make one the cause of another, than which nothing can be more absurd and unintelligible. Thus, for example, having observed that when we perceive by sight a certain round luminous figure, we at the same time perceive by touch the idea or sensation called *heat*, we do from thence conclude the sun to be the cause of heat. And in like manner perceiving the motion and collision of bodies to be attended with sound, we are inclined to think the latter an effect of the former.

33. The ideas imprinted on the senses by the Author of Nature are called *real things*: and those excited in the imagination being less regular, vivid and constant, are more properly termed *ideas*, or *images of things*, which they copy and represent. But then our sensations, be they never so vivid and distinct, are nevertheless *ideas*, that is, they exist in the mind, or are perceived by it, as truly as the ideas of its own framing. The ideas of

sense are allowed to have more reality in them, that is, to be more strong, orderly, and coherent than the creatures of the mind; but this is no argument that they exist without the mind. They are also less dependent on the spirit, or thinking substance which perceives them, in that they are excited by the will of another and more powerful spirit: yet still they are *ideas*, and certainly no *idea*, whether faint or strong, can exist otherwise than in a mind perceiving it.

34.   Before we proceed any farther, it is necessary to spend some time in answering objections which may probably be made against the principles hitherto laid down. In doing of which, if I seem too prolix to those of quick apprehensions, I hope it may be pardoned, since all men do not equally apprehend things of this nature; and I am willing to be understood by everyone. First then, it will be objected that by the foregoing principles, all that is real and substantial in Nature is banished out of the world: and instead thereof a chimerical scheme of ideas takes place. All things that exist, exist only in the mind, that is, they are purely notional. What therefore becomes of the sun, moon, and stars? What must we think of houses, rivers, mountains, trees, stones; nay, even of our own bodies? Are all these but so many chimeras and illusions on the fancy? To all which, and whatever else of the same sort may be objected, I answer, that by the principles premised, we are not deprived of any one thing in Nature. Whatever we see, feel, hear, or any wise conceive or understand, remains as secure as ever, and is as real as ever. There is a *rerum natura*, and the distinction between realities and chimeras retains its full force. This is evident from *Sect.* 29, 30, and 33, where we have shewn what is meant by *real things* in opposition to *chimeras*, or ideas of our own framing; but then they both equally exist in the mind, and in that sense are alike *ideas*.

35.   I do not argue against the existence of any one thing that we can apprehend, either by sense or reflexion. That the things I see with mine eyes and touch with my hands do exist, really exist, I make not the least question. The only thing whose existence we deny, is that which philosophers call matter or corporeal substance. And in doing of this, there is no damage done to the rest of mankind, who, I dare say, will never miss it. The atheist indeed will want the colour of an empty name to support his impiety; and the philosophers may possibly find, they have lost a great handle for trifling and disputation.

36.   If any man thinks this detracts from the existence or reality of things, he is very far from understanding what hath been premised in the plainest terms I could think of. Take here an abstract of what has been said. There are spiritual substances, minds, or human souls, which will or excite ideas in themselves at pleasure: but these are faint, weak, and unsteady in respect

of others they perceive by sense, which being impressed upon them according to certain rules or laws of Nature, speak themselves the effects of a mind more powerful and wise than human spirits. These latter are said to have more *reality* in them than the former: by which is meant that they are more affecting, orderly, and distinct, and that they are not fictions of the mind perceiving them. And in this sense, the sun that I see by day is the real sun, and that which I imagine by night is the idea of the former. In the sense here given of *reality*, it is evident that every vegetable, star, mineral, and in general each part of the mundane system, is as much a *real being* by our principles as by any other. Whether others mean anything by the term *reality* different from what I do, I entreat them to look into their own thoughts and see.[2]

37.   It will be urged that thus much at least is true, to wit, that we take away all corporeal substances. To this my answer is, that if the word *substance* be taken in the vulgar sense, for a combination of sensible qualities, such as extension, solidity, weight, and the like; this we cannot be accused of taking away. But if it be taken in a philosophic sense, for the support of accidents or qualities without the mind: then indeed I acknowledge that we take it away, if one may be said to take away that which never had any existence, not even in the imagination. . . .

Notes

1 As Berkeley understands it, this is Locke's doctrine to the effect that a general concept, like *triangle*, is an indefinite image formed by abstraction from particular ideas, such as perceptions of particular triangles. Berkeley insists, in the Introduction to the *Principles*, that all ideas are particular, though they may be put to general use by being made to 'stand for' other ideas. For example, I may use an idea of a particular triangle to represent triangles at large. Berkeley does not explain how the doctrine of materialism depends on that of abstract ideas. Presumably, though, the thought is this. If we do have an idea of matter or materiality at all, it must be an abstract one: since there are no abstract ideas, then we do not have such an idea.

2 This section records as robustly as any Berkeley's conviction that his idealism disposes of scepticism about the reality of physical objects. Many commentators, including Hume, think that Berkeley's denial of matter gives to the sceptic everything the latter could want. Berkeley's view, however, is that if a house simply is a collection of ideas perceived by us or by God, then its existence is as certain as that of ideas. There is, so to speak, no gap between ideas and objects of the kind the sceptic exploits in trying to cast doubt on a correspondence between the order of ideas and the order of things.

Immanuel Kant, *Critique of Pure Reason*, [second edition], Transcendental Aesthetic (§§1–3, 8)

From Immanuel Kant, *Critique of Pure Reason*, trans. Werner S. Pluhar. Indianapolis: Hackett Publishing Co., Inc., 1996, pp. 71–84, 94–104 (most notes omitted. Asterisked note is Kant's). Copyright © 1996 by Hackett Publishing Co., Inc. Reprinted by permission of Hackett Publishing Co., Inc. All rights reserved.

Immanuel Kant (1724–1804) perceived metaphysics in his day as a 'combat ground' on which rival thinkers were 'groping about' with no clear criteria for adjudicating among their competing systems. If what should be the greatest of the sciences is to overcome this 'shaky state of uncertainty and contradictions', its protagonists must first attend to the methodological question 'How is metaphysics possible?'. In the Introduction to his greatest work, *Critique of Pure Reason*, Kant converted this question into 'How are synthetic *a priori* judgements possible?'. These are judgements which, while necessarily true and so immune to refutation by experience, are not merely 'trivial' or analytic judgements guaranteed by the meanings of the concepts they contain. They include, for example, the principle that everything takes place according to the law of causality, as well as the truths of mathematics. Kant's revolutionary answer to the question of how such judgements are possible not only indicates the proper method for metaphysics, but is the key to the development of his own metaphysical system of Transcendental Idealism.

Much of Kant's enquiry concerns the *a priori* conditions for our *understanding* anything: but he sharply distinguishes these from the conditions for our having sensory experiences or 'intuitions'. The 'Transcendental Aesthetic', which has nothing to do with 'aesthetics' in the modern sense, attempts to establish the 'principles of *a priori* sensibility'. Kant's first central claim, here, is that the *a priori* conditions of the mind's intuitions of 'outer' objects and its own 'inner' states are space and time respectively. My selection focuses on the former (most of Kant's claims about time are closely analogous to those he makes about space, as §8 makes clear). The insistence that our experience of what is 'outer' must be spatial is not the dull point that what is spatially outside us gets experienced as such, but the contentious claim that objects which are 'outer' in the sense of being objective – distinct, that is, from our own 'inner' states – must be spatially locatable.[1]

Space, like time, has always been a topic of metaphysical interest, not least because of the puzzles about infinity it seems to generate. Kant himself addresses such issues later in the *Critique*, and in the Transcendental Aesthetic several of the points he makes about space are of interest in their own right – for example, his rejection of Leibniz's view that space is simply a relation between objects or their parts. But in the context of the present volume, it is the strategic place of Kant's discussion in his overall metaphysics which is crucial.

The startling conclusion he draws from his observations about space is that it is not a property of things as they are in themselves, but only 'the subjective condition of sensibility' under which objects are experienced by us. Hence it is 'only from the human standpoint' that we may speak of space, of extended things, and so on (B 42). Given how central a feature of the empirical world its spatial order surely is, then, if Kant's conclusion is correct, he is well on the way to establishing his general thesis that how this world must be is due to *our* 'imposition' of form and structure. Kant's conclusion may seem to put him on the side of Berkeley (chapter 10 above), and against Locke (chapter 8 above), by denying that space is a property of an external world. But Kant insists that he an 'empirical realist' about space, for there really are 'outer' objects, which must be spatial: it's just that, from the transcendental viewpoint, even 'outer' objects are 'appearances' of things in themselves, the nature of these latter being completely unknowable.

Kant deploys a number of arguments to establish the 'ideality' of space, and commentators differ as to which of these is the weightiest.[2] One is 'the argument from geometry' (B 41, 47ff), according to which Euclid's propositions are synthetic *a priori* truths – something they could not be if they were, *per impossibile*, descriptions of how things in themselves are. Another rests on the claim that 'through outer sense we are given nothing but mere relational presentations', and hence we cannot penetrate 'the intrinsic character belonging to the object in itself' (B 67).[3] But perhaps Kant's most powerful argument is what has been called 'the argument from elimination'.[4] There are only so many ways in which one could try to account for our *a priori* knowledge that objects

[1] P. F. Strawson, *The Bounds of Sense: an essay on Kant's* Critique of Pure Reason, London: Methuen, 1966, skilfully explains this and many other points.

[2] See the dispue between Strawson (*The Bounds of Sense*), and Henry E. Allison, *Kant's Transcendental Idealism*, New Haven: Yale University Press, 1983, over the weight to be attached to 'the argument from geometry', discussed below.

[3] Rae Langton, *Kantian Humility: our ignorance of things in themselves*, Oxford: Clarendon Press, 1998, puts this argument of Kant's to interesting use.

[4] See Allison, *Kant's Transcendental Idealism*.

are spatial – Leibniz's relational theory, for example. If, as Kant tries to show, all but his own account *definitely* fail then, like it or not, his must win the day.

Needless to say, Kant's arguments and conclusion have often been challenged. Certainly 'the argument from geometry' is open to the charge that Kant fails to distinguish between treating Euclid's theorems as uninterpreted, 'formal' consequences of definitions, and regarding them as physically interpreted accounts of reality. Treated one way, they are necessarily true, but only 'analytic'. Treated the other way, they are 'synthetic', but may not be true at all, let alone necessarily true. Other critics, while conceding that space and time may be necessary forms of our sensibility, are puzzled as to why this should rule out the possibility that they are *also* features of things in themselves.[5] Nevertheless, Kant's philosophy of space and time, like his wider metaphysics to which it is integral, continues to have its champions. Metaphysics, despite Kant's efforts, remains the 'combat ground' it was in his own day.

 ## Transcendental Aesthetic

§1

In whatever way and by whatever means a cognition may refer to objects, still *intuition* is that by which a cognition refers to objects directly, and at which all thought aims as a means. Intuition, however, takes place only insofar as the object is given to us; but that, in turn, is possible only – for us human beings, at any rate[1] – by the mind's being affected in a certain manner. The capacity (a receptivity) to acquire presentations as a result of the way in which we are affected by objects is called **sensibility**. Hence by means of sensibility objects are *given* to us, and it alone supplies us with *intuitions.* Through understanding, on the other hand, objects are *thought*, and from it arise *concepts*. But all thought must, by means of certain characteristics, refer ultimately to intuitions, whether it does so straightforwardly (*directe*) or circuitously (*indirecte*); and hence it must, in us [human beings], refer ultimately to sensibility, because no object can be given to us in any other manner than through sensibility.

B 34   The effect of an object on our capacity for presentation, insofar as we are
A 20   affected by the object, is *sensation*. Intuition that refers to the object through sensation is called *empirical* intuition. The undetermined object of an empirical intuition is called *appearance*.

---

[5] See, for example, Stefan Körner, *Kant*, Harmondsworth: Penguin, 1955.

Whatever in an appearance corresponds to sensation I call its *matter*; but whatever in an appearance brings about the fact that the manifold of the appearance can be ordered in certain relations I call the *form* of appearance. Now, that in which alone sensations can be ordered and put into a certain form cannot itself be sensation again. Therefore, although the matter of all appearance is given to us only a posteriori, the form of all appearance must altogether lie ready for the sensations a priori in the mind; and hence that form must be capable of being examined apart from all sensation.

All presentations in which nothing is found that belongs to sensation I call *pure* (in the transcendental sense of the term). Accordingly, the pure form of sensible intuitions generally, in which everything manifold in experience is intuited in certain relations, will be found in the mind a priori. This pure form of sensibility will also itself be called *pure intuition*. Thus, if   B 35
from the presentation of a body I separate what the understanding thinks in it, such as substance, force, divisibility, etc., and if I similarly separate from it what belongs to sensation in it, such as impenetrability, hardness, color, etc., I am still left with something from this empirical intuition,   A 21
namely, extension and shape. These belong to pure intuition, which, even if there is no actual object of the senses or of sensation, has its place in the mind a priori, as a mere form of sensibility.

There must, therefore, be a science of all principles of a priori sensibility; I call such a science *transcendental aesthetic*. It constitutes the first part of   B 36
the transcendental doctrine of elements, and stands in contrast to that [part of the] transcendental doctrine of elements which contains the principles of pure thought and is called transcendental logic.

Hence in the transcendental aesthetic we shall, first of all, *isolate* sensibil-   A 22
ity, by separating from it everything that the understanding through its concepts thinks [in connection] with it, so that nothing other than empirical intuition will remain. Second, we shall also segregate from sensibility everything that belongs to sensation, so that nothing will remain but pure intuition and the mere form of appearances, which is all that sensibility can supply a priori. In the course of that inquiry it will be found that there are two pure forms of sensible intuition, which are principles for a priori cognition: viz., space and time. We now proceed to the task of examining these.

Section I
Space

§2
Metaphysical Exposition of this Concept

By means of outer sense (a property of our mind) we present objects as outside us, and present them one and all in space. In space their shape, magnitude, and relation to one another are determined or determinable. By means of inner sense the mind intuits itself, or its inner state. Although inner sense provides no intuition of the soul itself as an object, yet there is a determinate form under which alone [as condition] we can intuit the soul's inner state. [That form is time.] Thus everything belonging to our inner determinations is presented in relations of time. Time cannot be intuited outwardly, any more than space can be intuited as something within us. What, then, are space and time? Are they actual beings? Are they only determinations of things, or, for that matter, relations among them? If so, are they at least determinations or relations that would belong to things intrinsically also, i.e., even if these things were not intuited? Or are they determinations and relations that adhere only to the form of intuition and hence to the subjective character of our mind, so that apart from that character these predicates cannot be ascribed to any thing at all? In order to inform ourselves on these points, let us first of all give an exposition of the concept of space. Now, by *exposition* (*expositio*) I mean clear (even if not comprehensive) presentation of what belongs to a concept; and such exposition is *metaphysical* if it contains what exhibits the concept as *given a priori*.

1.   Space is not an empirical concept that has been abstracted from outer experiences. For the presentation of space must already lie at the basis in order for certain sensations to be referred to something outside me (i.e., referred to something in a location of space other than the location in which I am). And it must similarly already lie at the basis in order for me to be able to present [the objects of] these sensations as outside and *alongside* one another, and hence to present them not only as different but as being in different locations. Accordingly, the presentation of space cannot be one that we take from the relations of outer appearance by means of experience; rather, only through the presentation of space is that outer experience possible in the first place.

2.   Space is a necessary a priori presentation that underlies all outer intuitions. We can never have a presentation of there being no space, even

A 23

B 38

A 24

though we are quite able to think of there being no objects encountered in
it. Hence space must be regarded as the condition for the possibility of
appearances, and not as a determination dependent on them. Space is an a
priori presentation that necessarily underlies outer appearances.

3.   Space is not a discursive or, as we say, universal concept of things as
such; rather, it is a pure intuition. For, first, we can present only one space;
and when we speak of many spaces, we mean by that only parts of one and
the same unique space. Nor, second, can these parts precede the one all-
encompassing space, as its constituents, as it were (from which it can be
assembled); rather, they can be thought only as *in it*. Space is essentially
one; the manifold in it, and hence also the universal concept of spaces as
such, rests solely on [our bringing in] limitations. It follows from this that,
as far as space is concerned, an a priori intuition of it (i.e., one that is not
empirical) underlies all concepts of space. By the same token, no geometric
principles – e.g., the principle that in a triangle two sides together are greater
than the third – are ever derived from universal concepts of *line* and *triangle*; rather, they are all derived from intuition, and are derived from it moreover a priori, with apodeictic certainty.

4.   We present space as an infinite *given* magnitude. Now it is true that
every concept must be thought as a presentation that is contained in an
infinite multitude of different possible presentations (as their common characteristic) and hence the concept contains these presentations *under itself.*
But no concept, as such, can be thought as containing an infinite multitude of presentations *within itself.* Yet that is how we think space (for all
parts of space, *ad infinitum*, are simultaneous). Therefore the original presentation of space is an a priori *intuition*, not a *concept.*

§3
Transcendental Exposition of the Concept of Space

By a *transcendental exposition* I mean the explication of a concept as a
principle that permits insight into the possibility of other synthetic a priori
cognitions. Such explication requires (1) that cognitions of that sort do
actually flow from the given concept, and (2) that these cognitions are
possible only on the presupposition of a given way of explicating that concept.

Geometry is a science that determines the properties of space synthetically and yet a priori. What, then, must the presentation of space be in
order for such cognition of space to be possible? Space must originally be
intuition. For from a mere concept one cannot obtain propositions that go

beyond the concept; but we do obtain such propositions in geometry (Introduction, V). This intuition must, however, be encountered in us a priori, i.e., prior to any perception of an object; hence this intuition must be pure rather than empirical. For geometric propositions are one and all apodeictic, i.e. linked with the consciousness of their necessity – e.g., the proposition that space has only three dimensions. But propositions of that sort cannot be empirical judgments or judgments of experience; nor can they be inferred from such judgments (Introduction, II).

How, then, can the mind have an outer intuition which precedes the objects themselves, and in which the concept of these objects can be determined a priori? Obviously, this can be so only insofar as this intuition resides merely in the subject, as the subject's formal character of being affected by objects and of thereby acquiring from them *direct presentation*, i.e., *intuition*, and hence only as form of outer *sense* in general.

Our explication of the concept of space is, therefore, the only one that makes comprehensible the *possibility of geometry* as a [kind of] synthetic a priori cognition. Any way of explicating the concept that fails to make this possibility comprehensible, even if it should otherwise seem to have some similarity to ours, can be distinguished from it most safely by these criteria.

A 26
B 42   ## Conclusions from the Above Concepts

(a) Space represents no property whatever of any things in themselves, nor does it represent things in themselves in their relation to one another. That is, space represents no determination of such things, no determination that adheres to objects themselves and that would remain even if we abstracted from all subjective conditions of intuition. For determinations, whether absolute or relative, cannot be intuited prior to the existence of the things to which they belong, and hence cannot be intuited a priori.

(b) Space is nothing but the mere form of all appearances of outer senses; i.e., it is the subjective condition of sensibility under which alone outer intuition is possible for us. Now, the subject's receptivity for being affected by objects precedes necessarily all intuitions of these objects. Thus we can understand how the form of all appearances can be given in the mind prior to all actual perceptions, and hence given a priori; and we can understand how this form, as a pure intuition in which all objects must be determined, can contain, prior to all experience, principles for the relations among these objects.

Only from the human standpoint, therefore, can we speak of space, of extended beings, etc. If we depart from the subjective condition under

which alone we can – viz, as far as we may be affected by objects – acquire
outer intuition, then the presentation of space means nothing whatso- B 43
ever. This predicate is ascribed to things only insofar as they appear to us, A 27
i.e., only insofar as they are objects of sensibility. The constant form of
this receptivity which we call sensibility is a necessary condition of all
relations in which objects are intuited as outside us; and if we abstract
from these objects, then the form of that receptivity is a pure intuition
that bears the name of space. We cannot make the special conditions of
sensibility to be conditions of the possibility of things, but only of the
possibility of their appearances. Hence we can indeed say that space encompasses all things that appear to us externally, but not that it encompasses all things in themselves, intuited or not, or intuited by whatever
subject. For we can make no judgment at all about the intuitions of other
thinking beings, as to whether they are tied to the same conditions that
limit our intuition and that are valid for us universally. If the limitation on
a judgment is added to the concept of the subject [term], then the judgment holds unconditionally. The proposition, All things are side by side
in space, holds under the limitation: if these things are taken as objects of
our sensible intuition. If I here add the condition to the concept and say,
All things considered as outer appearances are side by side in space, then
this rule holds universally and without limitation. Accordingly, our expo- B 44
sition teaches that space is *real* (i.e., objectively valid) in regard to every- A 28
thing that we can encounter externally as object, but teaches at the same
time that space is *ideal* in regard to things when reason considers them in
themselves, i.e., without taking into account the character of our sensibility. Hence we assert that space is *empirically real* (as regards all possible
outer experience), despite asserting that space is *transcendentally ideal,*
i.e., that it is nothing as soon as we omit [that space is] the condition of
the possibility of all experience and suppose space to be something underlying things in themselves.

Besides space, on the other hand, no other subjective presentation that is
referred to something external could be called an a priori objective presentation. For from none of them can we derive synthetic a priori propositions, as we can from intuition in space (§3). Hence, strictly speaking, ideality
does not apply to them, even though they agree with the presentation of
space inasmuch as they belong merely to the subjective character of the
kind of sense involved. They may belong, e.g., to the sense of sight, of
hearing, or of touch, by [being] sensations of colors, sounds, or heat. Yet
because they are mere sensations rather than intuitions, they do not allow
us to cognize any object at all, let alone a priori.

The only aim of this comment is to forestall an error: it might occur to B 45 someone to illustrate the ideality of space asserted above by means of examples such as colors or taste, etc. These are thoroughly insufficient for this, because they are rightly regarded not as properties of things, but merely as changes in ourselves as subjects, changes that may even be different in different people. For in this case, something that originally is itself only appearance – e.g., a rose – counts as a thing in itself in the empirical meaning of this expression, a thing in itself that in regard to color can nonetheless appear differently to every eye. The transcendental concept of appearances in space, on the other hand, is a critical reminder. It reminds us that nothing whatever that is intuited in space is a thing in itself, and that space is not a form of things, one that might belong to them as they are in themselves. Rather, what we call external objects are nothing but mere presentations of our sensibility. The form of this sensibility is space; but its true correlate, i.e., the thing in itself, is not cognized at all through these presentations, and cannot be. Nor, on the other hand, is the thing in itself ever at issue in experience. . . .

A 30

B 59   ## §8
General Comments on Transcendental Aesthetic

I.   In order to forestall any misinterpretation of our opinion regarding the basic character of sensible cognition as such, we must first explain as distinctly as possible what that opinion is.

A 42

What we have tried to say, then, is the following. All our intuition is nothing but the presentation of appearance. The things that we intuit are not in themselves what we intuit them as being. Nor do their relations in themselves have the character that they appear to us as having. And if we annul ourselves as subject, or even annul only the subjective character of the senses generally, then this entire character of objects and all their relations in space and time – indeed, even space and time themselves – would vanish; being appearances, they cannot exist in themselves, but can exist only in us. What may be the case regarding objects in themselves and apart from all this receptivity of our sensibility remains to us entirely unknown. All we know is the way in which we perceive them. That way is peculiar to us and does not necessarily have to apply to all beings, even though it applies necessarily to all human beings. Solely with that way of perceiving are we dealing here. Space and time are its pure forms; sensation as such as its matter. Only that way of perceiving can we cognize a priori, i.e., prior to all actual perception, and that is why it is called pure intuition. Sensation, on the other hand, is that component in our cognition on whose account it

B60

is called a posteriori cognition, i.e., empirical intuition. The forms [of intuition] attach to our sensibility with absolute necessity, no matter of what kind our sensations may be; the sensations can differ very much. Even if we could bring this institution of ours to the highest degree of distinctiveness, that would still not get us closer to the character of objects in themselves. For what we would cognize, and cognize completely, would still be only our way of intuiting, i.e., our sensibility; and we would always cognize it only under the conditions attaching to the subject originally: space and time. What objects may be in themselves would still never become known to us, not even through the most enlightened cognition of what alone is given to us, viz., their appearance.

   Hence we must reject the view that our entire sensibility is nothing but our confused presentation of things, a presentation that contains solely what belongs to them in themselves, but contains it only by way of an accumulation of characteristics and partial presentations that we do not consciously discriminate. For this view falsifies the concept of sensibility and of appearance, thus rendering the entire doctrine of sensibility useless and empty. The distinction between an indistinct and a distinct presentation is merely logical and does not concern the content. No doubt the concept of *rightness* as employed by common sense contains just the same as can be extricated from it by the most subtle speculation, except that in its common and practical use one is not conscious of the diverse presentations contained in that thought. But that does not entitle us to say that the common concept is sensible and contains a mere appearance. For rightness cannot be an appearance at all; rather, its concept lies in the understanding, and we present by it a character of acts (their moral character) which belongs to them in themselves. On the other hand, when a *body* is presented in intuition, this presentation contains nothing whatever that could belong to an object in itself. It contains, rather, merely the appearance of something, and the way we are affected by that something. This receptivity of our cognitive capacity is called sensibility; and even if we were to see through that appearance and to its very bottom, yet this receptivity remains as different as day and night from cognition of the object in itself.

   Hence the philosophy of Leibniz and [Christian] Wolff, by considering the distinction between what is sensible and what is intellectual as a merely logical one, has imposed an entirely wrong point of view on all investigations about the nature and origin of our cognitions. For plainly the distinction is transcendental, and does not concern merely the form of these cognitions, i.e., their distinctness or indistinctness, but concerns their origin and content. Hence sensibility does not merely fail to provide us with a

A 43

B 61

A 44

B 62

distinct cognition of the character of things in themselves; it provides us with none whatsoever. And once we remove our subjective character, then the presented object, along with the properties contributed to it by sensible intuition, is not to be found anywhere at all; nor can it possibly be found, because this subjective character is precisely what determines the form of that object as appearance.

A 45   It is true that we commonly make this distinction about appearances: we distinguish what attaches to their intuition essentially and holds for the sense of every human being in general, from what belongs to that intuition only contingently by being valid only for a special position of this or that sense, or for the special organization of that sense, but not valid for the relation of [the intuition to] sensibility in general. We then speak of the first kind of cognition as presenting the object in itself, and of the second as presenting only its appearance. This distinction, however, is only empirical. If (as is commonly done) we fail to go beyond it and do not (as we ought to do) regard that empirical intuition in turn as mere appearance, in which nothing whatever belonging to some thing in itself is to be found, then our transcendental distinction is lost. We then

B 63   believe after all that we cognize things in themselves, even though in the world of sense, however deeply we explore its objects, we deal with nothing whatever but appearances. Thus it is true, e.g., that when during a rain accompanied by sunshine we see a rainbow, we will call it a mere appearance, while calling the rain the thing in itself. And this is indeed correct, provided that we here take the concept of a thing in itself as meaning only something physical. We then mean by it something that in general experience, and in all its different positions in relation to the senses, is yet determined thus, and not otherwise, in intuition. But suppose that

A 46   we take this empirical something as such, and that – without being concerned about its being the same for the sense of every human being – we ask whether it presents also an object in itself (not whether it presents the rain drops, for these, as appearances, will already be empirical objects). In that case our question about the presentation's relation to the object is transcendental, and the answer is: Not only are these drops mere appearances; rather, even their round shape, and indeed even the space in which they fall, are nothing in themselves. They are, rather, mere modifications, or foundations, of our sensible intuition. The transcendental object, however, remains unknown to us.

Our second important concern in this transcendental aesthetic is that it should not merely gain some favor as a plausible hypothesis, but should be as certain and indubitable as can possibly be demanded of a theory that is to serve as an organon. In order to make this certainty fully evident, let us select some case that can render the validity of this organon obvious and can serve to clarify further what has been set forth in §3.

Suppose, then, that space and time are in themselves objective, and are conditions of the possibility of things in themselves. We then find, in the first place, that we encounter a large number of synthetic a priori propositions about both space and time – above all about space, which we shall therefore investigate here as our prime example. The propositions of geometry are cognized synthetically a priori and with apodeictic certainty. And so I ask: From where do you obtain such propositions, and on what does the understanding rely in order to arrive at such absolutely necessary and universally valid truths? There is no other way [to arrive at truths] than through concepts or through intuition. But these concepts and intuitions are both given either a priori or a posteriori. The a posteriori ones, i.e., empirical concepts as well as the empirical intuition on which they are based, can yield only such synthetic propositions as are likewise merely empirical, i.e., propositions of experience. As such, these propositions can never contain necessity and absolute universality; yet these are what characterize all geometric propositions.[2] The first and sole means of arriving at such cognitions is a priori, through mere concepts or through intuitions. From mere concepts, however, we clearly can obtain no synthetic cognition at all, but only analytic cognition. Just take the proposi- tion that two straight lines cannot enclose any space and hence do not permit [construction of], any figure, and try to derive it from the concept of straight lines and of the number two. Or take the proposition that three straight lines permit [construction of] a figure, and try similarly to derive it from these mere concepts. All your endeavor is futile, and you find yourselves compelled to have recourse to intuition, as indeed geometry always does. Hence you give yourselves an object in in- tuition. But of which kind is this intuition? Is it a pure a priori intuition or an empirical one? If it were an empirical intuition, then it could never turn into a universally valid proposition, let alone an apodeictic one; for experience can never supply anything like that. Hence you must give your object to yourselves a priori in intuition, and base your synthetic proposition on this object. Now suppose that there did not lie within you a power to intuit a priori; that this subjective condition were not, as regards its form, at the same time the universal a priori condition under which alone the object of this (outer) intuition is itself possible; and that the object (the triangle) were something in itself, even apart from any relation to yourselves as subject. If that were so, how could you say that what necessarily lies in [or belongs to] your subjective conditions for constructing a triangle must also belong necessarily to the triangle itself?

B 66   For, after all, you could not add to your concepts (of three lines) anything new (the figure) that would therefore have to be met with necessarily in the object, since this object would be given prior to your cognition rather than through it. Hence you could not synthetically a priori establish anything whatsoever about external objects if space (and similarly time) were not a mere form of your intuition, an intuition that a priori contains conditions under which alone things can be external objects for you – these objects being nothing in themselves, apart from these subjective conditions. Therefore the following is not merely possible – or

A 49   probable, for that matter – but indubitably certain: Space and time, as the necessary conditions of all (outer and inner) experience, are merely subjective conditions of all our intuition. Hence in relation to these conditions all objects are mere appearances, and are not given to us in this way on their own. And that is why much can be said a priori about these objects as regards their form, but not the least can ever be said about the thing in itself that may underlie these appearances.

II. This theory, according to which both outer and inner sense are ideal and hence all objects of the senses are mere appearances, can be confirmed superbly by the following observation. Whatever in our cognition belongs to intuition (excluding, therefore, what are not cognitions at all, i.e., both the feeling of pleasure and displeasure and the will) con

B 67   tains nothing but mere relations: of places in an intuition (extension), of change of places (motion), and of laws according to which this change is determined (motive forces). But what is present in that place, or what effect – besides the change of place – it produces in the things themselves, is not given to us by [what belongs to intuition]. Now through mere relations we do not, of course, cognize a thing in itself. Hence our judgment must surely be this: since through outer sense we are given nothing but mere relational presentations, outer sense can, by the same token, contain in its presentation only the relation of an object to the subject, but not the intrinsic character belonging to the object in itself. The same applies to inner intuition. For not only does the proper material in it, with which we occupy our mind, consist in presentations of *outer senses*, but the time in which we place these presentations, and which itself precedes the consciousness of them in experience and underlies, as formal condition, the way in which we place them within the mind, already contains relations: of succession, of simultaneity, and of what is simultaneous with succession (the permanent). Now, presentation that can precede all acts of thinking anything is intuition; and if this intuition contains nothing but relations then it is the form of intuition. But this form does not present anything except insofar as something is being placed

within the mind. Therefore this form can be nothing but the way in
which the mind is affected by its own activity – viz., this placing of its
presentation – and hence affected by itself; i.e., it is an inner sense insofar
as that sense's form is concerned. Whatever is presented through a sense
is, to that extent, always appearance. Hence either we must not grant
that there is an inner sense at all; or we must grant that the subject who
is the object of this sense can be presented through it only as appearance,
and not as he would judge himself if his intuition were self-activity only,
i.e., if it were intellectual intuition. What underlies this whole difficulty is
this: how can a subject inwardly intuit himself? But this difficulty is shared
by every theory. The consciousness of oneself (apperception) is the simple presentation of the *I*; and if through this consciousness by itself all
the manifold in the subject were given *self-actively*, then the inner intuition would be intellectual. But in man this consciousness requires also
inner perception of the manifold given in the subject beforehand; and
the way in which this manifold is given in the mind – viz., without spontaneity – must, for the sake of marking this distinction, be called sensibility. If the power to become conscious of oneself is to locate (apprehend)
what lies in the mind, then it must affect the mind; and only in that way
can it produce an intuition of itself. But the form of this intuition lies at
the basis beforehand in the mind; and this form determines, in the presentation of time, the way in which the manifold is [placed] together in
the mind. And thus this power does not intuit itself as it would if it
presented itself directly and self-actively; rather, it intuits itself according
to the way in which it is affected from within, and hence intuits itself as it
appears to itself, not as it is.

III. I am saying, then, that the intuition of external objects and the
self-intuition of the mind both present these objects and the mind, in
space and in time, as they affect our senses, i.e., as they appear. But I do
not mean by this that these objects are a mere *illusion*. For when we deal
with appearance, the objects, and indeed even the properties that we ascribe to them, are always regarded a something actually given – except
that insofar as the object's character depends only on the subject's way of
intuiting this given object in its relation to him, we do also distinguish
this object as *appearance* from the same object as object *in itself*. Thus
when I posit both bodies and my soul as being in accordance with the
quality of space and time, as condition of their existence, I do indeed
assert that this quality lies in my way of intuiting and not in those objects
in themselves. But in asserting this I am not saying that the bodies merely
seem to be outside me, or that my soul only *seems* to be given in my self-
consciousness. It would be my own fault if I turned into mere illusion

B 68

B 69

B 70   what I ought to class with appearance.* This is not, however, what happens if we follow our principle that all our sensible intuitions are ideal. On the contrary: it is when we attribute *objective reality* to those forms of presentation that we cannot prevent everything from being thereby transformed into mere *illusion*. For suppose that we regard space and time as properties that, as far as their very possibility is concerned, must be found in things in themselves. And now reflect on the absurdities in which we then become entangled, inasmuch as [we then have] two infinite things that must not be substances nor anything actually inhering in substances,

B 71   but that yet must be something existent – indeed, must be the necessary condition for the existence of all things – and must moreover remain even if all existing things are annulled. If we thus reflect on this supposition, then we can hardly blame the good *Berkeley* for downgrading bodies to mere illusion.[3] Indeed, even our own existence, which would in this way be made dependent on the self-subsistent reality of a nonentity such as time would be, would be transformed along with this time into nothing but illusion – an absurdity of which no one thus far has made himself guilty.

IV. In natural theology we think an object [viz. God] that not only cannot possibly be an object of intuition for us, but that cannot in any way be an object of sensible intuition even to itself. [When we think of God in this way,] we take great care to remove the conditions of time and space from all his intuition. (All his cognition must be intuition rather than *thought*, which always manifests limits.) But what right do we have to do this if we have beforehand turned space and time into forms of things in themselves – such forms, moreover, as are a priori conditions of the existence of things and hence would remain even if we had annulled the things themselves? For as conditions of all existence in general, they would have to be condi-

B 72   tions also of the existence of God. If we are not to make space and time objective forms of all things, then we are left with only one alternative: we

---

* The predicates of the appearance can be ascribed to the object itself in relation to our sense: e.g., to the rose, the red color or the scent. But what is mere illusion can never be ascribed as predicate to an object, precisely because illusion ascribes to the object taken *by itself* what belongs to it only in relation to the senses or in general to the subject – an example being the two handles intially ascribed to Saturn. If something is not to be met with at all in the object in itself, but is always to be met with in the object's relation to the subject and is inseparable from the presentation of the object, then it is appearance. And thus the predicates of space and time are rightly ascribed to objects of the senses, as such; and in this there is no illusion. Illusion first arises if, by contrast, I ascribe the redness to the rose *in itself*, or the handles to Saturn, or extension to all external objects *in themselves*, without taking account of – and limiting my judgment to – a determinate relation of these objects to the subject.

must make them subjective forms of our kind of intuition, inner and outer. Our kind of intuition is called sensible because it is *not original.* I.e., it is not such that through this intuition itself the existence of its object is given (the latter being a kind of intuition that, as far as we can see, can belong only to the original being). Rather, our kind of intuition is dependent on the existence of the object, and hence is possible only by the object's affecting the subject's capacity to present.

There is, moreover, no need for us to limit this kind of intuition – intuition in space and time – to the sensibility of man. It may be (though we cannot decide this) that any finite thinking being must necessarily agree with man in this regard. Yet even if this kind of intuition were thus universally valid, it would not therefore cease to be sensibility. It would remain sensibility precisely because it is derivative (*intuitus derivativus*) rather than original (*intuitus originarius*), and hence is not intellectual intuition. For the reason just set forth, intellectual intuition seems to belong solely to the original being, and never to a being that is dependent as regards both its existence and its intuition (an intuition that determines that being's existence by reference to given objects). This last remark, however, must be considered as included in our aesthetic theory only as an illustration, not as a basis of proof.

Concluding the Transcendental Aesthetic   B73

Thus in our pure a priori intuitions, space and time, we now have one of the components required for solving the general problem of transcendental philosophy: *How are synthetic propositions possible a priori?* When in an a priori judgment about space and time we want to go beyond the given concept, we encounter what cannot be discovered a priori in the given concept, but can indeed be so discovered in the intuition corresponding to that concept and can be combined with it synthetically. Because of this, however, such judgments can never reach beyond objects of the senses, and can hold only for objects of possible experience.

Notes

1 Here and elsewhere Kant's wording suggests that his thesis is limited to specifically *human* capacities and limitations. But in other places, it looks as if his claims are meant to apply to all rational creatures whose knowledge, unlike that of God's, requires experience.

2 This 'argument from geometry' is more fully expounded by Kant in his *Prolegomena to Any Future Metaphysics*, Manchester: Manchester University Press, 1953, pp. 36–51.

3 Berkeley, as we may see from chapter 10 above, would certainly reject the charge of 'downgrading bodies to mere illusion'. But whatever the propriety of Kant's use of the term 'illusion', his claim that Berkeley treats spatial properties as no different in status from, say, colours and smells, is accurate.

Arthur Schopenhauer, *The World as Will and Representation*, Vol. II, Chapter 18

12

12

From Arthur Schopenhauer, *The World as Will and Representation*, Vol. II, trans. E. F. J. Payne. Mineola: Dover Publications, Inc., 1966, pp. 191–200 (asterisked notes are the translator's).

The aspect of Kant's metaphysics which, in the years immediately following the publication of the *Critique*, was to cause most consternation was his doctrine of things in themselves. The unease was as much emotional as intellectual, for it was at best frustrating, at worst tragic, to learn that reality in itself is completely unknowable. Much effort was therefore devoted, by philosophers generally sympathetic to Kant, to dispensing with or amending this doctrine. Thus the so-called Absolute Idealists in Germany attempted to show that reality itself – and not just 'appearances' – is either a product of mind or, at any rate, 'mind-like' and knowable. Fichte, for example, wrote that 'there is no world that subsists on its own. Wherever we look, we see nothing but the reflection of our own inner activity'.[1]

Another German philosopher who equally admired Kant, Arthur Schopenhauer (1788–1860), offered a different solution from that of the Absolute Idealists – whom he vituperatively dubbed 'charlatans' – in his *The World as Will and Representation* (1819). (The chapter I have selected is from Volume II, a series of supplements, written a quarter of a century later, which are often more succinct and considered than the chapters of the original edition.) Schopenhauer agrees with Kant that the spatio-temporal world I experience is only 'my representation', since it is thoroughly 'conditioned by the subject' (Vol. I, p. 3). Indeed, he insists, in certain moods, that it is mere 'illusion' or, borrowing from the Indian philosophers he admired, *maya* (see chapter 5 above on Śaṁkara's philosophy). After all, Schopenhauer argues, the experienced world is one of individual things and persons, but individuation presupposes

---

[1] J. G. Fichte, *Introductions to the* Wissenschaftslehre *and Other Writings*, Indianapolis: Hackett, 1994, p. 145.

spatial criteria and space is, as Kant showed, only a condition of our sensibil-ity.[2]

Schopenhauer further agrees with Kant that there must also exist a realm of noumena or things in themselves. Otherwise, he urges, we should have to con-cede that the world is but an 'empty dream' (Vol. I, p. 99) – something it is impossible for us to do. Where he takes issue with Kant is over the alleged unknowability of things in themselves: hence the title of the chapter I have selected, 'On the possibility of knowing the thing-in-itself'. To be sure, we can-not know it either through perception or conceptual understanding: we can-not *represent* it. But Schopenhauer's crucial and original claim is that there is 'a way *from within*' to knowledge of the thing in itself. This is because we have direct, non-representational and non-inferential knowledge of *ourselves* as agents or subjects of *will*. The will is not just one faculty among others; rather, it is our very nature and essence, of which our conscious and rational activities are but manifestations, and not the autonomous processes we usually imag-ine. This a point which Schopenhauer begins to defend towards the end of Ch. 18 and elaborates in the immediately following one.

Subsequent chapters also defend the daring claim briefly made in Ch. 18 that not only are *we* essentially will, but that 'the inner nature of every thing is *will*'. The whole natural order, that is, should be seen as manifesting an under-lying will which is its 'inner principle'. Schopenhauer, therefore, is allied to those philosophers – from Heraclitus to Henri Bergson – for whom reality is to be understood not through such categories as object and property, but in terms of process, desire, force. His arguments may fail to persuade, but there is no denying that Schopenhauer powerfully expresses a vision which 'to some eyes, in some moods . . . seem[s] both compelling and authentic'.[3]

One puzzle critics may have concerns Schopenhauer's description of the will as the thing in itself. Part of his answer is that the will satisfies at least some of Kant's criteria for the noumenal. Negatively, it is something which we do not know through representation; positively, it is the precondition for the exist-ence of anything which we can represent. But part of his answer involves a concession to his critics. *Strictly*, what we can directly experience is not the will as it is in itself. For one thing, we experience it as operating in time, and time – like space – is not a dimension of the thing in itself. Nevertheless, having admitted that the will is not presented 'quite naked', Schopenhauer consoles himself that our knowledge of the will is 'the point where the thing-in-itself enters the phenomenon most immediately'. In knowing ourselves as will, that is, we get as close as we ever can to acquaintance with the thing in itself.

---

[2] See my 'Self and morality in Schopenhauer and Nietzsche', in C. Janaway (ed.), *Willing and Nothingness: Schopenhauer as Nietzsche's Educator*, Oxford: Clarendon Press, 1998.
[3] Patrick Gardiner, *Schopenhauer*, Harmondsworth: Penguin, 1963, p. 183.

The 'inner nature' of everything – the will – is, for Schopenhauer, not at all the rational 'Spirit' or 'Idea' which many Absolute Idealists posited as the underlying principle of both the natural world and human history. On the contrary, it is 'blind activity', so that everything which manifests it is caught up in a pointless, frenetic whirl. This includes ourselves, who are seen by Schopenhauer, in one commentator's apt phrase, as 'delusively individualized throbs of craving'.[4] It is this metaphysical vision which informs Schopenhauer's famous 'pessimism', his judgements that existence is a 'mistake' and that 'life . . . ought to disgust us' (Vol. II, Ch. 46). In Schopenhauer's philosophy, metaphysical truths are not dry abstractions, but the foundation of a total *Weltanschauung*.

Schopenhauer, On the Possibility of Knowing the Thing-in-Itself

Chapter 18

In 1836, under the title *Ueber den Willen in der Natur* [On the Will in Nature], I already published the really essential supplement to this book, which contains the most characteristic and important step of my philosophy, namely the transition from the phenomenon to the thing-in-itself, given up by Kant as impossible. We should make a great mistake if we tried to regard the statements of others, with which I have there associated my explanations, as the real and proper material and subject of that work, a work small in volume but important as regards its contents. On the contrary, those statements are merely the occasion from which I have started, and I have there discussed that fundamental truth of my teaching with greater distinctness than anywhere else, and brought it down to the empirical knowledge of nature. This has been done most exhaustively and stringently under the heading "Physical Astronomy"; so that I cannot hope ever to find a more correct and accurate expression of that core of my philosophy than what is there recorded. Whoever wishes to know my philosophy thoroughly and investigate it seriously must first take that chapter into consideration. Therefore all that is said in that small work would in general constitute the main subject-matter of the present supplements, if it had not to be excluded as having preceded them; whereas I here assume it to be known, since otherwise what is best would be missing.

---

[4] T. L. S. Sprigge, *Theories of Existence*, Harmondsworth: Penguin, 1984, p. 90.

First of all, I will make a few preliminary observations from a more general point of view as to the sense in which we can speak of a knowledge of the thing-in-itself, and of the necessary limitation of this sense.

What is *knowledge*? It is above all else and essentially *representation*. What is *representation*? A very complicated *physiological* occurrence in an animal's brain, whose result is the consciousness of a *picture or image* at that very spot. Obviously the relation of such a picture to something entirely different from the animal in whose brain it exists can only be a very indirect one. This is perhaps the simplest and most intelligible way of disclosing the *deep gulf between the ideal and the real*. This is one of the things of which, like the earth's motion, we are not immediately aware; the ancients, therefore, did not notice it, just as they did not observe the earth's motion. On the other hand, once first demonstrated by Descartes, it has ever since given philosophers no rest. But after Kant had at last shown most thoroughly the complete diversity of the ideal and the real, it was an attempt as bold as it was absurd, yet quite correctly calculated with regard to the power of judgement of the philosophical public in Germany and thus crowned with brilliant success, to try to assert the *absolute identity* of the two by dogmatic utterances referring to a so-called intellectual intuition. On the contrary, a subjective and an objective existence, a being for self and a being for others, a consciousness of one's own self and consciousness of other things, are in truth given to us immediately, and the two are given in such a fundamentally different way that no other difference compares with this. About *himself* everyone knows directly, about everything else only very indirectly. This is the fact and the problem.

On the other hand, it is no longer the essential point here, but one of secondary importance, whether, through further processes in the interior of the brain, universal concepts (*universalia*) are abstracted from the representations or pictures of perception that have arisen in the brain, for the purpose of further combinations, whereby knowledge becomes *rational*, and is then called *thinking*. For all such *concepts* borrow their contents only from the representation of perception, which is therefore *primary knowledge*, and thus is alone taken into consideration when we investigate the relation between the ideal and the real. Accordingly, it is evidence of a complete ignorance of the problem, or at any rate it is very inept, to want to describe this relation as that between *being* and *thinking*. In the first place, *thinking* has a relation only to *perceiving*, but *perceiving* has a relation to the *being-in-itself* of what is perceived, and this last is the great problem with which we are here concerned. On the other hand, empirical being, as it lies before us, is simply nothing but being-given in perception; but the relation of this to *thinking* is no riddle, for the concepts, and hence the immediate material of thinking, are obviously *abstracted* from perception, as no reasonable person can doubt. Incidentally, we can see how important the choice of expressions in philosophy is from the fact that the inept expression censured above, and the misunderstanding that has arisen from it, have become the foundation of the whole Hegelian pseudo-philosophy that has engrossed the attention of the German public for twenty-five years.

But if it should be said that "perception is already knowledge of the thing-in-itself, for it is the effect of that which exists outside us, and as this *acts*, so it *is*; its action is just its being"; then to this we reply: (1) that the law of causality, as has been sufficiently proved, is of subjective origin,[1] as is also the sensation of the senses from which the perception comes; (2) that time and space, in which the object presents itself, are likewise of subjective origin; (3) that, if the being of the object consists merely in its acting, this means that it consists merely in the changes produced by it in others; consequently, itself and in itself is nothing at all. Only of *matter* is it true, as I have said in the text and discussed in the essay *On the Principle of Sufficient Reason* at the end of §21, that its being consists in its acting, that it is through and through only causality, and thus is causality itself objectively perceived, but that it is thus nothing in itself (ἡ ὕλη τὸ ἀληθινὸν ψεῦδος, *materia mendacium verax*);* on the contrary, as an ingredient of the perceived object it is a mere abstraction, which by itself alone cannot be given in any experience. It will be fully considered later on in a chapter to itself. Yet the perceived object must be something *in itself*, and not merely *something for others*; for otherwise it would be positively only representation, and we should have an absolute idealism that in the end would become theoretical egoism, in which all reality disappears, and the world becomes a mere subjective phantasm. However, if, without questioning further, we stop altogether at the *world as representation*, then of course it is immaterial whether I declare objects to be representations in my head or phenomena that exhibit themselves in time and space, since time and space themselves are only in my head. In this sense, then, an identity of the ideal and the real might still be affirmed; yet since Kant, this would be to say nothing new. Moreover, the inner nature of things and of the phenomenal world would obviously not be exhausted in this way, but with it we should still always be only on the *ideal* side. The *real* side must be something *toto genere* different from the *world as representation*, namely that which things are *in themselves*; and it is this complete diversity between the ideal and the real that Kant has demonstrated most thoroughly.

* "Matter is a lie and yet true." [Tr.]

Locke had denied knowledge of things as they are in themselves to the senses; but Kant denied it also to the perceiving *understanding*. Under this name I embrace here what he calls *pure* sensibility and the law of causality that brings about empirical perception, in so far as this law is given *a priori*. Not only are both right, but it can also be seen quite directly that there is a contradiction in the assertion that a thing is known according to what it is in and by itself, in other words, outside our knowledge. For, as I have said, all knowing is essentially a making of representations; but my making of representations, just because it is mine, can never be identical with the being-in-itself of the thing outside me. The being in and by itself of every thing must necessarily be *subjective*. But in the representation of another, it exists just as necessarily as something *objective*, a difference that can never be entirely reconciled. For through this the whole mode of its existence is fundamentally changed; as something objective, it presupposes a foreign subject, and exists as the representation of that subject; moreover, as Kant has shown, it has entered forms foreign to its own nature, just because they belong to that foreign subject whose knowledge becomes possible only through them. If, absorbed in this reflection, I perceive, let us say, lifeless bodies of easily observable size and regular comprehensible form, and then attempt to conceive this spatial existence in its three dimensions as their being-in-itself, and consequently as the existence that is subjective to the things, then I at once feel the impossibility of the thing, since I can never think of those objective forms as the being that is subjective to the things. On the contrary, I become directly conscious that what I represent there is a picture or image, brought about in my brain and existing only for me as the knowing subject, and that this picture cannot constitute the ultimate, and therefore subjective, being-in-and-by-itself of even these lifeless bodies. On the other hand, I cannot assume that even these lifeless bodies exist simply and solely in my representation, but as they have unfathomable properties, and, by virtue of these, activity, I must concede them a *being-in-itself* of some kind. But this very inscrutability of the properties, pointing as it certainly does on the one hand to something existing independently of our knowledge, on the other hand gives the empirical proof that, because our knowledge consists only in the *framing of representations* by means of subjective forms, such knowledge always furnishes mere *phenomena*, not the being-in-itself of things. From this it can be explained that in all we know, a certain something remains hidden from us as being quite unfathomable, and we must confess that we are unable to understand even the commonest and simplest phenomena. For not merely do the highest productions of nature, namely living beings, or the *complicated* phenomena of the inorganic world remain inscrutable to us, but even every rock-crystal, even iron pyrites, are, by virtue of their crystallographical, optical, chemical, and electrical properties, an abyss of incomprehensibilities and mysteries for our searching consideration and investigation. This could not be so if we knew things as they are in themselves; for then at any rate the simpler phenomena, the path to whose properties was not barred to us by ignorance, would of necessity be thoroughly intelligible to us, and their whole being and inner nature could not fail to pass over into knowledge. Therefore it lies not in the defectiveness of our acquaintance with things, but in the very nature of knowledge itself. For if our perception, and thus the whole empirical apprehension of the things that present themselves to us, is already determined essentially and principally by our cognitive faculty and by its forms and functions, then it must be that things exhibit themselves in a manner quite different from their own inner nature, and that therefore they appear as through a mask. This mask enables us always merely to assume, never to know, what is hidden beneath it; and this something then gleams through as an inscrutable mystery. Never can the nature of anything pass over into knowledge wholly and without reserve; but still less can anything real be constructed *a priori*, like something mathematical. Therefore the empirical inscrutability of all the beings of nature is an *a posteriori* proof of the ideality, and merely phenomenal actuality, of their empirical existence.

In consequence of all this, on the path of *objective knowledge*, thus starting from the *representation*, we shall never get beyond the representation, i.e., the phenomenon. We shall therefore remain at the outside of things; we shall never be able to penetrate into their inner nature, and investigate what they are in themselves, in other words, what they may be by themselves. So far I agree with Kant. But now, as the counterpoise to this truth, I have stressed that other truth that we are not merely the *knowing subject*, but that *we ourselves* are also among those realities or entities we require to know, that *we ourselves are the thing-in-itself*. Consequently, a way *from within* stands open to us to that real inner nature of things to which we cannot penetrate *from without*. It is, so to speak, a subterranean passage, a secret alliance, which, as if by treachery, places us all at once in the fortress that could not be taken by attack from without. Precisely as such, the *thing-in-itself* can come into consciousness only quite directly, namely by *it itself being conscious of itself*; to try to know it objectively is to desire something contradictory. Everything objective is representation, consequently appearance, in fact mere phenomenon of the brain.

Kant's principal result may be summarized in its essence as follows: "All concepts which do not have as their basis a perception in space and time (sensuous perception), or in other words, have not been drawn from such a perception, are absolutely empty, that is to say, they give us no knowledge. But as perception can furnish only *phenomena*, not things-in-themselves, we too have absolutely no knowledge of things-in-themselves." I admit this of everything, but not of the knowledge everyone has of his own *willing*. This is neither a perception (for all perception is spatial), nor is it empty; on the contrary, it is more real than any other knowledge. Further, it is not *a priori*, like merely formal knowledge, but entirely *a posteriori*; hence we are unable to anticipate it in the particular case, but in this are often guilty of error concerning ourselves. In fact, our *willing* is the only opportunity we have of understanding simultaneously from within any event that outwardly manifests itself; consequently, it is the one thing known to us *immediately*, and not given to us merely in the representation, as all else is. Here, therefore, lies the datum alone capable of becoming the key to everything else, or, as I have said, the only narrow gateway to truth. Accordingly, we must learn to understand nature from ourselves, not ourselves from nature. What is directly known to us must give us the explanation of what is only indirectly known, not conversely. Do we understand, let us say, the rolling away of a ball when it has received an impulse more thoroughly than we understand our own movement when we have perceived a motive? Many may think so, but I say that the reverse is the case. However, we shall arrive at the insight that in both the occurrences just mentioned what is essential is identical, although identical in the same way as the lowest audible note of harmony is identical with the note of the same name ten octaves higher.

Meanwhile it is to be carefully noted, and I have always kept it in mind, that even the inward observation we have of our own will still does not by any means furnish an exhaustive and adequate knowledge of the thing-in-itself. It would do so if it were a wholly immediate observation. But such observation is brought about by the will, with and by means of corporization,[2] providing itself also with an intellect (for the purpose of its relations with the external world), and then through this intellect knowing itself in self-consciousness (the necessary reverse of the external world); but this knowledge of the thing-in-itself is not wholly adequate. In the first place, such knowledge is tied to the form of the representation; it is perception or observation, and as such falls apart into subject and object. For even in self-consciousness, the I is not absolutely simple, but consists of a knower (intellect) and a known (will); the former is not known and the latter is not knowing, although the two flow together into the consciousness of an I. But on this very account, this I is not *intimate* with itself through and through, does not shine through so to speak, but is opaque, and therefore remains a riddle to itself. Hence even in inner knowledge there still occurs a difference between the being-in-itself of its object and the observation or perception of this object in the knowing subject. But the inner knowledge is free from two forms belonging to outer knowledge, the form of *space* and the form of *causality* which brings about all sense-perception. On the other hand, there still remains the form of *time*, as well as that of being known and of knowing in general. Accordingly, in this inner knowledge the thing-in-itself has indeed to a great extent cast off its veils, but still does not appear quite naked. In consequence of the form of time which still adheres to it, everyone knows his *will* only in its successive individual *acts,* not as a whole, in and by itself. Hence no one knows his character *a priori,* but he becomes acquainted with it only by way of experience and always imperfectly. Yet the apprehension in which we know the stirrings and acts of our own will is far more immediate than is any other. It is the point where the thing-in-itself enters the phenomenon most immediately, and is most closely examined by the knowing subject; therefore the event thus intimately known is simply and solely calculated to become the interpreter of every other.

For in the case of every emergence of an act of will from the obscure depths of our inner being into the knowing consciousness, there occurs a direct transition into the phenomenon of the thing-in-itself that lies outside time. Accordingly, the act of will is indeed only the nearest and clearest *phenomenon* of the thing-in-itself; yet it follows from this that, if all the other phenomena could be known by us just as immediately and intimately, we should be obliged to regard them precisely as that which the will is in us. Therefore in this sense I teach that the inner nature of every thing is *will,* and I call the will the thing-in-itself. In this way, Kant's doctrine of the inability to know the thing-in-itself is modified to the extent that the thing-in-itself is merely not absolutely and completely knowable; that nevertheless by far the most immediate of its phenomena, distinguished *toto genere* from all the rest by this immediateness, is its representative for us. Accordingly we have to refer the whole world of phenomena to that one in which the thing-in-itself is manifested under the lightest of all veils, and still remains phenomenon only in so far as my intellect, the only thing capable of knowledge, still always remains distinguished from me as the one who wills, and does not cast off the knowledge-form of *time*, even with *inner* perception.

Accordingly, even after this last and extreme step, the question may still be raised what that will, which manifests itself in the world and as the world, is ultimately and absolutely in itself; in other words, what it is, quite apart from the fact that it manifests itself as *will*, or in general *appears*, that is to say, *is known* in general. This question can *never* be answered, because, as I have said, being-known of itself contradicts being-in-itself, and every-thing that is known is as such only phenomenon. But the possibility of this question shows that the thing-in-itself, which we know most immediately in the will, may have, entirely outside all possible phenomenon, determinations, qualities, and modes of existence which for us are abso-lutely unknowable and incomprehensible, and which then remain as the inner nature of the thing-in-itself, when this, as explained in the fourth book, has freely abolished itself as *will*, has thus stepped out of the phe-nomenon entirely, and as regards our knowledge, that is to say as regards the world of phenomena, has passed over into empty nothingness. If the will were positively and absolutely the thing-in-itself, then this nothing would be *absolute*, instead of which it expressly appears to us there only as a relative nothing.

I now proceed to supplement by a few relevant observations the estab-lishment, given in [Book 2 of Vol. I] as well as in the work *On the Will in Nature*, of the doctrine that what makes itself known in the most immedi-ate knowledge as will is precisely that which objectifies itself at different grades in all the phenomena of this world. I shall begin by producing a series of psychological facts proving first of all that in our own conscious-ness the *will* always appears as the primary and fundamental thing, and throughout asserts its pre-eminence over the intellect; that, on the other hand, the intellect generally turns out to be what is secondary, subordi-nate, and conditioned. This proof is the more necessary as all philosophers before me, from the first to the last, place the true and real inner nature or kernel of man in the *knowing* consciousness. Accordingly, they have con-ceived and explained the I, or in the case of many of them its transcendent hypostasis called soul, as primarily and essentially *knowing*, in fact *thinking*, and only in consequence of this, secondarily and derivatively, as *willing*. This extremely old, universal, and fundamental error, this colossal $\pi\rho\tilde{\omega}\tau o\nu$ $\psi\tilde{\epsilon}\tilde{\upsilon}\delta o\varsigma$ and fundamental $\dot{\upsilon}\sigma\tau\epsilon\rho o\nu$ $\pi\rho\acute{o}\tau\epsilon\rho o\nu$,* must first of all be set aside, and instead of it the true state of the case must be brought to perfectly distinct consciousness. However, as this is done for the first time here after thousands of years of philosophizing, some detailed account will not be out of place. The remarkable phenomenon that in this fundamental and essential point all philosophers have erred, in fact have completely reversed the truth, might be partly explained, especially in the case of the philoso-phers of the Christian era, from the fact that all of them aimed at present-ing man as differing as widely as possible from the animal. Yet they felt

---

* "The first false step." "Confusion of the earlier with the later, or of ground with conse-quent." [Tr.]

vaguely that the difference between the two was to be found in the intellect and not in the will. From this arose in them unconsciously the tendency to make the intellect the essential and principal thing, in fact to describe willing as a mere function of the intellect. Therefore the concept of a *soul*, as transcendent hypostasis, is not only inadmissible, as is established by the *Critique of Pure Reason*, but it becomes the source of irremediable errors by its establishing beforehand in its "simple substance" an indivisible unity of knowledge and of the will, the separation of which is precisely the path to truth. Therefore that concept can no longer occur in philosophy, but is to be left to German medical men and physiologists, who, laying aside scalpel and scoop, venture to philosophize with concepts they received when they were confirmed. They might perhaps try their luck with them in England. The French physiologists and zootomists have (till recently) kept themselves entirely free from this reproach.

The first consequence of their common fundamental error, which is very inconvenient to all these philosophers, is that, since in death the knowing consciousness obviously perishes, either they must admit death to be the annihilation of man, against which our inner nature revolts, or resort to the assumption of a continued existence of the knowing consciousness. For this a strong faith is required, since everyone's own experience has abundantly demonstrated to him the complete and general dependence of the knowing consciousness on the brain, and one can just as easily believe in a digestion without a stomach as in a knowing consciousness without a brain. My philosophy alone leads us out of this dilemma; in the first place it puts man's real inner nature not in consciousness, but in the will. This will is not essentially united with consciousness, but is related to consciousness, in other words to knowledge, as substance to accident, as something illuminated to light, as the string to the soundingboard; it comes into consciousness from within just as the corporeal world comes from without. Now we can grasp the indestructibility of this real kernel and true inner being that is ours, in spite of the obvious extinction of consciousness in death and its corresponding non-existence before birth. For the intellect is as fleeting and as perishable as is the brain, and is the brain's product, or rather its activity. But the brain, like the whole organism, is the product or phenomenon of, in short a secondary thing to, the will, and it is the will alone that is imperishable.[3]

Notes

1 Kant had argued in *Critique of Pure Reason* (B 232ff) that the law of causal-

ity does not apply to things in themselves, but expresses a condition on our capacity to experience an objective, empirical world.

2 Here there is a brief allusion to Schopenhauer's important claim that 'willing and acting are one', or that 'my body and my will are one' (Vol. I pp. 99ff). His point is that, in the case of human beings at least, acts of will are not 'inner' or immaterial mental acts which bring about bodily actions, but those very actions as experienced by the agent.

3 Critics have been justifiably puzzled by Schopenhauer's references to the role of the brain. Earlier he has spoken as if the reason why we can observe appearances or 'illusions', and only these, is that everything is filtered through the brain. But, as he in effect points out in the last sentence of the chapter, the brain is as much a phenomenon or appearance as anything else in the empirical order. In that case, it is hard to see how the brain can explain how that whole order is accessible to us.

John Stuart Mill, *An Examination of Sir William Hamilton's Philosophy*, Chapter 11

13

From John Stuart Mill, *An Examination of Sir William Hamilton's Philosophy and of the Principal Philosophical Questions Discussed in his Writings*, ed. J. M. Robson. Toronto: University of Toronto Press, 1979, pp. 177–87 (most notes omitted: asterisked note is Mill's).

In nineteenth-century Britain, hardly less than in Germany, metaphysical effort was devoted to dissolving or mitigating Kant's dichotomy between phenomena and unknowable things in themselves. Schopenhauer's identification of a partially knowable thing in itself with a cosmic will had little appeal for the leading British empiricist of the century, J. S. Mill (1806–73). Not only did this retain the idea of something beyond all possible perceptual experience, but the cosmic will was far too speculative a notion to be accepted by a philosopher for whom inductive generalization from observed data was the only legitimate form of inference.[1] Indeed, one of Mill's aims in the famous Chapter 11 of his *Examination* (1865), 'The psychological theory of the belief in an external world', is to expose the conviction that there are things in themselves as an illegitimate one to which people are, albeit for readily intelligible psychological reasons, unfortunately prone.

The chapter begins with a related issue which may seem to belong more to psychology than metaphysics: why do we believe in an external, material reality at all? Mill's target is those philosophers – mainly members of the Scottish 'commonsense school', and in particular Sir William Hamilton (1791–1856) – who held that this belief is an intuitive, non-inferential one. Against them, Mill argues that the belief is an 'acquired product', which we inevitably arrive at on the basis of our experiences or 'sensations' as governed by the laws of 'associationist' psychology, such as that a given sensation causes us to think of other sensations with which it has been regularly associated.

Without quite appreciating the change, Mill shifts to metaphysics once he

---

[1] Mill's accounts of inference and induction are expounded in his *A System of Logic*, London: Longman & Green, 1886.

explains *what* precisely it is we come to believe in as a result of our experience and psychology. 'Matter', he famously writes, 'may be defined [as] a Permanent Possibility of Sensation'. To believe there are external physical objects is to believe that, besides our actual sensations of colour, shape and so on, there are clusters of sensations we *would* experience under appropriate conditions. To such clusters we give names like 'table' and 'city'. So, for example, to hold that Calcutta exists, even though no one is currently experiencing the place, means that, under certain possible conditions, 'I should still have the sensations which, if now present, would lead me to affirm that Calcutta exists here and now'.

Mill, then, is what we would now call a 'phenomenalist', a philosopher for whom belief in an external world is *reducible* to beliefs concerning future and possible perceptual experiences. In effect, he is picking up on and elaborating a view briefly hinted at by Bishop Berkeley (see p. 166 above) – a view which, in Berkeley's case but not, of course, in Mill's, was superceded by an account of external reality in terms of the experiences God is having.

Mill is satisfied that a permanent possibility of sensation 'constitutes altogether our idea of external substance'. For example, it answers to our conviction that such substances are 'perdurable' – that they do not change in the way our actual sensations do. One might then expect Mill, like many later phenomenalists, to dismiss as entirely unmotivated and indeed as unintelligible the claim that external objects are unperceivable things in themselves. However, consistently or otherwise, this is not what he does: rather, he sees such a claim as one which ordinary people – and not just wayward metaphysicians – unsurprisingly, though illegitimately, tend to embrace. A main reason for this tendency is the natural, if unfortunate, psychological urge to move from the proper distinction between individual experiences and their causes to one between experience *as a whole* and its supposed cause. In Chapter 11, Mill does not make clear why this move is illegitimate, but his objection is grounded in his theory of inference according to which, as mentioned earlier, only inductive inference from observed cases to further, in principle, observable cases is permissible.[2] There is, within that theory, no room for a principle like that of 'inference to the best explanation' which some philosophers have invoked by way of support for postulating unobservable entities as the cause of our experience as a whole.

Mill's ontology of actual and possible sensations is a parsimonious one, but not as parsimonious as that of some later phenomenalists. For in the Appendix to Chapters 11 and 12, Mill baulks, with some evident disappointment, at attempting to reduce *minds* or *selves* to collections of sensations in the same

---

[2] A clear exposition of this point, and of Mill's views at large, is John Skorupski's in his *English-Language Philosophy 1750 to 1945*, Oxford: Oxford University Press, 1993, pp. 54ff.

manner that physical objects have been reduced to these. My mind, he argues, cannot be reduced to a cluster or, in Hume's phrase, 'bundle' of sensations, since any sensation properly allocated to that cluster must already be recognizable as *mine*. Hence, we are forced to 'ascribe a reality to the Ego – to my own Mind – different from that real existence as a Permanent Possibility, which is the only reality I acknowledge in Matter' (p. 208). There will, of course, be philosophers who feel that, despite Mill's own lively arguments, a robust sense of the reality of physical objects, as much as that of minds, resists any dissolution of them into mere possibilities of experience.

Mill, The Psychological Theory of the Belief in an External World

Chapter XI

We have seen Sir W. Hamilton at work on the question of the reality of Matter, by the introspective method, and, as it seems, with little result. Let us now approach the same subject by the psychological. I proceed, therefore, to state the case of those who hold that the belief in an external world is not intuitive, but an acquired product.

This theory postulates the following psychological truths, all of which are proved by experience, and are not contested, though their force is seldom adequately felt, by Sir W. Hamilton and the other thinkers of the introspective school.

It postulates, first, that the human mind is capable of Expectation. In other words, that after having had actual sensations, we are capable of forming the conception of Possible sensations; sensations which we are not feeling at the present moment, but which we might feel, and should feel if certain conditions were present, the nature of which conditions we have, in many cases, learnt by experience.

It postulates, secondly, the laws of the Association of Ideas. So far as we are here concerned, these laws are the following: 1st. Similar phænomena tend to be thought of together. 2nd. Phænomena which have either been experienced or conceived in close contiguity to one another, tend to be thought of together. The contiguity is of two kinds; simultaneity, and immediate succession. Facts which have been experienced or thought of simultaneously, recall the thought of one another. Of facts which have been experienced or thought of in immediate succession, the antecedent, or the thought of it, recalls the thought of the consequent, but not conversely. 3rd. Associations produced by contiguity become more certain and rapid by repetition. When two phænomena have been very often experienced in conjunction, and have not, in any single instance, occurred separately either in experience or in thought, there is produced between them what has been called Inseparable, or less correctly, Indissoluble Association: by which is not meant that the association must inevitably last to the end of life – that no subsequent experience or process of thought can possibly avail to dissolve it; but only that as long as no such experience or process of thought has taken place, the association is irresistible; it is impossible for us to think the one thing disjoined from the other. 4th. When an association has acquired this character of inseparability – when the bond between the two ideas had been thus firmly riveted, not only does the idea called up by association become, in our consciousness, inseparable from the idea which suggested it, but the facts or phænomena answering to those ideas come at last to seem inseparable in existence: things which we are unable to conceive apart, appear incapable of existing apart; and the belief we have in their coexistence, though really a product of experience, seems intuitive. Innumerable examples might be given of this law. One of the most familiar, as well as the most striking, is that of our acquired perceptions of sight. Even those who, with Mr. [Samuel] Bailey, consider the perception of distance by the eye as not acquired, but intuitive, admit that there are many perceptions of sight which, though instantaneous and unhesitating, are not intuitive. What we see is a very minute fragment of what we think we see. We see artificially that one thing is hard, another soft. We see artificially that one thing is hot, another cold. We see artificially that what we see is a book, or a stone, each of these being not merely an inference, but a heap of inferences, from the signs which we see, to things not visible. We see, and cannot help seeing, what we have learnt to infer, even when we know that the inference is erroneous, and that the apparent perception is deceptive. We cannot help seeing the moon larger when near the horizon, though we know that she is of precisely her usual size. We cannot help seeing a mountain as nearer to us and of less height, when we see it through a more than ordinarily transparent atmosphere.

Setting out from these premises, the Psychological Theory maintains, that there are associations naturally and even necessarily generated by the order of our sensations and of our reminiscences of sensation, which, supposing no intuition of an external world to have existed in consciousness, would inevitably generate the belief, and would cause it to be regarded as an intuition.

What is it we mean, or what is it which leads us to say, that the objects we perceive are external to us, and not a part of our own thoughts? We mean, that there is concerned in our perceptions something which exists when we are not thinking of it; which existed before we had ever thought of it, and would exist if we were annihilated; and further, that there exist things which we never saw, touched, or otherwise perceived, and things which never have been perceived by man. This idea of something which is distinguished from our fleeting impressions by what, in Kantian language, is called Perdurability; something which is fixed and the same, while our impressions vary; something which exists whether we are aware of it or not, and which is always square (or of some other given figure) whether it appears to us square or round – constitutes altogether our idea of external substance. Whoever can assign an origin to this complex conception, has accounted for what we mean by the belief in matter. Now all this, according to the Psychological Theory, is but the form impressed by the known laws of association, upon the conception or notion, obtained by experience, of Contingent Sensations; by which are meant, sensations that are not in our present consciousness, and individually never were in our consciousness at all, but which in virtue of the laws to which we have learnt by experience that our sensations are subject, we know that we should have felt under given supposable circumstances, and under these same circumstances, might still feel.

I see a piece of white paper on a table. I go into another room. If the phænomenon always followed me, or if, when it did not follow me, I believed it to disappear *è rerum naturâ* [from the natural order], I should not believe it to be an external object. I should consider it as a phantom – a mere affection of my senses: I should not believe that there had been any Body there. But, though I have ceased to see it, I am persuaded that the paper is still there. I no longer have the sensations which it gave me; but I believe that when I again place myself in the circumstances in which I had those sensations, that, when I go again into the room, I shall again have them; and further, that there has been no intervening moment at which this would not have been the case. Owing to this property of my mind, my conception of the world at any given instant consists, in only a small proportion, of present sensations. Of these I may at the time have none at all, and they are in any case a most insignificant portion of the whole which I apprehend. The conception I form of the world existing at any moment, comprises, along with the sensations I am feeling, a countless variety of possibilities of sensation: namely, the whole of those which past observation tells me that I could, under any supposable circumstances, experience at this moment, together with an indefinite and illimitable multitude of others which though I do not know that I could, yet it is possible that I might, experience in circumstances not known to me. These various possibilities are the important thing to me in the world. My present sensations are generally of little importance, and are moreover fugitive: the possibilities, on the contrary, are permanent, which is the character that mainly distinguishes our idea of Substance or Matter from our notion of sensation. These possibilities, which are conditional certainties, need a special name to distinguish them from mere vague possibilities, which experience gives no warrant for reckoning upon. Now, as soon as a distinguishing name is given, though it be only to the same thing regarded in a different aspect, one of the most familiar experiences of our mental nature teaches us, that the different name comes to be considered as the name of a different thing.

There is another important peculiarity of these certified or guaranteed possibilities of sensation; namely, that they have reference, not to single sensations, but to sensations joined together in groups. When we think of anything as a material substance, or body, we either have had, or we think that on some given supposition we should have, not some *one* sensation, but a great and even an indefinite number and variety of sensations, generally belonging to different senses, but so linked together, that the presence of one announces the possible presence at the very same instant of any or all of the rest. In our mind, therefore, not only is this particular Possibility of sensation invested with the quality of permanence when we are not actually feeling any of the sensations at all; but when we are feeling some of them, the remaining sensations of the group are conceived by us in the form of Present Possibilities, which might be realized at the very moment. And as this happens in turn to all of them, the group as a whole presents itself to the mind as permanent, in contrast not solely with the temporariness of my bodily presence, but also with the temporary character of each of the sensations composing the group; in other words, as a kind of permanent substratum, under a set of passing experiences or manifestations: which is another leading character of our idea of substance or matter, as distinguished from sensation.

Let us now take into consideration another of the general characters of our experience, namely, that in addition to fixed groups, we also recognise a fixed Order in our sensations; an Order of succession, which, when ascertained by observation, gives rise to the ideas of Cause and Effect, according to what I hold to be the true theory of that relation, and is on any theory the source of all our knowledge what causes produce what effects. Now, of what nature is this fixed order among our sensations? It is a constancy of antecedence and sequence. But the constant antecedence and sequence do not generally exist between one actual sensation and another. Very few such sequences are presented to us by experience. In almost all the constant sequences which occur in Nature, the antecedence and consequence do not obtain between sensations, but between the groups we have been speaking about, of which a very small portion is actual sensation, the greater part being permanent possibilities of sensation, evidenced to us by a small and variable number of sensations actually present. Hence, our ideas of causation, power, activity, do not become connected in thought with our sensations as *actual* at all, save in the few physiological cases where these figure by themselves as the antecedents in some uniform sequence. Those ideas become connected, not with sensations, but with groups of possibilities of sensation. The sensations conceived do not, to our habitual thoughts, present themselves as sensations actually experienced, inasmuch as not only any one or any number of them may be supposed absent, but none of them need be present. We find that the modifications which are taking place more or less regularly in our possibilities of sensation, are mostly quite independent of our consciousness, and of our presence or absence. Whether we are asleep or awake the fire goes out, and puts an end to one particular possibility of warmth and light. Whether we are present or absent the corn ripens, and brings a new possibility of food. Hence we speedily learn to think of Nature as made up solely of these groups of possibilities, and the active force in Nature as manifested in the modification of some of these by others. The sensations, though the original foundation of the whole, come to be looked upon as a sort of accident depending on us, and the possibilities as much more real than the actual sensations, nay, as the very realities of which these are only the representations, appearances, or effects. When this state of mind has been arrived at, then, and from that time forward, we are never conscious of a present sensation without instantaneously referring it to some one of the groups of possibilities into which a sensation of that particular description enters; and if we do not yet know to what group to refer it, we at least feel an irresistible conviction that it must belong to some group or other; *i.e.* that its presence proves the existence, here and now, of a great number and variety of possibilities of sensation, without which it would not have been. The whole set of sensations as possible, form a permanent background to any one or more of them that are, at a given moment, actual; and the possibilities are conceived as standing to the actual sensations in the relation of a cause to its effects, or of canvas to the figures painted on it, or of a root to the trunk, leaves, and flowers, or of a substratum to that which is spread over it, or, in transcendental language, of Matter to Form.

When this point has been reached, the Permanent Possibilities in question have assumed such unlikeness of aspect, and such difference of apparent relation to us, from any sensations, that it would be contrary to all we know of the constitution of human nature that they should not be conceived as, and believed to be, at least as different from sensations as sensations are from one another. Their groundwork in sensation is forgotten, and they are supposed to be something intrinsically distinct from it. We can withdraw ourselves from any of our (external) sensations, or we can be withdrawn from them by some other agency. But though the sensations cease, the possibilities remain in existence; they are independent of our will, our presence, and everything which belongs to us. We find, too, that they belong as much to other human or sentient beings as to ourselves. We find other people grounding their expectations and conduct upon the same permanent possibilities on which we ground ours. But we do not find them experiencing the same actual sensations. Other people do not have our sensations exactly when and as we have them: but they have our possibilities of sensation; whatever indicates a present possibility of sensations to ourselves, indicates a present possibility of similar sensations to them, except so far as their organs of sensation may vary from the type of ours. This puts the final seal to our conception of the groups of possibilities as the fundamental reality in Nature. The permanent possibilities are common to us and to our fellow-creatures; the actual sensations are not. That which other people become aware of when, and on the same grounds, as I do, seems more real to me than that which they do not know of unless I tell them. The world of Possible Sensations succeeding one another according to laws, is as much in other beings as it is in me; it has therefore an existence outside me; it is an External World.

If this explanation of the origin and growth of the idea of Matter, or External Nature, contains nothing at variance with natural laws, it is at least an admissible supposition, that the element of Non-ego which Sir W. Hamilton regards as an original datum of consciousness, and which we certainly do find in what we now call our consciousness, may not be one of its primitive elements – may not have existed at all in its first manifestations. But if this supposition be admissible, it ought, on Sir W. Hamilton's principles, to be received as true. The first of the laws laid down by him for the interpretation of Consciousness, the law (as he terms it) of Parsimony, forbids to suppose an original principle of our nature in order to account for phænomena which admit of possible explanation from known causes. If the supposed ingredient of consciousness be one which might grow up (though we cannot prove that it did grow up) through later experience; and if, when it had so grown up, it would, by known laws of our nature, appear as completely intuitive as our sensations themselves; we are bound, according to Sir W. Hamilton's and all sound philosophy, to assign to it that origin. Where there is a known cause adequate to account for a phænomenon, there is no justification for ascribing it to an unknown one.

And what evidence does Consciousness furnish of the intuitiveness of an impression, except instantaneousness, apparent simplicity, and unconsciousness on our part of how the impression came into our minds? These features can only prove the impression to be intuitive, on the hypothesis that there are no means of accounting for them otherwise. If they not only might, but naturally would, exist, even on the supposition that it is not intuitive, we must accept the conclusion to which we are led by the Psychological Method, and which the Introspective Method furnishes absolutely nothing to contradict.

Matter, then, may be defined, a Permanent Possibility of Sensation. If I am asked, whether I believe in matter, I ask whether the questioner accepts this definition of it. If he does, I believe in matter: and so do all Berkeleians. In any other sense than this, I do not. But I affirm with confidence, that this conception of Matter includes the whole meaning attached to it by the common world, apart from philosophical, and sometimes from theological, theories. The reliance of mankind on the real existence of visible and tangible objects, means reliance on the reality and permanence of Possibilities of visual and tactual sensations, when no such sensations are actually experienced. We are warranted in believing that this is the meaning of Matter in the minds of many of its most esteemed metaphysical champions, though they themselves would not admit as much: for example, of Reid, Stewart, and Brown.[1] For these three philosophers alleged that all mankind, including Berkeley and Hume, really believed in Matter, inasmuch as unless they did, they would not have turned aside to save themselves from running against a post. Now all which this manœuvre really proved is, that they believed in Permanent Possibilities of Sensation. We have therefore the unintentional sanction of these three eminent defenders of the existence of matter, for affirming, that to believe in Permanent Possibilities of Sensation is believing in Matter. It is hardly necessary, after such authorities, to mention Dr Johnson, or any one else who resorts to the *argumentatum baculinum* of knocking a stick against the ground.[2] Sir W. Hamilton, a far subtler thinker than any of these, never reasons in this manner. He never supposes that a disbeliever in what he means by Matter, ought in consistency to act in any different mode from those who believe in it. He knew that the belief on which all the practical consequences depend, is the belief in Permanent Possibilities of Sensation, and that if nobody believed in a material universe in any other sense, life would go on exactly as it now does. He, however, did believe in more than this, but, I think, only because it had never occurred to him that mere Possibilities of Sensation could, to our artificialized consciousness, present the character of objectivity which, as we have now shown, they not only can, but unless the known laws of the human mind were suspended, must necessarily, present.

Perhaps it may be objected, that the very possibility of framing such a notion of Matter as Sir W. Hamilton's – the capacity in the human mind of imagining an external world which is anything more than what the Psychological Theory makes it – amounts to a disproof of the theory. If (it may be said) we had no revelation in consciousness, of a world which is not in some way or other identified with sensation, we should be unable to have the notion of such a world. If the only ideas we had of external objects were ideas of our sensations, supplemented by an acquired notion of permanent possibilities of sensation, we must (it is thought) be incapable of conceiving, and therefore still more incapable of fancying that we perceive, things which are not sensations at all. It being evident however that some philosophers believe this, and it being maintainable that the mass of mankind do so, the existence of a perdurable basis of sensations, distinct from sensations themselves, is proved, it might be said, by the possibility of believing it.

Let me first restate what I apprehend the belief to be. We believe that we perceive a something closely related to all our sensations, but different from those which we are feeling at any particular minute; and distinguished from sensations altogether, by being permanent and always the same, while these are fugitive, variable, and alternately displace one another. But these attributes of the object of perception are properties belonging to all the possibilities of sensation which experience guarantees. The belief in such permanent possibilities seems to me to include all that is essential or characteristic in the belief in substance. I believe that Calcutta exists, though I do not perceive it, and that it would still exist if every percipient inhabitant were suddenly to leave the place, or be struck dead. But when I analyse the belief, all I find in it is, that were these events to take place, the Permanent Possibility of Sensation which I call Calcutta would still remain; that if I were suddenly transported to the banks of the Hoogly, I should still have the sensations which, if now present, would me to affirm that Calcutta exists here and now. We may infer, therefore, that both philosophers and the world at large, when they think of matter, conceive it really as a Permanent Possibility of Sensation. But the majority of philosophers fancy that it is something more; and the world at large, though they have really, as I conceive, nothing in their minds but a Permanent Possibility of Sensation, would, if asked the question, undoubtedly agree with the philosophers: and though this is sufficiently explained by the tendency of the human mind to infer difference of things from difference of names, I acknowledge the obligation of showing how it can be possible to believe in an existence transcending all possibilities of sensation, unless on the hypothesis that such an existence actually is, and that we actually perceive it.

The explanation, however, is not difficult. It is an admitted fact, that we are capable of all conceptions which can be formed by generalizing from the observed laws of our sensations. Whatever relation we find to exist between any one of our sensations and something different from *it*, that same relation we have no difficulty in conceiving to exist between the sum of all our sensations and something different from *them*. The differences which our consciousness recognises between one sensation and another, give us the general notion of difference, and inseparably associate with every sensation we have, the feeling of its being different from other things: and when once this association has been formed, we can no longer conceive anything, without being able, and even being compelled, to form also the conception of something different from it. This familiarity with the idea of something different from *each* thing we know, makes it natural and easy to form the notion of something different from *all* things that we know, collectively as well as individually. It is true we can form no conception of what such a thing can be; our notion of it is merely negative; but the idea of a substance, apart from its relation to the impressions which we conceive it as making on our senses *is* a merely negative one. There is thus no psychological obstacle to our forming the notion of a something which is neither a sensation nor a possibility of sensation, even if our consciousness does not testify to it; and nothing is more likely than that the Permanent Possibilities of sensation, to which our consciousness does testify, should be confounded in our minds with this imaginary conception. All experience attests the strength of the tendency to mistake mental abstractions, even negative ones, for substantive realities; and the Permanent Possibilities of sensation which experience guarantees, are so extremely unlike in many of their properties to actual sensations, that since we are capable of imagining something which transcends sensation, there is a great natural probability that we should suppose these to be it.

But this natural probability is converted into certainty, when we take into consideration that universal law of our experience which is termed the law of Causation, and which makes us mentally connect with the beginning of everything, some antecedent condition, or Cause. The case of Causation is one of the most marked of all the cases in which we extend to the sum total of our consciousness, a notion derived from its parts. It is a striking example of our power to conceive, and our tendency to believe, that a relation which subsists between every individual item of our experience and some other item, subsists also between our experience as a whole, and something not within the sphere of experience. By this extension to the sum of all our experiences, of the internal relations obtaining between its several parts, we are led to consider sensation itself – the aggregate whole of our sensations – as deriving its origin from antecedent existences transcending sensation. That we should do this, is a consequence of the particular character of the uniform sequences, which experience discloses to us among our sensations. As already remarked, the constant antecedent of a sensation is seldom another sensation, or set of sensations, actually felt. It is much oftener the existence of a group of possibilities, not necessarily including any actual sensations, except such as are required to show that the possibilities are really present. Nor are actual sensations indispensable even for this purpose; for the presence of the object (which is nothing more than the immediate presence of the possibilities) may be made known to us by the very sensation which we refer to it as its effect. Thus, the real antecedent of an effect – the only antecedent which, being invariable and unconditional, we consider to be the cause – may be, not any sensation really felt, but solely the presence, at that or the immediately preceding moment, of a group of possibilities of sensation. Hence it is not with sensations as actually experienced, but with their Permanent Possibilities, that the idea of Cause comes to be identified: and we, by one and the same process, acquire the habit of regarding Sensation in general, like all our individual sensations, as an Effect, and also that of conceiving as the causes of most of our individual sensations, not other sensations, but general possibilities of sensation. If all these considerations put together do not completely explain and account for our conceiving these Possibilities as a class of independent and substantive entities, I know not what psychological analysis can be conclusive.

It may perhaps be said, that the preceding theory gives, indeed, some account of the idea of Permanent Existence which forms part of our conception of matter, but gives no explanation of our believing these permanent objects to be external, or out of ourselves. I apprehend, on the contrary, that the very idea of anything out of ourselves is derived solely from the knowledge experience give us of the Permanent Possibilities. Our sensations we carry with us wherever we go, and they never exist where we are not; but when we change our place we do not carry away with us the Permanent Possibilities of Sensation: they remain until we return, or arise and cease under conditions with which our presence has in general nothing to do. And more than all – they are, and will be after we have ceased to feel, Permanent Possibilities of Sensation to other beings than ourselves. Thus our actual sensations and the permanent possibilities of sensation, stand out in obtrusive contrast to one another: and when the idea of Cause has been acquired, and extended by generalization from the parts of our experience to its aggregate whole, nothing can be more natural than that the

Permanent Possibilities should be classed by us as existences generically distinct from our sensations, but of which our sensations are the effect.*

The same theory which accounts for our ascribing to an aggregate of possibilities of sensation, a permanent existence which our sensations themselves do not possess, and consequently a greater reality than belongs to our sensations, also explains our attributing greater objectivity to the Primary Qualities of bodies than to the Secondary. For the sensations which correspond to what are called the Primary Qualities (as soon at least as we come to apprehend them by two senses, the eye as well as the touch) are always present when any part of the group is so. But colours, tastes, smells, and the like, being, in comparison, fugacious, are not, in the same degree, conceived as being always there, even when nobody is present to perceive them. The sensations answering to the Secondary Qualities are only occasional, those to the Primary, constant. The Secondary, moreover, vary with different persons, and with the temporary sensibility of our organs; the Primary, when perceived at all, are, as far as we know, the same to all persons and at all times.[3]

Notes

1 Thomas Reid (1710–96) was the leading representative of Scottish

* My able American critic, Dr H. B. Smith, contends . . . that these facts afford no proofs that objects *are* external to us. I never pretended that they do. I am accounting for our conceiving, or representing to ourselves, the Permanent Possibilities as real objects external to us. I do not believe that the real externality to us of anything, except other minds, is capable of proof. But the Permanent Possibilities are external to us in the only sense we need care about; they are not constructed by the mind itself, but merely recognised by it; in Kantian language, they are *given* to us, and to other beings in common with us. "Men cannot act, cannot live," says Professor [Alexander] Fraser, "without assuming an external world, in some conception of the term external. It is the business of the philosopher to explain what that conception ought to be. For ourselves we can conceive only – (1) An externality to our present and transient experience in *our own* possible experience past and future, and (2) An externality to our own conscious experience, in the contemporaneous, as well as in the past or future experience of *other minds.*" The view I take of externality, in the sense in which I acknowledge it as real, could not be more accurately expressed than in Professor Fraser's words. Dr Smith's criticisms continually go wide of the mark because he has somehow imagined that I am defending, instead of attacking, the belief in Matter as an entity *per se.* As when he says that my reasoning assumes, contrary to my own opinion, "an *à priori* necessity and validity of the law of cause and effect, or invariable antecedence and consequence." This might fairly have been said if I were defending the belief in the supposed hidden cause of our sensations: but I am only accounting for it; and to do so I assume only the tendency, but not the legitimacy of the tendency, to extend all the laws of our own experience to a sphere beyond our experience.

'commonsense philosophy', and Dugald Stewart (1735–1828) and Thomas Brown (1778–1820) were two of his main, if critical, followers.

2 An *argumentum baculinam* is literally an argument with a stick, hence an argument taking the form of a threat. The phrase hardly fits Dr Johnson's famous 'argument' against Berkeley's immaterialism, which consisted in kicking a stone.

3 Although this paragraph argues for a significant distinction between shape etc. on the other hand and colours, tastes, etc. on the other, it is not, of course, a defence of Locke's distinction between primary and secondary qualities, which was between those qualities in mind-independent objects which do and those which do not resemble our experiences of them (see chapter 8 above).

F. H. Bradley, *Appearance and Reality*, Chapters 13 and 14

From F. H. Bradley, *Appearance and Reality: a metaphysical essay*. Oxford: Clarendon Press, 1930 (9th impression), pp. 119–30, 140–42 (middle sections of Ch. 14 and some notes omitted: asterisked note is Bradley's). Reprinted by permission of Oxford University Press.

'[T]here is no being . . . outside of . . . psychical existence'. This stark statement by the leading 'Oxford Idealist', F. H. Bradley (1846–1924), in his magnum opus *Appearance and Reality* (1893), might sound to put him in the same camp as J. S. Mill (chapter 13 above). However, Bradley's idealism is of an entirely different stamp from Mill's atomistic phenomenalism, which Bradley saw as a pernicious doctrine intimately linked to an individualistic utilitarian ethics that he detested. (I omit the sections in Ch. 14 where he argues that his own metaphysics satisfies our moral aspirations.) Bradley's position has some affinity with that of the German Absolute Idealists, but still more with that of Śaṁkara (chapter 4 above), as T. S. Eliot, who wrote a dissertation on Bradley, and several modern Indian philosophers have noted.

Chapters 13–14, which succinctly state the kernel of Bradley's metaphysics, presuppose a number of earlier conclusions. The first is that a belief is true in virtue of its coherence with a total body of beliefs, and that its 'degree of truth' depends on how adequately it expresses this totality. Our everyday beliefs enjoy only a very limited degree of truth, since in affirming, say, that the cat is on the mat, I severely abstract elements from the whole of reality, thereby giving little indication of what that whole is.[1] The second is that it is perverse to regard the world as a collection of elements that are somehow related to one another. 'A relational way of thought . . . must give appearance, and not truth' (*Appearance and Reality*, p. 28). The notion of relations between a plurality of independent objects is, Bradley argues, incoherent. The argument,

---

[1] On degrees of truth, see Bradley's *Principles of Logic*, Oxford: Oxford University Press, 1883, and Richard Wollheim's discussion in his *F. H. Bradley*, Baltimore: Penguin, 1969, ch. 4.

reminiscent of Śaṁkara (see p. 86 above), is that the notion involves a regress. For the cat and the mat to be spatially related, there must be a further relation between the cat, the mat and that spatial relation – and so on.[2]

Combining these points, Bradley elaborates, in Ch. 13, his claim that plurality is only 'appearance', that reality as such, or the Absolute, is a single harmonious and systematic whole, within which each artificially abstracted element owes its identity to its place in that whole. Nothing, except that whole, enjoys the independence required to count as fully real. Echoes of Śaṁkara and, indeed, Spinoza (see chapter 7 above) are easy to hear.

This monistic claim, explains Bradley, only tells us of the 'form' of absolute reality. There remains the question, what is its 'matter' or nature? The unequivocal answer is that 'this matter is experience. . . . [To] be real . . . must be to fall within sentience'. The argument here is, perhaps, disappointingly curt, little more than a repetition of Berkeley's 'master argument' (see p. 166 above) to the effect that we can never succeed in thinking or imagining something unthought or unimagined. 'I can myself conceive of nothing else than the experienced.' Be that as it may, Bradley's own idealism is far removed from Berkeley's and Mill's. For him, experience is not the sum of atomic sense-data, perceptions and so on taking place in individual minds or subjects. Individual minds, no less than particular sense-data, are artificial abstractions from the essentially seamless unity of experience as a whole. The subject–object distinction, like that between different subjects, belongs to the realm of appearance.

What can be said about experience as a whole, the 'matter' of absolute reality? Very little, according to Bradley, since as soon as we try to think or speak about it we are bound to employ concepts and distinctions that distort its seamless character. Bradley does, however, think that, in certain kinds of familiar experiences, we get a glimmer or intimation of this whole. Thus, in 'mere feeling', where our experience is as yet unarticulated into subject and object, thought and will, and so on, there is a sense, however dark, of a 'unity which transcends and yet contains every manifold appearance'. Bradley, here, is reversing a whole tradition of western rationalism, according to which it is thought, not 'mere feeling', which provides access to the nature of reality. Indeed, one suspects that Bradley is a mystic *manqué*, hinting at, without (like Śaṁkara) endorsing, the possibility of a special experience of the oneness of reality.

Bradley was an immensely influential philosopher at the turn of the century, one whom philosophers rather more in fashion today, such as William James and Bertrand Russell, saw that they needed to take on and refute if

---

[2] For an excellent discussion of Bradley's account of relations, see Peter Hylton, *Russell, Idealism and the Emergence of Analytic Philosophy*, Oxford: Clarendon Press, 1990, pp. 48ff.

their own positions were to pass muster. It is to these positions that we turn in the following chapters of this volume.

Bradley, The General Nature of Reality

Chapter XIII

The result of our First Book has been mainly negative. We have taken up a number of ways of regarding reality, and we have found that they all are vitiated by self-discrepancy. The reality can accept not one of these predicates, at least in the character in which so far they have come. We certainly ended with a reflection which promised something positive. Whatever is rejected as appearance is, for that very reason, no mere nonentity. It cannot bodily be shelved and merely got rid of, and, therefore, since it must fall somewhere, it must belong to reality. To take it as existing somehow and somewhere in the unreal, would surely be quite meaningless. For reality must own and cannot be less than appearance, and that is the one positive result which, so far, we have reached.[1] But as to the character which, otherwise, the real possesses, we at present know nothing; and a further knowledge is what we must aim at through the remainder of our search. The present Book, to some extent, falls into two divisions. The first of these deals mainly with the general character of reality, and with the defence of this against a number of objections. Then from this basis, in the second place, I shall go on to consider mainly some special features. But I must admit that I have kept to no strict principle of division. I have really observed no rule of progress, except to get forward in the best way that I can.

At the beginning of our inquiry into the nature of the real we encounter, of course, a general doubt or denial. To know the truth, we shall be told, is impossible, or is, at all events, wholly impracticable. We cannot have positive knowledge about first principles; and, if we could possess it, we should not know when actually we had got it. What is denied is, in short, the existence of a criterion. I shall, later on, in Chapter xxvii, have to deal more fully with the objections of a thorough-going scepticism, and I will here confine myself to what seems requisite for the present.

Is there an absolute criterion? This question, to my mind, is answered by a second question: How otherwise should we be able to say anything at all about appearance? For through the last Book, the reader will remember, we were for the most part criticizing. We were judging phenomena and were condemning them, and throughout we proceeded as if the self-contradictory could not be real. But this was surely to have and to apply an absolute criterion. For consider: you can scarcely propose to be quite passive when presented with statements about reality. You can hardly take the position of admitting any and every nonsense to be truth, truth absolute and entire, at least so far as you know. For, if you think at all so as to discriminate between truth and falsehood, you will find that you cannot accept open self-contradiction. Hence to think is to judge, and to judge is to criticize, and to criticize is to use a criterion of reality. And surely to doubt this would be mere blindness or confused self-deception. But if so, it is clear that, in rejecting the inconsistent as appearance, we are applying a positive knowledge of the ultimate nature of things. Ultimate reality is such that it does not contradict itself; here is an absolute criterion. And it is proved absolute by the fact that, either in endeavouring to deny it, or even in attempting to doubt it, we tacitly assume its validity.

One of these essays in delusion may be noticed briefly in passing. We may be told that our criterion has been developed by experience, and that therefore at least it may not be absolute. But why anything should be weaker for having been developed is, in the first place, not obvious. And, in the second place, the whole doubt, when understood, destroys itself. For the alleged origin of our criterion is delivered to us by knowledge which rests throughout on its application as an absolute test. And what can be more irrational than to try to prove that a principle is doubtful, when the proof through every step rests on its unconditional truth? It would, of course, not be irrational to take one's stand on this criterion, to use it to produce a conclusion hostile to itself, and to urge that therefore our whole know-ledge is self-destructive, since it essentially drives us to what we cannot accept. But this is not the result which our supposed objector has in view, or would welcome. He makes no attempt to show in general that a psycho-logical growth is in any way hostile to metaphysical validity. And he is not prepared to give up his own psychological knowledge, which knowledge plainly is ruined if the criterion is *not* absolute. The doubt is seen, when we reflect, to be founded on that which it endeavours to question. And it has but blindly borne witness to the absolute certainty of our knowledge about reality.

Thus we possess a criterion, and our criterion is supreme. I do not mean to deny that we might have several standards, giving us sundry pieces of information about the nature of things. But, be that as it may, we still have an over-ruling test of truth, and the various standards (if they exist) are certainly subordinate. This at once becomes evident, for we cannot refuse to bring such standards together, and to ask if they agree. Or, at least, if a doubt is suggested as to their consistency, each with itself and with the rest, we are compelled, so to speak, to assume jurisdiction. And if they were guilty of self-contradiction, when examined or compared, we should con-demn them as appearance. But we could not do that if they were not sub-ject all to one tribunal. And hence, as we find nothing not subordinate to the test of self-consistency, we are forced to set that down as supreme and absolute.

But it may be said that this supplies us with no real information. If we think, then certainly we are not allowed to be inconsistent, and it is admit-ted that this test is unconditional and absolute. But it will be urged that, for knowledge about any matter, we require something more than a bare negation. The ultimate reality (we are agreed) does not permit self-contra-diction, but a prohibition or an absence (we shall be told) by itself does not amount to positive knowledge. The denial of inconsistency, therefore, does not predicate any positive quality. But such an objection is untenable. It may go so far as to assert that a bare denial is possible, that we may reject a predicate though we stand on no positive basis, and though there is noth-ing special which serves to reject. This error has been refuted in my *Princi-ples of Logic* (Book I, Chapter iii), and I do not propose to discuss it here. I will pass to another sense in which the objection may seem more plausible. The criterion, it may be urged, in itself is doubtless positive; but, for our knowledge and in effect, is merely negative. And it gives us therefore no information at all about reality, for, although knowledge is there, it cannot be brought out. The criterion is a basis, which serves as the foundation of denial; but, since this basis cannot be exposed, we are but able to stand on it and unable to see it. And it hence, in effect, tells us nothing, though there are assertions which it does not allow us to venture on. This objec-tion, when stated in such a form, may seem plausible, and there is a sense in which I am prepared to admit that it is valid. If by the nature of reality we understand its full nature, I am not contending that this in a complete form is knowable. But that is very far from being the point here at issue. For the objection denies that we have a standard which gives *any* positive knowledge, *any* information, complete or incomplete, about the genuine reality. And this denial assuredly is mistaken.

The objection admits that we know what reality *does*, but it refuses to allow us any understanding of what reality *is*. The standard (it is agreed) both exists and possesses a positive character, and it is agreed that this character rejects inconsistency. It is admitted that we know this, and the point at issue is whether such knowledge supplies any positive information. And to my mind this question seems not hard to answer. For I cannot see how, when I observe a thing at work, I am to stand there and to insist that I know nothing of its nature. I fail to perceive how a function is nothing at all, or how it does not positively qualify that to which I attribute it. To know only so much, I admit, may very possibly be useless; it may leave us without the information which we desire most to obtain; but, for all that, it is not total ignorance.

Our standard denies inconsistency, and therefore asserts consistency. If we can be sure that the inconsistent is unreal, we must, logically, be just as sure that the reality is consistent. The question is solely as to the meaning to be given to consistency. We have now seen that it is not the bare exclusion of discord, for that is merely our abstraction, and is otherwise nothing. And our result, so far, is this. Reality is known to possess a positive character, but this character is at present determined only as that which excludes contradiction.

But we may make a further advance. We saw (in the preceding chapter) that all appearance must belong to reality. For what appears is, and whatever is cannot fall outside the real. And we may now combine this result with the conclusion just reached. We may say that everything, which appears, is somehow real in such a way as to be self-consistent. The character of the real is to possess everything phenomenal in a harmonious form.

I will repeat the same truth in other words. Reality is one in this sense that it has a positive nature exclusive of discord, a nature which must hold throughout everything that is to be real. Its diversity can be diverse only so far as not to clash, and what seems otherwise anywhere cannot be real. And, from the other side, everything which appears must be real. Appearance must belong to reality, and it must therefore be concordant and other than it seems. The bewildering mass of phenomenal diversity must hence somehow be at unity and self-consistent; for it cannot be elsewhere than in reality, and reality excludes discord. Or again we may put it so: the real is individual. It is one in the sense that its positive character embraces all differences in an inclusive harmony. And this knowledge, poor as it may be, is certainly more than bare negation or simple ignorance. So far as it goes, it gives us positive news about absolute reality.

Let us try to carry this conclusion a step further on. We know that the real is one; but its oneness so far, is ambiguous. Is it one system, possessing diversity as an adjective; or is its consistency, on the other hand, an attribute of independent realities? We have to ask, in short, if a plurality of reals is possible, and if these can merely coexist so as not to be discrepant? Such a plurality would mean a number of beings not dependent on each other. On the one hand they would possess somehow the phenomenal diversity, for that possession, we have seen, is essential. And, on the other hand, they would be free from external disturbance and from inner discrepancy. After the inquiries of our First Book the possibility of such reals hardly calls for discussion. For the internal states of each give rise to hope-less difficulties. And, in the second place, the plurality of the reals cannot be reconciled with their independence. I will briefly resume the arguments which force us to this latter result.

If the Many are supposed to be without internal quality, each would forthwith become nothing, and we must therefore take each as being inter-nally somewhat. And, if they are to be plural, they must be a diversity somehow coexisting together. Any attempt again to take their together-ness as unessential seems to end in the unmeaning. We have no knowledge of a plural diversity, nor can we attach any sense to it, if we do not have it somehow as one. And, if we abstract from this unity, we have also there-with abstracted from the plurality, and are left with mere being.

Can we then have a plurality of independent reals which merely coexist? No, for absolute independence and coexistence are incompatible. Absolute independence is an idea which consists merely in one-sided abstraction. It is made by an attempted division of the aspect of several existence from the aspect of relatedness; and these aspects, whether in fact or thought, are really indivisible.

If we take the diversity of our reals to be such as we discover in feeling and at a stage where relations do not exist, that diversity is never found except as one integral character of an undivided whole. And if we forcibly abstract from that unity, then together with feeling we have destroyed the diversity of feeling. We are left not with plurality, but with mere being, or, if you prefer it, with nothing. Coexistence in feeling is hence an instance and a proof not of self-sufficiency, but of dependence, and beside this it would add a further difficulty. If the nature of our reals is the diversity found at a stage below relations, how are we to dispose of the mass of relational appearance? For that exists, and existing it must somehow qualify the world, a world the reality of which is discovered only at a level other than its own. Such a position would seem not easy to justify.

Thus a mode of togetherness such as we can verify in feeling destroys the independence of our reals. And they will fare no better if we seek to find their coexistence elsewhere. For any other verifiable way of togetherness must involve relations, and they are fatal to self-sufficiency. Relations, we saw, are a development of and from the felt totality. They inadequately express, and they still imply in the background that unity apart from which the diversity is nothing. Relations are unmeaning except within and on the basis of a substantial whole, and related terms, if made absolute, are forth-with destroyed. Plurality and relatedness are but features and aspects of a unity.

If the relations in which the reals somehow stand are viewed as essential, that, as soon as we understand it, involves at once the internal relativity of the reals. And any attempt to maintain the relations as merely external must fail.[2] For if, wrongly and for argument's sake, we admit processes and arrangements which do not qualify their terms, yet such arrangements, if admitted, are at any rate not ultimate. The terms would be prior and independent only with regard to *these* arrangements, and they would remain relative otherwise, and vitally dependent on some whole. And severed from this unity, the terms perish by the very stroke which aims to set them up as absolute.

The reals therefore cannot be self-existent, and, if self-existent, yet taken as the world they would end in inconsistency. For the relations, because they exist, must somehow qualify the world. The relations then must externally qualify the sole and self-contained reality, and that seems self-contradictory or meaningless.* And if it is urged that a plurality of independent beings may be unintelligible, but that after all some unintelligible facts must be affirmed – the answer is obvious. An unintelligible fact may be admitted so far as, first, it is a fact, and so far as, secondly, it has a meaning which does not contradict itself internally or make self-discrepant our view of the world. But the alleged independence of the reals is no fact, but a theoretical construction; and, so far as it has a meaning, that meaning contradicts itself, and issues in chaos. A reality of this kind may safely be taken as unreal.

We cannot therefore maintain a plurality save as dependent on the relations in which it stands. Or if desiring to avoid relations we fall back on the diversity given in feeling, the result is the same. The plurality then sinks to become merely an integral aspect in a single substantial unity, and the reals have vanished.

---

* To this brief statement we might add other fatal objections. There is the question of the reals' interaction and of the general order of the world. Here, whether we affirm or deny, we turn in a maze. The fact of knowledge plunges us again in a dilemma. If we do not know that the Many are, we cannot affirm them. But the knowledge of the Many seems compatible with the self-existence neither of what knows nor of what is known. Finally, if the relations are admitted to an existence somehow alongside of the reals, the sole reality of the reals is given up. The relations themselves have now become a second kind of real thing. But the connexion between these new reals and the old ones, whether we deny or affirm it, leads to insoluble problems.

The General Nature of Reality (*cont.*)

Chapter XIV

Our result so far is this. Everything phenomenal is somehow real; and the absolute must at least be as rich as the relative. And, further, the Absolute is not many; there are no independent reals. The universe is one in this sense that its differences exist harmoniously within one whole, beyond which there is nothing. Hence the Absolute is, so far, an individual and a system, but, if we stop here, it remains but formal and abstract. Can we then, the question is, say anything about the concrete nature of the system?

Certainly, I think this is possible. When we ask as to the matter which fills up the empty outline, we can reply in one word, that this matter is experience. And experience means something much the same as given and present fact. We perceive, on reflection, that to be real, or even barely to exist, must be to fall within sentience. Sentient experience, in short, is reality, and what is not this is not real. We may say, in other words, that there is no being or fact outside of that which is commonly called psychical existence. Feeling, thought, and volition (any groups under which we class psychical phenomena) are all the material of existence, and there is no other material, actual or even possible. This result in its general form seems evident at once; and, however serious a step we now seem to have taken, there would be no advantage at this point in discussing it at length. For the test in the main lies ready to our hand, and the decision rests on the manner in which it is applied. I will state the case briefly thus. Find any piece of existence, take up anything that any one could possibly call a fact, or could in any sense assert to have being, and then judge if it does not consist in sentient experience. Try to discover any sense in which you can still continue to speak of it, when all perception and feeling have been removed; or point out any fragment of its matter, any aspect of its being, which is not derived from and is not still relative to this source. When the experiment is made strictly, I can myself conceive of nothing else than the experienced. Anything, in no sense felt or perceived, becomes to me quite unmeaning. And as I cannot try to think of it without realizing either that I am not thinking at all, or that I am thinking of it against my will as being experienced, I am driven to the conclusion that for me experience is the same as reality. The fact that falls elsewhere seems, in my mind, to be a mere word and a failure, or else an attempt at self-contradiction. It is a vicious abstraction whose existence is meaningless nonsense, and is therefore not possible.

This conclusion is open, of course, to grave objection, and must in its consequences give rise to serious difficulties. I will not attempt to anticipate the discussion of these, but before passing on, will try to obviate a dangerous mistake. For, in asserting that the real is nothing but experience, I may be understood to endorse a common error. I may be taken first to divide the percipient subject from the universe; and then, resting on that subject, as on a thing actual by itself, I may be supposed to urge that it cannot transcend its own states. Such an argument would lead to impossible results, and would stand on a foundation of faulty abstraction. To set up the subject as real independently of the whole, and to make the whole into experience in the sense of an adjective of that subject, seems to me indefensible. And when I contend that reality must be sentient, my conclusion almost consists in the denial of this fundamental error. For if, seeking for reality, we go to experience, what we certainly do *not* find is a subject or an object, or indeed any other thing whatever, standing separate and on its own bottom. What we discover rather is a whole in which distinctions can be made, but in which divisions do not exist. And this is the point on which I insist, and it is the very ground on which I stand, when I urge that reality is sentient experience. I mean that to be real is to be indissolubly one thing with sentience. It is to be something which comes as a feature and aspect within one whole of feeling, something which, except as an integral element of such sentience, has no meaning at all. And what I repudiate is the separation of feeling from the felt, or of the desired from desire, or of what is thought from thinking, or the division – I might add – of anything from anything else. Nothing is ever so presented as real by itself, or can be argued so to exist without demonstrable fallacy. And in asserting that the reality is experience, I rest throughout on this foundation. You cannot find fact unless in unity with sentience, and one cannot in the end be divided from the other, either actually or in idea. But to be utterly indivisible from feeling or perception, to be an integral element in a whole which is experienced, this surely is itself to *be* experience. Being and reality are, in brief, one thing with sentience; they can neither be opposed to, nor even in the end distinguished from it.

I am well aware that this statement stands in need of explanation and defence. This will, I hope, be supplied by succeeding chapters, and I think it better for the present to attempt to go forward. Our conclusion, so far, will be this, that the Absolute is one system, and that its contents are nothing but sentient experience. It will hence be a single and all-inclusive experience, which embraces every partial diversity in concord. For it cannot be less than appearance, and hence no feeling or thought, of any kind, can fall outside its limits. And if it is more than any feeling or thought which we know, it must still remain more of the same nature. It cannot pass into another region beyond what falls under the general head of sentience. For to assert that possibility would be in the end to use words without a meaning. We can entertain no such suggestion except as self-contradictory, and as therefore impossible.

This conclusion will, I trust, at the end of my work bring more conviction to the reader; for we shall find that it is the one view which will harmonize all facts. And the objections brought against it, when it and they are once properly defined, will prove untenable. But our general result is at present seriously defective; and we must now attempt to indicate and remedy its failure in principle. . . .

. . . And hence, for the present at least, we must believe that reality satisfies our whole being. Our main wants – for truth and life, and for beauty and goodness – must all find satisfaction. And we have seen that this consummation must somehow be experience, and be individual. Every element of the universe, sensation, feeling, thought and will, must be included within one comprehensive sentience. And the question which now occurs is whether really we have a positive idea of such sentience. Do we at all know what we mean when we say that it is actual?

Fully to realize the existence of the Absolute is for finite beings impossible. In order thus to know we should have to be [it], and then *we* should not exist. This result is certain, and all attempts to avoid it are illusory. But then the whole question turns on the sense in which we are to understand 'knowing'. What is impossible is to construct absolute life in its detail, to have the specific experience in which it consists. But to gain an idea of its main features – an idea true so far as it goes, though abstract and incomplete – is a different endeavour. And it is a task, so far as I see, in which we may succeed. For these main features, to some extent, are within our own experience; and again the idea of their combination is, in the abstract, quite intelligible. And surely no more than this is wanted for a knowledge of the Absolute. It is a knowledge which of course differs enormously from the fact. But it is true, for all that, while it respects its own limits; and it seems fully attainable by the finite intellect.

I will end this chapter by briefly mentioning the sources of such knowledge. First, in mere feeling, or immediate presentation, we have the experience of a whole (Chapters ix, xix, xxvi, xxvii). This whole contains diversity, and, on the other hand, is not parted by relations. Such an experience, we must admit, is most imperfect and unstable, and its inconsistencies lead us at once to transcend it. Indeed, we hardly possess it as more than that which we are in the act of losing. But it serves to suggest to us the general idea of a total experience, where will and thought and feeling may all once more be one. Further, this same unity, felt below distinctions, shows itself later in a kind of hostility against them. We find it in the efforts made both by theory and practice, each to complete itself and so to pass into the other. And, again, the relational form, as we saw, pointed everywhere to a unity. It implies a substantial totality beyond relations and above them, a whole endeavouring without success to realize itself in their detail. Further, the ideas of goodness, and of the beautiful, suggest in different ways the same result. They more or less involve the experience of a whole beyond relations though full of diversity. Now, if we gather (as we can) such considerations into one, they will assuredly supply us with a positive idea. We gain from them the knowledge of a unity which transcends and yet contains every manifold appearance. They supply not an experience but an abstract idea, and idea which we make by uniting given elements. And the mode of union, once more in the abstract, is actually given. Thus we know what is meant by an experience, which embraces all divisions, and yet somehow possesses the direct nature of feeling. We can form the general idea of an absolute experience in which phenomenal distinctions are merged, a whole become immediate at a higher stage without losing any richness. Our complete inability to understand this concrete unity in detail is no good ground for our declining to entertain it. Such a ground would be irrational, and its principle could hardly everywhere be adhered to. But if we can realize at all the general features of the Absolute, if we can see that somehow they come together in a way known vaguely and in the abstract, our result is certain. Our conclusion, so far as it goes, is real knowledge of the Absolute, positive knowledge built on experience, and inevitable when we try to think consistently. We shall realize its nature more clearly when we have confronted it with a series of objections and difficulties. If our result will hold against them all, we shall be able to urge that in reason we are bound to think it true.

Notes

1 I take Bradley to mean two things in these rather confusing remarks. First, that while a merely apparent X is not a real X, its appearing as X is real enough. Second, given Bradley's doctrine of degrees of truth, experiencing an apparent aspect of the world is not necessarily, therefore, to be experiencing it in a totally unveridical way.
2 In Bradley's vocabulary, external relations – if there were any – would hold between independently existing and identifiable objects. According to him,

there are no such external relations. An internal relation between X and Y, on the other hand, is one that must obtain between them in order for them to *be* X and Y. Since everything is internally related to everything else, it follows that the identity of any one thing logically depends on its place within a 'harmonious' whole of things.

15 ▶ William James, 'The One and the Many'

From John J. McDermott (ed.), *The Writings of William James.* Chicago: University of Chicago Press, 1977, pp. 258–70 (some notes omitted; asterisked notes are James's).

An important bone of metaphysical contention in several earlier chapters of this anthology has been that of the unity *versus* plurality of the world. Is it a single Spinozan substance or an infinity of Leibnizian monads? An indivisible Bradleian Absolute or a collection of atomic Millian sensations? For the American psychologist and pragmatist philosopher, William James (1842–1910), the issue is not simply important but 'the most central of all philosophic problems', the 'most pregnant' one whose resolution has more implications for the rest of a philosopher's opinions than that of any other question.[1]

Although James notes, and without any animosity, a purely 'mystical', primarily 'eastern', version of monism, his focus is upon the more 'talkative and explicit' versions to be found in western philosophical literature. (Somewhat questionably, he associates monism and pluralism with rationalism and empiricism respectively.) The burden of argument, James holds, falls upon the monist – be he Spinoza, Bradley or James's American contemporary, Josiah Royce. Not only does science treat the world as composed of many, separable elements, but our commonsense experience is evidently that of a plural world. To show that such treatment or experience is deluded would be a difficult task.

In James's view, the usual monistic arguments quite fail to discharge this task. Both Spinoza's appeal to the nature of underlying substance and more recent idealist appeals to an indivisible experience present to a single 'noetic subject' verge on the meaningless, since these are hypotheses without testable, pragmatic consequences. He agrees, for example, with David Hume's criticism of the notion of material substance as an idle one which adds nothing of empirical significance to that of sensory data 'united by the imagination'.

---

[1] *Pragmatism* (1907), also in *The Writings of William James*, pp. 405–6. The present selection is from James's posthumously published *Some Problems of Philosophy. A Beginning of an Introduction to Philosophy* (1911).

This is not to say that no sense can ever be attributed to remarks like 'The world is one' or 'Reality is a unity'. They may, for example, be drawing attention to the systematic causal connections we find, or expect to find, among things. Or they may remind us that we are able to take the world as a whole as an object of thought and speculation. The problem is that, if this is what monism amounts to, it is no way incompatible with pluralism. Things need to be genuinely different from one another in order to be causally related, and the fact that we can think about the world as a whole does not mean that this whole is without genuinely distinguishable and separate items, intelligible independently of one another.

One might expect James to end here, content to conclude, as he almost does (p. 245 below), that, in so far as sense can be made of monistic claims, the debate between monists and pluralists is over something of a non-issue. '[T]he world is "one" in some respects, and "many" in others'. In contrast with some of his fellow pragmatists, however, James was, one might say, a highly 'generous' pragmatist, putting few restrictions on the kinds of pragmatic pay-off or advantages which might speak in support of a belief. It is not, therefore, irrelevant to James that the monistic thesis may bring with it a sense of 'stability and peace' and confer value and 'dignity' on the world.[2]

When considerations like these are introduced, James seems to suggest, there is no universally compelling rational resolution of the issue: for the competing positions are attractive to men of different stamps. Monism, with its portrait of a stable, integrated world will appeal to the 'more religious' person; pluralism, which emphasizes change and unpredictability, to the 'more moral' one, since it allows for 'melioristic' intervention by human beings in the course of events. Indeed, the crux of the debate, for James, comes to turn on the possibility of genuine 'novelty' in the world, something which is required for belief in a freedom of the will which is in turn necessary for adoption of an authentically moral point of view.[3] James leaves us in no doubt about his own, 'melioristic' and pluralistic sympathies, but it is a mark of his 'generous' pragmatism that he is appreciatively aware of opposed sympathies.

Like Spinoza, Fichte and Bradley before him, and in marked contrast with most later metaphysicians, James is a thinker for whom metaphysical issues are not to be finally divorced from the value that philosophical beliefs may have for the conduct of life.[4]

---

[2] See James's The Varieties of Religious Experience: A Study in Human Nature, New York: Longman, Green & Co., 1923, which copiously illustrates his 'generosity' in refusing to confine the 'experiences' which may support a belief to everyday sensory ones.

[3] James was helped out of a severe depression in 1870 by his newly-won conviction that freedom of the will genuinely exists. See his Diary entry for 30 April 1870, in The Writings of William James, pp. 7–8.

[4] See Hilary Putnam, Pragmatism: an open question, Oxford: Blackwell, 1995 for a defence of this aspect of James's thought.

James, The One and the Many

The full nature, as distinguished from the full amount, of reality, we now believe to be given only in the perceptual flux. But, though the flux is continuous from next to next, nonadjacent portions of it are separated by parts that intervene, and such separation seems in a variety of cases to work a positive disconnection. The latter part, may contain no element surviving from the earlier part, may be unlike it, may forget it, may be shut off from it by physical barriers, or whatnot. Thus when we use our intellect for cutting up the flux and individualizing its members, we have (provisionally and practically at any rate) to treat an enormous number of these as if they were unrelated or related only remotely, to one another. We handle them piecemeal or distributively, and look at the entire flux as if it were their sum or collection. This encourages the empiricist notion, that the parts are distinct and that the whole is a resultant.

This doctrine rationalism opposes, contending that the whole is fundamental, that the parts derive from it and all belong with one-another, that the separations we uncritically accept are illusory, and that the entire universe, instead of being a sum, is the only genuine unit in existence, constituting (in the words often quoted from d'Alembert) *'un seul fait et une grande vérité'* ['one single fact and one great truth'].

The alternative here is known as that between pluralism and monism. It is the most pregnant of all the dilemmas of philosophy, although it is only in our time that it has been articulated distinctly. Does reality exist distributively? or collectively? – in the shape of *eaches, everys, anys, eithers*? or only in the shape of an *all* or *whole*? An identical content is compatible with either form obtaining, the Latin *omnes*, or *cuncti*, or the German *alle* or *sämmtliche* expressing the alternatives familiarly. Pluralism stands for the distributive, monism for the collective form of being.

Please note that pluralism need not be supposed at the outset to stand for any particular kind or amount of disconnection between the many things which it assumes. It only has the negative significance of contradicting monism's thesis that there is absolutely *no* disconnection. The irreducible outness of *any*thing, however infinitesimal, from *any*thing else, in *any* respect, would be enough, if it were solidly established, to ruin the monistic doctrine.

I hope that the reader begins to be pained here by the extreme vagueness of the terms I am using. To say that there is 'no disconnection', is on the face of it simply silly, for we find practical disconnections without number. My pocket is disconnected with Mr. Morgan's bank-account, and King Edward VII's mind is disconnected with this book. Monism must mean that all such apparent disconnections are bridged over by some deeper absolute union in which it believes, and this union must in some way be more real than the practical separations that appear upon the surface.

In point of historical fact monism has generally kept itself vague and mystical as regards the ultimate principle of unity. To be One is more wonderful than to be many, so the principle of things must be One, but of that One no exact account is given. Plotinus simply calls it the One. 'The One is all things and yet no one of them. . . . For the very reason that none of them was in the One, are all derived from it. Furthermore, in order that they may be real existences, the One is not an existence, but the father of existences. And the generation of existence is as it were the first act of generation. Being perfect by reason of neither seeking nor possessing nor needing anything, the One overflows, as it were, and what overflows forms another hypostasis. . . . How should the most perfect and primal good stay shut up in itself as if it were envious or impotent? . . . Necessarily then something comes from it' [*Enneads*, Book V].

This is like the Hindoo doctrine of the Brahman, or of the Âtman. In the Bhagavat-gita the holy Krishna speaking for the One, says: "I am the immolation. I am the sacrificial rite. I am the libation offered to ancestors. I am the drug. I am the incantation. I am the sacrificial butter also. I am the fire. I am the incense. I am the father, the mother, the sustainer, the grandfather of the universe – the mystic doctrine, the purification, the syllable "Om" . . . the path, the supporter, the master, the witness, the habitation, the refuge, the friend, the origin, the dissolution, the place, the receptacle, the inexhaustible seed. I heat (the world) I withhold and pour out the rain. I am ambrosia and death, the existing and the non-existing. . . . I am the same to all beings. I have neither foe nor friend. . . . Place thy heart on me, worshipping me, sacrificing to me, saluting me' [*Bhagavadgita*, ch. iv].

I call this sort of monism mystical, for it not only revels in formulas that defy understanding,* but it accredits itself by appealing to states of illumination not vouchsafed to common men. Thus Porphyry, in his life of

---

* Al-Ghazzali, the Mohammedan philosopher and mystic, gives a more theistic version of essentially the same idea: 'Allah is the guider aright and the leader astray; he does what he wills and decides what he wishes; there is no opposer of his decision and no repeller of his decree. He created the Garden, and created for it a people, then used them in obedience. And he created the Fire, and created for it a people, then used them in rebellion. . . . Then he said, as has been handed down from the Prophet: "These are in the Garden, and I care not; and these are in the Fire, and I care not." So he is Allah, the Most High, the King, the Reality. He is not asked concerning what he does; but they are asked.' (D. B. MacDonald's translation, in *Hartford Seminary Record*, January, 1910.) Compare for other quaotations, W. James: *The Varieties of Religious Experience*, pp. 415–22.

Plotinus, after saying that he himself once had such an insight, when 68 years old, adds that whilst he lived with Plotinus, the latter four times had the happiness of approaching the supreme God and consciously uniting with him in a real and ineffable act.

The regular mystical way of attaining the vision of the One is by ascetic training, fundamentally the same in all religious systems. But this ineffable kind of Oneness is not strictly philosophical, for philosophy is essentially talkative and explicit, so I must pass it by.

The usual philosophic way of reaching deeper oneness has been by the conception of substance. First used by the Greeks, this notion was elaborated with great care during the Middle Ages. Defined as any being that exists *per se*, so that it needs no further subject in which to inhere (*Ens ita per se existens, ut non indigeat alio tamquam subjecto, cui inhaereat, ad existendum*) a 'substance' was first distinguished from all 'accidents' (which do require such a subject of inhesion – *cujus esse est inesse*). It was then identified with the 'principle of individuality' in things, and with their 'essence,' and divided into various types, for example into first and second, simple and compound, complete and incomplete, specific and individual, material and spiritual substances. God, on this view, is a substance, for he exists *per se*, as well as *a se*; but of secondary beings, he is the creator, not the substance, for once created, they also exist *per se* though not *a se*. Thus, for scholasticism, the notion of substance is only a partial unifier, and in its totality, the universe forms a pluralism from the substance-point-of-view.

Spinoza broke away from the scholastic doctrine. He began his 'Ethics' by demonstrating that only one substance is possible, and that that substance can only be the infinite and necessary God. This heresy brought reprobation on Spinoza, but it has been favored by philosophers and poets ever since. The pantheistic spinozistic unity was too sublime a prospect not to captivate the mind. It was not till Locke, Berkeley, and Hume began to put in their 'critical' work that the suspicion began to gain currency that the notion of substance might be only a word masquerading in the shape of an idea.*

Locke believed in substances, yet confessed that 'we have no such clear idea at all, but only an uncertain supposition of we know not what, which

---

* No one believes that such words as 'winter,' 'army,' 'house,' denote substances. They designate collective facts, of which the parts are held together by means that can be experimentally traced. Even when we can't define what groups the effects together, as in 'poison,' 'sickness,' 'strength,' we don't assume a substance, but are willing that the word should designate some phenomenal agency yet to be found out. Nominalists treat all substances after this analogy, and consider 'matter,' 'gold,' 'soul,' as but the names of so many grouped properties, of which the bond of union must be, not some unknowable substance corresponding to the name, but rather some hidden portion of the whole phenomenal fact.

we take to be the substratum, or support of those ideas we do not know' [see p. 144 above]. He criticized the notion of personal substance as the principles of self-sameness in our different minds. *Experientially* our personal identity consists, he said, in nothing more than the functional and perceptible fact that our later states of mind continue and remember our earlier ones.

Berkeley applied the same sort of criticism to the notion of bodily substance. 'When I consider,' he says, 'the two parts ("being" in general, and "supporting accidents") which make the signification of the words "material substance," I am convinced there is no distinct meaning annexed to them. . . . Suppose an intelligence without the help of external bodies to be affected with the same train of sensations that you are, imprinted in the same order, and with like vividness in his mind. I ask whether that intelligence hath not all the reason to believe the existence of corporeal substances, represented by his ideas, and exciting them in his mind, that you can possibly have for believing the same thing [see p. 172 above]. Certain *grouped sensations*, in short, are all that corporeal substances are *known-as*, therefore the only meaning which the word 'matter' can claim is that it denotes such sensations and their groupings. They are the only verifiable aspect of the word.

The reader will recognize that in these criticisms our own pragmatic rule is used. What difference in practical experience is it supposed to make that we have each a personal substantial principle? This difference, that we can remember and appropriate our past, calling it 'mine.' What difference that in this book there is a substantial principle? This, that certain optical and tactile sensations cling permanently together in a cluster. The fact that certain perceptual experiences do seem to *belong together* is thus all that the word substance means. Hume carries the criticism to the last degree of clearness. 'We have no idea of substance,' he says, 'distinct from that of a collection of particular qualities, nor have we any other meaning when we either talk or reason concerning it. The idea of a substance . . . is nothing but a collection of simple ideas that are united by the imagination and have a particular name assigned them by which we are able to recall that collection' [*Treatise on Human Nature*, I §6]. Kant's treatment of substance agrees with Hume's in denying all positive content to the notion. It differs in insisting that, by attaching shifting percepts to the permanent name, the category of substance unites them *necessarily* together, and thus makes nature intelligible. It is impossible to assent to this. The grouping of qualities becomes no more intelligible when you call substance a 'category' than when you call it a bare word.

Let us now turn our backs upon ineffable or unintelligible ways of accounting for the world's oneness, and inquire whether, instead of being a principle, the 'oneness' affirmed may not merely be a name like 'substance,' descriptive of the fact that certain *specific and verifiable connections* are found among the parts of the experiential flux. This brings us back to our pragmatic rule: Suppose there is a oneness in things, what may it be known-as? What differences to you and me will it make?

Our question thus turns upside down, and sets us on a much more promising inquiry. We can easily conceive of things that shall have no connection whatever with each other. We may assume them to inhabit different times and spaces, as the dreams of different persons do even now. They may be so unlike and incommensurable, and so inert towards one another, as never to jostle or interfere. Even now there may actually be whole universes so disparate from ours that we who know ours have no means of perceiving that they exist. We conceive their diversity, however; and by that fact the whole lot of them form what is known in logic as one 'universe of discourse.' To form a universe of discourse argues, as this example shows, no further kind of connection. The importance attached by certain monistic writers to the fact that any chaos may become a universe by being merely named, is to me incomprehensible. We must seek something better in the way of oneness than this susceptibility of being mentally considered together, and named by a collective noun.

What connections may be perceived concretely or in point of fact, among the parts of the collection abstractly designated as our 'world'?

There are innumerable modes of union among its parts, some obtaining on a larger, some on a smaller scale. Not all the parts of our world are united *mechanically*, for some can move without the others moving. They all seem united by *gravitation*, however, so far as they are material things. Some again of these are united *chemically*, while others are not; and the like is true of thermic, optical, electrical, and other *physical* connections. These connections are specifications of what we mean by the word oneness when we apply it to our world. We should not call it one unless its parts were connected in these and other ways. But then it is clear that by the same logic we ought to call it 'many' so far as its parts are disconnected in these same ways, chemically inert towards one another or non-conductors to electricity, light and heat. In all these modes of union, some parts of the world prove to be conjoined with other parts, so that if you choose your line of influence and your items rightly, you may travel from pole to pole without an interruption. If, however, you choose them wrongly, you meet with obstacles and non-conductors from the outset, and cannot travel at all. There is thus neither absolute oneness nor absolute manyness from the physical point of view, but a mixture of well-definable modes of both.

Moreover, neither the oneness nor the manyness seems the more essential attribute, they are co-ordinate features of the natural world.

There are plenty of other practical differences meant by calling a thing One. Our world, being strung along in time and space, has *temporal and spatial unity*. But time and space relate things by determinately sundering them, so it is hard to say whether the world ought more to be called 'one' or 'many' in this spatial or temporal regard.

The like is true of the *generic oneness* which comes from so many of the world's parts being similar. When two things are similar you can make inferences from the one which will hold good of the other, so that this kind of union among things, so far as it obtains, is inexpressibly precious from the logical point of view. But an infinite heterogeneity among things exists alongside of whatever likeness of kind we discover; and our world appears no more distinctly or essentially as a One than as a Many, from this generic point of view.

We have touched on the noetic[1] unity predicable of the world in consequence of our being able to mean the whole of it at once. Widely different from unification by an abstract designation, would be the concrete noetic union wrought by an all-knower of perceptual type who should be acquainted at one stroke with every part of what exists. In such an absolute all-knower idealists believe. Kant, they say, virtually replaced the notion of Substance, by the more intelligible notion of Subject. The 'I am conscious of it,' which on some witness's part must accompany every possible experience, means in the last resort, we are told, one individual witness of the total frame of things, world without end, amen. You may call his undivided act of omniscience instantaneous or eternal, whichever you like, for time is its object just as everything else is, and itself is not in time.

We shall find reasons later for treating noetic monism as an unverified hypothesis. Over against it there stands the noetic pluralism which we verify every moment when we seek information from our friends. According to this, everything in the world might be known by somebody, yet not everything by the same knower, or in one single cognitive act – much as all mankind is knit in one network of acquaintance, A knowing B, B knowing C, – Y knowing Z, and Z possibly knowing A again, without the possibility of anyone knowing everybody at once. This 'concatenated' knowing, going from next to next, is altogether different from the 'consolidated' knowing supposed to be exercised by the absolute mind. It makes a coherent type of universe in which the widest knower that exists may yet remain ignorant of much that is known to others.

There are other systems of concatenation besides the noetic concatenation. We ourselves are constantly adding to the connections of things, organizing labor-unions, establishing postal, consular, mercantile, railroad, tele-graph, colonial, and other systems that bind us and things together in ever wider reticulations. Some of these systems involve others, some do not. You cannot have a telephone system without air and copper connections, but you can have air and copper connections without telephones. You cannot have love without acquaintance, but you can have acquaintance without love, etc. The same thing, moreover, can belong to many systems, as when a man is connected with other objects by heat, by gravitation, by love, and by knowledge.

From the point of view of these partial systems, the world hangs together from next to next in a variety of ways, so that when you are off of one thing you can always be on to something else, without ever dropping out of your world. Gravitation is the only positively known sort of connection among things that reminds us of the consolidated or monistic form of union. If a 'mass' should change anywhere, the mutual gravitation of all things would instantaneously alter.

Teleological and aesthetic unions are other forms of systematic union. The world is full of partial purposes, of partial stories. That they all form chapters of one supreme purpose and inclusive story is the monistic conjecture. They *seem*, meanwhile, simply to run alongside of each other – either irrelevantly, or, where they interfere, leading to mutual frustrations, – so the appearance of things is invincibly pluralistic from this purposive point of view.

It is a common belief that all particular beings have one origin and source, either in God, or in atoms all equally old. There is no real novelty, it is believed, in the universe, the new things that appear having either been eternally prefigured in the absolute, or being results of the same *primordia rerum*, atoms, or monads, getting into new mixtures. But the question of being is so obscure anyhow, that whether realities have burst into existence all at once, by a single 'bang,' as it were; or whether they came piecemeal, and have different ages (so that real novelties may be leaking into our universe all the time), may here be left an open question, though it is undoubtedly intellectually economical to suppose that all things are equally old, and that no novelties leak in.

These results are what the Oneness of the Universe is *known-as*. They *are* the oneness, pragmatically considered. A world coherent in any of these ways would be no chaos, but a universe of such or such a grade. (The grades might differ, however. The parts, e.g., might have space-relations, but nothing more; or they might also gravitate; or exchange heat; or know, or love one another, etc.)

Such is the cash-value of the world's unity, empirically realized. Its total unity is the sum of all the partial unities. It consists of them and follows upon them. Such an idea, however, outrages rationalistic minds, which habitually despise all this practical small-change. Such minds insist on a deeper, more through-and-through union of all things in the absolute, 'each in all and all in each,' as the prior condition of these empirically ascertained connections. But this may be only a case of the usual worship of abstractions, like calling 'bad weather' the cause of to-day's rain, etc., or accounting for a man's features by his 'face,' when really the rain *is* the bad weather, is what you *mean* by 'bad weather,' just as the features are what you mean by the face.

To sum up, the world is 'one' in some respects, and 'many' in others. But the respects must be distinctly specified, if either statement is to be more than the emptiest abstraction. Once we are committed to this soberer view, the question of the One or the Many may well cease to appear important. The amount either of unity or of plurality is in short only a matter for observation to ascertain and write down, in statements which will have to be complicated, in spite of every effort to be concise.

The One and the Many (*continued*) – Values and Defects

We might dismiss the subject with the preceding chapter were it not for the fact that further consequences follow from the rival hypotheses, and make of the alternative of monism or pluralism what I called it on page [238], the most 'pregnant' of all the dilemmas of metaphysics.

To begin with, the attribute 'one' seems for many persons to confer a value, an ineffable illustriousness and dignity upon the world, with which the conception of it as an irreducible 'many' is believed to clash.

Secondly, a through-and-through noetic connection of everything with absolutely everything else is in some quarters held to be indispensable to the world's rationality. Only then might we believe that all things really do *belong* together, instead of being connected by the bare conjunctions 'with' or 'and.' The notion that this latter pluralistic arrangement may obtain is deemed 'irrational'; and of course it does make the world partly alogical or non-rational from a purely intellectual point of view.

Monism thus holds the oneness to be the more vital and essential element. The entire cosmos must be a consolidated unit, within which each member is determined by the whole to be just that, and from which the slightest incipiency of independence anywhere is ruled out. With Spinoza, monism likes to believe that all things follow from the essence of God as necessarily as from the nature of a triangle it follows that the angles are equal to two right angles. The whole is what yields the parts, not the parts the whole. The universe is *tight*, monism claims, not loose; and you must take the irreducible whole of it just as it is offered, or have no part or lot in it at all. The only alternative allowed by monistic writers is to confess the world's non-rationality – and no philosopher can permit himself to do that. The form of monism regnant at the present day in philosophic circles is *absolute idealism*. For this way of thinking, the world exists no otherwise than as the object of one infinitely knowing mind. The analogy that suggests the hypothesis here is that of our own finite fields of consciousness, which at every moment envisage a much-at-once composed of parts related variously, and in which both the conjunctions and the disjunctions that appear are there only in so far as we are there as their witnesses, so that they are both 'noetically' and monistically based.

We may well admit the sublimity of this noetic monism and of its vague vision of an underlying connection among all phenomena without exception.* It shows itself also able to confer religious stability and peace, and it invokes the authority of mysticism in its favor. Yet, on the other hand, like many another concept unconditionally carried out, it introduces into philosophy puzzles peculiar to itself, as follows:–

1. It does not account for our finite consciousness. If nothing exists but as the Absolute Mind knows it, how can anything exist otherwise than as that Mind knows it? That Mind knows each thing in one act of knowledge, along with every other thing. Finite minds know things without other things, and this ignorance is the source of most of their woes. We are thus not simply objects to an all-knowing subject: we are subjects on our own account and know differently from its knowing.

2. It creates a problem of evil. Evil, for pluralism, presents only the practical problem of how to get rid of it. For monism the puzzle is theoretical: How – if Perfection be the source, should there be Imperfection? If the world as known to the Absolute be perfect, why should it be known otherwise, in myriads of inferior finite editions also? The perfect edition surely was enough. How do the breakage and dispersion and ignorance get in?

3. It contradicts the character of reality as perceptually experienced. Of our world, change seems an essential ingredient. There is history. There are novelties, struggles, losses, gains. But the world of the Absolute is represented as unchanging, eternal, or 'out of time,' and is foreign to our powers either of apprehension or of appreciation. Monism usually treats the sense-world as a mirage or illusion.

---

* In its essential features, Spinoza was its first prophet, Fichte and Hegel were its middle exponents, and Josiah Royce is its best contemporary representative.

4. It is fatalistic. Possibility, as distinguished from necessity on the one hand and from impossibility on the other, is an essential category of human thinking. For monism, it is a pure illusion; for whatever is is necessary, and aught else is impossible, if the world be such a unit of fact as monists pretend.

Our sense of 'freedom' supposes that some things at least are decided here and now, that the passing moment may contain some novelty, be an original starting-point of events, and not merely transmit a push from elsewhere. We imagine that in some respects at least the future may not be co-implicated with the past, but may be really addable to it, and indeed addable in one shape *or* another, so that the next turn in events can at any given moment genuinely be ambiguous, i.e., possibly this, but also possibly that.

Monism rules out this whole conception of possibles, so native to our common-sense. The future and the past are linked, she is obliged to say; there can be no genuine novelty anywhere, for to suppose that the universe has a constitution simply additive, with nothing to link things together save what the words 'plus,' 'with,' or 'and' stand for, is repugnant to our reason.

Pluralism, on the other hand, taking perceptual experience at its face-value, is free from all these difficulties. It protests against working our ideas in a vacuum made of conceptual abstractions. Some parts of our world, it admits, cannot exist out of their wholes; but other, it says, can. To some extent the world *seems* genuinely additive: it may really be so. We cannot explain conceptually *how* genuine novelties can come; but if one did come we could experience *that* it came. We do, in fact, experience perceptual novelties all the while. Our perceptual experience overlaps our conceptual reason: the *that* transcends the *why*. So the common-sense view of life, as something really dramatic, with work done, and things decided here and now, is acceptable to pluralism. 'Free will' means nothing but real novelty; so pluralism accepts the notion of free will.

But pluralism, accepting a universe unfinished, with doors and windows open to possibilities uncontrollable in advance, gives us less religious certainty than monism, with its absolutely closed-in world. It is true that monism's religious certainty is not rationally based, but is only a faith that 'sees the All-Good in the All-Real.' In point of fact, however, monism is usually willing to exert this optimistic faith: its world is certain to be saved, yes, is saved already, unconditionally and from eternity, in spite of all the phenomenal appearances of risk.*

A world working out an uncertain destiny, as the phenomenal world

---

* For an eloquent expression of the monistic position, from the religious point of view, read J. Royce: *The World and the Individual*, vol. ii, lectures 8, 9, 10.

appears to be doing, is an intolerable idea to the rationalistic mind.

Pluralism, on the other hand, is neither optimistic nor pessimistic, but melioristic, rather. The world, it thinks, may be saved, on condition that its parts shall do their best. But shipwreck in detail, or even on the whole, is among the open possibilities.

There is thus a practical lack of balance about pluralism, which contrasts with monism's peace of mind. The one is a more moral, the other a more religious view; and different men usually let this sort of consideration determine their belief.

So far I have sought only to show the respective implications of the rival doctrines without dogmatically deciding which is the more true. It is obvious that pluralism has three great advantages:–

1. It is more 'scientific,' in that it insists that when oneness is predicated, it shall mean definitely ascertainable conjunctive forms. With these the disjunctions ascertainable among things are exactly on a par. The two are co-ordinate aspects of reality. To make the conjunctions more vital and primordial than the separations, monism has to abandon verifiable experience and proclaim a unity that is indescribable.

2. It agrees more with the moral and dramatic expressiveness of life.

3. It is not obliged to stand for any particular amount of plurality, for it triumphs over monism if the smallest morsel of disconnectedness is once found undeniably to exist. 'Ever not quite' is all it says to monism; while monism is obliged to prove that what pluralism asserts can in no amount whatever possibly be true – an infinitely harder task.

The advantages of monism, in turn, are its natural affinity with a certain kind of religious faith, and the peculiar emotional value of the conception that the world is a unitary fact.

So far has our use of the pragmatic rule brought us towards understanding this dilemma. The reader will by this time feel for himself the essential practical difference which it involves. The word 'absence' seems to indicate it. The monistic principle implies that nothing that is can in any way whatever be absent from anything else that is. The pluralistic principle, on the other hand, is quite compatible with some things being absent from operations in which other things find themselves singly or collectively engaged. *Which* things are absent from which other things, and *when*, – these of course are questions which a pluralistic philosophy can settle only by an exact study of details. The past, the present, and the future in perception, for example, are absent from one another, while in imagination they are present or absent as the case may be. If the time-content of the world be not one monistic block of being, if some part, at least, of the future, is added to the past without being virtually one therewith, or implicitly contained therein, then it is absent really as well as phenomenally and may be called an absolute novelty in the world's history in so far forth.

Towards this issue, of the reality or unreality of the novelty that appears, the pragmatic difference between monism and pluralism seems to converge. That we ourselves may be authors of genuine novelty is the thesis of the doctrine of free-will. That genuine novelties can occur means that from the point of view of what is already given, what comes may have to be treated as a matter of *chance*. We are led thus to ask the question: In what manner does new being come? Is it through and through the consequence of older being or is matter of chance so far as older being goes? – which is the same thing as asking: Is it original, in the strict sense of the word?

We connect again here with what was said [earlier]. We there agreed that being is a datum or gift and has to be begged by the philosopher; but we left the question open as to whether he must beg it all at once or beg it bit by bit or in instalments. The latter is the more consistently empiricist view.

Note

1 'Noetic' (from the Greek *noētos*) tends to mean, in modern philosophical parlance, that which is apprehended by the intellect rather than the senses. James is referring to that minimal unity the world possesses in virtue of our being able to regard it as a single object of thought.

16 Bertrand Russell, *The Philosophy of Logical Atomism*, Lecture VIII

From Bertrand Russell, *Logic and Knowledge: Essays 1901–1950*, ed. R. C. Marsh. London: George Allen & Unwin, 1956, pp. 269–81. Reprinted by permission of Routledge and The Bertrand Russell Peace Foundation.

Lecture VIII – the last of a series which Bertrand Russell (1872–1970) gave in London in 1918 – 'point[s] to a few of the morals' of the earlier lectures for 'various problems of metaphysics'. In fact, it provides a succinct presentation of the metaphysical aspects of the logical atomism which he and his former student, Ludwig Wittgenstein, had been developing during the preceding years. (Despite Russell's claim in the Preface to be 'explaining certain ideas . . . learnt from . . . Wittgenstein' (p. 177), it became clear, after the publication of the latter's *Tractatus Logico-Philosophicus*, that there were important differences between the views of the two men.)

As the name 'logical atomism' suggests, Russell's philosophy is a thoroughly pluralistic one, honouring 'the common-sense belief that there are many separate things' (p. 178).[1] Lecture VIII, however, is concerned to articulate a metaphysics which does not at all belong to plain common-sense. The central claim is that nothing fundamentally exists except 'ultimate simples', which turn out to be sense-data (the immediate, fleeting data of perception) and their simple properties (including relational properties). All 'the familiar objects of daily life: tables, chairs, Piccadilly Socrates, and so on' are at best 'logical fictions' (p. 253). While it would be too crude bluntly to deny the existence of the table I take myself to have been working at over the months, the table must be treated simply as a 'series' of related sense-data, not an 'ultimate' constituent of reality. What can be bluntly denied is that there is any empirical reason to postulate the existence, in any sense, of 'metaphysical entities' which, by their very nature, are never 'empirically given'.

---

[1] See Peter Hylton, *Russell, Idealism and the Emergence of Analytic Philosophy*, Oxford: Clarendon Press, 1990, for a good account of Russell's overcoming of his early flirtation with Bradley's idealist monism.

Russell's conclusions, then, are in the tradition of British empiricism.[2] He is, however, more ontologically generous than some of his predecessors in including qualities or properties, as well as sensory particulars, among the genuine constituents of reality. Russell's argument, which doesn't surface in Lecture VIII, is that any attempt to do away with universals, such as properties, requires the notion of similarity among particulars. But this itself is the notion of a relational property, and hence of a universal. In another respect, though, Russell is more parsimonious than, for example, John Stuart Mill (see chapter 13 above). For Russell, unlike Mill, shares the Humean view that the self is 'fiction', reducible to a series of experiences related to one another over time.

Given the debt of his conclusions to the empiricist tradition, Russell's originality resides less in these conclusions than in his arguments for them. Unlike earlier empiricists, he appeals, primarily, to the notion of meaning and other concepts of 'philosophical grammar'. In particular, Russell has argued in previous lectures that many, indeed nearly all, expressions which look like names – referring to genuine constituents of reality – are nothing of the sort. Rather, they are 'incomplete symbols', ultimately analysable into 'logically proper names' which do so refer. Provision of the form of such analyses is the purpose of Russell's famous 'theory of descriptions'.

This theory, as it stands, does not tell us *what* the constituents of reality referred to by genuine names are. But we can, Russell thinks, say this much: they are entities which the names *mean*, so that they must exist if the names are to be meaningful at all. From this it follows, he has argued, that the entities must be 'ultimate simples'. If they were not, the words standing for them could be analysed into simpler terms and so would not depend for their meaning on the actual existence of the entities. This still leaves the nature of the simples undetermined, and it is here that Russell's empiricist legacy comes into play. (It is here, too, where he parts company with Wittgenstein, who refuses to specify what entities count as ultimate simples.) Russell's reasoning is that – among particulars, at least – only sense-data fill the bill, for they alone are items whose existence one cannot be in error about and is therefore guaranteed in the very act of naming them, albeit with such descriptively uninformative names as 'this' and 'that'. For Russell, then, only the parsimonious, seemingly 'dry and dull', world of empiricism has the structure which corresponds to the structure of our language.

As an extra bonus, Russell briefly discusses William James's theory of 'neutral monism'. This is not monism in a sense which contradicts the pluralism we saw James defending in chapter 15 above. It is not the doctrine that reality is a single indivisible unity, but the denial that mind and matter are two different kinds of entity, and hence a denial of Cartesian dualism. For the 'neutral monist',

---

[2] See D. F. Pears, *Russell and the British Tradition in Philosophy*, London: Fontana, 1967, for a good account of Russell's relation to that tradition.

as Russell clearly explains on p. 259 below, the difference between mental and physical phenomena is a function of their 'arrangement'. Grouped in one way, they count as mental; grouped in another way, they count as physical. Russell is sympathetic to this theory, though he raises a couple of difficulties it faces. Three years later, he was to endorse it more emphatically, writing that 'the stuff of which the world of our experience is composed is . . . neither mind nor matter, but something more primitive'.[3]

▶ ▶ ▶   ## Russell, Excursus into Metaphysics: What There Is

I come now to the last lecture of this course, and I propose briefly to point to a few of the morals that are to be gathered from what has gone before, in the way of suggesting the bearing of the doctrines that I have been advocating upon various problems of metaphysics. I have dealt hitherto upon what one may call philosophical grammar, and I am afraid I have had to take you through a good many very dry and dusty regions in the course of that investigation, but I think the importance of philosophical grammar is very much greater than it is generally thought to be. I think that practically all traditional metaphysics is filled with mistakes due to bad grammar, and that almost all the traditional problems of metaphysics and traditional results – supposed results – of metaphysics are due to a failure to make the kind of distinctions in what we may call philosophical grammar with which we have been concerned in these previous lectures.

Take as a very simple example, the philosophy of arithmetic. If you think that 1, 2, 3, and 4, and the rest of the numbers, are in any sense entities, if you think that there are objects, having those names, in the realm of being, you have at once a very considerable apparatus for your metaphysics to deal with, and you have offered to you a certain kind of analysis of arithmetical propositions. When you say, e.g., that 2 and 2 are 4, you suppose in that case that you are making a proposition of which the number 2 and the number 4 are constituents, and that has all sorts of consequences, all sorts of bearings upon your general metaphysical outlook. If there has been any truth in the doctrines that we have been considering, all numbers are what I call logical fictions. Numbers are classes of classes, and classes are logical fictions, so that numbers are, as it were, fictions at two removes, fictions of fictions. Therefore you do not have, as part of the ultimate constituents of your world, these queer entities that you are inclined to call numbers. The same applies in many other directions.

[3] *The Analysis of Mind*, London: Allen & Unwin, 1921, p. 10.

One purpose that has run through all that I have said, has been the justification of analysis, i.e., the justification of logical atomism, of the view that you can get down in theory, if not in practice, to ultimate simples, out of which the world is built, and that those simples have a kind of reality not belonging to anything else. Simples, as I tried to explain, are of an infinite number of sorts. There are particulars and qualities and relations of various orders, a whole hierarchy of different sorts of simples, but all of them, if we were right, have in their various ways some kind of reality that does not belong to anything else. The only other sort of object you come across in the world is what we call *facts*, and facts are the sort of things that are asserted or denied by propositions, and are not properly entities at all in the same sense in which their constituents are. That is shown in the fact that you cannot name them. You can only deny, or assert, or consider them, but you cannot name them because they are not there to be named, although in another sense it is true that you cannot know the world unless you know the facts that make up the truths of the world; but the knowing of facts is a different sort of thing from the knowing of simples.

Another purpose which runs through all that I have been saying is the purpose embodied in the maxim called Occam's Razor. That maxim comes in, in practice, in this way: take some science, say physics. You have there a given body of doctrine, a set of propositions expressed in symbols – I am including words among symbols – and you think that you have reason to believe that on the whole those propositions, rightly interpreted, are fairly true, but you do not know what is the actual meaning of the symbols that you are using. The meaning they have *in use* would have to be explained in some pragmatic way: they have a certain kind of practical or emotional significance to you which is a datum, but the logical significance is not a datum, but a thing to be sought, and you go through, if you are analysing a science like physics, these propositions with a view to finding out what is the smallest empirical apparatus – or the smallest apparatus, not necessarily wholly empirical – out of which you can build up these propositions. What is the smallest number of simple undefined things at the start, and the smallest number of undemonstrated premises, out of which you can define the things that need to be defined and prove the things that need to be proved? That problem, in any case that you like to take, is by no means a simple one, but on the contrary an extremely difficult one. It is one which requires a very great amount of logical technique; and the sort of thing that I have been talking about in these lectures is the preliminaries and first steps in that logical technique. You cannot possibly get at the solution of such a problem as I am talking about if you go at it in a straightforward fashion with just the ordinary acumen that one accumulates in the course of reading or in the study of traditional philosophy. You do need this apparatus of symbolical logic that I have been talking about. (The description of the subject as symbolical logic is an inadequate one. I should like to describe it simply as logic, on the ground that nothing else really is logic, but that would sound so arrogant that I hesitate to do so.)

Let us consider further the example of physics for a moment. You find, if you read the works of physicists, that they reduce matter down to certain elements – atoms, ions, corpuscles, or what not. But in any case the sort of thing that you are aiming at in the physical analysis of matter is to get down to very little bits of matter that still are just like matter in the fact that they persist through time, and that they travel about in space. They have in fact all the ordinary everyday properties of physical matter, not the matter that one has in ordinary life – they do not taste or smell or appear to the naked eye – but they have the properties that you very soon get to when you travel toward physics from ordinary life. Things of that sort, I say, are not the ultimate constituents of matter in any metaphysical sense. Those things are all of them, as I think a very little reflection shows, logical fictions in the sense that I was speaking of. At least, when I say they are, I speak somewhat too dogmatically. It is possible that there may be all these things that the physicist talks about in actual reality, but it is impossible that we should ever have any reason whatsoever for supposing that there are. That is the situation that you arrive at generally in such analyses. You find that a certain thing which has been set up as a metaphysical entity can either be assumed dogmatically to be real, and then you will have no possible argument either for its reality or against its reality; or, instead of doing that, you can construct a logical fiction having the same formal properties, or rather having formally analogous formal properties to those of the supposed metaphysical entity and itself composed of empirically given things, and that logical fiction can be substituted for your supposed metaphysical entity and will fulfil all the scientific purposes that anybody can desire. With atoms and the rest it is so, with all the metaphysical entities whether of science or of metaphysics. By metaphysical entities I mean those things which are supposed to be part of the ultimate constituents of the world, but not to be the kind of thing that is ever empirically given – I do not say merely not being itself empirically given, but not being the *kind* of thing that is empirically given. In the case of matter, you can start from what is empirically given, what one sees and hears and smells and so forth, all the ordinary data of sense, or you can start with some definite ordinary object, say this desk, and you can ask yourselves, 'What do I mean by saying that this desk that I am looking at now is the same as the one I was looking at a week ago?' The first simple ordinary answer would be that it *is* the same desk, it is actually identical, there is a perfect identity of substance, or whatever you like to call it. But when that apparently simple answer is suggested, it is important to observe that you cannot have an empirical reason for such a view as that, and if you hold it, you hold it simply because you like it and for no other reason whatever. All that you really know is such facts as that what you see now, when you look at the desk, bears a very close similarity to what you saw a week ago when you looked at it. Rather more than that one fact of similarity I admit you know, or you may know. You might have paid some one to watch the desk continuously throughout the week, and might then have discovered that it was presenting appearances of the same sort all through that period, assuming that the light was kept on all through the night. In that way you could have established continuity. You have not in fact done so. You do not in fact know that that desk has gone on looking the same all the time, but we will assume that. Now the essential point is this: What is the empirical reason that makes you call a number of appearances, appearances of the same desk? What makes you say on successive occasions, I am seeing the same desk? The first thing to notice is this, that it does not matter what is the answer, so long as you have realized that the answer consists in something empirical and not in a recognized metaphysical identity of substance. There is something given in experience which makes you call it the same desk, and having once grasped that fact, you can go on and say, it is that something (whatever it is) that makes you call it the same desk which shall be *defined* as *constituting* it the same desk, and there shall be no assumption of a metaphysical substance which is identical throughout. It is a little easier to the untrained mind to conceive of an identity than it is to conceive of a system of correlated particulars, hung one to another by relations of similarity and continuous change and so on. That idea is apparently more complicated, but that is what is empirically given in the real world, and substance, in the sense of something which is continuously identical in the same desk, is not given to you. Therefore in all cases where you seem to have a continuous entity persisting through changes, what you have to do is to ask yourself what makes you consider the successive appearances as belonging to one thing. When you have found out what makes you take the view that they belong to the same thing, you will then see that that which has made you say so, is all that is *certainly* there in the way of unity. Anything that there may be over and above that, I shall recognize as something I cannot know. What I can know is that there are a certain series of appearances linked together, and the series of those appearances I shall define as being a desk. In that way the desk is reduced to being a logical fiction, because a series is a logical fiction. In that way all the ordinary objects of daily life are extruded from the world of what there is, and in their place as what there is you find a number of passing particulars of the kind that one is immediately conscious of in sense. I want to make clear that I am not *denying* the existence of anything; I am only refusing to affirm it. I refuse to affirm the existence of anything for which there is no evidence, but I equally refuse to deny the existence of anything against which there is no evidence. Therefore I neither affirm nor deny it, but merely say, that is not in the realm of the knowable and is certainly not a part of physics; and physics, if it is to be interpreted, must be interpreted in terms of the sort of thing that can be empirical. If your atom is going to serve purposes in physics, as it undoubtedly does, your atom has got to turn out to be a series of classes of particulars. The same process which one applies to physics, one will also apply elsewhere. The application to physics I explained briefly in my book on the *External World*, Chapters III and IV.[1]

I have talked so far about the unreality of the things we think real. I want to speak with equal emphasis about the reality of things we think unreal, such as phantoms and hallucinations. Phantoms and hallucinations, considered in themselves, are, as I explained in the preceding lectures, on exactly the same level as ordinary sense-data. They differ from ordinary sense-data only in the fact that they do not have the usual correlations with other things. In themselves they have the same reality as ordinary sense-data. They have the most complete and absolute and perfect reality that anything can have. They are part of the ultimate constituents of the world, just as the fleeting sense-data are. Speaking of the fleeting sense-data, I think it is very important to remove out of one's instincts any disposition to believe that the real is the permanent. There has been a metaphysical prejudice always that if a thing is really real, it has to last either forever or for a fairly decent length of time. That is to my mind an entire mistake. The things that are really real last a very short time. Again I am not denying that there *may* be things that last forever, or for thousands of years; I only say that those are not within our experience, and that the real things that we know by experience last for a very short time, one tenth or half a second, or whatever it may be. Phantoms and hallucinations are among those, among the ultimate constituents of the world. The things that we call real, like tables and chairs, are systems, series of classes of particulars, and the particulars are the real things, the particulars being sense-data when they happen to be given to you. A table or chair will be a series of classes of particulars, and therefore a logical fiction. Those particulars will be on the same level of reality as a hallucination or a phantom. I ought to explain in what sense a chair is a series of classes. A chair presents at each moment a number of different appearances. All the appearances that it is presenting at a given moment make up a certain class. All those sets of appearances vary from time to time. If I take a chair and smash it, it will present a whole set of different appearances from what it did before, and without going as far as that, it will always be changing as the light changes, and so on. So you get a series in time of different sets of appearances, and that is what I mean by saying that a chair is a series of classes. That explanation is too crude, but I leave out the niceties, as that is not the actual topic I am dealing with. Now each single particular which is part of this whole system is linked up with the others in the system. Supposing, e.g. I take as my particular the appearance which that chair is presenting to me at this moment. That is linked up first of all with the appearance which the same chair is presenting to any one of you at the same moment, and with the appearance which it is going to present to me at later moments. There you get at once two journeys that you can take away from that particular, and that particular will be correlated in certain definite ways with the other particulars which also belong to that chair. That is what you mean by saying – or what you ought to mean by saying – that what I see before me is a real thing as opposed to a phantom. It means that it has a whole set of correlations of different kinds. It means that that particular, which is the appearance of the chair to me at this moment, is not isolated but is connected in a certain well-known familiar fashion with others, in the sort of way that makes it answer one's expectations. And so, when you go and buy a chair, you buy not only the appearance which it presents to you at that moment, but also those other appearances that it is going to present when it gets home. If it were a phantom chair, it would not present any appearances when it got home and would not be the sort of thing you would want to buy. The sort one calls real is one of a whole correlated system, whereas the sort you call hallucinations are not. The respectable particulars in the world are all of them linked up with other particulars in respectable, conventional ways. Then sometimes you get a wild particular, like a merely visual chair that you cannot sit on, and say it is a phantom, a hallucination, you exhaust all the vocabulary of abuse upon it. That is what one means by calling it unreal, because 'unreal' applied in that way is a term of abuse and never would be applied to a thing that *was* unreal because you would not be so angry with it.

I will pass on to some other illustrations. Take a person. What is it that makes you say, when you meet your friend Jones, 'Why, this is Jones'? It is clearly not the persistence of a metaphysical entity inside Jones somewhere, because even if there be such an entity, it certainly is not what you see when you see Jones coming along the street; it certainly is something that you are not acquainted with, not an empirical datum. Therefore plainly there is something in the empirical appearances which he presents to you, something in their relations one to another, which enables you to collect all these together and say, 'These are what I call the appearances of one person', and that something that makes you collect them together is not the persistence of a metaphysical subject, because that, whether there be such a persistent subject or not, is certainly not a datum, and that which makes you say 'Why, it is Jones' is a datum. Therefore Jones is not constituted as he is known by a sort of pin-point ego that is underlying his appearances, and you have got to find some correlations among the appearances which are of the sort that make you put all those appearances together and say, they are the appearances of one person. Those are different when it is other people and when it is yourself. When it is yourself, you have more to go by. You have not only what you look like, you have also your thoughts and memories and all your organic sensations, so that you have a much richer material and are therefore much less likely to be mistaken as to your own identity than as to someone else's. It happens, of course, that there are mistakes even as to one's own identity, in cases of multiple personality and so forth, but as a rule you will know that it is you because you have more to go by than other people have, and you would know it is you, not by a consciousness of the ego at all but by all sorts of things, by memory, by the way you feel and the way you look and a host of things. But all those are empirical data, and those enable you to say that the person to whom something happened yesterday was yourself. So if you can collect a whole set of experiences into one string as all belonging to you, and similarly other people's experiences can be collected together as all belonging to them by relations that actually are observable and without assuming the existence of the persistent ego. It does not matter in the least to what we are concerned with, what exactly is the given empirical relation between two experiences that makes us say, 'These are two experiences of the same person'. It does not matter precisely what that relation is, because the logical formula for the construction of the person is the same whatever that relation may be, and because the mere fact that you can know that two experiences belong to the same person proves that there is such an empirical relation to be ascertained by analysis. Let us call the relation R. We shall say that when two experiences have to each other the relation R, then they are said to be experiences of the same person. That is a definition of what I mean by 'experiences of the same person'. We proceed here just in the same way as when we are defining numbers. We first define what is meant by saying that two classes 'have the same number', and then define what a number is. The person who has a given experience x will be the class of all those experiences which are 'experiences of the same person' as the one who experiences *x*. You can say that two events are co-personal when there is between them a certain relation *R*, namely that relation which makes us say that they are experiences of the same person. You can define the person who has a certain experience as being those experiences that are co-personal with that experience, and it will be better perhaps to take them as a series than as a class, because you want to know which is the beginning of a man's life and which is the end. Therefore we shall say that a person is a certain series of experiences. We shall not deny that there may be a metaphysical ego. We shall merely say that it is a question that does not concern us in any way, because it is a matter about which we know nothing and can know nothing, and therefore it obviously cannot be a thing that comes into science in any way. What we know is this string of experiences that makes up a person, and that is put together by means of certain empirically given relations, such, e.g., as memory.

I will take another illustration, a kind of problem that our method is useful in helping to deal with. You all know the American theory of neutral monism, which derives really from William James and is also suggested in the work of Mach, but in a rather less developed form. The theory of neutral monism maintains that the distinction between the mental and the physical is entirely an affair of arrangement, that the actual material arranged is exactly the same in the case of the mental as it is in the case of the physical, but they differ merely in the fact that when you take a thing as belonging in the same context with certain other things, it will belong to psychology, while when you take it in a certain other context with other things, it will belong to physics, and the difference is as to what you consider to be its context, just the same sort of difference as there is between arranging the people in London alphabetically or geographically. So, according to William James, the actual material of the world can be arranged in two different ways, one of which gives you physics and the other psychology. It is just like rows or columns: in an arrangement of rows and columns, you can take an item as either a member of a certain row or a member of a certain column; the item is the same in the two cases, but its context is different.

If you will allow me a little undue simplicity I can go on to say rather more about neutral monism, but you must understand that I am talking more simply than I ought to do because there is not time to put in all the shadings and qualifications. I was talking a moment ago about the appearances that a chair presents. If we take any one of these chairs, we can all look at it, and it presents a different appearance to each of us. Taken all together, taking all the different appearances that that chair is presenting to all of us at this moment, you get something that belongs to physics. So that, if one takes sense-data and arranges together all those sense-data that appear to different people at a given moment and are such as we should ordinarily say are appearances of the same physical object, then that class of sense-data will give you something that belongs to physics, namely, the chair at this moment. On the other hand, if instead of taking all the appearances that that chair presents to all of us at this moment, I take all the appearances that the different chairs in this room present to me at this moment, I get quite another group of particulars. All the different appearances that different chairs present to me now will give you something belonging to psychology, because that will give you my experiences at the present moment. Broadly speaking, according to what one may take as an expansion of William James, that should be the definition of the difference between physics and psychology.

We commonly assume that there is a phenomenon which we call seeing the chair, but what I call my seeing the chair according to neutral monism is merely the existence of a certain particular, namely the particular which is the sense-datum of that chair at that moment. And I and the chair are both logical fictions, both being in fact a series of classes of particulars, of which one will be that particular which we call my seeing the chair. That actual appearance that the chair is presenting to me now is a member of me and a member of the chair, I and the chair being logical fictions. That will be at any rate a view that you can consider if you are engaged in vindicating neutral monism. There is no simple entity that you can point to and say: this entity is physical and not mental. According to William James and neutral monists that will not be the case with any simple entity that you may take. Any such entity will be a member of physical series and a member of mental series. Now I want to say that if you wish to test such a theory as that of neutral monism, if you wish to discover whether it is true or false, you cannot hope to get any distance with your problem unless you have at your fingers' ends the theory of logic that I have been talking of. You never can tell otherwise what can be done with a given material, whether you can concoct out of a given material the sort of logical fictions that will have the properties you want in psychology and in physics. That sort of thing is by no means easy to decide. You can only decide it if you really have a very considerable technical facility in these matters. Having said that, I ought to proceed to tell you that I have discovered whether neutral monism is true or not, because otherwise you may not believe that logic is any use in the matter. But I do not profess to know whether it is true or not. I feel more and more inclined to think that it may be true. I feel more and more that the difficulties that occur in regard to it are all of the sort that may be solved by ingenuity. But nevertheless there *are* a number of difficulties;

there are a number of problems, some of which I have spoken about in the course of these lectures.[2] One is the question of belief and the other sorts of facts involving two verbs. If there are such facts as this, that, I think, may make neutral monism rather difficult, but as I was pointing out, there is the theory that one calls behaviourism, which belongs logically with neutral monism, and that theory would altogether dispense with those facts containing two verbs, and would therefore dispose of that argument against neutral monism. There is, on the other hand, the argument from emphatic particulars, such as 'this' and 'now' and 'here' and such words as that, which are not very easy to reconcile, to my mind, with the view which does not distinguish between a particular and experiencing that particular. But the argument about emphatic particulars is so delicate and so subtle that I cannot feel quite sure whether it is a valid one or not, and I think the longer one pursues philosophy, the more conscious one becomes how extremely often one has been taken in by fallacies, and the less willing one is to be quite sure that an argument is valid if there is anything about it that is at all subtle or elusive, at all difficult to grasp. That makes me a little cautious, and doubtful about all these arguments, and therefore although I am quite sure that the question of the truth or falsehood of neutral monism is not be solved except by these means, yet I do not profess to know whether neutral monism is true or is not. I am not without hopes of finding out in the course of time, but I do not profess to know yet.

As I said earlier in this lecture, one thing that our technique does, is to give us a means of constructing a given body of symbolic propositions with the minimum of apparatus, and every diminution in apparatus diminishes the risk of error. Suppose, e.g., that you have constructed your physics with a certain number of entities and a certain number of premises; suppose you discover that by a little ingenuity you can dispense with half of those entities and half of those premises, you clearly have diminished the risk of error, because if you had before 10 entities and 10 premises, then the 5 you have now would be all right, but it is not true conversely that if the 5 you have now are all right, the 10 must have been. Therefore you diminish the risk of error with every diminution of entities and premises. When I spoke about the desk and said I was not going to assume the existence of a persistent substance underlying its appearances, it is an example of the case in point. You have anyhow the successive appearances, and if you can get on without assuming the metaphysical and constant desk, you have a smaller risk of error than you had before. You would not necessarily have a smaller risk of error if you were tied down to *denying* the metaphysical desk. That is the advantage of Occam's Razor, that it diminishes your risk of error. Considered in that way you may say that the whole of our problem belongs rather to science than to philosophy. I think perhaps that is true, but I believe the only difference between science and philosophy is, that science is what you more or less know and philosophy is what you do not know. Philosophy is that part of science which at present people choose to have opinions about, but which they have no knowledge about. Therefore every advance in knowledge robs philosophy of some problems which formerly it had, and if there is any truth, if there is any value in the kind of procedure of mathematical logic, it will follow that a number of problems which had belonged to philosophy will have ceased to belong to philosophy and will belong to science. And of course the moment they become soluble, they become to a large class of philosophical minds uninteresting, because to many of the people who like philosophy, the charm of it consists in the speculative freedom, in the fact that you can play with hypotheses. You can think out this or that which *may* be true, which is a very valuable exercise until you discover what *is* true; but when you discover what is true the whole fruitful play of fancy in that region is curtailed, and you will abandon that region and pass on. Just as there are families in America who from the time of the Pilgrim Fathers onward had always migrated westward, toward the backwoods, because they did not like civilized life, so the philosopher has an adventurous disposition and likes to dwell in the region where there are still uncertainties. It is true that the transferring of a region from philosophy into science will make it distasteful to a very important and useful type of mind. I think that is true of a good deal of the applications of mathematical logic in the directions that I have been indicating. It makes it dry, precise, methodical, and in that way robs it of a certain quality that it had when you could play with it more freely. I do not feel that it is my place to apologize for that, because if it is true, it is true. If it is not true, of course, I do owe you an apology; but if it is, it is not my fault, and therefore I do not feel I owe any apology for any sort of dryness or dulness in the world. I would say this too, that for those who have any taste for mathematics, for those who like symbolic constructions, that sort of world is a very delightful one, and if you do not find it otherwise attractive, all that is necessary to do is to acquire a taste for mathematics, and then you will have a very agreeable world, and with that conclusion I will bring this course of lectures to an end.

Note

1 *Our Knowledge of the External World*, Allen & Unwin, 1914.
2 The two rather technical problems Russell mentions emerge from earlier

lectures. (a) In Lecture IV, he has discussed 'propositions involving two verbs', such as 'I believe that Socrates is wise'. The problem is whether such propositions record irreducible, *sui generis* mental facts. If they do, then these facts cannot also, in a different 'arrangement', be physical facts. Russell, however, allows the possibility of a 'behaviourist' analysis of such propositions which would remove the difficulty. (b) In Lecture II, Russell has argued that the only genuine logically proper names are terms like 'this' and 'that' when these are used, not to refer to a physical object, but 'to stand for an actual object of sense', a sense-datum. The difficulty, I take it, is that with 'This is red' so construed, it contrasts with the same words when used to state a fact about a physical object. The contrast seems to imply that there are two kinds of fact, sensory and physical, not one 'neutral' fact which, according to the arrangement it is placed in, could count as either mental or physical.

A. N. Whitehead, *Process and Reality*, Part I, Chapters 1 and 2 (selected sections)

From F. S. C. Northrop and M. W. Gross (eds), *Alfred North Whitehead: an anthology.* Cambridge: Cambridge University Press, 1953, pp. 567–72, 576–87 (some notes omitted; asterisked notes are Whitehead's).

Process and Reality: an essay in cosmology, the major work of the British emigré to Harvard, Alfred North Whitehead (1861–1947), emerged from the Gifford Lectures which he delivered in Edinburgh in 1927–8. Although Whitehead had been Bertrand Russell's collaborator on *Principia Mathematica*, these Lectures display not so much the influence of his earlier work on logic as that of the 'life philosophy' of Henri Bergson and of recent currents in physics, notably Einsteinian relativity theory and quantum mechanics. Like Bergson and contemporary physicists, Whitehead aimed to develop a theory of the universe which would dispense with the 'static', mechanical model of the world that still exerted an unfortunate grip, he believed, on most philosophers. The resulting metaphysics, highly influential in the United States, is known as 'Process philosophy' or, as Whitehead calls it in the following pages, 'the philosophy of organism'.

The Sections I have selected from *Process and Reality* give a fair idea of the shape of Whitehead's theory, but they also record his conception of 'speculative philosophy' or metaphysics. Despite the attacks being launched on the metaphysical enterprise by the logical positivists during the 1920s, Whitehead's view of the enterprise is unapologetically in the tradition of Hegel. Speculative philosophy provides a 'synoptic vision' of reality 'in terms of which every element of our experience can be interpreted'. While the sciences must be incorporated in this vision, it is the 'self-denial of thought' to suppose that they alone can provide it.

Like the positivists, however, Whitehead focuses attention on issues of meaning and language, and he outbids Russell in regarding everyday language – its subject–predicate structure, for example – as a poor guide to the nature of reality: 'no verbal statement is the adequate expression of a proposition'. A main reason for this is that every statement is 'elliptical', indicating far more by way of its relation to experience than it can actually state. This, in turn, is because experience and reality themselves are systematic wholes from which particular things and facts may only be artificially abstracted. To regard any such thing or fact as self-contained and independent is to commit 'the fallacy of misplaced concreteness'. This emphasis on the universe as being, not a collection of substances, but a totality of processes, within which everything is intimately interrelated, is the central thrust of 'Process philosophy'.[1]

Given this, it is unsurprising to find Whitehead criticizing Descartes' dualism, and even Spinoza's monism because of its sharp distinction between the two 'modes' of thought and extension (see pp. 123 above). Later in *Process and Reality*, and still more in Lecture 8 of *Modes of Thought* (1938), Whitehead insists on the continuity between human mental processes and ones going on at the 'merely' material level, and hence on the artificiality of any dualistic division.

The opening section of Ch. 2 introduces some of Whitehead's main terms of art: 'actual entity', 'nexus' and 'prehension'. Unlike some monists, Whitehead does not treat reality as a single indivisible whole. It contains 'actual entities', but these processes are 'drops of experience, complex and interdependent', related to one another in a 'nexus' or 'togetherness'. Instead of calling this relation 'causality', which might connote an excessive degree of separation among the related items, Whitehead speaks of 'prehension'. This, he explains, should be thought of on the model of psychological phenomena, like desire and appetite. There are echoes here, as Whitehead notes, of Leibniz's monadology, not least in the suggestion that primitive, unconscious 'mindlikeness' permeates the material universe (see chapter 9 above). However, in the words of one commentator, whereas Leibniz's monads are 'windowless', in having no contact with other monads, a Whiteheadian 'actual entity' is all window, for 'in an important sense [it] *is* its relations to other beings'.[2]

An area where Whitehead's thinking has had particular influence is the philosophy of religion: hence the emergence of the 'Process theology' associated with such figures as Charles Hartshorne.[3] The inspiration, here, is Whitehead's reference to the 'ultimate' and 'creative' character of reality as 'God': a reference he elsewhere justifies by attributing responsibility for 'importance, value, and ideal' to the 'creative' process. God, he makes clear, should not be thought of, in the manner of some monists, as an 'Absolute' enjoying a more 'eminent' reality than its 'accidents'. God, for Whitehead, is no way apart from reality or process itself.

---

[1] See Nicholas Rescher, 'The promise of process philosophy', in his *Baffling Phenomena*, Savage, MD: Rowman & Littlefield, 1991.
[2] Donald W. Sherburne, 'Whitehead, Alfred North', in *A Companion to Metaphysics*, ed. J. Kim and E. Sosa, *op. cit.*, p. 511.
[3] See E. H. Cousins (ed.), *Process Theology*, New York: Newman, 1971.

Whitehead, Part I – The Speculative Scheme

Chapter I   *Speculative Philosophy*

SECTION I

This course of lectures is designed as an essay in Speculative Philosophy. Its first task must be to define 'speculative philosophy,' and to defend it as a method productive of important knowledge.

Speculative Philosophy is the endeavor to frame a coherent, logical, necessary system of general ideas in terms of which every element of our experience can be interpreted. By this notion of 'interpretation' I mean that everything of which we are conscious, as enjoyed, perceived, willed, or thought, shall have the character of a particular instance of the general scheme. Thus the philosophical scheme should be coherent, logical, and, in respect to its interpretation, applicable and adequate. Here 'applicable' means that some items of experience are thus interpretable, and 'adequate' means that there are no items incapable of such interpretation.

'Coherence,' as here employed, means that the fundamental ideas, in terms of which the scheme is developed, presuppose each other so that in isolation they are meaningless. This requirement does not mean that they are definable in terms of each other; it means that what is indefinable in one such notion cannot be abstracted from its relevance to the other notions. It is the ideal of speculative philosophy that its fundamental notions shall not seem capable of abstraction from each other. In other words, it is presupposed that no entity can be conceived in complete abstraction from the system of the universe, and that it is the business of speculative philosophy to exhibit this truth. This character is its coherence.

The term 'logical' has its ordinary meaning, including 'logical' consistency, or lack of contradiction, the definition of constructs in logical terms, the exemplification of general logical notions in specific instances, and the principles of inference. It will be observed that logical notions must themselves find their places in the scheme of philosophic notions.

It will also be noticed that this ideal of speculative philosophy has its rational side and its empirical side. The rational side is expressed by the terms 'coherent' and 'logical.' The empirical side is expressed by the terms 'applicable' and 'adequate.' But the two sides are bound together by clearing away an ambiguity which remains in the previous explanation of the term 'adequate.' The adequacy of the scheme over every item does not mean adequacy over such items as happen to have been considered. It means that the texture of observed experience, as illustrating the philosophic scheme, is such that all related experience must exhibit the same texture. Thus the philosophic scheme should be 'necessary' , in the sense of bearing in itself its own warrant of universality throughout all experience, provided that we confine ourselves to that which communicates with immediate matter of fact. But what does not so communicate is unknowable, and the unknowable is unknown;* and so this universality defined by 'communication' can suffice.

This doctrine of necessity in universality means that there is an essence to the universe which forbids relationships beyond itself, as a violation of its rationality. Speculative philosophy seeks that essence.

SECTION II

Philosophers can never hope finally to formulate these metaphysical first principles. Weakness of insight and deficiencies of language stand in the way inexorably. Words and phrases must be stretched towards a generality foreign to their ordinary usage; and however such elements of language be stabilized as technicalities, they remain metaphors mutely appealing for an imaginative leap.

There is no first principle which is in itself unknowable, not to be captured by a flash of insight. But, putting aside the difficulties of language, deficiency in imaginative penetration forbids progress in any form other than that of an asymptotic approach to a scheme of principles, only definable in terms of the ideal which they should satisfy.

The difficulty has its seat in the empirical side of philosophy. Our datum is the actual world, including ourselves; and this actual world spreads itself for observation in the guise of the topic of our immediate experience. The elucidation of immediate experience is the sole justification for any thought; and the starting point for thought is the analytic observation of components of this experience. But we are not conscious of any clear-cut complete analysis of immediate experience, in terms of the various details which comprise its definiteness. We habitually observe by the method of difference. Sometimes we see an elephant, and sometimes we do not. The result is that an elephant, when present, is noticed. Facility of observation depends on the fact that the object observed is important when present, and sometimes is absent.

The metaphysical first principles can never fail of exemplification. We can never catch the actual world taking a holiday from their sway. Thus, for

---

* This doctrine is a paradox. Indulging in a species of false modesty, 'cautious' philosophers undertake its definition.

the discovery of metaphysics, the method of pinning down thought to the strict systematization of detailed discrimination, already effected by antecedent observation, breaks down. This collapse of the method of rigid empiricism is not confined to metaphysics. It occurs whenever we seek the larger generalities. In natural science this rigid method is the Baconian method of induction, a method which, if consistently pursued, would have left science where it found it. What Bacon omitted was the play of a free imagination, controlled by the requirements of coherence and logic. The true method of discovery is like the flight of an aeroplane. It starts from the ground of particular observation; it makes a flight in the thin air of imaginative generalization; and it again lands for renewed observation rendered acute by rational interpretation. The reason for the success of this method of imaginative rationalization is that, when the method of difference fails, factors which are constantly present may yet be observed under the influence of imaginative thought. Such thought supplies the differences which the direct observation lacks. It can even play with inconsistency; and can thus throw light on the consistent, and persistent, elements in experience by comparison with what in imagination is inconsistent with them. The negative judgment is the peak of mentality. But the conditions for the success of imaginative construction must be rigidly adhered to. In the first place, this construction must have its origin in the generalization of particular factors discerned in particular topics of human interest; for example, in physics, or in physiology, or in psychology, or in aesthetics, or in ethical beliefs, or in sociology, or in languages conceived as storehouses of human experience. In this way the prime requisite, that anyhow there shall be some important application, is secured. The success of the imaginative experiment is always to be tested by the applicability of its results beyond the restricted locus from which it originated. In default of such extended application, a generalization started from physics, for example, remains merely an alternative expression of notions applicable to physics. The partially successful philosophic generalization will, if derived from physics, find applications in fields of experience beyond physics. It will enlighten observation in those remote fields, so that general principles can be discerned as in process of illustration, which in the absence of the imaginative generalization are obscured by their persistent exemplification.

Thus the first requisite is to proceed by the method of generalization so that certainly there is some application; and the test of some success is application beyond the immediate origin. In other words, some synoptic vision has been gained.

In this description of philosophic method, the term 'philosophic generalization' has meant 'the utilization of specific notions, applying to a restricted group of facts, for the divination of the generic notions which apply to all facts.'

In its use of this method natural science has shown a curious mixture of rationalism and irrationalism. Its prevalent tone of thought has been ardently rationalistic within its own borders, and dogmatically irrational beyond those borders. In practice such an attitude tends to become a dogmatic denial that there are any factors in the world not fully expressible in terms of its own primary notions devoid of further generalization. Such a denial is the self-denial of thought.

The second condition for the success of imaginative construction is unflinching pursuit of the two rationalistic ideals, coherence and logical perfection.

Logical perfection does not here require any detailed explanation. An example of its importance is afforded by the role of mathematics in the restricted field of natural science. The history of mathematics exhibits the generalization of special notions observed in particular instances. In any branches of mathematics, the notions presuppose each other. It is a remarkable characteristic of the history of thought that branches of mathematics developed under the pure imaginative impulse, thus controlled, finally receive their important application. Time may be wanted. Conic sections had to wait for eighteen hundred years. In more recent years, the theory of probability, the theory of tensors, the theory of matrices are cases in point.

The requirement of coherence is the great preservative of rationalistic sanity. But the validity of its criticism is not always admitted. If we consider philosophical controversies, we shall find that disputants tend to require coherence from their adversaries, and to grant dispensations to themselves. It has been remarked that a system of philosophy is never refuted; it is only abandoned. The reason is that logical contradictions, except as temporary slips of the mind – plentiful, though temporary – are the most gratuitous of errors; and usually they are trivial. Thus, after criticism, systems do not exhibit mere illogicalities. They suffer from inadequacy and incoherence. Failure to include some obvious elements of experience in the scope of the system is met by boldly denying the facts. Also while a philosophical system retains any charm of novelty, it enjoys a plenary indulgence for its failures in coherence. But after a system has acquired orthodoxy, and is taught with authority, it receives a sharper criticism. Its denials and its incoherences are found intolerable, and a reaction sets in.

Incoherence is the arbitrary disconnection of first principles. In modern philosophy Descartes' two kinds of substance, corporeal and mental, illustrate incoherence. There is, in Descartes' philosophy, no reason why there should not be a one-substance world, only corporeal, or a one-substance world, only mental. According to Descartes, a substantial individual 'requires nothing but itself in order to exist.' Thus this system makes a virtue of its incoherence. But on the other hand, the facts seem connected, while Descartes' system does not; for example, in the treatment of the body-mind problem. The Cartesian system obviously says something that is true. But its notions are too abstract to penetrate into the nature of things.

The attraction of Spinoza's philosophy lies in its modification of Descartes' position into greater coherence. He starts with one substance, *causa sui*, and considers its essential attributes and its individualized modes, i.e. the '*affectiones substantiae*.' The gap in the system is the arbitrary introduction of the 'modes.' And yet, a multiplicity of modes is a fixed requisite, if the scheme is to retain any direct relevance to the many occasions in the experienced world.

The philosophy of organism is closely allied to Spinoza's scheme of thought. But it differs by the abandonment of the subject-predicate forms of thought, so far as concerns the presupposition that this form is a direct embodiment of the most ultimate characterization of fact. The result is that the 'substance-quality' concept is avoided; and that morphological description is replaced by description of dynamic process. Also Spinoza's 'modes' now become the sheer actualities; so that, though analysis of them increases our understanding, it does not lead us to the discovery of any higher grade of reality. The coherence, which the system seeks to preserve, is the discovery that the process, or concrescence, of any one actual entity involves the other actual entities among its components. In this way the obvious solidarity of the world receives its explanation.

In all philosophic theory there is an ultimate which is actual in virtue of its accidents. It is only then capable of characterization through its accidental embodiments, and apart from these accidents is devoid of actuality. In the philosophy of organism this ultimate is termed 'creativity'; and God is its primordial, non-temporal accident. In monistic philosophies, Spinoza's or absolute idealism, this ultimate is God, who is also equivalently termed 'The Absolute.' In such monistic schemes, the ultimate is illegitimately allowed a final, 'eminent' reality, beyond that ascribed to any of its accidents. In this general position the philosophy of organism seems to approximate more to some strains of Indian, or Chinese, thought, than to western Asiatic, or European, thought. One side makes process ultimate; the other side makes fact ultimate. . . .

SECTION V

Every science must devise its own instruments. The tool required for philosophy is language. Thus philosophy redesigns language in the same way that, in a physical science, pre-existing appliances are redesigned. It is exactly at this point that the appeal to facts is a difficult operation. This appeal is not solely to the expression of the facts in current verbal statements. The adequacy of such sentences is the main question at issue. It is true that the general agreement of mankind as to experienced facts is best expressed in language. But the language of literature breaks down precisely at the task of expressing in explicit form the large generalities – the very generalities which metaphysics seeks to express.

The point is that every proposition refers to a universe exhibiting some general systematic metaphysical character. Apart from this background, the separate entities which go to form the proposition, and the proposition as a whole, are without determinate character. Nothing has been defined, because every definite entity requires a systematic universe to supply its requisite status. Thus every proposition proposing a fact must, in its complete analysis, propose the general character of the universe required for that fact. There are no selfsustained facts, floating in nonentity. This doctrine, of the impossibility of tearing a proposition from its systematic context in the actual world, is a direct consequence of the fourth and the twentieth of the fundamental categoreal explanations which we shall be engaged in expanding and illustrating.[1] A proposition can embody partial truth because it only demands a certain type of systematic environment, which is presupposed in its meaning. It does not refer to the universe in all its detail.

One practical aim of metaphysics is the accurate analysis of propositions; not merely of metaphysical propositions, but of quite ordinary propositions such as 'There is beef for dinner today,' and 'Socrates is mortal.' The one genus of facts which constitutes the field of some special science requires some common metaphysical presupposition respecting the universe. It is merely credulous to accept verbal phrases as adequate statements of propositions. The distinction between verbal phrases and complete propositions is one of the reasons why the logicians' rigid alternative, 'true or false,' is so largely irrelevant for the pursuit of knowledge.

The excessive trust in linguistic phrases has been the well-known reason vitiating so much of the philosophy and physics among the Greeks and among the medieval thinkers who continued the Greek traditions. For example John Stuart Mill writes: 'They (the Greeks) had great difficulty in distinguishing between things which their language confounded, or in putting mentally together things which it distinguished; and could hardly combine the objects in nature, into any classes but those which were made for them by the popular phrases of their own country; or at least could not help fancying those classes to be natural, and all others arbitrary and artificial. Accordingly, scientific investigation among the Greek schools of speculation and their followers in the Middle Ages, was little more than a mere sifting and analysing of the notions attached to common language. They thought that by determining the meaning of words they could become acquainted with facts.'* Mill then proceeds to quote from Whewell a paragraph illustrating the same weakness of Greek thought.†

But neither Mill, nor Whewell, tracks this difficulty about language down to its sources. They both presuppose that language does enunciate well-defined propositions. This is quite untrue. Language is thoroughly indeterminate, by reason of the fact that every occurrence presupposes some systematic type of environment.

For example, the word 'Socrates,' referring to the philosopher, in one sentence may stand for an entity presupposing a more closely defined background than the word 'Socrates,' with the same reference, in another sentence. The word 'mortal' affords an analogous possibility. A precise language must await a completed metaphysical knowledge.

The technical language of philosophy represents attempts of various schools of thought to obtain explicit expression of general ideas presupposed by the facts of experience. It follows that any novelty in metaphysical doctrines exhibits some measure of disagreement with statements of the facts to be found in current philosophical literature. The extent of disagreement measures the extent of metaphysical divergence. It is, therefore, no valid criticism of one metaphysical school to point out that its doctrines do not follow from the verbal expression of the facts accepted by another school. The whole contention is that the doctrines in question supply a closer approach to fully expressed propositions.

The truth itself is nothing else than how the composite natures of the organic actualities of the world obtain adequate representation in the divine nature. Such representations compose the 'consequent nature' of God, which evolves in its relationship to the evolving world without derogation to the eternal completion of its primordial conceptual nature. In this way the 'ontological principle' is maintained [see p. 279 below] – since there can be no determinate truth, correlating impartially the partial experiences of many actual entities, apart from one actual entity to which it can be

---

* Cf. *Logic*, Book V, Ch. III.
† Cf. Whewell's *History of the Inductive Sciences*.

referred. The reaction of the temporal world on the nature of God is considered subsequently in Part V: it is there termed 'the consequent nature of God.'

Whatever is found in 'practice' must lie within the scope of the metaphysical description. When the description fails to include the 'practice,' the metaphysics is inadequate and requires revision. There can be no appeal to practice to supplement metaphysics, so long as we remain contented with our metaphysical doctrines. Metaphysics is nothing but the description of the generalities which apply to all the details of practice.

No metaphysical system can hope entirely to satisfy these pragmatic tests. At the best such a system will remain only an approximation to the general truths which are sought. In particular, there are no precisely stated axiomatic certainties from which to start. There is not even the language in which to frame them. The only possible procedure is to start from verbal expressions which, when taken by themselves with the current meaning of their words, are ill-defined and ambiguous. These are not premises to be immediately reasoned from apart from elucidation by further discussion; they are endeavours to state general principles which will be exemplified in the subsequent description of the facts of experience. This subsequent elaboration should elucidate the meanings to be assigned to the words and phrases employed. Such meaning are incapable of accurate apprehension apart from a correspondingly accurate apprehension of the metaphysical background which the universe provides for them. But no language can be anything but elliptical, requiring a leap of the imagination to understand its meaning in its relevance to immediate experience. The position of metaphysics in the development of culture cannot be understood without remembering that no verbal statement is the adequate expression of a proposition.

An old established metaphysical system gains a false air of adequate precision from the fact that its words and phrases have passed into current literature. Thus propositions expressed in its language are more easily correlated to our flitting intuitions into metaphysical truth. When we trust these verbal statements and argue as though they adequately analysed meaning, we are led into difficulties which take the shape of negations of what in practice is presupposed. But when they are proposed as first principles they assume an unmerited air of sober obviousness. Their defect is that the true propositions which they do express lose their fundamental character when subjected to adequate expression. For example consider the type of propositions such as 'The grass is green,' and 'The whale is big.' This subject-predicate form of statement seems so simple, leading straight to a metaphysical first principle; and yet in these examples it conceals such complex, diverse meanings.

SECTION VI

It has been an objection to speculative philosophy that it is over-ambitious. Rationalism, it is admitted, is the method by which advance is made within the limits of particular sciences. It is, however, held that this limited success must not encourage attempts to frame ambitious schemes expressive of the general nature of things.

One alleged justification of this criticism is ill-success: European thought is represented as littered with metaphysical systems, abandoned and un-reconciled.

Such an assertion tacitly fastens upon philosophy the old dogmatic test. The same criterion would fasten ill-success upon science. We no more retain the physics of the seventeenth century than we do the Cartesian philosophy of that century. Yet within limits, both systems express import-ant truths. Also we are beginning to understand the wider categories which define their limits of correct application. Of course, in that century, dog-matic views held sway; so that the validity both of the physical notions, and of the Cartesian notions, was misconceived. Mankind never quite knows what it is after. When we survey the history of thought, and likewise the history of practice, we find that one idea after another is tried out, its limi-tations defined, and its core of truth elicited. In application to the instinct for the intellectual adventures demanded by particular epochs, there is much truth in Augustine's rhetorical phrase, *Securus judicat orbis terrarum.*[2] At the very least, men do what they can in the way of systematization, and in the event achieve something. The proper test is not that of finality, but of progress.

But the main objection, dating from the sixteenth century and receiving final expression from Francis Bacon, is the uselessness of philosophic specu-lation. The position taken by this objection is that we ought to describe detailed matter of fact, and elicit the laws with a generality strictly limited to the systematization of these described details. General interpretation, it is held, has no bearing upon this procedure; and thus any system of general interpretation, be it true or false, remains intrinsically barren. Unfortu-nately for this objection, there are no brute, self-contained matters of fact, capable of being understood apart from interpretation as an element in a system. Whenever we attempt to express the matter of immediate experi-ence, we find that its understanding leads us beyond itself, to its contem-poraries, to its past, to its future, and to the universals in terms of which its definiteness is exhibited. But such universals, by their very character of universality, embody the potentiality of other fact with variant types of definiteness. Thus the understanding of the immediate brute fact requires its metaphysical interpretation as an item in a world with some systematic relation to it. When thought comes upon the scene, it finds the interpretations as matters of practice. Philosophy does not initiate interpretations. Its search for a rationalistic scheme is the search for more adequate criticism, and for more adequate justification, of the interpretations which we perforce employ. Our habitual experience is a complex of failure and success in the enterprise of interpretation. If we desire a record of uninterrupted experience, we must ask a stone to record its autobiography. Every scientific memoir in its record of the 'facts' is shot through and through with interpretation. The methodology of rational interpretation is the product of the fitful vagueness of consciousness. Elements which shine with immediate distinctness, in some circumstances, retire into penumbral shadow in other circumstances, and into black darkness on other occasions. And yet all occasions proclaim themselves as actualities within the flux of a solid world, demanding a unity of interpretation.

Philosophy is the self-correction by consciousness of its own initial excess of subjectivity. Each actual occasion contributes to the circumstances of its origin additional formative elements deepening its own peculiar individuality. Consciousness is only the last and greatest of such elements by which the selective character of the individual obscures the external totality from which it originates and which it embodies. An actual individual, of such higher grade, has truck with the totality of things by reason of its sheer actuality; but it has attained its individual depth of being by a selective emphasis limited to its own purposes. The task of philosophy is to recover the totality obscured by the selection. It replaces in rational experience what has been submerged in the higher sensitive experience and has been sunk yet deeper by the initial operations of consciousness itself. The selectiveness of individual experience is moral so far as it conforms to the balance of importance disclosed in the rational vision; and conversely the conversion of the intellectual insight into an emotional force corrects the sensitive experience in the direction of morality. The correction is in proportion to the rationality of the insight.

Morality of outlook is inseparably conjoined with generality of outlook. The antithesis between the general good and the individual interest can be abolished only when the individual is such that its interest is the general good, thus exemplifying the loss of the minor intensities in order to find them again with finer composition in a wider sweep of interest.

Philosophy frees itself from the taint of ineffectiveness by its close relations with religion and with science, natural and sociological. It attains its chief importance by fusing the two, namely, religion and science, into one rational scheme of thought. Religion should connect the rational generality of philosophy with the emotions and purposes springing out of existence in a particular society, in a particular epoch, and conditioned by particular antecedents. Religion is the translation of general ideas into particular thoughts, particular emotions, and particular purposes; it is directed to the end of stretching individual interest beyond its self-defeating particularity. Philosophy finds religion, and modifies it; and conversely religion is among the data of experience which philosophy must weave into its own scheme. Religion is an ultimate craving to infuse into the insistent particularity of emotion that non-temporal generality which primarily belongs to conceptual thought alone. In the higher organisms the differences of tempo between the mere emotions and the conceptual experiences produce a life-tedium, unless this supreme fusion has been effected. The two sides of the organism require a reconciliation in which emotional experiences illustrate a conceptual justification, and conceptual experiences find an emotional illustration.

This demand for an intellectual justification of brute experience has also been the motive power in the advance of European science. In this sense scientific interest is only a variant form of religious interest. Any survey of the scientific devotion to 'truth,' as an ideal, will confirm this statement. There is, however, a grave divergence between science and religion in respect to the phases of individual experience with which they are concerned. Religion is centred upon the harmony of rational thought with the sensitive reaction to the percepta from which experience originates. Science is concerned with the harmony of rational thought with the percepta themselves. When science deals with emotions, the emotions in question are percepta and not immediate passions – other people's emotion and not our own; at least our own in recollection, and not in immediacy. Religion deals with the formation of the experiencing subject; whereas science deals with the objects, which are the data forming the primary phase in this experience. The subject originates from, and amid, given conditions; science conciliates thought with this primary matter of fact; and religion conciliates the thought involved in the process with the sensitive reaction involved in that same process. The process is nothing else than the experiencing subject itself. In this explanation it is presumed that an experiencing subject is one occasion of sensitive reaction to an actual world. Science finds religious experiences among its percepta; and religion finds scientific concepts among the conceptual experiences to be fused with particular sensitive reactions.

The conclusion of this discussion is, first, the assertion of the old doctrine that breadth of thought reacting with intensity of sensitive experience stands out as an ultimate claim of existence; secondly, the assertion that empirically the development of self-justifying thoughts has been achieved by the complex process of generalizing from particular topics, of imaginatively schematizing the generalizations, and finally by renewed comparison of the imagined scheme with the direct experience to which it should apply.

There is no justification for checking generalization at any particular stage. Each phase of generalization exhibits its own peculiar simplicities which stand out just at that stage, and at no other stage. There are simplicities connected with the motion of a bar of steel which are obscured if we refuse to abstract from the individual molecules; and there are certain simplicities concerning the behaviour of men which are obscured if we refuse to abstract from the individual peculiarities of particular specimens. In the same way, there are certain general truths, about the actual things in the common world of activity, which will be obscured when attention is confined to some particular detailed mode of considering them. These general truths, involved in the meaning of every particular notion respecting the actions of things, are the subject matter for speculative philosophy.

Philosophy destroys its usefulness when it indulges in brilliant feats of explaining away. It is then trespassing with the wrong equipment upon the field of particular sciences. Its ultimate appeal is to the general consciousness of what in practice we experience. Whatever thread of presupposition characterizes social expression throughout the various epochs of rational society, must find its place in philosophic theory. Speculative boldness must be balanced by complete humility before logic, and before fact. It is a disease of philosophy when it is neither bold nor humble, but merely a reflection of the temperamental presuppositions of exceptional personalities.

Analogously, we do not trust any recasting of scientific theory depending upon a single performance of an aberrant experiment, unrepeated. The ultimate test is always widespread, recurrent experience; and the more general the rationalistic scheme, the more important is this final appeal.

The useful function of philosophy is to promote the most general systematization of civilized thought. There is a constant reaction between specialism and common sense. It is the part of the special sciences to modify common sense. Philosophy is the welding of imagination and common sense into a restraint upon specialists, and also into an enlargement of their imaginations. By providing the generic notions philosophy should make it easier to conceive the infinite variety of specific instances which rest unrealized in the womb of nature.

Chapter II   The Categoreal Scheme

SECTION I

This chapter contains an anticipatory sketch of the primary notions which constitute the philosophy of organism. The whole of the subsequent discussion in these lectures has the purpose of rendering this summary intelligible, and of showing that it embodies generic notions inevitably presupposed in our reflective experience – presupposed, but rarely expressed in explicit distinction. Four notions may be singled out from this summary, by reason of the fact that they involve some divergence from antecedent philosophical thought. These notions are, that of an 'actual entity,' that of a 'prehension,' that of a 'nexus,' and that of the 'ontological principle.' Philosophical thought has made for itself difficulties by dealing exclusively in very abstract notions, such as those of mere awareness, mere private sensation, mere emotion, mere purpose, mere appearance, mere causation. These are the ghosts of the old 'faculties,' banished from psychology, but still haunting metaphysics. There can be no 'mere' togetherness of such abstractions. The result is that philosophical discussion is enmeshed in the fallacy of 'misplaced concreteness.'* In the three notions – actual entity, prehension, nexus – an endeavour has been made to base philosophical thought upon the most concrete elements in our experience.

'Actual entities' – also termed 'actual occasions' – are the final real things of which the world is made up. There is no going behind actual entities to find anything more real. They differ among themselves: God is an actual entity, and so is the most trivial puff of existence in far-off empty space. But, though there are gradations of importance, and diversities of function, yet in the principles which actuality exemplifies all are on the same level. The final facts are, all alike, actual entities; and these actual entities are drops of experience, complex and interdependent.

In its recurrence to the notion of a plurality of actual entities the philosophy of organism is through and through cartesian. The 'ontological principle' broadens and extends a general principle laid down by John Locke in his *Essay* (Bk. II, Ch. XXIII, Sec. 7), when he asserts that 'power' is 'a great part of our complex ideas of substances.' The notion of 'substance' is transformed into that of 'actual entity'; and the notion of 'power' is tranformed into the principle that the reasons for things are always to be found in the composite nature of definite actual entities – in the nature of God for reasons of the highest absoluteness, and in the nature of definite temporal

---

* Cf. my *Science and the Modern World*, Ch. III [also in the Whitehead *Anthology*].

actual entities for reasons which refer to a particular environment. The ontological principle can be summarized as: no actual entity, then no reason.

Each actual entity is analysable in an indefinite number of ways. In some modes of analysis the component elements are more abstract than in other modes of analysis. The analysis of an actual entity into 'prehensions' is that mode of analysis which exhibits the most concrete elements in the nature of actual entities. This mode of analysis will be termed the 'division' of the actual entity in question. Each actual entity is 'divisible' in an indefinite number of ways, and each way of 'division' yields its definite quota of prehensions. A prehension reproduces in itself the general characteristics of an actual entity: it is referrent to an external world, and in this sense will be said to have a 'vector character'; it involves emotion, and purpose, and valuation, and causation. In fact, any characteristic of an actual entity is reproduced in a prehension. It might have been a complete actuality; but, by reason of a certain incomplete partiality, a prehension is only a subordinate element in an actual entity. A reference to the complete actuality is required to give the reason why such a prehension is what it is in respect to its subjective form. This subjective form is determined by the subjective aim at further integration, so as to obtain the 'satisfaction' of the completed subject. In other words, final causation and atomism are interconnected philosophical principles.

With the purpose of obtaining a one-substance cosmology, 'prehensions' are a generalization from Descartes' mental 'cogitations,' and from Locke's 'ideas,' to express the most concrete mode of analysis applicable to every grade of individual actuality. Descartes and Locke maintained a two-substance ontology – Descartes explicitly, Locke by implication. Descartes, the mathematical physicist, emphasized his account of corporeal substance; and Locke, the physician and the sociologist, confined himself to an account of mental substance. The philosophy of organism, in its scheme for one type of actual entities, adopts the view that Locke's account of mental substance embodies, in a very special form, a more penetrating philosophic description than does Descartes' account of corporeal substance. Nevertheless, Descartes' account must find its place in the philosophic scheme. On the whole, this is the moral to be drawn from the *Monadology* of Leibniz. His monads are best conceived as generalizations of contemporary notions of mentality. The contemporary notions of physical bodies only enter into his philosophy subordinately and derivatively. The philosophy of organism endeavours to hold the balance more evenly. But it does start with a generalization of Locke's account of mental operations.

Actual entities involve each other by reason of their prehensions of each other. There are thus real individual facts of the togetherness of actual entities, which are real, individual, and particular, in the same sense in which actual entities and the prehensions are real, individual, and particular. Any such particular fact of togetherness among actual entities is called a 'nexus' (plural form is written 'nexūs'). The ultimate facts of immediate actual experience are actual entities, prehensions, and nexūs. All else is, for our experience, derivative abstraction.

The explanatory purpose of philosophy is often misunderstood. Its business is to explain the emergence of the more abstract things from the more concrete things. It is a complete mistake to ask how concrete particular fact can be built up out of universals. The answer is, 'In no way.' The true philosophic question* is, How can concrete fact exhibit entities abstract from itself and yet participated in by its own nature?

In other words, philosophy is explanatory of abstraction, and not of concreteness. It is by reason of their instinctive grasp of this ultimate truth that, in spite of much association with arbitrary fancifulness and atavistic mysticism, types of Platonic philosophy retain their abiding appeal; they seek the forms in the facts. Each fact is more than its forms, and each form 'participates' throughout the world of facts. The definiteness of fact is due to its forms; but the individual fact is a creature, and creativity is the ultimate behind all forms, inexplicable by forms, and conditioned by its creatures.

Notes

1 The 'categoreal explanations' referred to are:
   (iv) '. . . it belongs to the nature of a "being" that it is a potential for every "becoming"' (p. 590), and
   (xx) 'to "function" means to contribute determination to the actual entities in the nexus of some actual world' (p. 593).
2 The sense of Augustine's remark is that a judgement which has the general consensus of mankind can be trusted.

* In this connection I may refer to the second chapter of my book *The Principle of Relativity* (Cambridge University, 1922) [also in the Whitehead *Anthology*].

Martin Heidegger, *Being and Time* (§§14–15, 19, 21)

From Martin Heidegger, *Being and Time*, trans. J. Macquarrie and E. Robinson. Oxford: Blackwell, 1962, pp. 91–102, 122–3, 128–34 (some passages and most notes omitted; asterisked note is the translators').

The texts usually chosen from the writings of the German philosopher Martin Heidegger (1889–1976) to illustrate his metaphysical views – the Introduction to *Being and Time* (1927), for example, or the lecture 'What is metaphysics?' – are ones in which he talks *about* the task of metaphysics or ontology. (In his later work, Heidegger, like the logical positivists but for different reasons, uses the term 'metaphysics' pejoratively.)[1] I have preferred, however, to choose some sections from *Being and Time* where Heidegger is engaged *in* ontology – in presenting part of his own account of the world and reality, and in contrasting that account with a more traditional one exemplified by, above all, Descartes.

That traditional ontology, Heidegger reasonably claims, is centred on the notion of *substance*. The world is a collection of logically independent substances, with objective properties which we can observe or cognize: a world of things 'present-at-hand' (*vorhanden*), in his terminology. That conception, of course, had been criticized by earlier writers including, as we have seen in previous chapters of this book, Bradley and Whitehead. Heidegger's rejection of it is, however, a distinctly original one. To understand it, we need to be acquainted with what has preceded the chapter of *Being and Time*, 'The Worldhood of the World', from which my selections are taken.

The purpose of the book is to address 'the question of Being', one which, Heidegger believes, philosophers have generally failed to do. They have focused on beings or entities, and not on the Being of these. (In Heidegger's jargon, they have focused on 'ontical' questions about the properties of beings, not the 'ontological' issue of their Being.) By 'Being' he means 'that

[1] See, e.g., his 'Letter on humanism', in *Martin Heidegger: Basic Writings*, ed. D. F. Krell, London: Routledge & Kegan Paul, 1978.

which determines entities as entities, that on the basis of which entities are already understood' (*Being and Time*, pp. 25–6). If we are to uncover these very general conditions for anything to be encountered or understood as the thing it is, enquiry should begin with those special beings – human beings, roughly – who have some grasp, however implicit and incohate, of those conditions. Heidegger prefers to speak of *Dasein*, his name for the kind of existence enjoyed by human beings. Reflection on *Dasein* soon reveals that its fundamental aspect is not knowledge or theoretical reason, but its 'Being-in-the-world' as an engaged, purposeful agent. (Being *in* the world, Heidegger emphasizes, is no mere matter of being spatially located in a universe.) The notion of the world that *Dasein* is 'in' must, therefore, be clarified if we are to progress towards uncovering the nature of Being, that 'basis' on which entities are encountered and understood. The world, as he puts it, is an '*existentiale*' of *Dasein*, one of the necessary structural components in its analysis.

That world, Heidegger insists, is not all a collection of substances or things 'present-at-hand'. Rather it is a world of 'equipment' (*Zeug*), of things 'ready-to-hand' (*zuhanden*), variously involved in our purposeful projects. We experience the world about us, in the first instance, as containing hammers, signposts, workshops, and the like, and not as mere lumps of spatially extended stuff. The world which *Dasein* is 'in' is a vast 'relational totality' of 'significance', in which things are what they are in virtue of their meaningful relations to each other and to ourselves. That we 'primordially' encounter the world in this way is not, moreover, a contingent matter: unless we did so, nothing would 'light up' for us, 'stand out' and hence be an object for attention and exploration. The 'present-at-hand' world of traditional ontology is, therefore, parasitic on the 'ready-to-hand' one of everyday engagement.

The defects of that traditional ontology are exposed in §21, where Heidegger argues that, on Descartes' account, it would be impossible to explain how we have any 'access' to the world, how things could 'show up' for us. It is hopeless, moreover, to construe 'ready-to-hand' things, like hammers, as 'really' being mere material lumps to which we subsequently and 'subjectively' attach some value or purpose. The bifurcation of our experience of, say, a hammer into an 'objective' perception of it as something with its cultural 'skin off' and an evaluation of that thing's purpose is entirely untrue to the phenomenology of our encounter with 'equipment'.

Heidegger's discussion raises many questions. One concerns how, given our 'primordial' experience of the world as 'equipment', we ever manage to attain the 'objective' standpoint – that of the scientist, say – from which we look at and examine things in isolation from their involvement with our projects and purposes. Heidegger addresses this question in §16, where he argues that regarding things as merely 'present-at-hand' emerges as a result of various 'break-

Jowns' in our usual, engaged dealings with things.[2] Without denying that an 'objective' standpoint is possible, Heidegger insists, however, that this stand-point is a derivative one and has no claim to be that from which things are experienced as they are in themselves. Another critical question is whether Heidegger, despite his protests, is not, after all, confusing 'genetic', 'anthropological' issues concerning *how* we come to experience and describe things with ontological ones concerning *what* fundamentally it is that we encounter.[3] This is a question which continues to divide his admirers and detractors.

Heidegger, The Worldhood of the World

◀ ◀ ◀

III

63

¶ *14. The Idea of the Worldhood of the World in General*

Being-in-the-world shall first be made visible with regard to that item of its structure which is the 'world' itself. To accomplish this task seems easy and so trivial as to make one keep taking for granted that it may be dispensed with. What can be meant by describing 'the world' as a phenomenon? It means to let us see what shows itself in 'entities' within the world. Here the first step is to enumerate the things that are 'in' the world: houses, trees, people, mountains, stars. We can *depict* the way such entities 'look', and we can give an *account* of occurrences in them and with them. This, how-ever, is obviously a pre-phenomenological 'business' which cannot be at all relevant phenomenologically. Such a description is always confined to en-tities. It is ontical. But what we are seeking is Being. And we have formally defined 'phenomenon' in the phenomenological sense as that which shows itself as Being and as a structure of Being.

Thus, to give a phenomenological description of the 'world' will mean to exhibit the Being of those entities which are present-at-hand within the world, and to fix it in concepts which are categorial.[1] Now the entities within the world are Things – Things of Nature, and Things 'invested with value'. Their Thinghood becomes a problem; and to the extent that the Thinghood of Things 'invested with value' is based upon the Thinghood of Nature, our primary theme is the Being of Things of Nature – Nature as

For a good account of this and many other points, see Hubert L. Dreyfus, *Being-in-the-World: a commentary on Heidegger's* Being and Time, *Division I*, Cambridge, MA: MIT Press, 1991.
  The charge of only 'doing anthropology' was made, early on, by Edmund Husserl. See my *Existentialism: a reconstruction*, Oxford: Blackwell, 1999 (revised edition), ch. 4, p. 64.

such. That characteristic of Being which belongs to Things of Nature (substances), and upon which everything is founded, is substantiality. What is its ontological meaning? By asking this, we have given an unequivocal direction to our inquiry.

But is this a way of asking ontologically about the 'world'? The problematic which we have thus marked out is one which is undoubtedly ontological. But even if this ontology should itself succeed in explicating the Being of Nature in the very purest manner, in conformity with the basic assertions about this entity, which the mathematical natural sciences provide, it will never reach the phenomenon that is the 'world'. Nature is itself an entity which is encountered within the world and which can be discovered in various way and at various stages.

Should we then first attach ourselves to those entities with which Dasein proximally and for the most part dwells – Things 'invested with value'? Do not these 'really' show us the world in which we live? Perhaps, in fact, they show us something like the 'world' more penetratingly. But these Things too are entities 'within' the world.

Neither the ontical depiction of entities within-the-world nor the ontological Interpretation of their Being is such as to reach the phenomenon of the 'world.' In both of these ways of access to 'Objective Being', the 'world' has already been 'presupposed', and indeed in various ways.

Is it possible that ultimately we cannot address ourselves to 'the world' as determining the nature of the entity we have mentioned? Yet we call this entity one which is "within-the-world". Is 'world' perhaps a characteristic of Dasein's Being? And in that case, does every Dasein 'proximally' have its world? Does not 'world' thus become something 'subjective'? How, then, can there be a 'common' world 'in' which, nevertheless, we *are*? And if we raise the question of the 'world', *what* world do we have in view? Neither the common world nor the subjective world, but *the worldhood of the world as such*. By what avenue do we meet this phenomenon?

'Worldhood' is an ontological concept, and stands for the structure of one of the constitutive items of Being-in-the-world. But we know Being-in-the-world as a way in which Dasein's character is defined existentially. Thus worldhood itself is an *existentiale*. If we inquire ontologically about the 'world', we by no means abandon the analytic of Dasein as a field for thematic study. Ontologically, 'world' is not a way of characterizing those entities which Dasein essentially is *not*; it is rather a characteristic of Dasein itself. This does not rule out the possibility that when we investigate the phenomenon of the 'world' we must do so by the avenue of entities within-the-world and the Being which they possess. The task of 'describing' the world phenomenologically is so far from obvious that even if we do no more than determine adequately what form it shall take, essential ontological clarifications will be needed.

This discussion of the word 'world', and our frequent use of it have made it apparent that it is used in several ways. By unravelling these we can get an indication of the different kinds of phenomena that are signified, and of the way in which they are interconnected.

1. "World" is used as an ontical concept, and signifies the totality of those entities which can be present-at-hand within the world.

2. "World" functions as an ontological term, and signifies the Being of those entities which we have just mentioned. And indeed 'world' can become a term for any realm which encompasses a multiplicity of entities: for instance, when one talks of the 'world' of a mathematician, 'world' signifies the realm of possible objects of mathematics.

3. "World" can be understood in another ontical sense – not, however, as those entities which Dasein essentially is not and which can be encountered within-the-world, but rather as that '*wherein*' a factical Dasein as such can be said to 'live'. "World" has here a pre-ontological existentiell signification.[2] Here again there are different possibilities: "world" may stand for the 'public' we-world, or one's 'own' closest (domestic) environment.

4. Finally, "world" designates the ontologico-existential concept of *worldhood*. Worldhood itself may have as its modes whatever structural wholes any special 'worlds' may have at the time; but it embraces in itself the *a priori* character of worldhood in general. We shall reserve the expression "world" as a term for our third signification. If we should sometimes use it in the first of these senses, we shall mark this with single quotation marks.

The derivative form 'worldly' will then apply terminologically to a kind of Being which belongs to Dasein, never to a kind which belongs to entities present-at-hand 'in' the world. We shall designate these latter entities as "belonging to the world" or "within-the-world".

A glance at previous ontology shows that if one fails to see Being-in-the-world as a state of Dasein, the phenomenon of worldhood likewise gets *passed over*. One tries instead to Interpret the world in terms of the Being of those entities which are present-at-hand within-the-world but which are by no means proximally discovered – namely, in terms of Nature. If one understands Nature ontologico-categorially, one finds that Nature is a limiting case of the Being of possible entities within-the-world. Only in some definite mode of its own Being-in-the-world can Dasein discover entities as Nature. This manner of knowing them has the character of depriving the world of its worldhood in a definite way. 'Nature', as the categorial aggregate of those structures of Being which a definite entity encountered within-

65

the-world may possess, can never make *worldhood* intelligible. But even the phenomenon of 'Nature', as it is conceived, for instance, in romanticism, can be grasped ontologically only in terms of the concept of the world – that to say, in terms of the analytic of Dasein.

When it comes to the problem of analysing the world's worldhood ontologically, traditional ontology operates in a blind alley, if, indeed, it sees this problem at all. On the other hand, if we are to Interpret the worldhood of Dasein and the possible ways in which Dasein is made worldly, we must show *why* the kind of Being with which Dasein knows the world is such that it passes over the phenomenon of worldhood both ontically and ontologically. But at the same time the very Fact of this passing-over suggests that we must take special precautions to get the right phenomenal point of departure for access to the phenomenon of worldhood, so that it will not get passed over.

Our method has already been assigned. The theme of our analytic is to be Being-in-the-world, and accordingly the very world itself; and these are to be considered within the horizon of average everydayness – the kind of Being which is *closest* to Dasein. We must make a study of everyday Being-in-the-world; with the phenomenal support which this gives us, something like the world must come into view.

That world of everyday Dasein which is closest to it, is the *environment*. From this existential character of average Being-in-the-world, our investigation will take its course towards the idea of worldhood in general. We shall seek the worldhood of the environment (environmentality) by going through an ontological Interpretation of those entities within-the-*environment* which we encounter as closest to us. The expression "environment" [Umwelt] contains in the 'environ' ["um"] a suggestion of spatiality. Yet the 'around' ["Umherum"] which is constitutive for the environment does not have a primarily 'spatial' meaning. Instead, the spatial character which incontestably belongs to any environment, can be clarified only in terms of the structure of worldhood. From this point of view, Dasein's spatiality, of which we have given an indication in Section 12, becomes phenomenally visible.[3] In ontology, however, an attempt has been made to start with spatiality and then to Interpret the Being of the 'world' as *res extensa*. In Descartes we find the most extreme tendency towards such an ontology of the 'world', with, indeed, a counter-orientation towards the *res cogitans* – which does not coincide with Dasein either ontically or ontologically. The analysis of worldhood which we are here attempting can be made clearer if we show how it differs from such an ontological tendency. Our analysis will be completed in three stages: (*A*) the analysis of environmentality and worldhood in general; (*B*) an illustrative contrast between our analysis of worldhood and Descartes' ontology of the 'world'; (*C*) the aroundness of the environment, and the 'spatiality' of Dasein.*

A. Analysis of Environmentality and Worldhood in General

¶ 15. The Being of the Entities Encountered in the Environment

The Being of those entities which we encounter as closest to us can be exhibited phenomenologically if we take as our clue our everyday Being-in-the-world, which we also call our "*dealings*" in the world and *with* entities within-the-world. Such dealings have already dispersed themselves into manifold ways of concern. The kind of dealing which is closest to us is as we have shown, not a bare perceptual cognition, but rather that kind of concern which manipulates things and puts them to use; and this has its own kind of 'knowledge'. The phenomenological question applies in the first instance to the Being of those entities which we encounter in such concern. To assure the kind of seeing which is here required, we must first make a remark about method. 67

In the disclosure and explication of Being, entities are in every case our preliminary and our accompanying theme; but our real theme is Being. In the domain of the present analysis, the entities we shall take as our preliminary theme are those which show themselves in our concern with the environment. Such entities are not thereby objects for knowing the 'world' theoretically; they are simply what gets used, what gets produced, and so forth. As entities so encountered, they become the preliminary theme for the purview of a 'knowing' which, as phenomenological, looks primarily towards Being, and which, in thus taking Being as its theme, takes these entities as its accompanying theme. This phenomenological interpretation is accordingly not a way of knowing those characteristics of entities which themselves are; it is rather a determination of the structure of the Being which entities possess. But as an investigation of Being, it brings to completion, autonomously and explicitly, that understanding of Being which belongs already to Dasein and which 'comes alive' in any of its dealings with entities. Those entities which serve phenomenologically as our preliminary theme – in this case, those which are used or which are to be found in the course of production – become accessible when we put ourselves into the position of concerning ourselves with them in some such way. Taken strictly, this talk about "putting ourselves into such a position"

---

* *A* is considered in Sections 15–18; *B* in Sections 19–21; *C* in Sections 22–24.

is misleading; for the kind of Being which belongs to such concernful dealings is not one into which we need to put ourselves first. This is the way in
which everyday Dasein always *is*: when I open the door, for instance, I use
the latch. The achieving of phenomenological access to the entities which
we encounter, consists rather in thrusting aside our interpretative tenden-
cies, which keep thrusting themselves upon us and running along with us,
and which conceal not only the phenomenon of such 'concern', but even
more those entities themselves *as* encountered of their own accord *in* our
concern with them. These entangling errors become plain if in the course
of our investigation we now ask which entities shall be taken as our preliminary theme and established as the pre-phenomenal basis for our study.

68   One may answer: "Things." But with this obvious answer we have perhaps already missed the pre-phenomenal basis we are seeking. For in ad-
dressing these entities as 'Things' (*res*), we have tacitly anticipated their
ontological character. When analysis starts with such entities and goes on
to inquire about Being, what it meets is Thinghood and Reality. Ontological explication discovers, as it proceeds, such characteristics of Being as
substantiality, materiality, extendedness, side-by-side-ness, and so forth.
But even pre-ontologically, in such Being as this, the entities which we
encounter in concern are proximally hidden. When one designates Things
as the entities that are 'proximally given', one goes ontologically astray,
even though ontically one has something else in mind. What one really has
in mind remains undetermined. But suppose one characterizes these 'Things'
as Things 'invested with value'? What does "value" mean ontologically?
How are we to categorize this 'investing' and Being-invested? Disregard-
ing the obscurity of this structure of investiture with value, have we thus
met that phenomenal characteristic of Being which belongs to what we
encounter in our concernful dealings?

The Greeks had an appropriate term for 'Things': πράγματα [pragmata]
– that is to say, that which one has to do with in one's concernful dealings
(πρᾶξις) [praxis]. But ontologically, the specifically 'pragmatic' character
of the πράγματα is just what the Greeks left in obscurity; they thought of
these 'proximally' as 'mere Things'. We shall call those entities which we
encounter in concern "*equipment*".[4] In our dealings we come across equipment for writing, sewing, working, transportation, measurement. The kind
of Being which equipment possesses must be exhibited. The clue for doing
this lies in our first defining what makes an item of equipment – namely, its
equipmentality.

Taken strictly, there 'is' no such thing as *an* equipment. To the Being of
any equipment there always belongs a totality of equipment, in which it
can be this equipment that it is. Equipment is essentially 'something in-

order-to' . . . . A totality of equipment is constituted by various ways of the 'in-order-to', such as serviceability, conduciveness, usability, manipulability.

In the 'in-order-to' as a structure there lies an *assignment* or *reference* of something to something. Only in the analyses which are to follow can the phenomenon which this term 'assignment' indicates be made visible in its ontological genesis. Provisionally, it is enough to take a look phenomenally at a manifold of such assignments. Equipment – in accordance with its equipmentality – always is *in terms of* its belonging to other equipment: ink-stand, pen, ink, paper, blotting pad, table, lamp, furniture, windows, doors, room. These 'Things' never show themselves proximally as they are for themselves, so as to add up to a sum of *realia* and fill up a room. What we encounter as closest to us (though not as something taken as a theme) is the room; and we encounter it not as something 'between four walls' in a geometrical spatial sense, but as equipment for residing. Out of this the 'arrangement' emerges, and it is in this that any 'individual' item of equip-   69 ment shows itself. *Before* it does so, a totality of equipment has already been discovered.

Equipment can genuinely show itself only in dealings cut to its own measure (hammering with a hammer, for example); but in such dealings an entity of this kind is not *grasped* thematically as an occurring Thing, nor is the equipment-structure known as such even in the using. The hammering does not simply have knowledge about the hammer's character as equipment, but it has appropriated this equipment in a way which could not possibly be more suitable. In dealings such as this, where something is put to use, our concern subordinates itself to the "in-order-to" which is constitutive for the equipment we are employing at the time; the less we just stare at the hammer-Thing, and the more we seize hold of it and use it, the more primordial does our relationship to it become, and the more unveiledly is it encountered as that which it is – as equipment. The hammering itself uncovers the specific 'manipulability' of the hammer. The kind of Being which equipment possesses – in which it manifests itself in its own right – we call *"readiness-to-hand"*. Only because equipment has *this* 'Being-in-itself' and does not merely occur, is it manipulable in the broadest sense and at our disposal. No matter how sharply we just *look* at the 'outward appearance' of Things in whatever form this takes, we cannot discover anything ready-to-hand. If we look at Things just 'theoretically', we can get along without understanding readiness-to-hand. But when we deal with them by using them and manipulating them, this activity is not a blind one; it has its own kind of sight, by which our manipulation is guided and from which it acquires its specific Thingly character. Dealings with equipment subordinate themselves to the manifold assignments of the 'in-order-to'. And the sight with which they thus accommodate themselves is *circumspection*.

'Practical' behaviour is not 'atheoretical' in the sense of "sightlessness". The way it differs from theoretical behaviour does not lie simply in the fact that in theoretical behaviour one observes, while in practical behaviour one *acts*, and that action must employ theoretical cognition if it is not to remain blind; for the fact that observation is a kind of concern is just as primordial as the fact that action has *its own* kind of sight. Theoretical behaviour is just looking, without circumspection. But the fact that this looking is non-circumspective does not mean that it follows no rules: it constructs a canon for itself in the form of *method*.

The ready-to-hand is not grasped theoretically at all, nor is it itself the sort of thing that circumspection takes proximally as a circumspective theme. The peculiarity of what is proximally ready-to-hand is that, in its readiness-to-hand, it must, as it were, withdraw in order to be ready-to-hand quite authentically. That with which our everyday dealings proximally dwell is not the tools themselves. On the contrary, that with which we concern ourselves primarily is the work – that which is to be produced at the time; and this is accordingly ready-to-hand too. The work bears with it that referential totality within which the equipment is encountered.

The work to be produced, as the *"towards-which"* of such things as the hammer, the plane, and the needle, likewise has the kind of Being that belongs to equipment. The shoe which is to be produced is for wearing (footgear); the clock is manufactured for telling the time. The work which we chiefly encounter in our concernful dealings – the work that is to be found when one is "at work" on something – has a usability which belongs to it essentially; in this usability it lets us encounter already the "towards-which" for which *it* is usable. A work that someone has ordered *is* only by reason of its use and the assignment-context of entities which is discovered in using it.

But the work to be produced is not merely usable for something. The production itself is a using *of* something for something. In the work there is also a reference or assignment to 'materials': the work is dependent on leather, thread, needles, and the like. Leather, moreover is produced from hides. These are taken from animals, which someone else has raised. Animals also occur within the world without having been raised at all; and, in a way, these entities still produce themselves even when they have been raised. So in the environment certain entities become accessible which are always ready-to-hand, but which, in themselves, do not need to be produced. Hammer, tongs, and needle, refer in themselves to steel, iron, metal, mineral, wood, in that they consist of these. In equipment that is used,

'Nature' is discovered along with it by that use – the 'Nature' we find in natural products.

Here however, "Nature" is not to be understood as that which is just present-at-hand, nor as the *power of Nature*. The wood is a forest of timber, the mountain a quarry of rock; the river is water-power, the wind is wind 'in the sails'. As the 'environment' is discovered, the 'Nature' thus discovered is encountered too. If its kind of Being as ready-to-hand is disregarded, this 'Nature' itself can be discovered and defined simply in its pure presence-at-hand. But when this happens, the Nature which 'stirs and strives', which assails us and enthralls us as landscape, remains hidden. The botanist's plants are not the flowers of the hedgerow; the 'source' which the geographer establishes for a river is not the 'springhead in the dale'.

The work produced refers not only to the "towards-which" of its usability and the "whereof" of which it consists: under simple craft conditions it also has an assignment to the person who is to use it or wear it. The work is cut to his figure; he 'is' there along with it as the work emerges. Even when goods are produced by the dozen, this constitutive assignment is by no means lacking; it is merely indefinite, and points to the random, the average. Thus along with the work, we encounter not only entities ready-to-hand but also entities with Dasein's kind of Being – entities for which, in their concern, the product becomes ready-to-hand; and together with these we encounter the world in which wearers and users live, which is at the same time ours. Any work with which one concerns oneself is ready-to-hand not only in the domestic world of the workshop but also in the *public world*. Along with the public world, the *environing Nature* is discovered and is accessible to everyone. In roads, streets, bridges, buildings, our concern discovers Nature as having some definite direction. A covered railway platform takes account of bad weather; an installation for public lighting takes account of the darkness, or rather of specific changes in the presence or absence of daylight – the 'position of the sun'. In a clock, account is taken of some definite constellation in the world-system. When we look at the clock, we tacitly make use of the 'sun's position', in accordance with which the measurement of time gets regulated in the official astronomical manner. When we make use of the clock-equipment, which is proximally and inconspicuously ready-to-hand, the environing Nature is ready-to-hand along with it. Our concernful absorption in whatever work-world lies closest to us, has a function of discovering; and it is essential to this function that, depending upon the way in which we are absorbed, those entities within-the-world which are brought along in the work and with it (that is to say, in the assignments or references which are constitutive for it) remain discoverable in varying degrees of explicitness and with a varying circumspective penetration.

The kind of Being which belongs to these entities is readiness-to-hand. But this characteristic is not to be understood as merely a way of taking them, as if we were talking such 'aspects' into the 'entities' which we proximally encounter, or as if some world-stuff which is proximally present-at-hand in itself were 'given subjective colouring' in this way. Such an Interpretation would overlook the fact that in this case these entities would have to be understood and discovered beforehand as something purely present-at-hand, and must have priority and take the lead in the sequence of those dealings with the 'world' in which something is discovered and made one's own. But this already runs counter to the ontological meaning of cognition, which we have exhibited as a *founded* mode of Being-in-the - world. To lay bare what is just present-at-hand and no more, cognition must first penetrate *beyond* what is ready-to-hand in our concern. *Readiness-to-hand is the way in which entities as they are 'in themselves' are defined ontologico-categorially.* Yet only by reason of something present-at-hand, 'is there' anything ready-to-hand. Does it follow, however, granting this thesis for the nonce, that readiness-to-hand is ontologically founded upon presence-at-hand?

72   But even if, as our ontological Interpretation proceeds further, readiness-to-hand should prove itself to be the kind of Being characteristic of those entities which are proximally discovered within-the-world, and even if its primordiality as compared with pure presence-at-hand can be demonstrated, have all these explications been of the slightest help towards understanding the phenomenon of the world ontologically? In interpreting these entities within-the-world, however, we have always 'presupposed' the world. Even if we join them together, we still do not get anything like the 'world' as their sum. If, then, we start with the Being of these entities, is there any avenue that will lead us to exhibiting the phenomenon of the world? . . .

89   **B. A Contrast between our Analysis of Worldhood and Descartes' Interpretation of the World**

Only step by step can the concept of worldhood and the structures which this phenomenon embraces be firmly secured in the course of our investigation. The Interpretation of the world begins, in the first instance, with some entity within-the-world, so that the phenomenon of the world in general no longer comes into view; we shall accordingly try tó clarify this approach ontologically by considering what is perhaps the most extreme form in which it has been carried out. We not only shall present briefly the basic features of Descartes' ontology of the 'world', but shall inquire into its presuppositions and try to characterize these in the light of what we have hitherto achieved. The account we shall give of these matters will enable us to know upon what basically undiscussed ontological 'founda- tions' those Interpretations of the world which have come after Descartes – and still more those which preceded him – have operated.

Descartes sees the *extensio* as basically definitive ontologically for the world. In so far as extension is one of the constituents of spatiality (accord- ing to Descartes it is even identical with it), while in some sense spatiality remains constitutive for the world, a discussion of the Cartesian ontology of the 'world' will provide us likewise with a negative support for a positive explication of the spatiality of the environment and of Dasein itself. With regard to Descartes' ontology there are three topics which we shall treat: 1. the definition of the 'world' as *res extensa* (Section 19); 2. the foundations of this ontological definition (Section 20); 3. a hermeneutical discussion of the Cartesian ontology of the 'world' (Section 21). The considerations which follow will not have been grounded in full detail until the '*cogito sum*' has been phenomenologically destroyed.

¶ 19. The Definition of the 'World' as res extensa

Descartes distinguishes the '*ego cogito*' from the '*res corporea*'. This dis- tinction will thereafter be determinative ontologically for the distinction between 'Nature' and 'spirit'. No matter with how many variations of con- tent the opposition between 'Nature' and 'spirit' may get set up ontically, its ontological foundations, and indeed the very poles of this opposition, remain unclarified; this unclarity has its proximate roots in Descartes' dis- tinction. What kind of understanding of Being does he have when he de- fines the Being of these entities? The term for the Being of an entity that is in itself, is "*substantia*". Sometimes this expression means the *Being* of an   90 entity as substance, *substantiality*, at other times it means the entity itself, *a substance*. That "*substantia*" is used in these two ways is not accidental; this already holds for the ancient conception of οὐσία [ousia] . . .

¶ 21. Hermeneutical Discussion of the Cartesian Ontology of the 'World'

The critical question now arises: does this ontology of the 'world' seek the phenomenon of the world at all, and if not, does it at least define some entity within-the-world fully enough so that the worldly character of this entity can be made visible in it? *To both questions we must answer "No".* The entity which Descartes is trying to grasp ontologically and in principle with his "*extensio*", is rather such as to become discoverable first of all by going through an entity within-the-world which is proximally ready-to-hand – Nature. Though this is the case, and though any ontological characterization of this *latter* entity within-the-world may lead us into obscurity, even if we consider both the idea of substantiality and the meaning of the "*existit*" and "*ad existendum* " which have been brought into the definition of that idea, it still remains possible that through an ontology based upon a radical separation of God, the "I", and the 'world', the ontological problem of the world will in some sense get formulated and further advanced. If, however, this is not possible, we must then demonstrate explicitly not only that Descartes' conception of the world is ontologically defective, but that his Interpretation and the foundations on which it is based have led him to *pass over* both the phenomenon of the world and the Being of those entities within-the-world which are proximally ready-to-hand.

In our exposition of the problem of worldhood (Section 14), we suggested the importance of obtaining proper access to this phenomenon. So in criticizing the Cartesian point of departure, we must ask which kind of Being that belongs to Dasein we should fix upon as giving us an appropriate way of access to those entities with whose Being as *extensio* Descartes equates the Being of the 'world'. The only genuine access to them lies in knowing [Erkennen], *intellectio*, in the sense of the kind of knowledge [Erkenntnis] we get in mathematics and physics. Mathematical knowledge is regarded by Descartes as the one manner of apprehending entities which can always give assurance that their Being has been securely grasped. If anything measures up in its own kind of Being to the Being that is accessible in mathematical knowledge, then it *is* in the authentic sense. Such entities are those *which always are what they are*. Accordingly, that which can be shown to have the character of something that *constantly remains*, makes up the real Being of those entities of the world which get experienced. That which enduringly remains, really *is*. This is the sort of thing which mathematics knows. That which is accessible in an entity *through mathematics*, makes up its Being. Thus the Being of the 'world' is, as it were, dictated to it in terms of a definite idea of Being which lies veiled in the concept of substantiality, and in terms of the idea of a knowledge by which *such* entities are cognized. The kind of Being which belongs to entities within-the-world is something which they themselves might have been permitted to present; but Descartes does not let them do so. Instead he prescribes for the world its 'real' Being, as it were, on the basis of an idea of Being whose source has not been unveiled and which has not been demonstrated in its own right – an idea in which Being is equated with constant

presence-at-hand. Thus his ontology of the world is not primarily determined by his leaning towards mathematics, a science which he chances to
esteem very highly, but rather by his ontological orientation in principle
towards Being as constant presence-at-hand, which mathematical knowledge is exceptionally well suited to grasp. In this way Descartes explicitly
switches over philosophically from the development of traditional ontology to modern mathematical physics and its transcendental foundations.

The problem of how to get appropriate access to entities within-the-
world is one which Descartes feels no need to raise. Under the unbroken
ascendance of the traditional ontology, the way to get a genuine grasp of
what really is has been decided in advance: it lies in *voεῖν* [noeen] – 'beholding' in the widest sense; *διavoεῖν* [dianoeen] or 'thinking' is just a more
fully achieved form of *voεῖν* and is founded upon it. *Sensatio* (*αἴσθησις*)
[aesthesis], as opposed to *intellectio*, still remains possible as a way of access
to entities by a beholding which is perceptual in character; but Descartes
presents his 'critique' of it because he is oriented ontologically by these
principles.

Descartes knows very well that entities do not proximally show themselves in their real Being. What is 'proximally' given is this waxen Thing
which is coloured, flavoured, hard, and cold in definite ways, and which
gives off its own special sound when struck. But this is not of any importance ontologically, nor, in general, is anything which is given through the
senses. . . . The senses do not enable us to cognize any entity in its Being;
they merely serve to announce the ways in which 'external' Things within-
the-world are useful or harmful for human creatures encumbered with bod- 97
ies. . . . they tell us nothing about entities in their Being. . . .

If we subject Descartes' Interpretation of the experience of hardness and
resistance to a critical analysis, it will be plain how unable he is to let what
shows itself in sensation present itself in its own kind of Being, or even to
determine its character (Cf. Section 19).

Hardness gets taken as resistance. But neither hardness nor resistance is
understood in a phenomenal sense, as something experienced in itself whose
nature can be determined in such an experience. For Descartes, resistance
amounts to no more than not yielding place – that is, not undergoing any
change of location. So if a Thing resists, this means that it stays in a definite
location relatively to some other Thing which is changing its location, or
that it is changing its own location with a velocity which permits the other
Thing to 'catch up' with it. But when the experience of hardness is Interpreted this way, the kind of Being which belongs to sensory perception is
obliterated, and so is any possibility that the entities encountered in such
perception should be grasped in their Being. Descartes takes the kind of

Being which belongs to the perception of something, and translates it into the only kind he knows: the perception of something becomes a definite way of Being-present-at-hand-side-by-side of two *res extensae* which are present-at-hand; the way in which their movements are related is itself a mode of that *extensio* by which the presence-at-hand of the corporeal Thing is primarily characterized. Of course no behaviour in which one feels one's way by touch can be 'completed' unless what can thus be felt has 'closeness' of a very special kind. But this does not mean that touching and the hardness which makes itself known in touching consist ontologically in different velocities of two corporeal Things. Hardness and resistance do not show themselves at all unless an entity has the kind of Being which Dasein – or at least something living – possesses.

Thus Descartes' discussion of possible kinds of *access* to entities within-the-world is dominated by an idea of Being which has been gathered from a definite realm of these entities themselves.

98   The idea of Being as permanent presence-at-hand not only gives Descartes a motive for identifying entities within-the-world with the world in general, and for providing so extreme a definition of their Being; it also keeps him from bringing Dasein's ways of behaving into view in a manner which is ontologically appropriate. But thus the road is completely blocked to seeing the founded character of all sensory and intellective awareness, and to understanding these as possibilities of Being-in-the-world. On the contrary, he takes the Being of 'Dasein' (to whose basic constitution Being-in-the-world belongs) in the very same way as he takes the Being of the *res extensa* – namely, as substance.

But with these criticisms, have we not fobbed off on Descartes a task altogether beyond his horizon, and then gone on to 'demonstrate' that he has failed to solve it? If Descartes does not know the phenomenon of the world, and thus knows no such thing as within-the-world-ness, how can he identify the world itself with certain entities within-the-world and the Being which they possess?

In controversy over principles, one must not only attach oneself to theses which can be grasped doxographically; one must also derive one's orientation from the objective tendency of the problematic, even if it does not go beyond a rather ordinary way of taking things. In his doctrine of the *res cogitans* and the *res extensa*, Descartes not only *wants to formulate* the problem of 'the "I" and the world'; he claims to have solved it in a radical manner. His *Meditations* make this plain. (See especially Meditations I and VI.) By taking his basic ontological orientation from traditional sources and not subjecting it to positive criticism, he has made it impossible to lay bare any primordial ontological problematic of Dasein; this has inevitably obstructed his view of the phenomenon of the world, and has made it possible for the ontology of the 'world' to be compressed into that of certain entities within-the-world. The foregoing discussion should have proved this.

One might retort, however, that even if in point of fact both the problem of the world and the Being of the entities encountered environmentally as closest to us remain concealed, Descartes has still laid the basis for characterizing ontologically that entity within-the-world upon which, in its very Being, every other entity is founded – material Nature. This would be the fundamental stratum upon which all the other strata of actuality within-the-world are built up. The extended Thing as such would serve, in the first instance, as the ground for those definite characters which show themselves, to be sure, as qualities, but which 'at bottom' are quantitative modifications of the modes of the *extensio* itself. These qualities, which are themselves reducible, would provide the footing for such specific qualities as "beautiful", "ugly", "in keeping", "not in keeping", "useful", "useless". If one is oriented primarily by Thinghood, these latter qualities must be taken as non-quantifiable value-predicates by which what is in the first instance just a material Thing, gets stamped as something good. But with this stratification, we come to those entities which we have characterized ontologically as equipment ready-to-hand. The Cartesian analysis of the 'world' would thus enable us for the first time to build up securely the structure of what is proximally ready-to-hand; all it takes is to round out the Thing of Nature until it becomes a full-fledged Thing of use, and this is easily done.

But quite apart from the specific problem of the world itself, can the Being of what we encounter proximally within-the-world be reached ontologically by this procedure? When we speak of material Thinghood, have we not tacitly posited a kind of Being – the constant presence-at-hand of Things – which is so far from having been rounded out ontologically by subsequently endowing entities with value-predicates, that these value-characters themselves are rather just ontical characteristics of those entities which have the kind of Being possessed by Things? Adding on value-predicates cannot tell us anything at all new about the Being of goods, *but would merely presuppose again that goods have pure presence-at-hand as their kind of Being.* Values would then be determinate characteristics which a Thing possesses, and they would be *present-at-hand.* They would have their sole ultimate ontological source in our previously laying down the actuality of Things as the fundamental stratum. But even pre-phenomenological experience shows that in an entity which is supposedly a Thing, there is something that will not become fully intelligible through Thinghood alone. Thus

99

the Being of Things has to be rounded out. What, then does the Being of values or their 'validity' . . . really amount to ontologically? And what does it signify ontologically for Things to be 'invested' with values in this way? As long as these matters remain obscure, to reconstruct the Thing of use in terms of the Thing of Nature is an ontologically questionable undertaking, even if one disregards the way in which the problematic has been perverted in principle. And if we are to reconstruct this Thing of use, which supposedly comes to us in the first instance 'with its skin off', does not this always require *that we previously take a positive look at the phenomenon whose totality such a reconstruction is to restore?* But if we have not given a proper explanation beforehand of its ownmost state of Being, are we not building our reconstruction without a plan? Inasmuch as this re-

100   construction and 'rounding-out' of the traditional ontology of the 'world' results in our reaching the same *entities* with which we started when we analysed the readiness-to-hand of equipment and the totality of involvements, it seems as if the *Being* of these entities has in fact been clarified or has at least become a *problem*. But by taking *extensio* as a *proprietas*, Descartes can hardly reach the Being of substance; and by taking refuge in 'value'-characteristics we are just as far from even catching a glimpse of Being as readiness-to-hand, let alone permitting it to become an ontological theme.

Descartes has narrowed down the question of the world to that of Things of Nature as those entities within-the-world which are proximally accessible. He has confirmed the opinion that to *know* an entity in what is supposedly the most rigorous ontical manner is our only possible access to the primary Being of the entity which such knowledge reveals. But at the same time we must have the insight to see that in principle the 'roundings-out' of the Thing-ontology also operate on the same dogmatic basis as that which Descartes has adopted.

We have already intimated in Section 14 that passing over the world and those entities which we proximally encounter is not accidental, not an oversight which it would be simple to correct, but that it is grounded in a kind of Being which belongs essentially to Dasein itself. When our analytic of Dasein has given some transparency to those main structures of Dasein which are of the most importance in the framework of this problematic, and when we have assigned to the concept of Being in general the horizon within which its intelligibility becomes possible, so that readiness-to-hand and presence-at-hand also become primordially intelligible ontologically for the first time, only then can our critique of the Cartesian ontology of the world (an ontology which, in principle, is still the usual one today) come philosophically into its own.

To do this, we must show several things. . . .

1. Why was the phenomenon of the world passed over at the beginning of the ontological tradition which has been decisive for us (explicitly in the case of Parmenides), and why has this passing-over kept constantly recurring?
2. Why is it that, instead of the phenomenon thus passed over, entities within-the-world have intervened as an ontological theme?
3. Why are these entities found in the first instance in 'Nature'?
4. Why has recourse been taken to the phenomenon of value when it has seemed necessary to round out such an ontology of the world?[5]

In the answers to these questions a positive understanding of the *problematic* of the world will be reached for the first time, the sources of our failure to recognize it will be exhibited, and the ground for rejecting the traditional ontology of the world will have been demonstrated.

101

The world and Dasein and entities within-the-world are the ontologically constitutive states which are closest to us; but we have no guarantee that we can achieve the basis for meeting up with these as phenomena by the seemingly obvious procedure of starting with the Things of the world, still less by taking our orientation from what is supposedly the most rigorous knowledge of entities. Our observations on Descartes should have brought us this insight. . . .

Notes

1 Heidegger does not make it clear until a bit later that the view expressed in this paragraph is not his own, but the one he will be criticizing.
2 'Existential' and 'existentiell' are Heideggerian terms of art. Dreyfus, *Being-in-the-World, op. cit.*, p. 20, explains them as follows: '*Existential* understanding is a worked-out understanding of the ontological structures of existence, that is, of what it is to be Dasein. *Existentiell* understanding is an individual's understanding of his or her own way to be, that is, of what he or she is'.
3 In that section, and also in Sections 23–4, Heidegger explains how different *Dasein*'s 'spatiality' is from that of 'present-at-hand' objects. For example, someone's being in his office is not a matter, merely, of a geometrical relationship to walls etc. Often, the relevant sense of 'in' is like the one intended when we speak of someone being in the world of fashion or showbusiness.
4 The German word is '*Zeug*', which can mean tool, instrument *etc.* Heidegger, though, uses it in a collective sense. It should be stressed that, for him, even

'things in Nature' are originally encountered as significant 'equipment', e.g., the wood as 'a forest of timber'.

5 *Being and Time*, which remained uncompleted, does not address all these questions. They were, however, to become the focus of many of Heidegger's later writings.

Index

THE CUBAN EMBARGO

The Domestic Politics of an
American Foreign Policy

Patrick J. Haney & Walt Vanderbush

UNIVERSITY OF PITTSBURGH PRESS

Published by the University of Pittsburgh Press, Pittsburgh, Pa. 15260

Copyright © 2005, University of Pittsburgh Press
Manufactured in the United States of America

Printed on acid-free paper

10 9 8 7 6 5 4 3 2 1

Library of Congress Cataloging-in-Publication Data

Haney, Patrick Jude.

The Cuban embargo : the domestic politics of an American foreign policy / Patrick J. Haney and Walt Vanderbush.

p. cm.

Includes bibliographical references and index.

ISBN 0-8229-5863-5 (pbk. : alk. paper)

1. Economic sanctions, American—Cuba. 2. United States—Foreign economic relations—Cuba. 3. Cuba—Foreign economic relations—United States. I. Vanderbush, Walt. II. Title.

HF1500.5.U5H36 2005

327.1'17—dc22

2004015828

Contents

Preface

IN THIS BOOK we explore the politics behind U.S. foreign policy toward Cuba and how the dynamics that drive policy toward the island have changed since 1980. Many analyses of the U.S. embargo policy focus on the stability of that policy over time. It is hard to argue with this view: the embargo has been in place since the Eisenhower administration. But we have been drawn more to the story of impressive change that lies just beneath the surface stability of the embargo. And this is why we begin by focusing on the Reagan years: the period when the Cuban American National Foundation (CANF) was founded, a time when the president used the threat from Cuba as an instrument to focus attention on the broader threat from communism in the hemisphere, and an era when the executive began to reach out to private groups to help move a new assertive anticommunist foreign policy. The Reagan administration's partnership with CANF and its charismatic leader, Jorge Mas Canosa, was a key part of this strategy; and it was successful in terms of helping to strengthen pro-embargo forces and to tighten the embargo, at least in the short run. But over time the political dynamics set in motion in the 1980s would serve to erode both presidential control of Cuba policy and the embargo policy itself. By the time that George W. Bush was sworn in as the forty-third president of the United States, control over the embargo had shifted to Congress, when the embargo policy was codified into law in 1996 in the controversial Helms-Burton legislation. In addition, Congress had moved to allow some commerce between the United States and Cuba and had taken control of the ban against open travel by Americans to Cuba—a ban that seems on its last leg. And now the strongest opponents of the strict embargo policy are not liberal Democrats, but a mix of free traders and conservative farm state legislators from both parties. A lot has changed since Ike and JFK imposed the embargo, and the changes will likely continue for the next administration. The goal of this book is to understand these changing dynamics, the rushing river underneath the frozen surface of the embargo.

We began to write together on American foreign policy toward Cuba because it was a subject of mutual interest to a student of U.S. foreign policy and a specialist on Latin America who found themselves together in a small college town in southwestern Ohio. Our work began by exploring the creation of CANF in order to see how the real story of its birth and growth, and its links to the new Reagan administration, pushed our conventional view of the role of ethnic interest groups in foreign policy. A conference paper turned into an article, and at the urging of our colleague Phil Brenner we next turned our attention to the politics of Cuba policy in the 1990s and how that had changed starting with the Reagan years. A scholar-practitioner recently said to us by email that studying Cuba policy is an addicting topic that defies logic. It's certainly addicting. And we've been trying to understand the complicated logic that has developed around Cuba policy over time. This book has been our primary vehicle for doing so.

This project is a collective effort, and we have many people to thank. We have given papers at many conferences since our first American Political Science Association panel in 1997 and would like to thank the other panelists and discussants who have helped us along the way. Earlier versions of some of the work that we present here have appeared in print, and we would like to thank the editors and reviewers of these pieces for all their help. We published some of the material on the emergence of CANF in the 1980s in *International Studies Quarterly* (June 1999), and an article on Cuba and the first Clinton administration in *Political Science Quarterly* (Fall 1999). We also published a case study on Helms-Burton in a collection of cases edited by Ralph Carter for CQ Press, *Contemporary Cases in U.S. Foreign Policy: From Trade to Terrorism* (2002). We also published an article with Phil Brenner on the period between 1998 and 2001 in *International Studies Perspectives* (2002), a revised version of which appears in the newest edition of Eugene Wittkopf and James M. McCormick's reader, *The Domestic Sources of American Foreign Policy* (2003). We also published a paper about the late 1990s in the journal *Congress and the Presidency* (2002).

Many individuals in and out of government were gracious with their time (once they realized we were at the *other* Miami we think they thought we couldn't do much harm), including especially Jose Sorzano, Richard Nuccio, Richard V. Allen, Steve Vermillion, Elliot Abrams, the Honorable Lincoln Diaz-Balart, and Dan Fisk. We particularly benefited from the period that Dan Fisk was out of government and was able to provide us many insights, as well as having time to write on this topic himself.

We have many colleagues to thank for all their help, including Phil Brenner, Ralph Carter, Gillian Gunn Clissold, Doug Foyle, Ole Holsti, Peter Kornbluh, Lynn Kuzma, Bill Mandel, Chuck Myers, Keith Shimko, Maria de los Angeles Torres, and Eugene Wittkopf. At Miami University we appreciate the support from the College of Arts and Science and the Department of Political Science and wish to thank Ryan Barilleaux, Sheila Croucher, Chris Kelley, Phil Russo, Melanie Ziegler, and the many graduate and undergraduate assistants who have helped us out along the way. We would like to thank Nathan MacBrien and the staff of the University of Pittsburgh Press, our copy editor Leslie Evans, and the anonymous reviewers of the manuscript, all of whom were very helpful with this project. And on a personal note we would like to thank each other, and Mac and Joe for their hospitality at key moments in the life of this project. Finally, we want to thank our families and our spouses, Kristin and Maureen, for all their patience and support. All these people have helped make this a better book; all remaining weaknesses are solely ours.

Abbreviations

AID	Agency for International Development
AIPAC	American Israel Public Affairs Committee
CANF	Cuban American National Foundation
CDA	Cuba Democracy Act
CFA	Citizens for America
CFR	Council on Foreign Relations
CIPE	Center for International Private Enterprise
CSIS	Center for Strategic International Studies
Excom	Executive Committee of the NSC
FTI	Free Trade Union Institute
JCS	Joint Chiefs of Staff
LIBERTAD	Cuban Liberty and Democratic Solidarity Act
MPLA	Popular Movement for the Liberation of Angola
NAFTA	North American Free Trade Agreement
NED	National Endowment for Democracy
NEPL	National Endowment for the Preservation of Liberty
NPR	National Public Radio
NSC	National Security Council
NSDD 77	National Security Decision Directive 77
OAS	Organization of American States
S/LPD	State Department Office of Public Diplomacy for Latin America and the Caribbean
UNITA	National Union for Total Independence (Angola)
USIA	U.S. Information Agency
WTO	World Trade Organization

THE CUBAN EMBARGO

Introduction

The Changing Politics of the Cuban Embargo

THE U.S. EMBARGO of Cuba began under President Eisenhower in 1960, was tightened after the end of the cold war in 1991, and was codified into law during the Clinton administration in the controversial 1996 Cuban Liberty and Democratic Solidarity Act (LIBERTAD), known as "Helms-Burton" for its sponsors. While on the surface there is clearly an impressive amount of policy continuity here, we try to show in this book that starting in the Reagan administration and continuing to this day the dynamics that drive U.S.-Cuba policy have changed greatly since the 1950s. The embargo is still with us; a simple look through the Code of Federal Regulations makes that clear. But the embargo has some holes in it, and sooner or later the embargo will fall. It may fall because Castro's eventual death leads to a new democratic government (though this is far from preordained). Or it may fall because an American president asks Congress to lift the embargo by repealing its legislative foundations (which is hard to imagine, certainly in the case of George W. Bush). It may also fall because Congress abruptly decides, even with Castro still in power, to remove the embargo (also not likely). A more likely scenario is that the embargo will wither away, eroding over time as a growing bipartisan coalition in Congress, made up of a patchwork of farm state legislators, probusiness and free trade Republicans, liberal Democrats who have always disliked the embargo, and even libertarian-minded members, continues to move successfully to end parts of the embargo. Limited sales of food and medicine to the island having already been allowed, loosening the ban on travel to Cuba, for example, could provide Cuba with more hard currency that could facilitate even more commerce. In fact, a movement to end the travel ban has been active for some time now. And even at a time when a wide range of factors would seem to work against such activism, the movement by this disparate group of legislators to challenge Cuba policy is intensifying.

The embargo of Cuba is not a monolith; rather, it is made up of several components: restrictions on travel to and from the island and on the sale of goods and services there, bans on investment in business ventures, constraints on immigration, limits on journalists and scholars going to Cuba, caps on how much money can be sent to family members in Cuba, and the like. Everything from what you can sell to Cuba to who can visit and how they can legally get there to how many cigars you can bring back is part of the embargo. In the last decade we have seen significant efforts to open the wall of the embargo one brick, one issue, at a time. What is particularly striking about this is not that it is happening, but how and why it is happening. Rather than the usual dynamic in which one side presses for change while the other attempts to maintain the status quo, the efforts to loosen the embargo have occurred at the same time that other legislative changes have tightened the embargo. We try to show here that the vulnerability of the embargo policy is actually, and perhaps ironically, rooted in past initiatives that were undertaken for the purpose of protecting and strengthening the embargo and presidential control over it. The codification of the economic sanctions in Helms-Burton in 1996 and the codification of the ban on travel in 2000 by embargo proponents have actually opened up Cuba policy to congressional activism in opposition to the embargo. If the various parts of the policy were still in the domain of the chief executive, President George W. Bush's longstanding support for the embargo certainly suggests that any changes would be unlikely while he was in office. Even more ironic, the interest group founded at the beginning of the Reagan presidency to strengthen the proembargo forces and increase the president's control over policy toward Cuba, the new Cuban American National Foundation (CANF), has over the longer term contributed first to the executive branch's loss of foreign policy prerogative and more recently to the movement in the direction of more normal relations with Cuba.

Our goal with this book is to examine the changing politics of U.S. policy toward Cuba and to show how the dynamics that drive policy have evolved over time. While most people are aware that there are occasional interactions between Cubans and Americans such as the baseball games in 1998 between the Cuban national team and the Baltimore Orioles, and a high-profile visit to the island by former President Carter in 2002, the extent of our current relationship may be not so widely known. Many would likely be surprised that thousands of Americans, an estimated 135,000 in 2002, visit Cuba legally each year with "licenses" that allow them to travel to Cuba and spend money there;[1] or that U.S. companies sold over $150 million worth of food and medicine to the island in 2002; or that Cuban Americans send annually, and legally, perhaps as much as $1 billion in the form of family remittances.[2] In this sense and others, the embargo has already been weakened. Here we provide an analysis of the changing political forces that have contributed to the evolution of Cuba policy that has developed even though the embargo remains.

We examine the changing dynamics behind U.S. foreign policy making toward Cuba by way of an extended study of relations with the island. While the U.S. embargo policy has remained relatively stable since the 1959 Cuban revolution, the dynamics that produce Cuba policy have changed dramatically over time. In the early years following the Cuban revolution, the president dominated the process of making U.S. policy toward Cuba, such as imposing the embargo and ordering the ill-fated invasion at the Bay of Pigs. Through much of the cold war period, the president and his advisers made Cuba policy, like most foreign policy, largely out of public view and away from domestic pressures. By the late 1970s and early 1980s, however, control over the process of making Cuba policy began to shift from the firm control of the president and into an arena that includes a variety of other actors as well, most notably Congress and interest groups. With these new groups now engaged, the debate over Cuba policy became as likely to focus on questions of economics, trade, and human rights, as on national defense and security. Today, the many components of Cuba policy are not so much driven by any one actor as they are pushed by several forces. Furthermore, all of these actors would appear to be more porous and open to influence from outside forces than ever before.

The irony of this situation, of course, is that the complicated political environment that surrounds Cuba policy was in part constructed by the presidency as a way to reassert executive control over foreign policy that had been lost to an increasingly aggressive Congress in the wake of Vietnam and Watergate. For example, as we discuss in greater detail later, the 1980 Reagan presidential campaign team and the new administration that followed helped sponsor the formation of CANF as an ally to lobby Congress, especially Democrats in the House of Representatives, for tougher policies on Cuba as part of their overall strategy to take the cold war to Latin America more aggressively. This alliance proved to be a powerful partnership for President Reagan. But the short-term gain for the president has turned out to be a long-term problem, contributing to a political environment around Cuba policy that is even more decentralized and harder to control. By 1991 President Bush and the now powerful CANF were on opposing sides of Cuba legislation, the Cuban Democracy Act. And the efforts of CANF to land a Cuban American in Congress—culminating in the election of Ileana Ros-Lehtinen (R-FL) in 1989, of Lincoln Diaz-Balart (R-FL) and Robert J. Menendez (D-NJ) in 1992, and Mario Diaz-Balart (R-FL) in 2002—would contribute to a Congress that was more interested in and assertive on Cuba policy than ever before, and a Congress that had resident experts on Cuba. President Clinton responded by facilitating the activism of economic interest groups on the other side in order to fend off initiatives promoted by Cuban Americans and their allies in Congress that threatened presidential prerogative in Cuba policy. Clinton appeared to have successfully resisted congressional attempts to further entrench the embargo policy until two Brothers to the Rescue planes were shot down early in 1996. Brothers to the Rescue had been formed in 1991 to conduct flights over the Florida Straits to search for people fleeing Cuba by boat or raft; eventually, the group began to also post anti-Castro leaflets and would occasionally drop them by air into Cuba. When the planes were shot down, the Clinton administration decided that it was politically necessary to give in to demands by pro-embargo members of Congress to codify the sanctions against Cuba. In the postcodification period, the economic interest groups that mobilized to strengthen one president's position on Cuba policy now work with their own legislative allies to promote policies that Clinton's successor would prefer not to see reach his desk. Over time, presidents' political and institutional interests have helped to create a quite complex policy-making environment for the embargo against Cuba. From the Reagan administration until today, the battles over Cuba policy have as much to do with who controls that policy as they do with the shape of the policy.

The fractured political environment that surrounds Cuba policy may reflect a broader change in U.S. foreign policy making. We suggest that while Cuba policy may be an extreme case of a struggle between the White House, Congress, and a broad set of societal actors to control the policy agenda, it is not unique. That is, we do not subscribe to a notion of Cuban exceptionalism, in which policy toward the island is simply explained as the inevitable power of a relatively large and strategically located Cuban American community that is able to effectively dictate the terms of the U.S. relationship to the island. From our perspective, the Cuba case has some distinct characteristics, including aspects of the role played by Cuban Americans, but it also shares important policy-making similarities with other cases. While we study the changing political and institutional dynamics behind Cuba policy, the actors and processes we analyze may be relevant to a broader set of cases of U.S. foreign policy making as we embark on a new century.

At first glance the addition of new actors, the broadening of the debate beyond security to include economic factors, and the more public nature of Cuba policy making over time may seem to be expected changes triggered by the demise of the cold war. The foreign policy agenda has become broader since the fall of the Soviet Union and the end of overarching threat of nuclear annihilation. And since foreign policy is no longer the nearly exclusive realm of the life-and-death realities of cold war nuclear Armageddon, it may be "safe" for actors beyond the president to get involved. Even after the attacks of September 11, 2001 led to a renewed war on terrorism, which has become the centerpiece of U.S. foreign policy, the foreign policy agenda, and the coalition of those who sought to move it, still remained much broader than during the cold war. As the dividing line between foreign and domestic policy becomes blurrier, we would expect Congress and interest groups to become more engaged in trying to steer the ship of state.[3] And certainly with the end of the cold war Cuba policy became as much a question of foreign economic policy as one of national security, with the Department of Defense itself admitting in 1997 that Cuba poses no significant military threat to the United States.[4] Thus we would expect to see some significant involvement of actors beyond the executive in trying to shape policy toward the island. Further bolstering this view that the end of the cold war led to a shift in the foreign policy-making environment, the fall of the Soviet Union ignited at least two vigorous rounds of debate about the future of the U.S. embargo policy toward Cuba: one that began with the Soviet Union's demise and a wave of democratization through Latin America,[5] and another in 1998 as President Clinton contemplated appointing a commission to study and make recommendations about U.S.-Cuba policy.[6]

We argue that while the end of the cold war may have intensified changes already underway in the U.S. foreign policy-making system with respect to Cuba policy it did not initiate these changes. Cuba policy began to elude the firm grip of the executive as early as the 1970s, and by the 1980s the center of Cuba policy activity had clearly begun to shift away from the White House. The cold war presidency of Ronald Reagan changed the nature of policy making toward Cuba more dramatically than the end of the cold war. To be sure, the fall of the Soviet Union and other developments associated with that time contributed to the changing dynamic of U.S. policy toward Cuba. But it was domestic political battles that began before and continued after the end of the cold war that more significantly altered the nature and location of Cuba policy making. Today, if a center exists at all it resides in Congress, which codified the long-standing embargo policy into law in Helms-Burton. Any significant shift in the core of the embargo must now go through Congress.

We show in this book that the policy-making process behind U.S.-Cuba policy has evolved considerably since the original implementation of the embargo in the early 1960s, despite the relative apparent continuity of that policy over the last four decades. We track the emergence and activity of different domestic political forces, focusing particularly on the increasingly assertive nature of Congress and interest groups and the progressively more porous nature of the policy process. Today's embargo policy is far different from the one imposed by Presidents Eisenhower and Kennedy; a mix of executive, legislative, and domestic societal forces all combine to craft the embargo policy, and developments far away from the Florida straits add pressure as well. We try to provide here an analysis of these changing dynamics.

This project is informed by two sometimes distinct sets of literature: the substantive study of U.S. policy toward Cuba, and the analysis of the role of domestic political institutions, societal groups, and electoral politics in making American foreign policy. There is a wide literature that tracks the history of U.S. policy toward Cuba.[7] Strong on history and substance, and each with its own angle on U.S.-Cuba relations, this literature tends not to focus on the changing political, electoral, and institutional roots of Cuba policy in the ways we attempt to do here. Two studies are especially worth noting in this regard. In a recent article, William LeoGrande examines U.S. policy toward Cuba through the "two-level game" framework, whereby he examines the interplay between domestic politics over Cuba policy on the one hand and the politics of international diplomacy on the other.[8] While we do not explicitly use the same model, we do try to build on LeoGrande's general theoretical approach to understanding Cuba policy as emerging from a nexus of domestic and global interests. The recent book by Morris Morley and Chris McGillion *Unfinished Business* also provides an interesting look at Cuba policy.[9] In explaining the continued existence of the embargo, they focus particularly on the 1990s and on how, in their view, the cold war never really ended with respect to Cuba. While our focus is longer in terms of time and more broadly on Cuba policy as a result of changing political and institutional dynamics in the United States, we share their emphasis on the domestic political roots of foreign policy. They focus largely on the continuity of the embargo. Our focus on the policy-making process—over a longer period of time—leads us to find some significant evolution in the politics that surround Cuba policy, and even some important changes to the embargo itself.

Research on the domestic sources of U.S. foreign policy has largely not focused on the Cuba case, and studies of Cuba policy often do not analyze the full range of domestic political dynamics behind it. Our approach is to merge the study of the substance of Cuba policy with a focus on the domestic politics that underlie that policy. We draw especially on research that examines the relative power of Congress, the president, and interest groups in making foreign policy.[10] Particularly interesting here are a variety of new books that explore how the end of the cold war may have altered long-established patterns of U.S. foreign policy making.[11] This new research, which explores a broad variety of cases and issues, tends to show that the foreign policy agenda of the United States is more diverse than the predominant security focus of the cold war and that a broader set of actors is engaged in policy making today than was the case during the heart of the cold war. The executive is today more fragmented, foreign policy is more complicated and diverse, and Congress is both more engaged and also more open to political forces in foreign policy than perhaps ever before.[12] While this work is theoretically rich and diverse and focuses on a wide range of cases, relatively little attention has been given to the case of U.S. policy toward Cuba. We try to address this gap through an extended study of Cuba policy.

In the first chapter we cover the history of U.S. policy toward Cuba policy through the heart of the cold war, from the 1959 revolution to the end of the 1970s. We examine how the "imperial" president, working in concert with other members of the executive branch and select congressional leaders, controlled Cuba policy and crafted plans such as the embargo policy itself, the failed invasion at the Bay of Pigs, the Soviet submarine minicrisis at Cienfuegos, and the Soviet Brigade episode. The executive branch dominated policy making during this period, though with the selective use of the public sphere to shift the policy-making calculus at times, a harbinger of things to come later.

In chapters 2 and 3 we focus on developments during the Reagan administration. Chapter 2 largely deals with the new Cuban American National Foundation (CANF), formed in part to help promote a more hard-line position toward Cuba specifically and Latin America generally. We track the birth and evolution of CANF over the decade into a powerful lobbying group, as it takes on various functions historically performed solely within the public sector and gains influence with executive agencies and Congress. The second of our chapters on the Reagan years covers both specific developments in Cuba policy and the role played by Cuba and CANF in policy toward Latin America more generally. We examine the administration's pursuit of a program of public diplomacy, marking an important turning point in the emergence of a foreign policy-making strategy that targets the U.S. public. While members of the administration creatively avoided public or even congressional oversight to pursue some aspects of its foreign policy in the 1980s, they also institutionalized the attempt to rally public support for administration policy. In combination with the role played by CANF, other public-private partnerships developing in the 1980s fundamentally changed the nature of foreign policy making toward Cuba. This, in concert with a new view of the role of Cuba, Latin America, and the Caribbean in the cold war signals a real shift in politics of Cuba policy.

Chapter 4 focuses on Cuba policy in the George Herbert Walker Bush administration and the rise of congressional activism in this area, along with the continuing importance of CANF. It is in this period that the executive-sponsored CANF took on a life of its own and was able to influence candidate Clinton and then President Bush during the 1992 presidential campaign to support tightening the Cuban embargo with the Cuba Democracy Act (CDA). Here we show the emerging importance for post–cold war foreign policy making toward Cuba of electoral politics (especially in Florida and New Jersey) and campaign contributions.

Chapters 5 and 6 explore the political dynamics of Cuba policy during the Clinton administration. Chapter 5 discusses the first Clinton term, during which the president seemed to prefer not to engage Cuba policy. Clinton suffered a backlash, however, against a prospective executive branch nominee, a new wave of immigration from Cuba, and the shooting down of planes flown by Brothers to the Rescue over the Florida Straits by the Cuban Air Force, helping lead to the passage of the Cuban Liberty and Democratic Solidarity Act of 1996. Helms-Burton would not just tighten the embargo but also codify it into law and seemingly solidify the centrality of Congress—and of several entrepreneurial members of Congress—in the Cuba policy process. The president was forced to react to a variety of public actors who by now had significant roles in Cuba policy making. The nuanced responses by the executive, and the public nature of the decision making, indicate a new complexity of the policy-making process. Then in chapter 6, cowritten with Philip Brenner, we analyze the ways that President Clinton struck back, seeking to regain some of the institutional power he ceded by signing Helms-Burton. We show how the chief executive creatively interpreted Helms-Burton as giving him the power to make significant adjustments to Cuba policy. We explore the dynamic of the very public struggle among an assertive president, a few powerful entrepreneurs in Congress, and an increasingly wide range of interest groups (and a weakened CANF). We also show how Congress reacted to these efforts with its own brand of complicated assertiveness in the form of a new codification, at the same time as an increasing bipartisan willingness to loosen the embargo.

Chapter 7 focuses on the dynamics behind Cuba policy in the George W. Bush administration. We discuss the electoral dynamics of Cuba policy during the close 2000 election (and recount), the new Bush foreign policy team, and the approach to Cuba that has emerged from the White House and from Congress. Even though Bush is committed to the embargo and in large part has Cuban American voters to thank for his victory in Florida in the 2000 election, we have nevertheless seen few of the substantive changes in Cuba policy to date that one might expect given the administration's statements and personnel. And we also witnessed a renewal of some sales of agricultural products to Cuba. All this takes place in the context of a dramatically different interest group environment than existed twenty years ago and as the congressional ground under the embargo is slowly but surely shifting.

We conclude by drawing together the trends we track throughout to show how domestic political forces tend to dominate Cuba policy making today. We argue that understanding these dynamics is essential to understanding the roots of Cuba policy. Our view is that the ground on which the embargo policy is now built, ground cultivated in the 1980s, is eroding. We argue that this erosion is caused in no small part because the political dynamics that were set in motion during the Reagan years as a way, ironically, to tighten the embargo and to strengthen the hand of the president intensified in the following years and have now boomeranged on the White House and on the embargo itself. We think that understanding the changing political dynamics involved in crafting Cuba policy is essential to understanding U.S. foreign policy toward the island today and may shed light on cases well beyond Cuba.

The Making of an Embargo

U.S.-Cuban Relations, 1959–1980

THE UNITED STATES and Cuba share a complicated and interconnected history. A full examination of this history, particularly of the
preembargo (and pre–Cuban revolution) period, is beyond the scope of
this book, which focuses on the politics of Cuba policy from the Reagan
administration to the present.[1] We try here, however, to orient readers, especially those less familiar with the background of U.S.-Cuban relations,
to the dynamics of U.S.-Cuba policy from the time of the Cuban revolution to the election of Ronald Reagan. Following the rise of Fidel Castro,
U.S. presidents from Eisenhower through Carter struggled to find ways
to isolate Castro and Cuba and to force Castro's demise. When Cuba
moved inside the Soviet sphere as the U.S. embargo took hold, the embargo became embedded in the politics of the cold war. The U.S. had long
been Cuba's major trading partner; now the Soviet Union would become
her main supporter. This early cold war period was also the era of the rise
of the Imperial President, a time when presidents, working with select
members of the executive branch and a few congressional leaders, made

Cuba policy with little intrusion from other domestic actors. From the imposition of the embargo by Executive Order, to the failed invasion at the Bay of Pigs, through failed attempts at restoring more normal relations during the détente of the 1970s, the president largely called the shots on Cuba policy during this period. The Eisenhower administration decided to end U.S. support for Cuban dictator Fulgencia Batista, but as Castro's communist positions took shape Ike eventually not only put in place the U.S. embargo policy but also set in motion plans for covert operations aimed against Castro and his government. As the embargo began under Eisenhower, we will discuss this period in a little more detail than the others in this chapter. President Kennedy presided over the failure at the Bay of Pigs but nonetheless continued efforts, as he tightened the embargo, to covertly topple Castro. President Johnson not only continued Kennedy's policy toward Cuba, he intensified the effort to isolate Cuba in the hemisphere. Near the end of the Nixon administration, and in the Ford and Carter administrations, some efforts were undertaken to ease relations with Cuba. The politics of Cuba policy, and the players who had access to power over that policy, began to change in this period. Congress became more engaged, and U.S. business interests began to suggest that there would be economic benefits to ending the embargo. Ultimately, these moves toward more normal relations ended with Cuban military adventures in Africa. Presidents made Cuba policy in this period, though their hold on the process was slipping as the 1980s approached. Below, we review the historical highlights of this period and draw attention to the ways that the dynamic of presidential control over Cuba policy began to evolve.

Eisenhower's Break

The U.S. relationship with Cuba was a complicated one. The Platt Amendment guaranteed a measure of U.S. control over affairs on the island from 1903 until Franklin Roosevelt ended the policy in 1934. A series of trade agreements and sugar acts then gave Cuban sugar producers favorable access to the U.S. market, but they also tied the Cuban economy to this single commodity and this market, giving the United States impressive leverage over Cuba. An estimated 80 percent of Cuba's hard foreign currency came from the sugar trade with the Unites States. And U.S. corporations controlled much of the sugar industry on the island.[2]

During its first term in office, the Eisenhower administration provided reasonably consistent support for Cuban President Batista, but inadequate information and unfortunate decisions plagued them from 1956 until Castro's forces took power on January 1, 1959. A key example of their confusion was that the new U.S. ambassador to Cuba in 1957, Earl E. T. Smith, had Wall Street experience but no diplomatic background; he did not even speak Spanish.[3] Ambassador Smith supported Batista and distrusted Castro more than many in the Eisenhower administration, particularly within the State Department.[4] In Washington, a vague sentiment emerged that the best possible outcome to the growing insurgency in Cuba would entail a continuity of *Batistianismo* without Batista. Not surprisingly, it proved easier to undermine longtime client Batista than to reverse the momentum generated by Castro's forces while Washington hoped for a non-Batista and non-Castro solution. Arms shipments to Cuba were suspended in mid-March 1958, and not long after a meeting in which Smith informed Batista that the U.S. government would no longer support him, the dictator fled the island on New Year's Eve that year, ushering Castro into power.

From the U.S. recognition of the new Cuban government on January 7, 1959, until the time that President Eisenhower broke diplomatic relations with Cuba in January 1961, the anti-Castro position grew steadily within the Eisenhower administration. Some of that sentiment was clearly due to a number of developments on the island. During the first month in power, the revolutionary government permitted the Communist party to operate freely, and it began a series of trials that led to the execution of a number of former officials in the Batista regime. These decisions, as well as Castro's declaration that he would head the country without elections, set the context for the Cuban president's trip to the United States in April 1959. While much of his tour, sponsored by the American Society of Newspaper Editors, was received favorably,[5] Castro's meeting with Vice President Nixon had the greatest impact on U.S. policy. On the basis of a meeting in which Nixon concluded that the

Cuban president was either "incredibly naïve" or a completely disciplined communist, the vice president later wrote: "I became a leading advocate for efforts to overthrow Castro."[6]

Castro's announcement that he would pursue agrarian reform on the island set new actors in and out of the U.S. government into motion. Property owners, particularly sugar growers, paid a heavy financial price and communicated their desire for action against Cuba to the Eisenhower White House.[7] Along with U.S. property holders, increasing numbers of Cubans fled the island following the May expropriation of farmlands greater than one thousand acres. By the fall of 1959 congressional and media criticism of the U.S. policy of "cautious" diplomacy was becoming more widespread.[8] But Eisenhower's problem, as biographer Stephen Ambrose notes, was that while Cuba was important to U.S. foreign policy, it was not *that* important in relative terms. Ike was not yet ready to invest significant resources in driving Castro from power, and he was certainly not going to send in the Marines.[9]

The public face of cautious diplomacy masked the more aggressive activity the Eisenhower administration was beginning to undertake to support Castro's opponents on the island and in exile. In a National Security Council (NSC) meeting, Vice President Nixon proposed support for an exile force that would be armed for military intervention against Castro.[10] While that idea was put on hold then, the Central Intelligence Agency (CIA) pursued related activities over the next several months, including smuggling Castro opponents out of Cuba and sending arms to known opposition forces in Cuba.[11] Ike's mood toward Castro, and with it support for a more aggressive policy toward the Cuban leader, would begin to change by late 1959 and early 1960, however.

Late in October 1959, Eisenhower approved a plan from the State Department and CIA to support Castro's opponents in Cuba, including raids by Cuban exiles against the island from U.S. territory. These initial plans ultimately led to a March 17, 1960, Oval Office meeting where President Eisenhower approved the outlines of a plan for covert action against the Castro government. Among the specifics of that plan were the creation of a radio station to broadcast into Cuba; a covert intelligence and action organization within Cuba; and the beginning of training for a paramilitary force outside Cuba that could be deployed into that country.[12] Eisenhower especially emphasized the need for finding a Cuban leader living in exile who could be recognized to form a new government.[13]

These plans for covert action against Cuba were made by the president and his close advisers largely without congressional consultations or public notice. But Congress was not inactive in the spring and summer of 1960. A proposal emerged from the House Foreign Affairs Committee at the end of March to terminate U.S. economic aid to Cuba unless the president determined that assistance was "in the national and hemispheric interest."[14] That bill passed both houses and was ultimately signed by the president. Eisenhower also wanted Congress to grant him the flexibility to unilaterally alter the existing sugar quota, which he eventually got. The covert operations, including the attempts to sabotage sugar production, were now supplemented by the prospect of formal economic sanctions.

Meanwhile, Eisenhower and Castro engaged in a series of back and forth steps that would ultimately lead to the end of U.S. diplomatic relations with Cuba. In October 1960, Eisenhower prohibited U.S. oil refineries in Cuba from refining Soviet crude oil, drastically cut the Cuban sugar quota, and imposed an economic embargo on all trade with Cuba except food and medicine. U.S. officials expected that Cuban-American trade would fall from $1.1 billion in 1957 to about $100 million; U.S. direct investment in Cuba would fall from more than $900 million to nothing.[15] For his part, Castro confiscated U.S. oil refineries, nationalized U.S.-owned and other foreign-owned property, and ordered the U.S. embassy staff to be dramatically cut back. While European allies may have urged Eisenhower to appear reasonable and moderate, he needed to project a tough image to discourage other Cubas from emerging in the hemisphere, and the domestic political incentives nearly all pointed toward getting tough on Castro. Congress received Ike's initiatives (those they knew about) "uncritically for the most part."[16] The real forcefulness of Eisenhower's Cuba policy—sabotage and the training of a Cuban exile invasion force—would not become widely known until after he left office. The initiative behind U.S.-Cuba policy clearly rested in the White House, as might have been expected. While the media may have helped shape U.S. public opinion toward accepting Castro as a reasonable figure by way of the famous Castro interview by Herbert Matthews of the *New York Times* in the Sierra Madre mountains, there is little evidence of concern for or use of the media on the part of Eisenhower administration officials as they debated the Castro-Batista dilemma in the months leading up to Castro's victory. A reasonable argument could be made that the narrow circle of influence lacked expertise on Cuba while policy was firmly in Ike's hands at this time.

The Eisenhower administration had made a key move in U.S. foreign policy in 1960 by placing anticommunism in the central position. While Ike and his advisers could not be sure that Castro posed much of an immediate threat to U.S. security and interests in Latin America, they became convinced that if allowed to go unchecked Castro's Cuba would pose such problems down the road. Eisenhower himself was unsure that sanctions would have much impact on Castro, but he pressed on in order to encourage Castro's opponents and to make a statement about U.S. power and credibility. Eisenhower ended diplomatic relations with Cuba on January 3, 1961, and suspended trade with the island, invoking the Trading with the Enemy Act, a few days later. While perhaps naively hoping to provoke Castro into overreacting, Eisenhower nevertheless had clearly staked U.S. policy toward the island as linked to the broad goals of anticommunism and defense of American hegemony and power in the region.[17] The embargo policy had been born, and the path toward the Bay of Pigs was being built.

President Kennedy and Dangerous Relations

When President Kennedy was sworn in as president he inherited invasion plans that were already well under way. The new president largely provided continuity both in terms of policy and the way that foreign policy decisions were made. Declassified documents of the Bay of Pigs, and conferences with key figures from both the U.S. and Soviet sides in the post–cold war years, have provided a wealth of information regarding U.S. decision making during the key Cuba-related events of the Kennedy presidency and has provided the basis for important recent books.[18] President Kennedy continued Eisenhower's use of a fairly small circle of advisers on Cuba before signing on to the ill-fated exile-invasion plan.[19] Experts on Cuba were notable by their absence as the invasion plan was discussed.[20] Rather, wide deference was given to military and intelligence experts,[21] though the Department of State offered some political objections.[22] President Kennedy's concern about public opinion centered mostly on his desire for plausible deniability of the U.S. role behind the exile invasion out of concern for domestic, Latin American, and world reaction.[23]

The fourteen hundred or so Cuban exiles who landed on the morning of April 17, 1961, were quickly overwhelmed by the waiting Cuban military. Always something of an open secret, given the difficulty of secretly training several hundred Cuban refugees, the April 15 strike by eight refugee-flown B-26s against the Cuban air force had put the Cubans on full alert. When President Kennedy canceled air support for the early morning landing on April 17, it was clear that the exile invasion force would face a formidable military defense in Cuba. In the end, some two hundred of the invaders were killed and more than twelve hundred were captured by the Cubans in what can only be described as a major foreign policy disaster.

Following the failure at the Bay of Pigs, the Kennedy administration was faced with the task of reconstructing its Cuba policy. Interestingly, the goal of overthrowing Castro was not changed. By August 1961, President Kennedy had approved a new CIA program of covert actions against Cuba. With a budget of more than $5 million, the CIA was to engage in propaganda activities in Cuba and throughout Latin America, as well as covert activities directed at the economy and continued support for paramilitary forces.[24] Ultimately, the various ideas about covert intelligence and sabotage activities were brought together in November as Operation Mongoose, a project headed by General Edward Landsdale.[25] In 1962 approximately $50 million was spent in covert operations, including hit-and-run attacks against sugar cane fields, harbors, and power stations.[26] Exiles played a prominent role in the program, but they proved to be quite independent in the field, making unauthorized raids that included attacking Soviet vessels twice.[27]

Congress became increasingly active following the Bay of Pigs and sought to pass a Cuban trade embargo bill. During hearings before a House committee in August 1961, officials from various departments in the executive branch argued that the proposed bill would constrain the president's flexibility to conduct foreign policy and react to changing circumstances.[28] On the Senate side, James Eastland (D-MS), chairman of the Senate Judiciary Committee, "was prepared to use his subcommittee as a rival foreign office to the State Department." Senators Barry Goldwater (R-AZ) and George Smathers (D-FL) were also prominent Senate voices on the subject of Cuba policy. Senator Smathers, in particular, sought to assume a role "as an expert on U.S.-Cuban relations. . . . There was no senator more often quoted on the Cuba story in 1959–1961 than George Smathers."[29] Although the activities of Congress put officials from the executive branch in uncomfortable positions at times, the important decisions were clearly still in the hands of Kennedy and his advisers. Successful pressure on the Organization of American States (OAS) to suspend Cuban membership and a ban of all Cuban imports and reexports of U.S. goods from third countries were among the products of administration work in early 1962.

Given that the Cuban missile crisis was essentially a U.S.-Soviet crisis, the decision-making process during that period is tangential to this story. Still, the Kennedy preference for small meetings with select executive branch advisers over full NSC sessions, or consultation with congressional leaders, played itself out most famously during the October 1962 meetings with the Executive Committee of the NSC (Excom).[30] The circle of individuals was kept very small, and secrecy (even in the sense of agreeing not to disclose aspects of the meeting and negotiations in the future) was paramount. There is some evidence of battles within the executive bureaucracy about policy toward Cuba, of course, as information about Soviet military activity on the island became known. Kennedy did apparently use press statements strategically as a means of countering the proponents of more aggressive actions against Castro.[31] The absence of a role for legislative input was a point of resentment for some, including Senator William Fulbright.[32] One way that members of Congress did play a role during the crisis was to serve as unfavorable comparisons—as advocates of invasion less reasonable than the president, Kennedy could compare them to himself in discussions with the Soviet leadership, for example.[33]

There was no relaxation of Cuba policy during President Kennedy's remaining year in office following the successful outcome of the missile crisis. In fact, Kennedy tightened the diplomatic and economic squeeze on Cuba in 1963 by prohibiting travel to or financial transactions with Cuba by U.S. citizens; in July he ordered all Cuban assets in the United States frozen. The era of presidential dominance over Cuba policy continued.

Johnson, Cuba, and Communism

President Johnson kept Kennedy's key foreign policy advisers after he rose to the White House following Kennedy's assassination, and he maintained a clear focus on both the island itself and, perhaps more important, on preventing another Cuba from happening. H. W. Brands called that latter objective, "Johnson's fidelphobia."[34] The effort to isolate Cuba remained a high priority. Less than a year after assuming power, the Johnson administration registered a notable success with the July 1964 vote by OAS members to impose economic sanctions and break diplomatic relations with Cuba by a 15-4 vote.[35] From 1964 until the end of Johnson's second term, only Mexico among the countries of Latin America maintained full diplomatic relations with Cuba. Johnson encouraged the rest of the West to likewise isolate Cuba.[36]

Consistent with President Johnson's efforts to isolate Cuba was an emphasis on preventing another Cuba in the hemisphere. Assistant Secretary of State for Inter-American Affairs Thomas Mann reflected that interest in a March 1964 statement that came to be known as the Mann Doctrine. In order to lessen the chances for future communist penetration into Latin America, the United States would henceforth place a higher priority on political stability and economic growth than on democratization. This policy played out in U.S. relations with Brazil in 1964 and the Dominican Republic in 1965. In Brazil, that nation's army did most of the work removing a chief executive who the Johnson administration believed leaned farther to the left than was appropriate. While the extent of U.S. promotion behind the scenes of President Goulart's removal is not entirely clear, we do know that the Johnson administration quickly endorsed the interim military government's legitimacy, sent emergency aid, and declared the change as constitutional, precluding the need for formal diplomatic recognition.[37]

The situation in the Dominican Republic was not as smooth; President Johnson used the U.S. military to block the ascension of a potential left of center government in 1965. To guarantee public support in the United States for the invasion, Johnson promoted the idea that Castro was behind the troublesome developments that led to U.S. intervention. In May 1965, well before the full-scale invasion of the Dominican Republic,

Johnson noted that the United States would use "every resource at our command to prevent the establishment of another Cuba in the hemisphere."[38]

The Johnson administration officials initially moved away from some of their predecessor's more controversial policies, such as assassination attempts on Castro and CIA-sponsored sabotage inside Cuba—efforts they increasingly saw as ineffective. In practice, though, the administration continued some operations against the sugar crop in Cuba, as well as attempts to sabotage products destined for Cuba from overseas ports.[39] With neither an overt nor covert military solution on the agenda, President Johnson made tightening, widening, and enforcing the economic sanctions against Cuba the focus of his policy.

During the early Vietnam years, Congress mostly supported Johnson's foreign policy decisions. Critiques from legislators were most notable for their exceptionalism. Senator Fulbright stepped up his criticism of U.S.-Cuba policy. The chair of the Senate Foreign Relations Committee called for policy change in a famous "Old Myths and New Realities" speech in early 1964. He argued that U.S. efforts to overthrow and isolate Castro had failed and that the United States should realize that Castro was a "distasteful nuisance but not an intolerable danger."[40] The other real challenge to the president was from lawmakers who sought to strengthen the economic sanctions against Cuba and countries that traded with it in ways that the White House opposed because the steps would limit President Johnson's flexibility in relations with allies.[41] In general, Congress deferred to and supported Johnson's Cuba policy.

With the exception of the American Israel Public Affairs Committee (AIPAC), which had played a role in foreign policy toward the Middle East since the 1950s, interest groups were not central foreign policy players during Johnson's presidency. An increase in activism by a variety of interest groups on both domestic and foreign issues in the mid-1960s, however, was beginning to affect the policy-making process. The civil rights and anti–Vietnam War movements were the vanguard of this new mobilization, but soon a wide array of groups followed.[42]

The principal foreign policy crisis that the Johnson administration dealt with in relation to Cuba involved migration.[43] In October 1965, about three thousand Cubans left the island from Camarioca in the initial "boatlift" to the United States. While there is some evidence that the Florida

congressional delegation encouraged the Johnson administration to consider economic and social costs on the state as it developed a response,[44]
policy was made by an ad hoc task force in the executive branch. The policy it formulated, including the beginning of the Freedom Flights program in early November 1965 (some 250,000 Cubans would come to the
United States under the auspices of the program by 1971), was accepted in
large part uncritically by Congress.[45] In 1966, President Johnson signed
the Cuban Adjustment Act that allowed more than 100,000 Cubans in the
United States to apply for permanent residence. The president chose to
enact this policy through the attorney general's authority on immigration
matters, rather than seek a bill from a Congress that would have likely
been fully supportive, keeping control over Cuba policy inside the executive branch.[46]

Nixon and Cuba

Regardless of the number of Third World hot spots, neither President
Nixon nor his chief foreign policy adviser, Henry Kissinger, was predis-
posed to focus on north-south relations. Rather, their preference was to
work with the Great Powers—both in the East and West.[47] Nixon and
Kissinger saw Latin America as a region of lesser importance that therefore should be ignored when possible and coerced when necessary. That
sort of sentiment would allow Kissinger to famously note that just because the Chileans voted for Socialist Salvador Allende they should not
have to live with the consequences. Kissinger was brutally honest in conceding that he neither knew very much about Latin America nor worried
about that lack of information.[48] President Nixon himself had a number
of personal experiences and relationships that made it hard for him to
ignore the region, whatever his own East-West predisposition may have
been. A disastrous trip through South America as vice president in the
1950s, the role Cuba played in the 1960 presidential election he had lost,
and even his close friend, Cuban American Bebe Rebozo, all made him
sensitive to the presence of left-wing movements in Latin America.

The Nixon administration undertook a review of U.S.-Cuba policy
relatively early on. Nixon apparently told an adviser about Castro: "There'll

be no change toward that bastard while I'm President." Both Nixon and Kissinger supported a renewal of covert operations against Castro.[49] Nixon and his advisers generally saw Cuba as the same kind of problem as did previous administrations. As the Deputy Assistant Secretary of State for Inter-American Affairs Robert Hurwitch told Congress in July 1969, "The Cuban government has not abandoned nor renounced its policies of engaging in subversion in the hemisphere. With respect to Cuba's military ties with the Soviet Union, we found even less reason to alter our policy toward Cuba."[50]

1970 was a critical year for U.S.-Latin American relations. Socialist Salvador Allende was elected president in Chile, and intelligence suggested that the Soviets were building a submarine base in Cuba. The Chilean issue was addressed through covert action. What to do about the construction at Cienfuegos in Cuba was more complicated. Kissinger was very angry about the construction and what it potentially represented—a large increase in the strategic capability of the Soviet nuclear fleet in the Western Hemisphere.[51] President Nixon, however, did not wish this to develop into a crisis that would endanger détente with the Soviets.[52] While the issue was settled without a major crisis and by most accounts satisfactorily for U.S. interests, it is an important case here because the policy-making dynamics over the issue of Cienfuegos appear in retrospect to signal an important shift in the nature of U.S. foreign policy making that would come to greater fruition later.

On September 9, 1970, intelligence information indicated that a Soviet flotilla, including a ship carrying two barges presumed to be for servicing nuclear subs, had arrived at Cienfuegos. Within a week, U-2 spy planes revealed construction activity at the site. CIA Director Richard Helms updated Kissinger on September 18 following an unrelated meeting. Kissinger was particularly taken with the photos of a soccer field near the Cienfuegos harbor and argued that the fact that Cubans play baseball not soccer was in itself conclusive evidence that the Soviets were constructing some sort of naval facility in the area. "Those soccer fields could mean war," he later told Nixon's Chief of Staff, H. R. "Bob" Haldeman.[53] Kissinger was perhaps wrong about Cuban interest in soccer, but he was right about the construction of some sort of submarine base on the southern coast of the island.

The executive branch was divided about how to respond. Nixon and the State Department did not want a public "crisis" with the Soviets and believed that the issue could be resolved in quiet negotiations. Kissinger, the Defense Department, and the Joint Chiefs of Staff (JCS) believed that the Soviet construction was a serious threat that demanded an aggressive response. Overarching all of this, policy makers knew that if the information about Soviet activity in Cuba were to enter the public arena, there was the distinct possibility that public outrage would follow and a crisis would be unavoidable. On September 16, two days before he saw the photographs of the soccer fields, Kissinger commented to *New York Times* columnist C. L. Sulzberger about "Soviet horsing around in Cuba."[54] On September 25, Sulzberger broke the news, noting the appearance of a naval installation under construction in Cienfuegos, to serve Soviet submarines.[55] But the initial, and presumably subsequent, "leaks" from Kissinger served a purpose. As a Kissinger biographer argued, "faced with a President who would not take the tough road, Kissinger treated him like any other bureaucratic enemy, and leaked to the press."[56]

After Sulzberger's column, a sense of at least mild urgency emerged in Congress and in the public at large. Articles appeared in newspapers almost daily, and Nixon's preferred approach of quiet diplomacy became a politically unacceptable strategy. In Congress, Florida Democrat Dante Fascell used his position as chair of a House subcommittee to call for a quick U.S. response, and Senator Frank Church (D-ID) announced that the Senate Foreign Relations Subcommittee on Western Hemispheric Affairs would hold a closed hearing to review the "potentially serious development" in Cuba.[57] For a few weeks the Nixon administration was under attack from two sides. Some in Congress and the media demanded a response to the serious threat posed by the Cienfuegos "crisis"; others skeptically charged Nixon with trying to get political benefits out of a relatively insignificant development.[58]

In the end, as Nixon wrote in his memoirs, "After some face-saving delays, the Soviets abandoned Cienfuegos."[59] Nixon believed that this was a foreign policy success. It was also, however, an example of the strategic use of information leaked to the public by an important player in the decision-making circle in order to shift the terms of debate. Certainly, the circle of decision makers remained small during Cienfuegos, but here we see new actors, especially Congress, acting in new arenas, in the public eye, entering the Cuba policy-making picture.

Even without the prompt of construction at Cienfuegos, Congress was willing to view Cuba within a cold war context that framed the Cuba question not in terms of whether the island nation should be isolated by the United States, but rather how aggressively the executive and legislature should be in extending the embargo. Generally, Nixon's and Kissinger's cold war rhetoric resonated in a Congress where voices such as those of Dante Fascell advocated even more aggressive action against communist Cuba. As Nixon's first term wore on, though, some Democrats began to question Cuba policy. Ted Kennedy (D-MA) was a prominent voice, noting the administration's "outdated and unrealistic" approach. And in a precursor to the debate almost three decades later, Kennedy suggested that treating China and Cuba as analogous cases was appropriate, given that recent overture by President Nixon toward communist China.[60]

During Nixon's shortened second term, congressional challenges to Cuba policy picked up steam. In 1971 and 1972, several senators, including William Fulbright (D-AR) and Charlie Mathias (R-MD), made speeches, introduced resolutions, and generally challenged the administration's policy on Cuba. The "Wednesday Group," a small block of moderate and liberal Republican members of the House, even recommended that the economic blockade of Cuba be lifted.[61] By the mid-1970s, members of Congress sometimes traveled to Cuba to personally assess U.S. policy. In 1974, Senators Claiborne Pell (D-RI) and Jacob Javits (R-NY) visited the island; the following year, during the Ford presidency, Charles Whalen (R-OH) was the first House member known to have traveled to postrevolution Cuba.[62] Philip Brenner suggests that the dynamic between the executive and the legislature over the Cuba issue at the time was characterized by examples of independent activity on the part of particular members of Congress within the context of an executive who mixed anti-Cuban rhetoric with just enough support for the activities of antiembargo legislators at key junctures.[63]

Near the end of the Nixon presidency, Secretary of State Kissinger began a process aimed at the potential normalization of relations with Cuba. In June 1974, Kissinger approved a trip by staff members from the Senate Foreign Relations Committee; he also sent a message to Castro by way of U.S. journalists; and he appointed an advocate of normalization, William D. Rogers, to the position of Assistant Secretary of State for Inter-American Affairs.[64] The combination of public and private moves by Kissinger suggested that an opening to Cuba might follow the China opening; Cuban activity in Africa would lead President Ford to reconsider such a move. While U.S. policy toward Cuba remained essentially the same when Nixon left office as it had been when he arrived, it was in this period that new dynamics around Cuba policy began to emerge, dynamics that would take greater hold later.

Ford, Carter, and Castro

President Nixon's resignation in August 1974 elevated Vice President Gerald R. Ford to the presidency at a potentially favorable time for normalizing U.S.-Cuban relations. The planning process for secret talks in Washington and New York between U.S. and Cuban officials was well underway. When those talks began in November 1974, the U.S. side was represented by William Rogers, assistant secretary of state, and Lawrence Eagleburger, assistant to the secretary of state—two reasonably high ranking officials who were thought to be sympathetic to normalization. In the post-Vietnam Congress, some conservatives such as Senator Bennett Johnston (D-LA) and Representative John Breaux (D-LA), seeing the potential economic benefits for their state in the event of a trade opening, joined liberal voices interested in policy change. Johnston and Breaux visited Cuba in November 1974 and returned touting the potential market for Louisiana-grown rice.[65] Dante Fascell (D-FL) and his House allies presented a formidable obstacle to significant policy change, although an organizational change in the House committee structure diluted his influence somewhat. The Foreign Affairs Committee, chaired by Fascell, was renamed the Committee on International Relations, and the new subcommittees were based on function rather than geography. The embargo fell under the International Trade and Commerce Subcommittee. Its chairman, Jonathan Bingham (D-NY), supported revoking the president's authority to continue the embargo.[66] In the international arena, Nixon's opening to China and moves toward détente with the Soviets seemed a favorable background, if not a precedent, for President Ford should he want to move in a similar direction on Cuba. And in July 1975, the OAS voted to lift the organization's collective sanctions against Cuba.[67]

Following the OAS vote Ford modified the embargo in several ways and announced his intentions to negotiate with the Cuban government on the question of normalized relations.[68] Changes to the embargo included ending the ban on trade by third-country subsidiaries, as long as goods were "nonstrategic" and were produced with minimal U.S. components; allowing third-country ships to bunker at U.S. ports; and the elimination of the prohibition of foreign aid to countries whose ships or planes transported goods to or from Cuba.[69]

Relations with Cuba went steadily downhill from this high point at the end of summer in 1975, primarily because of Castro's decision to deploy several thousand Cuban troops to Angola to bolster the forces of the MPLA, or Popular Movement for the Liberation of Angola, which were the most Marxist forces involved in the Angolan civil war. The United States gave covert assistance to the UNITA (National Union for Total Independence) forces in the civil war. Just before Christmas of 1975, Ford announced that the possibility of improving U.S.-Cuban relations had been eliminated by the Cuban military involvement in Africa, as well as support for the Puerto Rican independence movement.[70] Within forty-eight hours, Castro vowed continued support for both movements.[71] Even though Kissinger exhorted Congress to take action against Cuba for its African adventures, Congress largely dismissed such rhetoric and voted to ban covert military aid to Angola in January 1976 over the appeals of the president and the secretary of state. As Ambrose notes, this action was an "example of Congress taking charge of foreign policy in a way unthinkable" in previous administrations.[72] Congress and the president were largely silent on Cuba policy the rest of the year. By the time President Carter took office in 1977, congressional interest in changing course on Cuba had all but disappeared, and in general the momentum seemed to have shifted away from any openings.

When President Jimmy Carter took office, he seemed intent on using his position to shift direction on a number of foreign policy issues. The new chief executive moved quickly to put his own imprint on U.S. policy toward Latin America, particularly in relations with Panama and Cuba.

In the case of Panama, Carter struggled to convince Congress (and the public) that returning the Canal was the right thing to do. While less sure of public sentiment with regard to Cuba policy, the Carter administration did fear a political backlash if talks with that country received too much publicity.[73] Within the administration, Secretary of State Cyrus Vance seemed to favor normalizing relations, while National Security Adviser Zbigniew Brzezinski had strong reservations.[74]

During Carter's first year as president he made a series of moves aimed at undoing his predecessors' policies. In March Carter lifted the restrictions on travel to Cuba by U.S. citizens and allowed them to spend up to $100 on Cuban goods during any single visit. A month later, a fishing rights and maritime boundaries agreement was signed. Finally "interests sections" were opened in Washington and Havana to serve functions typically undertaken by ambassadors and embassies. The NSC also discontinued its blacklisting of foreign ships engaged in Cuba trade. These moves were significant enough that Wayne Smith, director of the Office of Cuban Affairs in the State Department, assumed that the president would shortly proceed in the near future to end the embargo entirely.[75]

There were favorable signs of ending the embargo coming from Capitol Hill as well. In 1977 a basketball team from South Dakota traveled to the island, accompanied by the state's senators, George McGovern and James Abourezk. Upon their return, the legislators argued for ending at least the embargo on food and medicine. President Carter offered some support, suggesting that he would not oppose congressional movement in that direction.[76] Other positive signs that same year included a visit to Cuba by Senate Foreign Relations Chairman Frank Church, and hints from U.S. businesses that they would benefit from doing business in Cuba.[77]

Cuba's move into Ethiopia in 1978 threatened to halt the momentum. Brzezinski, dubious about the diplomatic openings, used the military adventure to great effect in the struggle between the NSC and State. While the president was still the controlling actor in foreign policy making, others —inside and outside the executive—attempted to influence policy in increasingly public ways. Brzezinski, for example, described in the press only as a "high ranking administration official," promoted the view that Cubans were expanding their military presence in Cuba. Reminiscent of Kissinger's leaks in 1970, he thus put the administration in a position of being essentially "trapped by its own rhetoric."[78] Secret administration negotiations with Cuba were subverted by the public escalation of words condemning the Soviet, and Cuban, role in Africa.

The domestic political climate surrounding the Panama Canal Treaty negotiations also shrunk Carter's space to operate on Cuba. Carter had prioritized the Panama Canal and used considerable political capital taking the issue to the U.S. public and Congress. By the time he gained a difficult victory on a 68-32 vote in April 1978, Carter was on the defensive in the face of conservative attacks about his administration's concessions and general weakness in foreign relations. Critics argued that not only were there Cuban soldiers threatening U.S. interests in Africa, but the Soviet military was offering an unanswered challenge to the United States in Cuba itself. Allegations were focused on the arrival of twenty-three Soviet MiG fighter-bombers in 1978, and in the following year, a combat brigade.[79]

The "discovery" of a Soviet military brigade in the summer of 1979, whose existence had been known to U.S. officials as far back as 1963, occurred at a difficult time politically for the Carter administration. A spring coup in Grenada and the Nicaraguan Sandinista success in July of that same year suggested that Latin America might be vulnerable to movements from the Left. A difficult battle for the ratification of SALT II in Congress, and the prospect of a tough right-wing Republican challenge in the 1980 presidential elections, complicated the political dynamic even further. [80]

Carter lost control of the Soviet brigade story. Senator Richard Stone (D-FL) went public with the story at a Senate Foreign Relations Committee hearing on July 17. With assurances from CIA Director Stansfield Turner and Secretary of Defense Harold Brown at the hearing that nothing new had been found in Cuba, Senator Church (D-ID) went on record with a statement later in the day that no significant Soviet military activity was taking place on the Caribbean island.[81] Still, the intelligence community's monitoring of military exercises in Cuba the following month led to a CIA report confirming that the Soviet troops in Cuba constituted a combat brigade.[82] That report was then leaked into media hands.[83] When Senator Church called a news conference to announce the combat brigade, a foreign policy crisis emerged almost entirely out of incomplete intelligence reports, politically sensitive legislators, and relatively obscure Washington media reports. The president was on the sidelines as the story played out in a very public way.

Electoral considerations entered into Senator Church's decision to go public. A liberal Democrat who had voted for the Panama Canal treaty, running in conservative Idaho, Church was clearly vulnerable to a 1980 challenge.[84] In fact an ad running against him showed him in Cuba smoking cigars with Castro.[85] The move by Senator Stone (D-FL) to go public with information about the brigade also suggests the emerging role of the Cuban exile community in Florida as a domestic political factor shaping the dispute not just over the brigade, but over U.S. policy toward Cuba more generally. Finally, in September, the Carter administration seized the agenda back from Congress and the exiles by announcing the discovery of information the U.S. government had had for approximately seventeen years.[86]

Although this crisis ended anticlimactically,[87] a number of trends in the way U.S.-Cuba policy was made were becoming apparent. Members of Congress were becoming more assertive on issues of foreign policy. The Cuban exile community, largely absent from policy circles since the Bay of Pigs, began to emerge as a political force as parts of the exile community recognized that they needed to rethink their strategy from covert forceful acts against Castro (and each other) toward Washington lobbying. [88] And the link between the U.S. and Cuban governments atrophied. In fact, the failure of the United States to protest terrorist acts against Cuba and unwillingness to discuss immigration questions played a role in the subsequent Mariel boatlift crisis of 1980.[89]

As boats began to leave from the port at Mariel in late April, it quickly became apparent that a major problem was at hand. During the first week of exodus, April 21–27, the 6,053 departing Cubans represented a larger number than the total who left during a 1965 boatlift from Camarioca; by the second week more than 1,000 people a day were leaving. While the Carter administration was certainly distracted at the time by the Iran hostage situation among other things, their decision-making process was clearly flawed. During an election year, a classically intermestic issue (that is, an issue with both domestic and international political implications) such as immigration posed a real challenge. In dealing with the international component—negotiations with Cuba—the NSC sought to take control of the policy and in doing so effectively excluded the "Cuba experts" from the process.[90] Domestically, the president faced serious economic problems and was confronted by legislators and the public, including those who sought to link the question of the Cuban exodus with Haitian refugees. Ultimately, the boatlift ended, but not before more than 100,000 *Marielitos* had reached U.S. shores.

By late spring of 1980, the list of issues other than Mariel that President Carter had to answer for in order to be reelected—from energy prices and an economic slowdown (the national malaise) to the hostages in Iran and the flurry of setbacks in Afghanistan and Nicaragua—had grown so long that Cuba may not have mattered. But in the Soviet brigade and Mariel crises, we do see a turning point in the foreign policy-making process. It was during the Carter administration that actors began to mobilize who would become increasingly significant players in the future. Congress became more assertive, and Cuban American groups with ties to the Reagan campaign began to form what would become the powerful Cuban American National Foundation. Finally, the effort to take unsettled policy debates to the public's ears, as CNN began to broadcast, hinted at the more public nature foreign policy making would take in the near future. It would be left for the winner in that presidential election year, Ronald Reagan, to make his own mark in broadening the scope and nature of foreign policy making even further in the 1980s.

The people and the governments of the United States and Cuba have been tied together in a complicated political history. As the Eisenhower administration put the economic embargo of Cuba into place and successive administrations followed suit, the politics that shaped American policy toward the island started to become more complicated as well. As the 1980s began, a new era of the politics of U.S.-Cuba policy was born, an era of executive dominance partnered with new ethnic interest group activism. The politics of Cuba policy would never again be as simple as they were during the Eisenhower years.

The Reagan Administration
and the Cuban American
National Foundation

THE REAGAN CAMPAIGN and administration had plans to overhaul U.S.
policy toward Latin America, and policy toward Cuba was a key part
of their plans. But Congress, and especially the Democrat-controlled House
of Representatives, posed a major hurdle to the administration's aim of
taking a more aggressively anticommunist stance in the hemisphere. Congress had become far more active in the foreign policy arena since Vietnam and Watergate, and the Reagan team wanted and sought help on the
Hill. Toward this end, the new Cuban American National Foundation
(CANF) would become a strategic partner for the Reagan administration.

Studies of American foreign policy often pay little attention to the role
and power of ethnic interest groups—how state actors either work with
or resist such groups, and how the state may try to use such groups to advance policy goals.[1] This indifference is perhaps understandable; early
studies showed these groups to have little influence, and the cold war contributed to a foreign policy-making process that was largely dominated by
the president. Interest group activity in foreign policy seemed relatively

unimportant with a few notable exceptions.[2] One such exception is attention to the role of the American Israel Public Affairs Committee (AIPAC), which is often seen as a unique example of a powerful ethnic interest group.[3] But after the Soviet Union fell and Congress became more engaged, the foreign policy-making process perhaps opened up to the dynamics that analysts have long said characterized domestic politics, including interest group activity.[4] Eric Uslander, for example, argues that there has been a sharp increase in the number and assertiveness of interest groups in foreign policy as the distinction between "foreign" and "domestic" policy has eroded, and he notes that the most prominent foreign policy lobby groups are ethnic interest groups.[5] Other recent studies seem to agree.[6]

No examination of the politics of Cuba policy can ignore the importance of CANF. The case of CANF, especially during the 1980s—its origins, its web of relationships with the government even during the cold war, and its role as a near coexecutor of policy—suggests that ethnic interest group activity is not new and may be far more complex than is commonly understood. Here, we examine the origins and activities of CANF in the 1980s as a window into the foreign policy-making process. We begin by exploring the birth and growth of CANF, including the conditions of its founding and its range of activities during the 1980s, paying particular attention to the web of public-private relationships created in the making of U.S.-Cuba foreign policy during the Reagan years. We then assess the importance of the CANF case for our understanding of the role of ethnic interest groups in U.S. foreign policy and the changing nature of U.S. foreign policy making more generally, drawing attention to the political strategy of forging a partnership with an interest group, at least in part, in order to reassert executive control over foreign policy.

The Birth and Growth of the Cuban American National Foundation

A series of agreements with Cuba in the first year of the Carter presidency seemed to mark the beginning of a new era of U.S.-Cuban relations as the two governments reestablished diplomatic interaction by setting up "interests sections" in Washington and Havana. The situation deteriorated over the next few years, however, as disputes arose over Cuban troops in Angola, the 1979 "discovery" of a Soviet brigade in Cuba, and the 1980 Mariel boatlift. As a result relations between the United States and Cuba were at least as strained when Carter left office as when he arrived. While the president was dealing with a series of policy setbacks in Latin America and elsewhere, right-wing critics of Carter were formulating a set of policies that Republican presidential candidate Ronald Reagan found compelling.

Support for a new hard line in Central America generally began to emerge, which included calls for tough steps against Cuba including the possibility, if other steps failed to unseat Castro, of a "war of national liberation" on the island."[7] In 1979 Jeane Kirkpatrick, Reagan's future UN ambassador, authored an article that defined and identified "totalitarian" regimes, such as Cuba under Castro.[8] Discussions of foreign policy in the Reagan 1980 presidential campaign regularly drew connections between Moscow and the revolutionary movements in Central America and Cuba.[9] Still, when President Reagan took office in 1981, he faced a Congress and general public that did not yet perceive the same crisis as his campaign and others had articulated. Reagan was also facing an institutional struggle for control over foreign policy. Congress had become increasingly active, or at least combative, in foreign affairs since Vietnam and Watergate.[10] If the Reagan administration were to move aggressively in Central America and the Caribbean, some effort to counter public apprehension would be necessary. To roll back communism abroad, an ideological counteroffensive within the United States, and within Congress, would be necessary.[11] Concerning the Reagan view of Central America generally, Elliot Abrams has said, "We had a policy. We arrived in office with a policy. . . . The operative problem for those of us on the inside was—how do you get Congress to vote the money you want for El Salvador first and later Nicaragua?"[12]

The 1980s marked a change in the approach by Cuban Americans attempting to challenge Castro's government as well. In general, exile groups were previously active only in southern Florida, where very occasional commando-type raids against the island were supplemented by localized politicking. Even in Miami, the exile right was generally fragmented, certainly lacking any visible organizational cohesion. And in Washington, D.C., there was "simply no organized voice" for a group that "had learned the costs of being out of the loop during the Ford and Carter years."[13] In addition to organizational weakness, the Cuban community suffered from a perception that at least a segment of the exiles were still involved in questionable covert activities. A flurry of bombings attributed to Cuban exiles in the second half of the 1970s, combined with the Mariel situation, was increasingly affecting public sentiment about the Cuban American community.[14] Jorge Mas Canosa, a founding member and longtime executive director of CANF, told the *Miami Herald* in 1986 that "We had to take the fight out of Calle Ocho and Miami Stadium and into the center of power . . . we had to stop commando raids and concentrate on influencing public opinion and governments."[15]

In an impressive concert of interests, the Reagan team and some Cuban Americans were thus both faced with the need to shift public perceptions on related issues at the same time. And both the Reagan administration and a Cuban American lobby had much to gain from the other's success in shaping public views about Cuba. This was not entirely new. Even before the Reagan administration, it is clear that the U.S. government was interested in the politics of the Cuban exile community. Maria de los Angeles Torres notes that declassified State Department documents lay out plans to weaken the more moderate leaders in the community who were not considered sufficiently anti-Castro and pro-American.[16] Sheila Croucher argues that the positive portrayals of early Cuban refugees were partly rooted in claims issued by individuals and agencies within the U.S. government to serve particular cold war political objectives.[17] By the time of the 1980 presidential campaign, a general perception of Cuban American economic success (at least somewhat a function of federal government assistance) and right-wing political views held sway.

What was new from the beginning of the Reagan campaign and administration was the central role of Cuba as a security threat in Central America and the Caribbean. An alliance with exiles from the island, who were themselves intent on maintaining pressure on Castro, certainly made sense. Torres argues "key Republicans had been eyeing the Cuban American community as early as 1980. This was especially the case among members of the New Right, whose ideology coincided with the conservatism many Cuban Americans had shown in their past involvement on foreign policy issues." She notes that Roger Fontaine, one of the coauthors of the

Santa Fe Report that reflected much of the tone of the Reagan campaign toward Cuba and Latin America, and later an adviser on Latin America at the NSC for Reagan, "asserted that what was needed in Washington was a strong, conservative Cuban American lobby."[18]

A number of different versions of the founding of the Cuban American National Foundation in 1980–1981 have appeared in the literature. Jorge Mas Canosa has claimed that the impetus for CANF was the idea of a few Cuban Americans, acting on their own, without help from any Reagan supporters: "It was my idea that I discussed with a few friends and we decided to carry it out." These friends included Pepe Hernandez, Raul Masvidal, and Carlos Salman.[19] Early reporting of CANF generally described the founding members as "three Miami businessmen" (Mas, Masvidal, and Salman), even if sometimes noting the coincidence that it was "formed the month Mr. Reagan took office."[20]

Masvidal, who left CANF following a series of disputes with Mas, recalls a different version of the organization's founding. He claims that the original push for CANF's formation came from Richard V. Allen, Reagan's first National Security Adviser. Masvidal adds that Richard Allen told him that with Reagan's election, "There will be a new opportunity for Cuban Americans. I suggest you copy the Israeli lobby, and I will help you. You should lobby both branches of government."[21] According to Masvidal, "the National Security Council wanted to start an organization that would help popularize the Reagan administration's policies. And so was born the Cuban American National Foundation."[22] Torres picks up on this connection. She argues, "just months after the 1980 election, a group of Cuban American businessmen and ideologues formed the Cuban American National Foundation (CANF). Its first meetings were held at National Security Council offices in Washington as part of the administration's effort to build citizen diplomacy for its projects. Jorge Mas Canosa, a Cuban exile, was brought on board by NSC employee Richard Allen to help organize the foundation."[23]

The prominent role of Reagan administration officials in the creation of CANF is presumed in most media reporting of the organization. For example, Gaeton Fonzi's research leads him to conclude definitively that the "CIA veteran, Richard Allen . . . came up with the idea that the Cuban exiles could be organized as an effective tool to promote the President's aggressive Latin American policy."[24] Carla Anne Robbins writes that Allen "suggested setting up a lobby group along the lines of the powerful [AIPAC]."[25] Newspaper accounts have been similar. The *New York Times* and *Washington Post* use some variation of "at the behest of the Reagan administration" or "with encouragement from Richard Allen" to refer to the circumstances of the birth of CANF.[26] The *Miami Herald* even referred to CANF as "the brainchild of Richard Allen."[27]

Richard Allen's recent recollection is close to that of Masvidal. Allen remembers having discussions with Mas around the time of the 1980 election, during which he noted that the Cuban Americans could be more effective than they had been to that point. To that end, he suggested that Mas study how Israel and Taiwan had been successful, with the idea that Cuban Americans could model themselves on those cases. Allen notes that it was "not an official suggestion," but that he and other members were clearly receptive to such an organizational effort by Mas, Masvidal, and Salman. Facing a Democrat-controlled House of Representatives that would need to be persuaded to support Reagan administration policies, any assistance from the Cuban community would be welcomed by the new administration. [28] Awareness of the unusual conditions of CANF's founding and close relationship with the Reagan administration seem to persist even to today. A former Clinton administration official close to Cuba policy said in an interview that the Reagan administration "made" CANF, and a former Senate Republican staff member who worked on Cuba policy noted the way CANF appeared to have been "blessed" by the Reagan administration in the 1980s.[29]

The Reagan administration's approach to Latin America coincided almost perfectly with the worldview of the new CANF leadership, and ideological compatibility was important for CANF's success.[30] Similarly to Reagan's position, Mas and CANF were committed to opposing Castro on the island and anywhere Cuban troops or allies were found. According to CANF's own literature, its initial objective was to establish an organization that "would challenge the myths propagated by the Cuban government, through the objective analysis and reporting of conditions in Cuba, of Castro's repressive dictatorship and destructive international policies, while promoting the ideals of respect for human rights and self-determination for the Cuban people."[31] Reagan administration interests in Central America or even Africa would naturally be served as a consequence of CANF activity in gathering and disseminating information about Castro's "destructive international policies."

Ronald Reagan argues in his memoirs, "one of the greatest frustrations during those eight years was my inability to communicate to the American people and to Congress the seriousness of the threat we faced in Central America."[32] The Cuban Americans in CANF were clearly not among the Americans that Reagan needed to convince. An argument that surfaced in a February 23, 1981, State Department White Paper that noted "definitive evidence of the clandestine military support given by the Soviet Union, Cuba, and their communist allies to Marxist-Leninist guerrillas' trying to overthrow the Salvadoran government" certainly was compatible with the anti-Castro commitment of Mas and friends.[33] For his entire presidency, Reagan would hold to the argument that the region's instability was a function of Castro's and his Sandinista allies' support for revolutionaries in El Salvador and Guatemala. CANF was an "educational" organization more than willing to spread the word about Castro's threat in this hemisphere. An "independent" lobbying group of Cuban Americans was potentially very valuable to an administration intent on generating much needed "public consensus."[34] For the Cuban Americans, the support from the Reagan administration for their cause was equally important.

CANF took the advice to model its organization on AIPAC to heart. The organization included legally separate entities, which allowed them to divide their resources between both tax-exempt educational and lobbying activities. Local chapters throughout the country, which could develop active ties to individual members of Congress, were another part of the AIPAC model adapted by CANF. AIPAC reportedly "trained CANF staff in tactics for transforming a foreign policy issue into a domestic one that would be susceptible to interest group pressure."[35] Even a lawyer with AIPAC experience, Bernard Barnett, helped Mas set up CANF with the same principles he had used with the Israeli lobby.[36] Perhaps most important, CANF is structured like AIPAC—into separate research, lobbying, and funding organizations. Money is contributed through the Free Cuba political action committee, lobbying is done by the foundation, and CANF itself serves a research and education function. While the leadership of these three entities indicates the interlocking nature of the organization's branches, the distinctions allowed CANF, like AIPAC, to receive government funds and maintain a tax-exempt status. The subsequent relationships formed by CANF with the government and the success of their lobbying efforts suggest that the Cuban group has surpassed the organization on which they modeled themselves.[37]

CANF leaders are particularly sensitive to arguments that they are somehow playing by different rules than other ethnic interest groups. The executive director in the early 1990s, Jacqueline Tillman, says that CANF "play(s) on the playing field as it was constructed."[38] Jose Sorzano, another former executive director, was similarly resentful of the claim made by some that "somehow or another Cuban Americans were playing by ad hoc rules that are different than for everyone else." He noted that during his time with Jeane Kirkpatrick at the United Nations, not a week went by without some American interest group lobbying them about their particular issues. People join organizations and try to influence government policy. That is how the system is supposed to work.[39] As executive director, Francisco "Pepe" Hernandez explained on Adam Smith's Money World: "we are learning from the system. This is exactly what makes the American system so great. And it is that small, very intensely interested groups should go to their government and lobby them and tell them how they feel about it. And after all, we are 1.5 million Americans."[40]

A potential problem with Hernandez's argument is that not all of the 1.5 million Cuban Americans were members, or even supporters, of CANF. And some of those not affiliated with CANF were quite politically active. More militant groups such as Alpha 66 and Omega 7 continued to advocate armed attacks against the island during the Reagan and Bush years.[41] During those two administrations there were also anti-Castro Democrats who did not work with CANF but lobbied their party's congressional members from Florida and New Jersey to increase the economic pressure on Cuba. On the other side, a group of politically active Cubans were labeled as *dialogueros* as a result of their desire to increase communication with Castro. While their numbers were small, their publications—such as *Areito*—and the fact that several held positions as intellectuals in and out of universities allowed them some voice on Cuba policy.[42] Among this variety of active groups, however, CANF held a unique and privileged relationship with the federal government during the 1980s.

Torres argues, "the Republican strategy of fundamentally altering the course of U.S. foreign policy toward Latin America was accompanied by a domestic electoral strategy that included reaching out to Latinos. The Republicans were keenly ideological in their approach to politics and, as such, understood the impact of symbolism. Hence, not only did they accept Cuban exiles as supporters, but they also promoted many of them to key policy positions within the government. Many officials had close links to CANF, such as Jose Sorzano and Otto Reich, for example."[43] From the beginning, then, it would appear that the Reagan administration encouraged and supported the emergence and growth of CANF as a smart political move to help further its policy interests. As Andres Oppenheimer has observed, "Whether CANF was born as an effort by Cuban exiles to influence Washington or vice versa is an open question."[44] What is perhaps most striking about this observation is not that it occurred, but rather that our typical understanding of the rise of such groups does not, perhaps, include such a pattern.

CANF's Policy Activities and Relationships

The political activities of CANF in the 1980s show a continuation of this pattern of cooperation over Cuba policy between the Reagan administration and CANF. The development of Radio/TV Marti, the role of CANF in dispersing some National Endowment for Democracy funds, and the "Operation Exodus" program all hint at wide access to, and perhaps even private control over, some public entities. Furthermore, CANF has been active in policy areas beyond Cuba in ways that exceed standard interest group information gathering and dissemination in the attempt to influence the policy agenda.

Radio and TV Marti

At the same time that discussions over the organization of Cuban exiles into a new organization were taking place, support for new government-sponsored radio broadcasts to the island was developing. A number of public and private efforts to broadcast had been undertaken in the 1960s and 1970s, but by 1980 only scattered clandestine operations were left. The Santa Fe Report called for a "Radio Free Cuba," which would "beam objective information to the Cuban people."[45] That same year the Campaign for a Democratic Majority, chaired by Senators Moynihan (D-NY) and Jackson (D-WA), released a report advocating, "a Radio Free Cuba of the intelligence, imagination, and skill of Radio Free Europe."[46] In June 1981 Thomas O. Enders, Reagan's nominee for assistant secretary of state for inter-American affairs, said that the Reagan administration was planning several new measures to confront Cuba, including a radio project.[47] Within several months of taking office, President Reagan created the Presidential Commission on Broadcasting to Cuba via executive order. Jorge Mas Canosa and another Cuban American were put on the commission that also included notable right-wing philanthropists Joseph Coors and Richard Mellon Scaife. The Reagan team must have known this was a confrontational policy initiative, since the CIA warned as much in August 1981.[48] In September 1981, Richard Allen announced that the administration would ask Congress to fund Radio Marti.[49] (The Reagan administration also appears to have begun broadcasts by a clandestine station, Radio Caiman, run by the CIA and transmitted from Central America from 1985 until 1994.[50])

Again, different interpretations on the respective roles of the Reagan administration and Cuban American leadership in policy development have been made. Mas claims that he had pursued the goal of establishing Radio Marti during the Carter years: "Doing lobbying in Congress, talking to senators and congressman to advocate the establishment of a radio-free Cuba."[51] Kenneth Skoug, a Foreign Service officer at the time, concurred that "Radio Marti had been fathered intellectually by the Cuban American National Foundation."[52] In support of that argument, Constantine Menges writes that during the Reagan campaign Mas came to him with the idea of radio broadcasts and he personally passed on the request for the presidential candidate to endorse the idea.[53] Brenner suggests that at least from the perspective of some in the Cuban government, Radio Marti was a "symbolic reward" to Cuban American supporters of Reagan's presidential campaign.[54] Mas himself, when asked whether the Foundation was the major force behind Radio and TV Marti, answered affirmatively.[55] On this issue, CANF's own Web site takes some credit for Radio

Marti, noting, "In addition to having our own radio station, La Voz de la Fundación, for transmissions to the island, we led the effort to establish the U.S. Information Agency's Radio Martí (1985) and TV Martí (1990), the official U.S. broadcasting operations of uncensored and unbiased news and programming for the Cuban people."[56]

While the notion of collaboration between ideologically compatible private and public sector representatives still fits generally into the academic literature about the influence of interest groups on policy, the post-policy-making role of CANF with Radio Marti and the U.S. Information Agency (USIA) offers a greater challenge to the assumed activity by ethnic interests. In October of 1983, President Reagan signed into law the bill that led to the first broadcast by Radio Marti in May 1985. Interestingly, the State Department wanted to delay the start of broadcasts until it had time to perform more "damage control," but Reagan was swayed by the USIA's director Charles Wick, who argued, at the urging of Mas Canosa, that everything was in place for broadcasts to begin.[57]

The chair of the Advisory Committee for Cuban Broadcasting at the time was Jorge Mas Canosa; Ernesto Betancourt, the first director of Radio Marti, was responsible for day-to-day operations. Betancourt, who resigned in 1990 following a number of conflicts with Mas, suggests that CANF and its leader had tremendous influence over the management of Radio Marti. In a statement to the congressional advisory board well after his resignation, Betancourt argued, "USIA has practically abdicated control of the stations to an exile group. . . . A key foreign policy instrument is being subordinated to political considerations."[58] While generally portraying Mas and CANF in a quite favorable light, Kenneth Skoug offers a similar interpretation of the organization's "great influence on its personnel selection and day-to-day operation."[59] And the director of the USIA, under whose authority Radio Marti falls, concedes, "Mas Canosa has exerted, from time to time, rather inordinate influence."[60] Of course, that influence may be only logical, as foundation president Hernandez suggests above. In a similar vein to the argument cited earlier about the 1.5 million intensely interested Americans, he claims: "Isn't it fair that if we produce or generate 80 percent of the news related to Cuba in this community, we should get 80 percent of the air time?"[61]

Mas held the chairmanship of the Advisory Committee continuously from his original appointment until his death in 1997. Radio Marti's annual budget during those years was in the $12–15 million range, and one critic sees that money as an example of U.S. taxpayer money funding what is "virtually a Cuban exile propaganda organ."[62] The focus of Radio Marti would also be broadened to include Cubans in Angola by May 1987. Mas himself, when he visited Angolan rebel group UNITA leader Jonas Savimbi in 1988, arranged to have UNITA's radio stations play Radio Marti's tapes.[63]

In order to put even more pressure on Castro, Mas proposed the idea of TV Marti in 1988. Despite much difference of opinion in Congress and serious logistical problems, Mas "twisted every political arm he could reach" and got the station funded.[64] Working with the White House and sympathetic Senator Lawton Chiles (D-FL), as well as ultimate bill sponsor Ernest Hollings (D-SC),[65] he was able to secure a ninety-day "trial" appropriation of $7.5 million without committee hearings in Congress.[66] Although the early-morning broadcasts were mostly jammed by Cuba, President Bush pronounced the trial period a success, and the jammed broadcasts continue to the present. By 1990, TV Marti began regular broadcasts under its own yearly budget of another $16 million.

Both the Radio and TV Marti bills were passed over the objections of significant domestic opposition. The National Association of Broadcasters, for example, feared retaliation from Cuba and thus lobbied against the bills. Ethnic interest groups are likely to have more success in "opposition-less" issues, defined as cases where there is agreement over ends but disagreement over means to that end.[67] While there is not usually a strong ethnic group in opposition to CANF, there have been vocal proponents of different strategies to effect political change in Cuba. In the case of Radio and TV Marti, we see general support for the idea of trying to engender political change in Cuba, but disagreement over the use of these information outlets as the appropriate means to that end. At more than $30 million per year, the combined budgets of the two Martis are a significant taxpayer contribution to the dissemination of information to Cuban citizens. While the extent of CANF control over that budget may be subject to some debate, we saw above a number of government officials, including former directors of Radio Marti and of the USIA—who share the Cuban exile's opposition to the Castro government—who are on record suggesting that the group exerted significant influence over the information broadcast by the two stations that the organization helped to create. Furthermore, a 1992 study by the Government Accounting Office also criticized TV Marti for its lack of balance and over promotion of the views of CANF.[68] For our purposes the important point is that there exists among both friends and critics of the ethnic interest group a consensus about CANF influence over wholly government-funded media operations, influence that appears to have been welcomed by the Reagan administration. This kind of relationship appears exceptional given the lack of recognition of such a possibility in the standard interest groups in foreign policy literature.

National Endowment for Democracy

CANF also developed a special relationship with the National Endowment for Democracy (NED). The standard explanation for the origins of the NED is that following a Reagan speech in 1982 introducing the idea of government financial support for democracy movements in other countries, a bipartisan study group was formed that recommended the creation of a National Endowment. That entity was to fund only organizations that did not engage in partisan activities and were expected to work outside the United States. Representative Dante Fascell (D-FL), a member of the study group, introduced the enabling legislation in Congress and then became the first director of the NED board. When one of the first grants issued by the NED went to a CANF-affiliated organization, some raised questions about the organization's links to Fascell and about the Cuban American group's role in bringing the bill through Congress.[69] For example, Peter Stone suggests that one of CANF's first lobbying successes was helping the Reagan administration create the NED.[70] Fonzi writes that Mas got one of his loyal representatives (Fascell) to sponsor the bill creating the NED.[71] Because of congressional restrictions on the use of such money, CANF was forced to create new organizations that could accept grants from the NED, such as the European Coalition for Human Rights in Cuba.

Mas testified during his suit against the *New Republic* that CANF did not receive any NED money. Rather, he claimed that the money "passed through" the foundation and that while serving this supportive function,

CANF did not request and "never kept a penny" for its administrative costs.[72] Most have not accepted Mas's distinction of pass-through grants and have concluded that the Cuban American group effectively captured several hundred thousand dollars in NED funding.[73] There were a number of other private organizations that served as conduits for NED funds, but CANF's role seems exceptional. By one calculation, the endowment gave some $780,000 in grants to Cuban human rights groups linked to the foundation between its 1984 start and 1990.[74] Another source argues that by 1988 CANF had received nearly $400,000 in NED funds and suggests not coincidentally that the National Coalition for a Free Cuba reported that over the same period its members had donated nearly the same amount to political campaigns.[75] When asked about the CANF relationship with the NED, Elliott Abrams noted that, given the friends CANF had in the government, they were probably able to claim an "informal veto" over NED programming directed toward Cuba.[76] Again in this case we see an early CANF role in policy making that over time seems to evolve into effective control over a government entity's dealings with Cuba, control that was welcomed by the administration—a pattern that pushes our standard conception of the role of such groups in foreign policy.

Immigration and Naturalization Service

Another institutional link was forged between CANF and the government during the Reagan years through Operation Exodus, also referred to as the Private Sector Initiative, when for the first time in U.S. history the refugee process was privatized. CANF was given the responsibility of processing the entrance of Cuban exiles from third countries. According to Mas, more than ten thousand exiles entered the United States during the time that CANF ran the program. Mas claims that the program never cost U.S. taxpayers "a penny"; indeed, CANF originally helped some with adjustment expenses.[77] And CANF's Web site maintains, "One of CANF's exodus support programs collected and distributed millions of dollars to reunite more than 10,000 Cuban refugees in third countries with family in the U.S. at no cost to U.S. taxpayers."[78] But in 1991 the organization became eligible to receive $588 of federal funds for each immigrant. And during the same year, the Department of Human Health and Services authorized $1.7 million for two thousand more Cubans under another Cuban Exodus Relief Fund program. As Jane Franklin notes, the refugee arrangement had both financial and membership benefits for CANF.[79] Certainly, Cuban Americans with relatives in third countries whom they hoped to bring to the United States were able to recognize that being on good terms with CANF was in their interest.

Irrespective of the possible monetary benefits, we know of no other private organization that currently has or ever had such an arrangement with the Immigration and Naturalization Service (INS). Such control over refugee resettlement is a remarkable power for a government to cede to a private organization. The standard literature on ethnic interest groups in foreign policy does not account for CANF's power in this arena, where critics say CANF has "created a government-sanctioned immigration and naturalization service of its own."[80]

From the Local to the Global

While CANF is best known for its influence in Washington on U.S.-Cuba policy, the organization and its members were active in Miami and other parts of Florida as well. Mas's personal wealth was partly a product of state and county contracts won by Church and Tower, the company of which he was the CEO. The "former milkman and shoe salesman" became a multimillionaire through projects such as building jails and laying underground cable for Southern Bell.[81] Mas and other Cuban Americans were able to parlay the success of their economic enterprises into greater political influence in South Florida. In the mid-1980s, Cuban Americans won positions as city manager and mayor of Miami, and then in 1990 as superintendent of Dade County schools. Longtime Mayor Xavier Suarez was himself a CANF board member, who actively supported Mas's attack and boycott of the *Miami Herald* after the newspaper's editorial opposition to CANF-supported policy in the early 1990s.[82] Mas is known for taking on not just the Miami media, but also city officials who did not do his bidding. The CANF leader apparently challenged one city commissioner, Joseph Corollo, to a duel after he derailed a real estate deal with Mas's company worth more than $100 million. Although that commissioner suggested water pistols as an attempt to defuse the conflict, Mas ultimately backed a challenger in the next elections who handily defeated Corollo. CANF's widespread local political influence was particularly important given the significance of Florida in the national political picture.

As another example of CANF's activism, Torres argues that in order to influence the development of ideas, CANF created "a fund that would match state spending on Cuban studies at Florida International University (FIU), a state school. After a long battle FIU refused the offer, and the program went to the University of Miami, a private institution. CANF also tried to set the cultural agenda for the Cuban émigré community by actively promoting the denial of visas to any performing artists from the island."[83]

The political and policy activities of CANF have over time also extended to foreign policy issues beyond U.S.-Cuban relations. On the contentious issue of aid to the Contras in Nicaragua, for example, the Cuban American right was a natural ally of the Reagan administration. Mas claimed that his involvement in supporting the Nicaraguan Contras was relatively minimal: "I talked to a few Congressmen and Senators on behalf of military assistance to the contras."[84] That probably understates the role of CANF and Mas in supporting the Reagan administration's policy in Nicaragua. For example, Mas's name appeared in Oliver North's notebooks connected to a request for money.[85] (The record is not entirely clear on whether Mas actually gave any money to the cause.) The *Miami Herald* reports, "The Cuban lobby had been part of the administration's lobbying team for contra aid."[86] In April 1984, CANF sponsored a two-day conference in Miami to encourage congressional support for aid to the anti-Communist forces in Central America.[87] And William Robinson notes the role of CANF, among a number of private groups, as having been part of U.S. "intervention" in the Nicaraguan elections.[88]

Mas and CANF were even more aggressive on the question of Angola, where Cuban troops had joined the battle against Jonas Savimbi and UNITA. By one account, Mas told a story of vacationing in Key West in 1984. When he thought about the forty thousand Cuban troops that had been sent to Angola, Mas came up with the idea to repeal the Clark

Amendment,[89] which specifically prohibited the U.S. government from funding the insurgency in Angola. Congressional allies of CANF, such as Representative Claude Pepper (D-FL), helped to push the repeal through Congress. Peter Rodman argues that Pepper "became an ardent advocate of repeal" of the amendment once he learned that Castro's troops were there. Pepper's district was composed of about 40 percent Cuban Americans (and his seat, once empty, would be won by a Cuban American, Ileana Ros-Lehtinen). [90] There is general agreement the Reagan administration was relatively passive during this process: "The essence of the matter is that the [Reagan administration] did not actively seek repeal of [the Clark Amendment], while the U.S. Congress, which had lately specialized in denying presidents flexibility in overseas interventions, repealed it anyway."[91] Some time after the Reagan administration had authorized aid for Savimbi, CANF sponsored a visit to the U.S. by the Angolan rebel leader.

On the other hand, the 1990 visit to Miami by South African Nelson Mandela met with protest from Cuban Americans angered by his link to Castro.[92] More evidence of the global reach of CANF is that the 1989 visit by Boris Yeltsin to Miami was paid for largely by CANF.[93] Mas then visited Moscow with U.S. Secretary of State James A. Baker in September 1991; soon after, CANF opened an office in Moscow.[94]Again, this activity suggests a more complex relationship among CANF, Congress, and the executive than that which is normally attributed to ethnic interest groups. CANF focused its efforts on issues pertaining to Cuba, if indirectly, and in many ways (e.g., the repeal of the Clark Amendment) was active in setting the policy agenda.

Assessing CANF in the 1980s

The case of the Cuban American National Foundation presents a complicated pattern of political activities that the standard interest group literature is hard pressed to explain. The emergence of CANF has various explanations, in particular the emphasis on policy entrepreneurs and the importance of group leadership.[95] Jorge Mas Canosa, by all accounts, was an exceptional figure in his ability to organize, lead, fundraise, and lobby.

Still, the story seems more complicated than that. CANF was formed on the basis of ideas and interests shared by group leaders and government actors—a symbiotic relationship.[96] But even this formulation may fail to account for the way that CANF's growth and activities were not only welcomed but also sponsored by the executive.

One thing is certain: CANF tried to emulate and even perfect the model established by AIPAC. "Like AIPAC, CANF set up separate research, lobbying, and PAC divisions. Like AIPAC, CANF has a clear agenda and pursues it aggressively. And like AIPAC, CANF is known for playing hard-ball politics."[97] The CANF case seems to confirm the suggestion that a unified organization, money, lobbying skill, and a cohesive constituency that votes in a bloc are key to the success of an ethnic interest group.[98] CANF is characterized by each of these features. It has also been proposed that the ability to appeal to American symbols is an important part of an ethnic interest group's resource base.[99] CANF enjoys this advantage as well; who can be against "freedom"? The notion that an ethnic interest group is more likely to be influential when it shares the policy preferences of the president is certainly part of the story of CANF, especially in the 1980s.[100] Here CANF seems to prove the point that "the closer an organization was to the foreign policy objectives of the United States, the more resources it would have."[101]

The argument that ethnic groups need to assimilate into the United States but retain an identification with the homeland—true of many diasporas—would seem to cut both ways with respect to Cuban Americans and CANF. In one sense, Cuban Americans have very much assimilated into the United States—the very heart of the "Cuban success story."[102] Jorge Mas Canosa was not alone among Cubans who came to the United States with little and who have prospered here. But in another sense Cuban Americans in the 1980s had not assimilated into the United States as other such groups. Many see themselves as "exiles" rather than "immigrants" and retain a hope of returning to their homeland when Castro (under whatever circumstances) leaves. The community largely lives and does business in Spanish, which has brought it into some conflict with others, in Miami in particular. For example, Mas himself said, "I have never assimilated. I never intended to. I am a Cuban first. I live here only as an extension of

Cuba. I live a Cuban life here. My friends, my social activities, they are all Cuban." Mas also noted that he spoke only Spanish in his "Cuban house."[103]

Another proposition that appears problematic here is the suggestion that an ethnic interest group will be more successful when its preference is widely shared or when its opposition is weak and divided. In some sense, we see this in the CANF case. Even though there is opposition in the public and Congress to CANF's policy preferences toward Cuba, and there is division in the Cuban American community over the issue as well, in the 1980s, at least, CANF seemed to have the playing field largely to itself in terms of organized interest group activism. Elliott Abrams recalls from his experience in the Reagan administration that CANF was "light years" ahead of other groups in terms of money, electoral placement, and lobbying skills.[104]

Yet, the CANF case seems more complicated than that. From its founding CANF played a role in the larger campaign by the Reagan administration to portray Central America and the Caribbean in a different way than Congress and a majority of the public viewed the region. CANF's success, even while having a political stance at variance with the general public, seems to stand in opposition to the view that issue salience and compatibility with the public are key factors in predicting interest group influence.[105] A key to understanding CANF's success, then, from its founding and range of activities including Radio and TV Marti, is recognizing the way CANF was working in concert with the Reagan administration to pursue common aims. The CANF case is an example of how the State can encourage the birth and growth of an ethnic interest group and incorporate it into the formal foreign policy apparatus.[106] This flow of influence— the influence of the executive on CANF—is in some ways more striking and probably more important than the flow that is observed by the standard view that tries to track the influence of a group on a policy. Torres argues, "the political possibilities available to CANF are a product of its relationship to individuals and policies in the federal government" and that the origins of CANF's power are related to its link to the state.[107] In each of the policy areas examined here the political success of CANF was derived in part from the way it was empowered by the Reagan administration and was a product of "shared initiative."

A Unique and Symbiotic Relationship

The case of the Cuban American National Foundation during the 1980s provides a valuable lens with which to view our conceptions of ethnic interest group activity in U.S. foreign policy. Much of what we see in this case challenges our standard view of the types of relationships ethnic interest groups built with government during the cold war. The birth of CANF itself would seem extraordinary. While there are a variety of schools of thought about interest group formation, we are unaware of any that posit the kinds of close links that this case exhibits between the executive and the would-be group at its origin. AIPAC, for example, was founded in no small part to lobby the legislative branch for aid to Israel, similar to CANF's formation in part to lobby Congress on Cuba policy. However, unlike AIPAC, the idea for which emerged out of the American Jewish community, the impetus for CANF seems to have emerged as much from the new Reagan team as it did from the Cuban American community.

Once formed, CANF's activities are perhaps most notable for the pattern of power sharing with the executive that they exhibit. CANF seems to have not only lobbied for Radio and TV Marti, but appears to have largely run the show at both outlets in the 1980s. CANF enjoyed an early and tight relationship with the NED, perhaps earning an informal veto over its programs directed at Cuba. CANF appears to have developed a unique relationship with the INS in handling immigration from Cuba. The organization seems to have set the agenda to repeal the Clark Amendment as a way to combat Cuba in Angola when neither Congress nor the Reagan administration had taken up the issue and was involved in helping define the debate about the Contras. What is perhaps most striking about this record is not the list of targets and successes but the web of relationships that was built among CANF and several government agencies and the executive—a web that seems to stretch our conventional understanding of what was possible for ethnic interest groups in the cold war.

In a reflection on the politics of Cuba policy and the strategies and activities of CANF, Richard Allen notes, "you won't find this in the textbooks." He argues that with CANF and Cuba policy we see a necessary merging of politics and policy: that when the Reagan administration sought support for its policies, it needed a well-organized group like CANF to pressure the Democrat-controlled Congress and the public.[108] The record discussed above, and Allen's recollections, suggest that a more complex understanding of the role of ethnic interest groups in U.S. foreign policy is required than we normally acknowledge. Studies often are framed in terms of whether interest groups win, rather than trying to understand how they work to build relationships with the government and how they may be supported by the state in pursuit of common goals.

The 1980s saw the emergence of CANF as a key actor in U.S.-Cuba policy and as one of the most influential groups of its kind in Washington. While its "success" may be unsurprising given its resources, organizational characteristics, and the compatibility of its views with the executive, the distinctiveness of this case is in the collaborative relationship between state and societal actors during the Reagan presidency. We argue that the key to understanding CANF's power in the 1980s is recognizing the mutual relationships and power sharing it enjoyed with the government and the way the executive welcomed this. There is not necessarily anything sinister about this; it would seem to be not only legal but also politically expedient for all sides. But it does stretch our common understandings of the roles and relations of ethnic interest groups in foreign policy making. The story of CANF in the 1980s is at least as much about the Reagan administration's attempt to "privatize" foreign policy and build and support societal groups to help promote its policies, as it is about CANF. This pattern of power sharing is made more striking because of the way the standard ethnic interest group literature has largely missed it.

If one of the goals of the Reagan administration was to help develop a Cuban American interest group that would help lobby the Hill for tougher foreign policies toward Cuba in particular, and Latin America in general, they were certainly successful. The Reagan-CANF partnership helped shift U.S. foreign policy toward the island, and the region, to the Right, and control of that policy to the White House. But this would end up to be a short-term win for President Reagan, and perhaps a longer-term loss for the presidency, in terms of being able to exercise control over Cuba policy. CANF was able to "build and use resources in ways that gave them independence from the U.S. government."[109] Such independence was fine as long as CANF and the president agreed on policy initiatives, but the harmony of interests that existed in the 1980s would prove more elusive as the cold war came to an end. And CANF's rise also served to motivate other groups, with views on Cuba policy across the political spectrum, and to move Congress, to also try to seize the initiative on Cuba policy. Independent and entrepreneurial Cuban Americans would be elected to Congress in 1989 and 1992, further complicating matters. The patterns set in motion in the 1980s, patterns meant to heighten executive control over foreign policy, would begin to shift policy power toward CANF and Congress in the Bush administration.

The Reagan Administration, Cuba, and the Cold War

MOST ANALYSES OF the Reagan administration's foreign policy toward Latin America are dominated by discussions of the Central American cases, particularly Nicaragua and El Salvador.[1] We argue that the Cuba case, however, was central to the debate about U.S. policy in the region during the 1980s. CANF worked together with the Reagan administration to pursue their common cold war agendas. The Reagan administration and CANF agreed that leftist governments in Central America and the Caribbean needed to be confronted vigorously, both those that already existed, as in Cuba and Nicaragua, and those that might come to power, as in El Salvador. In order to pursue this end, it was important to strongly challenge Castro and the Cuban Revolution as an essential part of justifying intervention in other countries in the region. The Reagan administration needed Cuba in order to make the "Moscow to Havana to Managua" link that would validate the aid to the Contras fighting the Sandinistas in Nicaragua, the invasion of Grenada, and even support for the Salvadoran government. Cracking down on communism in Cuba, and attacking leftist governments or movements elsewhere in the hemisphere, were intertwined in the Reagan administration's policy of bringing the cold war to the region in a more assertive way. It followed logically, then, that the Reagan administration would craft a hard-line approach to relations with both Cuba and governments or movements sympathetic to the Castro government.

We see the Reagan administration as a key point in the development of the politics of policy toward Cuba. We take this view not just because the Reagan team changed the substantive nature of U.S.-Latin American relations, but even more important because it was during this period that the foreign policy-making process that created Cuba policy appeared to change quite dramatically. We have discussed the blurring of the distinction between the private and the public in the case of CANF. While the Cuban American interest group may be the best example of the privatization of foreign policy, it is certainly not the only one. Other groups developed new alliances with the government through such programs as the National Endowment for Democracy (NED). Think tanks grew rapidly in number and influence during the 1980s, particularly those sympathetic to President Reagan on the political right. Opponents of Reagan's foreign policies also mobilized around issues ranging from nuclear weapons to aid for the Contras. Congress became increasingly more engaged in foreign policy as well. In the end, however, an executive branch willing to use innovative means was able to successfully drive the foreign policy agenda during nearly all of Reagan's two terms. In the example of Cuba, as well as in the U.S. approach to cases the Reagan administration linked to Moscow through Havana, we can see evidence of the hard-line substance of the president's policies, and changes in the foreign policy-making process, during the 1980s. It was in this era that the White House would begin to craft Cuba policy on new grounding, a foundation that we will see later has ironically assured the long-term loss of executive control over the embargo and perhaps even the weakening of the embargo itself.

Reagan's Hard-Line Approach

During the 1980 presidential campaign, Ronald Reagan was critical of the foreign policy approach of President Carter in Latin America and elsewhere. According to Reagan and other right-wing critics, Carter's failure to recognize and defend U.S. interests in Latin America helped produce the return of the Panama Canal, the "loss" of Nicaragua to the Sandinistas, and the strength of the Salvadoran revolutionaries. Support for a new hard line in Central America was articulated by the Committee of Santa Fe, whose 1980 report, *A New Inter-American Policy for the Eighties,* faulted Carter for ignoring the Soviet threat in the Western Hemisphere. This view put Cuba at the center of U.S. problems in the region. The report advocated steps toward Cuba that were "frankly punitive": Cuban diplomats must leave Washington; aerial reconnaissance must be resumed; tourist dollars must be shut off; and the 1977 fishing agreement should be reassessed. Arguing that Cuba must be held liable for its policies of aggression in the Americas, the report suggests that the U.S. government establish a Radio Free Cuba as part of a campaign to provide "objective information" to the Cuban people. Finally, the report urged, "If propaganda fails, a war of national liberation against Castro must be launched."[2] Another influential voice on the right was that of Jeane Kirkpatrick, Reagan's future UN ambassador, who authored the 1979 *Commentary* article that drew the distinction between authoritarian and totalitarian regimes, such as Castro's Cuba and later Sandinista Nicaragua.

The influence of the Committee of Santa Fe and Kirkpatrick, a senior fellow at the American Enterprise Institute at the time, reflect the growing role played by nongovernmental think tanks and others private sector actors in the policy-making process. As a private citizen, however, Reagan had made known his own views on the threat posed by Cuba well before the Committee of Santa Fe formally began its discussions. In a series of radio addresses he made during the second half of the 1970s, he criticized Cuba for having produced "tens of thousands of political prisoners" and for the meager food rations available to much of the population. U.S. politicians who sought to normalize relations with the island, such as Senators James Abourezk (D-SD), Frank Church (D-ID), and George McGovern (D-SD), were attacked for their naïveté about the situation on the island.[3] By the time of the 1980 presidential election campaign, candidate Reagan was making arguments very similar to those put forth by the Committee of Santa Fe and Kirkpatrick. In a radio interview, for example, he argued that "The troubles in Nicaragua bear a Cuban label . . . there is no question but that most of the rebels are Cuban-trained, Cuban-armed, and dedicated to creating another communist country in this hemisphere."[4]

Cuba played a central role, then, in the Reagan administration's effort to construct in the mind of the public a particular type of crisis in Central America, and Cuban Americans with similar views were among the administration's most effective and loyal allies. Reagan's views on the threat posed to U.S. interests by Cuba and Central America were not as widely held, however, among the rest of the general public. If the Reagan administration were to move aggressively in Central America once he took office, some effort to counter public suspicion would be necessary. In order to roll back communism, an ideological counteroffensive within the United States was necessary as well. That effort would entail both innovative public relations efforts by government officials and interesting alliances by the Reagan administration with groups and individuals operating in the private sector.

During the 1980s, the issue of U.S. policy toward Cuba was not as contentious among the general public or in Congress as was the issue of U.S. relations with Nicaragua and El Salvador. For the purposes of the Reagan administration, however, Cuba needed to represent a threat to U.S. interests both in terms of the repressive conditions on the island and the support that nation provided for revolutions on the left in Central America, the Caribbean, and Africa. Public justification of the Grenada intervention, aid and support for the Salvadoran government (and military), and the need to finance the Contra force in Nicaragua all rested in part on the essential goal of not allowing "another Cuba." The public rationalizations also proposed and assumed the essential role of Cuba in supporting the organization of the left in each of those countries.

Selling Congress and the general public on the Cuba threat to the hemisphere was a priority from the beginning of President Reagan's first term in office. An ambitious research paper was presented to the Subcommittee on Western Hemisphere Affairs of the Senate Foreign Relations Committee by the Department of State in December 1981 laying out Cuba's "support for violence in Latin America." Within the report, there were separate discussions of five Central American, four Caribbean, and four South American countries. As is pointed out in the preface, though, "Cuba is most active in Central America, where its immediate goals are to exploit and control the revolution in Nicaragua and to induce the overthrow of the Governments of El Salvador and Guatemala."[5]

The problem that the Reagan administration confronted with respect to implementing a more aggressive policy in Latin America was that both the general public and Congress had been, to some extent, influenced by romanticized images of Nicaragua, El Salvador, and even Cuba, produced by what the new administration saw as naive Carter administration officials and the so-called liberal media. As the Committee of Santa Fe argued in its report, "Coverage of Latin American political reality by the U.S. media is both inadequate and displays a substantial bias favoring proponents of radical socio-economic transformation of the less developed countries along collectivist lines." The committee recommended, "U.S. policy formulation must insulate itself from propaganda appearing in the general and specialized media which is inspired by forces explicitly hostile to the United States."[6] Several authors of the report later joined the Reagan White House, including Roger Fontaine as the Latin American specialist on the National Security Council staff, Lt. General Gordon Sumner as the Assistant Secretary of State for Inter-American Affairs, and Lewis Tambs as ambassador to Colombia and later Costa Rica. Among the most important changes in the nature of foreign policy making during the Reagan administration were those explicitly related to this private committee's recommendation that the U.S. government must counter the private media's "propaganda."

To set the context for their more aggressive policies in Central America and the Caribbean, in the first month that they were in office, the Reagan team's strategy was to combine public statements about the Soviet threat with leaked stories to the media about the Soviet-Cuban role in the region. The *New York Times* ran stories in February about the Soviet-El Salvador arms pipeline, based on administration leaks to set the stage for the release later that month of the Reagan White Paper, *Communist Interference in El Salvador*. Along with the report, several documents (in Spanish) were released to support the document's conclusions. Mark Hertsgaard argues that the release was a "fantastic public relations coup for the State Department as reporters in effect reduced themselves to human transmission belts, disseminating propaganda that would later be revealed to be false."[7] Jimmy Carter's press secretary, Hodding Carter, went even further: "The White Paper was swallowed whole and regurgitated in a fashion not equaled since the Johnson Administration's White Paper on

Vietnam 15 years ago."[8] The immediate reaction of the press suggests they had not learned their lesson, contrary to what might be expected, from the mainstream media's uncritical acceptance of the similarly named papers offered by President Johnson to justify a policy that had already been enacted. Soon after, challenges to both the documents and the paper's conclusions were being offered by critical press on the left; by June, even the *Wall Street Journal* had criticized the paper's accuracy and challenged the authenticity of the documents on which the report was based.[9] But by the time the credibility of the White Paper had been successfully attacked, the document had served the purpose of reinforcing the idea that the Soviets and Cubans had successfully infiltrated Central America. Even as the Reagan administration was waging this successful ideological counteroffensive against what it saw as a biased media, the president was secretly signing the authorization of covert operations in Central America. By the time that Ronald Reagan publicly acted at the beginning of April to permanently cut off the economic aid to Nicaragua that had been suspended by Carter at the end of his own term, both the battles for U.S. public opinion and aid for Nicaraguan rebels had been engaged by the executive branch.

These actions emanating from the chief executive reflect the advantage that the president has in setting the context for both the debate in Congress and coverage by the media. Potential congressional opponents were forced into a reactive mode, even though the public as a whole was quite wary of the president's approach to Central America.[10] Direct policy relations with Cuba received relatively little congressional or media attention at the beginning of the Reagan presidency. Within a few weeks of Reagan's taking office, the U.S. government did expel a diplomat at the Cuban Interests section, accusing him of encouraging businesses to trade with the island.[11] The Senate voted 84-0 later in the year to prohibit the use of any U.S. government funds to promote trade with Cuba. That unanimous support for the current embargo policy was only slightly qualified by a resolution requesting that the president "consider the full range of economic and diplomatic options" in his dealings with all of the nations of the Caribbean.[12]

Although there is evidence that some members of the Reagan administration were advocates of more aggressive action toward Cuba during the first year of his presidency, particularly Secretary of State Alexander Haig, the executive branch largely used Cuba as justification for its aggressive policies in Central America. Even with the use of Cuba, public audiences around the country still did not receive government officials' defenses of the new policy favorably. William LeoGrande points out that the hostile receptions prompted the State Department's Foreign Service Institute to begin classes teaching their spokespeople how to defend the president's Central American policy in public.[13] To facilitate that public relations campaign, both the State Department and National Security Council ratcheted up the attack on Cuba at the end of 1981. The State Department issued a report in November on Cuban subversion in the region that included the position that Grenada had been turned into "a virtual client" of Havana.[14] In the NSC, Reagan signed National Security Decision Directive 17, authorizing a $20 million plan to organize Nicaraguan rebels to fight against "the Cuban presence and Cuban-Sandinista support structure in Nicaragua and elsewhere in Central America" that same month.[15] At the same November NSC meeting, the need for a "public diplomacy" program focused on Latin America was discussed.[16] Both the U.S. government support for the Salvadoran government and the rebels in Nicaragua continued to generate significant opposition among the U.S. public at the time. The Reagan administration continued to blame a media and population that did not see Central America and the Caribbean from a cold war perspective in which governments and movements were either with the United States or with the enemy—the Soviet Union and Cuba.

Public Diplomacy

The momentum for a public diplomacy program that would counter the perceived media softness toward the communist threat in Central America and the Caribbean grew by the second year of the Reagan presidency. In April 1982, a top secret NSC document outlined new policy recommendations for Central America and Cuba. Here, the NSC began to advocate a "concerted public information effort," because "We continue to have serious difficulties with U.S. public and Congressional opinion, which jeopardizes our ability to stay the course."[17] Two months later, President Reagan gave a speech to Parliament in Great Britain, in which he proposed a new emphasis on the global promotion of democratic institutions as a central U.S. foreign policy strategy. This public introduction of the new effort was followed less than a week later by the circulation within the Reagan administration of a document entitled "Project Democracy: Proposals for Action." Robert Parry has pointed out that the proposal called for the incorporation of nongovernmental organizations into the promotion of foreign policy; these vehicles include Freedom House, the Trilateral Commission, the Twentieth Century Fund, wealthy individuals, and defense contractors.[18] The selling of foreign policy to the public by the Reagan administration was gradually becoming more sophisticated. The development of CANF was an important step in the promotion of the Reagan agenda, but the task of shifting the foreign policy debate about the Americas would require opening a number of different fronts. Private groups and public sector figures were able to affect the debate about U.S. foreign policy in the region. As William Robinson points out, even before the formalization of public diplomacy, the National Endowment of Democracy, and other coordinated attempts to gain support for Reagan's policies in the region, the administration had registered the important success of moving "the entire spectrum of 'acceptable' U.S. policies to the right."[19] The sorts of right-wing arguments made by the Committee of Santa Fe and Jeane Kirkpatrick during the Carter presidency were now close to becoming the centrist assumptions at the root of the Central American policy debate.

Top officials took a number of opportunities to attack Cuba and its influence in Central America during the Reagan administration's first couple of years in office. Vice President Bush gave a talk before the Council of the Americas in June 1981, in which he argued: "Cuba brings to the hemisphere the ideology of the Soviet Union with a commitment to spread totalitarianism in its own image and to extend Soviet-Cuban influence." At the same meeting, Assistant Secretary of State for Inter-American Affairs Thomas O. Enders (perceived to be a moderate voice within the Reagan team) described Nicaragua as Cuba's "forward base of operations."[20] Given the strong rhetoric coming from people like Bush, Haig, and even Enders, as well as aggressive U.S. naval maneuvers in the Caribbean in both 1981 and 1982, the relatively mild tightening of the embargo policy during those years did not receive much attention. In September 1981, the president signed an executive order creating the Presidential Commission on Broadcasting to Cuba. The Commission's work would bear fruition some four years later with the launching of Radio Marti. The Reagan administration also threatened to enforce the embargo more strictly by confiscating imported goods containing Cuban nickel; and in 1982, the travel ban was reinstated by means of prohibiting the spending of dollars in Cuba by all U.S. citizens except academics, journalists, and exiles visiting their families.[21] In effect, that tightening of the restrictions in travel was a reinstitution of the policy that had been in effect from 1963 until Carter's 1977 easing of the ban. Reagan also allowed the fishing agreement with Cuba signed during his predecessor's term to lapse around the same time. These changes caused such little stir partly because the likely opponents of the embargo were focused on what seemed to be the main event in Central America.

The president signed National Security Decision Directive 77 on January 14, 1983, formalizing the development of this new public diplomacy activity to be undertaken within the National Security Council. Walter Raymond, a veteran of CIA covert action, left his position in the intelligence agency to manage the new diplomacy effort targeting both domestic and international publics. A classified strategy paper produced by the Central American Public Diplomacy Task Force in May 1983 pointed out that an "apathetic," if not "hostile" U.S. public, "serious opposition in Congress," and unfriendly press coverage, combined to create problems for foreign policy makers.[22] What was necessary was a coordinated effort to change the public perceptions held of governments and rebels in Nicaragua and El Salvador to better reflect the Reagan administration's view of Central America's pivotal role in the cold war. The Salvadoran situation was initially the more pressing for the Reagan administration's domestic propaganda operation. As the paper argued, "Our public diplomacy effort must be directed to: obtaining congressional support for economic and security assistance [in El Salvador and] to foster a climate of editorial and public opinion that will encourage congressional support of administration policy."[23]

The State Department Office of Public Diplomacy for Latin American and the Caribbean (S/LPD) emerged from the task force managed by

Raymond. The first head of that Office of Public Diplomacy was Otto Reich, a Cuban-born bureaucrat with experience at the Agency for International Development (AID) and the School of the Americas.[24] Under Reich, the Public Diplomacy Office pursued a variety of overt and covert strategies aimed at shaping the debate over Reagan's Central American policy. As a Cuban American, Reich helped to make the symbolic link between his country of birth and the need for the United States to play a role in Nicaragua and El Salvador. Arranging talks and lectures by State Department officials or producing published documents explaining developments in Central America from the U.S. government's perspective for circulation to domestic and foreign audiences were representative of the straightforward and overt aspect of the office's work. During its first year of operation, S/LPD booked more than 1,500 different speaking engagements, distributed materials to some 1,600 college libraries, and sent information to 520 political science faculties, as well as more than one hundred editorial writers and a comparable number of religious organizations. Television personalities on such shows as *The McLaughlin Group* and *This Week with David Brinkley* were given "special attention."

When reporting that ran contrary to the administration's view of events in Central America and the Caribbean did appear in the mainstream media, Reich and others in his office responded aggressively. A memo from Secretary of State George Shultz to the president described how Reich had spent a total of three hours with a CBS correspondent and the network's Washington Bureau Chief. In it, Shultz notes that Reich had seen a CBS documentary that "was unbalanced and conveyed a deceptive image favorable to the guerrillas and distorting of U.S. and El Salvadoran Government goals and tactics in the conflict." Everyone at CBS was reported to be "very cordial and cooperative with Ambassador Reich." According to the secretary of state, this example "has been repeated dozens of times over the past few months."[25] Another case that has frequently been noted was Reich's attempt to convince National Public Radio (NPR) to correct its "bias" against U.S. policy in Central America. He suggested to editors at NPR that he would have all of NPR's programs monitored.[26] As was noted in the Iran-Contra report, Reich's goal was to make sure that the media and others realized that "attacking the President was no longer cost free."[27] It certainly appears that in the view of Reich, the choices in Central America were very straightforward. You were with the president, the Contras, and the Salvadoran government, or you were with the Sandinistas, the FMLN in El Salvador, and their Soviet and Cuban sponsors. Any media criticism of the former or support for the latter put them on the wrong side.

Bringing in Private Supporters

While the aggressive attempts by the Reagan administration and its public diplomacy program to shape media coverage as a means of gaining public and congressional support for its policies went beyond the efforts by any previous administration, it was the relationships developed during the process, with private organizations, that may have been most innovative. As we suggested earlier, an increasing number of private organizations on the political right were growing in terms of resources and importance during the 1980s. The emphasis for analysts of foreign policy making is usually on CANF, which was becoming probably the second most influential ethnic interest group after the Jewish-American lobby during the 1980s. But other private organizations, whose birth and emergence on to the political scene were less directed by the government, began to take on a new role in the policy-making process as well. Citizens for America (CFA) was a pro-Contra lobbying group that also had special access to the Reagan White House. Reich was asked during his deposition for the Senate Select Committee on Iran-Contra about an NSC memo that listed nine names: two from NSC (Oliver North and Walter Raymond), two from State (Otto Reich and Jonathan Miller), one from the Department of Defense (Nestor Sanchez), two from International Business Communications[28] (Frank Gomez and Rich Miller), and two from CFA (Jeff Bell and Jack Abramson).[29] While Reich claimed to be unclear as to the memo in question, it certainly implied a sort of public-private coordination that had been relatively rare before the Reagan years. The Office of Public Diplomacy, shut down based on its "use of federal funds for publicity or propaganda uses not authorized by Congress,"[30] was the only governmental entity to be entirely closed in the aftermath of Iran-Contra. State Department officials suggested that they would be reorganizing the office, by distributing functions and officials to other areas of the department.[31] Robert Kagan, the S/LPD director who succeeded Otto Reich, remained a senior adviser to Elliott Abrams. The impact of public diplomacy practices on foreign policy making would be much more long lasting than the office itself. Since Iran-Contra, private groups may not have raised significant amounts of money for arming combatants that one branch of the U.S. government could not convince another were worthy of military assistance. But they have certainly continued to try to manipulate the media, lobby the legislature, and defeat members of Congress whose policy positions deviate from their own.

When President Reagan signed NSDD 77, he authorized a "quasi-governmental institute" that would be formally incorporated as the NED by congressional act in November 1983. Consistent with the recommendation offered by the Committee of Santa Fe report, Congress directed the NED to pass on funds to groups in the private sector, rather than spending any money directly. According to the original proposal put before Congress, money was to be funneled primarily through four institutes: the Republican Party's National Republican Institute for International Affairs; the Democratic Party's National Democratic Institute for International Affairs; the AFL-CIO's Free Trade Union Institute (FTI); and the Chamber of Commerce's Center for International Private Enterprise (CIPE). As with the Office of Public Diplomacy, the NED was defended as an opening up of policy-making activities to the general public. While the legal status of the NED is that of nongovernmental, in practice Congress wholly funds it and all grants are approved by the State Department.[32]

Opposition to the NED was offered by those opposing both the private sector conduits for the taxpayer funds and the activities that some of those private groups pursued. In particular, the party institutes were seen as potential conflicts of interest, and a contribution to a specific candidate in a Panamanian election was thought to be inappropriate. Over the years, the opponents of the NED were able to reduce the budget of the agency. Endowment advocates, however, offered unqualified praise. Board member Orrin Hatch (R-UT) defended its budget during one of the yearly debates: "We are talking abut $18 million being used to spread democratic principles around the world to offset the $3 to $4 billion expenditure being used by the Soviets to work against democracy all over the world. . . . The National Endowment for Democracy is making a tremendous impact for the forces of freedom worldwide."[33] At the end of Reagan's second term, George Will described the NED as "one of this decade's good deeds" and then went on to link spending by the Endowment to the record high percentage of the world's population living in countries classified as free by Freedom House.[34]

CANF played an important role in deciding on the grants made to "promote democracy" in Cuba. In the case of the Cuban Americans and other private organization activities, the public sector was able to influence outcomes while maintaining some ambiguity about the government's control over the use of money to influence political outcomes in foreign countries. In the process, certain like-minded groups in the private sector were promoted by the Reagan administration. Those organizations' ability to act domestically was clearly enhanced by the privileged relationship with and resources provided by the federal government. In addition to that somewhat indirect effect on the domestic political arena, the NED also funded the academic publication, *Journal of Democracy*. Although academic journals do not play a central role in the Washington foreign policy debate, the government-funded journal commissions articles that promote a certain representation of democracy and in some small way influences the academic debates on democratization in Latin America and elsewhere. While the relationship to the NED is clearly noted in the journal, the public-private interaction is consistent with the argument that the Reagan presidency marked an innovative blurring of that distinction.

The Iran-Contra investigation produced evidence of government relationships with private groups during the Reagan years that were clearly illegal; a number of officials in the executive branch coordinated activities that had been expressly prohibited by congressional legislation. For our purposes, however, it is those relationships that did not rise to the level of illegality that are an even more important legacy of the Reagan presidency. The symbiotic relationship between CANF and the executive branch appears to have been perfectly legal. Both the ethnic interest group and the Reagan administration benefited from the interaction between the two. Other groups on the political right-wing developed special relationships with the government during the Reagan years as well. Membership in and donations to a private organization whose agenda was compatible with the president led to audiences with members of the administration up to and including the president. Armed with information and encouragement from those meetings, "Right-wing groups used a full array of lobbying tools and public relations methods, seeking to influence public opinion with advertising, appearances on television and radio talk shows, and op-ed articles. Right-wing groups also targeted selected members of Congress, flooding offices with petitions and postcards." Amy Fried suggests that for "tactical reasons," these groups frequently advocated actions more extreme than the president's own public positions. Referring to the debate over policy toward Nicaragua, she writes: "Group leaders were aware that taking a hard-line position made Reagan's views look like a moderate and reasonable compromise and so could help the administration obtain funds for the contras."[35] In the case of Cuba during this time, there are certainly hard-liners in South Florida whose advocacy of invading the island would make Reagan's approach to the island seem almost prudent. To the extent that the executive branch coordinated private groups' activities but took care to keep its role secret, both Congress and the public were put at a disadvantage in the foreign policy-making debate. Once mobilized and supported, of course, those same private organizations would potentially develop into more independent actors who might challenge rather than support a future president.

Not all of the efforts by the Reagan administration to shape public perceptions about Latin America and policies toward the region were so covert or even novel. Reagan's speeches, effectively making use of the traditional bully pulpit advantages held by the president, played a role in framing the struggle in Central America and the Caribbean as one between the "evil empire" (and its Cuban or Nicaraguan proxies) and "freedom fighters" such as the Contras, CANF, and the anticommunist Salvadoran government. The president's vision was clear, and the Soviet-Cuban link was at the center of his argument. He warned, "If we do not act promptly and decisively in defense of freedom, new Cubas will arise from the ruins of today's conflicts. We will face more totalitarian regimes, tied militarily to the Soviet Union; more regimes exporting subversion."[36] A March 1983 address to the nation is also representative of the public use of strong rhetoric supplemented by aerial photographs supporting the administration's perception of a security threat in the region. The four photos the president showed were labeled "Soviet Communications Intelligence Facility" in Lourdes, Cuba; "Soviet MIGs" in western Cuba; "Soviet Weaponry" at Sandino Airfield, Nicaragua; and "Airfield under Construction" at Point Salines, Grenada. In his speech, he maintained: "The Soviet-Cuban militarization of Grenada, in short, can only be seen as power projection into the region. And it is in this important economic and strategic area that we're trying to help the Governments of El Salvador, Costa Rica, Honduras, and others in their struggles for democracy against guerrillas supported through Cuba and Nicaragua."[37] The invasion of Grenada and removal of the center-left government seven months later provided such "public relations dividends" to the Reagan presidency that it was described as a "propaganda windfall."[38]

Gradual Deterioration of U.S.-Cuban Relations

In 1983 and 1984, Cuba still seemed to be more important to the Reagan administration as a justification for its policies in Grenada, Nicaragua, and El Salvador than as a direct issue for policy making. While a government official such as Elliott Abrams would complain that the media was not portraying the Cuban president as "one of the most vicious tyrants of our time," there did not appear to be any inclination on the part of the Reagan team to focus too much attention on new policy toward the island. Salvadoran President Duarte provided a taped message for *Face the Nation* in which he suggested that he would not be appearing live because "some kind of death squad organized in Cuba has just arrived to make a suicide attempt to kill me."[39] The Cuban connection he mentioned certainly added weight to the Reagan administration's attempt to frame the struggles in Central America as ultimately rooted in the Soviet-Cuban connection. Congress did approve Radio Marti in 1983, and President Reagan added his signature in October. The election year of 1984 included the help of Hollywood in Reagan's public diplomacy effort. *Red Dawn* was based on a scenario in which Cuban, Soviet, and Nicaraguan troops had invaded the southwestern United States and had to be fought off by a small group of U.S. teenage "freedom fighters."[40] A month after the election, an immigration agreement with Cuba was reached. Cuba would accept 2,764 Marielitos and the United States would take 3,000 political prisoners and up to 20,000 immigrants per year from the island.[41] When Radio Marti began broadcasting in May 1985, Castro responded by rescinding support for the immigration agreement. President Reagan responded with a decree that for all practical purposes barred any Cuban from entering the United States.[42]

Other developments in the first year of Reagan's second term suggested at least the possibility of new debate around the Cuba policy. Fidel Castro gave several interviews that were covered by different media outlets. In February, the *MacNeil-Lehrer News Hour* broadcast a three-part interview with the Cuban president; in March part of Dan Rather's six-hour interview with Castro was broadcast on *60 Minutes*; and in August even *Playboy* magazine featured interviews of President Castro by three different interviewers.[43] On June 30, *New York Times* editor Karl E. Meyer wrote about his recent trip to Cuba and called for an end to the U.S. embargo. Even before that flurry of media attention, three U.S. representatives had visited the island, with several business people along as "advisers."[44] The members of the House, as well as a delegation from the National Conference of Catholic Bishops, who visited the island around the same time, returned calling for negotiations to improve relations. The Reagan administration countered those developments with aggressive speeches about the region, including the State of the Union address and the March release of White Paper #3: "The Soviet-Cuban Connection."[45]

In the early part of 1987, U.S.-Cuban relations were at what one analyst described as "their lowest ebb since the 1962 missile crisis." In January, Jose Sorzano moved from the position of CANF president to take a job in the administration as director of Latin American affairs for the NSC. While Cuba denied U.S. officials the right to land charter planes loaded with cargo for the Interests Section in Havana, the United States pushed a resolution in the United Nations condemning the Cuban government's human rights policies. In July, Cuban television broadcast a documentary that detailed U.S. espionage activities on the island.[46] Somewhat surprisingly, however, on November 19 the United States and Cuba concluded immigration talks by restoring the 1984 agreement that had been suspended as Cuba's response to Radio Marti. In the U.S. Congress, legislators from both houses introduced legislation that would allow the sale of some foodstuffs to Cuba. The bills were handily defeated in both 1987 and 1988. Close to the end of his second term, President Reagan did sign a trade act that eliminated the existing requirement for licensing of printed material, recordings, and other media products imported from Cuba.[47]

The Reagan Foreign Policy Legacy

Some analysts were starting to discuss the Reagan impact on foreign policy making while he was still in office. Once the Iran-Contra story broke, those who had opposed the application of the Reagan Doctrine to Latin America were able to attack not only the substance of the policies but also the methods employed by the administration in the making and implementation of policy. In a prominent *Foreign Affairs* article, Arthur Schlesinger Jr. wrote: "The Reagan Doctrine has made covert action its chosen instrument and has thereby made secrecy, deceit and mendacity the foundation of American foreign policy."[48] Parry and Kornbluh concluded their article in *Foreign Policy* the following year with a similar point: "Deception then becomes the coin of the realm, and irrationality, spawned by the acceptance of propaganda as truth, dictates the most sensitive judgments of U.S. foreign-policymakers."[49]

During the Reagan years, neither the press nor the public was up to the task of providing a check on a deceptive and secretive president. Leslie Janka, a Reagan press officer, candidly describes the administration's strategy as based on the idea that "the media will take what we feed them. . . . They've got to write their story every day. You give them their story, they'll go away. As long as you come in there every day, hand them a well-packaged, premasticated story in the format they want, they'll go away. . . . You give them the line of the day, you give them press briefings, you give them facts, access to people who will speak on the record. . . . And you do that long enough, they're going to stop bringing their own stories, and stop being investigative reporters of any kind, even modestly so."[50] The other part of this strategy was to covertly undermine the credibility of those investigative reporters who discover information contrary to the official press briefings.

Reagan officials dealt with Congress then as an adversary without a legitimate claim to play a role in making foreign policy. Reflecting back on the Reagan years, Elliott Abrams makes the point succinctly: "One of the reasons we fought as hard as we did was we thought that what the Democratic leadership in Congress was doing was really constitutionally illegitimate in addition to being wrong with respect to Central America."[51] There is more than a little irony in Abrams's challenge of the constitutionality of Congress, given his own admission to having lied to that body. But it is clear that whether lying to Congress or acting as if the Boland Amendment, the law that prohibited further funding of the Nicaraguan Contras, did not exist, the executive branch did not see the legislature as a partner in foreign policy making, but as an opponent to be defeated by any means necessary.

The Iran-Contra scandal exposed a new sort of link between public institutions and private groups. In the focus on the arms for hostages deal and the funding of the Contras in general, however, the larger trend of such integration within the foreign policy-making process during the 1980s remained largely hidden. Beyond the solicitation of funds to evade the Boland Amendment, the role played by a variety of private groups to try to influence policy on a security issue marked an important change. As Cynthia Arnson and Philip Brenner point out, the Council for Inter-American Security declared that it spent $2.84 million in the effort to pass the executive branch's request for $100 million in aid to the Contras in 1986 alone. Noting other examples of even larger contributions by such groups as the National Endowment for the Preservation of Liberty (NEPL), the same analysts argue that the work by the various interest groups was "buttressed, encouraged, and even coordinated by the White House."[52] That coordination, which included the participation of Reagan, North, and others in the private groups' fundraising efforts, is similar to the symbiotic relationship between CANF and the Reagan administration.

The rise of the New Right in the 1980s was associated with the growth in both the number and funding levels of right-wing think tanks over the course of the decade. While their activity in economic policy issues, such as regulation domestically and trade internationally, was well documented, the idea that these groups would become such key players in foreign policy was not as widely discussed. If anything, the portrayal of interest group activity in Central America tended to assume large numbers of nongovernmental organizations opposing the Reagan administration and making their policy-making efforts more difficult. However, Amy Fried argues convincingly: "By 1983 and 1984, the contra cause was in full gear, and conservative groups were fully activated. Right-wing groups used a full array of lobbying tools and public relations methods, seeking to influence public opinion with advertising, appearances on television and radio talk shows, and op-ed articles. Right-wing groups also targeted selected members of Congress, flooding offices with petitions and postcards."[53] This collaboration with think tanks and other private organizations marked a significant change from the executive branch approach to the leading foundations and think tanks that David Newsom argues "were seen as enemies" by the Nixon administration. Part of that shift certainly had to do with the growth of right-wing think tank options since the Nixon presidency. By 1980, the American Enterprise Institute had grown to a staff of 135 and a budget of $10.4 million from 19 and $1 million a decade earlier. The Heritage Foundation, which was founded in 1973, had an annual income of $7 million in 1980 but grew to $18 million by the end of the 1980s.[54] While the numbers are not quite as dramatic, other groups on the right such as the Cato Institute and the Center for Strategic International Studies (CSIS) grew in importance during the Reagan years. What made these groups all the more successful was that they were "linked together in an informal, syndicated network, and [had] interlocking boards and umbrella organizations."[55]

Assessing the Reagan Years

In the end, what we saw happen during the Reagan years was the simultaneous privatization of some aspects of foreign policy making and an effort to build public support for foreign policy in large part through this energizing of private groups as the president's new partners. In its most extreme moments, officials in the Reagan administration coordinated private groups that engaged in promoting, funding, and implementing policies advocated by the executive branch of government. The Committee of Santa Fe (a private group, of course) had previewed the effectiveness of just such a strategy in 1980. While the excesses of the Reagan administration's privatization of foreign policy were discovered, and some were eliminated as a result, the trend toward the blurring of public and private was not interrupted. Some of the main characters in the Reagan administration and the governmental relationships with supportive private groups would return to prominence during the George W. Bush presidency.

The embargo with Cuba was strengthened in a variety of ways during the Reagan years. CANF and Cuban American influence generally were institutionalized in the foreign policy-making process. Radio Marti marked a particularly important development for the hard-line Cuban American community, but other programs were developed, such as the NED, which were also government-funded vehicles that served the interests of CANF and other embargo supporters. While that group of Cuban Americans was working closely with the Reagan administration through this range of interesting relationships, the U.S. embargo policy itself was becoming more restrictive. Constraints on travel were reinstated, and previous agreements between the two countries were allowed to lapse. Perhaps most important, the perception that the very existence of the Castro government posed a serious threat to the United States was further entrenched during an effective campaign by the Reagan administration. By means of White Papers, the Public Diplomacy program, and Reagan's own public words, the cold war hawks successfully used Cuba as a large part of the justification for interventions throughout Latin America in the 1980s.

By the end of President Reagan's second term, U.S. policy toward Cuba had come a long way from resting on decisions made behind closed doors by presidents and their close advisers as we saw in the Eisenhower era. Cuba policy was clearly placed in a wider context of U.S.-Latin American relations by the Reagan administration. Interest groups on both sides increased their presence in the debates about policy toward Latin American. The Reagan administration worked very closely with private groups that shared its position on developments in the region as a means of countering both congressional opposition and organizations outside government that opposed its foreign policy. From the initial influence of the Committee of Santa Fe on the ideas and policies of the Reagan administration, to the incorporation of nongovernmental organizations such as CANF or Freedom House into the policy-making process, to the role played by wealthy individuals in funding the Nicaraguan Contras, there was a wide range of public-private partnerships in U.S. policy toward Latin America during the 1980s. This mobilization clearly increased the ability of the executive branch to pursue its policy agenda while Reagan was president. CANF and Cuba played a vital role in the Reagan administration's policy toward Latin America. The unintended consequence of this effort is that succeeding chief executives would find that once activated, these groups' loyalty to their own interests would transcend any loyalty to the branch of government that sponsored their initial growth in influence. In the specific case of Cuba policy, the privatization begun in the Reagan era for the purpose of strengthening both the hands of the president and the embargo itself would later become a force that tied the hands of future presidents. And once energized, a range of interest groups and active members of Congress would become increasingly engaged on the side of stripping presidential power over Cuba policy and loosening the embargo itself. By 1992 President George Herbert Walker Bush would feel the heat that Reagan had helped create.

The Rise of Congress and
the Fall of the Cold War

The George H. W. Bush Administration

THE 1989 INAUGURATION of George Herbert Walker Bush as president of the United States seemed to give hope to both sides in the debate over U.S. policy toward Cuba as the cold war began to wind down.
Those who wished to see better relations between the United States and
Cuba could point to Bush as more pragmatic than President Reagan, and
thus perhaps more likely to deal with Castro's Cuba during a time of great
international change.[1] Even the Santa Fe group, whose strong positions on
Central America and Cuba bolstered the Reagan campaign and administration earlier, had now come to see Castro's fall as inevitable and to propose
that the United States should develop relations with "younger government
functionaries [in Cuba] as a way to identify potential reformers."[2] Others
wished Bush would tighten the embargo on Cuba.[3] Those who wished the
United States to retain—and even tighten—its embargo of Cuba could
point to Bush's close political and fund-raising ties to CANF as evidence
that he was with them.[4] And one of Bush's sons, Jeb, in hopes of starting a
political career had moved to Florida where he had close ties with conser-

74

vative Miami Cubans.[5] For the most part the Bush administration tried to keep Cuba policy on the back-burner, though it generally continued the Reagan approach to the island and to CANF. But the Bush administration would ultimately struggle to retain control of Cuba policy in the face of an increasingly aggressive Congress. The Bush administration is an interesting bridge between the Reagan administration and the Clinton team, between the cold war era and the post–cold war world, and between an era of Cuba policy dominated by the executive and CANF and a period where the president and Congress regularly, and openly, clashed over policy toward the island.

We begin by briefly discussing the relationship between Congress and the president in the area of foreign policy. Then we focus on the development of key components of Cuba policy in the first Bush administration: Radio and TV Marti, the immigration issues that would start to bring Cuba policy to the Bush administration's front-burner, the election of Cuban Americans to Congress that would increase Congressional activism on Cuba policy, and ultimately the Cuban Democracy Act that was forced on an unwilling president in part by an entrepreneurial Congress, the interest group the previous president helped to spawn, and the realities of electoral politics.

Our findings show that the initiative behind Cuba policy during the Bush administration was slowly, but surely, shifting from the White House to Capitol Hill. While this trend may have begun even during the cold war, following Vietnam and Watergate, it began to accelerate as the cold war came to a close. It is perhaps common to portray policy makers as "hostages" of the Cuban American National Foundation (CANF),[6] and it is certainly the case that during the Reagan administration CANF enjoyed broad access and power. The evidence suggests that starting during the Bush administration the politics of Cuba policy became far more complicated than simply domination by CANF. Through much of the 1980s Cuba policy was largely driven by presidential prerogative and interest group power; by the end of Bush's lone term, Cuba policy was not so much being driven as it was being pushed by several actors, including interest groups, the president, and assertive members of Congress. Ironically, some of these forces would ultimately evolve into the core that would move to loosen or end embargo. It is in this period that the power over the embargo enjoyed by Congress and CANF begins to expand—though aimed at tightening the embargo. These forces, once unleashed, will eventually boomerang and cut away at the U.S. embargo policy.

Congress, the President, and Foreign Policy

Since our examination of the changing politics of U.S. policy toward Cuba is informed by debates about the relative power of different actors in U.S. foreign policy, it is worth briefly discussing some of the debates in the literature about this issue. During at least the first two decades following World War II, a scholarly consensus existed that the "imperial president" ran U.S. foreign policy. As Cecil Crabb and Pat Holt describe it, for example, the situation in the mid-1960s was one "of virtually unchecked presidential authority in diplomacy."[7] Examples of presidential primacy in the making of U.S. policy toward Latin America during the quarter-century following World War II abound. The exile invasion of Cuba, military intervention in the Dominican Republic, covert activities in Guatemala and Chile, and even sponsored assassination plots against Latin American leaders were products of the dominant executive branch.[8] Randall Ripley and James Lindsay suggest that the list of actors relevant to understanding U.S. foreign and defense policy as late as the mid-1970s included only the president and the national security bureaucracy.[9]

But with the turn against the imperial presidency that followed Vietnam and Watergate came a new era of congressional activism in the foreign policy arena.[10] In addition to the scholarly assessment, executive branch officials up to and including presidents have complained about the new constraints emanating from the legislature. In referring to the ways that Congress had broadened its powers in foreign relations, President Ford argued: "The pendulum has swung so far that you could almost say we have moved from an imperial Presidency to an imperiled Presidency."[11] More recently, scholars have suggested that the cold war's demise has led to a "new tug-of-war" between the branches,[12] leading to "a fundamental change in executive-legislative relations of foreign policy."[13] And with the end of the cold war, this trend has likely intensified. Bert Rockman, for example, argues, "the post–cold war environment has changed the nature of policy priorities and has required organizational adaptation and refocusing. Formerly peripheral organizational players are now at the core. The central players of the past no longer exclusively determine the agenda. Trade, commercial, financial, economic, and even regulatory issues now play a much larger independent role in U.S. policy than they did in the bipolarized world of the cold war."[14]

Contributing to the change in the balance of power between Congress and the president was the loss of the executive's near monopoly over information—among the branch's most important resources.[15] In the last two decades, more opportunities have developed for individual members of Congress to engage in what John Tierney refers to as "policy entrepreneurialism."[16] Representatives and senators may gain credibility on the basis of acquired expertise over a certain nation or region and as a result exert disproportionate influence on issues within "their" perceived domains.

The capacity of Congress to influence policy in a struggle with the president may vary by issue area. Ripley and Lindsay argue that Congress is likely to have the least influence in "crisis" policy making, somewhat more in "strategic" policy, and the most effect over "structural" issues (which largely mirror domestic spending issues).[17] And Jeremy Rosner agrees that congressional assertiveness varies from issue to issue: In traditional national security concerns or threats, including policies with probable domestic economic impact, the executive is likely to have the balance of power; with nontraditional issues, such as human rights, Congress is more likely to exert influence.[18] Economic sanctions, in particular, are an area to expect increased activism by Congress.[19] Congressional activity may also vary in response to the ways that the international environment gives rise to critical foreign policy issues.[20]

Scholars such as Barbara Hinckley challenge this position and argue that the increase in congressional activity is "less than meets the eye."[21] After all, "the fact remains that the president is still in charge of American foreign policy."[22] Or, as Roger Hilsman describes it, the president is the "decision maker of last resort."[23] In general, the literature on the relative importance of the president and Congress in making foreign policy still sides with the executive branch. While there has been a resurgence of congressional activism in foreign policy, the balance of power—especially in crisis and strategic policy making—favors the president. Harold H.

Koh argues that presidents almost always win foreign policy competitions with Congress for a variety of factors inherent to the institution of the presidency, such as executive initiative. Other reasons focus on congressional attributes and behaviors, such as general congressional acquiescence that shows itself in legislative myopia, weak bill drafting, lack of effective tools to restrain the executive, and lack of political will to engage in foreign policy disputes.[24] Louis Fisher and Gordon Silverstein both argue that there has actually been a large shift of authority over war powers and other foreign policy areas since the Second World War to the president. That shift, they both argue, has been facilitated by Congress itself, which has been only too willing to hand authority to the executive, or to give power over as an unintended consequence of congressional action.[25]

But there is an important caveat here: In structural policy, such as trade policy, Congress plays a significant role in steering the ship of state. And the Constitution's commerce clause clearly gives Congress power over trade agreements and the power to initiate legislation, including sanctions legislation.[26] Policy toward Cuba in the wake of the cold war is as much or more a matter of trade policy as national security policy. All this suggests that while Cuba policy may be unique in the extent to which domestic political forces beyond the White House are central players, to some extent by design following the Reagan administration approach, the Cuba case was not a total outlier as George H. W. Bush became president.

Cuba on the Back-Burner

U.S. policy toward Cuba had long emerged largely out of international circumstances, Cuba's strategic position in the cold war, and presidential preference. Richard Nixon noted in 1973, for example, "We do not intend to lecture countries on their internal structure, either in cases like the Philippines at present, or that of the communist countries. Our concern is for foreign policy behavior and we will aid dictatorships if it is in our interest to do so. Our opposition to Cuba, the USSR and PRC has been based on their external policy of aggression and subversion. When they modify those policies, we will modify our policy toward them."[27]

While the embargo was meant to isolate and contain Cuba (if not lead to the overthrow of the Castro government), American presidents also

wanted Castro to remove Cuban forces from Africa and to stop foment-
ing revolution in Central America. But changing international circumstances would alter Cuba's position in the world; the goals of U.S. policy
toward Cuba would also change.

The end of the cold war and the fall of the Soviet Union had enormous repercussions for Cuba as Cuba lost its greatest trade partners practically overnight. By the late 1980s, Soviet economic and military aid may
have combined to account for 20 percent of Cuba's gross domestic product.
Nearly 75 percent of Cuba's trade was with the Soviets by 1989; almost 90
percent was with other socialist countries. But Mikhail Gorbachev began to
reduce Soviet aid to Cuba for both domestic and foreign policy reasons.[28]
The impact on Cuba would be enormous. Between 1989 and 1992, for example, total imports to the island dropped by 75 percent,[29] and petroleum
imports from Russia fell by more than two-thirds between 1988 and 1992.[30]
Cuba's economy shrank by perhaps one-third between 1990 and 1993.[31] In
1990 the German government announced that all aid to Cuba that used to
flow from the former East Germany would be halted.[32] Soviet foreign aid
to Cuba, which had amounted to about 25 percent of all Soviet foreign
aid, about $21 billion, and all subsidized trade between the Soviet Union,
now Russia, and Cuba also came to an end.[33] Having lost its major trading
partners, Cuba appeared more vulnerable than ever.

In light of these new developments the Bush administration tried to
simultaneously keep the pressure on Cuba, and even increase it, while
keeping Cuba policy out of the path of other, more important, foreign policy concerns. The prevailing sentiment was that Castro could not possibly
survive these new developments, so his departure was only a matter of time.
The Bush administration began to shift U.S. demands of Cuba, "moving
the goalposts," as the price for ending the embargo. Now, beyond demanding modification of Cuba's foreign policy, the Bush administration began
to verbally push for domestic reform on the island: free and fair elections
under international supervision and respect for human rights at home.[34]
Still, Cuba was not a priority for the Bush administration. As a senior Bush
administration official said, "We have beefed up our rhetoric, but getting
rid of Castro is not a front-burner policy, because we recognize that the
Cuban system is tied to one individual. Once that individual passes, we
think the system will change, as it has elsewhere."[35] A Pentagon officer re-
counted to *Newsweek*, "The word we've gotten is, 'Don't even waste your

time on a new policy for Cuba.' It's a nonissue."[36] The prevailing sentiment seemed to be that with Soviet aid gone, and democracy sweeping the hemisphere—even in places like Nicaragua and Panama (both during the Bush administration)—Castro's fall was imminent. "Two down and one to go," State Department spokeswoman Margaret Tutwiler told the press after Nicaraguan elections in 1990.[37]

In this environment, it did not seem to make sense to the Bush administration to take steps toward Cuba that would alienate allies, like Europe, and potential allies, like Russia. Since Castro's fall was seen as inevitable, the new administration's "time was better sent on other endeavors."[38] Bills like the Mack Amendment, which was offered for three straight years starting in 1989 and which sought to tighten the embargo by prohibiting foreign subsidiaries of U.S. firms from doing business with Cuba, promised to make Cuba policy less about Cuba and more about our allies: so the Bush administration opposed such moves. The U.S. State Department sent a cable to embassies in Brussels, Ottawa, and Paris in September 1989 arguing, "We permit [subsidiary trade] because we recognize that attempting to apply our embargo to third countries will lead to unproductive and bitter trade disputes with our allies."[39] But with the fall of Cuba as a national security issue, and the rise of Cuba policy as a trade issue in the wake of the cold war, domestic pressures from Congress and interest groups began to increasingly impinge on the executive primacy of Cuba policy that presidents had previously enjoyed. Bush could keep Cuba policy in the background for a while, but not forever.

Radio and TV Marti

The Reagan-CANF partnership on Radio Marti continued into the Bush administration. The Reagan administration and CANF worked closely together on a range of initiatives in the 1980s, including the creation of Radio Marti, a government-sponsored radio station aimed at Cuba analogous to Radio Free Europe or Radio Liberty. Having first asked for a bill in September 1981, in October 1983 President Reagan signed into law the bill that led to the first broadcast by Radio Marti in May 1985. Jorge Mas Canosa would serve as chairman of the Radio Marti advisory board from its inception until his death and play a key role with the station. The political partnership between CANF and the radio station, or the significant control of the station by CANF, led the first director of Radio Marti, Ernesto Betancourt, to resign in 1990 following a number of conflicts with Mas. Betancourt argued in frustration, "USIA has practically abdicated control of the stations to an exile group. . . . A key foreign policy instrument is being subordinated to political considerations."[40] The disagreement between Betancourt and Mas seemed to be over CANF control of both Radio and TV Marti. Mas allegedly told a TV Marti correspondent that if George Bush were elected president in 1989, Mas would "get rid of" Betancourt.[41] Betancourt quit rather than be moved to a new job at USIA.[42]

The original proposal for TV Marti came from Mas himself; serious discussions about such a station began in 1988. The new Bush administration supported the station, seeing it as a way to press its agenda of domestic political and human rights reform in Cuba. By 1990 TV Marti was broadcasting regularly and was regularly being jammed by the Cuban government. Nevertheless, in January 1991 the President's Advisory Board for Cuba Broadcasting, headed by Mas, declared the station "a success both technically and in terms of American foreign policy."[43] A USIA study of broadcasts in the spring of 1990 concluded that as many as 28 percent of Cubans in and around Havana could watch TV Marti without interruption. But a Government Accounting Office (GAO) report that examined that data found it unreliable and pointed to a study by the U.S. Interests Section in Havana that found that as few as 1 percent of Cubans in the target area could actually watch the broadcasts.[44] Nevertheless Bush stood firmly behind the project. In April 1990 Bush told a group of broadcasters, "The voice of freedom will not be still as long as there is an America to tell the truth."[45] Presidential and CANF support notwithstanding, in 1991 and 1992 Congress became increasingly divided on continued funding for TV Marti. Each year, however, the station survived the budget ax. The 1992 vote to save TV Marti in the 1993 appropriations bill was close in the House: 215-181. One House member who opposed funding the station, Chester Atkins (D-MA), argued, "TV Marti is the Peter Sellers-inspired plan to overthrow Cuba by broadcasting TV sitcoms between 3:30 and 6 in the morning."[46] Supporters like Rep. Ileana Ros-Lehtinen (R-FL), herself a Cuban American, argued that even if the broadcasts do not reach any viewers, Castro must spend valuable money to block the signals.[47] Also in 1993 the Cuba Broadcasting advisory board recommended that the offices for Radio and TV Marti move from Washington, D.C., to Miami, which many saw as a way to enhance even further CANF's control over the stations.[48] (The offices were moved in 1996.) At the same time, though, an independent panel began increased scrutiny of TV Marti with respect to the fairness of its broadcasts to show the diversity of Cuban American community opinion.[49] In 1995 a USIA investigation found "pervasive influence by anti-Castro lobbyist Jorge Mas Canosa in management of the station and in news coverage that deliberately misrepresented U.S. policy toward Cuba."[50] The television broadcasts are still on the air and are rarely seen by anyone in Cuba. Over time Radio and TV Marti have received nearly $350 million in federal funding.

CANF's Growing Independence

We previously discussed some of the ways during the Reagan administration that CANF became an increasingly independent player, though always in ways that suited the interests of the Reagan administration, such as CANF's activism on the Clark Amendment. This pattern would continue in the Bush administration and in some ways intensify. The interests of CANF and the executive during the early Bush years largely coincided on matters such as Radio and TV Marti, though it is worth noting that Mas Canosa and CANF's allies in Congress spurred TV Marti.[51] Many of these allies were cultivated over a long period of time; between 1982 and 1992, CANF's Political Action Committee (the Free Cuba PAC) donated more than $1 million to congressional candidates.[52] Another area where CANF and the Bush administration seemed to work together was on pressing Cuba about domestic political reform and human rights. Bush had already signaled that this would be a new yardstick by which to judge the U.S.-Cuban relationship, and it again came to the fore on the appointment of a U.S. representative to the UN Human Rights Commission in 1989. Bush had singled out the longtime political prisoner in Cuba, Armondo Valladeres, as a hero of his during one of the televised presidential debates in 1988. Valladeres had close ties to CANF and other strongly anti-Castro groups. Bush's appointment of Valladeres to this key post was a way to continue to pressure Cuba, in this case through an international organization, regarding the Bush administration's new emphasis on human rights violations in Cuba.[53]

Jacqueline Tillman, a former CANF executive director who had been deputy director of Latin American affairs at the NSC before coming to the Foundation, has said, "the foundation has a habit of saying it 'drives' U.S. policy on Cuba and 'drives' President Bush."[54] The White House actually paid little attention to Cuba policy. "The President is letting himself be pushed by external forces because he is comfortable about the direction in which they are pushing him," a White House official said. The Bush administration has in effect "delegated Cuba policy to an active congressional group, inspired by domestic lobbies, that regularly pushes the administration into a position of aggressive posturing."[55] For an administration that expected Castro's fall to follow that of other dictators in the hemisphere, and for whom Cuba policy was not a top priority, this is perhaps not a surprising pattern.

Cuba Policy to the Front-Burner

Cuba policy moved to the Bush administration's front-burner for two reasons. First, Haitian exiles were fleeing en masse but were largely being returned to Haiti, which raised the specter of a double standard relative to Cuban exiles who gained easy entry to the United States.[56] Second, Congress—now including Cuban American members—became more engaged in this area in ways that did not always coincide with the interests of the Bush administration. Ultimately, Congress formulated the Cuban Democracy Act (CDA) following hearings before a House committee in 1991.[57] Both of these items would haunt President Bush through the 1992 election.

Double Standards

On September 29, 1991, a violent coup deposed Haiti's first elected leader, Jean-Bertrand Aristide. The economic and political conditions in Haiti contributed to a large increase in Haitians fleeing to the United States. But under a plan put into effect in September 1981, Haitians would be interdicted at sea, and those not qualifying for political refugee status would be returned to Haiti, in order not to give an incentive for mass migration to the United States. Few Haitians picked up at sea attained such status. From the start of the program until the September 1991 coup, the United States intercepted approximately twenty-three thousand Haitians at sea, but only twenty-eight were eligible for asylum. In the two months following the coup, two thousand more were interdicted and nearly all returned to Haiti. This immigration crisis drew attention to the anomaly of how Cubans who flee their island are treated under U.S. immigration law. Under the Cuban Adjustment Act of 1966, Cubans who reached the United States were automatically granted asylum.[58] The attention of the Haiti crisis helped draw Cuba policy into the public domain.

Congressional Activism on Cuba Policy

Cuban Americans in Congress

In 1989 Cuban American Ileana Ros-Lehtinen (R-FL) took her seat in the House of Representatives, the seat long held by Democrat Claude Pepper, representing Florida's Eighteenth District. Previously a state senator and elected in 1982 as the first Hispanic woman in the Florida legislature, the special election held in August 1989 led to Ros-Lehtinen being the first Cuban American in Congress (she was born in Havana in 1952 and came to the United States when she was seven). Ros-Lehtinen was CANF's candidate and a member of the Foundation; Jeb Bush was her campaign manager.[59] The race received a great deal of national and party attention. GOP National Chairman Lee Atwater spoke to a CANF meeting that summer and argued that the seat should go to a Cuban American.[60] President Bush went to Florida to campaign for her (and some say to draw attention to her campaign manager).[61] In September 1989 several subcommittees of the House Foreign Affairs Committee held one of a series of hearings on U.S. policy toward Cuba. Ros-Lehtinen, though not a member of the committee, was nevertheless welcomed to the hearing by the chairman and played an active role in the discussion.[62] In a later discussion on Cuba policy as a member of the Foreign Affairs Committee, she would play an active role in the hearings, noting Cuba as her native homeland, and thus claiming special experience and expertise with the subject.[63] Cuba policy now had a watchdog inside Congress.

The arrival of Ros-Lehtinen added a new dimension to the view of Cuba policy from Congress, and two fellow Cuban Americans soon joined her in the House in 1993. Lincoln Diaz-Balart was born in Cuba in 1959 and came to the United States in 1963. He was a Republican member of the Florida House, first elected in 1986, and took Ros-Lehtinen's empty seat in the Florida Senate in 1989. He was elected to the U.S. House of Representatives in 1992 representing Florida's redrawn Twenty-first District. He also then took a seat on the House Foreign Affairs Committee.[64] Robert Menendez's parents were Cuban immigrants. A Democrat, Menendez served as mayor of Union City, New Jersey, and was a state legislator. He was elected to the U.S. House also in 1992, representing New Jersey's new Thirteenth District.[65]

The arrival of these three Cuban Americans in Congress contributed to a new congressional activism in Cuba policy with which the president would have to deal and also coincided with the emergence of electoral politics as an important force on Cuba policy. While these members and CANF worked together closely, the House members by definition had a range of prerogative and power that changed the nature of the relationship between CANF and Congress. These Cuban Americans did not need to lobby Congress; they were *in* Congress. Increasingly the object of CANF lobbying, and of the Cuban American House members' persuasion, was not Congress but the president, who did not always see eye to eye with the group or the increasingly aggressive Congress on Cuba policy. One way this lobbying emerged was during Ros-Lehtinen's first campaign over the case of Dr. Orlando Bosch. Bosch was in jail in Venezuela from 1976 to 1987, having been linked to the 1976 bombing of a Cuban jetliner that killed seventy-three people. He was acquitted several times, but his ties to political violence and terrorism against several countries, notably Cuba, caught the attention of the U.S. Department of Justice. When he came to Miami in 1988, Bosch was arrested on a parole violation from an earlier offense in the United States. The Justice Department decided to deport Bosch. The case became a great controversy when anti-Castro forces in Miami, who viewed Bosch as a hero in the fight against Castro, moved to free Bosch in the United States. Among those arguing against the government's decision was

Ros-Lehtinen and her campaign manager, Jeb Bush; Ros-Lehtinen apparently urged the president to stop the deportation.[66] Bosch was released and now lives in Miami.[67] But the Bosch case is just one small example of the president getting backed into a corner by Cuban American influence, now including Cuban American members of Congress.

Cuban Democracy Act

Beginning in 1989 Connie Mack (R-FL) offered a bill for three consecutive years that would prohibit foreign subsidiaries of U.S. firms from trading with Cuba. Bush administration officials consistently opposed the Mack Amendment during that period. In July 1991 Bernard Aronson, assistant secretary of state for inter-American affairs, testified before Congress that "The ban on subsidiaries of U.S. multi-nationals would create a foreign policy problem with a lot of allies who rightly believe that that would be an assertion of U.S. law into their territory and who would be prepared to retaliate in direct ways. Our analysis is that the benefits that we would gain in terms of embargo enforcement are relatively minimal."[68] The Mack Amendment was defeated easily in 1991, as it was in previous years, showing that while Congress was becoming more active they were not yet able to countervail against the executive.

In early 1992 the impetus came from the other side of the aisle, as first Congressman Robert Torricelli (D-NJ) and then Senator Bob Graham (D-FL) introduced the Cuban Democracy Act (CDA) in their respective chambers. Richard Nuccio, Torricelli's aide, has been described as the "intellectual force" behind the CDA legislation;[69] he drafted the bill in July 1991.[70] Torricelli first unveiled his bill in an op-ed piece in the *Los Angeles Times* in August 1991. In it he accused the Bush administration of not moving swiftly enough to force change in Cuba and for not really having a Cuba policy. "The Bush Administration and I do not differ on Cuba's list of offenses. But citing them does not constitute a policy," he argued.[71] Showing the domestic political bind that the Bush administration was in, a *Newsweek* story quoted Mas Canosa as saying, "Goddam it, we've got to do *something*" [to tighten pressure on Castro]. The authors go on to note:

> Members of Congress who agree propose to increase the economic
> pressure. Neoconservatives and Democrats who need Cuban-American

votes want to tighten the embargo by preventing U.S. subsidiaries from trading with Cuba. All this leaves the president in the middle, wishing Cuba would just go away, at least until [the election]. The Cuban-American community so far backs him and Bush won't disrupt that by relaxing the embargo. He also knows that more coercive measures would be foolhardy. So he hopes to stand pat. But the rhetoric is confusing. On one hand, Bush says the United States has no aggressive intentions toward Cuba. On the other, he pacifies the Cuban-American community with predictions that Castro will fall. The question is whether anti-Castro forces are willing to watch what he says, not what he does.[72]

The CDA had two tracks, which were sometimes referred to as "carrots and sticks." One focus of the measure—similar to the Mack Amendment—was to increase the economic pressure on Cuba by shutting off trade with foreign subsidiaries of U.S. multinationals and making it more difficult for ships that had made Cuban stops to enter U.S. ports. This would close the de facto loosening of the embargo that followed as the Cuba economy opened to the rest of the world following the fall of the Soviet Union.[73] The other focus was to try to reach out to the Cuban people by making communication and family visits to Cuba easier. CANF played a prominent role throughout the legislative process of this bill. Torricelli had developed close ties to the interest group, although his own New Jersey district had almost no Cuban Americans. In a future statewide race for the U.S. Senate, however, Cuban American support would be quite helpful. Among the original twenty-two House sponsors of the CDA, fourteen had received total donations from the CANF PAC of more than $1000.[74] From its partisan roots in the Reagan White House, CANF diversified its party links while making considerable inroads in the legislative branch, which was ascending in policy importance. The episode also shows CANF's growing independence from the executive that once sponsored it.

Jorge Dominguez has suggested that Torricelli's proposal was part of a "Democratic Party campaign strategy," to force the hand of the Bush administration on a bill that had bipartisan support in Congress and CANF support in Florida and New Jersey.[75] A Democratic aide was quoted as suggesting that most of the Democrats backing the bill were hoping that President Bush would veto it.[76] At first it looked as if exactly that would happen. A month after the bill was introduced in Congress, Bush shared the dais with Mas at a $1000-a-plate dinner for the reelection campaign and yet offered no endorsement of the pending legislation.[77] In April, Robert Gelbard, principal deputy assistant secretary of state for inter-American affairs, offered several objections to the CDA before Congress. Among the most important to the administration (foreshadowing future debates) was that the bill would cost the U.S. diplomatically and impinge "on the President's constitutionally mandated powers to conduct foreign affairs."[78] Both Canada and the European Community warned the Bush administration that the CDA would damage relations between the United States and its allies and lead to reprisals.[79]

The outcome of the CDA was not to be determined on the basis of a balance of national interests or constitutional questions about executive power but rather by the domestic politics of a presidential campaign. Within a few days of the fund-raiser referred to above, where Bush did not endorse the CDA, Mas had dinner with Stephen Solarz (D-NY) and evidently offered to provide help for Clinton's presidential campaign if he decided to endorse the CDA.[80] Clinton adviser George Stephanopoulos and Torricelli negotiated Clinton's acceptance of the CDA.[81] With a campaign short of funds, an interest in being competitive in Florida against President Bush in the general election, and even a Rodham family connection to the Cuban American community in Florida, candidate Clinton signed on in Miami with the simple statement: "I have read the Torricelli-Graham bill and I like it."[82] That short statement capped a day in which the candidate raised $275,000 from Cuban Americans in Coral Gables and Miami.

Even though Clinton's acceptance of the CDA did not lead to an electoral victory in Florida, the Clinton campaign team saw the politics of it favorably. A former Clinton administration official familiar with the campaign explains, "the point was not to win a majority of the Cuban vote but to get a bunch of campaign money, to outflank Bush on the Right, and to make Bush spend time and money in Florida, which should be a gimme state for Republicans." Furthermore, they were "not just thinking about one election, but also about building an electoral coalition for the future by breaking up the solid South and getting the Reagan Democrats back.

Clinton got 20 percent of the Cuban vote in 1992, compared to 5 percent for 1988 Democrat Candidate Michael Dukakis—all because of the endorsement, a good deal. And they made inroads to the [Cuban] community and CANF and Mas." The Clinton team also liked the hard-soft policy side of the CDA: "get hard with the regime but open to the people and allow for freedom to change the embargo with political change in Cuba. This would allow for responding to and working with a Castro-led regime that led the transition to democracy and human rights in Cuba, allowing the President to adjust the embargo accordingly."[83]

When word of Clinton's decision to sign on to the CDA reached the Bush camp, they tried to cut their political losses; The *Miami Herald* reports that President Bush told advisers, "I will not be upstaged on Cuba by Bill Clinton." A few days after the Clinton announcement, President Bush announced new restrictions at U.S. ports on ships carrying Cuban goods and then began to work with Congress on fashioning the CDA that he would sign into law only a couple of weeks before the election. Advocates of increasing the economic pressure on Cuba—inside and outside of Congress—got a bill that marked a significant step beyond anything that working with the Reagan administration had produced. The bill's advocates also believed that it offered a way to facilitate an opening directly to the Cuban people. As the Bush presidency came to an end, CANF had been able to use its money and votes to influence a sitting president to support a policy toward Cuba that he had previously argued was unnecessary, if not harmful, to U.S. interests, and constitutionally problematic.[84] CANF played a prominent role in the creation and adoption of the CDA as its political partnership with the Republican executive branch of the 1980s was shifting to an alliance that included Democrats on the Hill. Beyond CANF, though, the rising importance of Capitol Hill in U.S.-Cuba policy making can be seen. In this case Congress began to emerge as a more independent player than in the 1980s. Further, the dynamics of presidential electoral politics intervened in unexpected ways to improve the bill's fortunes, as a presidential candidate loomed large in the policy-making process. Indeed, the CDA can be seen as the first of a pattern of moves whereby "Congress and Cuban groups [CANF] bring such bills in election years to back the administration into a corner."[85]

The Domestic Roots of U.S.-Cuba Policy

The story of Cuba policy in the Bush years shows how broad domestic political calculations began in earnest to push Cuba policy. The power of the executive to control Cuba policy, which the Reagan administration largely did with its partner, CANF, began to significantly diminish during the Bush administration. CANF began to constrain the president, as the interest group that rose to prominence in no small part because of the support of the White House, began to be another force that pushed on the executive. With the end of the cold war, the embargo was kept in place during the Bush years largely due to "powerful domestic factors."[86] As Glastris has noted, "the Cuban-American lobby has become more powerful domestically in part because Cuba has become less powerful internationally."[87] Dario Moreno of Florida International University notes that without compelling strategic interests at stake, it has in fact become "easy to surrender to the Cuban-American lobby."[88]

But more important, Congress became increasingly aggressive in this area. Robert Salisbury anticipates this development, noting, "in the Congress of the late 1980s interest groups are virtually awash in access but often subordinate in influence."[89] CANF's subordination to an aggressive Congress starts to develop in this period. This is not so say that CANF did not continue to be a central player in crafting Cuba policy. As Elliott Abrams, former assistant secretary of state for inter-American affairs, said in 1992,"You don't want the foundation attacking you. An attack from the foundation would hurt you more than an attack by any other Cuban group, and so you avoid it."[90] But it is to say that in this period CANF became a less dominant actor in shaping U.S. policy toward Cuba as Congress largely overtook CANF's roles as policy initiator and watchdog. CANF remained a central force, now often checking the executive rather than working in tandem with it.

One possible interpretation of the CDA story is that it marks the ultimate success of an ethnic interest group that had been driving U.S.-Cuba policy since CANF's origins in the early Reagan years. While tempting, this explanation is clearly not sufficient. CANF supported the CDA, but Congress wrote it and pushed it, and Clinton's acceptance of the CDA made sense on many levels—as did Bush's reversal. Entrepreneurial members of Congress began to usurp many of the functions once performed more exclusively by the executive and CANF. A small number of influential members of Congress began to play a surprisingly important role in shaping U.S. policy toward Cuba during this period. This is consistent with other foreign policy issues where various members of Congress have stood out "by virtue of their persistence, expertise, or cleverness."[91] No longer was it accurate to see CANF and the president as taking on Congress on Cuba policy; now it was as often the opposite.

The link between Cuba policy and electoral concerns emerged in this period as well. Cuba policy played a key role in the election of Ileana Ros-Lehtinen and even pitted the Justice Department's position on a deportation against that of the president's son. During the 1992 presidential campaign, electoral politics and fund-raising realities led to support for the CDA by Governor Clinton, whose team saw the bill as both good politics and good policy,[92] and by President Bush, reversing his earlier position.

The electoral and interinstitutional dynamics that began to contribute to the shape of U.S. policy toward Cuba by the end of the Bush years would mature quickly into a significant force with which President Clinton would have to deal. The struggle for control of U.S. policy toward the island, just starting during the Bush administration, was about to really heat up. And it began even before Clinton took office.

The Road to Helms-Burton

The First Clinton Administration

B Y THE TIME William Jefferson Clinton took the oath of office in January 1993, Cuba policy rested firmly inside the complex dynamics of domestic politics. Following the 1992 Cuban Democracy Act, the initiative behind Cuba policy in the first Clinton administration largely moved out of the White House and onto Capitol Hill. While this trend began before the end of the cold war, it accelerated in the years following its demise. In this period it was perhaps common to argue that policy makers were hostages to the Cuban American National Foundation,[1] a forceful supporter of the embargo, but the evidence suggests that the politics of Cuba policy are more complicated than that. Through the 1980s Cuba policy was largely driven by presidential prerogative and interest group power. By the 1990s Cuba policy was not so much driven as it was *pushed* by several actors, including interest groups and the president. But by the end of Clinton's first term, the initiative on Cuba policy rested squarely on Capitol Hill. With the strictures of the Cuban Liberty and Democratic Solidarity Act of 1996, or Helms-Burton, changes in the core of Cuba policy—the embargo—must go through Congress. If some members of Congress were riding high after their success with the CDA, they had no idea how much higher they would get—with a little help from the Cuban Air Force.

Cuba Policy As Clinton Comes to Washington

Even though Clinton's acceptance of the CDA during the 1992 campaign did not lead to an electoral victory in Florida that year, the Clinton campaign team saw the politics of it favorably. The Clinton team also liked the hard-soft policy side of the CDA, which would "get hard with the regime but open to the people and allow for freedom to change the embargo with political change in Cuba. This would allow for responding to and working with a Castro-led regime that led the transition to democracy and human rights in Cuba, allowing the President to adjust the embargo accordingly."[2] While the Clinton team would try to move forward under the CDA, even before taking office Clinton would learn a lesson about the domestic politics of Cuba policy.

Mario Baeza and Clinton's First Year

President-elect Clinton did not appear immediately interested in rewarding the Cuban American community in Miami with appointed positions as he began to put together his administration. Mario Baeza was a black Cuban American lawyer with a leading Manhattan firm, Debevoise and Plimpton, and a graduate of Harvard Law School. Baeza was friendly with both Clinton transition team Co-Chair Vernon Jordan and Democratic National Committee Chair and Commerce Secretary-Designate Ron Brown. His specialty was Latin American privatization. Baeza's family left Cuba in 1958, and the Clinton transition team apparently, if mistakenly, thought the move to appoint Baeza to the job of assistant secretary of state for inter-American affairs would be well received by the Cuban American community.[3] It may also have reflected an interest in a different constituency, African Americans, and perhaps even a more pressing issue in Latin America: trade. The Clinton transition team apparently did not do all of its homework before reaching the decision on Baeza. An abbreviated interview process made it likely that the White House was unaware of Baeza's recent visit to Cuba as part of a Mexican conference on investment prospects on the island.[4] In addition, key Democratic members of Congress, such as Robert Torricelli, were not consulted about the choice. Torricelli, whose backyard was adjacent to Baeza's, did not know the Cuban American lawyer and offered the initial opposition to his proposed nomination.[5] Cuban Americans in Congress were unhappy with the potential nominee as well. Lincoln Diaz-Balart (R-FL), for example, said that his constituents were "very, very concerned" about Baeza. Nor was CANF consulted about Baeza, and it quickly mobilized against the presumed antiembargo lawyer. In particular, the interest group encouraged its new allies in the Democratic Party to register their opposition with the president and his transition team. The rapid response, "a sudden blizzard of opposition,"[6] was successful, and Baeza's name was literally crossed out on the list of nominees that was faxed to the Hill.[7] The interest group sponsored by the executive had become a major player in checking its former partner.

Clinton's last-minute removal of Baeza was only one of several times that the president backed off in the face of vocal opposition to a proposed or actual nominee. Still, the ability of CANF and perhaps its most supportive Democratic member of Congress to derail the nomination is noteworthy. The conflict over Baeza's nomination suggested to the foreign policy community that Cuba policy "was being waged largely outside of government circles."[8] One writer, Dick Kirschten, described the blocking of the proposed appointment as a "chit" called in by Clinton's "Miami benefactors." The perceived influence of CANF over presidential appointments by the first Democrat to hold that office in more than a decade gave some indication that Cuba was not a place where the Clinton administration intended to immediately challenge the status quo of Cuba policy. In Alexander Watson Clinton ultimately selected a compromise candidate for the position at the State Department.[9] The choice of Richard Nuccio as his top assistant met with strong CANF approval. Nuccio, as Torricelli's aide, had been described as the "intellectual force" behind the CDA legislation.[10] The executive's appointment prerogative was here constrained by Congress and by the interest group that was sponsored by an earlier president to be a presidential ally on the Hill. Times had changed.

Throughout the first year of the Clinton presidency, the administration's occasional public statements were consistent on the need to stay the course on Cuba and on the utility of the CDA. In November 1993, for example, President Clinton argued that his Cuba policy was working, stating that "gestures of openness that have come out of the Castro regime in the last several months have been the direct result of our policy of pressure and firmness." He went on to note, "no Democrat in my life time, in the White House at least, has come close to taking the strong position I have on this, agreeing with the Cuban American community."[11] Assistant Secretary Watson made his first major policy statement at an October 1993 CANF-hosted luncheon, where he voiced support for the CDA and went on to claim that Clinton had no plan "to soften" policy toward Cuba.[12] Following Jesse Jackson's Christmas Day call to end the "suffering" caused by the embargo, Watson countered, "We will continue our diplomatic, political, and economic isolation of the Cuban government and maintain our economic embargo as a form of leverage."[13]

Clinton kept up a good public front of support for the embargo. Yet, a number of officials within the administration had previously made arguments about the need to reevaluate, if not change, U.S. policy toward Cuba. According to one critic of the Clinton administration: "On the entire Clinton foreign policy team—Bill (and Hillary); Anthony Lake and Richard Feinberg at the National Security Council; Warren Christopher, Strobe Talbott, and Tarnoff at the State Department—there isn't one single person who favors a hard line against Castro."[14] Clinton's continued support for the embargo can be seen at least in part as a result of the ongoing influence of CANF and the growing importance of congressional and electoral calculations, especially in Florida, in making Cuba policy.

Immigration Crisis

A new series of attempts by Cubans to leave the island began in the summer of 1994. Initially, the departures were largely by means of commandeering ships. Hijackings of tugboats, ferries, and even a Navy passenger transport ship took place in the Bay of Havana between July 13 and August 8. The hijackers were occasionally assisted by the U.S. Coast Guard and later given political asylum in Miami.[15] Frustrated by the government's actions and accusing the United States of encouraging the departures,

Castro announced that henceforth Cubans were free to leave the island, and thousands of *balseros,* or rafters, proceeded to leave on whatever small rafts they could construct. Clinton, sensitized by his own problems with rioting *Marielitos* in 1980 when he was governor of Arkansas, was confronted with an immigration crisis during the first campaign season of his presidency. Not only were the midterm elections in play, but Democratic Governor Lawton Chiles of Florida was in a difficult race for reelection against Jeb Bush.

By 1994 immigration questions were capable of generating pressure nearly as intense as that from hard-liners on Cuba policy, and there was a much larger domestic constituency likely to be engaged at some level by the issue. This was the year that California voters, for example, overwhelmingly approved Proposition 187, which would deny education and nonemergency medical care to undocumented immigrants. Some referred to the Cuban rafters arriving in Florida that summer as part of a "slow motion Mariel." While the White House attempted to downplay the seriousness of the issue, Governor Chiles feared that the exodus would accelerate and firmly requested federal action. When the administration did not respond, Chiles claimed that the federal government was "in denial" and declared a state of emergency in Florida.[16]

At a press conference on the morning of August 18, Attorney General Janet Reno denied that any thought was being given to reexamining Cuban refugee policy. Some thirteen hours later an announcement was made by Reno that the nearly three-decades-long policy of granting asylum automatically to all arriving Cubans was being ended and that any rafters would henceforth be detained by the U.S. government. The process that led to this decision was apparently rather haphazard. The new policy appears to have been crafted in an afternoon meeting of President Clinton's top foreign policy advisers, although no experts on Cuba, or Latin America in general, were present. Clinton, who had not attended the meeting, endorsed the group's consensus to reverse the current policy. He had apparently still not discussed the change directly with any of his Cuba or Latin America specialists. One reporter notes, "There's little evidence . . . that Clinton was deeply involved in the unsystematic process by which the policy toward Cuba was dramatically reshaped. It doesn't appear that he ever heard his advisers debate the pros and cons of his choices in a structured setting."[17] The following day, President Clinton ordered the Coast Guard to intercept the balseros and transport them to the U.S. Naval Base at Guantanamo. The 1966 Cuban Adjustment Act had been effectively repealed; Cuban migrants would no longer automatically receive political refugee status, and the new "wet foot/dry foot" policy was born, whereby Cubans would still receive special status if they reached shore but not if intercepted at sea (with "wet feet").

Reaction to the new policy by the majority of Cuban Americans was one of shock and outrage.[18] President Clinton met the following night with Mas and other Cuban Americans, as well as Governor Chiles and Miami officials, as part of what was referred to as "operation mollification."[19] At the meeting, Mas pushed for policy responses up to and including a naval blockade. After a second meeting on the morning of August 20, President Clinton announced a series of new sanctions that limited cash remittances and visits to the island and authorized an increase in the broadcasting to the island by TV and Radio Marti. With these concessions in hand, Mas was able to return to Miami and offer support for the overall package of changes in policy. One analyst suggests that the measures instituted by Clinton marked the hard-liners' most important victory in years.[20] Another interpretation was that administration officials had decided upon the new restrictions prior to the meetings, and therefore CANF did not "gain anything that the president was not willing to give."[21] Either way, the president acted aggressively and placated both Governor Chiles and CANF, and he had not apparently lessened his chances of winning the state of Florida in 1996.

Such a policy balanced competing domestic political pressure reasonably well, but it did not address the situation in Cuba itself. If anything, the new limits on remittances and visits may have increased the motivation for Cubans to leave. Castro made no attempt to halt the exodus, and Cubans continued to take to the seas, apparently undeterred by the prospect of spending some time at Guantanamo. As the number of Cubans held at the naval base and elsewhere grew, it became clear that negotiations with the Castro government were going to be necessary. On September 1, those talks opened in New York City. A little over a week later, the United States and Cuba issued a joint communiqué that included reference to the interests both countries had in keeping rafters from undertaking dangerous trips to sea. The United States for its part agreed to provide at least twenty thousand visas a year for legal immigrants, and the Cuban government committed itself to preventing citizens from leaving the island illegally for the United States.

The long-term status of Cubans held at Guantanamo, or what to do with those who might flee the island in the future, was not resolved by the September 1994 accord. Additional secret discussions were held between U.S. and Cuban officials that eventually produced the May 2, 1995 migration agreement. The joint statement by the two governments that day announced a U.S. policy of returning to Cuba any Cubans who are found at sea or who enter the Guantanamo naval base illegally. Clinton defended the decision as necessary to an audience of Cuban Americans in June: "I know that many of you have questions about aspects of this policy. Yet, the simple truth is that there is no realistic alternative. We simply cannot admit all Cubans who seek to come here. We cannot let people risk their lives on open seas in unseaworthy rafts. And we cannot sentence thousands of young men to live in limbo at Guantanamo."[22]

That decision ended the more than three decades of providing automatic political asylum and unrestricted access to the United States for Cubans fleeing postrevolution Cuba. With this change it became clear that CANF and Mas were no longer the driving force behind policy toward Cuba. The administration did not consult Mas before the day the announcement was made, and it appears that he and other members of CANF were unaware of the secret negotiations between Alarcon and Tarnoff that led to the May 2 announcement.[23] Demonstrations by Cuban Americans were widespread in the aftermath of the announcement, and even within the administration the policy change led to the resignations of two top officials in the State Department's Office of Cuban Affairs. Cuba policy was clearly a function of a much more complex pattern of politics than it had been during the Reagan-Bush years. While Congress had become more engaged in making strategic policy toward Cuba, in this crisis it was not a key player—as we might expect. Still, President Clinton faced new pressures from domestic constituencies in this crisis, regarding the immigration issue, state level elections, and even budget considerations about the mounting expense at Guantanamo. Finally, CANF's access to the executive branch was no longer guaranteed, and President Clinton unilaterally changed a significant part of the U.S. policy toward Cuba. That unilateral action increased the skepticism about Clinton's dedication to a tough embargo, and the Republican success in the 1994 elections that led to Republican majorities in the House and Senate weakened the position of those Clinton administration officials who might have been interested in at least softening the embargo. The outcomes of the 1994 elections also strengthened the hand of those in Congress who opposed such a shift.

The Helms-Burton Act

On February 24, 1996, Cuban Air Force MiG jetfighters shot down two unarmed planes that had flown across the Florida Straits toward Cuba, killing four Cuban Americans: three U.S. citizens and one U.S. resident.[24] The planes were operated by members of the group Brothers to the Rescue, who fly over the waters separating Florida and Cuba watching for rafters, and who have also been known to fly over Cuba from time to time to drop anti-Castro leaflets. [25] Following the shootdown, on March 12, President Bill Clinton signed into law the Cuban Liberty and Democratic Solidarity Act of 1996.[26] The measure tightened the long standing U.S. embargo of Cuba that had previously existed by executive order and codified it into law.

As Clinton signed Helms-Burton, he said, "Today I sign [the bill] with a certainty that it will send a powerful, unified message from the United States to Havana, that the yearning of the Cuban people for freedom must not be denied." He continued, "The legislation I sign today further tightens that embargo. It sends a strong message to the Cuban Government. We will not tolerate attacks on United States citizens and we will stand with those both inside and outside Cuba who are working for a peaceful transition to freedom and democracy." He concluded by saying that he signed the bill "in the name of the four men who were killed when their planes were shot down on February 24: Armando Alejandre, Carlos Costa, Mario de la Pena, and Pablo Morales. In their memory, I will continue to do everything I can to help the tide of democracy that has swept our entire hemisphere finally, finally reach the shores of Cuba."[27]

The road to passage of this law was not as simple as it might at first appear. Indeed, at one point Clinton's Secretary of State, Warren Christopher, argued that he would urge President Clinton to veto the bill should it ever come before him, and that was a softer version of the bill than the one Clinton ultimately signed.

Momentum Builds and Fades

The impetus for a new legislative initiative had begun to emerge even before the 1994 elections. Many on the Hill were frustrated that Castro had survived the wave of democratization that had swept Latin America. Furthermore, some Republicans were concerned that Clinton was not doing enough to try to remove Castro from power in Cuba. From the perspective of Dan Fisk, a key former Republican Senate committee staffer who worked for Senator Jesse Helms (R-NC) during this period, Clinton had run to the right of President Bush on the CDA, only then to either ignore Cuba policy or to send signals of rapprochement. The contrast of Cuba policy with Clinton's Haiti policy—where Clinton invested significant time and resources and even committed to a military solution in 1994, although it was not ultimately necessary, to remove a dictator and restore democracy—frustrated many in Congress too. The view from some on the Hill was that Haiti and Cuba were both countries with dictatorships, but Clinton seemed interested only in dethroning Haiti's rulers. A key force in the Haiti case, though, was the activism of the Congressional Black Caucus, which kept national attention on the issue. And Senator Helms and others decided that similar activism by a different group of legislators was needed on Cuba.[28] It was in this context that the Cuban Liberty and Democratic Solidarity Act, LIBERTAD for short, or "Helms-Burton" for its sponsors—Helms in the Senate and Dan Burton (R-IN) in the House—began to take shape.

Helms-Burton picked up steam in early 1995 at the direction of Senator Helms, the new chairman of the Senate Foreign Relations Committee. Dan Fisk was the point man on the legislation directed at driving Castro from Cuba. Fisk constructed the bill by bringing together all the pieces of Cuba legislation that had been floating around the Hill over the past few years. He also formed a coalition of staffers from the House and Senate to review these past initiatives and to plan this new bill.[29] Notably absent from the drafting coalition was CANF. While CANF was the biggest and most important lobby group in town on Cuba policy, and the drafting coalition wanted CANF's partnership in pushing the bill once drafted, the autonomous role in Cuba policy for Congress and some of its key members —especially the three Cuban Americans—was growing.

The original idea was to add Helms-Burton onto some other bill, but pressure and momentum caused Senator Helms to unveil Helms-Burton as a freestanding bill in February 1995. It included several controversial components to tighten and expand the embargo of Cuba. Perhaps most controversial was the bill's "Title III" that would give U.S. nationals the right to sue in U.S. courts foreign companies that "traffic" in stolen property in Cuba. Title III of the bill states, "any person that . . . traffics in property which was confiscated by the Cuban government on or after January 1, 1959, shall be liable to any United States national who owns the claim to such property for money damages." With this, a foreign company that does business in Cuba on or with property of U.S. nationals that was seized following the Cuban Revolution could be taken to court for a financial settlement. This "extraterritorial" nature of the bill was highly controversial: its standing in international law was questioned by many, and it promised to pose diplomatic headaches for the president even bigger than the ones Bush feared from the CDA. For example, Canadian officials offered a strong protest of Title III by way of a letter to the U.S. State Department in April, declaring that this part of Helms-Burton "would constitute an illegitimate intrusion upon third countries."[30]

Also controversial was "Title IV" of the bill, which would deny visas to executives of foreign companies "trafficking" (doing business) in confiscated properties in Cuba. Title IV directs that "The Secretary of State shall deny a visa to, and the Attorney General shall exclude from the United States, any alien who the Secretary of State determines is a person who . . . traffics in confiscated property, a claim to which is owned by a United States national." As Helms-Burton was moving through Congress in the spring and summer, it is important to note, others took more direct action to challenge Castro as boats and small airplanes made periodic runs toward Cuba from Miami.

Hearings in the House were marked by suspicion about the Clinton administration's intentions toward Cuba. Administration witnesses were grilled about an article in the *Washington Post* that claimed an internal

National Security Council paper suggested the embargo of Cuba be lifted.[31] This was compounded by leaks from the administration and from abroad that the Clinton team was considering loosening or lifting the embargo.[32] Clinton's unilateral move to lift the economic embargo of Vietnam and to normalize relations in 1994–1995, and his actions to reverse U.S. policy on automatically granting asylum to fleeing Cubans during the 1994 immigration crisis, also suggested to congressional proponents of the Cuban embargo that they might need to restrain the president in this area. Lincoln Diaz-Balart (R-FL), for example, was very concerned that the Clinton administration was going to normalize relations with Cuba before political reforms might be enacted there. He says he received a variety of signals that suggested this intention, including one from a British diplomat who told him they had been assured by the Clinton people that the president would normalize relations after the 1996 elections.[33] Another House member, Dana Rohrbacher (R-CA), adopted harsher rhetoric when he described the foreign corporations using appropriated property in Cuba as "the scum of the globe."[34] And from the Senate side, Jesse Helms received wild applause in Miami in April with phrases like, "Time to go, Castro," and "Hasta la bye bye, Fidel."[35]

The administration came out publicly against Helms-Burton. In an April 1995 interview on CNN, President Clinton argued that it was unnecessary because of the existing CDA.[36] Undersecretary of State for Political Affairs Peter Tarnoff testified against the bill in the Senate because it would limit the president's flexibility in conducting foreign affairs. He, like Clinton, argued that the two tracks of the CDA were sufficient.[37] Secretary of State Warren Christopher sent a letter that argued against the bill to Speaker of the House Newt Gingrich the day before the House vote. Christopher wrote that if Helms-Burton were passed he would urge the president to veto it on the grounds that it was overly inflexible for dealing with the rapidly developing situation in Cuba. He also opposed Title III as counterproductive.[38] A congressional opponent of the bill, Charles Rangel (D-NY), was certain of the ultimate fate of the bill, saying on the House floor: "This will never become law in this country, and you know it. It is going to be vetoed, and it will not be overridden. You know and I know that this is theatrics, and it will never become law."[39] Nevertheless, the

House passed LIBERTAD by a count of 294-130 on September 21, and action moved to the Senate—where passage promised to be more difficult.

According to Fisk, Clinton himself never actually threatened to veto Helms-Burton, leaving it to the State Department to try to keep the bill from ever reaching his desk. Since there was no "heavy-handed White House presence" against the bill, its proponents in the Senate did not think Helms-Burton was necessarily a "killer" for Clinton.[40] A former administration official confirmed that their strategy was not to threaten a veto but rather to prevent the bill from ever getting to the president without having to issue a veto threat.[41] The administration also tried to "expand the scope" of the conflict by cultivating corporate opposition to the bill. On October 6, Chief of Staff Leon Panetta and Clinton's foreign policy advisers met with a group of about fifty U.S. corporate executives about taking a trip to Cuba. The problem with this potential visit was that according to Treasury Department regulations, only certain categories of U.S. citizens and residents may legally travel to the island. Groups typically receiving special "licenses" to travel to Cuba include journalists and academics.[42] To meet these restrictions, the executives, including heads of Time Warner, Hyatt Hotels, General Motors, and Zenith, were then classified as "journalists" and went to Cuba to meet with Castro.[43] Diaz-Balart challenged the one-day trip to Cuba by these executives: "there is an abhorrent, unscrupulous, carefully planned strategy by administration officials to use the business community as a means of putting pressure on Congress."[44] Senator Phil Gramm (R-TX) described Clinton's maneuvers as "putting out the welcome mat to Castro instead of tightening the noose around his aging neck."[45]

Despite a plea by Senator Bob Graham (D-FL) by way of an earlier "Dear Colleague" letter to Senate Democrats urging their support of the bill,[46] attempts to move Helms-Burton toward a Senate vote failed twice in mid-October 1995. As Clinton and corporate opposition grew more forceful, support for Helms-Burton faltered. In the meantime Clinton moved forward under the two tracks of the CDA. At Freedom House, President Clinton announced his intention to tighten enforcement of the embargo but to also take steps to promote democracy on the island. He announced measures to expand contacts between people in the two countries, including the opening of news bureaus, relaxed travel restrictions, and more activities by U.S. nongovernmental organizations in Cuba. He announced a new grant for Freedom House as a first of its kind effort to fund NGO work in Cuba on behalf of democracy and human rights.[47]

Unable to move the bill as it was, the Senate removed controversial Titles III and IV. Even though Helms-Burton had passed overwhelmingly in the House, the president seemed poised to win the showdown. Once the bill passed the Senate in its weakened form, Helms-Burton seemed dead as it went to Conference Committee to resolve the differences between the House and Senate versions of the bill. The very future of the embargo looked bleak to some.

While this was unfolding in Washington, D.C., the events in the Florida Straits intervened. Regularly flying missions over the waters between Cuba and Florida, Brothers to the Rescue were also reportedly flying over Cuba on occasion to drop anti-Castro leaflets. Tension over these flights rose by February 1996 as the Cuban government became increasingly angry. Bringing the tension to a dramatic and tragic crescendo, Cuban Air Force jets shot down two small unarmed Brothers to the Rescue planes over the Florida Straits on February 26, 1996—killing four people and breathing new life into the Helms-Burton Act.[48]

Helms-Burton's Second Chance

The shootdown produced a strong reaction from some in Congress and reinvigorated support for Helms-Burton. Ros-Lehtinen characterized the shootdown as "an act of war" and called for a naval blockade.[49] On February 26 Clinton condemned the attack and ordered a number of actions directed against Cuba. He asked Ambassador Madeleine Albright to seek condemnation of Cuba's actions at the United Nations, and he announced his interest in having Congress pass a bill to provide compensation for the family members of those killed. He ordered Radio Marti to extend its efforts, ended air travel between the United States and Cuba, and placed restrictions on the travel of Cuban officials in the United States. He also announced his intention to reach an agreement with Congress on Helms-Burton as the advantage now clearly shifted to the Hill.[50] At a strategy meeting the next day that was attended by Burton, Diaz-Balart, Patrick

Kennedy (D-RI), Menendez, Ros-Lehtinen, Torricelli, and others, Titles III and IV were put back in the bill. And Diaz-Balart insisted that a new measure be added as well: codification of the embargo into law. This move, inserted into Title I of the bill, would take the full body of the U.S. embargo policy toward Cuba—that until now had existed by Executive Order—and establish it as law. Title I, § 102(h), states that "The economic embargo of Cuba, as in effect on March 1, 1996, including all restrictions under part 515 of Title 31, Code of Federal Regulations, shall be in effect upon enactment of this Act." Thereafter, Congress would have to repeal or alter the law if the embargo were to be ended in the future (as Clinton did earlier with Vietnam). Diaz-Balart said he would insist on codification and that he wanted their support; they all agreed.[51]

From the perspective of congressional supporters of Helms-Burton, Clinton now had no choice but to accept the bill because it was "the only game in town."[52] A House staffer noted that the shootdown "changed everything" and left the administration "no position to bargain."[53] Patrick Kennedy argued, "Now is not the time to relax on Castro. Shooting down unarmed civilian planes is just one more in an escalating and disturbing pattern of human rights violations by the Castro regime, desperately clinging to power in its final days." Diaz-Balart, adopting a populist tone at the same press conference, said, "Sometimes Main Street's got to . . . speak up and [tell] Wall Street where to go."[54] Even Richard Nuccio, then the president's Special Adviser for Cuba Policy, admitted that "President Castro created a veto-proof majority for the Helms-Burton bill."[55]

The next morning the congressional activists presented their revised plan to Nuccio and the administration. At eight o'clock in the morning on February 28 in Robert Menendez's office, the coalition from the Hill met with several members of the administration, including Nuccio. As Diaz-Balart recalls, the administration emphasized that they wanted to include in the legislation a presidential "waiver" for Title III that would, essentially, allow the president to sign the bill but then waive its enforcement at least temporarily for reasons of "national security." They negotiated most of the day on this issue. When the issue of codification was brought up, the Clinton team objected on the grounds that it was "new" to the bill. Diaz-Balart then asked, "Well, are you going to lift the embargo?" When the Clinton team said that they would not, Diaz-Balart's response was,

"Good, then we have no problem; next issue." This go-round happened a few times through the day, but Diaz-Balart argues that there was never any negotiation on this point, plus the Clinton team seemed more concerned with Title III, for which they ultimately got a form of a waiver.[56] The waiver in Title III states that "the President may suspend the right to bring an action under this title . . . for a period of not more than 6 months if the President determines in writing to the appropriate congressional committees at least 15 days before suspension takes effect that such suspension is necessary to the national interests of the United States and will expedite a transition to democracy in Cuba."[57]

When it came time to negotiate on Title IV, for which the Clinton administration also wanted waivers, Diaz-Balart recalls that Torricelli "played the bad guy and said there would be no waiver there." He further notes that the Clinton team had virtually no bargaining power and few options. "What were they going to do, veto a bill after a terrorist government's air force shot down American citizens? Not even Qadhafi has done exactly that."[58] Fisk agrees that the deal was "you get waivers on Title III, and we get codification."[59]

The Clinton team then assembled to decide how to proceed. The group included Attorney General Janet Reno, Secretary of Defense William J. Perry, Secretary of State Warren Christopher, Chairman of the Joint Chiefs of Staff General John M. Shalikasvili, Director of Central Intelligence John Deutch, and others. As they discussed the policy issues, none of them appeared to know about the codification provision; when they were told about it, they objected on the grounds that it took away too much prerogative from the president and they wondered about its constitutionality. Political advisers George Stephanopoulos and Leon Panetta overruled the policy people and argued that Clinton should sign the bill because his administration could be weakened politically if they vetoed it following such a dramatic event. President Clinton's reelection chances could also be hurt 'if he were to anger the politically strong Cuban American population in Florida and New Jersey, and signing the bill would make him look "tough." When National Security Adviser Anthony Lake agreed, the policy discussion was over; political calculations carried the day. Rather than argue against codification, the Clinton team focused on the waivers to Title III so they could explain their reversal on the bill and salve the allies, who were not going to take well to Title III. They then said they would sign the bill.[60]

Not everyone was happy about the deal. Charles Rangel assessed the new law: "This bill has nothing to do with Castro; it has everything to do with our friends and our voters in Florida."[61] Senator Dodd warned that the bill "totally ties the hands of this president and future presidents to respond flexibly to change in Cuba when it comes."[62] Representative Hamilton shared this concern and argued that codification would "lock in the president of the United States in the conduct of foreign policy."[63] Beyond these concerns, critics of the bill continued to worry about how Helms-Burton would set the United States and its allies at odds over the extraterritorial nature of the bill. Supporters of the bill nevertheless argued that international opposition should not affect U.S. policy making, however. Paul Coverdell (R-GA) declared, "We can't retreat because this is disruptive to some of our European allies." Ileana Ros-Lehtinen added, "The United States must stop hiding behind international public opinion and stop wavering."[64] The cosponsor of the bill, Dan Burton, concluded that agreement on Helms-Burton "makes it clear that Fidel Castro and his blood-soaked, dictatorial, corrupt tyranny is about to end."[65] After the new bill passed both houses, Clinton signed Helms-Burton on March 12, 1996, saying it "will send a powerful, unified message from the United States to Havana, that the yearning of the Cuban people for freedom must not be denied."[66]

In the future, Clinton might waive Title III, but the ultimate question of Cuba policy—the embargo—was now codified into law.

The Domestic Roots of U.S.-Cuba Policy

The pattern of the first Clinton administration shows how broad domestic political calculations have come to push Cuba policy. During Clinton's campaign in 1992, electoral politics and the realities of fundraising led to support for the CDA. Once in office, when raised, Cuba policy often fell to the president's political advisers rather than the policy experts. In the Baeza case, when Clinton miscalculated—whether due to poor information or an oversight—he quickly reversed himself even if it meant crossing out

Baeza's name on a list of nominees. In a single afternoon in 1994, the Cuban Adjustment Act—and thirty years of preferential treatment for Cuban migrants—was repealed when different domestic inputs entered the Clinton political calculus. In the case of Helms-Burton, the shootdown of the Brothers to the Rescue plane altered the political equation, and opposition to a weaker bill became support for an even stronger bill almost overnight.

One interpretation of these events is that, with the exception of the immigration policy change that CANF opposed, they mark the ultimate success of an ethnic interest group that had been driving U.S.-Cuba policy since its origins in the early Reagan years. This explanation, however interesting, misses the mark. CANF supported the CDA, but Clinton's acceptance of the CDA made sense on many levels. While CANF opposed the Baeza appointment, so too did many on the Hill who acted to have his name removed. CANF opposed the immigration policy change and was in fact excluded from the policy process in that case. CANF was excluded from the drafting of Helms-Burton, though welcomed as a lobbyist on its behalf. CANF lobbying was largely unsuccessful until the Cuban Air Force changed everything. U.S.-Cuba policy in the first Clinton term was rooted in a complex pattern of politics in which the money, votes, and institutional links of CANF mattered, but the larger domestic political calculus of the president mattered even more. Further, entrepreneurial members of Congress usurped many of the functions once performed more exclusively by the executive and CANF. A small number of influential members of Congress appear to play a surprisingly important role in shaping U.S. policy toward Cuba. This is consistent with other foreign policy issues where various members of Congress have stood out "by virtue of their persistence, expertise, or cleverness."[67]

Reflecting on the policy process evident in the cases, we reach a number of other conclusions as well. First, the executive decision-making process was noteworthy for the haphazard nature of meetings and consultation that preceded policy choices. This can be seen especially in the Baeza and immigration cases, but it is also apparent in the Helms-Burton case following the shootdown. Second, electoral calculations figured prominently in the decision by then-candidate Clinton to support the CDA and later in the immigration reversal by President Clinton. Cuba as a "foreign" policy issue came to be infused with more "domestic" political content in this period, and the importance of elections, interest groups, and Congress increased. While the president could still act with great prerogative during the immigration crisis, even this had to be managed domestically.

Third, during the crisis that followed the 1996 shootdown the balance of power shifted from the president to assertive policy entrepreneurs in Congress. This move may be particularly striking because it happened during a crisis, exactly the kind of situation in which we would expect the president's policy advantage over Congress to be greatest. The belief of the president and his political advisers that they needed to respond to the pressures brought to bear by Congress (and the Cuban Air Force) can help explain why Clinton signed on to Helms-Burton. It is still striking to note, however, that Clinton accepted codification of Cuba policy, which cuts into the heart of the foreign policy prerogative of the presidency, largely without a fight. The shifting of the locus of Cuba policy to Capitol Hill with the passage of Helms-Burton is especially significant for students of U.S. foreign policy. The initiative behind Helms-Burton was in part a product of the 1994 elections and an interest by some in Congress to stop what was perceived as a drift in Cuba policy.[68] Clinton and his advisers consistently opposed the bill because they saw it as unnecessary and as an encroachment on presidential authority in foreign policy. After the shootdown, Clinton negotiated waivers for Title III but accepted codification and thus surrendered significant foreign policy prerogative to the legislature. Now any actor, including a president, who would try to change the core of U.S. policy toward Cuba—the embargo—must recognize that the path to do so runs through Capitol Hill. While the executive might still make lesser changes—and there is some debate in Congress about his right to do even that—following Helms-Burton, Congress appeared to retain control over the heart of U.S. foreign policy toward Cuba. And by this time it had become clear that struggles between the president and Congress, and the assertiveness of Cuban Americans and other policy entrepreneurs in the Legislature, were likely to matter as much as developments on the island of Cuba itself, for the direction of Cuba policy.

The President Strikes Back

WITH PHILIP BRENNER

THE PASSAGE OF the Cuban Liberty and Democratic Solidarity Act in 1996 would seem to have put to rest the academic debate over which branch controls Cuba policy. Helms-Burton codified the U.S. embargo of Cuba into law and thus appeared to put Congress in the driver's seat on making—and changing—Cuba policy. But in the years since President Clinton signed Helms-Burton there have been a number of moves on Cuba policy that suggest the struggle over control of Cuba policy is far from settled.

In order to explain the changing politics of making policy toward Cuba, and the continuing struggle between the branches over policy toward the island, we discuss here the key policy developments that emerged between the passage of Helms-Burton and the end of Bill Clinton's second term, which included a second congressional codification in 2000. We analyze how these changes came about and assess what these developments show about the relationship between Congress and the executive on Cuba policy, and more generally about these two branches as foreign policy makers operating in an evolving interest group environment. We argue that while the policy preferences that key players hold are important, there are also notable institutional interests that have led each branch to vie for control of Cuba policy. Having signed away significant authority over the embargo in Helms-Burton, Clinton acted to reassert executive power in clever ways. Congress has since acted to tighten its institutional grip on Cuba policy, even as it has become more fractured on the wisdom of the embargo. We also note the way that global developments and pressures continue to influence the debate about policy toward Cuba. With the end of the cold war and the decline of Cuba as a security threat, Cuba policy has become increasingly "domesticated:"[1] it is now safe to argue about policy toward the island, and that makes it seem even more likely that we would see congressional activism here. But the pattern of congressional and presidential activism is curious and contains elements of both inter-branch and intrabranch conflict.[2] And the political environment in which Cuba policy is made began to change rapidly in the late 1990s.

Cuba Policy after Helms-Burton

The intent of Helms-Burton was clearly spelled out in the conference committee report on the bill: the economic embargo of Cuba was to remain in effect until a democratically elected government comes to power, a government that, among other things, could not include Fidel or Raul Castro. The president may then come to Congress to seek an end to the embargo.[3] Concerning the codification component, the report states that "all economic sanctions in force on March 1, 1996, shall remain in effect until they are either suspended or terminated.[4] The report went on to note, "It is not the intent of this section to prohibit executive branch agencies from amending existing regulations to tighten economic sanctions on Cuba."[5] Although Clinton could waive Title III, the ultimate question of Cuba policy—the embargo—was clearly codified into law. Helms-Burton seemed to mark a key shift in foreign policy power by transferring control over the embargo to Congress. We show how President Clinton tried over time to loose these bonds, if not slip them altogether, and how Congress responded with its own measures—some that hardened the embargo, some that softened it. We argue that President Clinton's efforts in the post-Helms-Burton era were not only based on his policy preferences toward Cuba but also, and perhaps more important, rooted in an attempt to regain executive power over foreign policy that he appeared to have signed away in Helms-Burton's codification of the embargo into law. His efforts focused on three areas: waiving Title III, generally not enforcing Title IV, and expanding the limited licensing power left in the bill in order to pursue new initiatives toward Cuba and alter the shape of, if not the existence of, the embargo. Each of these steps shows how vigorous executive power in this area can be, even when it appears that Congress has acted decisively.[6]

Waiving Title III

Under the compromise between the administration and the bill's supporters that created Title III's waiver mechanism, the president may waive or suspend the right to bring suit for six months and may renew the waiver each six months, "if the President determines and reports in writing to the appropriate congressional committees at least 15 days before the suspension takes effect that such suspension is necessary to the national interests of the United States and will expedite a transition to democracy in Cuba."[7]

Congress sought to set this waiver apart from other "national security" waivers. In fact, Congress explicitly rejected the president's proposal that the waiver could be used if it "is important to the national interests of the United States, including expediting a transition to democracy in Cuba." The conference committee did not want the "transition to democracy" component to be only one of many items the president would weigh when deciding whether to use the waiver; rather, the committee wanted this to be the central issue involved. Indeed, the committee went on to argue that in their view "under current circumstances the President could not in good faith determine that the suspension of the right of action is either 'necessary to the national interests of the United States' or 'will expedite a transition to democracy in Cuba.' In particular, the committee believes that it is demonstrably not the case that suspending the right of action will expedite a transition to democracy in Cuba."[8] The drafters of Helms-Burton frankly did not think Clinton would use the waivers because they did not think the president could show progress toward a democratic transition in Cuba.[9] Helms himself, following Clinton's first use of the waiver in July 1996, [10] argued angrily that he had intended the bill to be "Clinton Proof."[11]

In July 1996 Clinton announced that effective August 1 he would allow Title III to come into force. However, Clinton also announced that he would exercise the Title III enforcement waiver, thus suspending or preventing suits from being brought under Helms-Burton. Clinton argued that this move put companies doing business in Cuba with expropriated American property "on notice" that they faced the prospect of significant liability in U.S. courts, while buying time to work on this issue with allies, who were angry about the extraterritorial nature of the legislation.[12]

Clinton waived enforcement of Title III again in January 1997. Justifying the waiver, Clinton argued that he had "decided to make maximum use of Title III to increase pressure on the Castro regime by working with our allies—not against them—to accelerate change in Cuba." He noted, "the international community is more united behind the cause of freedom in Cuba than ever before in the 38-year history of Castro's oppressive regime." Clinton cited the "Common Position" adopted by the European Union for reform in Cuba as evidence of this new international consensus. He also noted that leaders from Latin America, Spain, and Portugal, meeting at the Ibero-American Summit in Santiago in November, called for democracy and full respect for human rights in Cuba; they emphasized Cuba's isolation as the hemisphere's only nondemocratic nation. He further argued that activity by nongovernmental actors had increased.[13] Clinton continued to exercise the waiver each six months throughout his presidency, announcing the final waiver on January 17, 2001.[14]

Largely Ignoring Title IV

Title IV instructs the secretary of state and attorney general to prevent any third-country national (or a member of that person's family) from entering the United States if that person has confiscated or "trafficked" in confiscated property in Cuba to which there is an existing claim by a U.S. national.[15] The clear intent of Title IV was to deter further economic activity in Cuba by foreign companies and to induce divestment by companies currently doing business on the island.[16]

Contrary to Clinton's assertion that Title IV was the subject of "aggressive implementation,"[17] it was, in fact, applied only selectively.[18] The primary targets of enforcement were executives of the Canadian firm Sherritt International. In July 1996, seven members of that company received official letters from the U.S. government informing them that they and their family members would not be allowed to legally enter the country.[19] The government also sent warning letters to executives of the Mexican firm Grupo Domos and the Italian company Stet International.[20] Grupo Domos, which was a partner in the Cuban telephone company, eventually relinquished its stake therein; the weak peso and other financial difficulties were probably as important as the threat posed by Helms-Burton in the Mexican company's decision to withdraw from the island.[21] Stet, also a telecommunications company, "immunized" itself against Helms-Burton by agreeing to compensate ITT for its confiscated assets.[22] By March 1999, a State Department official testified that only officials with Sherritt Corporation (fifteen by now) and the Israeli BM group were being excluded from the United States as a result of Title IV.[23] Given that initial estimates ran from one hundred to two hundred joint ventures that were trafficking in confiscated property,[24] the small number of companies targeted certainly suggests that the Clinton administration practiced a de facto waiver of Title IV.

While we believe that the chief executive's policy and institutional interests are important parts of explaining the Clinton administration's implementation decisions on both Title III and IV, it is also clear that global interests and pressures played roles as well. Among Cuba's largest trading partners were the other members of the North American Free Trade Agreement (NAFTA)—Canada and Mexico. Denial of visas or suits against Canadian and Mexican businesses would seem to directly conflict with NAFTA provisions prohibiting such restraints on trade. While Mexico and Canada largely limited themselves to rhetorical denunciation of LIBERTAD, the Canadian parliament did pass a law in 1996 making it illegal for a Canadian corporation to adhere to the terms of Helms-Burton. The law has never been invoked, but that sort of development would potentially pose a significant threat to the future of NAFTA itself.

The Clinton administration also worked to reach agreement with the European Union not to enforce Helms-Burton against European companies.[25] The administration was involved in negotiations with European allies over LIBERTAD's sanctions from the time of the bill's passage in 1996. In 1997 the administration agreed to seek changes in the law to eliminate extraterritorial provisions in return for an EU promise to curtail trade with Cuba. But its failure to obtain congressional approval of the changes renewed the EU's criticisms of U.S. policy.[26] At stake was the very basis of the World Trade Organization (WTO). The administration responded to attacks on LIBERTAD with the assertion that the WTO charter allowed trade sanctions for "national security" reasons. If left standing, this stratagem would open a loophole in the WTO through which any country could ignore the new global trading regime when it suited their interests. It was an approach U.S. allies wanted to discourage. European trade partners of the United States argued that the extraterritorial elements of Helms-Burton and the 1992 Torricelli Bill fundamentally conflicted with the free trade goals of the WTO. Significantly, their views were articulated by corporate leaders in the United States such as retired Chrysler chairman Lee Iacocca and real estate developer Mort Zuckerman, and the major corporations that supported Americans for Humanitarian Trade with Cuba and USA*Engage.[27] Officials of U.S.-based global corporations thus conveyed international pressures in the process of promoting their own economic interests in eliminating global trade sanctions. Critical articles and editorials in the major print media, including business-oriented publications such as *The Economist* and *Wall Street Journal,* reflected a frustration with what business chiefs saw as an outmoded policy.[28]

Expanding Licensing Power

The president was given some limited licensing power to revise the sanctions that were codified when Helms-Burton was enacted. Using "sense of the Congress" language, less powerful than statutory language, under certain circumstances the president may reinstitute licenses (1) to allow people in the United States to send money to their families in Cuba and (2) to allow travel to Cuba by U.S. residents who have family members there.[29] The reinstitution of remittances is premised on reforms in Cuba to allow small businesses to operate freely; the reinstitution of family travel is based on the Cuban government's release of political prisoners and the recognition of fundamental freedoms such as the right of association.

Clinton used this limited licensing power to relax a number of the restrictions placed on access to Cuba that were imposed following the Brothers to the Rescue shootdown. The first of these steps followed the pope's 1998 visit to the island.[30] Clinton announced the resumption of licensing direct humanitarian charter flights to Cuba; the establishment of new licensing arrangements to permit Cuban Americans and Cuban families living in the United States to send humanitarian remittances to their families in Cuba at the level of $300 per quarter, as was permitted until 1994; and the facilitation of licensing for the sale of medicines and medical supplies and equipment to Cuba.[31] Once again, we see these actions by the president as rooted in both his interest in reasserting control over a policy that had been codified by Congress and in responding to the new pressures posed by the pope's upcoming criticism of the U.S. embargo. In a series of masses across the island during his January visit, the pontiff found common ground with Castro in a critique of global capitalism's blind market forces, and he pointedly called for an end to "oppressive economic measures—unjust and ethically unacceptable—imposed from outside the country."[32] The pope's visit further undermined international acquiescence in the embargo, and several South American countries signed trade pacts with Cuba over the following months. Caribbean countries gave Castro a hero's welcome at a summit in which the region's leaders signed a free trade agreement.[33]

The administration also reached an agreement in mid-1998 to let Cuban airliners fly over the United States en route to Canada. The agreement was reached days before the UN's International Civil Aviation Organization was due to rule on the dispute. The United States was expected to lose its case because the "national security exception" would likely not be upheld, given that the U.S. Defense Department itself admitted that Cuba posed no significant threat to the United States. [34] The executive branch continued to modify Cuba policy in a context shaped by the codification of the embargo, the president's institutional interests, and external pressures.

In January 1999, Clinton announced a second set of unilateral actions "toward the Cuban people," including: increased support for Radio and TV Marti; expansion of remittances by allowing any U.S. resident to send limited funds to individual Cuban families and independent organizations; expansion of people-to-people contact through two-way exchanges among academics, athletes, scientists, and others; authorization of the sale of food and agricultural inputs to independent nongovernmental entities such as family restaurants, religious groups, and private farmers; authorization of charter passenger flights to cities in Cuba other than Havana and from some cities in the United States other than Miami; and finally, a pledge to establish direct mail service to Cuba.[35] After announcing these initiatives, Clinton scuttled a widely-supported plan to assemble a bipartisan commission on U.S.-Cuba policy.[36]

While Clinton admitted that he was prevented "from lifting the embargo without the support of Congress"[37] and that his steps on Cuba were "clearly circumscribed" by Helms-Burton,[38] his moves in March 1998 and in January 1999 nevertheless seemed to go well beyond what the bill permitted. In particular, the proposed sale of food to Cubans suggested a president who was willing to push the envelope of the possible. As for the source of this authority, James Dobbins, a Clinton White House official, argued in 1999 that the language in Helms-Burton " codified the embargo, and at the same time it codified the president's licensing power; that is, it codified a process by which there was an embargo to which exceptions could be granted on a case-by-case basis, by the president, in cases in which it was deemed to be consistent with U.S. policy."[39] Another interpretation would be that the president was ignoring Helms-Burton and instituting measures that seemed to flow more from Track II of the CDA than LIBERTAD. After all, by rejecting the proposed commission to review policy, the politically astute president may have been seeking a way to give something to those he had disappointed. The words of one State Department official suggest a calculus of that sort: "We did not want to use up political capital in naming a commission that would probably not be effective. . . . We felt it was more realistic to split the difference."[40] Later reports suggested that electoral politics played a prominent role in the decision to reject the call for a policy review. Senator Bob Graham and Vice President Al Gore recognized that the commission would be doing its work in the middle of the 2000 presidential campaign and that the Democratic nominee would be hard pressed to overcome the presumed Cuban American backlash in Florida.[41]

Proembargo forces in Congress were certainly glad that the president had rejected the commission idea, but generally they reacted negatively to what they saw as Clinton's unfaithfulness to the language and intent of

Helms-Burton. Taken as a whole, the waivers of Title III, failure to aggressively enforce Title IV, and tinkering with the embargo itself by expanding the president's licensing power clearly angered the advocates of rigorous economic sanctions and seemed to show the limits of congressional power over Cuba policy, even with a codified embargo. There were, however, others in Congress who opposed the embargo for a variety of reasons who were becoming mobilized in the post-Helms-Burton atmosphere. When Congress began to react to the president's actions following Helms-Burton, it did not do so as a unified institution.

Congress Replies

The White House portrayed its reforms as responses to the pope's visit and his urging the United States to act in support of the church and other nongovernmental groups in Cuba.[42] While that representation may have provided the president additional political space to challenge a codified policy, there were still objections registered by members of Congress. One congressional staffer argued, "it was not clear that Clinton has the authority himself to allow direct flights, since the ban is covered under the legislation, which does not allow special waivers [for flights]."[43] Representative Diaz-Balart weighed in by declaring that "We are not going to let Clinton proceed along the path of normalization."[44] On CNN, Ileana Ros-Lehtinen lamented that congressional initiatives to tighten the embargo risked becoming "nothing more than historical documents to be examined by graduate students for their dissertations because the Clinton administration does not enforce the law." She went on to argue, "We believe that these initiatives are not authorized by law."[45] Their challenge did not prevent those changes from taking place. The Cuban American supporters of the embargo were somewhat more successful at holding off the growing momentum in Congress itself to end some sanctions on Cuba.

Gambits in 1999

Even as President Clinton was tinkering with aspects of the embargo, legislators interested in access to the Cuban market for U.S. products developed momentum around their own bills to authorize food and drug sales.

In the House, the Freedom to Market Act was introduced in May 1999. That bill required the General Accounting Office to report on the impact and effectiveness of economic sanctions imposed by the United States and would prohibit the imposition of unilateral sanctions on exports of agricultural products or medical supplies. Given the influence of the three Cuban American members of Congress, the battle in the House for this bill was decidedly uphill. In May, George Nethercutt (R-WA) offered an amendment in the House Appropriations Committee to lift all unilateral sanctions on food and medicine; it failed 28-24.[46] Opposed to the amendment, Diaz-Balart argued: "I recognize that the agriculture community in the United States is going through difficult economic times. . . . But I do not think taxpayer-financed trade with terrorist states is an appropriate way to try to help U.S. farmers."[47] At the end of July, the House Appropriations Committee rejected another amendment that would have lifted sanctions on the sale of food and medicine.[48]

Support for lifting the sanctions on food and drug sales was more widespread in the Senate, and opposition to the change was also far less committed. While Democrats such as Christopher Dodd (D-CT) had a long record of opposing the embargo against Cuba on human rights grounds, Republicans from farm states were clearly the leaders of the new anti-sanctions efforts in the Senate. In January 1999 John Ashcroft (R-MO) introduced the Selective Agriculture Embargoes Act of 1999 that would place new obstacles in the way of any president who wanted to embargo the export of agricultural commodities. Among his cosponsors were Democrats and conservative Midwestern and Western Republicans. Chuck Hagel (R-NE) and Conrad Burns (R-MT) each made statements in support of the bill on the day of its introduction.[49] Ashcroft and Burns, it should be noted, both faced tough reelection campaigns in 2000. The bill would have served the dual purpose of providing potential economic benefits to exporting farmers and giving new leverage to the Senate over the president's imposition of sanctions. Less than a month later, Senator Ashcroft introduced the Food and Medicine for the World Act of 1999, which even more clearly sought to constrain the president's ability to unilaterally impose sanctions. The bill required "the approval of Congress of the imposition of any new unilateral agricultural sanction, or any new unilateral sanction with respect to medicine, medical supplies, or medical equipment, against a foreign country."[50] Once again, the list of cosponsors was bipartisan.

At this point, members of Congress were increasingly divided on the issue of sanctions. On the one hand, Congress's own Helms-Burton imposed strict sanctions on Cuba and codified the embargo into law in a way that only Congress could change. On the other hand, Ashcroft's proposals sought to put barriers in the way of executive-imposed sanctions. While members of Congress were increasingly split over the wisdom of sanctions generally, and over the future of the Cuban embargo specifically, what a majority of members of Congress could come together on was the move to wrest control of this type of foreign policy from the executive. As summer approached, developments in and out of the Senate suggested some momentum behind the reexamination of economic sanctions, including toward Cuba. Arlen Specter (R-PA) made a visit to Cuba at the beginning of June that included a long set of meetings with Castro. Soon after, the Clinton administration announced that it would be sending Coast Guard and State Department officials to meet with their Cuban counterparts.[51] American Farm Bureau president Dean Kelckner led a trip to Cuba in May, and the president of the U.S. Chamber of Commerce, Tom Donohue, made his own visit in July.[52] Upon his return Donohue argued on the op-ed pages of the *Washington Post* for lifting the embargo.[53] In the midst of these visits, Senator Ashcroft announced that he would seek to pass the Food and Medicine for the World Act as an amendment to the Agriculture Appropriations Bill.[54] By the end of June, there were fourteen antisanctions pieces of legislation pending in the House and eleven in the Senate; six were Cuba specific.[55]

Torricelli, Helms, and the two senators from Florida, Democrat Bob Graham and Republican Connie Mack, led the Senate opposition to any change in the embargo of Cuba. Helms tried to eliminate Ashcroft's amendment on August 3 by moving to table it, but he lost that vote 28-70.[56] Still, Torricelli, with close ties to the Cuban American community in Florida and New Jersey, and Helms were able to persuade Ashcroft to modify his amendment by adding an annual licensing provision that would apply to those on the State Department's annual list of terrorist countries. While that concession led some proembargo lawmakers to declare victory, they later admitted that the amendment represented an erosion of the U.S. embargo against Cuba. A provision that was reportedly "hastily redrafted in the Senate cloakroom" would have allowed U.S. banks to finance the sale of food or medical supplies to Cuba and would have eliminated the need for U.S. firms to verify how the medical products were being used.[57] In a press release that day, Ashcroft noted that in addition to protecting "the nation's hard-pressed farmers from being victimized in diplomatic disputes with foreign leaders," the bill would also "require the President to obtain congressional approval before the U.S. implements new trade sanctions that include food or medicine."[58] Leading farm state Senators Daschle (D-SD) and Dorgan (D-ND) left the following week for a meeting with Fidel Castro and other Cuban officials. Daschle claimed that the trip was intended to highlight the Senate's passage of that August 4 amendment to the agricultural spending bill.[59]

The Clinton administration was opposed to the constraints that they believed the House's Freedom to Market Act placed on the president. Under Secretary of State Stuart Eizenstat argued before the House Agriculture Committee that the bill would "impose inflexible procedural hurdles" on the president and that the executive branch also needed "broad national interest waiver authority."[60] The administration generally reacted cautiously to the developments in the Senate as well. Administration officials were not quoted to any great extent in the media on the subject of the Ashcroft amendment, with the comment by a spokesperson that the White House was "prepared to work with Congress" on the crafting of the final wording of the bill representative of the ambiguity coming from the executive branch.[61] A spokesman for the National Security Council said later that the president was willing to listen to "credible ideas" about the sale of food and medical supplies to Cuba.[62] But suggesting that the White House had no intention of leading on the issue, one administration official emphasized: "There's no hidden agenda of normalization. There's no hidden agenda of lifting the embargo."[63]

With the Clinton administration largely on the sidelines, a Senate and House conference committee was appointed in September to review a number of amendments, including the Ashcroft Food and Medicine for the World Act. As a member of the Agricultural Subcommittee of Appropriations in the House, George Nethercutt introduced his own amendment to the Ashcroft amendment, which included removal of the licensing requirement and an allowance for government financing of sales. The House conference members approved the amendment, but then some in the Republican leadership made an attempt to eliminate Cuba from the bill. The Senate conferees demanded inclusion of Cuba, however, and sent the bill back for final House approval. At that point, Tom DeLay, an opponent of the Ashcroft amendment that appeared ready to pass out of conference, ordered the conference committee to be shut down after its only meeting.[64]

When the conference committee reconvened on September 21, Representatives Diaz-Balart and Ros-Lehtinen had persuaded Republican leaders of both houses to "tie sales to Cuba to free elections, the release of all Cuban political prisoners and the legalization of political parties and nongovernmental labor unions."[65] Proembargo forces were still unable to win majority support in the conference, however, leading to an impasse. Divisions within Congress cut across party and ideological lines in atypical ways. With farm state legislators and a strong majority of congressional Democrats as backers of the efforts to facilitate the sale of goods to Cuba, the Cuban American members of the House were left dependent on Republican leadership in both houses to support the embargo. Ashcroft represented the wing of the Republican Party that had been nearly automatic on questions of the embargo of Cuba over the years, and the Missouri senator had strongly supported Helms-Burton; his change of position is notable. DeLay continued to work hard to beat back the Ashcroft amendment. According to a congressional aide, the Texas representative proposed adding as much as $700 million in farmer aid to the bill in exchange for dropping the Cuba sanctions component of the agricultural package.[66] In the end, Republican leaders DeLay and Senator Trent Lott (R-MS) succeeded in stripping the Cuba provision from the agricultural bill before the October 1 deadline, even though indications were that a majority of the conference committee members favored the sanctions proposal.[67] In the aftermath, fellow Republicans in the Senate led the attack on the leadership's tactics. Ashcroft described the methods used as "autocratic,"[68] and Hagel criticized the "base intimidation" by a "small elite cabal."[69]

Given the Clinton administration's low profile during the congressional debates, the president was largely able to avoid criticism from either side of the issue. The CANF leadership, for example, did not blame the executive branch for raising the issues, but rather the organization's Washington director declared that the issue "has absolutely been pushed onto the radar screen by the ag lobby groups."[70] Business, church, and academic groups opposed to the embargo had become more actively involved in this area. When the pope openly criticized U.S. sanctions during his January 1998 visit to Cuba, these groups increased their efforts. Americans for Humanitarian Trade with Cuba, an organization of prominent former U.S. officials and corporate leaders founded in January 1998, gained former House Ways and Means Committee chair Sam Gibbons (D-FL) as a member soon after the pope's visit.[71] The U.S. Catholic Conference, which had opposed the U.S. embargo since 1972, once again asked the U.S. government to take a fresh look at its Cuba policy.[72] USA*Engage, a group of more than six hundred companies founded in 1997 to promote engagement and trade rather than economic sanctions with rival nations, called for a reappraisal of U.S. policy toward Cuba. In the academic and journalistic communities, a wave of antiembargo rhetoric and activity continued to grow. Editorials from newspapers across the political spectrum criticized the embargo.

In October 1998 former Republican Secretaries of State Henry Kissinger, George P. Shultz, and Lawrence Eagleburger, and Senators John Warner (R-VA) and Christopher Dodd (D-CT) led a bipartisan group in proposing that Clinton create a commission to review U.S. policy toward Cuba. In the background, the Council on Foreign Relations (CFR) had organized an independent task force that was expected to issue a report in early 1999 with recommendations for relaxing the embargo significantly.[73]

By rejecting the commission and offering business and political leaders some relaxation of the embargo, President Clinton simultaneously tried to satisfy proembargo interests and mollify critics of Cuba policy. But his January 1999 announcement itself opened the door to more pressure on both the legislative and executive branches from interest groups. In a sense, the Clinton administration did what the Reagan administration had done in fostering the power of CANF. It used a classic formula of expanding the scope of conflict to change the balance of political power, as political scientist E. E. Schattschneider explained forty years earlier.[74] By reframing the debate to focus on trade, he brought new and powerful groups into the process of shaping Cuba policy and made the administration itself vulnerable to pressure. This enabled the administration, and Congress, to assert that it was responding to legitimate pressures as it changed the policy. The

Clinton administration had already begun this process of expanding the circle of debate in 1994–1995, seeking to find counterpressures to embargo hard-liners. That process began to bear fruit in 1998–2000. For example, twenty members of the American Farm Bureau, which came out against the embargo for the first time in January 1999, received permission to visit Cuba in May of the same year. Upon their return, the group's president, Dean Kleckner, testified before the Senate that the "embargo or sanction does long-term harm to farmers and the agricultural economy."[75] As the issue of sanctions became framed as one of trade instead of ethnic politics, the electoral interests of farm state senators and representatives brought new voices to the antiembargo movement. Ultimately, though, the 1999 legislative attempts to relax the embargo failed. A few Cuban American representatives continued to wield impressive power over the Cuba sanctions, even in the face of engagement by significant economic interest groups and their own congressional allies. As a Missouri newspaper editorialized when it was clear that the legislation would not pass in 1999: "It's preposterous that Florida lawmakers can dispense such hardship to midwestern farmers."[76]

Legislative Efforts in 2000

Before Congress could begin debate on the embargo again, the entire country learned the name Elian Gonzalez. On Thanksgiving Day, a five-year-old Cuban boy was discovered clinging to an inner tube a few miles off the Florida coast. While few politicians on either side of the embargo debate distinguished themselves during the several months spent discussing the fate of Elian, his presence in the United States hurt the embargo supporters more than the critics. The young boy provided the American public with a new Cuban face to replace Fidel Castro's. The seeming irrationality of Cuba policy became personified by the difficulty in reuniting a sympathetic little boy with his father. In addition, the stalemate further damaged the credibility of the anti-Castro lobby, which defied public sentiment in trying desperately to keep the boy from returning to Cuba. Their intransigence raised questions about what seemed to be excessive influence of Cuban Americans over U.S. foreign policy. In the spring of 2000, Senator Hagel made the critique very explicitly: "You can no longer hold America's interests captive to a small group of political interests, and that's essentially what the Cuban American community has been doing."[77] Near the same time, even Jesse Helms appeared to be more open to the sale of farm products. His Foreign Relations Committee approved the Ashcroft position by voice vote at the end of March as a part of the Technical Assistance, Trade Promotion and Anti-Corruption Act of 2000. A section included in that act directed the president to terminate any unilateral agricultural or medical sanctions in effect and required the president to seek congressional approval for any future sanctions on food or medicine. On the House side, DeLay sponsored an amendment to eliminate the sanctions language from the appropriations bill, but his proposal was defeated.[78] It certainly seemed as if Elian Gonzalez had made it easier for legislators to vote against the Cuba lobby and for a rapprochement with Cuba.[79]

Similar bills that would allow the sale of food and medicine to countries currently sanctioned by the United States cleared committees in both houses and went to their respective floors by the middle of May. Negotiations in the House were particularly contentious, in large part because Republican leaders there gave veto power over any agreement to Cuban American representatives Diaz-Balart and Ros-Lehtinen.[80] The Miami Republicans worked their colleagues during May and June to alter the language in the House version of the bill. While CANF was clearly not a major player at this point, the organization did sponsor television advertisements in the districts of key house members, including George Nethercutt.[81] Nethercutt, who defeated House Speaker Thomas Foley in 1994, had broken his promise to leave after three terms and was embroiled in a difficult race for reelection at the time. Nethercutt formerly endorsed the embargo, but his views had obviously changed. Among other things, the Washington Wheat Commission estimated that if sanctions on Cuba, Libya, Syria, and Iraq were lifted U.S. farmers could export nearly $500 million in additional wheat.[82] By the end of June, a compromise was reached in the House; the bill would forbid the use of U.S. government credits in sales to Cuba and at the same time toughen the existing travel ban. The deal was opposed by DeLay,[83] but not all of the proembargo forces were entirely disappointed. Ros-Lehtinen claimed: "This agreement is much better for us than current law. No credits for Castro and no tourism either."[84]

The Clinton administration kept a low profile as these bills made their way through Congress in large part because they had such mixed feelings about the bills. An administration official argued that they were not "averse" to modifying the sanctions on some countries, but they did oppose this legislation "on the ground that it interferes with the president's ability to make foreign policy."[85] White House Press Secretary Joe Lockhart said in late June that Clinton supports "the main thrust of the measure," but that the president "needs flexibility, as the steward of our foreign policy, to implement the policy."[86] Still, Nethercutt was not concerned about a possible presidential veto,[87] noting in June, "I think members of both parties would resist any veto."[88] Clinton's aides privately admitted that he would sign the bill if it passed.[89]

Given the breadth and depth of the bipartisan congressional support for allowing food and medicine sales to Cuba, the ability of those committed Cuban American legislators to get both the stipulation that no U.S. government or private sector financing would be used for the purchase of these products, and the codification of the travel ban into the final appropriations bill in October, was fairly remarkable. That Congress moved to restrict the president's ability to unilaterally impose sanctions is equally notable. With those additions (and a variety of sweeteners added to the final bill), the House voted 340-75 and the Senate 86-8 to approve the changes in sanctions policy toward Cuba that ultimately made up Title IX of the FY2001 Agriculture Appropriations Bill. Some of those who supported lifting sanctions altogether were disappointed in the final bill. As Senator Dorgan (D-ND) suggested, "The hard-liners won out on the Cuba issue."[90]

The president signed the bill less than a month before the 2000 election. The bill's new constraints on the president's ability to impose sanctions, and codification of another aspect of U.S.-Cuba policy, were part of the Clinton legacy that the new president would inherit.

When Policy and Interests Collide

Helms-Burton promised to put Congress at the center of the process that creates Cuba policy. But we argue that President Clinton's moves after signing Helms-Burton can be seen in no small part as an effort to retake lost terrain. Not being in a position to veto the bill following the shoot-down, and having gained the waiver for Title III, the administration set about to turn apparent weakness into strength. While Clinton certainly had policy interests at stake vis-à-vis the island,[91] after Helms-Burton the administration also had significant institutional interests at stake. Having seemingly lost control over the shape of U.S. embargo policy toward Cuba, Clinton needed to act in order to restore presidential authority over a key foreign policy issue—and perhaps to prevent this dynamic from spreading to other substantive foreign policy issues.

In broad form, the Clinton strategy can be seen as early as in his signing statement of the bill. Clinton announced in his written statement (though not in his spoken remarks) that he would treat various parts of Helms-Burton as "precatory," and thus "not derogating from the President's authority to conduct foreign policy."[92] The items Clinton argued he would take as precatory included a section of the bill (§ 201) that clearly stated what the policy of the United States is toward a democratic transition in Cuba.[93] Clinton used such language only twelve times in signing statements, rarely in such a sweeping way as here.[94] He argued that the bill's codification provision—§ 102(h)—imposed "overly rigid constraints" on foreign policy making; and he expressed dissatisfaction that there was no waiver provision for Title IV. Alan J. Kreczko, special assistant to the president and legal adviser for the National Security Council during this period, reports that this language emerged less from the administration's concern about Cuba policy than it did from a "preserve the president's institutional prerogatives policy,"[95] setting the stage for future moves by Clinton that would be as much about regaining power as they were about policy toward the island.

By invoking this term as he signed Helms-Burton, Clinton signaled his likely future infidelity to the bill's strictures. Congress perhaps should have seen it coming, but the bill's intent concerning the substance of U.S. policy toward Cuba was clearly stated, and the codification of the embargo into law was equally clear. What supporters of the bill did not count on (and what the bill's detractors, even those who ultimately voted for the bill, under the circumstances, may have been hoping for) was the room some readings of the bill left for presidential authority on all matters up to the ultimate question of the embargo. Clinton's steps on Titles III and IV, and his use of licenses, combined to try to erode Congress's codification of the embargo and to reassert presidential authority.

While Clinton was correct to the extent that he understood his role to be one of conducting the foreign policy of the United States, we would argue that he was incorrect in assuming that he should be able to unilaterally determine what that foreign policy is in a situation where, as with Helms-Burton, Congress has clearly spoken on the matter. Lawrence Tribe argues, "Although the President alone can act in foreign affairs, the content of presidential options is defined partly—and increasingly—by congressional enactments and limited by constitutional strictures. Hence, while it may be symbolically correct to say that the President is the sole national 'actor' in foreign affairs, it is not accurate to label the President the sole national policy maker."[96] Furthermore, the Constitution clearly gives Congress the power to regulate foreign commerce and to play a dominant force in trade legislation. The Constitution grants to Congress the power to regulate tariffs and foreign commerce, while the president enjoys no comparable authority to direct international trade. According to Wilson: "In the area of foreign commerce . . . Congress is given more respect by the courts. While Congress will be allowed to delegate its foreign commerce power to the president if it so chooses, the courts have held that power over foreign commerce ultimately rests with the legislative branch and with that branch alone." [97] The line of court cases in this domain suggests that when Congress has clearly spoken on a matter involving trade, the president is limited to conducting U.S. foreign policy according to that mandate.[98]

One of the first cases to deal with the relative powers of Congress and the president in the trade legislation context was *Little v. Barreme* in 1804.[99] In that case, Congress passed a bill that authorized the president to seize U.S. ships headed to French ports. President Thomas Jefferson, however, ordered that ships heading both to and from French ports could be seized. A ship's captain who followed these orders of the president found himself in court, and the Supreme Court ruled against him even though he acted in accordance with a presidential order. According to the court, Congress had taken care to specifically identify ships sailing "to" French ports in the statute, and thus in ordering the seizure of vessels to or from French ports, the president was reconstructing the language of the legislation. Implicit in the court's opinion is the notion that once Congress has spoken clearly on an issue, as by enacting legislation, the president is not at liberty to rewrite that legislation according to his own views on the wisdom of that particular policy.

Similarly in the 1953 case of *United States v. Guy W. Capps, Inc.,* the Fourth Circuit invalidated a presidential action that contradicted a trade statute passed by Congress. The court explained that "the power to regulate foreign commerce is vested in Congress, not in the executive or the court."[100] As late as 1986 the Supreme Court reiterated its commitment to congressional preeminence in matters relating to international trade in the case of *Japan Whaling Association v. American Cetacean Society.* In that case, which dealt with a law passed by Congress that directed the president to take steps to stop the whaling practices of states, the Supreme Court was clear that the president "may not act contrary to the will of Congress when exercised within the bounds of the Constitution. If Congress has directly spoken to the precise issue in question, if the intent of Congress is clear, that is the end of the matter." In that particular case, the majority allowed the president to exercise discretion that seemed contrary to the will of Congress but said it allowed such discretion "unless the legislative history of the enactment shows with sufficient clarity that the agency construction is contrary to the will of Congress."[101] While there may have been a lack of clarity in the record on the whaling case, one would be hard pressed to find such ambiguity in the text or history of Helms-Burton. Like President Jefferson in *Little v. Barreme*, Clinton attempted to reconstruct an otherwise clear congressional enactment after he signed Helms-Burton into law. The fact that Helms-Burton is premised on the U.S. embargo of Cuba, a type of trade legislation, means that the president should be constrained by the choices Congress has constitutionally made. In this case he seems to have felt no such constraints.

While policy preferences are certainly an important element in understanding the complex dynamics of the Cuba policy-making process, they are not sufficient to convince the president to take such a position in opposition to the clear intent of Congress and to the bill he willingly signed. To get there, we must also take into account the important institutional interests at stake. During this period, Congress as an institution certainly stayed engaged on Cuba policy as well. It was not the executive branch that drove the issue of ending some sanctions on Cuba; this emerged from

Congress, backed by relatively new agribusiness interests. Clearly, the perceived reduction of external security threats with the demise of the Soviet Union has allowed economic constituencies to seek influence over foreign policy without fearing the same backlash as was possible during the cold war.[102] The end of the cold war allowed Cuba policy, to a large extent, to become as much a domestic issue as a foreign policy issue, thus opening it to a range of forces far broader than we normally see in classic "security" policy making. Other international developments were important too. Falling global commodity prices gave farmers and their representatives the motivation and justification for their attempts to secure new markets for their constituents' goods. Members of Congress facing difficult reelection bids at the end of the decade in those farm states were among the leading actors promoting food sales to Cuba. The argument about the value of free trade as a means of promoting political democratization is an aspect of the dominant neoliberal ideology and helped to provide some cover for those who might be accused of being interested only in their own economic benefits. At the same time, the dominant interest group supporting the embargo, the Cuban American National Foundation, experienced a relative decline in its power. But as we saw, the Cuban American members of the House retained significant power even in the face of embargo opposition alliances in Congress that cut across party and political lines in surprising ways. The closeness of the vote in Florida to decide President Clinton's successor in 2000, however, reminded the United States that the Cuban American community was likely to continue to play an important role in both U.S. domestic politics and foreign policy making for some time to come.

George W. Bush and the
Struggle for Control

T HE 2000 ELECTION seemed to offer little difference between the two
major-party presidential candidates on Cuba policy. Neither ticket
was oriented toward lifting, or easing, the embargo.[1] In Florida, Gore
probably hoped that with the help of Joe Lieberman, a long time hard-
line supporter of the embargo, he might offset the Bush family's statewide
connections to Cuban Americans. But even though Gore's public position
on Cuba and Elian Gonzalez mirrored that of his opponent, his association with the Clinton-Reno actions toward the Cuban boy likely penalized
the sitting vice president. The Cuban American leadership in Miami cam-
paigned tirelessly for George W. Bush as they tried to turn the election
into a referendum on Clinton's Elian policy.[2] George W. Bush received
nearly $115,000 in contributions from Cuban Americans compared to Al
Gore's $28,000 (Clinton had received about twice that much in 1996, nearly
as much as Bob Dole).[3] In Miami-Dade County Cuban Americans make
up about one-third of the population. About half of the estimated 800,000
exiles there are registered to vote. Of that number roughly 85 percent are

registered Republicans. Democratic voters still outnumber Republicans in the county, but Cuban Americans are the single largest voting bloc in South Florida; they vote in high numbers and have much power and financial clout. In the end Gore carried the county, but he did so by only 39,000 votes, well below Clinton's 1996 margin in the county of 117,000 votes. It would not be hard to conclude the Elian cost Gore the election; he made Gore pay in the recount too. Alex Penelas, the attractive Democratic Cuban American mayor of the county and Gore supporter, pulled a disappearing act, and the recount effort in Miami-Dade County fell under the control of the Republican Party, urged on by the Cuban Americans. Even if they were not fully responsible for Bush's ultimately taking office, the Cuban Americans claimed credit. Delfin Gonzalez, the brother of Lazaro, at whose house Elian stayed, told the *Miami Herald,* "if it wasn't for Elian George Bush would not have won the presidency." Other Cuban American leaders in Florida echoed this view.[4]

From the Victor Come the Spoils?

When President Bush took office in January 2001, most observers assumed that Cuba policy in the executive branch would be driven by the president's desire to show appreciation to the Cuban American voters, whose support had been essential in such a close Florida election. The two Cuban American members of Congress from Florida were also expected to gain influence with the chief executive, based on their help with Florida and longstanding relationships to the Bush family. This perceived appreciation and influence suggested the embargo could be tightened under the new president. Other forces seemed to imply that Cuba policy could change but in the opposite direction. In Congress there was considerable support for weakening the embargo policy: a majority favored eliminating the restriction on travel, and many preferred allowing more and easier trade. Economic interest groups working with antiembargo allies in Congress remained a strong force. The opposition to the embargo was also expected to benefit from the weakening and moderating of the most important proembargo interest group, CANF. Ironically, one of the great accomplishments of the proembargo forces—codification of the embargo—now actually made the sanctions policy more vulnerable than if the executive branch, headed by George Bush, retained control.

President Bush did still have an important role to play in Cuban policy making, of course, and his Cuban American allies were hoping for more support than they received from Bill Clinton. At a minimum the new president was expected to publicly support the embargo policy, but there was also room for Bush to be much tougher on the margins of Cuba policy than his predecessor had been. Among the issues in play to varying degrees were travel, remittances, support for opposition groups in Cuba, and the sale of food and medicine. Bush might consider undoing some of the reforms that Clinton instituted during his second term, or he could simply propose tightening the existing embargo regulations in these areas. Some sentiment even existed to overturn the Clinton policy of returning to the island Cubans caught at sea, the so-called wet foot/dry foot policy that emerged from the 1994 immigration crisis. The president could also appoint representatives of the hard-line Cuban American community, or at least those who had been strong and consistent advocates of the embargo policy, to his new administration. And clearly, President Bush could ensure the enforcement of the existing laws: specifically the full enforcement of Title IV of Helms-Burton, which could be applied to more companies doing business in Cuba, and the end of the waivers of Title III. The words of Bush administration officials certainly suggested that the new president had every interest in delivering for the Cuban American hard-liners. Describing their agenda for Cuba, a senior administration official said, "our number one priority is to do nothing that could adversely affect the reelection of Jeb Bush as Governor of Florida." And Anne Louise Bardach argues that while Bush is a free trader at heart, his political adviser Karl Rove "has urged him to fully accommodate exile hard-liners in return for electoral victories for both his brother and himself."[5]

For the most part, however, the early part of the Bush administration was characterized by policy continuity rather than the blanket adoption of the hard-line Cuban American community wish list. There was symbolic support to be sure. For example, Bush's first major speech on Cuba came at the White House during a ceremony to mark Cuban Independence Day. While U.S. presidents traditionally mark the occasion of the May 20, 1902, withdrawal of the nation's forces from Cuba, the 2001 East Room ceremony was described as a "much more elaborate affair" than usual, with attendance by Colin Powell and Condoleezza Rice; Gloria Estefan sang the Cuban national anthem.⁶ In addition to the ceremony's symbolic value, the president promised to fight any attempt to weaken the sanctions. But there was little substantive movement; in the first few months, the Bush administration proposed no new initiatives on Cuba.

Within six months of taking office, Bush had to deal with Helms-Burton and the Title III dilemma. If driven solely by electoral calculations, presumably the decision would be easy. By not waiving the toughest provision of Helms-Burton, the president would make it absolutely clear to the Cuban American community that, unlike President Clinton, he would take their side even when there were potential costs (such as alienating major trading partners). As the *Financial Times,* an important European financial newspaper, argued, "There is only one argument for not waiving Title III—as Mr. Clinton did from the moment Helms-Burton took effect —and it is based on the most short sighted domestic political calculation. It is that unblocking the provision would win approval from the small but vocal Cuban American community, above all in the electoral pivot state of Florida. In all other respects, such a decision would be deplorable."⁷

Bush did choose to continue to exercise the waiver. In Clinton-like fashion, Bush softened the blow to his Cuban American supporters: he formally announced that he would put forth hard-line Cuban American Otto Reich for a State Department position as part of a package of Cuba policy statements that included increased support for Radio Marti, a promise to tighten travel restrictions on U.S. citizens, and increased funds for dissidents on the island.⁸ Still, some described the combined announcements in terms such as "a setback for the Cuban exile lobby and its Congressional allies."⁹ The Republican Cuban American members of Congress offered mild public support for the president, but New Jersey Democrat Robert Menendez went on the attack: "On his first opportunity to show his true colors, the president was dishonest and weak, and has failed the Cuban people seeking political, social and economic freedom."¹⁰ Nor did Bush do much to strengthen enforcement of Title IV. Except for a Panamanian-based subsidiary of an Israeli company, only the executives and children of the Canadian mining company Sherritt International were on the U.S. Title IV blacklist: "For President Bush, the Canadian company will continue to serve as proof that his administration means business, without taking action against European companies, which he dare not do."[11] What we have then is a proembargo president anxious to preserve Cuban American votes, but who seems to be constrained by potential European opposition to aggressive enforcement of U.S. law. President Bush's tenure has not otherwise suggested that he will weigh the sentiment of "old Europe" too heavily in his decision making.

Both the tragic events of September 11 and the damage wrought on Cuba by Hurricane Michelle affected U.S.-Cuba policy later that year. The Cuban government was quick to offer its sympathy and assistance to the United States after the terrorist attacks. Perhaps not surprisingly, the Bush administration did not take them up on the offer and instead gave some new attention to Cuba's place on the list of terrorism-sponsoring states (along with Iran, Iraq, Syria, Libya, North Korea, and Sudan). In the face of Hurricane Michelle's impact on his country a couple of months later, Castro decided to take advantage of the opportunity to buy $10 million in food and medical supplies from the United States —a chance he earlier had rejected, saying Cuba had no intention of buying even "a single grain of rice or a single aspirin."[12] When major companies such as Archer Daniels Midland and Cargill signed agreements to deliver food, it might have seemed like a first step toward the eventual end of the embargo. That optimism was tempered by an executive branch decision in January 2002 to deny travel licenses to a group of agricultural representatives, including two former U.S. secretaries of agriculture. President Bush's first year in office included some of these largely symbolic gestures to the proembargo forces, but on the whole the change in presidents did not yield substantially different U.S. policy toward Cuba.

President Bush's reward of the Cuban American community may be strongest in the area of appointments. But not all of his appointments were popular among Cuban Americans. Attorney General John Ashcroft had opposed economic sanctions in general and supported the sale of food to Cuba during his time as a Missouri senator. Colin Powell's writings and comments in recent years suggested sympathy for lifting the embargo with Cuba. Career diplomat John Maisto was chosen to deal with Latin American affairs at the National Security Council, disappointing advocates of a tougher policy toward Cuba.[13] Offsetting those sorts of choices was the administration's secretary of housing and urban development, Mel Martinez, the first Cuban American to serve in the cabinet and a "Pedro Pan" child.[14] Martinez was cochairman of Bush's 2000 campaign in Florida, and he had been very critical of Clinton's, and Gore's, position on Elian Gonzalez.[15] In fact, he hosted Elian's trip to Disney World.[16] Interestingly, the Cuban American cabinet member's brother, Rafael Martinez, was later nominated by the Bush administration to serve as a representative on the Organization of American States' Inter-American Commission on Human Rights, although he lost out in the vote cast by member nations at the end of the organization's annual meetings in 2003. It marked the first time that the United States was excluded from representation on the influential human rights organization.[17]

In a position directly related to U.S.-Cuba policy, Otto Reich as the choice to be assistant secretary of state for Western Hemisphere affairs was probably the most controversial of the new president's foreign policy choices. A less well-known Cuban American, Colonel Emilio Gonzalez, was also appointed to handle the Cuba portfolio at the National Security Council.[18] Reich had engaged in "prohibited covert propaganda" as the head of the Office of Public Diplomacy in the Reagan years. Lincoln Diaz-Balart, though, referred to the selection as a "brilliant choice," Ileana Ros-Lehtinen described Reich as "a man of integrity and a man of principle," and Bob Graham was said to be "very supportive of the Reich nomination."[19] But there was considerable opposition, much of it casting the choice as one driven solely by electoral interests of the president and his brother. Lissa Weinmann, executive director of Americans for Humanitarian Trade with Cuba, argued that the Reich appointment indicated that "the political needs of Jeb Bush in Florida are interfering with the circumspect approach to foreign policy-making."[20] The St. Petersburg Times held a similar view: "Bush was rewarding Florida's Cuban American community for helping him win the presidency. At the same time, the president was thought to be boosting his re-election prospects in 2004 and those of his brother, Governor Jeb Bush, this year."[21] Beyond his Iran-Contra background, after the September 11 some in the media noted Reich's links to "terrorism" by way of his association with Orlando Bosch.[22] Faced with stiff congressional opposition, Bush ultimately gave Reich a "recess appointment" that would run until just after Jeb Bush's successful reelection.[23] Reich used his first post-appointment public appearance, in March 2002, to make his position on U.S.-Cuba policy clear: "We are not going to help Fidel Castro stay in power by opening up our markets to Cuba." He argued that the United States could promote a transition on the island by "not throwing a lifeline to a failed, corrupt, dictatorial, murderous regime."[24]

Challenges to the Embargo

At approximately the same time that Reich made his first official statement on Cuba, a number of other events suggested new momentum for the anti-embargo forces. Retired U.S. Army General Barry McCaffrey visited Cuba and later told reporters that Cuba represents "zero threat to the United States."[25] Next, Cuba announced that it would make further U.S. food purchases, following up on the sales after Hurricane Michelle.[26] Members of the House opposed to the U.S. embargo formed a new working group to promote greater openings toward Cuba, including lifting the travel ban and easing the process for selling food to the island.[27] Finally, former president Carter announced that he would travel to Cuba later in the year.[28]

The Bush administration hit back on Cuba shortly before Carter's May trip. John Bolton, under secretary of state for arms control, accused Cuba of producing germs for use in biological warfare in a speech before the Heritage Foundation in Washington. Diaz-Balart welcomed Bolton's words as beginning "to put into the proper perspective the debate about Cuba, a terrorist state with biological weapons 90 miles from the shores of the United States."[29] By lumping Cuba together with other rogue states just one tier below the "axis of evil," the Bush administration may have been acting to shore up support in Miami for Jeb Bush's ongoing gubernatorial campaign. After all, Diaz-Balart and Ros-Lehtinen had recently made two unfulfilled requests of the Bush administration: to deny Carter permission to visit and to fire Secretary of the Treasury O'Neill for his comments that he would prefer to use the resources of his department to track down terrorists than to chase down U.S. visitors to Cuba.[30] Carter made his own statement upon his return, concluding an op-ed article: "I would like to see unrestricted trade and visitation between Cuba and the United States, as would most Americans and a strong and growing group of Cuban immigrants in Miami. Until this goal is politically possible, we should take other, more modest steps toward reconciliation."³¹

President Bush took the occasion of the centennial anniversary of Cuban independence to make his own announcement on Cuba policy. He vowed to maintain the embargo and travel restrictions, while proposing mild changes in people-to-people contact between the two nations. He announced new scholarships for Cubans to study in the United States, greater aid to Cuban civil society by way of religious and nongovernmental organizations, a willingness to resume direct mail service between the two countries, and efforts to modernize Radio and TV Marti.³² On the whole, the statement still did not appear to mark any sort of dramatic shift in U.S.-Cuba policy.

Movement to change U.S.-Cuba policy was continuing in the legislature. During President Bush's first year in office, the House of Representatives voted by an impressive 240-186 margin to prohibit the Treasury Department from spending money to enforce the travel ban. The Senate version of Treasury's appropriations bill did not include that provision, and the restriction was not included in the House-Senate conference report on the bill. In the post–September 11 atmosphere, the challengers to the embargo were reluctant to push the controversial provision. The antiembargo forces in Congress, however, went back on the offensive in 2002. At a Cuban Trade Conference held in Mexico early in the year, a member of the Cuba Working Group, Joanne Emerson (D-MO), argued that "there are five major opponents in the House" to opening the embargo: Republican Whip Tom DeLay; Ros-Lehtinen and Diaz-Balart; Cuban American Bob Menendez (D-NJ); and Richard Gephardt (D-MO).³³ Representative Jeff Flake (R-AZ) challenged the assumption that domestic political calculations would always favor the embargo: "U.S. business, tourism and farm-state politics are overtaking Miami politics on this issue."³⁴ Flake has spearheaded congressional efforts to ease the embargo. The Arizona congressman's amendment to lift a cap on the amount of money U.S. citizens can send to Cubans was approved by a vote of 243-169. A new vote to block the Treasury Department from enforcing travel restrictions, including issuing fines to U.S. citizens who travel to Cuba illegally, won 262-167. Only a vote to effectively end the economic embargo was defeated by a count of 226-204.[35] The congressional votes came less than two weeks after a joint letter from Secretary of Treasury Paul O'Neill and Secretary of State Colin Powell had been sent to the Committee on Appropriations of the House strongly opposing any loosening of the embargo.[36] On the day of the votes, White House spokesman Ari Fleischer said that the president would veto the appropriations bill if the Cuba provisions were attached.[37] Even in the face of such a clear message from the executive branch, members of the House continued to challenge the embargo.

The 2002 Elections

The first ever U.S. Food and Agribusiness Exposition was scheduled to take place in Havana at the end of September, only six weeks before the first major elections in the United States since the 2000 debacle. A number of business leaders and Governor Jesse Ventura of Minnesota were planning to attend the expo. Apparently trying to check the momentum that such a high profile event might give to the antiembargo forces, a Bush administration official charged that Cuba was harming the U.S. "war on terror." Dan Fisk, deputy assistant secretary of state for the Western Hemisphere, added that the Castro government was "impeding our efforts to defeat terrorism" by giving U.S. officials "fabricated" information.[38] "Make no mistake about it," said Fisk, who helped draft Helms-Burton while on the staff of Senator Helms, "Castro aids terrorism and aids terrorists."[39] Whether true or not, the effort to continue to associate Cuba with the rogue states sponsoring terrorism could also help counter congressional support for easing the embargo policy with the island. And the aggressive charges of support for terrorism would be welcomed among hard-line Cuban Americans voting for governor of Florida only a couple of months later.

The embargo was a key issue in the election for a newly created Florida congressional seat where the Republican Mario Diaz-Balart, brother of Lincoln, was running against another Cuban American, Annie Betancourt. Betancourt, the widow of a Bay of Pigs veteran, argued that the embargo "has failed miserably," although she did not explicitly call for an end to the embargo. In a district that Diaz-Balart had helped to create as a state senator, a number of factors worked against Betancourt. Registered Republican voters outnumbered Democrats by 43-35, and the well-connected Diaz-Balart outspent Betancourt by a ratio of more than six to one.[40] Early optimism about Betancourt's chances faded by November, and in the end Mario Diaz-Balart easily won the seat to become the fourth Cuban American in Congress. Hard-liners in the Cuban American community were quick to claim the significance of that district vote: "Mario's victory, in particular, is a response to those who say the exile community's mentality has changed and the younger generations do not support the sanctions against Fidel Castro," noted a spokeswoman for the Cuban Freedom Council.[41] In the governor's race, the president's brother comfortably defeated Democratic challenger Bill McBride.

Attempting to build on the November electoral success for their cause, Ileana Ros-Lehtinen and Lincoln Diaz-Balart sent a letter to President Bush urging him to announce his intention to resubmit Otto Reich to the Senate as soon as possible.[42] In January 2003, however, the Bush administration announced that it would not renominate Reich to the top State Department position on Latin America but would instead make him a "special envoy for Western Hemisphere initiatives." Richard Lugar's (R-IN) becoming chair of the Senate Foreign Relations Committee, combined with Colin Powell's apparent discomfort with Reich, led the Bush administration to give Reich a position that did not require Senate confirmation. Roger Noriega, the former top policy aide to the Senate Foreign Relations Committee when Jesse Helms was chair, was nominated by Bush to take the assistant secretary position in the State Department. With Noriega, the Cuban American community was certainly getting someone with longstanding support for the hard-line approach to relations with Cuba. Ros-Lehtinen, whose letter only a few weeks earlier had noted how important it was that Reich be renominated to the position, was quoted as saying that Noriega was a "wonderful addition to the State Department team," adding that Otto Reich was getting a job that was "just what he wants."[43] Reich announced in June 2004 that he would be leaving the administration for "personal and financial reasons." Still, Bush had once again passed on an opportunity to demonstrate with a controversial action that he was as hard-line on Cuba policy as Diaz-Balart and Ros-Lehtinen.

Both Sides Face New Challenges

It was not long after the election that the hard-liners in the Cuban American community were confronted with a new issue. The Varela Project was an initiative by opposition leaders in Cuba to use a clause in the nation's constitution to permit a referendum if at least ten thousand signatures were presented to the National Assembly. After having submitted more than the necessary number of signatures, the project received significant global attention. Oswaldo Paya received the European parliament's Sakharov prize at the end of 2002 and met with both the Spanish prime minister and the pope during a trip that eventually led him to the United States. Given the assumption behind the project that democratic reform can and should come from a movement inside Cuba, the Miami hard-liners have viewed Paya and the Varela Project with distrust. The Cuban dissident opposes the embargo, putting him further at odds with Miami hard-liners. During his U.S. visit he met with Secretary of State Colin Powell, who stated his "admiration" for the activist.[44] Having moved in a prodialogue direction in recent years, CANF also offered its support for Paya. The Cuban American members of Congress and their allies, however, were critical.[45] The decision to meet with Paya at such a high level suggests that the administration was willing to risk letting some Cuban American leaders become "more openly dissatisfied with Bush."[46] During the buildup prior to the invasion of Iraq, for which "democratization" was offered as one of the ostensible goals, meeting with a prodemocracy activist from Cuba may have been more important than placating some of the hard-liners in Little Havana.

By meeting with Paya, however, the Bush administration was acting in a way consistent with the majority of Cuban Americans according to recent polls. The *Miami Herald* published a poll that suggested a majority of Cuban Americans were in favor of dialogue generally and that they were supportive of the Varela project, in particular. The Schroth and Associates survey suggested that 59 percent of Cuban Americans supported the project and only 23 percent were opposed. A separate poll by Sergio Bendixen released at the same time found even greater community support for the project. The Schroth poll also indicated that 54 percent of respondents supported CANF dialogue with high-level Cuban officials, not including Fidel or Raul Castro. Finally, though, when directly asked their position on the embargo itself, 60 percent supported and 28 percent opposed the economic sanctions.[47]

In response, the Cuban American members of Congress attacked the polls' accuracy. After all, the finding that the Miami Cubans overwhelmingly believed the island's dissidents were more important than exile leaders in promoting democracy in Cuba was a direct challenge to the hard-liners. Diaz-Balart suggested that the pollsters' interest was to undermine the political power of Cuban Americans: "That political power bothers them so much that what they are doing is attacking us, attacking the strength we have by sowing confusion and intrigue."[48] At a rally in Little Havana at the end of March, Diaz-Balart told a crowd of tens of thousands of demonstrators there to support the Bush policy on Iraq and to make a link between Fidel Castro and Saddam Hussein: "All those people going around with their little surveys should take a look at Calle Ocho." At least one analyst offered a more nuanced interpretation of the dynamic: "On big-ticket items, such as the embargo, the three Congress members are right: The exile community hasn't changed. . . . On issues from travel to humanitarian aid, food sales and support for dissidents, there is a much more varied position than what was reflected at the rally."[49]

That rally came only a few days after the Bush administration announced some reforms to the embargo. The more restrictive changes were in the area of travel permits. Licenses for educational travel would be limited to those directly related to course work, closing what some saw as a loophole for solidarity groups to falsely declare the purpose of their visit as educational. But on the other side, there was a substantial increase in household remittances, up to $3,000 per quarter from the previous limit of $300. Also, new licenses would be made available to independent organizations engaged in humanitarian activities—from construction to education. These changes appeared to be consistent with proposals the president had made in May 2002. While they seemed relatively balanced, the president of the U.S.-Cuba Trade and Economic Council, a group opposed to the embargo, went so far as to describe the net effect as easing the embargo: "Overall, these changes are expansive, these are not constrictive."[50]

Fidel Strikes Back?

At the same time the Bush administration was announcing these changes, developments on the island presented a new challenge to those seeking to ease the embargo. The Cuban government arrested several dozen dissidents in mid-March 2003. Government statements accompanying the arrests implicated James Cason, who heads the United States' Interests Section in Havana. Cason was said to have attended meetings of dissidents in Cuba and to have provided them with financial and other resources (including opening his offices and home to Castro's opponents).[51] Accusing Cason of trying "to foment the internal counterrevolution," a statement from the Cuban government read: "No nation, no matter how powerful, has the right to organize, finance and serve as a center for subverting the constitutional order."[52] Complicating the situation on the island were several hijackings of planes and a ferry, at the end of March and the beginning of April, by those seeking to enter the U.S.

The Cuban government moved aggressively. After short trials, Cuban courts handed down sentences ranging from six to twenty-eight years to dozens of activists. After an even quicker secret trial, the Cuban government sentenced the three men who hijacked the ferry to the death penalty and gave life sentences to four others who used weapons to help the hijackers take control of the boat. Among the analyses of the Cuba crackdown were suggestions that Castro was once again attempting to subvert any move toward easing the U.S. embargo toward his country. As Bardach pointed out, this was only the most recent of Castro's provocations at a time when there was a move in the direction of normalizing relations.[53] Senator Max Baucus (D-MT) made a similar claim in his April 30 statement in support of ending the Cuba travel ban: "In my view it is because Castro wants the embargo to continue."[54] Others, such as Andres Oppenheimer and William LeoGrande, preferred to link the repression to growing political and economic difficulties facing the Castro regime.[55]

While the developments in Cuba were assumed by most to be a setback for the embargo opponents, the Cuba Working Group and others attempted to spin the crackdown as an argument for policy change. Jeff Flake, sponsor of a bill to ease the travel ban, argued, "The crackdown happened not under our proposed policy but under the policy we had for 42 years. We need a lot more American voices in Cuba, not fewer."[56] In an op-ed article a few weeks later, Flake quoted Oswaldo Paya in support of his position: "We appeal to all foreigners who come to our country as tourists to show solidarity, to take part in demonstrations. To support the opening up of Cuba."[57] In the Senate, a bipartisan group presented legislation to legalize travel by U.S. citizens to Cuba, the Freedom to Travel to Cuba Act (S.950). Officials in the Bush administration, however, suggested that movement to tighten the embargo was a more appropriate response. According to anonymous U.S. government sources, the Bush administration was considering suspending remittances to family members in Cuba and direct flights to the island.[58] A founder of Human Rights Watch countered: "An influx of American people and ideas would be far more threatening to Cuban officials than any tightening of the embargo that the Bush administration is contemplating."[59] In a meeting with Bush administration officials, CANF further complicated the situation for the president. The interest group advocated greater support for TV and Radio Marti, as well as more money to assist dissidents in Cuba, but they argued at the same time against more restrictions on travel and remittances.[60]

The Bush administration was clearly in a difficult spot at the beginning of summer. Nearly all of the responses available entailed potential political costs. To not increase pressure on the Cuban government would alienate hard-liners in Miami. Restrictions on travel or remittances would alienate moderates within the community. A change of immigration policy ran the risk of unleashing a new flow of Cubans from the island, leading to some backlash from non-Cuban Floridians. When fourteen Cuban diplomats based in the United States were expelled in mid-May, it might have been interpreted as a response to the events in Cuba; the Bush administration argued, however, that they were kicked out as a result of their activities in the United States. Either way, that action probably entailed no political costs to the U.S. president in the Cuban American community, but neither could anyone in his administration claim that it would somehow hasten the fall of Castro in Cuba. When the 101st anniversary of Cuba's independence from Spain produced no new initiatives from the Bush administration, it seemed to confirm a strategy of not risking the political costs that might result if the president delivered the Cuban American hard-liners' wish list. The president did symbolically meet with a group of former political prisoners and relatives of the recently imprisoned dissidents. The Republican Cuban American members of Congress did not attend the meeting and offered a short, relatively neutral statement about the president's lack of action. Democrat Robert Menendez, though, was very critical, accusing Bush of "continuing a policy of appeasement" and failing to back up his rhetoric with actions.[61] Elsewhere in the world, the response to the crackdown in Cuba was quite vigorous. On the left, some intellectuals in Latin America, including longtime friend Carlos Fuentes, broke publicly with Castro. Cuba's largest foreign investor and trading partner, the European Union, decided to restrict diplomatic contacts and cultural exchanges with the island nation.[62]

In the United States, advocates of new openings with Cuba waited very little time after the Castro repression before renewing their efforts to change the embargo policy. Within a week of the administration's decision not to ratchet up the pressure on the Cuban government, Senator Baucus (D-MT) put a hold on Roger Noriega's nomination as the assistant secretary of state for the Western Hemisphere in an attempt to force a vote on the Senate floor for his bill to ease U.S. restrictions on travel to Cuba.[63] Outside the government, representatives of agricultural interest groups continued to suggest that trade and travel posed a greater challenge to Castro than did the embargo. A rice farmer from Texas pointed out that Cuba consumes more rice than his own state and went on to suggest: "I believe the simplest and best way to change Cuba to democracy is to sell our goods there and let Americans go down there and mingle with the Cubans."[64] Trade breakthroughs did continue during the summer, notably the arrival of the first U.S.-flagged commercial vessel to arrive in Havana harbor since 1961. *Helen III* left Mobile, Alabama, with a U.S. crew and a cargo of newsprint and timber and entered the Cuban harbor on July 11. Although the ship's captain had to make a phone call to be sure that the Cubans had fully paid for the goods before the cargo could be unloaded, yet another dent in the embargo had been made.[65]

Soon after the *Helen III* arrived in Cuba, the *Gaviota 16* left a Cuban port under the control of twelve hijackers and would-be migrants to the United States. Captured at sea by the U.S. Coast Guard, the dozen Cubans responsible for stealing the government boat were returned to their home country to stand trial. As part of the agreement between the two governments, none of the hijackers could be given a harsher sentence than ten years in prison. Once again, the anti-Castro hardliners in the United States were enraged with the Bush administration's decision to return what they described as "freedom seeking" refugees. The Diaz-Balart brothers and Ros-Lehtinen held a joint news conference at which Lincoln declared: "This act of infamy in coordination with the Cuban tyranny is a condemnable monstrosity."[66] The U.S. government's apparent attempt to deter future departures from the island did not appear to have any immediate effect. Only a couple of days later, a 1951 Chevy flatbed truck—mounted on a pontoon of oil drums, with another dozen Cubans aboard—was stopped at sea by the Coast Guard on its way to Key West.

At its annual board meeting, CANF leaders raised the stakes for the Bush administration policy of returning Cubans picked up at sea, particularly the hijackers. Referring to the Bush administration, Jorge Mas Santos, CANF's chairman and son of founder Jorge Mas Canosa, said: "This will cost them. They can't count on the support of our community if they don't fulfill their promises. This administration until now has done absolutely nothing to fulfill the promises they made to this community." After taking the opportunity to attack Lincoln Diaz-Balart for his inability to influence the Bush administration on the issue, Mas went on to outline the four things CANF would like to see Bush deliver on Cuba: a change in the wet foot/dry foot policy; more resources devoted to Radio and TV Marti; greater financial assistance for dissidents in Cuba; and an indictment of Fidel for crimes against humanity.[67] Even the president's brother offered a rare public critique of the administration policy. According to Florida Governor Jeb Bush, returning the hijacking suspects was "just not right."[68] A number of Democrats sought to take advantage of the Cuban American anger over the Bush administration return of the hijackers. Senator Bill Nelson (D-FL) gave the keynote speech at the CANF meetings for the second consecutive year, and he later said that he would call for a congressional investigation into the negotiations between the Bush administration and the Castro government.[69] Presidential candidate Joe Lieberman (D-CT) attacked President Bush even more aggressively, arguing that his decision to return the would-be refugees marked an "abandonment of American values."[70]

Lieberman's comments suggested the possibility of a Democratic candidate's taking a page from Clinton's 1992 playbook by running to the right of President Bush on Cuba policy. Lieberman had a history of working closely with the hard-line Cuban American community. Their support was important in his successful Senate challenge of incumbent Lowell Weicker, and Lieberman had consistently supported CANF since taking office. That strategy of running to the right of Bush on Cuba, however, would be unlikely to matter during the Democratic primaries. If anything, voters in states with an interest in agricultural exports to Cuba would be more likely to determine who gets the Democratic nomination than Cuban Americans in south Florida.

Still, most Democratic candidates approached the Cuba issue with the intent of minimizing any differences between their own policy preferences and those of President Bush. For example, Senator John Edwards (D-NC) held a series of meetings with Cuban American leaders in Miami nearly two years before the 2004 election was to be held. An attendee of the meetings suggested: "It looks like [Edwards] looked at the numbers and realized that the only way to win Florida is to get a substantial amount of Cuban voters."[71] John Kerry (D-MA) was another Democratic candidate whose views on Cuba policy seemed to shift over time in the direction of greater support for the embargo. Kerry said in a *Meet the Press* interview that he favored keeping sanctions in place, comments that seemed at odds with his words during a 2000 *Boston Globe* interview, in which Kerry suggested that a reassessment of the embargo policy was "way overdue" and that the "politics of Florida" were the only reason for Cuba's being treated differently from other nations such as China.[72] Howard Dean was also accused of a late conversion to support for the embargo—an August 2003 headline in the *Miami Herald* read: "Democratic contender Dean alters Cuba stand."[73] General Wesley Clark, while speaking to reporters in South Florida in December 2003, seemed to leave a little space between the Bush administration's policy and that which might be followed if he were to become president: "In general embargoes normally, usually, they don't work, and they certainly haven't worked in the case of Cuba as far as ending the Castro regime. . . . We don't want to give a gift to Fidel Castro. But we do want to help the Cuban people achieve the same rights as everybody else in the hemisphere."[74]

While the Democratic candidates worked on their Cuba policy stances, President Bush had his own electoral calculations to make as well. After the return of the hijackers to Cuba in July, Bush did make an effort to respond to some of the requests from the exile community. Long time allies of the hard-liners in the exile community, such as Roger Noriega, Dan Fisk, and Otto Reich, went to Miami for consultations with exile leaders. While refusing to be drawn into the debate over the wet foot/dry foot policy, the Bush administration representatives did promise to devote the time and resources necessary to "modernize" Radio and TV Marti.[75] Within the state of Florida, however, evidence of Cuban American discontent with the Bush administration's overall approach to Cuba continued to be manifest. A number of Republican state lawmakers sent a letter to the White House suggesting that if the Bush administration did not change course on Cuba policy, "we cannot guarantee that in next year's election Cuban Americans will provide Republican candidates for federal office the unprecedented levels of support garnered in past elections."[76] A *Miami Herald* editorial offered its own set of policy recommendations: allow Cubans stopped at sea access to attorneys; improve Radio and TV Marti technology to overcome jamming; indict the Cuban MiG pilots who downed the planes in 1996; and work with European and Latin American governments to jointly pressure the Cuban government in the area of human rights.[77] Only a few days later, government officials formally announced that TV Marti would begin transmitting by satellite, and federal prosecutors put forth murder indictments for a Cuban general and two crew members of the MiG that shot down the Brothers to the Rescue planes in 1996.[78]

The Bush administration certainly had the 2004 presidential election in mind when responding to the criticism from Florida by CANF, state lawmakers, Miami-Dade County Republicans, the *Miami Herald,* and Governor Bush. In choosing to deliver on the indictment and satellite transmission of TV Marti, the White House opted for a relatively safe course. The moves would likely receive little attention outside of Florida, and they ran little risk of controversy within the increasingly divided Cuban American community itself. A Republican president such as George Bush would do what was necessary to maintain the Cuban American vote, but if thinking largely of electoral interests, he would prefer to avoid any more dramatic and controversial gestures. Indicting a few Cubans had no significant political costs; taking on wet foot/dry foot, on the other hand, would likely alienate other Latino and non-Latino voters in South Florida. As one staffer on Capitol Hill was quoted: "It was the Karl Rove traditional strategy of putting out fires but not going too far to upset other constituencies."[79]

The recurring issue of the travel ban raised the possibility that the White House would have to take a more public stance on a divisive question than Bush or Rove might prefer. President Bush warned that he would veto any legislation that lifted the ban on travel to Cuba, but the administration preferred not to have to break out the veto stamp (at the end of 2003 he had yet to veto a bill). The politics of the travel ban are especially tricky. More than 60 percent of Cuban Americans support easing travel restrictions according to one poll,[80] and the House of Representatives has opposed the ban on travel for the last two years. Although down from the 262-177 vote of 2002, a clear majority (227-188) of the House voted on September 9, 2003, to ease restrictions on travel to Cuba. While the Bush administration's veto threat may have cut into the margin slightly, the crackdown by the Castro regime earlier in the year probably played the greater role in the change from the previous year.

Jeff Flake (R-AZ) offered the amendment that would cut the federal funds for enforcement of the travel ban, suggesting: "If the U.S. is serious about undermining Castro and bringing democratic reforms to Cuba, the best thing we can do is lessen Castro's control over the island by allowing Americans to travel to Cuba."[81] Supporters came from both parties, however, and the interests driving their votes varied considerably. Some represented farm states and saw increased travel and trade with Cuba as desirable for their constituents; others rejected the idea of government limits on travel by U.S. citizens from a libertarian perspective; some opposed economic sanctions as a generally ineffective means of promoting political change; and longstanding liberal Democratic opponents of the embargo added their votes.

Agricultural interests in the United States apparently saw lifting the travel ban as one more step in opening Cuba to more trade. In the year since an unprecedented September 2002 food and agribusiness exhibition in Havana, the Cubans imported some $250 million worth of food and agricultural products from the United States. While that total constituted about 20 percent of Cuba's food imports in 2002, the U.S. agroindustry saw an opportunity to increase their share of that market considerably.[82] President Bush chose the anniversary of the 1868 beginning of the Cuban struggle for independence from Spain to announce a move in the opposite direction to that preferred by a clear majority of Congress. As the first of what he described as several new initiatives toward Cuba, Bush said: "we are strengthening enforcement of those travel restrictions to Cuba that are already in place." And to that end, he announced: "I've instructed the Department of Homeland Security to increase inspections and shipments to and from Cuba." The U.S. president went on to suggest that we would increase the numbers of Cubans allowed to emigrate here legally and establish "a commission for the assistance to a free Cuba" headed by Colin Powell and Mel Martinez (Cuban-born secretary of housing and urban development) to plan for the post-Castro period.[83]

President Bush's political advisers, including his brother, saw these initiatives as sufficient to placate a restless Cuban American community in Florida. Governor Jeb Bush said, "The president's support is strong in the Cuban American community. And as the policy is unveiled, that strength will solidify."[84] The response within the Miami community was much more measured. As one analyst, Damien Fernandez, commented: "He's tiptoeing around the margins. . . . The question is one of heightened expectations. For many in the Cuban American community, it's 'We voted for you; you won Florida; you promised—where are the deliverables.'"[85]

Less than two weeks after Bush announced his new initiatives, the U.S. Senate voted 59-36 to block spending to enforce the travel restrictions to Cuba with language identical to that of the House. Those voting to prohibit enforcement included thirty-nine Democrats, nineteen Republicans, and one independent. In 1999, the last time the Senate had an opportunity to vote on the travel restrictions, the move to ease the limits lost fifty-five to forty-three. Of the sixteen more votes in 2003 for lifting the ban, thirteen were from Senators who switched their position from the previous vote.[86]

Given the continuing momentum at the national level for easing the embargo, and a growing sense that limits on travel and remittances to Cuba were becoming unpopular even in the Cuban American community, it was hard to imagine that President Bush would be willing to make the travel ban the basis of his first veto. Ann Louise Bardach argues that Bush has to run the risk of losing Cuban American moderates and other voters, because "though Cuban exiles have a multiplicity of political views, the extreme right wing still controls the political leadership and electoral machinery of Miami-Dade, along with the vitally important Spanish-language radio stations." Suggesting that the Bush administration was both looking forward and paying back, she goes on: "Bush is unlikely to have forgotten that it was Miami exile radio that summoned rowdy protesters to the canvassing board during the 2000 presidential recount. And Miami-Dade County officials decided to shut the recount down."[87]

We would not normally expect a House-Senate conference committee formed to consider a spending bill to tamper with the travel ban, given that it passed both houses with identical language. But House Majority leader Tom DeLay (R-TX), a strong supporter of the embargo, stacked the committee, giving ten of the seventeen slots for the House to those in favor of the ban. Of the seventeen Senate conferees, however, fourteen were opponents of the ban.[88] As the conference committee began its discussions, Joni Scott—who had received a "pre-penalty" notice from the Treasury Department warning her of an impending $10,000 fine for a 1999 trip during which she distributed hundreds of Bibles in Cuba—met with lawmakers. The forty-three-year-old Republican who teaches at a Christian school explained that in talking to Republican representatives she discovered that they were reluctant to embarrass President Bush: "This trip has been an eye-opener . . . [GOP staff members were] honest enough to say they were sympathetic but realistic—that they can't afford a veto."[89]

In the end, President Bush did not need to use the veto. At a late night meeting of staffers, the provision was quietly removed from the bill. The backroom maneuvering irritated both Democrats and conservative Republicans. A staffer for a Massachusetts Democrat was quoted as saying: "The fact that it could be undermined is mind-blowing, and more reminiscent of the Politburo than Congress." While not as aggressive, an analyst from the Heritage Foundation noted: "The administration takes a hard line meant to please a certain crowd in Miami."[90] The Republican sponsor of the bill, Jeff Flake, concluded: "Disgusting. Politics have triumphed again over principle. For the same reason we will never have a rational farm policy as long as presidential campaigns begin in Iowa, we will never have a rational Cuba policy as long as presidential campaigns are perceived to end in Florida."[91]

President Bush continued to look for ways to shore up the Cuban American vote in Florida during the first half of the 2004 presidential election year. The president's Commission for Assistance to a Free Cuba, which had been formed the previous fall, released its report in May 2004. The commission called for tightening the embargo by limiting family visits, redefining family to mean only immediate family, and reducing the amount of money that could be spent during family visits. Other recommendations ranged from spending additional money on NGOs, public diplomacy, and efforts to build democracy, to a more aggressive pursuit of Title IV visa sanctions.[92] In the end, President Bush took a number of their suggestions and announced new limits on family travel and remittances, as well as a $45 million increase in funds to promote a democratic transition on the island.[93]

A month after the president's announcement, as we make our final revisions to this book, the political impact of these initiatives is unclear. Some analysts in South Florida have suggested that the moves would cost Bush votes from moderate members of the exile community who find it more difficult to travel to Cuba and to help members of their family still living on the island.[94] Perhaps in response to that potential loss of support, the Bush administration did not immediately move to enforce the restrictions on travel and spending by Cuban Americans.[95] Nevertheless the restrictions are set to come into force in July. Bush's Democratic opponent John Kerry has criticized these restrictions.

Curious Continuity in Cuba Policy

What is perhaps most striking about Cuba policy in the lead up to George W. Bush's 2004 campaign for reelection is the similarity between this president's approach and that pursued by Bill Clinton. This is not to suggest that Clinton and Bush have equal political and personal commitments to the embargo. Clinton gave mixed signals on Cuba throughout his political career, and his support for the CDA and acceptance of Helms-Burton seemed based more on short-term political benefits than a long-term commitment to economic sanctions against the island. President Bush (and his brother Jeb), on the other hand, has embraced the hard-line Cuban American community for years and has never wavered in his support for the embargo. Our conclusion is not that President Bush is somehow less committed to the embargo than previously assumed, or that he has undergone a recent conversion, but that the dynamics around Cuba policy in the early twenty-first century are such that holding the line is as much as a hard-line president is able to accomplish.

We have seen a greater presence for Cuban Americans in the Bush administration to this point, including the controversial Otto Reich. While these appointments have symbolic significance when compared to the Clinton aborted nomination of someone like Mario Baeza, Reich served only the one-year recess appointment before the chief executive chose to sideline the former Public Diplomacy official, rather than risk a Senate confirmation battle. In terms of overall relations with Cuba, we have not seen any inclination yet on the part of President Bush to overturn controversial Clinton reforms such as the wet foot/dry foot immigration policy. Some may have been surprised that President Bush has not at least moved to aggressively enforce either Title III or Title IV of Helms-Burton. To do so, however, would have risked considerable backlash not just internationally, but also from most business groups, free traders, and other congressional opponents of the embargo. Within Congress, the disparate group of members who support easing the embargo has grown to the point where even a president as strongly supportive of the embargo as Bush may not be able to do more than play defense on Cuba policy. If he were to move in the direction of tightening the embargo, it would run the risk of mobilizing even more members of Congress to the other side. There is home for nearly any member of Congress in a group that already includes Jeff Flake (R-AZ), Ron Paul (R-TX), Chuck Hagel (R-NE), Charles Rangel (D-NY), and Chris Dodd (D-CT). The Cuban Americans in Congress and President Bush have their hands full.

The complete collapse of the embargo is perhaps not imminent. After all, there are developments over the last few years that would seem nearly ideal for the hard-line supporters of the embargo. Florida's electoral votes were never more important than they were in 2000. No president has ever been as indebted to the state of Florida, nor has one been as personally connected to hard-line Cuban Americans. A fourth Cuban American has been elected to the House after a campaign that included a heavy focus on his support for the embargo. Castro has executed hijackers, jailed dozens of dissidents, and in the process given his U.S.-based opponents plenty of ammunition with which to attack those who would advocate lifting the embargo. But in the end, the early review of the Bush presidency is that even with developments this favorable, about the best the embargo supporters can hope for is continuity from the Clinton years in the substance of Cuba policy. There have certainly been some symbolically significant words and gestures for embargo supporters from President Bush. But given the overall momentum against the embargo, the president and his Cuban American allies will be lucky to continue to hold the line. The cultivation of interest groups around Cuba policy in the 1980s and the assertiveness of Congress on the Cuban embargo in the 1990s have evolved from blanket support for the embargo to a rising tide of support for its easing. The political dynamics set in motion starting in the Reagan White House have come of age—ironically to undermine the embargo policy they were developed to strengthen. Presidents should be careful what they wish for.

Conclusion

A STANDARD INTERPRETATION OF U.S.-Cuba policy from the 1959 Cuban revolution to the present would focus on the apparent continuity. For more than forty-five years, Fidel Castro has remained in power, and now long after the end of the cold war and the threat from the Soviet Union the United States still wages a cold war with Cuba through the embargo that began under Dwight Eisenhower.[1] Even Castro sounded this theme recently when at the end of a five-and-a-half-hour speech in early 2004 he suggested that President George W. Bush has plans to assassinate him.[2] While we know of no evidence that such a plan exists, the Bush administration has demonstrated a willingness to attack unfriendly authoritarian governments elsewhere and has spoken suggestively about a possible biological weapons capacity in Cuba that could make Castro nervous. And if nothing else, the Castro accusation is an indication of the level of hostility that still exists between the two governments. In terms of domestic politics in the United States, the electoral importance of Florida and presumably the bloc of Cuban American voters there appear to be more important than ever. Neither Senator John Kerry, the 2004 Democratic presidential candidate, nor President Bush has shown any inclination to deviate much from the embargo policy toward Cuba.

On the surface, Cuba policy is seemingly caught in the same time warp that visitors to the island frequently suggest characterizes the island nation's streets and neighborhoods. We have argued here, however, that under the surface of an apparently frozen embargo a number of significant changes have taken place over the last couple of decades in U.S.-Cuba policy, changes both in terms of the outlines of the policy—what is permitted within the context of the embargo—and in terms of how this policy is constructed. We argue that the Reagan presidency marked a significant turning point in the policy-making process. The Reagan team used the communist threat from Cuba as a vehicle to draw attention to the perceived broader communist threat in the hemisphere and built alliances with new private actors interested in Cuba policy. Ironically, the long term impact of the Reagan administration's efforts was to lay the groundwork for the ultimate erosion of the embargo policy itself as Congress and new societal groups, which would by the late 1990s and early 2000s begin to turn against the embargo, gained a foothold in the Cuba policy-making process.

In the spring of 2003, following Castro's crackdown on dissidents, a CANF spokesman said: "The overwhelming position of our board is that the U.S. should not react to Castro's provocation."[3] A little more than two decades after the Reagan administration sponsored the development of a hard-line organization of Cuban Americans to help it ratchet up the pressure on Cuba and the Latin American left, and only a few years after some in Miami called for a new blockade of Cuba, or even a military strike, following the 1996 Brothers to the Rescue shootdown, that same group now serves as a moderating check on the U.S. president. While the policy that the Reagan administration secured with the help of CANF remains largely the same twenty some years later, the evolution of the most prominent Cuban American interest group is one part of the dramatically changed dynamics surrounding the making of U.S.-Cuba policy. While it is important to understand the changed nature of CANF, and of the interest group environment that surrounds Cuba policy, interest groups are only

one of several key components of the changing politics of the Cuban embargo. In this book we have tracked the developments around the embargo policy; here, we conclude by highlighting several dynamics that run
throughout the book and that are driving the politics of the embargo.

Changing Interest Group Environment

Starting in the 1980s, the Cuban American National Foundation has been
a central player in crafting Cuba policy. Founded in 1981 at the urging of
Reagan administration officials, CANF quickly built a web of relationships in the executive that extended into Central America and Africa policy
as well as Cuba policy. It also had bipartisan ties with several influential
members of Congress who sponsored CANF-backed legislation. Robert
Torricelli (D-NJ) was a harsh critic of the Reagan approach to Latin America and had visited Cuba and met Castro in 1987, but by 1991 Torricelli
had come around to the "correct view" on Cuba.[4] Subsequent to his 1987
trip, Torricelli received nearly $240,000 from Cuban American PACS and
individuals—ranking him all time second, behind Ileana Ros-Lehtinen
and ahead of Bob Menendez and Lincoln Diaz-Balart.[5] In 1988 Joe Lieberman ran against Republican incumbent, and embargo critic, Lowell
Weicker. He took in nearly $30,000 in donations from Cuban-related
groups and individuals and beat Weicker by ten thousand votes. During
the last twenty years, only two Republicans outside of New Jersey or
Florida received similar or more Cuban American money in an election
cycle as Lieberman: Jesse Helms (R-NC) received $63,427 in 1996; Dan
Burton (R-IN) took in $28,500 that same year.[6] Lieberman is the fifteenth
largest recipient of Cuban American donations among all candidates for
Congress and the White House.[7] CANF certainly spread its money around,
funding opportunistic Democrats, helping Cuban American candidates in
both parties, and rewarding staunchly anti-Castro Republicans such as
Helms and Burton.

It is worth noting, however, that the evidence about CANF and the
power of political contributions is far from conclusive. From 1982 through
the 2000 election cycle, CANF's Free Cuba PAC gave more than $1.6 mil-
lion to candidates for political office. While no one would scoff at that sort

of money, it pales in comparison to the sixty-seven Pro-Israel PACS tracked by the Center for Responsive Politics, which gave over $16 million in the same period.[8] And the Cuban American giving rate has gone down in recent cycles, perhaps mirroring the general drop in CANF power.[9] A recent study finds that between 1999 and February 2002 Cuban Americans gave about $1.8 million in political contributions and that about 70 percent of that total was given by the two brothers who run the Flo-Sun Sugar Company, Alfonso (a Democrat) and Jose (a Republican) Fanjul. The total contributions were split between the two major parties, with Republicans getting slightly more than Democrats.[10] Cuban-related giving is certainly important and in cases such as Torricelli's may have been decisive, but we see the bipartisan donations by Cuban Americans as playing a relatively small role in the overall picture. It is frankly easier to explain positions on Castro by people like Helms, Burton, and Lieberman as more consistent with their general foreign policy views than as the result of campaign contributions.[11] And the money available to members of Congress from the economic interest groups opposed to the embargo is far greater than that being handed out by Cuban Americans in the 1990s.

Reflecting on the development of CANF over the last twenty-plus years, it's clear that the group moved well beyond its partnership with the executive branch after President Reagan left office. The interest group successfully promoted the election of Cuban Americans to the U.S. House of Representatives, and then it effectively played presidential candidate Clinton against a sitting president to help pass the CDA in 1992. But the elections of those Cuban American members of Congress and President Clinton led to a situation in which CANF was occasionally relegated to the sidelines. We saw that diminished role for CANF as early as the 1994 immigration agreement and certainly during the negotiations over Helms-Burton in 1995–1996. In Clinton's second term, the death of Mas, and then 1998 media reports about CANF links to terrorist Luis Posada Carriles and exiles indicted for plotting to assassinate Fidel,[12] accelerated the shift in influence from the interest group to Diaz-Balart, Ros-Lehtinen, and Menendez in Congress. Following the resignations of several board members and the resolution of the Elian Gonzalez saga, a weakened CANF leaned toward a more moderate position within the Cuban American community. Its advocacy of dialogue, support for the Varela project, and opposition to any toughening of the embargo has actually put them in a potentially adversarial position vis-a-vis the Bush administration. In the end, only the chief executive that sponsored its founding, Ronald Reagan, unambiguously benefited from CANF activism on Cuba policy. Future presidents were forced to contend with varying degrees of opposition from a relatively autonomous CANF.

In making its case for the embargo, CANF was faced over time with an increasing number of business, church, and academic groups on the other side of the debate. We argued that the emergence of some of these groups was by design of the executive branch. President Clinton sought to develop domestic counterweights to CANF and proembargo forces in Congress by helping to reframe Cuba policy as a trade issue instead of as an issue of ethnic politics. In doing so, Clinton helped antiembargo forces to bring the electoral interests of farm state senators and representatives into the mix on Cuba policy. Throughout the 1990s, business and farming interests mobilized to achieve access to markets from which they were previously excluded by U.S. government economic sanctions, such as Cuba. These groups in turn developed links to members of Congress, whose constituents would economically benefit from the loosening or end of the embargo or were ideologically committed to "free" trade. "I need to stand up for the farmers in my district," Washington's George Nethercutt stated plainly.[13] In the end, unlikely bipartisan alliances emerged in both the House and the Senate to challenge restrictions on U.S. access to Cuba and its markets. In the wake of falling global commodity prices and the U.S. growing trade deficit with the rest of the world, the agroindustry made a case for trade with Cuba that was increasingly difficult to refute.

Pharmaceutical companies added their voice to the chorus against the embargo in 2000. House passage of permanent normal trading relations with China, a communist country whose human rights record is worse than Cuba's, vitiated the logic of arguments put forth by embargo proponents. The changed circumstances became most evident when Senator Helms, the arch Castro foe and author of LIBERTAD, tacitly dropped his opposition to easing the embargo. In March 2000 he allowed the Senate Foreign Relations Committee to authorize sales of food and medicine to Cuba.[14] The end of the cold war has generated a relative decline in the importance of traditional security interests, which appears to have opened the door to greater interest group activism over foreign policy, as Eric Uslander has argued convincingly.[15] Cuba is no longer a security issue, and so by 2000 the farm lobby was able to combine with former government officials who represented global corporations to transform much of the debate about the embargo from one centered on ethnic politics to one focused on international trade.

The Struggle for Control of the Embargo

Since the 1992 CDA and Helms-Burton, Congress has largely controlled Cuba policy. In that presidential election year, Congress passed a controversial piece of substantive foreign policy legislation in the CDA, legislation President Bush (at least initially) opposed. When Helms-Burton ultimately passed, with a little help from the Cuban Air Force, Congress wrote the embargo policy into law; and they codified even more in 2000. Congress would appear to be in the center square on Cuba policy. As Dan Fisk noted, "policy toward Cuba runs through Capitol Hill as much as, if not more than, through the Oval Office."[16] Still, the preeminent role for Congress that we might expect, given these developments, has perhaps not developed. Presidents, if highly motivated, can find ways to get around Congress, as Clinton did by 1998 and 1999. The record of the last decade shows an impressive amount of congressional activism on Cuba policy and on trade policy more generally, but it also highlights the limits of congressional activism and the strength of the executive, even in an area where Congress has acted clearly to try to constrain the president. We would argue that Cuba policy is not so much driven by any one actor but is pushed along by an increasingly broad array of actors with varying goals and both policy and institutional interests.

The 2000 codification bill highlights this. In the end Congress passed a bill that codified the existing ban on U.S. citizens' travel to Cuba and restricted the president's ability to impose sanctions, adding yet more constraints on the executive branch's ability to make foreign policy, especially Cuba policy. Noting this congressional activism is easy; assessing its significance is trickier. The ability of a core of Cuba policy hard-liners on the Hill to codify the embargo into place in 1996 is impressive. And the capacity of this group to shape the final bill in 2000 is just as noteworthy, given the breadth of the actual support in Congress for allowing the unconstrained sale of food and medicine to Cuba. Not only was the credit restriction placed on the sale, but as an added bonus the prohibition of travel was codified. These proembargo representatives, led by the Cuban Americans, wielded significant power over the fate of U.S.-Cuba policy in this period. At first glance this influence is perhaps not surprising, particularly in the circumstances of the first codification. But by 2000 the politics of Cuba policy had begun to shift significantly. If the combined forces of farm state legislators, liberal members of Congress who have long opposed the embargo, and an ever increasing number of business organizations are unable to wrest control of Cuba policy back from a few Cuban American members of the House, even given the electoral implications of Florida and New Jersey, we may have to reassess our assumptions about how foreign policy making takes place. At the same time, though, one must note that the travel ban was not the only significant foreign policy action embedded in the 2000 bill: it also sought to restrict the president's hands when using sanctions as a foreign policy tool. This action appears to be a significant step for Congress in asserting its authority over trade policy. How significant this step turns out to be in practice remains to be seen. Helms-Burton looked airtight, but as we saw it turned out to be fairly porous.

In recent books, Louis Fisher and Gordon Silverstein each make compelling arguments that since World War II the president has garnered significant unilateral control over much of foreign policy and war power, often with the unwitting (and even witting) help of Congress.[17] We agree that Cuba policy largely fit into this trend during the cold war, but in the period that we study here Cuba policy has become more domesticated—more porous and open to forces outside the executive office, including an increasingly assertive Congress. Congress has acted to retain significant authority over Cuba policy: the embargo itself, the travel ban, and the financing of some food and medicine sales. In the process Congress has restricted the president's ability to unilaterally impose sanctions on other countries. President Clinton showed the limits of congressional action and the strength of the executive following Helms-Burton—the kind of strength that Fisher and Silverstein document. When a president's actions seem to defy the intent of legislation (whether the War Powers Act or Helms-Burton),

Congress has historically found it very difficult to prevent or sanction the action.[18] Nevertheless, after Helms-Burton no president can unilaterally end the embargo of Cuba as, for example, President Clinton did with Vietnam. While a smaller step than its drafters perhaps imagined, Helms-Burton does nevertheless guarantee Congress an important role in settling the ultimate question of the embargo.

President Bush's task with Cuba policy making has perhaps been even more difficult than Reagan's Central America and Cuba policy making given the nature of the opposition Bush has faced. President Reagan's opposition in Congress and the public was nearly all to his political left: both moderates and liberals, predominantly Democrats. In the current Cuba policy debate, Bush has also faced economic interest groups whose politics may be quite conservative and whose votes are as likely to be Republican as Democratic. In particular, large agroindustrial interests have aggressively entered the debate about selling food to Cuba. In December 2001, the first direct shipment of food from the United States since the beginning of the embargo arrived at Cuban ports. Since that time, the Cuban government has continued to pay cash for agricultural products from a number of different states and many of the largest food companies.

We see a number of similarities between the foreign policy-making process in the George W. Bush administration generally and the process during the Reagan years. The appointment of several Reagan officials by President Bush certainly contributed to that impression. Otto Reich, Eliot Abrams, John Negroponte, and Admiral John Poindexter played important roles in making and carrying out the Reagan policy toward Latin America. As we have seen from President Bush's approach to foreign policy since the events of September 11, 2001, the world is characterized as divided between "us" and "them." From our discussion of the Reagan years, we can see similarities between the Reagan administration's diplomacy in Central America and the Bush approach to the Middle East. There are "freedom fighters" and those who "hate freedom" in the Bush administration's world view. Any opponents of that characterization are at least naive and perhaps something worse. As was the case for the Reagan administration, the Bush officials believe that the executive branch should be free to make and conduct its foreign policy without interference from Congress, the domestic public, or the global community. While those actors have not been able to constrain President Bush in his making of policy toward a country such as Iraq, we have argued here that, perhaps surprisingly, relations toward Cuba are far less easily controlled.

The Cuban Americans in Congress and their allies in the House leadership have withstood further efforts to weaken the embargo over the last couple of years. But bills continue to emerge and generate considerable support in Congress. We see the strong, existing opposition in Congress to at least parts of the embargo as likely to continue to grow. But the Cuban American members of Congress suggest that with a sympathetic president and congressional leaders as allies, they will be able to continue to resist those challenges. As Ros-Lehtinen responded when asked about a new working group of House members opposed to the Cuba embargo: "As long as we have George W. Bush in the White House, their efforts will continue to be failed ones."[19] The problem for embargo supporters is that the center of Cuba policy is no longer in the White House. And congressional opposition to the embargo, with prodding from a range of economic interest groups and cover from a new generation of moderate Cuban Americans, has already changed the more than four-decade-old sanctions policy and is trying to loosen it even more.

Is Cuba Policy Unique?

Analysts sometimes see Cuba as an exceptional case of U.S. foreign policy because of the domestic political interests involved. Opponents of the embargo from across the political spectrum have argued that, especially in the post–cold war period, it serves neither U.S. nor Cuban interests, implying there is some unique explanation for this one example of foreign policy irrationality. They suggest that a small group of intensely committed Cuban Americans have held the country hostage to an outdated policy as a result of their intense beliefs, geographical concentration, and considerable economic resources. As we have shown in this book, however, the story is far more complicated. In fact, a range of forces is involved in pushing Cuba policy, and these forces have been evolving over the last twenty-five years just as the embargo policy itself has evolved. Furthermore, the dynamics involved in Cuba policy—which seem to many to be unique—

are perhaps typical of U.S. foreign policy in the post–cold war era more generally.

The Cuba case indicates that in the wake of the cold war foreign policy may be becoming more domesticated over time, thus allowing Congress and interest groups easier access to the policy process. The case indicates that ethnic interest groups, as well as other organized interests, can success-fully set their sights on policy influence—particularly on Capitol Hill.[20] The Cuba case may look unique in that it is highly salient to a number of constituencies in crosscutting ways. Long the domain of the president and the Cuban American National Foundation, now an array of members of Congress, with powerful constituencies and interest groups behind them, vie with the president to control Cuba policy. But there are other cases that suggest at least a potentially similar complexity in the executive-legislative relationship. Policies to promote trade, whether with Africa or the Ameri-cas, are likely to engage a broad range of crosscutting constituencies that will prompt a heavy dose of congressional activism. Sanctions policies are also likely to mobilize constituencies from energy companies to farmers and human rights groups, and with them, Congress. Issues such as aid to Colombia, where the drug trade, security, and human rights are all involved—or Mexico, including issues from immigration to trade, secu-rity, the environment, and human rights—might ultimately mobilize as wide an array of groups in and out of Congress as Cuba policy. In this sense we see the case of the politics of Cuba policy not so much as an ex-treme case but more as a bellwether of the potential future of the politics of U.S. foreign policy.

Even in recent cases of using the military, the area of foreign policy where the executive branch seems to maintain the upper hand, we see ev-idence of effective ethnic and other interest group mobilization. President Clinton's decision to intervene aggressively in Haiti to restore President Aristide to his elected office was at least partly a response to pressure from African Americans. Randall Robinson and the TransAfrica Forum lob-bied vigorously for intervention, and Robinson's hunger strike drew con-siderable attention to the situation in Haiti. The Congressional Black Caucus weighed in with a president indebted to African American voters. In President George W. Bush's invasion of Iraq, the executive branch ap-pears to have worked closely with the Iraqi exile community. In that case, no one explains the invasion of Iraq as a result of pressure from the Iraqi-American community, but we have observed members of that ethnic group in important (and controversial) relationships with government officials. The tactic of comparing Saddam Hussein to Hitler is reminiscent of the demonization of Fidel Castro. We might speculate about domestic counterweights too, where energy companies weigh in on sanctions against Iraq, Iran, and Libya, in ways similar to the agroindustrial lobby on Cuba policy. Again, the dynamics in the Cuba case are somewhat different from those in Haiti or Iraq, but the point is that there are enough similarities to suggest that Cuba is not the exceptional case that some make it out to be.

We also see a trend that has some generalizability in the way that the public and private have been blurred at times in the formation and implementation of Cuba policy. In its attempt to sell the new "war on terrorism," the Bush administration seemed to be working from an old Reagan administration playbook. Charlotte Beers, with a successful private sector career as an advertising executive, was appointed by President Bush to head a new public diplomacy initiative and to help "rebrand" U.S. foreign policy.[21] Beers, who left the under secretary of state for public diplomacy position in the spring of 2003, had previously served as the chairman of both J. Walter Thompson and Ogilvy & Mather, successfully promoting products ranging from Uncle Ben's Rice to American Express. The Pentagon hired a Washington, D.C., public relations firm a few weeks after the September 11 attacks to promote the U.S. government's activities in Afghanistan and around the globe. The Rendon Group has a history of working for the U.S. government in the Middle East, including a reported $23 million that the firm was paid by the CIA to improve the image of a group of Iraqis opposed to Saddam Hussein.[22] In Latin America, Rendon played roles in both President Aristide's return to power in Haiti during the Clinton administration and the Panama invasion under the first President Bush.[23] In another example, William Bennett, education secretary and drug czar under Reagan, heads Americans United for Victory over Terrorism, which seeks to maintain public support for the war on terrorism and to combat dissent in places like college campuses, editorial pages, and television.[24] Senior advisers to the group include Frank Gaffney (former assistant secretary of defense in the Reagan administration who worked for Richard Perle), and James Woolsey (formerly Clinton's Director of Central Intelligence and a public advocate for extending the war to Iraq).[25] Relationships between the government and technically private organizations, which include former government officials actively working to promote a specific foreign policy agenda, are every bit as important and interesting in the current Bush presidency as they were during the Reagan years. The recent shift toward a reliance on private military contractors to carry out "mission sensitive" tasks in Iraq are but another example of the privatization of foreign policy that we see emerging in the Reagan years.[26] The symbiotic relationship between CANF and the Reagan administration was an early example of a partnership between private organizations and the government, but it is not the only such example. Indeed, these partnerships may be becoming more common over time.

Concluding Thoughts on the Politics of the Cuban Embargo

One trend that is clear in the period we survey here is the introduction of new actors and greater complexity into the foreign policy-making process. We described the relatively closed environments in which Presidents Eisenhower and Kennedy met with a few close advisers to decide on such moves as the invasion at the Bay of Pigs. Following Vietnam and Watergate, Congress became much more engaged in making foreign policy. By the 1980s, the Reagan administration sought support from private groups and organizations as a means to counter the new influence and power of their congressional opponents. In the 1990s, congressional activism was such that in the case of Cuba policy, a few entrepreneurial members successfully took away presidential prerogative with the Helms-Burton codification of the embargo. Now, the future of the core of Cuba policy, the embargo, is in the hands of the legislative branch of government. The chain of events that led from an executive-sponsored ethnic interest group to a Cuban American presence in a more assertive Congress to the introduction of other powerful economic interest groups into the fray included a number of unintended consequences. If we are right, the erosion of the embargo becomes understandable as the unintended and unforeseen outcome of a number of decisions made by embargo supporters to maintain and strengthen the economic sanctions on Cuba. Dynamics set in motion to bolster presidential control over a tightened embargo have begun to boomerang on both the White House and the embargo itself.

The survival of the embargo for more than four decades has been impressive and perhaps surprising in many ways. But while the embargo still stands, the ground it is built on has been shifting. Already there are significant holes in the embargo as increased trade between the United States and Cuba has begun and Cuban Americans visit and send money to the island in impressive amounts. And the movement to continue to loosen the travel ban, often seen as a backdoor way to further erode the embargo because with more hard currency from U.S. tourists in Cuba Castro could buy more goods under existing law without the United States bothering to end the embargo, has been resilient. Within a few months of Castro's repressive actions in the spring of 2003, a majority of the members of Congress, from both parties and quite different political perspectives, voted to lift the travel ban. Even retiring Representative Dick Armey (R-TX) added his voice to the antiembargo movement in comments made at a trade promotion event in Kansas. He suggested that restrictions on travel and trade would last at most another year and strongly implied that he supported the elimination of those restrictions. Most interestingly, he explained his previous support for the embargo as based on his own district's not having enough of an economic stake in trade with Cuba to offset his friendship with the Cuban American representatives from Florida: "What you see in the House of Representatives and what you see by way of individual votes —my own is an example—is loyalties to your friends. . . . Sometimes on an issue like Cuba, my particular loyalty to Lincoln Diaz-Balart and Ileana Ros-Lehtinen is not counterbalanced by focused interest in my district."[27] Armey's admission that he apparently put his friendship with a couple of colleagues above his own belief that a different policy was in the United States' interest certainly complicates the attempt by analysts to explain the U.S.-Cuba policy-making process. Armey's words were in a sense endorsed recently by Colin Powell's chief of staff, who described the embargo as the "dumbest policy on the face of the earth."[28] While Armey's "one-year" prediction has been proven wrong, his words, at the very least, add weight to an argument that much more than presidential preferences, Cuban American voters, and Florida's electoral votes drive the embargo debate.

Cuba policy under President Bush has certainly been affected by his political advisers' calculations about Cuban American voters, just as such concerns have influenced all chief executives during the time of the modern embargo, but that it is only one of many factors that currently shape U.S. foreign policy. American economic interests, including both the larger desire to maintain global trade momentum and the particular interests of various domestic economic groups, are also part of the story. Furthermore, we see institutional interests on display as members of the legislature compete with the executive for control over policy, regardless of the various policy preferences that seem to exist within each of the branches. The dynamics in Congress itself, including the willingness of some members to defer to policy entrepreneurs (or friends) like Diaz-Balart and Ros-Lehtinen, play a role in the Cuban policymaking process as well. Finally, the broader context of U.S. foreign policy seems to be influencing Cuba policy to some extent. The discussion of terrorism, democratization, and an axis of evil elsewhere in the world help set the context for contemporary relations with the Castro government in Cuba.

We conclude on a speculative note as we look toward the 2004 election. The time-tested strategy by most Democrat candidates trying to win the state of Florida in a national election has been to stake out a position on Cuba that is relatively indistinguishable from their Republican opponents. Certainly that strategy has worked for current Democratic Senators Bill Nelson and Robert Graham, and President Clinton won the state several months after signing Helms-Burton in 1996. It is possible, though, that this calculus could change in Florida. While the hard-line Cuban Americans in Congress and Florida generally continue to argue that both parties need to do their bidding or risk a backlash at the voting booth, for Democratic presidential candidates, at least, that may be more bark than bite. Bill Clinton won the White House in 1992 without Florida, and in 2000 Al Gore apparently had more Florida voters attempt to cast votes for him than George Bush, even though the Democratic candidate received only a small minority of the Cuban American vote. A Democratic candidate who can accurately capture some of the thirty-four hundred Buchanan voters in Palm Beach County, or some of the over-votes in Jacksonville, could win Florida with no greater Cuban American participation than Gore. But Gore tried to not allow much light between himself and Bush on Cuba, his ties to Clinton, Reno, and Elian, notwithstanding. The real question for a Democratic candidate is whether there is a way to win while going in a different direction.

It is at least possible that a Democratic candidate could do better in Florida by arguing for small changes to the embargo, as younger Cuban Americans are less wedded to the hard embargo, and as the state's non-Cuban Hispanic vote increases rapidly. At the very least, that would seem a more promising approach than giving the appearance of pandering to the Cuban Americans (as some think Gore did in the Elian affair). A Democratic presidential candidate might take a more nuanced position on the embargo—in favor of more travel, continued family remittances, and no limits on the sale of food and medicine to Cuba, perhaps, while maintaining diplomatic isolation and other elements of the economic embargo, particularly prohibiting the import of Cuban goods to the United States—and find that there is a net gain in Florida, much less the rest of the country. Of the roughly 80 percent of Cuban American voters who supported Bush in 2000, it is at least possible that 10 percent of them could be convinced that opening up Cuba to travel and greater sales of agriculture might be more effective than the current policy. Some polls have certainly suggested that more Cuban Americans in Florida support those policy changes than supported Gore in 2000. And there are some signs that part of this kind of strategy might be put in play this year as the Bush administration places tighter limits on family travel and remittances while the Kerry campaign seems to oppose these initiatives. [29] Such an approach, especially one that urges more food sales to Cuba, might even get a candidate a few more votes among farmers in Iowa or libertarians in New Hampshire.[30] And we should remember that other issues are also in play in Florida: the prescription drug benefit, the war in Iraq, and amnesty for undocumented workers, to name just a few, could all cut for or against the president and have little or nothing to do with Cuba. We also must remember that Florida is not the only state in play for the 2004 election, and a plan that replays the 2000 election while winning Florida may not be the best strategy for a Democratic candidate. It may be a better plan to cede Florida and go after Ohio, Arizona, and Nevada—with or without a focus on easing the embargo. Even if the Democratic candidate decides that the path to victory in Florida goes through Miami-Dade County, where Gore won only 53 percent of the vote in 2000 (compared to 67 percent in Broward County), it need not go through Cuban Americans as much as it used to.[31]

Finally, some have suggested that this may be the last presidential election during the era of the Cuban embargo. Writing recently in *Time* magazine, for example, Tim Padgett suggests, "even Cuban exiles in Miami, the strongest backers of the 41-year old embargo, say they don't expect the travel ban to survive much beyond next year's presidential election—that is, once George W. Bush no longer needs Florida's votes."[32] As we have discussed, the politics of Cuba policy, to the extent that they have a trend line, seem to us to be moving away from the embargo for a variety of economic, political, institutional, and electoral reasons. This election may be the last great hurrah for embargo hard-liners as they hold out the prize of Florida's electoral votes, or the embargo may go out with a whimper at some future point. But however it ultimately recedes, the days of the strong U.S. embargo of Cuba are numbered in large part because the political dynamics set in motion in the 1980s have come of age in ways that have undermined presidential control over the embargo, and the embargo policy itself.

Notes

1. Introduction

1. Christina Hoag, "Bush Shuts Door Clinton Left Ajar to U.S. Visitors," *Miami Herald,* April 18, 2003, p. 1C.

2. Jose De Cordoba, "U.S. Contends with Potent New Force on Cuba: Moderate Miami Exiles," *Wall Street Journal,* April 29, 2003, p. A14.

3. Rebecca K. C. Hersman, *Friends and Foes,* p. 14; Philip Brenner, Patrick J. Haney, and Walt Vanderbush, "Intermestic Interests and U.S. Policy toward Cuba."

4. See "The Cuban Threat to National Security," http://www.defenselink.mil/pubs/cubarpt.htm (accessed June 2, 2004).

5. For example, see Wayne Smith, "Shackled to the Past"; Gail DeGeorge with Douglas Harbrecht, "Warmer Winds Are Blowing from Washington to Havana"; Peter Hakim, "It's Time to Review U.S. Cuba Policy," p. 47; "Curbing Castro," *The Economist,* October 28, 1995, pp. 17–18; "Lift the Embargo," *Wall Street Journal,* August 26, 1994, p. A10; "Isolating Cuba Hasn't Worked," *Chicago Tribune,* August 23, 1994, section 1, p. 14; Susan Kaufman Purcell, "Cuba's Cloudy Future"; and "The Cuban Illusion"; Charles Lane, "TRB from Washington"; Michael G. Wilson, "Hastening Castro's Downfall." For other views, see Bob Benenson, "Dissonant Voices Urge Clinton to Revise Policy on Cuba"; Saul Landau, "Clinton's Cuba Policy"; David Rieff, "Cuba Refrozen."

6. See U.S. Congress, Senate Committee on Foreign Relations and House Committee on International Relations, Staff Report, *Cuba at the Crossroads;* http://www.uscubacommission.org/; Bernard W. Aronson and William D. Rogers, *U.S.-Cuban Relations in the 21st Century;* Edward Gonzalez and Richard A. Nuccio, eds., *The RAND Forum on Cuba.*

7. Newer books about U.S.-Cuba policy include Donna Rich Kaplowitz, *Anatomy of a Failed Embargo;* Jane Franklin, *Cuba and the United States;* Peter Schwab, *Cuba;* Kenneth N. Skoug, *The United States and Cuba Under Reagan and Shultz;* Thomas G. Paterson, *Contesting Castro;* Joaquin Roy, *Cuba, the United States, and the Helms-Burton Doctrine;* Anne Louise Bardach, *Cuba Confidential;* and Maria de los Angeles Torres, *In the Land of Mirrors.* Less recent works include Wayne Smith, *The Closest of Enemies;* Louis A. Perez, *Cuba and the United States;* and Philip Brenner, *From Confrontation to Negotiation.*

8. For a recent analytical work that seeks to explain U.S.-Cuba policy, see William LeoGrande, "From Havana to Miami."

9. Morris H. Morley and Chris McGillion, *Unfinished Business.*

10. For example, Cecil V. Crabb Jr. and Pat M. Holt, *Invitation to Struggle;* E. E.

Schattschneider, *The Semi-Sovereign People;* various editions of Eugene R. Wittkopf and James M. McCormick, eds., *The Domestic Sources of American Foreign Policy;* James M. Lindsay, *Congress and the Politics of U.S. Foreign Policy;* Randall B. Ripley and James M. Lindsay, eds., "How Congress Influences Foreign and Defense Policy"; Cynthia J. Arnson, *Crossroads;* David Gary Adler and Larry N. George, eds., *The Constitution and the Conduct of American Foreign Policy.*

11. See, e.g., James M. Scott, ed., *After the End;* Ripley and Lindsay, *U.S. Foreign Policy after the Cold War;* Brigitte L. Nacos, Robert Y. Shapiro, and Pierangelo Isernia, eds., *Decisionmaking in a Glass House;* David A. Deese, ed., *The New Politics of American Foreign Policy;* Thomas E. Mann, ed., *A Question of Balance;* Jeremy D. Rosner, *The New Tug-of-War;* Robert Y. Shapiro, Martha Joynt Kumar, and Lawrence R. Jacobs, eds., *Presidential Power.*

12. Hersman, *Friends and Foes,* pp. 10–14.

2. The Making of an Embargo

1. See Louis A. Perez, *Cuba and the United States;* Perez, *Cuba under the Platt Amendment, 1902–1934;* Jules R. Benjamin, The United States and Cuba; Morris H. Morley, Imperial State and Revolution; and Philip Brenner, *From Confrontation to Negotiation,* among others, for a more detailed background.

2. See Stephen G. Rabe, *Eisenhower and Latin America,* pp. 119–20.

3. Mark T. Gilderhus, *The Second Century,* p. 166.

4. Robert E. Welch Jr., *Response to Revolution,* pp. 30–31.

5. See Rabe, *Eisenhower and Latin America,* pp. 123–24.

6. Peter Kornbluh, ed., *Bay of Pigs Declassified,* p. 267.

7. Morley, *Imperial State and Revolution,* pp. 82–83.

8. Jules R. Benjamin, *The United States and the Origins of the Cuban Revolution,* p. 185; Welch, *Response to Revolution,* p. 31.

9. Stephen E. Ambrose, *Eisenhower,* p. 556 (emphasis in original).

10. Maria de los Angeles Torres, *In the Land of Mirrors,* p. 55.

11. Benjamin, *The United States and the Origins of the Cuban Revolution,* p. 188; see also William B. Breuer, *Vendetta.*

12. Kornbluh, *Bay of Pigs Declassified,* pp. 267, 269.

13. Ambrose, *Eisenhower,* p. 557.

14. Morley, *Imperial State and Revolution,* p. 88.

15. Rabe, *Eisenhower and Latin America,* p. 163.

16. Morley, *Imperial State and Revolution,* p. 126.

17. Rabe, *Eisenhower and Latin America,* pp. 130, 164, 174–75.

18. See Mark J. White, ed., *The Kennedys and Cuba;* Kornbluh, *Bay of Pigs Declassified;* James G. Blight and Philip Brenner, *Sad and Luminous Days.*

19. David Kaiser, "Men and Policies," p. 13.

20. See Wayne Smith, *The Closest of Enemies,* p. 71, who argues that "none of the men sitting around the table had first hand knowledge of Cuba, and they failed to consult

with those who did. . . . Consulting them might have made a difference, for they would have killed the notion that a popular uprising would occur." See also Welch, *Response to Revolution,* p. 68.

21. Welch, *Response to Revolution,* p. 71.

22. Kornbluh, *Bay of Pigs Declassified,* p. 288.

23. For example, see McGeorge Bundy's memo to the president February 8, 1961, attributing the State Department's wariness to United Nations' and Latin American political reactions. In Kornbluh, *Bay of Pigs Declassified,* p. 288.

24. White, *The Kennedys and Cuba,* pp. 62–65.

25. See Kornbluh, *Bay of Pigs Declassified,* pp. 325–27, for a detailed discussion.

26. Kai Bird, *The Color of Truth,* p. 242.

27. Morley, *Imperial State and Revolution,* p. 152.

28. Morley, *Imperial State and Revolution,* pp. 188–89.

29. Welch, *Response to Revolution,* pp. 105, 109–10.

30. Kaiser, *Men and Policies,* p. 19.

31. Philip Zelikow, "American Policy and Cuba, 1961–1963," p. 328.

32. Haynes Johnson and Bernard M. Gwertzman, *Fulbright,* p. 182.

33. White, in *The Kennedys and Cuba,* p. 182, points out the comparison made at one point to a speech by Senator Homer Capehart (R-IN), for example.

34. H. W. Brands, *The Wages of Globalism,* p. 31.

35. William Walker, "The Struggle for the Americas," p. 75.

36. Morley, *Imperial State and Revolution,* p. 306.

37. Gilderhus, *The Second Century,* p. 190.

38. Brands, *Wages of Globalism,* p. 58.

39. Walker, "The Struggle for the Americas," pp. 66–67.

40. Speech quoted in Johnson and Gwertzman, *Fulbright,* pp. 187–88.

41. Morley, *Imperial State and Revolution,* pp. 215–18.

42. See the discussion of this rise in activism by Tony Smith, *Foreign Attachments,* p. 91.

43. The so-called water crisis that came out of the Cuban government's shutoff of the water supply to the U.S. naval base at Guantanamo Bay was resolved quickly.

44. David W. Engstrom, *Presidential Decision Making Adrift,* p. 22.

45. Engstrom, *Presidential Decision Making Adrift,* p. 23, suggests that looking through the Congressional Record at the time he could find only one criticism.

46. Engstrom, *Presidential Decision Making Adrift,* p. 30.

47. Gilderhus, *The Second Century,* p. 195.

48. Seymour M. Hersh, *The Price of Power,* p. 263.

49. Morley, *Imperial State and Revolution,* pp. 247–48.

50. Quoted in Morley, *Imperial State and Revolution,* p. 248.

51. Stephen E. Ambrose, *Nixon,* p. 381.

52. Gilderhus, *The Second Century,* p. 197.

53. H. R. Haldeman, with Joseph DiMona, *The Ends of Power,* pp. 85–86. See also Raymond L. Garthoff, "Handling the Cienfuegos Crisis"; and Patrick J. Haney, "Soccer Fields and Submarines in Cuba."

54. Haney, "Soccer Fields and Submarines," p. 76.

55. C. L. Sulzberger, "Ugly Clouds in the South," *New York Times*, September 25, 1970, p. 43.

56. Hersh, *The Price of Power*, p. 254.

57. John W. Finney, "Rivers Cites Soviet Power in New Defense Fund Plea," *New York Times*, September 29, 1970, p. 3.

58. For example, Bernard Gwertzman, "Moscow Scoffs at Sub-Base Issue," *New York Times*, October 1, 1971, p. 1, notes the *Times of London's* skeptical coverage of the issue.

59. Nixon, *RN*, p. 489.

60. Morley, *Imperial State and Revolution*, p. 280.

61. Philip Brenner, *The Limits and Possibilities of Congress*, p. 45.

62. Torres, *In the Land of Mirrors*, p. 91.

63. Philip Brenner, *From Confrontation to Negotiation*.

64. Pamela S. Falk, "U.S.- Cuba Negotiations," p. 169.

65. Morley, *Imperial State and Revolution*, p. 284.

66. Brenner, *The Limits and Possibilities of Congress*, p. 47.

67. "Chronology of Cuban Affairs, 1958–1998," http://www.state.gov/www/regions/wha/cuba_chronology.html.

68. Jane Franklin, *Cuba and the United States*, p. 119.

69. Morley, *Imperial State and Revolution*, p. 277.

70. Franklin, *Cuba and the United States*, p. 123.

71. "Chronology of Cuban Affairs, 1958–1998."

72. Stephen E. Ambrose, *Rise to Globalism*, p. 277.

73. Engstrom, *Presidential Decision Making Adrift*, p. 44.

74. See Gilderhus, *The Second Century*, p. 206, on Vance's advocacy; and Smith, *The Closest of Enemies*, p. 100, on Brzezinski's reservations.

75. Smith, *The Closest of Enemies*, p. 118.

76. Smith, *The Closest of Enemies*, p. 108.

77. Falk, "U.S.- Cuba Negotiations," p. 171.

78. Smith, *The Closest of Enemies*, pp. 126, 142.

79. Gilderhus, *The Second Century*, p. 206.

80. Robert A. Strong, *Working in the World*, p. 210.

81. Smith, *The Closest of Enemies*, p. 184.

82. Strong, *Working in the World*, p. 214, suggests this report as the first time the modifier "combat" was used.

83. Strong, *Working in the World*, p. 215.

84. Morley, *Imperial State and Revolution*, p. 265.

85. Gloria Duffy, "Crisis Mangling," p. 78.

86. Cyrus Vance, *Hard Choices*, p. 362.

87. David D. Newsom, *The Soviet Brigade in Cuba*.

88. See Maxine Molyneaux, "The Politics of the Cuban Diaspora in the United States," pp. 288–310.

89. Engstrom, *Presidential Decision Making Adrift*, p. 53.

90. Engstrom, *Presidential Decision Making Adrift*, pp. 138, 72.

3. The Reagan Administration and the Cuban American National Foundation

1. David Skidmore and Valerie M. Hudson, "Establishing the Limits of State Autonomy." Thanks also to an anonymous reviewer for helping us with this formulation.

2. See Stephen A. Garrett, "Eastern European Ethnic Groups and American Foreign Policy"; Abdul Aziz Said, *Ethnicity and U.S. Foreign Policy;* Mohammed E. Ahrari, ed., *Ethnic Groups and U.S. Foreign Policy*, pp. xi–xxi; and a series of articles in *Foreign Policy*.

3. See U.S. Congress, House of Representatives, Committee on Foreign Affairs, *Executive-Legislative Consultation on Foreign Policy*, p. 46; Bernard C. Cohen, *The Public's Impact on Foreign Policy;* Thomas M. Franck and Edward Weisband, *Foreign Policy by Congress,* p. 187; Paul Findley, *They Dare to Speak Out,* p. 25; David H. Goldberg, *Foreign Policy and Ethnic Interest Groups;* Mitchell G. Bard, "The Role of Ethnic Interest Groups on American Middle East Policy"; J. A. Nathan and J. K. Oliver, *Foreign Policy Making and the American Political System,* chapter 11.

4. See A. DeConde, *Ethnicity, Race, and American Foreign Policy;* Abraham F. Lowenthal, "U.S. Policy toward Latin America"; David W. Dent, "Interest Groups."

5. Eric M. Uslander, "All Politics Are Global," pp. 370–73.

6. For example, see Rochelle L. Stanfield, "Ethnic Politicking"; Cynthia J. Arnson and Philip Brenner, "The Limits of Lobbying"; Elizabeth S. Rogers, "The Conflicting Roles of American Ethnic and Business Interests in the U.S. Economic Sanctions Policy"; Richard Bernstein and Ross H. Munro, "The New China Lobby"; David J. Vidal, *Defining the National Interest;* Paul Glastris, "Multicultural Foreign Policy in Washington."

7. Committee of Santa Fe, *A New Inter-American Policy for the Eighties,* pp. 43–44.

8. Jeane J. Kirkpatrick, "Dictatorship and Double Standards."

9. Holly Sklar, *Washington's War on Nicaragua.*

10. See, e.g., I. M. Destler, "Dateline Washington"; Leslie H. Gelb and Anthony Lake, "Washington Dateline"; John G. Tower, "Congress versus the President"; Lee H. Hamilton and Michael H. Van Dusen, "Making Separation of Powers Work."

11. William I. Robinson and Kent Norsworthy, *David and Goliath,* p. 21; John Spicer Nichols, "The Power of the Anti-Fidel Lobby." See also Robert Parry and Peter Kornbluh, "Iran-Contra's Untold Story."

12. Elliot Abrams, "Public Opinion and Reagan Policy," pp. 106–7.

13. Jane Franklin, *Cuba and the United States,* pp. 170–71.

14. Joan Didion, *Miami,* pp. 99–101.

15. Alfonso Chardy, "Mas Canosa Built Solid Foundation," *Miami Herald,* November 24, 1977, pp. A–11; see also Cathy Booth, "The Man Who Would Oust Castro," *Time,* October 26, 1992, pp. 56–57; Scott Sleek, "Mr. Mas Goes to Washington"; Gaeton Fonzi, "Who Is Jorge Mas Canosa?"

16. Maria de los Angeles Torres, "Autumn of the Cuban Patriarchs," p. 24.

17. Sheila L. Croucher, "The Success of the Cuban Success Story," p. 369.

18. Maria de los Angeles Torres, *In the Land of Mirrors,* p. 115.

19. Jorge Mas Canosa, deposition from *Mas Canosa v. New Republic, Inc., and Ann Louise Bardach,* pp. 1101–2.

20. Reginald Stuart, "Miami's Community of Republican Cubans Awaits Reagan with Excitement," *New York Times,* May 20, 1983, pp. A–15.

21. John Newhouse, Reporter at Large, "Socialism or Death," p. 76.

22. Anne Louise Bardach, "Our Man in Miami," p. 21.

23. Torres, *In the Land of Mirrors,* p. 115.

24. Fonzi, "Who Is Jorge Mas Canosa?" p. 121.

25. Carla Anne Robbins, "Dateline Washington," p. 172.

26. Larry Rohter, "An Exile's Empire: A Special Report," *New York Times,* May 8, 1995, pp. A–1; Lee Hockstader and William Booth, "Cuban Exiles Split on Life After Castro: Miami Groups in Bitter Conflict over Who Might Be in Charge," *Washington Post,* March 10, 1992, pp. A–1.

27. Christopher Marquis, "Mas Canosa Dead at 58," *Miami Herald,* November 24, 1997, pp. A–1.

28. Richard V. Allen, telephone interview with the author, November 25, 1997.

29. Telephone interviews with the author on June 1, 1998, and June 16, 1998.

30. Trice, *Interest Groups and the Foreign Policy Process;* Fernandez, "From Little Havana to Washington, D.C."

31. This text was on the CANF Web site in its "about CANF" section as late as 1997. The site has since been revised: http://www.canfnet.org.

32. Ronald Reagan, *An American Life,* p. 471.

33. Robert A. Pastor, "The Reagan Administration," p. 6.

34. Christopher Simpson, *National Security Directives of the Reagan and Bush Administrations,* p. 363.

35. Philip Brenner and Saul Landau, "Passive Aggressive," p. 18.

36. Pat Jordan, "After Fidel, Mr. Mas?" *Los Angeles Times,* May 3, 1992, pp. MAG 23, 71.

37. Newhouse, "Socialism or Death," p. 76.

38. Sleek, "Mr. Mas Goes to Washington," p. 36.

39. Jose Sorzano, telephone interview with the author, October 15, 1997.

40. Francisco Hernandez, *Adam Smith's Money World,* PBS, from Lexis/Nexis, transcript #1124, May 4, 1995.

41. Andres Oppenheimer, *Castro's Final Hour,* pp. 104, 324.

42. Maria de los Angeles Torres, "Will Miami Fall Next?"; David Rieff, *The Exile,* pp. 18–19.

43. Torres, *In the Land of Mirrors,* p. 121.

44. Oppenheimer, *Castro's Final Hour,* p. 329.

45. Committee of Santa Fe, p. 46.

46. Howard H. Frederick, *Cuban-American Radio Wars.*

47. Jon Elliston, ed., *Psywar on Cuba,* p. 215.

48. CIA, National Foreign Assessment Center, "Radio Jamming Policy in the East Bloc," August 13, 1981, cited in Elliston, *Psywar,* pp. 216–17.

49. John M. Goshko, "U.S., Accusing Castro of Lying to Populace, Plans New Radio to 'Tell the Truth' to Cuba," *Washington Post,* September 24, 1981, p. A40; Ellison, *Psywar,* p. 219.

50. Elliston, *Psywar,* p. 227; BBC, "Clandestine, Unofficial and Satellite Broadcasts," July 23, 1993; Gary Dexter, "The Anti-Castro Broadcasters."

51. Mas Canosa, deposition, p. 321.

52. Kenneth N. Skoug, *The United States and Cuba under Reagan and Shultz,* p. 201.

53. Constantine C. Menges, *Inside the National Security Council,* p. 218.

54. Philip Brenner, *From Confrontation to Negotiation,* p. 39.

55. Mas Canosa, deposition, p. 757.

56. http://www.canfnet.org/About/aboutmain.htm.

57. Ellison, *Psywar,* p. 227; Menges, *Inside the National Security Council,* p. 219.

58. Patrick J. Kiger, *Squeeze Play,* p. 71.

59. Skoug, *The United States and Cuba under Reagan and Shultz,* p. 201.

60. Kiger, *Squeeze Play,* p. 72. By being placed under the USIA, Radio Marti was distinct from both Radio Free Europe and Radio Liberty, which were governed by the Board for International Broadcasting. Given the fear by some in Congress that it would become an exile propaganda instrument, the station was to be operated out of Washington, where theoretically it could be closely supervised.

61. Larry Rohter, "Miami's Cuban Exiles May Lose TV Station," *New York Times,* July 10, 1993, pp. A–7.

62. Wayne Smith, "Pirating Radio Marti."

63. Elliston, *Psywar,* p. 231; Celia W. Dugger, "Radio Marti to Broadcast in Africa Programs Aimed at Cuban Troops," *Miami Herald,* April 6, 1988, p. 1B.

64. Richard V. Allen, quoted in Alvin A. Snyder, *Warriors of Disinformation,* p. 241; Elliston, *Psywar,* p. 241.

65. Which is in and of itself interesting since there are few Cuban Americans in South Carolina, indicating the scope of CANF in Congress.

66. Fonzi, "Who Is Jorge Mas Canosa?" p. 89.

67. See Paul Y. Watanabe, *Ethnic Groups, Congress, and American Foreign Policy,* p. 60.

68. Robbins, "Dateline Washington," p. 165.

69. The motivation of the Reagan administration to create the NED emerged from concerns well beyond Cuba, though. For a good discussion of this, see Elizabeth Cohn, *Idealpolitik in U.S. Foreign Policy.* The connection to Cuba policy fits as part of a broader interest in the administration to privatize parts of foreign policy, and the NED was one such instrument that was used for many policies, including Cuba policy. Our thanks to Phil Brenner for helping to clarify this point.

70. Peter H. Stone, "Cuban Clout," p. 452.

71. Fonzi, "Who Is Jorge Mas Canosa?" p. 119.

72. Mas Canosa, deposition, p. 253.

73. John Spicer Nichols, "The Power of the Anti-Fidel Lobby"; Stone, "Cuban Clout"; Franklin, *Cuba and the United States,* pp. 295–96.

74. Larry Rohter, "Cuban Exiles Try to Stop PBS Show," *New York Times,* October 13, 1992, pp. A–15; Torres, *In the Land of Mirrors,* p. 146.

75. Nichols, "The Power of the Anti-Fidel Lobby," pp. 389–92; Torres, *In the Land of Mirrors,* pp. 116–17.

76. Elliot Abrams, telephone interview with the author, October 8, 1997.

77. Mas Canosa, deposition, p. 201.

78. http://www.canfnet.org/About/aboutmain.htm.

79. Franklin, *Cuba and the United States,* p. 243; Torres, *In the Land of Mirrors,* p. 144.

80. Newhouse, "Socialism or Death," p. 77.

81. Sleek, "Mr. Mas Goes to Washington," p. 40.

82. Rieff, *The Exile*, pp. 91–100.

83. Torres, *In the Land of Mirrors,* p. 144. For more on CANF's power, see Americas Watch, "Dangerous Dialogue."

84. Mas Canosa, deposition, p. 535.

85. See Linda Robinson, "After Castro Moves Out"; Jane Franklin, "The Exiles in Miami Call the Shots in Washington," p. 21; Patrick J. Kiger, *Squeeze Play,* pp. 30–31.

86. Celia Dugger, "Cuban Lobby Scales to the Top of Capitol Hill," *Miami Herald,* April 11, 1988, p. 1A.

87. Franklin, *Cuba and the United States,* p. 202.

88. William I. Robinson, *Promoting Polyarchy,* p. 96.

89. Fonzi, "Who Is Jorge Mas Canosa?" p. 119.

90. Peter Rodman, *More Precious than Peace,* p. 365. See also James M. Scott, *Deciding to Intervene,* p. 130.

91. Rodman, *More Precious than Peace,* p. 364.

92. Sheila L. Croucher, *Imagining Miami,* pp. 142–71.

93. Oppenheimer, *Castro's Final Hour,* p. 365; Jane Franklin, "Cuba," p. 21.

94. T. Elaine Carey, "Cuban Exiles Plan Office in Moscow," *The Atlanta Constitution,* October 9, 1991, pp. A–2.

95. Terry M. Moe, *The Organization of Interests;* Kay Lehman Schlozman and John T. Tierney, *Organized Interests and American Democracy*, chapter 4; Jack L. Walker, "The Origins and Maintenance of Interest Groups."

96. Watanabe, *Ethnic Groups, Congress, and American Foreign Policy.*

97. Sleek, "Mr. Mas Goes to Washington," p. 38.

98. Martin Weil, "Can the Blacks Do for Africa What the Jews Did for Israel?"; Said, *Ethnicity and U.S. Foreign Policy;* Tierney, "Congressional Activism in Foreign Policy"; Vidal, *Defining the National Interest.*

99. Weil, "Can the Blacks Do for Africa What the Jews Did for Israel?"

100. Trice, *Interest Groups and the Foreign Policy Process;* Fernandez, "From Little Havana to Washington, D.C."

101. Torres, *In the Land of Mirrors,* pp. 183–84.

102. Croucher, "The Success of the Cuban Success Story."

103. Jordan, "After Fidel, Mr. Mas?" p. 71.

104. Elliot Abrams, telephone interview with the author, October 8, 1997.

105. Skidmore, "The Politics of National Security Policy"; Vidal, *Defining the National Interest.*

106. Again, thank you to an anonymous reviewer for helping to clarify this.

107. Torres, *In the Land of Mirrors,* pp. 183–84.

108. Richard V. Allen, telephone interview with the author, November 25, 1997.

109. Torres, *In the Land of Mirrors,* pp. 183–84.

4. The Reagan Administration, Cuba, and the Cold War

1. Representative of the strong body of work dealing with Reagan and Central America are: Cynthia J. Arnson, *Crossroads;* Peter Kornbluh, *Nicaragua;* William M. LeoGrande, *Our Own Backyard;* William I. Robinson and Kent Norsworthy, *David and Goliath;* and Holly Sklar, *Washington's War on Nicaragua.*

2. Committee of Santa Fe, *A New Inter-American Policy for the Eighties,* pp. 43–44.

3. See the radio addresses collected in Ronald Reagan, *Reagan on Cuba.* In particular, "Castro's Games," pp. 7–8; "Castro in Africa," pp. 9–10; "Castro's Political Prisoners," p. 11; and "Fidel Castro: Denounced by His Own Sister," pp. 15–16, make the above points. All of those commentaries were made in 1976–1977.

4. Quoted in Sklar, *Washington's War on Nicaragua,* p. 57.

5. U.S. Department of State, Bureau of Public Affairs, "Cuba's Renewed Support for Violence in Latin America," p. 2.

6. Committee of Santa Fe, *A New Inter-American Policy for the Eighties,* p. 19.

7. Mark Hertsgaard, *On Bended Knee,* p. 111.

8. Quoted in Sklar, *Washington's War on Nicaragua,* p. 67.

9. *Wall Street Journal,* June 8, 1981, p. 1.

10. One example of this public sentiment was a Gallup poll in May 1981 that found that 38 percent disapproved of the president's policy in Central America, while 30 percent approved. See William LeoGrande, *Our Own Backyard,* p. 97.

11. Jane Franklin, *Cuba and the United States,* p. 166.

12. Donna Rich Kaplowitz, *Anatomy of a Failed Embargo,* pp. 131–32.

13. LeoGrande, *Our Own Backyard,* p. 97.

14. Morris H. Morley, *Imperial State and Revolution,* p. 328.

15. James M. Scott, *Deciding to Intervene,* pp. 160–61.

16. LeoGrande, *Our Own Backyard,* p. 146.

17. Sklar, *Washington's War on Nicaragua,* p. 243.

18. From Reagan administration records cited by Robert Parry, *Lost History,* pp. 47–48.

19. William I. Robinson, *Promoting Polyarchy,* p. 21.

20. Quoted in Robert C. Armstrong, "We Built It, We Paid for It, It's Ours," pp. 29–31.

21. Philip Brenner, "The Thirty-Year War," p. 19.

22. Parry, *Lost History,* p. 51.

23. Cited in Parry, *Lost History,* p. 52.

24. In chapter 7, we take up the 2001 nomination and the January 2002 recess appointment of Reich to be the State Department's highest ranking official for Latin American affairs.

25. "Memorandum/ For: the President/ From: George P. Shultz/ Subject: News Coverage of Central America," drafted April 15, 1984. Available at www.gwu.edu/~nsarchiv/NSAEBB/NSAEBB40/.

26. Among the places this story has been discussed is Robert Parry and Peter Kornbluh, "Iran-Contra's Untold Story."

27. U.S. Congress, *Report of the Congressional Committees Investigating the Iran-Contra Affair,* p. 34.

28. International Business Communications had a number of links to the Office of Public Diplomacy. According to U.S. Congress, *Report of the Congressional Committees Investigating the Iran-Contra Affair,* p. 87, the group received more than $440,000 in contracts from the S/LPD.

29. Deposition of Otto J. Reich, p. 839.

30. U. S. Congress, *Report of the Congressional Committees Investigating the Iran-Contra Affair,* p. 34.

31. "Washington Talk: Briefing," *New York Times,* December 30, 1987, p. B6.

32. William I. Robinson, *Promoting Polyarchy,* p. 93.

33. Norman Kempster, "Troubled Foundation; Democracy—Export Stirs Controversy," *Los Angeles Times,* February 6, 1986, p. 1.

34. George Will, "Seed Money for Democracy," *Washington Post,* December 18, 1988, p. C7.

35. Amy Fried, *Muffled Echoes,* pp. 132–33.

36. From Public Papers of the President: Ronald Reagan, U.S. Government Printing Office, February 16, 1982, p. 325, cited in Cynthia Weber, *Faking It,* p. 70.

37. President Ronald Reagan, "Peace and National Security."

38. Mark Hertsgaard, *On Bended Knee,* p. 211.

39. Jane Franklin, *Cuba and the United States,* pp. 206, 201.

40. "Operation Red Dawn" would be the code name for the raid by U.S. soldiers that led to the capture of Saddam Hussein almost two decades later. Making clear the link to the earlier movie, U.S. troops took the name of the U.S. students' guerrilla resistance group in identifying Iraqi locations as Wolverine I and Wolverine II. A problem with the analogy is that the U.S. troops are the occupier in Iraq rather than the guerrillas resisting occupation as the Wolverines were in the movie. See Timothy Noah, "Good Mission, Bad Name," online at http://slate.msn.com/id/2092608/.

41. Franklin, *Cuba and the United States,* p. 208.

42. Brenner, "The Thirty-Year War," p. 20.

43. Franklin, *Cuba and the United States,* pp. 210, 211, 214–15.

44. Kenneth N. Skoug Jr., *The United States and Cuba under Reagan and Shultz,* p. 84. Skoug's skepticism about the "large delegation of businessmen billed as 'advisers'" to one of the representatives is apparent.

45. Peter Kornbluh, *Nicaragua,* p. 170.

46. Brenner, "The Thirty-Year War," p. 20.

47. See the "State Department Chronology," at http://www.state.gov/www/regions/wha/cuba_chronology.html.

48. Arthur Schlesinger Jr., "A Democrat Looks at Foreign Policy," p. 270.

49. Parry and Kornbluh, "Iran-Contra's Untold Story," p. 30.

50. In Hertsgaard, *On Bended Knee,* p.52.

51. Elliott Abrams, "Public Opinion and Reagan Policy," p.109.

52. Cynthia Arnson and Philip Brenner, "The Limits of Lobbying," pp. 203–4.

53. Fried, *Muffled Echoes,* p.132.

54. David D. Newsom, *The Public Dimension of Foreign Policy,* pp. 112, 152, 113.

55. Robinson and Norsworthy, *David and Goliath,* p. 90.

5. The Rise of Congress and the Fall of the Cold War

1. See, e.g., R. J. Kurz, "Bush's First Stand."

2. Maria de los Angeles Torres, *In the Land of Mirrors*, p. 130.

3. See, e.g., "A Reagan Doctrine?" *National Review*, January 27, 1989, pp. 12–13.

4. See, e.g., Wayne Smith, "Washington and Havana"; Gillian Gunn, *Cuba in Transition*, pp. 18–21; Donna Rich Kaplowitz, *Anatomy of a Failed Embargo*, pp. 145–69.

5. Gunn, *Cuba in Transition*, pp. 18–19.

6. See, e.g., "The Fading of Fidel," *The Economist*, January 17, 1998, p. 13; and Walter Russell Mead, "Mutual Assured Stupidity"; cf. Kaplowitz, *Anatomy of a Failed Embargo*.

7. Cecil V. Crabb Jr. and Pat M. Holt, *Invitation to Struggle*, p. 269.

8. Stephen G. Rabe, "The Presidency."

9. Randall B. Ripley and James M. Lindsay, "Foreign and Defense Policy in Congress," pp. 3–14.

10. For example, see Thomas W. Franck and Edward Weisband, *Foreign Policy by Congress*; Philip Brenner, *The Limits and Possibilities of Congress;* Cynthia J. Arnson, *Crossroads;* John T. Tierney, "Congressional Activism in Foreign Policy"; Thomas E. Mann, ed., *A Question of Balance.* See also Anthony King, ed., *The New American Political System*; Richard E. Neustadt, *Presidential Power and the Modern Presidents*, pp. 234–37.

11. Crabb and Holt, *Invitation to Struggle*, p. 268.

12. Jeremy D. Rosner, *The New Tug-of-War*, p. 11.

13. James M. Lindsay, "End of an Era," pp. 177–78. See also Rebecca K. C. Hersman, *Friends and Foes*.

14. Bert A. Rockman, "The Presidency and Bureaucratic Change after the Cold War," p.36.

15. Crabb and Holt, *Invitation to Struggle*, p. 19.

16. Tierney, "Congressional Activism in Foreign Policy," p. 104.

17. James M. Lindsay and Randall B. Ripley, "How Congress Influences Foreign and Defense Policy," pp. 19–22. See also Ralph G. Carter, "Congressional Trade Politics, 1985–1995"; and Rosner, *The New Tug-of-War*, pp. 2–3.

18. Rosner, *The New Tug-of-War*, pp. 2–3.

19. A. Cooper Drury, "U.S. Presidents and the Use of Economic Sanctions," p. 639.

20. Marie T. Henehan, *Foreign Policy and Congress*.

21. Barbara Hinckley, *Less Than Meets the Eye*.

22. Crabb and Holt, *Invitation to Struggle*, p. 1.

23. Roger Hilsman, *The Politics of Policy Making in Defense and Foreign Affairs*, p. 18.

24. Harold H. Koh, "Why the President Almost Always Wins in Foreign Affairs," pp. 158–80.

25. Louis Fisher, *Congressional Abdication on War and Spending;* Gordon Silverstein, *Imbalance of Powers*.

26. See Ralph G. Carter, "Congressional Trade Politics, 1985–1995"; and Rosner, *The New Tug-of-War*, pp. 2–3.

27. General Brent Scowcroft memo to Richard Nixon, "The President's Meeting

with Ambassador John Scali," February 13, 1973, President's Office Files, Box 91, cited in Richard Reeves, *President Nixon,* pp. 572–73.

28. Susan Kaufman Purcell, "Cuba's Cloudy Future," pp. 113–30.

29. Patrick J. Kiger, *Squeeze Play,* p. 38.

30. William LeoGrande, "The United States and Cuba after the Cold War," p. 5.

31. Kaplowitz, *Anatomy of a Failed Embargo,* p. 145.

32. "Cuban Crisis," *The Independent* (London), November 17, 1990, p. 10.

33. "Soviets To Slash Foreign Aid, Defense Spending Next Year," *Miami Herald,* November 27, 1990, p. A7; Statement of Robert S. Gelbard, p. 218. See also Kaplowitz, *Anatomy of a Failed Embargo,* pp. 145–47.

34. Statement of Bernard Aronson, pp. 92–93; Morris H. Morley and Chris McGillion, *Unfinished Business;* Ann Devroy, "U.S. Employs 'Verbal Policy' in Attempt to Isolate Castro," *Washington Post,* April 3, 1990, p. A13; Maria Christina Garcia, *Havana USA,* p. 163; see also Kaplowitz, *Anatomy of a Failed Embargo,* pp. 147–48.

35. Quoted in Devroy, "U.S. Employs 'Verbal Policy' in Attempt to Isolate Castro."

36. Quoted in Tom Maslund, "Running against Fidel," *Newsweek,* March 9, 1992, p. 44.

37. Quoted in Philip Brenner and Saul Landau, "Passive Aggressive," p. 14.

38. Jorge I. Dominguez, "U.S. Policy toward Cuba in the 1980s and 1990s," p. 172.

39. "Cuba Sanctions Amendment in the State Authorization Bill," from U.S. Department of State to embassies abroad, September 1989, quoted in Kaplowitz, *Anatomy of a Failed Embargo,* p. 151.

40. Quoted in Kiger, *Squeeze Play,* p. 71. See also Kenneth N. Skoug, *The United States and Cuba under Reagan and Shultz,* p. 201.

41. Jay Mallin, quoted in Jon Elliston, ed., *Psywar on Cuba,* p. 271.

42. Kiger, *Squeeze Play,* p. 71.

43. President's Advisory Board for Cuba Broadcasting, "Special Report on TV Marti," p. 1. See also Elliston, *Psywar on Cuba,* p. 250.

44. U.S. Government Accounting Office, "Broadcasts to Cuba"; Ellison, *Psywar on Cuba,* pp. 250–56.

45. James Gerstenzang, "Bush to Keep Pushing TV Marti, Notes Fears of U.S. Broadcasters," *Los Angeles Times,* April 3, 1990, p. A14.

46. "Rollcall," *Los Angeles Times,* August 9, 1992, p. J10.

47. Paul Anderson, "TV Marti Gets Last Minute Reprieve in House Vote," *Miami Herald,* July 31, 1992, p. A3.

48. Alfonso Chardy, "TV Radio Marti HQ May Move to Miami," *Miami Herald,* December 4, 1992, p. B2.

49. Mimi Whitefield, "Panel Meets to Review TV Marti," *Miami Herald,* December 12, 1992, p. A24.

50. David Adams, "On the Air, but under Fire," *St. Petersburg Times,* March 27, 2001, p. 1A.

51. Fonzi, "Who Is Jorge Mas Canosa?" p. 89; Brenner and Landau, "Passive Aggressive," p. 18; Kaplowitz, *Anatomy of a Failed Embargo,* p. 134. See also *The Cuban Connection: Cuban-American Money in U.S. Elections, 1979–2000,* Center for Responsive Politics, 2001, online at: http://www.opensecrets.org/pubs/cubareport/index.asp.

52. Peter Slevin, "Washington Gives Cuban Foundation Clout, Legitimacy"; Kaplowitz, *Anatomy of a Failed Embargo,* p. 134.

53. Torres, *In the Land of Mirrors,* pp. 130–31.

54. Peter Slevin, "Washington Gives Cuban Foundation Clout, Legitimacy"; Kaplowitz, *Anatomy of a Failed Embargo,* p. 134.

55. Quoted in Brenner and Landau, "Passive Aggressive," p. 18.

56. U.S. Congress, *Cuban and Haitian Immigration.*

57. U.S. Congress, *Cuba in a Changing World,* p. 154. For the first public statement of the Cuban Democracy Act, see Robert G. Torricelli, "Let Democracy Shine through an Open Door," *Los Angeles Times,* August 18, 1991, p. M5.

58. U.S. Congress, *Cuban and Haitian Immigration.* See also William M. LeoGrande, *The United States and Cuba after the Cold War,* pp. 7–8.

59. Garcia, *Havana USA,* p. 156; Torres, "Will Miami Fall Next?" pp. 34–35; Torres, *In The Land of Mirrors,* p. 123.

60. Laura Parker, "Cuban-Americans Lead in Races for House Seat; Pepper Long Represented Miami District," *Washington Post,* July 30, 1989, P. A3.

61. Maralee Schwartz and Ann Devroy, "Bush's Florida Trip May Help Son Shine," *Washington Post,* August 8, 1989, p. A15.

62. U.S. Congress, *Cuba and the United States,* pp. 201, 308–9, 323, 392–93.

63. U.S. Congress, *Consideration of the Cuban Democracy Act of 1992,* pp. 4–5.

64. For a biography of Diaz-Balart, see http://www.house.gov/diaz-balart/bio.htm (accessed June 9, 2004).

65. Jerry Gray, "Hudson County a Harbinger of a New Hispanic Influence," *New York Times,* February 23, 1991, p. 27; Wayne King, "The 1992 Elections: New Jersey-U.S. House Races; All 10 Incumbents Win Re-election, and Democrats Keep Majority in Delegation," *New York Times,* November 4, 1992, p. B15; http://menendez.house.gov/leadership/.

66. Jeffrey Schmalz, "Furor over Castro Foe's Fate Puts Bush on Spot in Miami," *New York Times,* August 16, 1989, p. A1; "Bush Exhorts Castro to Reform 'More Openness, More Freedom' Demanded of Cuban Leader," *St. Louis Post-Dispatch,* April 7, 1989, p. 12A; President Wants Havana to Join Wave of Openness," *Los Angeles Times,* August 16, 1989, p. A2; Maureen Dowd, "Bush Plans First TV Speech Devoted to Drug War," *New York Times,* August 17, 1989, p. A21.

67. Sue Anne Pressley, "Among Miami's Cuban-Americans, Terrorism Is a Familiar Story; Tactics Used by—and Against—Castro Still Stir Debate in Exile Community," *Washington Post,* September 25, 2001, p. A10.

68. See U.S. Congress, *Cuba in a Changing World,* p. 128.

69. Kiger, *Squeeze Play,* p. 34.

70. Richard A. Nuccio, telephone interview with the author, July 30, 1998; the name "Cuban Democracy Act" was used in a bill Jorge Mas Canosa presented in his testimony before Congress in July, 1991. See U.S. Congress, *Cuba in a Changing World,* pp. 154–55.

71. Robert G. Torricelli, "Let Democracy Shine through an Open Door."

72. Quoted in Tom Masland with Spencer Reiss, Douglas Waller, and Marcus Mabry, "Running Against Fidel," *Newsweek,* March 9, 1992, p. 44.

73. Richard A. Nuccio, July 30, 1998.

74. Peter H. Stone, "Cuban Clout," p. 451.

75. Dominguez, "U.S. Policy toward Cuba in the 1980s and 1990s," p. 172.

76. In Carla Robbins, "Dateline Washington," pp. 165–66.

77. Jane Franklin, *Cuba and the United States,* p. 290.

78. U.S. Congress, *Consideration of the Cuban Democracy Act of 1992,* p. 359.

79. "Bush Warned by EC That Torricelli Bill Could Hurt Relations," *Miami Herald,* October 9, 1992, p. A6; "Canada Warns U.S.-Owned Subsidiaries," *Miami Herald,* October 10, 1992, p. A20.

80. Franklin, *Cuba and the United States,* p. 290.

81. Former Clinton administration official, telephone interview with the author, June 1, 1998.

82. Ann Bardach, "Our Man in Miami," *The New Republic,* October 3, 1994, p. 20.

83. Former Clinton administration official, telephone interview with the author, June 1, 1998. And in fact Clinton won Florida in 1996 (and some think Gore won it in 2000). See also David Rieff, "Cuba Refrozen."

84. Quoted in Tom Fiedler, "How Candidates Were Squeezed on Castro Policy," *Miami Herald,* April 26, 1992, p. 1C.

85. Former Clinton administration official, telephone interview with the author, June 1, 1998.

86. Gillian Gunn, *Cuba in Transition,* p. 13.

87. Paul Glastris, "Multicultural Foreign Policy in Washington," p. 35.

88. Quoted in Glastris, "Multicultural Foreign Policy in Washington."

89. Robert H. Salisbury, "The Paradox of Interest Groups in Washington—More Groups, Less Clout," p. 214.

90. Peter Slevin, "Washington Gives Cuban Foundation Clout, Legitimacy."

91. Tierney, "Congressional Activism in Foreign Policy," 111.

92. Richard Nuccio, telephone interview with the author, July 30, 1998.

6. The Road to Helms-Burton

1. See "The Fading of Fidel," *The Economist,* January 17, 1998, p. 13; Walter Russell Mead, "Mutual Assured Stupidity"; Donna Rich Kaplowitz, *Anatomy of a Failed Embargo.*

2. Former Clinton administration official, telephone interview with the author, June 11, 1998; see also David Rieff, "Cuba Refrozen."

3. Pamela Constable, "Cuban Americans Protest Clinton Pick," *Boston Globe,* January 20, 1993, p. 5.

4. Jorge I. Dominguez, "U.S. Policy toward Cuba in the 1980s and 1990s," pp. 173–74.

5. Former Clinton administration official, telephone interview with the author, June 1, 1998.

6. Quoted in Constable, "Cuban Americans Protest Clinton Pick."

7. Constable, "Cuban Americans Protest Clinton Pick"; see also Dick Kirschten,

"Capitol Hill Watch," p. 295; Mimi Whitefield and Christopher Marquis, "Cuban Concerns May Threaten Lawyer's Shot at Top Latin Post"; John M. Goshko, "Controversy Erupts on Latin America Post; Cuba Exiles, Black Caucus Are at Odds," *Washington Post*, January 23, 1993, p. A4; George Gedda, "The Cuba Lobby," pp. 25–26; and Morris Morley and Chris McGillion, *Unfinished Business*, p. 54.

8. Saul Landau, "Clinton's Cuba Policy," p. 36.

9. Dick Kirschten, "Guantanamo, Si; Otherwise, No," p. 1198.

10. Patrick J. Kiger, *Squeeze Play,* p. 34.

11. William Jefferson Clinton, "Media Roundtable on NAFTA," p. 2350.

12. Jane Franklin, *Cuba and the United States,* p. 324.

13. Ben Barber, "U.S. Policy toward Cuba Shows Signs of Change," *Christian Science Monitor,* December 29, 1993, p. 6.

14. Elliott Abrams, "Castro's Latest Coup," p. 37.

15. Jesus Arboleya, *Havana Miami*, pp. 56–57.

16. Jonathan C. Smith, "Foreign Policy for Sale?" pp. 207, 212.

17. Burt Solomon, "Clinton's Fast Break on Cuba . . . or Foreign Policy on the Fly," pp. 2044–45.

18. In "From Exiles to Immigrants," p. 87, David Rieff describes Cuban Miami as "stupefied." And in "Foreign Policy for Sale?" p. 215, Jonathan Smith writes that the reaction of the Cuban American community "was first one of shock, then one of anger."

19. Philip Brenner and Peter Kornbluh, "Clinton's Cuba Calculus," p. 35.

20. Maria Cristina Garcia, *Havana USA,* p. 168.

21. Smith, "Foreign Policy for Sale?" p. 217.

22. William Jefferson Clinton, "Remarks to the Cuban American Community," p. 1138.

23. Peter Kornbluh, "Cuba No Mas," p. 745.

24. See Walt Vanderbush and Patrick J. Haney, "Policy toward Cuba in the Clinton Administration."

25. See Carl Nagin, "Backfire."

26. Public Law 104-114, March 12, 1996, codified at U.S. Code 22 (1996), § 6021.

27. William Jefferson Clinton, "Remarks on Signing the Cuban Liberty and Democratic Solidarity (LIBERTAD) Act of 1996," p. 478.

28. Dan Fisk, telephone interview with the author, June 16, 1998.

29. See Kiger, *Squeeze Play*, chapter 5. See also Dick Kirschten, "Raising Cain."

30. Steven Greenhouse, "Allies of U.S. Seek to Block Bill on Cuba," *New York Times,* April 13, 1995, p. A9.

31. See U.S. Congress, *Cuban Liberty and Democratic Solidarity Act*, pp. 31–34.

32. Fisk, telephone interview with the author, June 16, 1998. See also U.S. Congress, *Cuban Liberty and Democratic Solidarity Act,* p. 76.

33. The Honorable Lincoln Diaz-Balart (R-FL), telephone interview with the author, July 2, 1998.

34. "Cuba: Congressional Vindictiveness at Work," *Minneapolis Star Tribune,* August 25, 1995, p. 18A.

35. David Adams, "Cuban Exiles Cheer Helms," *St. Petersburg Times,* April 18, 1995, p. 2A.

36. William Jefferson Clinton, "Interview with Wolf Blitzer and Judy Woodruff on CNN," pp. 624–25.

37. U.S. Congress, *Cuban Liberty and Democratic Solidarity Act,* pp. 16–30.

38. See Warren Christopher, Secretary of State, to Newt Gingrich, Speaker of the House, *Congressional Record.* Contrary to the assertion by Andreas Lowenfeld that "The President had indicated that he would veto the Helms-Burton bill if it reached his desk" (which can be cited from Christopher's letter rather than any presidential statement), Clinton himself never threatened to veto Helms-Burton. This strategy was confirmed by an administration official close to Cuba policy as well as by Dan Fisk in the Senate: former Clinton administration official, telephone interview with the author, June 1, 1998; Dan Fisk, telephone interview with the author, June 16, 1998. See also Andreas F. Lowenfeld, "Agora," p. 419; Kiger, *Squeeze Play,* p. 54.

39. William L. Roberts, "Bill to Tighten Embargo on Cuba Passes House by a Wide Margin."

40. Fisk, telephone interview with the author, June 16, 1998.

41. Former Clinton administration official, telephone interview with the author, June 1, 1998.

42. For more detail on these regulations, see http://www.state.gov/www/regions/wha/cuba/travel.html. See also http://www.treas.gov/offices/eotffc/ofac/sanctions/sanctguide-cuba.html.

43. Kiger, *Squeeze Play,* 54; Christopher Marquis, "New Clinton Strategy Eases Rules on Travel, Cultural Ties to Cuba," *Tampa Tribune,* October 6, 1995, p. 1; and Norman Pearlstine, "To Our Readers."

44. Mark Matthews, "Congress Divided on Clinton Move to Thaw Cuba Policy," *Baltimore Sun,* October 7, 1995, p. 9A.

45. William L. Roberts, "Clinton Draws Mixed Review on Cuba Policy," p. 2A.

46. Pamela Falk, "U.S.-Cuba Deal Seems Close to Fruition," *Denver Post,* October 19, 1995, p. B7.

47. William Jefferson Clinton, "Remarks at a Freedom House Breakfast," pp. 1780–81.

48. See Nagin, "Backfire."

49. Nancy Mathis, "New Sanctions against Cuba; U.S. Plans Action after 2 Civilian Planes Downed," *Houston Chronicle,* February 26, 1996, p. A1.

50. William Jefferson Clinton, "Remarks Announcing Sanctions against Cuba following the Downing of Brothers to the Rescue Airplanes," pp. 381–82. See also Nagin, "Backfire."

51. Diaz-Balart, telephone interview with the author, July 2, 1998.

52. Fisk, telephone interview with the author, June 16, 1998.

53. Steve Vermillion, from the office of the Honorable Lincoln Diaz-Balart, telephone interview with the author, June 19, 1998.

54. "Press Conference: Reaction to Cuban Shootdown of Civilian Aircraft," Federal News Service, February 27, 1996.

55. Quoted in Carroll J. Doherty, "Planes' Downing Forces Clinton to Compromise on Sanction," p. 565.

56. Diaz-Balart, telephone interview with the author, July 2, 1998.

57. Cuban Liberty and Democratic Solidarity Act of 1996, Public Law 104-1145, March 12, 1996, codified at U.S. Code 22, § 6085.

58. Diaz-Balart, telephone interview with the author, July 2, 1998.

59. Fisk, telephone interview with the author, June 16, 1998.

60. Former Clinton administration official, telephone interview with the author, June 1, 1998. See also Nagin, "Backfire," p. 34; Richard A. Nuccio, "Cuba; A U.S. Perspective," pp. 16–17, 27 n. 9.

61. "House, in 336–86 Vote, Passes Bill Increasing Economic Sanctions on Cuba," *Buffalo News,* March 7, 1996, p. 4A.

62. "Clinton, Congress, Agree on Bill to Hit Cuba," *Montreal Gazette,* February 29, 1996, p. B1.

63. "House, in 336–86 Vote, Passes Bill Increasing Economic Sanctions on Cuba," *Buffalo News,* March 7, 1996, p. 4A.

64. Helen Dewar, "Clinton, Hill Agree on Cuba Sanctions; New Curbs May Be Enacted Next Week," *Washington Post,* February 29, 1996, p. A16.

65. "Hearing of the House International Relations Committee: Cuba Shootdown Incident," *Federal News Service,* February 29, 1996.

66. William Jefferson Clinton, "Remarks on Signing the Cuban Liberty and Democratic Solidarity (LIBERTAD) Act of 1996," pp. 478–79.

67. John T. Tierney, "Congressional Activism in Foreign Policy," p. 111.

68. Fisk, telephone interview with the author, June 16, 1998.

7. *The President Strikes Back*

1. Thanks to an anonymous reviewer for coining this term.

2. Thanks to Bill Mandel for helping us conceptualize this.

3. U.S. Congress, Committee of Conference, Report 104-468, *Cuban Liberty and Democratic Solidarity (LIBERTAD) Act of 1996,* pp. 27–30. Hereafter Conference Committee Report.

4. Conference Committee Report, p. 45.

5. Conference Committee Report, pp. 45–46.

6. See Walt Vanderbush and Patrick J. Haney, "Clinton, Congress, and Cuba Policy between Two Codifications," pp. 171–94; and Philip Brenner, Patrick J. Haney, and Walt Vanderbush, "The Confluence of Domestic and International Interests," pp. 192–208.

7. 22 U.S.C. 6085 § 306(c)(1)(b) and § 306(c)(2).

8. Conference Committee Report, p. 65.

9. In addition, they did not believe Clinton would risk the political costs in Florida and New Jersey of making the first waiver announcement close to the 1996 elections. Steve Vermillion, from the office of Lincoln Diaz-Balart, telephone interview with the author, February 8, 1999.

10. William Jefferson Clinton, "Statement on Action on Title III of the Cuban Liberty and Democratic Solidarity (LIBERTAD) Act of 1996," pp. 1265–1266. To help coordinate efforts with allies concerning Cuba, Clinton also appointed Stuart Eizenstat

to serve as special representative of the president and secretary of state for the promotion of democracy in Cuba. See William Jefferson Clinton, "Statement on Efforts to Bring Democracy to Cuba," pp. 1455–56.

11. Jesse Helms, "Helms Slams Decision to Waive Cuba Provision," Congressional press releases, July 16, 1996.

12. William Jefferson Clinton, "Statement on Action on Title III of the Cuban Liberty and Democratic Solidarity (LIBERTAD) Act of 1996," pp. 1265–66. See William Jefferson Clinton, "Statement on Efforts to Bring Democracy to Cuba," pp. 1455–56.

13. See William Jefferson Clinton, "Statement on Action on Title III of the Cuban Liberty and Democratic Solidarity (LIBERTAD) Act of 1996," pp. 3–4.

14. William Jefferson Clinton, "Statement on Suspending Title III of the Cuban Liberty and Democratic Solidarity (LIBERTAD) Act of 1996," p. 138. President George W. Bush has continued to invoke the waiver.

15. 22 U.S.C. 6091.

16. Conference Committee Report, p. 66.

17. William Jefferson Clinton, "Statement on Review of Title III of the Cuban Liberty and Democratic Solidarity (LIBERTAD) Act of 1996," p. 1383.

18. The Clinton administration showed a little more interest in Title IV in 1999; see Juan O. Tamayo, "U.S. Poised to Bar Execs of Firm Operating in Cuba," *Miami Herald,* July 3, 1999, p. A12; Tim Golden, "U.S., Avoiding Castro, Relaxes Rules on Cuba," *New York Times,* July 7, 1999, p. A1.

19. See John M. Kirk and Peter McKenna, *Canada-Cuba Relations,* pp. 168–69; Carla Anne Robbins and Jose de Cordoba, "Sherritt Officials to Be Barred from U.S.," *Wall Street Journal,* July 11, 1996, p. A11.

20. See John Pearson, "Just Who's Getting Punished Here?"

21. See Larry Rohter, "Mexican Conglomerate Abandons Cuban Phone Venture," *New York Times,* June 30, 1997, p. D2.

22. Guy de Jonquie'res, "Keeping the Lid on Helms-Burton: U.S. and EU Warn That Talks May Prove Complicated," *The Financial Times,* July 31, 1997, p. 4.

23. Statement of Michael E. Ranneberger.

24. Craig Auge, "Title IV of the Helms-Burton Act."

25. Joaquin Roy, "Europe"; Joaquin Roy, *Cuba, The United States, and the Helms-Burton Doctrine;* Dan Balz, "U.S. Eases Stand on Cuba, Iran Sanctions," *Washington Post,* May 19, 1998, p. A15.

26. Wayne S. Smith, "European Union-U.S. Understanding Fails to Resolve Dispute over Helms-Burton Act."

27. Mimi Whitefield, "Execs Visiting Cuba Nothing New," *Miami Herald,* October 6, 1995, p. A10; Christopher Marquis, "New Voices Join Call to End Cuba Embargo at Same Time Others Push for Trade Ban to Be Tightened," *Miami Herald,* June 14, 1995, p. A10.

28. "Curbing Castro," *The Economist,* October 28, 1995, pp. 17–18; "Lift the Embargo," *Wall Street Journal,* August 26, 1994, p. A10; "Isolating Cuba Hasn't Worked," *Chicago Tribune,* August 23, 1994, section 1, p. 14.

29. 22 U.S.C. 6042 §112.

30. On the day that the pope arrived in Cuba, a story broke in the U.S. press about a White House intern named Monica, dampening media attention on the visit. See, e.g., "Clinton Denies Affair with Intern, Cover-up Attempt," *CNN: All Politics,* January 21, 1998, http://cnn.com/ALLPOLITICS/1998/01/21/clinton.starr.am/.

31. William Jefferson Clinton, "Statement on Cuba," pp. 475–76.

32. Steve Fainaru, "In Cuba, Awe and Exhilaration," *Boston Globe,* January 26, 1998, p. A1.

33. "Cuba, Chile Sign Trade Pact," *Rocky Mountain News,* August 22, 1998, p. A49; Canute James, "Caricom in Trade Deal with Dominican Republic," *Financial Times,* August 24, 1998, p. 4; "Britain Says It's Eager to Trade with Cuba," *Journal of Commerce,* November 5, 1998, p. A3.

34. See Christopher Marquis, "Cuba May Be Allowed to Fly over U.S. Territory," *Miami Herald,* June 16, 1998, http://www.defenselink.mil/pubs/cubarpt.htm.

35. William Jefferson Clinton, "Statement on United States Policy toward Cuba," pp. 7–8.

36. See, e.g., Thomas W. Lippman, "Group Urges Review of Cuba Policy," *Washington Post,* November 8, 1998, p. A10; and the commission's Web site at http://uscubacommission.org/index.html (accessed June 9, 2004).

37. William Jefferson Clinton, "Remarks and a Question and Answer Session at a Democratic National Committee Dinner in New York City," p. 27.

38. William Jefferson Clinton, "The President's News Conference with Prime Minister Prodi (of Italy)," pp. 801–8.

39. Special State Department Briefing: U.S.-Cuba Relations, *Federal News Service,* January 5, 1999.

40. Jim Hoagland, "Tiptoeing 'Round a Relic," *Washington Post,* January 7, 1999, p. A25.

41. Juan Tamayo, "How the Battle on Cuba Led to Easing Restrictions," January 10, 1999, p. A1.

42. In the media reporting, at least one article began: "At the urging of Pope John Paul II." Steven Erlanger, "U.S. to Ease Curbs on Relief to Cuba and Money to Kin," *New York Times,* March 20, 1998, p. A1.

43. Quoted in Erlanger, "U.S. to Ease Curbs on Relief to Cuba and Money to Kin."

44. Quoted in Christopher Marquis, "U.S. to Cut Sanctions on Cuba," *Pittsburgh Post-Gazette,* March 20, 1998, p. A1.

45. CNN Early Edition, January 5, 1999, Transcript # 99010503V08.

46. Emily Church, "Agriculture Bill Moves to House Floor, Where Fights Are Likely over Farm Aid, Other Amendments," p. 1218.

47. "Lawmakers Reject Attempt to Ease Unilateral Sanctions," Associated Press, May 20, 1999.

48. Miles A. Pomper, "Senate Votes to Halt Food Sanctions," p. 1962.

49. Congressional Record, January 27, 1999, p. 51027.

50. Congressional Record, February 11, 1999, p. 51439.

51. Juan O. Tamayo, "U.S. Officials to Visit Cuba, Discuss Cooperative Efforts in Drug War," *Miami Herald,* June 19, 1999, p. A9.

52. Karen DeYoung, "U.S. Businesses Encouraged to Explore Trade with Cuba," *Washington Post,* July 28, 1999, p. A1.

53. Thomas J. Donohue, "Market Foothold in Cuba," *Washington Post,* July 26, 1999, p. A19.

54. Press release by Senator John Ashcroft, Federal Document Clearing House, Inc., June 24, 1999.

55. Karen DeYoung, "U.S. Businesses Encouraged to Explore Trade with Cuba," *Washington Post,* July 28, 1999, p. A1.

56. Pomper, "Senate Votes to Halt Food Sanctions," p. 1962.

57. Christopher Marquis, "Senate Supports Sales of Food to Cuba if President OKs Them," *Miami Herald,* August 6, 1999, p. 27A.

58. Press release by Senator John Ashcroft, Federal Document Clearing House, Inc., August 3, 1999.

59. Miles Pomper, "Farm-State Democrats' Visit to Cuba Highlights Debate over Whether to Ease Embargo," p. 2067.

60. Statement by Stuart E. Eizenstat.

61. Thomas W. Lippman, "Senate Votes to Lift an Embargo on Cuba; Measure to End Most Unilateral Export Bans Would Allow Food, Medicine Sales," *Washington Post,* August 7, 1999, p. A15.

62. "Clinton Open to Talks on Lifting Cuba Food Embargo," August 17, 1999, CNN, found at CubaNet CubaNews, //64.21.33.164/cnews/y99/ago99/18e8.htm.

63. Esther Schrader and Mike Clary, "Cold War Curtain around Cuba Parting Slowly," *Los Angeles Times,* August 21, 1999, p. A12.

64. "History of U.S.-Cuba Policy," the U.S.-Cuba Commission Web site www .uscubacommission.org/htm/history.htm.

65. Ana Radelat, "Debate on U.S. Sales in Cuba Rekindled," *Miami Herald,* September 22, 1999, found at http://64.21.33.164/cnews/y99/sep99/22e9.htm.

66. Alex Canizares, "Texas Rice Farmers Push to Reopen Cuban Trade," *Houston Chronicle,* September 25, 1999, p. Business 1.

67. Jake Thompson, "Hagel Faults Lott for Allowing Sanctions Issue to Be Dropped," *Omaha World-Herald,* September 30, 1999, p. 4.

68. Deirdre Shesgreen, "Negotiators Stop Effort by Ashcroft to Ease Some Trade Sanctions," *St. Louis Post-Dispatch,* October 1, 1999, p. A16.

69. Thompson, "Hagel Faults Lott for Allowing Sanctions Issue to Be Dropped."

70. Philip Brasher, "Farmers Spur Lawmakers to Seek Ease on Cuba Sanctions," Associated Press, September 21, 1999.

71. Christopher Marquis, "Coalition Will Urge End to Cuba Embargo," *Miami Herald,* January 14, 1998, p. 10A; Louis Jacobson, "Gibbons Fights the Cuban Embargo," p. 300.

72. Christopher Marquis, "Bishops Urge U.S. to Ease Cuban Sanctions," *Miami Herald,* February 3, 1998, p. 5A.

73. The task force ultimately called for a number of steps to be taken to engage the Cuban people directly without lifting the embargo. See Bernard W. Aronson and William D. Rogers, *U.S.-Cuban Relations in the 21st Century.* The task force issued a second report in November 2000 that reiterated its call for opening trade between the

United States and Cuba. See Morris Morley and Chris McGillion, *Unfinished Business,* chapter 4.

74. E. E. Schattschneider, *The Semi-Sovereign People,* chapter 2.

75. Lizette Alvarez, "U.S. Farm Groups Join Move to Ease Cuba Embargo," *New York Times,* May 24, 2000, p. A8; Ana Radelat, "Farm Lobby Pushes to End Ban on Food Sales to Cuba, Other Nations," *Miami Herald,* July 5, 1999, p. A1.

76. "Florida's Dictatorship," editorial, *St. Louis Post-Dispatch,* October 8, 1999, p. C20.

77. Peter Wallsten, "Elian Case Forces a Fresh Look at Cuban American Influence," p. 827.

78. Adriel Bettelheim, "Agriculture Spending Bills Host Debates on Tobacco, International Sanctions," p. 1109.

79. Karen DeYoung, "Can Elian Case Alter U.S.-Cuban Dynamic? Custody Fight Renews Debate on Relations," *Washington Post,* May 2, 2000, p. A04.

80. Miles Pomper and Adriel Bettelheim, "Easing Up on 'Rogue' Cuba," p. 1510.

81. Dan Freedman, "Anti-Castro Group Backs Embargo on Cuba Trade," *Seattle Post-Intelligence,* June 15, 2000, p. A16, located at www.seattlepi.com/national/sanc15 .shtml.

82. Kevin Galvin, "State Farmers May Benefit from Fight over Cuban Boy," *Seattle Times,* May 10, 2000, p. A1.

83. Eliza Newlin Carney, "Blows for the Hammer," p. 2232.

84. "Don't Count Cuba Sales Anytime Soon," editorial, *Seattle Post-Intelligence,* June 30, 2000, p. A18, located at www.seattlepi.com/opinion/cued1.shtml.

85. Eric Pianin, "Move to Ease Sanctions on Cuba Gains Ground," *Washington Post,* May 12, 2000, p. A28.

86. Bob Deans, "Cuba Trade Deal Likely," *Atlanta Journal Constitution,* June 28, 2000, p. 1A.

87. The only reference to a veto threat we could find is in "Cuba Sanctions Eased: Clinton Vows to Veto Bill Easing Restrictions," *Newsday,* New York, July 22, 2000, p. A12: "The administration has threatened to veto [the bill]." We see this as anomalous, especially since there is no quotation in the article indicating disagreement on the bill at the level of a veto threat.

88. Quoted in Stephen Fidler and Pascal Fletcher, "House Agrees Cuba Food Deal," *Financial Times,* June 28, 2000, p. 13.

89. Bill Nichols, "House Measure Would Loosen Cuba Embargo GOP Leaders Oppose Plan for Some Sales," *USA Today,* June 16, 2000, p. 8A; Jenalia Moreno, "Bill to Let Cubans Buy U.S. Food Nears Passage," *Houston Chronicle,* October 18, 2000, p. 1.

90. Philip Brasher, "Senate OKs Bill Slightly Easing Cuba Trade Embargo," *Seattle Post-Intelligence,* October 19, 2000, www.seattlepi.com/national/cong196.shtml.

91. Daniel W. Fisk, "Cuba"; Vanderbush and Haney, "Policy toward Cuba in the Clinton Administration."

92. William Jefferson Clinton, "Statement on Signing the Cuban Liberty and Democratic Solidarity (LIBERTAD) Act of 1996," pp. 479–80.

93. The other parts Clinton announced he would take as precatory include §104(a), which calls for "Continued Opposition to Cuban Membership in International Finan-

cial Institutions"; §109(b), which says, "The President shall take the necessary steps to encourage the Organization of American States to create a special emergency fund for the explicit purpose of deploying human rights observers, election support, and election observation in Cuba"; §113, which states, "The President shall instruct all United States Government officials who engage in official contacts with the Cuban Government to raise on a regular basis the extradition of or rendering to the United States all persons residing in Cuba who are sought by the United States Department of Justice for crimes committed in the United States;" § 201, which calls for "U.S. Policy toward a Transition Government and a Democratically Elected Government in Cuba"; §202(e), which instructs the President "(1) to seek to obtain the agreement of other countries and of international financial institutions and multilateral organizations to provide to a transition government in Cuba, and to a democratically elected government in Cuba, assistance comparable to that provided by the United States under this Act; and (2) to work with such countries, institutions, and organizations to coordinate all such assistance programs"; and §202(f), "The President shall take the necessary steps to communicate to the Cuban people the plan for assistance developed under this section."

94. According to a search of the online version of the *Weekly Compilation of Presidential Documents,* they are: Foreign Relations Authorization Act, FY 94 and 95 (4/30/94): HR 2333, Public Law # 103-236; LIBERTAD (3/12/96): HR 927, Public Law # 104-114; National Defense Authorization Act, FY 97 (9/23/96): HR 3230, Public Law # 104-201; Holocaust Victims Redress Act (2/20/98): S 1564, Public Law # 105-158; International Religious Freedom Act of 1998 (10/27/98): HR 2431, Public Law # 105-292; Veterans Entrepreneurship and Small Business Development Act of 1999 (8/17/00): H.R. 1568, Public Law # 106-50; An Act to Locate and Secure the Return of Zachary Baumel, a United States Citizen, and Other Israeli Soldiers Missing in Action (11/8/99): H.R. 1175, Public Law # 106-89; Floyd D. Spence National Defense Authorization Act for FY 2001 (10/30/00): H.R. 4205, Public Law # 106-398; Global AIDS and Tuberculosis Relief Act of 2000 (8/19/00): H.R. 3519, Public Law # 106-264; Consolidated Appropriations Act, FY 2001 (12/21/00): H.R. 4577, Public Law # 106-554; Assistance for International Malaria Control Act (12/27/00): S. 2943, Public Law # 106-570; Omnibus Indian Advancement Act (12/27/00): H.R. 5528, Public Law #106-568. For comparison, according to a Lexis-Nexis Academic Universe Search of the Public Papers of the President, President Bush used the term "precatory" ten times during his administration, including once for the bill that included the Cuban Democracy Act. It appears that President Reagan may have used it only once, in 1987.

95. Telephone interview with the author, June 18, 2002.

96. Laurence H. Tribe, *American Constitutional Law,* p. 219.

97. Theresa Wilson, "Who Controls International Trade?" p. 163.

98. See Patrick J. Haney, Maureen P. Haney, and Walt Vanderbush, "Clinton's Other Infidelity."

99. 6 U.S. (2 Cranch) 170 (1804).

100. 204 F.2d (1953), pp. 655, 658.

101. 478 U.S. 221 (1986), quotations at p. 233.

102. Bert A. Rockman, "Reinventing What for Whom?" p. 145.

8. George W. Bush and the Struggle for Control

1. William D. Hartung, "Quick on the Trigger."

2. Anne Louise Bardach, *Cuba Confidential,* p. 306.

3. "Cuban-American Contributions to Presidential Candidates (by Cycle)," available at http://www.opensecrets.org/pubs/cubareport/presreceipts.asp (accessed June 10, 2004).

4. Bardach, *Cuba Confidential,* pp. 306–12, 317.

5. Bardach, *Cuba Confidential,* p. 321–22.

6. Karen DeYoung, "President against Relaxing Cuban Economic Sanctions," *Washington Post,* May 19, 2001, p. A5.

7. "Bush and Cuba," *Financial Times* (London), July 16, 2001, p. 16.

8. Karen DeYoung, "Bush Continues a Clinton Policy on Cuba," *Washington Post,* July 17, 2001, p. A10.

9. Christopher Marquis, "Bush Forgoes Trying to Bar Cuba Deals by Foreigners," *New York Times,* July 17, 2001, p. A8.

10. Tim Johnson and Nancy San Martin, "Bush: Ban on Cuba Lawsuits Remains," *Miami Herald,* July 17, 2001.

11. "Cuban Embargo Outlives Intent; U.S. Making an Example of Sherritt," *Toronto Star,* July 18, 2001, p. E01.

12. Tim Johnson, "U.S. Farmers Elated over Cuba Trade," *Miami Herald,* November 16, 2001, p. 16A.

13. Karen DeYoung, "More U.S. Aid Sought for Cuban Dissidents," *Washington Post,* March 8, 2001, p. A16.

14. From 1960 to 1962, between ten thousand and fifteen thousand Cuban children were sent out of the country by parents who apparently feared a rumor that the Cuban state would take over parental authority from them. This flight of children was described as Operation Peter/Pedro Pan.

15. Curtis Krueger, "Bush Cabinet: Housing Nominee's Rise Began in Borrowed Home," *St. Petersburg Times,* January 17, 2001, p. 1A.

16. Bardach, *Cuba Confidential,* p. 318.

17. Larry Rohter, "O.A.S. Votes against U.S. Candidate for Human Rights Group," *New York Times,* June 12, 2003, p. A11.

18. Juan Tamayo, "Miamian Will Help Oversee Cuba Policy," *Miami Herald,* January 26, 2002, p. 14A.

19. Carol Rosenberg, "Controversial Envoy Picked for Top Latin Affairs Post," *Miami Herald,* March 23, 2001, p. 1A.

20. Shawn Zeller, "The Bush Brothers' Cuban Connection," p. 717.

21. Paul de la Garza, "Bush Sidesteps Senate, Appoints Reich, Scalia," *St. Petersburg Times,* January 12, 2002, p. 5A.

22. Bosch eventually entered the U.S. illegally. In 1989 the Justice Department, citing reports from both the FBI and CIA of Bosch's "terrorist" activities, ruled that he should be deported. See Duncan Campbell, "Bush Appointee Linked to Terrorism," *The Guardian,* November 28, 2001, available at http://www.guardian.co.uk/Archive/Article/0,4273,4308826,00.html.

23. See Miles A. Pomper, "Recess Appointments by Bush for Conservatives Reich, Scalia," p. 126. Recess appointments are usually reserved for noncontroversial cases, but not always so. For background on some Reagan recess appointments, see Steven Pressmen, "Reagan's Recess Appointments Rankle Hill," p. 1698. Clinton also was involved in some controversial appointments, notably Bill Lann Lee as assistant attorney general for civil rights and James C. Hormel, who is openly gay, as ambassador to Luxembourg. See Karen Foerstel, "Recess Appointments: A Risky Game," p. 2824.

24. Associated Press, "Reich Promises Opposition to Castro," March 23, 2002.

25. "Retired U.S. General Says Cuba Not Threat, Urges Links," *Miami Herald,* March 4, 2002, p. 7A.

26. Tim Johnson, "Cuba to Buy $17 Million in Grain from U.S. Company," *Miami Herald,* March 5, 2002, p. 1A.

27. Peter Slevin, "Pursuing an Opening to Cuba," *Washington Post,* March 9, 2002, p. A5.

28. Alfonso Chardy, "Carter to Visit Cuba; He'll Be 1st Ex-president There since '59," *Miami Herald,* March 23, 2002, p. 1A.

29. Judith Miller, "Washington Accuses Cuba of Germ-Warfare Research," *New York Times,* May 7, 2002, p. A6.

30. Carol Rosenberg, "Pair Asked Bush to Block Carter's Trip," *Miami Herald,* May 7, 2002, p. 1A.

31. Jimmy Carter, "Openings to Cuba: We Must Find a Common Ground," *Washington Post,* May 24, 2002, p. A35.

32. George W. Bush, "Remarks Announcing the Initiative for a New Cuba."

33. "Legislative Strategy on Cuban Trade Reform? One Step at a Time," Michigan Farm Bureau press release, February 1, 2002, www.michiganfarmbureau.com/press/releases/cuba-reform.html.

34. Tim Padgett, "What Castro Wants," p. 8.

35. Tim Johnson, "House Votes to Ease Ban on Travel to Cuba," *Miami Herald,* July 24, 2002, p. 1A.

36. "Bush Administration Opposes Legislative Efforts to Amend Cuba Policy," July 11, 2002, letter available at Washington File, U.S. Department of State, http://usinfo.state.gov/topical/pol/terror/02071606.htm.

37. Eric Green, "Bush Administration Reiterates That U.S. Policy on Cuba Remains Unchanged," July 25, 2002, Washington File, U.S. Department of State, http://usinfo.state.gov/topical/pol/terror/02072500.htm.

38. Frank Davies and Juan O. Tamayo, "Cuba Hampers War on Terror, U.S. Says," *Miami Herald,* September 18, 2002, p. 1A.

39. Keith Epstein, "U.S. Says Cuba Misled Terror Probe," *Tampa Tribune,* September 18, 2002, p. 1.

40. David Cazares, "Congressional Candidate in Miami-Dade Urges New Cuba Policy," *Sun-Sentinel,* October 16, 2002, p. 1B.

41. Carlos Rojas Lindsay, "Cuban American Victories in Florida Ensure Cuban Embargo," *Financial Times* (London), November 6, 2002.

42. "Support Reich Publicly," letter from Ros-Lehtinen and Diaz-Balart, available

at www.broward.com/mld/miamiherald/2002/11/30/news/opinion/4633009.htm (posted on November 30, 2002).

43. Paul Richter, "Bush Sidesteps Controversy Naming Top Diplomat," *Los Angeles Times,* January 10, 2003, p. A23.

44. Andres Oppenheimer, "Meeting of Powell, Cuban Activist Signals Change," *Miami Herald,* January 9, 2003, p. 8A.

45. This moderation of CANF, or at least movement toward dialogue, followed some of the public relations and organizational problems around the Elian case. The departure of board members that we mentioned earlier probably had something to do with differences over the CANF support for Paya and the Varela Project. The new leaders, Mas Santos (the son of Mas Canosa) and Joe Garcia (executive director), are both only thirty-nine years old and may represent a new generation of those born after the Cuban revolution.

46. "Paya's Visit, Reich's Reassignment Signal Quiet Shift on Cuba," *Washington Post,* January 9, 2003, available at www.washingtonpost.com/ac2/wp-dyn/A33166-2003jan9.

47. Andrea Elliott and Elaine De Valle, "Cubans in Exile Split on Policy," *Miami Herald,* February 13, 2003, p. 1A.

48. David Adams, "Cuban Exiles Bend toward Reform," *St. Petersburg Times,* February 25, 2003, p. 1A.

49. Nancy San Martin, "Thousands Rally on Calle Ocho," *Miami Herald,* March 30, 2003, p. 1B.

50. Nancy San Martin, "Rules Changed on Cuba Trips," *Miami Herald,* March 25, 2003, p. 3A.

51. "Crackdown: An American Envoy Tugs Castro's Beard," *The Economist,* March 22, 2003, p. 34.

52. Duncan Campbell, "International Roundup: U.S. Envoy to Cuba 'Urged on Rebels,'" *The Guardian,* March 20, 2003, p. 19.

53. Ann Louise Bardach, "A Purge with a Purpose," *New York Times,* April 13, 2003, Sec. 4, p. 13.

54. Max Baucus, "Floor Statement on Cuba Travel Ban Legislation," April 30, 2003, from The Center for International Policy's Cuba Project, available at www .ciponline.org/cuba/travel/cipo43003travelbill.htm.

55. William LeoGrande, "Castro's Iron Fist Suggests a Brittle Grip on Power," *Los Angeles Times,* May 9, 2003, p. B15; Andres Oppenheimer, "Cuban Repression Linked to Hard Times," *Miami Herald,* April 13, 2003, p. 1A.

56. David Gonzalez, "Cuban Crackdown on Critics Stalls a Drive to Ease U.S. Embargo," *New York Times,* April 13, 2003, p. A1.

57. Jeff Flake, "How to Hurt Castro," *New York Times,* May 12, 2003, p. A25.

58. Alfonso Chardy, "U.S. Ready in Case of Major Exodus from Cuba," *Miami Herald,* April 20, 2003, p. 1A.

59. Jeri Laber, "Stop Playing into Castro's Hands," *Washington Post,* May 1, 2003, p. A27.

60. Marika Lynch, "Exile Group Urges Boosting Cuba Broadcasts," *Miami Herald,* May 2, 2003, p. 14A.

61. Paul Richter, "Bush Stays Put on Cuba Policy," *Los Angeles Times,* May 21, 2003, p. A4.

62. Carol J. Williams, "Cuba Finds Crackdown on Dissent Has a Price," *Los Angeles Times,* July 20, 2003, p. A1.

63. Tim Johnson, "Senator Blocks Diplomat Nominee to Force Cuba Move," *Miami Herald,* May 28, 2003, p. 3A. Noriega was ultimately confirmed by the Senate at the end of July.

64. Mike Williams, "Cuban Repression Stalls Trade Ties; But Farm Groups Still Favor Ending 40-Year-Old Embargo," *Atlanta Journal-Constitution,* June 8, 2003, p. 1B.

65. John Rice, "Historic Arrival in Havana Harbor," *Miami Herald,* July 12, 2003, p. 6A.

66. Nancy San Martin, "U.S. Returns to Cuba Dozen Who Took Boat," *Miami Herald,* July 22, 2003, p. 1A.

67. Oscar Corral, "CANF Outraged by Return of Dozen Cubans," *Miami Herald,* July 27, 2003, p. 1B.

68. Peter Wallsten, "Cubans' Return 'Just Not Right,' Gov. Bush Says," *Miami Herald,* August 1, 2003, p. 1A.

69. Nancy San Martin, "Nelson Questions Return of 12 to Cuba," *Miami Herald,* July 29, 2003.

70. Peter Wallsten, "Lieberman Rips Bush in Attempt to Woo Cubans, *Miami Herald,* July 30, 2003, p. 1A.

71. Steve Miller, "Edwards Eyes Cubans for Potential Support," *Washington Times,* November 22, 2002, p. A4.

72. Peter Wallsten, "Keep Cuba Sanctions, Democratic Presidential Candidate Kerry Says," *Miami Herald,* September 1, 2003, p. A1.

73. Peter Wallsten, "Democratic Contender Dean Alters Cuba Stand," *Miami Herald,* August 26, 2003, p. A1.

74. Peter Wallsten, "Clark Hints He Would Explore Cuba Ties," *Miami Herald,* December 3, 2003, p. 1B.

75. Andres Oppenheimer, "Dangers in Cuba Policy Shift Seen," *Miami Herald,* August 7, 2003, p. 3A.

76. John-Thor Dahlburg, "Fla. Lawmakers Warn Bush on Cuba Policy," *Los Angeles Times,* August 12, 2003, p. 16.

77. "For Coherent Cuba Policy: President Bush Has Been Distracted," editorial, *Miami Herald,* August 17, 2003, p. L4.

78. John-Thor Dahlburg, "U.S. Indicts Cuban Airmen in 1996 Deaths," *Los Angeles Times,* August 22, 2003, p. A19.

79. Tim Johnson and Nancy San Martin, "White House Urged Charges in 1996 Cuba Shoot-Down," *Miami Herald,* August 30, 2003, p. 1A.

80. Cynthia Carris Alonso, "The Travel Industry's Push to Unlock Cuba."

81. Paul Richter, "House Votes to Ease Travel to Cuba," *Los Angeles Times,* September 10, 2003, p. A9.

82. Nancy San Martin, "U.S. Exports Account for Largest Chunk of Food Product Purchases," *Miami Herald,* October 1, 2003, p. 8A.

83. George W. Bush, "Remarks on Cuba."

84. Frank Davies, "Bush Vows to Push Castro Harder," *Miami Herald,* October 11, 2003, p. 1A.

85. Damian Fernandez, director of the Cuban Research Institute at Florida International University. Quoted in Elisabeth Bumiller, "Bush Promises Cuban Americans to Keep Up Pressure on Castro," *New York Times,* October 11, 2003, p. A5.

86. Christopher Marquis, "Senate Approves Easing of Curbs on Cuba Travel," *New York Times,* October 24, 2003, p. A6.

87. Ann Louise Bardach, "Bush Passes on Cuban Exiles' Right," *Los Angeles Times,* October 26, 2003, p. M3.

88. Frank Davies, "Cuba Travel Battle Looms," *Miami Herald,* October 31, 2003, p. 14A.

89. Frank Davies, "Teacher Facing Trip Penalty Lobbies against Cuba Ban," *Miami Herald,* November 13, 2003, p. 11A.

90. Christopher Marquis, "Bush's Allies Plan to Block Effort to Ease Ban on Cuban Travel," *New York Times,* November 13, 2003, p. A1.

91. Al Kamen, "Photo Op Becomes an Oops," *Washington Post,* November 14, 2003, p. A27.

92. For the full Report to the President: Commission for Assistance to a Free Cuba, see: http://www.state.gov/p/wha/rt/cuba/commission/2004/ (accessed 06/10/2004).

93. Nancy San Martin and Karl Ross, "Bush to Tighten Cuba Sanctions, Seek New Funds, *Miami Herald,* May 7, 2004, p. 1A.

94. Luisa Yanez, "Policy on Cuba Will Cost Bush Votes, Group Warns," *Miami Herald*, May 11, 2004, p. 5B.

95. For example, Jeff Tyler, "Getting Along with Cuba," *National Public Radio: Marketplace*, June 8, 2004, available at http://marketplace.publicradio.org/shows/2004/06/08_mpp.html (accessed June 10, 2004).

9. Conclusion

1. See Donna Rich Kaplowitz, *Anatomy of a Failed Embargo;* Morris H. Morley and Chris McGillion, *Unfinished Business.*

2. Nancy San Martin, "Bush, Exiles Plotting to Kill Me, Castro Says," *Miami Herald,* January 31, 2004, p. 1A.

3. Jose De Cordoba, "U.S. Contends with Potent New Force on Cuba: Moderate Miami Exiles," *Wall Street Journal,* April 29, 2003, p. A14.

4. Patrick J. Kiger, *Squeeze Play,* p. 34; Jorge Mas Canosa, Deposition, p. 420.

5. Kiger, *Squeeze Play,* p. 34; Center for Responsive Politics, available at http://www.opensecrets.org/pubs/cubareport/toprecipients.asp.

6. Center for Responsive Politics, http://www.opensecrets.org/pubs/cubareport/congressreceipts.asp.

7. Center for Responsive Politics, http://www.opensecrets.org/pubs/cubareport/appendix.asp.

8. Center for Responsive Politics, http://www.opensecrets.org/pubs/cubareport/comparisons.asp.

9. Center for Responsive Politics, http://www.opensecrets.org/pubs/cubareport/free.asp.

10. Alfredo Corchado, "Study Details How Cuban Exiles Have Aided Key U.S. Lawmakers," *Dallas Morning News,* May 20, 2002, p. A1. The study was conducted by Cynthia Thomas. See http://www.tristrategies.com/news/dallasmn.html.

11. A staffer involved with Cuba legislation argues as much, noting that his boss was a hard-liner on Castro long before CANF started making campaign contributions; telephone interview with the author, June 10, 1998.

12. Ann Louise Bardach and Larry Rohter, "A Bomber's Tale: Decades of Intrigue; Life in the Shadows, Trying to Bring Down Castro," *New York Times,* July 13, 1998, p. A1.

13. Karen DeYoung and Eric Pianin, "Congressional Mood Shifts on Cuba Trade Ban," *Washington Post,* May 23, 2000, p. A01.

14. "Senate Panel Clears Sales of Food to Cuba," *Chicago Sun-Times,* March 24, 2000, p. 30.

15. Eric M. Uslander, "All Politics Are Global."

16. Daniel W. Fisk, "Cuba," p. 94. Fisk has since joined the administration, working at the State Department on, among other things, Cuba policy.

17. Louis Fisher, *Congressional Abdication on War and Spending;* Gordon Silverstein, *Imbalance of Powers.*

18. Nor have the courts been particularly helpful in restraining the president, although they have been more willing to do so in the area of trade legislation than war powers (as discussed in more detail in chapter 6). See, e.g., *Little v. Barreme* (1804), *United States v. Guy W. Capps, Inc.* (1953), and *Japan Whaling Association v. American Cetacean Society* (1986). Thanks to Maureen Haney for her help with this.

19. Peter Slevin, "Pursuing an Opening to Cuba," *Washington Post,* March 9, 2002, p. A5.

20. Tony Smith, *Foreign Attachments,* p. 130. See also Yossi Shain, *Marketing the American Creed Abroad.*

21. Naomi Klein, "America Is Not a Hamburger: President Bush's Attempts to Rebrand the United States Are Doomed," *The Guardian,* March 14, 2002, p. 19.

22. "PR Firm Hired to Explain War to Rest of World," *Seattle Times,* October 19, 2001, p. A6.

23. Andrew Miga, "Hub-Linked PR Firm Off to War—Feds Award Rendon Propaganda Contract," *Boston Herald,* February 20, 2002, p. 8.

24. Walter Shapiro, "Anti-Anti-War Crowd Dreams Up a Disloyal Opposition," *USA Today,* March 13, 2002, p. 5A.

25. See the group's Web site at http://www.avot.org.

26. See, e.g., James Flanigan, "In Iraq, Army of Private Contractors Is Set to Stay Entenched," *Los Angeles Times*, May 23, 2004, p. C1.

27. Paul Richter, "Armey Urges End to Cuba Sanctions," *Los Angeles Times,* August 9, 2002, p. A1.

28. Wil S. Hylton, "Casualty of War," *GQ Magazine*, June, 2004, p. 236.

29. Lesley Clark and Elaine De Valle, "Bush, Kerry Spark Renewed Cuba Debate," *Miami Herald,* June 7, 2004, available at http://www.miami.com/mld/miamiherald/8861704.htm.

30. See Katharine Q. Seelye, "Shift in States May Give Bush Electoral Edge," *New York Times,* December 2, 2003, p. A24. See also Robert David Sullivan, "Beyond Red and Blue," *Commonwealth* (Winter 2003): online exclusive, available at http://www .massinc.org/commonwealth/new_map_exclusive/beyond_red_blue.html.

31. Sullivan, "Beyond Red and Blue"; see also Thomas F. Schaller, "A Route for 2004 That Doesn't Go Through Dixie," *New York Times,* November 16, 2003, p. B1.

32. Tim Padgett, "Preparing for a Mass Exodus—Into Cuba?" *Time,* December 22, 2003, p. 35.

Bibliography

Government documents are listed separately, following the primary bibliography.

Abrams, Elliot. "Castro's Latest Coup." *National Review,* June 12, 1995, p. 37.
———. "Public Opinion and Reagan Policy: Administration Commentaries." In *Public Opinion in U.S. Foreign Policy: The Controversy over Contra Aid,* edited by Richard Sobel, pp. 105–22. Lanham, MD: Rowman and Littlefield, 1993.
Adler, David Gary, and Larry N. George, eds. *The Constitution and the Conduct of American Foreign Policy.* Lawrence: University Press of Kansas, 1996.
Ahrari, Mohammed E., ed. *Ethnic Groups and U.S. Foreign Policy.* New York: Greenwood, 1985.
Alonso, Cynthia Carris. "The Travel Industry's Push to Unlock Cuba." *Business Week,* August 27, 2003, available at www.businessweek.com/bwdaily/dnflash/aug2003/nf20030827_7686_db039.htm.
Ambrose, Stephen E. *Eisenhower: The President.* New York: Simon & Schuster, 1984.
———. *Nixon.* Vol. 2. New York: Simon & Schuster, 1989.
———. *Rise to Globalism: American Foreign Policy Since 1938.* New York: Penguin Books, 1993.
Americas Watch. *Dangerous Dialogue: Attacks on Freedom in Miami's Cuban Exile Community.* Human Rights Watch Report B407 (August 1992).
Arboleya, Jesus. *Havana Miami: The U.S.-Cuba Migration Conflict.* Melbourne: Ocean Press, 1996.
Armstrong, Robert C. "'We Built It, We Paid for It, It's Ours.'" *NACLA, Report on the Americas* 15 (July–August 1981): pp. 25–35.
Arnson, Cynthia J. *Crossroads.* New York: Pantheon Books, 1989.
Arnson, Cynthia, and Philip Brenner. "The Limits of Lobbying: Interest Groups, Congress, and Aid to the Contras." In *Public Opinion in U.S. Foreign Policy: The Controversy over Contra Aid,* edited by Richard Sobel, pp. 191–220. Lanham, MD: Rowman and Littlefield, 1993.
Aronson, Bernard W., and William D. Rogers. *U.S.-Cuban Relations in the 21st Century: A Follow-on Report of an Independent Task Force Sponsored by the Council on Foreign Relations.* New York: Council on Foreign Relations, 2001.
Aronson, Bernard W., and William D. Rogers. *U.S.-Cuban Relations in the 21st Century: Report of an Independent Task Force Sponsored by the Council on Foreign Relations.* New York: Council on Foreign Relations, 1999.
Auge, Craig. "Title IV of the Helms-Burton Act: A Questionable Secondary Boycott." *Law and Policy in International Business* 28, 2 (Winter 1997): pp. 575–91.
Bard, Mitchell G. "The Role of Ethnic Interest Groups on American Middle East Policy."

In *The Domestic Sources of American Foreign Policy: Insights and Evidence,* 2nd ed., edited by Eugene R. Wittkopf, pp. 79–94. New York: St. Martin's, 1994.

Bardach, Anne Louise. *Cuba Confidential: Love and Vengeance in Miami and Havana.* New York: Random House, 2002.

———. "Our Man in Miami." *The New Republic,* October 3, 1994, pp. 20–25.

Benenson, Bob. "Dissonant Voices Urge Clinton to Revise Policy on Cuba." *CQ Weekly Report,* August 24, 1994, p. 2498.

Benjamin, Jules R. *The United States and Cuba: Hegemony and Dependent Development, 1880–1934.* Pittsburgh: University of Pittsburgh Press, 1977.

———. *The United States and the Origins of the Cuban Revolution.* Princeton: Princeton University Press, 1990.

Bernstein, Richard, and Ross H. Munro. "The New China Lobby." In *The Domestic Sources of American Foreign Policy: Insights and Evidence,* 3rd ed., edited by Eugene R. Wittkopf and James M. McCormick, pp. 71–84. Lanham, MD: Rowman and Littlefield, 1998.

Bettelheim, Adriel. "Agriculture Spending Bills Host Debates on Tobacco, International Sanctions." *CQ Weekly Report,* May 13, 2000, p. 1109.

Bird, Kai. *The Color of Truth: McGeorge Bundy and William Bundy, Brothers in Arms: A Biography.* New York: Simon & Schuster, 1998.

Blight, James G., and Philip Brenner. *Sad and Luminous Days: Cuba's Struggle with the Superpowers after the Missile Crisis.* Lanham, MD: Rowman & Littlefield, 2002.

Booth, Cathy. "The Man Who Would Oust Castro." *Time,* October 26, 1992, pp. 56–57.

Brands, H. W. *The Wages of Globalism: Lyndon Johnson and the Limits of American Power.* New York: Oxford University Press, 1995.

Brenner, Philip. *From Confrontation to Negotiation: U.S. Relations with Cuba.* Boulder: Westview, 1988.

———. *The Limits and Possibilities of Congress.* New York: St. Martin's, 1983.

———. "The Thirty-Year War." *NACLA, Report on the Americas* 24 (November 1990): pp. 17–20.

Brenner, Philip, and Peter Kornbluh. "Clinton's Cuba Calculus." *NACLA, Report on the Americas* 29 (September/October 1995): pp. 33–39.

Brenner, Philip, and Saul Landau. "Passive Aggressive." *NACLA, Report on the Americas* 24 (November 1990): pp. 13–25.

Brenner, Philip, Patrick J. Haney, and Walt Vanderbush. "The Confluence of Domestic and International Interests: U.S. Policy toward Cuba, 1998–2001." *International Studies Perspectives* 3 (2002): pp. 192–208.

———. "Intermestic Interests and U.S. Policy Toward Cuba." In *The Domestic Sources of American Foreign Policy: Insights and Evidence,* 4th ed., edited by Eugene R. Wittkopf and James M. McCormick, pp. 67–84. Lanham, MD: Rowman and Littlefield, 2003.

Breuer, William B. *Vendetta: Fidel Castro and the Kennedy Brothers.* New York: Wiley, 1997.

Carney, Eliza Newlin. "Blows for the Hammer." *National Journal,* July 8, 2000, p. 2232.

Carter, Ralph G. "Congressional Trade Politics, 1985–1995." *Congress and the Presidency* 26 (Spring 1999): pp. 61–76.

Church, Emily. "Agriculture Bill Moves to House Floor, Where Fights Are Likely over Farm Aid, Other Amendments." *CQ Weekly Report,* May 22, 1999, p. 1218.

Cohen, Bernard. *The Public's Impact on Foreign Policy.* Boston: Little, Brown, 1973.

Cohn, Elizabeth. *Idealpolitik in U.S. Foreign Policy: The Reagan Administration and the U.S. Promotion of Democracy.* Unpublished Ph.D. dissertation, American University, 1995.

Committee of Santa Fe. *A New Inter-American Policy for the Eighties,* edited by Lewis Tambs. Washington, DC: Council for Inter-American Security, 1980.

Crabb, Cecil V. Jr., and Pat M. Holt. *Invitation to Struggle: Congress, the President and Foreign Policy,* 4th ed. Washington, DC: Congressional Quarterly, 1992.

Croucher, Shelia L. *Imagining Miami: Ethnic Politics in a Postmodern World.* Charlottesville: University of Virginia Press, 1997.

———. "The Success of the Cuban Success Story: Ethnicity, Power, and Politics." *Identities* 2, 4 (1996): pp. 351–84.

DeConde, A. *Ethnicity, Race, and American Foreign Policy.* Boston: Northeastern University Press, 1992.

Deese, David A., ed. *The New Politics of American Foreign Policy.* New York: St. Martin's, 1994.

DeGeorge, Gail, and Douglas Harbrecht. "Warmer Winds Are Blowing from Washington to Havana." *Business Week,* August 2, 1993, p. 42.

Dent, David W. "Interest Groups." In *U.S.-Latin American Policymaking: A Reference Handbook,* edited by David W. Dent, pp. 129–62. Westport, CT: Greenwood Press, 1995.

Destler, I. M. "Dateline Washington: Congress As Boss?" *Foreign Policy* 42 (Spring 1981): pp. 167–80.

Dexter, Gary. "The Anti-Castro Broadcasters." *Popular Communications,* October 1993, pp. 22–31.

Didion, Joan. *Miami.* New York: Simon & Schuster, 1987.

Doherty, Carrol J. "Planes' Downing Forces Clinton to Compromise on Sanction." *CQ Weekly Report,* March 2, 1996, p. 565.

Dominguez, Jorge I. "U.S. Policy toward Cuba in the 1980s and 1990s." *The Annals of the American Academy of Political and Social Science* 533 (May 1994): pp. 165–76.

Drury, A. Cooper. "U.S. Presidents and the Use of Economic Sanctions." *Presidential Studies Quarterly* 30 (December 2000): pp. 623–42.

Duffy, Gloria. "Crisis Mangling and the Cuban Brigade." *International Security* 8, 1 (Summer 1983): pp. 67–87.

Elliston, Jon, ed. *Psywar on Cuba: The Declassified History of U.S. Anti-Castro Propaganda.* Melbourne: Ocean Press, 1999.

Engstrom, David W. *Presidential Decision Making Adrift: The Carter Administration and the Mariel Boatlift.* Lanham, MD: Rowman & Littlefield, 1997.

Falk, Pamela S. "U.S.-Cuba Negotiations: The Continuing Stall." In *Reversing Relations with Former Adversaries: U.S. Foreign Policy after the Cold War,* edited by C. Richard Nelson and Kenneth Weisbrode, pp. 164–88. Gainesville: University Press of Florida, 1998.

Fernandez, Damian J. "From Little Havana to Washington, D.C.: Cuban Americans and U.S. Foreign Policy." In *Ethnic Groups and U.S. Foreign Policy,* edited by Mohammed E. Ahrari, pp. 115–34. Westport, CT: Greenwood Press, 1987.

Findley, Paul. *They Dare to Speak Out: People and Institutions Confront Israel's Lobby.* Chicago: Lawrence Hill Books, 1989.

Fisher, Louis. *Congressional Abdication on War and Spending.* College Station: Texas A&M Press, 2000.

Fisk, Daniel W. "Cuba: The End of an Era." *The Washington Quarterly* 24 (Winter 2001): pp. 93–107.

Foerstel, Karen. "Recess Appointments: A Risky Game." *CQ Weekly Report,* November 27, 1999, p. 2824.

Fonzi, Gaeton. "Who Is Jorge Mas Canosa?" *Esquire,* January 1993, pp. 86–89, 119–22.

Foreign Policy 60 (1985), series of articles.

Franck, Thomas M., and Edward Weisband. *Foreign Policy by Congress.* New York: Oxford University Press, 1979.

Franklin, Jane. *Cuba and the United States: A Chronological History.* Melbourne: Ocean Press, 1997.

———. "The Exiles in Miami Call the Shots in Washington." *The Progressive* 57, 7 (July 1993): pp. 18–22.

Frederick, Howard H. *Cuban-American Radio Wars.* Norwood, NJ: Ablex Publishing, 1986.

Fried, Amy. *Muffled Echoes: Oliver North and the Politics of Public Opinion.* New York: Columbia University Press, 1997.

Garcia, Maria Christina. *Havana USA: Cuban Exiles and Cuban-Americans in South Florida, 1959–1994.* Berkeley: University of California Press, 1996.

Garrett, Stephen A. "Eastern European Ethnic Groups and American Foreign Policy." *Political Science Quarterly* 93 (1978): pp. 301–23.

Garthoff, Raymond L. "Handling the Cienfuegos Crisis." *International Security* 8, 1 (Summer 1983): pp. 46–66.

Gedda, George. "The Cuba Lobby." *Foreign Service Journal* 70, 6 (June 1993): pp. 25–26.

Gelb, Leslie H., and Anthony Lake. "Washington Dateline: Watergate and Foreign Policy." *Foreign Policy* 12 (Fall 1973): pp. 176–88.

Gilderhus, Mark T. *The Second Century: U.S.-Latin American Relations since 1889.* Wilmington, DE: Scholarly Resources Books, 2000.

Glastris, Paul. "Multicultural Foreign Policy in Washington." *U.S. News and World Report,* July 21, 1997, pp. 30–35.

Goldberg, David H. *Foreign Policy and Ethnic Interest Groups: American and Canadian Jews Lobby for Israel.* New York: Greenwood, 1990.

Gonzalez, Edward, and Richard A. Nuccio, eds. *The RAND Forum on Cuba.* Conference Proceedings 146. Santa Monica, CA: Rand, 1999.

Gunn, Gillian. *Cuba in Transition: Options for U.S. Policy.* New York: Twentieth Century Fund, 1993.

Hakim, Peter. "It's Time to Review U.S. Cuba Policy." *Brookings Review* 13 (Winter 1995): p. 47.

Haldeman, H. R. with Joseph DiMona. *The Ends of Power.* New York: Times Books, 1978.

Hamilton, Lee H., and Michael H. Van Dusen. "Making Separation of Powers Work." *Foreign Affairs* 57, 1 (Fall 1978): pp. 17–39.

Haney, Patrick J. "Soccer Fields and Submarines in Cuba: The Politics of Problem Definition." *Naval War College Review* 4 (Autumn 1997): pp. 67–84.

Haney, Patrick J., Maureen P. Haney, and Walt Vanderbush. "Clinton's Other Infidelity: Signaling, Ignoring, and Disobeying Helms-Burton." In *Executing the Constitution: Putting the President Back into the Constitution,* edited by Christopher S. Kelley. Book manuscript under review.

Haney, Patrick J., and Walt Vanderbush. "The Helms-Burton Act: Congress and Cuba Policy." In *Contemporary Cases in U.S. Foreign Policy: From Terrorism to Trade,* edited by Ralph G. Carter, pp. 270–90. Washington, DC: CQ Press, 2002

Haney, Patrick J., and Walt Vanderbush. "The Role of Ethnic Interest Groups in U.S. Foreign Policy: The Case of the Cuban American National Foundation." *International Studies Quarterly* 43 (1999): pp. 939–59.

Hartung, William D. "Quick on the Trigger." *The Progressive* 64 (November 2000): online at http://www.progressive.org/wh1100.htm.

Henehan, Marie T. *Foreign Policy and Congress: An International Relations Perspective.* Ann Arbor: University of Michigan Press, 2000.

Hersh, Seymour M. *The Price of Power: Kissinger in the White House.* New York: Summit Books, 1983.

Hersman, Rebecca K. C. *Friends and Foes: How Congress and the President Really Make Foreign Policy.* Washington, DC: Brookings, 2000.

Hertsgaard, Mark. *On Bended Knee: The Press and the Reagan Presidency.* New York: Shocken Books, 1989.

Hilsman, Roger. *The Politics of Policy Making in Defense and Foreign Affairs.* New York: Harper & Row, 1971.

Hinckley, Barbara. *Less Than Meets the Eye: Foreign Policy Making and the Myth of the Assertive Congress.* Chicago: University of Chicago Press, 1994.

Hylton, Wil S. "Casualty of War." *GQ Magazine,* June 2004, pp. 226–232, 235–236.

Jacobson, Louis. "Gibbons Fights the Cuban Embargo." *National Journal,* February 7, 1998, p. 300.

Johnson, Haynes, and Bernard M. Gwertzman. *Fulbright: The Dissenter.* Garden City, NY: Doubleday, 1968.

Kaiser, David. "Men and Policies: 1961–1969." In *The Diplomacy of the Crucial Decade,* edited by Diane B. Knuz. New York: Columbia University Press, 1994.

Kaplowitz, Donna Rich. *Anatomy of a Failed Embargo: U.S. Sanctions against Cuba.* Boulder: Lynne Rienner, 1998.

Kiger, Patrick J. *Squeeze Play: The United States, Cuba, and the Helms-Burton Act.* Washington, DC: The Center for Public Integrity, 1997.

King, Anthony, ed. *The New American Political System.* Washington, DC: AEI Press, 1978.

Kirk, John M., and Peter McKenna. *Canada-Cuba Relations: The Other Good Neighbor Policy.* Gainesville: University Press of Florida, 1997.

Kirkpatrick, Jeane J. "Dictatorship and Double Standards." *Commentary* 68 (1979): pp. 34–45.

Kirschten, Dick. "Capitol Hill Watch." *National Journal,* January 30, 1993, p. 295.

―――. "Guantanamo, Si; Otherwise, No." *National Journal,* May 13, 1995, p. 1198.

―――. "Raising Cain." *National Journal,* July 1, 1995, pp. 1714–17.

Koh, Harold H. "Why the President Almost Always Wins in Foreign Affairs." In *The Constitution and the Conduct of Foreign Policy,* edited by David Gray Adler and Larry N. George, pp. 158–82. Lawrence: The University Press of Kansas, 1996.

Kornbluh, Peter. "Cuba No Mas." *The Nation,* May 29, 1995, p. 745.

―――. *Nicaragua: The Price of Intervention: Reagan's Wars against the Sandinistas.* Washington, DC: Institute for Policy Studies, 1987.

Kornbluh, Peter, ed. *Bay of Pigs Declassified: The Secret CIA Report on the Invasion of Cuba.* New York: The New Press, 1998.

Kurz, R. J. "Bush's First Stand." *Hemisphere* 2 (Fall 1989): pp. 4–5.

Landau, Saul. "Clinton's Cuba Policy: A Low-Priority Dilemma." *NACLA, Report on the Americas* 26 (May 1993): pp. 35–37.

Lane, Charles. "TRB from Washington." *New Republic,* February 6, 1998, pp. 6, 41.

LeoGrande, William M. "From Havana to Miami: U.S. Cuba Policy As a Two-Level Game." *Journal of Interamerican Studies and World Affairs* 40 (Spring 1998): pp. 67–86.

―――. *Our Own Backyard: The United States in Central America, 1977–1992.* Chapel Hill: University of North Carolina Press, 1998.

―――. *The United States and Cuba after the Cold War: The 1994 Refugee Crisis.* Washington, DC: Institute for the Study of Diplomacy, 1995.

Lindsay, James M. *Congress and the Politics of U.S. Foreign Policy.* Baltimore: Johns Hopkins University Press, 1994.

―――. "End of an Era: Congress and Foreign Policy after the Cold War." In *The Domestic Sources of American Foreign Policy: Insights and Evidence,* 3rd ed., edited by Eugene R. Wittkopf and James M. McCormick, pp. 173–84. Lanham, MD: Rowman & Littlefield, 1999.

Lindsay, James, and Randall B. Ripley. "How Congress Influences Foreign and Defense Policy." In *Congress Resurgent: Foreign and Defense Policy on Capitol Hill,* edited by James Lindsay and Randall Ripley, pp. 17–36. Ann Arbor: University of Michigan Press, 1999.

Lowenfeld, Andreas F. "Agora: The Cuban Liberty and Democratic Solidarity (LIBERTAD) Act: Congress and Cuba: The Helms-Burton Act." *American Journal of International Law* 90 (July 1996): pp. 419–34.

Lowenthal, Abraham F. "U.S. Policy toward Latin America." In *U.S. Foreign Policy: The Search for a New Role,* edited by Robert J. Art and Seyom Brown, pp. 358–82. New York: Macmillan, 1993.

Mann, Thomas E., ed. *A Question of Balance: The President, Congress and Foreign Policy.* Washington, DC: Brookings, 1990.

Mas Canosa, Jorge. Deposition from *Mas Canosa v. The New Republic, Inc., and Ann Louise Bardach,* testimony, January 10, February 20–21, April 10–11, 1996. United States District Court for the Southern District of Florida. Case Number: 94-2681-CIV.

Masland, Tom. "Running against Fidel." *Newsweek,* March 9, 1992, p. 44.

Mead, Walter Russell. "Mutual Assured Stupidity: Washington's Cuba Policy Is Made in Miami." *The New Yorker,* March 11, 1996, pp. 9–10.

Menges, Constantine C. *Inside the National Security Council: The True Story of the Making and Unmaking of Reagan's Foreign Policy.* New York: Simon & Schuster, 1988.

Moe, Terry M. *The Organization of Interests.* Chicago: University of Chicago Press, 1980.

Molyneaux, Maxine. "The Politics of the Cuban Diaspora in the United States." In *The United States and Latin America: The New Agenda,* edited by Victor Bulmer-Thomas and James Dunkerley, pp. 287–310. London: Institute for Latin American Studies, 1990.

Morley, Morris H. *Imperial State and Revolution: The United States and Cuba, 1952–1986.* London: Cambridge University Press, 1987.

Morley, Morris H., and Chris McGillion. *Unfinished Business: America and Cuba after the Cold War, 1989–2001.* New York: Cambridge University Press, 2002.

Nacos, Brigitte L., Robert Y. Shapiro, and Pierangelo Isernia, eds. *Decisionmaking in a Glass House: Mass Media, Public Opinion, and American and European Foreign Policy in the 21st Century.* Lanham, MD: Rowman & Littlefield, 1994.

Nagin, Carl. "Backfire." *The New Yorker,* January 26, 1998: pp. 30–35.

Nathan, J. A., and J. K. Oliver. *Foreign Policy Making and the American Political System.* Baltimore: Johns Hopkins University Press, 1994.

Neustadt, Richard E. *Presidential Power and the Modern Presidents.* New York: Free Press, 1990.

Newhouse, John. Reporter at Large. "Socialism or Death." *New Yorker,* April 27, 1992, pp. 52–83.

Newsom, David D. *The Public Dimension of Foreign Policy.* Bloomington: Indiana University Press, 1996.

———. *The Soviet Brigade in Cuba.* Bloomington: Indiana University Press, 1987.

Nichols, John Spicer. "The Power of the Anti-Fidel Lobby." *The Nation,* October 24, 1988, pp. 389–92.

Nixon, Richard N. *RN: The Memoirs of Richard Nixon.* New York: Simon & Schuster, 1990.

Nuccio, Richard A. "Cuba: A U.S. Perspective." In *Transatlantic Tensions: The United States, Europe, and Problem Countries,* edited by Richard N. Haass, pp. 7–28. Washington, DC: Brookings, 1990.

Oppenheimer, Andres. *Castro's Final Hour.* New York: Simon & Schuster, 1992.

Padgett, Tim. "Preparing for a Mass Exodus—Into Cuba?" *Time,* December 22, 2003, p. 35.

———. "What Castro Wants." *Time,* May 27, 2002, p. 8.

Parry, Robert. *Lost History: Contras, Cocaine, the Press and Project Democracy.* Arlington, VA: The Media Consortium, 1999.

Parry, Robert, and Peter Kornbluh. "Iran-Contra's Untold Story." *Foreign Policy* 72 (Summer 1988): pp. 3–30.

Pastor, Robert A. "The Reagan Administration: On Its Own Petard." In *United States Policy in Latin America: A Quarter Century of Crisis and Challenge, 1961–1986,* edited by John D. Martz. Omaha: University of Nebraska Press, 1988.

Paterson, Thomas G. *Contesting Castro.* New York: Oxford University Press, 1994.

Pearlstine, Norman. "To Our Readers." *Time,* October 25, 1995, p. 4.

Pearson, John. "Just Who's Getting Punished Here?" *Business Week International Editions,* June 17, 1996, p. 28.

Perez, Louis A. *Cuba and the United States: Ties of Singular Intimacy,* 3rd ed. Athens: University of Georgia Press, 2003.

———. *Cuba under the Platt Amendment, 1902–1934.* Pittsburgh: University of Pittsburgh Press, 1986.

Pomper, Miles A. "Farm-State Democrats' Visit to Cuba Highlights Debate over Whether to Ease Embargo." *CQ Weekly Report,* September 4, 1999, p. 2067.

———. "Recess Appointments by Bush for Conservatives Reich, Scalia." *CQ Weekly Report,* January 12, 2002, p. 126.

———. "Senate Votes to Halt Food Sanctions." *CQ Weekly Report,* August 7, 1999, p. 1962.

Pomper, Miles, and Adriel Bettelheim. "Easing Up on 'Rogue' Cuba: New Label, New Policy." *CQ Weekly Report,* June 24, 2000, p. 1510.

Pressmen, Steven. "Reagan's Recess Appointments Rankle Hill." *CQ Weekly Report,* July 14, 1984, p. 1698.

Purcell, Susan Kaufman. "Cuba's Cloudy Future." *Foreign Affairs* 69, 3 (Summer 1990): pp. 113–30.

———. "The Cuban Illusion: Keeping the Heat on Castro." *Foreign Affairs* 75, 3 (May/June 1996): pp. 159–61.

Rabe, Stephen G. *Eisenhower and Latin America: The Foreign Policy of Anticommunism.* Chapel Hill: The University of North Carolina Press, 1988.

———. "The Presidency." In *U.S.-Latin American Policymaking,* edited by David W. Dent, pp. 248–76. Westport, CT: Greenwood Press, 1995.

Reagan, Ronald. *An American Life.* New York: Simon & Schuster, 1990.

———. *Reagan on Cuba: Selected Statements by the President.* Washington, DC: Cuban American National Foundation, 1986.

Reeves, Richard. *President Nixon: Alone in the White House.* New York: Simon & Schuster, 2001.

Rieff, David. "Cuba Refrozen." *Foreign Affairs* 75 (July/August 1996): pp. 62–75.

———. *The Exile: Cuba in the Heart of Miami.* New York: Simon & Schuster, 1993.

———. "From Exiles to Immigrants." *Foreign Affairs* 74 (July/August 1995): pp. 76–90.

Ripley, Randall B., and James M. Lindsay. "Foreign and Defense Policy in Congress: An Overview and Preview." In *Congress Resurgent: Foreign and Defense Policy on Capitol Hill,* edited by Randall B. Ripley and James M. Lindsay, pp. 3–16. Ann Arbor: University of Michigan Press, 1993.

———. *U.S. Foreign Policy after the Cold War.* Pittsburgh: University of Pittsburgh Press, 1997.

Robbins, Carla Anne. "Dateline Washington: Cuban-American Clout." *Foreign Policy* 88 (1992): pp. 162–82.

Robinson, Linda. "After Castro Moves Out." *U.S. News and World Report,* May 4, 1992, p. 44.

Roberts, William L. "Bill to Tighten Embargo on Cuba Passes House by a Wide Margin." *Journal of Commerce,* September 22, 1995, p. 8A.

————. "Clinton Draws Mixed Review on Cuba Policy." *Journal of Commerce,* October 10, 1995, p. 2A.

Robinson, William I. *Promoting Polyarchy: Globalization, U.S. Intervention and Hegemony.* New York: Cambridge University Press, 1996.

Robinson, William I., and Kent Norsworthy. *David and Goliath: The U.S. War against Nicaragua.* New York: Monthly Review, 1987.

Rockman, Bert A. "The Presidency and Bureaucratic Change after the Cold War." In *U.S. Foreign Policy after the Cold War,* edited by Randall B. Ripley and James M. Lindsay, pp. 21–41. Pittsburgh: University of Pittsburgh Press, 1997.

————. "Reinventing What for Whom? President and Congress in the Making of Foreign Policy." *Presidential Studies Quarterly* 30 (March 2000): pp. 133–54.

Rodman, Peter. *More Precious Than Peace: The Cold War and the Struggle for the Third World.* New York: Scribner, 1994.

Rogers, Elizabeth S. "The Conflicting Roles of American Ethnic and Business Interests in the U.S. Economic Sanctions Policy: The Case of South Africa." In *The Limits of State Autonomy: Societal Groups and Foreign Policy Formulation,* edited by David Skidmore and Valerie M. Hudson, pp. 185–204. Boulder: Westview Press, 1993.

Rosner, Jeremy D. *The New Tug-of-War: Congress, the Executive Branch, and National Security.* Washington, DC: Carnegie Endowment for International Peace, 1995.

Roy, Joaquin. *Cuba, the United States, and the Helms-Burton Doctrine.* Gainesville: University Press of Florida, 2000.

————. "Europe: Cuba, the U.S. Embargo, and the Helms-Burton Law." In *Transatlantic Tensions: The United States, Europe, and Problem Countries,* edited by Richard N. Haass, pp. 29–47. Washington, DC: Brookings, 1999.

Said, Abdul Aziz. *Ethnicity and U.S. Foreign Policy.* New York: Praeger, 1981.

Salisbury, Robert H. "The Paradox of Interest Groups in Washington—More Groups, Less Clout." In *The New American Political System,* 2nd ed., edited by Anthony King, pp. 203–39. Washington, DC: AEI Press, 1990.

Schattschneider, E. E. *The Semi-Sovereign People.* New York: Rinehart and Winston, 1960.

Schlesinger, Arthur Jr. "A Democrat Looks at Foreign Policy." *Foreign Affairs* 66, 2 (Winter 1987/1988): pp. 263–83.

Schlozman, Kay Lehman, and John T. Tierney. *Organized Interests and American Democracy.* New York: Harper & Row, 1986.

Schwab, Peter. *Cuba: Confronting the U.S. Embargo.* New York: St. Martin's, 1990.

Scott, James M. *Deciding to Intervene: The Reagan Doctrine and American Foreign Policy.* Durham: Duke University Press, 1996.

Scott, James M., ed. *After the End: Making U.S. Foreign Policy in the Post–Cold War World.* Durham: Duke University Press, 2001.

Shain, Yossi. *Marketing the American Creed Abroad.* New York: Cambridge University Press, 1999.

Shapiro, Robert Y., Martha Joynt Kumar, and Lawrence R. Jacobs, eds. *Presidential Power: Forging the Presidency for the Twenty-First Century.* New York: Columbia University Press, 2000.

Silverstein, Gordon. *Imbalance of Powers*. New York: Oxford University Press, 1997.

Simpson, Christopher. *National Security Directives of the Reagan and Bush Administrations*. Boulder: Westview Press, 1995.

Skidmore, David. "The Politics of National Security Policy: Interest Groups, Coalitions, and the Salt II Debate." In *The Limits of State Autonomy,* edited by David Skidmore and Valerie Hudson, pp. 205–36. Boulder: Westview Press, 1993.

Skidmore, David, and Valerie Hudson. "Establishing the Limits of State Autonomy: Contending Approaches to the Study of State-Society Relations and Foreign Policy-Making." In *The Limits of State Autonomy: Societal Groups and Foreign Policy Formulation,* edited by David Skidmore and Valerie Hudson, pp. 1–24. Boulder: Westview Press, 1993.

Sklar, Holly. *Washington's War on Nicaragua*. Boston: South End Press, 1988.

Skoug, Kenneth N. *The United States and Cuba under Reagan and Shultz: A Foreign Service Officer Reports*. Westport, CT: Praeger, 1996.

Sleek, Scott. "Mr. Mas Goes to Washington." *Common Cause Magazine* 17, 1 (January/February 1991): pp. 37–40.

Smith, Jonathan C. "Foreign Policy for Sale? Interest Group Influence on President Clinton's Cuba Policy, August 1994." *Presidential Studies Quarterly* 28 (Winter 1998): pp. 207–20.

Smith, Tony. *Foreign Attachments: The Power of Ethnic Groups in the Making of American Foreign Policy*. Cambridge: Harvard University Press, 2000.

Smith, Wayne. *The Closest of Enemies: A Personal and Diplomatic Account of U.S.-Cuban Relations since 1957*. New York: Norton, 1987.

———. "European Union-U.S. Understanding Fails to Resolve Dispute over Helms-Burton Act." *International Policy Report* (March 1999), available at http://ciponline.org/199031pr.htm.

———. "Pirating Radio Marti." *The Nation,* January 27, 1997, p. 21.

———. "Shackled to the Past: The United States and Cuba." *Current History* 95 (February 1996): pp. 9–54.

———. "Washington and Havana: Time for Dialogue." *World Policy Journal* 7, 3 (Summer 1990): pp. 557–73.

Snyder, Alvin A. *Warriors of Disinformation: American Propaganda, Soviet Lies, and the Winning of the Cold War*. New York: Arcade Publishing, 1995.

Solomon, Burt. "Clinton's Fast Break on Cuba . . . or Foreign Policy on the Fly." *National Journal,* September 3, 1994, p. 2044.

Stanfield, Rochelle L. "Ethnic Politicking." *National Journal,* December 30, 1989, pp. 3096–99.

Stone, Peter H. "Cuban Clout." *National Journal,* February 20, 1993, p. 452.

Strong, Robert A. *Working in the World: Jimmy Carter and the Making of American Foreign Policy*. Baton Rouge: Louisiana State University Press, 2000.

Sullivan, John D. Discussion. In *Public Diplomacy: USA versus USSR,* edited by Richard F. Staar. Stanford: Hoover Institution Press, Stanford University, 1986.

Tierney, John T. "Congressional Activism in Foreign Policy: Its Varied Forms and Stimuli." In *The New Politics of American Foreign Policy,* edited by David A. Deese, pp. 102–30. New York: St. Martin's, 1994.

Torres, Maria de los Angeles. "Autumn of the Cuban Patriarchs." *The Nation,* December 1, 1997, p. 24.

————. *In the Land of Mirrors: Cuban Exile Politics in the United States.* Ann Arbor: University of Michigan Press, 1999.

————. "Will Miami Fall Next?" *NACLA, Report on the Americas* 24 (November 1990): pp. 29–30.

Tower, John G. "Congress versus the President: The Formulation and Implementation of American Foreign Policy." *Foreign Affairs* 60, 2 (Winter 1982): pp. 229–46.

Tribe, Laurence H. *American Constitutional Law,* 2nd ed. Mineola, NY: Foundation Press, 1988.

Trice, Robert H. *Interest Groups and the Foreign Policy Process: U.S. Policy in the Middle East.* Beverly Hills, CA: Sage, 1976.

Uslander, Eric M. "All Politics Are Global: Interest Groups in the Making of Foreign Policy. In *Interest Group Politics,* 4th ed., edited by Allan J. Cigler and Burdett A. Loomis, pp. 369–91. Washington, DC: CQ Press, 1995.

Vance, Cyrus. *Hard Choices: Critical Years in America's Foreign Policy.* New York: Simon & Schuster, 1983.

Vanderbush, Walt, and Patrick J. Haney. "Clinton, Congress, and Cuba Policy between Two Codifications: The Changing Executive-Legislative Relationship in Foreign Policy Making." *Congress and the Presidency* 29 (Autumn 2002): pp. 171–94.

————. "Policy toward Cuba in the Clinton Administration." *Political Science Quarterly* 144 (Fall 1999): pp. 387–408.

Vidal, David J. *Defining the National Interest: Minorities and U.S. Foreign Policy in the 21st Century, a Conference Report.* New York: Council on Foreign Relations, 1996.

Walker, Jack L. "The Origins and Maintenance of Interest Groups." *American Political Science Review* 77 (1983): pp. 390–406.

Walker, William. "The Struggle for the Americas: The Johnson Administration and Cuba." In *The Foreign Policies of Lyndon Johnson: Beyond Vietnam,* edited by H. W. Brands, pp. 61–97. College Station: Texas A&M Press, 1999.

Wallsten, Peter. "Elian Case Forces a Fresh Look at Cuban-American Influence." *CQ Weekly Report,* April 8, 2000, p. 827.

Watanabe, Paul Y. *Ethnic Groups, Congress, and American Foreign Policy.* Westport, CT: Greenwood Press, 1984.

Weber, Cynthia. *Faking It: U.S. Hegemony in a "Post-Phallic" Era.* Minneapolis: University of Minnesota Press, 1999.

Weil, Martin. "Can the Blacks Do for Africa What the Jews Did for Israel?" *Foreign Policy* 15 (Summer 1974): pp. 109–22.

Welch, Robert E. Jr. *Response to Revolution: The United States and the Cuban Revolution, 1959–1961.* Chapel Hill: The University of North Carolina Press, 1985.

White, Mark J., ed. *The Kennedys and Cuba: The Declassified Documentary History.* Chicago: Ivan R. Dee, 1999.

Whitefield, Mimi, and Christopher Marquis. "Cuban Concerns May Threaten Lawyer's Shot at Top Latin Post." *Journal of Commerce,* January 21, 1993, p. 12A.

Wilson, Michael G. "Hastening Castro's Downfall." The Heritage Foundation *Back-*

grounder 904 (July 2, 1992), available at http://www.heritage.org/Research/LatinAmerica/BG904.cfm (accessed June 10, 2004).

Wilson, Theresa. "Who Controls International Trade? Congressional Delegation of the Foreign Commerce Power." *Drake Law Review* 47 (1998).

Wittkopf, Eugene R., and James M. McCormick, eds. *The Domestic Sources of American Foreign Policy: Insights and Evidence.* Lanham, MD: Rowman & Littlefield, 1988.

Zelikow, Philip. "American Policy and Cuba, 1961–1963." *Diplomatic History* 24, 2 (Spring 2000): pp. 317–34.

Zeller, Shawn. "The Bush Brothers' Cuban Connection." *National Journal,* March 10, 2001, p. 717.

Government Documents

Bush, George W. "Remarks Announcing the Initiative for a New Cuba." *Weekly Compilation of Presidential Documents* 38 (May 20, 2002): pp. 852–54.

———. "Remarks on Cuba." *Weekly Compilation of Presidential Documents* 39, 41 (October 10, 2003): pp. 1366–68.

Christopher, Warren, Secretary of State. Letter to Newt Gingrich, Speaker of the House, *Congressional Record* (September 20, 1995): p. H9352.

Clinton, William Jefferson. "Interview with Wolf Blitzer and Judy Woodruff on CNN." *Weekly Compilation of Presidential Documents* 31 (April 14, 1995): pp. 624–25.

———. "Media Roundtable on NAFTA." *Weekly Compilation of Presidential Documents* 29 (November 12, 1993): p. 2350.

———. "Remarks and a Question and Answer Session at a Democratic National Committee Dinner in New York City." *Weekly Compilation of Presidential Documents* 34 (January 8, 1998): p. 27.

———. "Remarks Announcing Sanctions against Cuba Following the Downing of Brothers to the Rescue Airplanes." *Weekly Compilation of Presidential Documents* 32 (February 26, 1996): pp. 381–82.

———. "Remarks at a Freedom House Breakfast." *Weekly Compilation of Presidential Documents* 31 (October 6, 1995): p. 1780–81.

———. "Remarks on Signing the Cuban Liberty and Democratic Solidarity (LIBERTAD) Act of 1996." *Weekly Compilation of Presidential Documents* 32 (March 12, 1996): p. 478.

———. "Remarks to the Cuban-American Community." *Weekly Compilation of Presidential Documents* 31 (June 30, 1995): p. 1138.

———. "Statement on Action on Title III of the Cuban Liberty and Democratic Solidarity (LIBERTAD) Act of 1996." *Weekly Compilation of Presidential Documents* 32 (July 16, 1996): pp. 1265–66.

———. "Statement on Action on Title III of the Cuban Liberty and Democratic Solidarity (LIBERTAD) Act of 1996." *Weekly Compilation of Presidential Documents* 33 (January 3, 1997): pp. 3–4.

———. "Statement on Cuba." *Weekly Compilation of Presidential Documents* 34 (March 20, 1998): pp. 475–76.

———. "Statement on Efforts to Bring Democracy to Cuba." *Weekly Compilation of Presidential Documents* 32 (August 16, 1996): pp. 1455–56.

———. "Statement on Review of Title III of the Cuban Liberty and Democratic Solidarity (LIBERTAD) Act of 1996." *Weekly Compilation of Presidential Documents* 35 (July 16, 1999): p. 1383.

———. "Statement on Signing the Cuban Liberty and Democratic Solidarity (LIBERTAD) Act of 1996." *Weekly Compilation of Presidential Documents* 32 (March 12, 1996): pp. 479–80.

———. "Statement on Suspending Title III of the Cuban Liberty and Democratic Solidarity (LIBERTAD) Act of 1996." *Weekly Compilation of Presidential Documents* 37 (January 17, 2001): p. 138.

———. "Statement on United States Policy toward Cuba." *Weekly Compilation of Presidential Documents* 35 (January 5, 1999): pp. 7–8.

———. "The President's News Conference with Prime Minister Prodi (of Italy)." *Weekly Compilation of Presidential Documents* 34 (May 6, 1998): pp. 801–8.

Congressional Record. Senate. 106th Congress, 1st session. Vol. 145, pt. 15 (January 27, 1999).

Congressional Record. Senate. 106th Congress, 1st session. Vol. 145, pt. 25 (February 11, 1999).

Deposition of Otto J. Reich. Hearing. U.S. Congress. U.S. Senate. Select Committee on Secret Military Assistance to Iran and to Nicaraguan Opposition. July 15, 1987. Available at www.gwo.edu/~nsaebb/nsaebb40.

President's Advisory Board for Cuba Broadcasting. "Special Report by the Advisory Board for Cuba Broadcasting on TV Marti": presented to President George H. W. Bush, January 1991.

Reagan, Ronald. "Peace and National Security." Presidential address to the nation (March 23, 1983). United States Department of State, Bureau of Public Affairs, Washington, DC, Current Policy No. 472.

Statement of Bernard Aronson. Hearing. U.S. Congress. House of Representatives. Committee on Foreign Affairs. Subcommittees on Europe and the Middle East, and on Western Hemisphere Affairs. *Cuba in a Changing World: The United States-Soviet-Cuba Triangle.* 102nd Congress, 1st session. July 11, 1991 (Washington, DC: GPO, 1991), pp. 92–93.

Statement of Michael E. Ranneberger, Coordinator for the Office of Cuban Affairs. U.S. Congress. Subcommittee on Western Hemisphere of the House International Relations Committee. 106th Congress, 1st session. March 24, 1999 (Washington, DC: GPO, 1999).

Statement of Robert S. Gelbard. Hearing. U.S. Congress. House of Representatives. Committee on Ways and Means. Subcommittee on Trade. *Cuban Democracy Act of 1992* and *Withdrawal of MFN Status from the Federal Republic of Yugoslavia.* 102nd Congress, 2nd session. August 10, 1992 (Washington, DC: GPO), p. 218.

Statement of Stuart E. Eizenstat, Under Secretary for Economic, Business, and Agricultural Affairs, U.S. Department of State. U.S. Congress. House of Representatives. Committee on Agriculture. 106th Congress, 1st session. Federal News Service, June 9, 1999.

U.S. Congress. House of Representatives. Committee on Foreign Affairs. *Consideration of the Cuban Democracy Act of 1992.* 102nd Congress, 2nd session. March 18, 1992. Washington, DC: GPO, 1993.

————. House of Representatives. Committee on Foreign Affairs. Subcommittees on Human Rights and International Organizations, Western Hemisphere Affairs, and International Economic Policy and Trade. *Cuba and the United States: Thirty Years of Hostility and Beyond.* 101st Congress, 1st session. September 20, 1989. Washington, DC: GPO, 1989.

————. House of Representatives. Committee on Foreign Affairs. Subcommittees on Europe and the Middle East, and on Western Hemisphere Affairs. *Cuba in a Changing World: The United States-Soviet-Cuba Triangle.* 102nd Congress, 1st session. April 30, July 11 and 31, 1991. Washington, DC: GPO, 1991, p. 154.

————. House of Representatives. Committee on the Judiciary. Subcommittee on International Law, Immigration, and Refugees. *Cuban and Haitian Immigration.* 102nd Congress, 1st session. November 20, 1991. Washington, DC: GPO, 1992.

————. Lee H. Hamilton, Chairman, House Select Committee, and Daniel K. Inouye, Chairman, Senate Select Committee. *Report of the Congressional Committees Investigating the Iran-Contra Affair.* 100th Congress, 1st session. H. Report No. 100-433, S. Report. No. 100-216, November 13, 1987. Washington, DC: GPO, 1992, p. 34.

————. House of Representatives. Committee on Foreign Affairs. *Executive-Legislative Consultation on Foreign Policy: Strengthening Foreign Policy Information Sources for Congress.* Washington, DC: GPO, 1982, p. 46.

————. House of Representatives. Committee on International Relations. Subcommittee on the Western Hemisphere. *The Cuban Liberty and Democratic Solidarity (LIBERTAD) Act of 1995.* 104th Congress, 1st session. March 16, 1995. Washington, DC: GPO, 1995, pp. 31–34.

————. Senate Committee on Foreign Relations and House Committee on International Relations. Staff Report. *Cuba at the Crossroads: The Visit of Pope John Paul II and Opportunities for U.S. Policy*, March 4, 1998.

————. Senate. Committee on Foreign Relations. Subcommittee on Western Hemisphere and Peace Corps Affairs. *Cuban Liberty and Democratic Solidarity Act.* 104th Congress, 1st session. May 22 and June 14, 1995. Washington, DC: GPO, 1995.

————. Committee of Conference. *Cuban Liberty and Democratic Solidarity (LIBERTAD) Act of 1996.* 104th Congress, 2nd session. Report 104–468, March 1, 1996. Washington, DC: GPO, 1996.

U. S. Department of State. Bureau of Public Affairs. *Cuba's Renewed Support for Violence in Latin America.* Washington DC, Special Report No. 90, December 14, 1981.

U.S. General Accounting Office. *Broadcasts to Cuba: TV Marti Surveys Are Flawed.* GAO/NSIAD-90-252, August 9, 1990.

Index

Carter administration, 26–30; loosening of embargo by, 27; Reagan criticism of, 54–55
Carter, Jimmy, 3, 137–38
Cason, James, 143
Castro, Fidel: on alleged assassination attempts, 155; early rule of, 13; and Hurricane Michelle aid, 135; interviews during Reagan administration, 68; meeting of corporate executives with, 103; and migration during Clinton administration, 96, 97; Nixon's meeting with, 13–14; Specter's meetings with, 120; U.S. trip of, 13
Castro, Raul, 111
Cato Institute, 71
CDA. *See* Cuban Democracy Act
Center for International Private Enterprise (CIPE), of Chamber of Commerce, 64
Center for Strategic International Studies (CSIS), 71
Central America: Cuba and, in Reagan administration, 53, 56–57, 72–73; public opinion opposed to Reagan on, 58, 59; Reagan administration, 33, 37, 53–63
Central Intelligence Agency (CIA): Carter administration, 28; clandestine radio broadcasts by, 40; Eisenhower administration, 14; and Iraq, 165; Kennedy administration, 17
Chile, 21
Chiles, Lawton, 42, 96–97
China, 24, 159
Christopher, Warren, 95, 99–100, 102, 106
Church and Tower, 45
Church, Frank, 23, 27, 28–29, 55
Cienfuegos, Cuba, 22–23
Citizens for America (CFA), 63
Clark Amendment, 46–47
Clark, Wesley, 147
Clinton administration, 92–130; and Brothers to the Rescue planes, 4–5, 99, 104; Congressional response to, 118; domestic politics and Cuba policy, 93–99, 107–9, 159; first, 92–109; and Helms-Burton Act, 99–109, 111–18, 126–29, 191–92n93; and licensing power, 115–18; second, 110–30
Clinton, Hillary, 95
Clinton, William Jefferson (Bill): Cuban

American campaign contributions to, 131; and Cuban Democracy Act, 88–89, 93; and Helms-Burton Act, 168
Coast Guard, 95, 97, 120, 145–46
cold war: continuation in Cuba policy of, 7; Cuba policy during, 24; end of, and Cuba policy, 6, 79; Reagan administration, 53–73
Colombia, 164
Commission for Assistance to a Free Cuba, 151–52
Committee of Santa Fe, 57, 60, 72, 74. See also *Santa Fe Report* (Fontaine)
Communist Interference in El Salvador (Reagan White Paper), 57–58
Communist party: early actions under Castro of, 13; Eisenhower administration and foreign policy emphasis on, 16
Congress: Bush (George H. W.) administration, 84–91; Bush (George W.) administration, 138–39, 149–51; Clinton administration, 92–93, 99–109, 118–26; Cuba policy activism of, 84–91; Cuban Americans in, 84–86, 101, 119, 124, 134, 140, 142, 145, 167; division concerning embargo, 119–20, 149–51, 167; Eisenhower administration, 15; executive branch versus, 76–78, 160–63; Ford administration, 26; influence of a few members of, 91, 108, 161; as initiator of Cuba policy, 92–93, 99–109, 160; Johnson administration, 20–21; Kennedy administration, 17–18; lobbying of, 31; members' trips to Cuba, 24, 27, 68, 120; Nixon administration, 23–24; Reagan administration, 70; reorganization of committees in, 25
Congressional Black Caucus, 100, 164
Contras, 46, 59, 70
Coors, Joseph, 40
Corollo, Joseph, 45
Council for Inter-American Security, 70
Council on Foreign Relations, 123
Coverdell, Paul, 107
covert operations against Cuba: Eisenhower administration, 14; Kennedy administration, 16–17; Nixon administration, 22
Crabb, Cecil, 76
Croucher, Sheila, 34
Cuba: agrarian reform in, 14; Air Force

downing of U.S. planes, 4–5, 99, 104, 148; Cienfuegos submarine base, 22–23; military actions in Africa of, 12, 26, 27–28; nationalization of U.S. interests by, 15, 101; recent crackdowns in, 143–45; Soviet dependence of, 79. *See also* Cuba policy

Cuba policy: Bush (George H. W.) administration and power shift in, 75; domestic roots of, 90–91; hard-line approach to, 33, 54–59; Reagan administration as key point in, 6, 54, 72–73, 156; relation to other foreign policy of, 163–66. *See also* embargo

Cuba Working Group, 138, 143

Cuban Adjustment Act, 21, 84, 97

Cuban American National Foundation (CANF), 33–52; birth and growth of, 30, 33–39; Bush (George H. W.) administration and, 74–75, 82–83; Bush (George W.) administration and, 144, 146; Clinton administration and, 94–95, 97–98, 108; and Cuban American representatives, 85; and Cuban Democracy Act, 87–89; development of, 158; on embargo relaxation, 122–23, 125; and ethnic interest group politics, 47–52; and executive branch, 4; Helms-Burton Act and, 100–101; and immigration, 44–45; independence of, 82–83, 90, 159; moderation of, 156, 158–59, 195n45; and NED, 43–44, 65; organizational structure of, 37–38; political contributions of, 157–58; political influence of, 45–47; and Radio Marti, 40–42, 80–82; Reagan administration and, 30, 34–37, 39–45, 49–53, 72–73, 159; and TV Marti, 41–43, 81–82; unforeseen effects of, 3; and Varela Project, 141, 195n45

Cuban Americans: assimilation of, 48; Bush (George W.) administration and, 133–37, 144–46, 148, 150–52; and Clinton immigration policy, 97–98; in Congress, 84–86, 101, 119, 124, 134, 140, 142, 145, 167; disarray before CANF among, 33–34; and Elian Gonzalez, 124–25; emergence into political power of, 29; and Lieberman, 147; political contributions of, 157–58; self-perception as exiles of, 48; support for Clinton

from, 88–89; and 2000 election, 131–32, 151; in 2004 election, 168–69; and Varela Project, 141

Cuban Democracy Act (CDA), 4, 83, 86–89, 93–95, 102–3, 160

Cuban Exodus Relief Fund, 45

Cuban Freedom Council, 140

Cuban Liberty and Democratic Solidarity Act (LIBERTAD) (1996). *See* Helms-Burton Act (1996)

Cuban missile crisis, 18

Daschle, Tom, 121

Dean, Howard, 147

Defense Department: Bush (George W.) administration, 165; Nixon administration, 23; on post–cold war Cuba, 6, 116; Reagan administration, 63

DeLay, Tom, 122, 125, 138, 151

Deutch, John, 106

Diaz-Balart, Lincoln, 4, 85, 94, 102, 103, 104–6, 118, 119, 122, 125, 136, 137, 138, 140, 142, 146, 157, 158, 167

Diaz-Balart, Mario, 4, 139–40, 146

Dobbins, James, 117

Dodd, Christopher, 107, 119, 123, 153

Dole, Bob, 131

domestic politics and Cuba policy, 6, 7–8; Clinton administration, 93–99, 107–9; George H. W. Bush administration, 90

Dominguez, Jorge, 87

Dominican Republic, 19–20

Donohue, Tom, 120

Dorgan, Byron, 121, 126

Duarte, Jose Napoleon, 67

Dukakis, Michael, 89

Eagleburger, Lawrence, 25, 123

Eastland, James, 17–18

economic interest groups: Clinton and, 4; and Congress, 5. *See also* agricultural industry; energy companies; pharmaceutical companies; trade policy

Edwards, John, 147

Eisenhower administration, 12–16; anti-Castro sentiments in, 13–14; Batista abandoned by, 13; cautious diplomacy of, 14; communism as central nemesis of, 16; covert operations under, 14; economic actions of, 1, 15–16

Eizenstat, Stuart, 121
El Salvador, 37, 57
electoral politics and Cuba policy: Clinton, 108–9; Clinton-Bush campaign, 88–91; contributions to candidates, 157–58; Democrats in 2004, 147–48, 168–69; Diaz-Balart and House election, 139–40; George W. Bush, 133, 148–49, 151–52; Gore, 117; Gore-Bush campaign, 136; 2004 election, 168–70
embargo: components of, 2; control over, 3–4; Cuban Democracy Act and, 87; expansion of debate on, 123–24, 159; future of, 1–2, 168–70; Helms-Burton Act and, 99–109; political actors in, 5–7, 30, 123–24, 130; recent challenges to, 137–39, 145, 167; Wednesday Group's recommendation to lift, 24. *See also* Cuba policy; travel ban; *under individual administrations*
Emerson, Joanne, 138
Enders, Thomas O., 40, 60
Estefan, Gloria, 134
Ethiopia, 27
ethnic interest groups, 30–31; CANF as model for, 48–52; CANF versus, 38; effectiveness of, 164–65; variety of Cuban, 38. *See also* Cuban American National Foundation
European Coalition for Human Rights in Cuba, 43
European Union, 113, 114–15, 141, 145
executive branch: Clinton's attempts to restore control to, 110–30; imperial presidency, 11–12, 76; legislative branch versus, 76–78, 160–63; power over embargo in, 3
exiles. *See* Cuban Americans

Fanjul, Alfonso, 158
Fanjul, Jose, 158
Fascell, Dante, 23, 24, 25, 43
Feinberg, Richard, 95
Fernandez, Damien, 150
Fisher, Louis, 78, 161
Fisk, Dan, 100, 103, 106, 139, 148, 160
Flake, Jeff, 138, 143–44, 149, 151–52, 153
Fleischer, Ari, 139
Florida International University (FIU), 46
Flo-Sun Sugar Company, 158

Foley, Thomas, 125
Fontaine, Roger, 34–35, 57
Fonzi, Gaeton, 35, 43
Food and Medicine for the World Act, 119–22
Ford administration, 25–26
Ford, Gerald, 76
foreign policy: Cuba policy as instructive for, 163–66; democracy promotion worldwide, 60; diversity of actors influencing, 8, 55, 166–68; executive versus legislative branches concerning, 128–29; imperial presidency and, 76; influenced by a few congressional members, 91, 108, 161; Reagan legacy in, 69–71; think tank role in, 55. *See also* Cuba policy; embargo; trade policy
Franklin, Jane, 45
Free Cuba political action committee, 37, 82, 157–58
Free Trade Union Institute, of AFL-CIO, 64
Freedom Flights, 21
Freedom House, 60, 65, 103–4
Freedom to Market Act, 119, 121
Freedom to Travel to Cuba Act, 144
Fried, Amy, 66, 71
Fuentes, Carlos, 145
Fulbright, William, 18, 20, 24

Garcia, Joe, 195n45
Gelbard, Robert, 88
Gephardt, Richard, 138
Germany, 79
Gingrich, Newt, 102
Goldwater, Barry, 18
Gonzalez, Elian, 124–25, 131–32, 136, 158, 195n45
Gorbachev, Mikhail, 79
Gore, Al, 117, 131–32, 168
Graham, Bob, 86, 103, 117, 120, 136, 168
Grenada, 28, 59, 66–67
Grupo Domos, 114
Guantanamo naval base, 97–98

Hagel, Chuck, 119, 122, 124–25, 153
Haig, Alexander, 59
Haiti, 83–84, 100, 164, 165
Haldeman, H. R. "Bob," 22
Hamilton, Lee, 107
Hatch, Orrin, 64–65

Helms, Jesse, 100–102, 113, 125, 140, 157, 158, 159
Helms, Richard, 22
Helms-Burton Act, 92, 99–109, 111–18, 120, 126–29, 160, 191–92n93; codification of embargo in, 1, 6, 105–7, 109, 160–61; licensing powers in, 115–18; Title III of, 101, 102, 104, 105–7, 112–13, 134; Title IV of, 101, 104, 105–6, 113–15, 134
Heritage Foundation, 137, 151
Hernandez, Francisco "Pepe," 35, 38, 41
Hollings, Ernest, 42
Homeland Security Department, 150
Human Rights Watch, 144

Ibero-American Summit (Santiago, 1996), 113
immigration: CANF and, 44–45; Carter administration and Mariel boat lift, 29–30; Clinton administration, 95–99; Haiti and, 83–84; Johnson administration, 20–21; Reagan administration, 68–69
Immigration and Naturalization Service (INS), 45
information leaks: Clinton administration, 102; Kissinger and, 23; Reagan administration and, 57
interest groups: changing environment for, 157–60; on embargo relaxation, 123–24; independent action of, 73; influence on government-funded programs of, 43; Johnson administration, 20; pro-Israel, 158 (see also American Israel Public Affairs Committee); Reagan administration and increasing power of, 63–67, 70–73. See also economic interest groups; ethnic interest groups
interests sections, 27, 32, 81, 143
International Business Communications, 63
Iran-Contra affair, 62, 63, 65, 69–70
Iraq, invasion of, 164–65

Jackson, Henry M. "Scoop," 40
Jackson, Jesse, 95
Japan Whaling Association v. American Cetacean Society (1986), 129
JCS. See Joint Chiefs of Staff
Jefferson, Thomas, 128
John Paul II, 116, 118, 123, 141

Johnson administration, 19–21; economic actions of, 20; isolation of Cuba under, 19; White Papers on Vietnam, 58
Joint Chiefs of Staff (JCS), 23
Justice Department, 85–86

Kennedy administration, 16–18; covert operations under, 16–17; and Cuban missile crisis, 18; economic actions of, 18
Kennedy, Patrick, 104–5
Kennedy, Ted, 24
Kerry, John, 147, 152, 156, 169
Kirkpatrick, Jeane, 33, 38, 55, 60
Kissinger, Henry, 21–26, 123
Kreczko, Alan J., 127

Lake, Anthony, 95, 106
Landsdale, Edward, 17
Latin America: Cuba policy shaped by concerns over, 15–16; Johnson administration involvement in, 19–20; Nixon and Kissinger on, 21. See also Central America; individual countries
leaks. See information leaks
LeoGrande, William, 7, 59, 143
Lieberman, Joe, 131, 146–47, 157, 158
Little v. Barreme (1804), 128
lobbying. See interest groups
Lott, Trent, 122
Lugar, Richard, 140

Mack Amendment, 80, 86, 87
Mack, Connie, 86, 120
Maisto, John, 135
Mandela, Nelson, 47
Mann Doctrine, 19
Mariel boatlift crisis, 29–30, 96
Martinez, Mel, 136, 150
Martinez, Rafael, 136
Mas Canosa, Jorge: and Angola, 46–47; on assimilation, 48–49; CANF's formation and, 34–37; and Clinton, 88, 97–98; and Contras, 46; and George H. W. Bush, 86, 88; and immigration, 44–45; as Mas Santos' father, 146; Moscow visit of, 47; and NED, 43–44; personal finances of, 45; political influence of, 45–46; and Radio Marti, 40–42, 80–82; and TV Marti, 42, 81–82
Mas Santos, Jorge, 146, 195n45

munity, 34; early acceptance of Castro, 15; Kennedy's concern for, 17; on Reagan Central America policy, 58, 59; Reagan concern for, on Central America, 33–34, 56–57
Puerto Rico, 26

radio: broadcasts to Cuba, 39–40, 55; and 2000 election, 151. *See also* Radio Marti
Radio Caiman, 40
Radio Free Cuba, 40, 55
Radio Marti, 40–42, 61, 68, 80–82, 97, 104, 116, 134, 138, 144, 148, 177n60
Rangel, Charles, 102, 107, 153
Raymond, Walter, 61–62, 63
Reagan administration, 31–73; CANF and, 30, 34–37, 39–45, 49–53, 72–73, 159; Central America policy of, 33, 37, 53–63, 72–73; cold war policies of, 53–73; versus Congress, 70; covert operations in Central America, 58, 69; deterioration of Cuban relations under, 67–69; foreign policy legacy of, 69–71; hard-line approach to Cuba, 54–59; political use of nongovernmental actors by, 60; power over embargo sought by, 4; private support sought by, 63–67, 70–73; public diplomacy on Central America, 59–64; significance for Cuba policy of, 6, 54, 72–73, 156; similarity to George W. Bush of, 162, 165–66
Reagan, Ronald: on Central America, 37, 66–67; Cuba criticism of, 55
Rebozo, Bebe, 21
recess appointments, 136, 194n23
Red Dawn (film), 67–68, 180n40
Reich, Otto, 39, 62–63, 134, 136, 140, 148, 153, 162
remittances, 115–16, 142, 152
Rendon Group, 165
Reno, Janet, 96, 106
Rice, Condoleezza, 134
right-wing groups, during Reagan administration, 65–66, 70–71
Robinson, Randall, 164
Rogers, William D., 25
Rohrbacher, Dana, 102
Roosevelt, Franklin, 12
Ros-Lehtinen, Ileana, 4, 47, 81, 84–86, 91,

104, 105, 107, 118, 122, 125, 136, 137, 138, 140, 146, 157, 158, 163, 167
Rove, Karl, 133, 149

Salman, Carlos, 35–36
SALT II treaty, 28
Sandinistas, 28, 37
Santa Fe group. *See* Committee of Santa Fe
Santa Fe Report (Fontaine), 34–35, 40, 55, 57, 64
Savimbi, Jonas, 42, 47
Scaife, Richard Mellon, 40
School of the Americas, 62
Selective Agriculture Embargoes Act, 119
Shalikasvili, John M., 106
Sherritt International, 114, 134
Shultz, George, 62, 123
S/LPD, 61–64
Smathers, George, 18
Smith, Adam, 38
Smith, Earl E. T., 13
Smith, Wayne, 27
Solarz, Stephen, 88
Sorzano, Jose, 38, 39, 68
Soviet Union: Carter administration actions of, 28–29; Central America and, 57; Cienfuegos submarine base, 22–23; Cuban missile crisis, 18
Specter, Arlen, 120
State Department: Bush (George H. W.) administration, 80; Clinton administration, 98, 102–3, 117, 120; and Cuban American community, 34; on Cuban influence in Latin America, 56; Eisenhower administration, 14; Kennedy administration, 17; Nixon administration, 23; Office of Public Diplomacy for Latin America and the Caribbean (S/LPD), 61–64; and Radio Marti, 41; Reagan administration, 34, 37, 41, 56, 57–58, 59, 61–64; and Reagan Central America policy, 59; release of false information by, 57; White Paper on El Salvador, 37, 57–58
Stephanopoulos, George, 88, 106
Stet International, 114
Stone, Peter, 43
Stone, Richard, 28–29
Suarez, Xavier, 45
sugar industry, 12–13, 15